Greenhill Books

The Greenhill
Armoured Fighting Vehicles
Data Book

The Greenhill
Armoured Fighting Vehicles
Data Book

Ian V. Hogg

Greenhill Books, London
Stackpole Books, Pennsylvania

The Greenhill Armoured Fighting Vehicles Data Book
First published in 2000 by
Greenhill Books, Lionel Leventhal Limited,
Park House, 1 Russell Gardens, London NW11 9NN
and
Stackpole Books,
5067 Ritter Road, Mechanicsburg, PA 17055, USA

British Library Cataloguing in Publication Data
Hogg, Ian V. (Ian Vernon), 1926–
The Greenhill armoured fighting vehicles data book
1. Armoured vehicles, Military – History
I. Title   II. Armoured fighting vehicles data book
623.7'475

ISBN 1-85367-391-9

Library of Congress Cataloging-in-Publication Data
Hogg, Ian V., 1926–
The Greenhill armoured fighting vehicles data book / Ian V. Hogg.
p.   cm.
Includes index.
ISBN 1-85367-391-9
1. Armored vehicles, Military. I. Title.

UG446.5 .II895 2000
623.7'475--dc21   00-037191

Edited and designed by Donald Sommerville
Printed and bound in Singapore by Kyodo Printing Company

Contents

List of Illustrations

Attempting to illustrate every vehicle listed in this volume would produce a massive and ridiculously expensive book. Instead, the illustrations have been chosen partly to show the progression of designs, but principally to show design features and expressions which are used in describing the vehicles in the body of the book.

Introduction

The first time I ever fired an artillery piece (Northover Projector and Smith Gun excepted) was against a tank target on Exmoor, and I soon discovered an aptitude for the business. Since then I have always had a fond regard for tanks – as targets, that is – and have kept a watchful eye on what the rascals are up to. And, of course, by extension, I have watched the rise and rise of what I have chosen here to call 'Infantry Armour' – APCs, MICVs, IFVs, whatever they are calling them this week – because I sometimes think that they are the true inheritors of the mantle of the tanks of 1916 which were, let us not forget, designed to help the infantry on to their objective and not, as some tank protagonists seemed to think in the 1930s, to go off to a remote corner of the battlefield and have a private scrap with the other side's tanks. Less glamorous, perhaps, are the various mechanical marvels that I have called 'Special Purpose Vehicles' but bridging, mine clearing and all the other varieties of combat engineering are often essential if all the other types are to be able to do their work.

Armoured cars and reconnaissance vehicles of various sorts are a fourth category; the 'poor relations of the tank', as a non-military acquaintance of mine calls them, and that seems to be a common belief. It is not true, of course; they are comparing bananas with coconuts. There are things to be done on the battlefield for which you need something quiet and nimble, and these machines exhibit some brilliant technology in getting a quart into a pint pot.

And, bringing up the rear, the self-propelled gun, assault gun, tank destroyer... whatever you choose to call a piece of autonomous artillery. I have had a soft spot for SP guns ever since a Sexton pulled my gun tractor out of the mud of Imber Ranges on a winter's day many years ago.

It is a sobering thought that every vehicle in this book – and there are more than 800 of them – has been designed and built within the lifetime of men and women still living. That there are still men who can look you in the eye and tell you that they watched the Tank Mark 1 lumbering across the mud of Flanders all those years ago. If you bear that in mind, the sheer number and diversity of vehicles listed here will surprise you, even shock you. Another thing to ponder on is the estimate that about 70% of the vehicles in this book never saw action nor ever will see it. A reference book restricted to AFVs that have actually fired in anger and been shot at would be slender indeed.

This is not a narrative of the history of the tank, nor is it an attempt to give a complete description of every vehicle. The aim on view is simply to provide, in one volume, the basic data on armoured fighting vehicles since the first armoured cars trundled out at the beginning of the century. In order to keep the book within a reasonable size, I have been strict in defining the contents – armoured fighting vehicles. An anti-aircraft gun on the back of a three-ton truck may be a fighting vehicle, but it is not armoured, nor is a Jeep festooned with machine guns. Ambulances and ammunition carriers may be armoured but they are not fighting vehicles, and so on. There are borderline cases – bridgelayers and mine clearing tanks are included because they have to do their particular thing in the middle of the action, and very often have to put up some sort of a fight in the process. So if some particular favourite of yours does not appear, think about it on those lines and you will probably see why. Another no-go area is the parade of prophecies which have emanated from Russia over the past few years; separation of fact from fiction has always been difficult in that part of the world, and today it is almost impossible, and rather than foster illusions I have ignored several dubious offerings. (And incidentally I use Russia throughout to cover the tsarist, the communist and the modern eras.)

There are also grounds for dispute over the allocation of some vehicles between 'reconnaissance' and 'infantry armour' or between 'tanks' and 'reconnaissance', but this has been done on the basis of how their owners use or used them or, in the case of those not taken up by the military, how their designers intended them to be used.

The information provided has been collected from a wide variety of sources; wherever possible the source has been an official document or manual, or maker's brochure, vehicle handbook and so on. For some of the very scarce and old tanks the full specification is impossible to find and I have had to make do with extracting figures from journals and newspaper reports. They may be found to disagree with other published figures, and this is very often due to miscalculation when shifting from metric to Imperial measure in days gone by when the pocket calculator was not even a dream.

Within the five categories the vehicles are listed by the name commonly used and cross-referenced by any other title they may have had. Tanks which did not have distinctive names are listed by numbers or whatever their owners used; but there are certain broad exceptions. For example, the first British tanks of 1916–18 are simply listed as 'Tank Mark XX', the British light tanks of the 1930s as 'Light Tank Mark XX' and the numbered series of German tanks 1933–45 are all to be found under 'Panzer'. In any case, there are numerous cross-references and a comprehensive index which may be resorted to for the hard ones. I might also point out that I have given up the use of Roman numerals in distinguishing Mark numbers; the British Army abandoned the practice almost 60 years ago and I see no reason for perpetuating it. The purists will say that it is the correct nomenclature: I disagree – the nomenclature is Mark One. How you choose to indicate the 'One' is not an issue.

A note on Japanese nomenclature: the type number of Japanese tanks produced before 1945 comes from the last two digits of the year of adoption in the Japanese calendar. Fortunately the last digit is the same as the equivalent year in the Western calendar, and the system was introduced in 1920s. Thus the Type 89 dates from 1929, Type 94 from 1934, and the Type 0 from 1940. In more recent times, from 1960 onwards, the type number is the last two digits of the year in the Western calendar. And while on the subject of dates, note that the date given at the start of the descriptive paragraph in various entries is the date of introduction for those vehicles which saw military service, or the date of design for those which did not.

Note that, unless stated otherwise, 'ton' means the Imperial ton of 2,240 pounds, not the short (US) ton of 2,000lb or the metric tonne of 1,000kg/2,204.6lb. 'Gallon' likewise means the Imperial gallon of 4.55 litres, not the US gallon of 3.78 litres. Note also that the performance figures are those of the manufacturer or authority, and are not necessarily borne out in service life. Manufacturers' figures will often be optimistic, but not invariably so. The maximum speed of an Alvis Scorpion is officially given as 55mph/88km/hr but I once saw one overtaking a petrified woman in a Mercedes-Benz on a German *Autobahn*, and you don't do that at 55 miles an hour…

Each section of the book is accompanied by a data table. The tables in the tanks, infantry armour and reconnaissance vehicles chapters are arranged in ascending order of gross weight, so that vehicles of a similar weight and size can be seen together more easily. The SP gun table is arranged in ascending order of weapon calibre. The tables are largely self-explanatory, though at the head of the various sections are notes on conventions used within them.

Several friends have produced odd pieces of information but I would particularly like to thank Peter Chamberlain and Chris Ellis for raiding their files for some of the more elusive details of early armoured vehicles. Caroline Johnson of the National Motor Museum, Beaulieu, and Helene Trebinska kindly helped find details of various early manufacturing companies.

Glossary and Abbreviations

AEV
Armoured Engineer Vehicle.

AIFV
Armoured Infantry Fighting Vehicle.

AMC France
Auto-mitrailleuse de Combat: armoured car (*auto-mitrailleuse* is literally machine-gun carrier).

AMD France
Auto-mitrailleuse de Découverte: armoured car (*découverte* = discovery).

AML France
Auto-mitrailleuse Lourde: heavy armoured car.

AMR France
Auto-mitrailleuse de Reconnaissance: armoured car.

AMX France
Atelier de Construction d'Issy-les-Moulineaux; a manufacturer of armoured vehicles.

AP
Armour Piercing; applied to projectiles. In small arm calibres 'AP' is a sufficient description, meaning a hard-cored bullet. In artillery calibres it needs to be qualified. **AP Shot** is a solid projectile, relying upon kinetic energy alone to penetrate; **AP Shell** is hollow and contains explosive and a delayed-action fuze, and relies upon kinetic energy to penetrate and pass beyond the armour and upon explosive energy to detonate within the tank and cause damage.

The abbreviation **AP** is also used as part of the description in specific types of ammunition listed below.

APC
Armoured Personnel Carrier.

APC
AP Capped; shot with a soft steel cap over the point which acts as a shock absorber on impact and assists penetration.

APCBC
APC shot with a thin metal Ballistic Cap over the penetrative cap.

APC/HE
AP Capped shell.

APC-I
APC shell with incendiary filling.

APCNR
AP Composite Non-Rigid. Similar to APCR but the surround is designed so as to be compressed when fired down a gun barrel with a tapering bore, so that the ratio of weight to diameter is more favourable to flight when the shot leaves the muzzle. Commonly called 'squeeze-bore'.

APCR
AP Composite Rigid. An insert projectile consisting of a core of tungsten carbide or other dense material, built up to calibre with a light alloy casing, thus giving a light projectile to develop high velocity.

APC-T
APC with tracer.

APDS
Armour Piercing Discarding Sabot. A form of AP shot which consists of a heavy penetrative core of a diameter considerably smaller than the calibre of the gun, supported in a light alloy casing of calibre diameter. The casing is designed to break up in the bore but support the core until it leaves the muzzle, after which the pieces of casing fall away leaving the core to travel to the target. A method of developing very high velocity. Used with rifled guns.

APFSDS
Armour Piercing Fin Stabilised Discarding Sabot. Similar to APDS but the core is longer and provided with fins. For use with smoothbore guns.

APHE
Armour piercing, high explosive; synonymous with AP Shell.

AP-I
Armour Piercing, Incendiary. AP shot, shell or small arm bullet with a small quantity of incendiary material incorporated in the construction.

AP-T
AP shot, shell or bullet with tracer.

APX France
Atelier de Construction de Puteaux. French ordnance factory in the suburbs of Paris.

ARE France
Atelier de Construction de Roanne. Principal French factory for tanks and other armoured vehicles, at Roanne, 50 miles NW of Lyon.

ARL France
Atelier de Construction de Rueil.

ArmdC UK
Armoured Car.

ARV
Armoured Recovery Vehicle.

ATGW
Anti-Tank Guided Weapon.

Ausf Germany
Ausführung. This is one of those words which can mean several slightly different things according to the context in which it appears. In the context of tanks, the best translation is 'batch', since it always means a production run of a tank to a specific pattern. 'Mark' or 'model' is not an accurate equivalent, since a particular mark of tank could be made this week, then nothing for a year, and then more of the same mark or model. Under the German system, the second lot would have a different Ausf letter because they would be a different production batch.

AVLB USA
Armoured Vehicle-Launched Bridge

'A' Vehicle UK
Descriptive category covering all armoured vehicles – tanks, SP guns, carriers, APCs etc.

AVRE UK
Armoured Vehicle, Royal Engineers; specialised assault engineer tank with demolition equipment etc.

Ballistic shaping
A term describing the shaping of a tank hull and/or turret with a view to deflecting attacking shot and not presenting any flat vertical surface for attack.

'B' Vehicle UK
Descriptive category covering all non-armoured vehicles, trucks, cars, tractors etc. Literally, any 'soft' vehicle.

Belleville Spring
A type of spring occasionally used in tank suspensions; takes the form of a concave washer, and when stacked concave face to concave face, convex to convex, forms a rudimentary and very stiff coil spring. Also found under the racer rings of heavy guns and tank turrets; they support the normal weight, allowing it to rotate on the roller race, but when the gun fires the Belleville springs compress and the gun or turret sits firmly down on the gun carriage or the tank hull, relieving the rollers of pressure and thus avoiding flattening them.

BLR Spain
Blindado Ligero des Ruedas: Wheeled light armoured vehicle

BMR Spain
Blindado Medio des Ruedas: Wheeled medium armoured vehicle

Bore evacuator
Another term for 'fume extractor', which see.

Bore sighting
Method of ensuring the the gun barrel and the sight both point at the same thing. See the entry on 'Muzzle reference' for a brief explanation of bore-sighting.

BT Russia
Bystrochodny Tankovy: fast tank, as in 'BT-7', etc.

BTS Russia
Bronetankovy Tyagach Sridny: medium armoured tractor, a form of Armoured Recovery Vehicle.

CA Italy
Carro Armato: armoured vehicle.

CET UK
Combat Engineer Tractor.

CEV USA
Combat Engineer Vehicle.

CKD UK/USA
Completely Knocked Down; a term descriptive of vehicles exported or supplied to other countries in a dismantled condition to save shipping space. As in 'The armoured cars were shipped CKD to Mombasa.'

CP
Concrete-piercing (artillery shells).

CTRA Spain

Carro de Transporte Sobre Rodas amfibio: wheeled amphibious scout car.

CV Italy

Carro Veloce: fast vehicle.

DCA France

Défense Contre Avions: anti-aircraft.

DEFA France

Direction d'Étude et Fabrication des Armements.

DIVADS USA

Divisional Air Defense gun system.

DU

Depleted Uranium. An exceptionally heavy and hard metal used for the penetrative cores of various types of armour-piercing ammunition. It is not radioactive to any significant extent, but is pyrophoric – on striking and penetrating it usually breaks up into fragments, which spontaneously ignite and thus act as an incendiary agent if any portion of the target is inflammable.

EBG France

Engin Blindé du Génie: engineer armoured vehicle

EBR France

Engin Blindé de Reconnaissance: armoured reconnaissance vehicle.

EPC France

Engin Principal de Combat: main battle tank.

ERFB

Extended Range, Full Bore. An artillery projectile with tapering head shape and stub wings giving additional aerodynamic lift during flight.

ERA

Explosive Reactive Armour.

ERFB-BB

Extended Range, Full Bore, Base Bleed. As ERFB but with a smokeless powder cache in the base which burns to fill the void behind the shell base with gas and thereby reduce aerodynamic drag,

Faceted

Refers to the shaping of a turret or hull in a series of small angular, flat plates so as to present surfaces likely to deflect shot. usually in designs where casting the component is to be avoided for some reason, but the best ballistic shape is desirable. Comparable, in a way, to modern 'stealth' technology for deflecting radar signals.

Fascine

A large, round, bundle of split wood, longer than the width of a tank, and tightly bound with chains or wire ropes. The bundle was carried by a tank and dropped into a ditch, trench or similar gap to permit tanks to cross; one or more fascines would be dropped in, as required, until the top of the fascine was close to the level of the surrounding ground and the tank could then drive across.

FT UK

Flame-Thrower.

FTF UK

Flame-Thrower Fluid – the inflammable liquid discharged by flame-throwers.

Fume Extractor

A device to ensure that the gases left behind in the gun after firing are sucked out through the muzzle before the breech is opened, so that they do not enter the gun turret during reloading. It consists of a hollow sleeve around the barrel about midway to two-thirds along its length and connected to the bore by several holes sloping back from the direction of the muzzle, up into the sleeve. On firing, the high pressure gas behind the projectile rushes up these ports and fills the sleeve. As soon as the projectile leaves the muzzle, the pressure in the barrel drops, leaving the high pressure gas in the sleeve to leak out through the sloping holes. Since these are pointing forward, this sets up a current of air towards the muzzle, which sucks out any fumes from the rest of the barrel and expels them.

FV UK

Fighting Vehicle. Followed by a number, it forms the developmental nomenclature of any British 'A' vehicle and is occasionally retained after its entry into service; an example was the FV432 armoured personnel carrier. This was actually called 'Trojan' when it entered service, but there were objections from the Trojan Motor Company, a near-moribund light car firm, and the name was dropped; no other name was ever officially given, and it remained the FV432 throughout its long career.

Glacis Plate

The (usually) sloped plate forming the upper surface of the front of a tank. Sloping it gives the driver better visibility and also deflects shot.

GMC USA

Gun Motor Carriage: self-propelled gun.

HE

High Explosive. The standard projectile for most artillery.

HEAT

High Explosive, Anti-Tank. An armour-defeating projectile using explosive energy in the form of a shaped charge.

HECP

High Explosive, Concrete Piercing. Similar to AP Shell but optimised for use against reinforced concrete fortifications.

HE/Frag

High Explosive, Fragmentation. All HE shells burst and deliver fragments, but some are optimised to produce more fragments and less blast so as to make them more effective in the anti-personnel role.

HE-I

High Explosive, Incendiary. A projectile popular for use with light air defence weapons.

HE-I-T

HE, Incendiary, Tracer.

HEP

High Explosive, Plastic. HE shell with thin walls filled with plastic explosive. On striking a tank the walls collapse and the explosive sticks to the tank and detonates, blowing off a scab of metal from the inside surface of the armour. American term for what the British call HESH (*qv*) and the Germans call 'Quetschkopf'.

HEPF

High Explosive, Pre-Fragmented. A type of artillery shell in which fragments – balls or slugs of steel or tungsten – are packed, generally in a plastic matrix, around the inside of the shell wall. The shell is then filled with high explosive. On detonation, the metal balls or slugs add to the quantity of anti-personnel/anti-materiel fragments and, being pre-formed, are all of optimum weight.

HERA

High Explosive, Rocket Assisted, of artillery shells.

HESH

High Explosive, Squash-Head. The same as HEP above.

HE-T

High Explosive, Tracer. Anti-personnel, anti-materiel shell for use by tank guns It is provided with a tracer element to aid the commander in directing fire.

HMC USA

Howitzer Motor Carriage: self-propelled howitzer.

HVAP

High Velocity, Armour Piercing. An armour-piercing shot consisting of a heavy tungsten or DU core inside a lightweight full calibre body. It does not discard any part nor change its shape during flight.

ICM

Improved Conventional Munition.

IFV

Infantry Fighting Vehicle.

Kfz Germany

Kraftfahrzeug: motor vehicle. Generally applied to any German military 'soft' vehicle.

KwK Germany

Kampfwagen Kanone: tank gun.

L/

Calibre length notation for a gun. A 75mm L/50 gun will be 50 x 75mm long. All other things being equal, the longer the gun the higher the velocity and hence the greater the range and penetration.

Laser Detection and Warning system.

An electronic sensing device on a tank or other vehicle which is activated when struck by a laser beam, as from a laser-guided missile or a laser illuminator. It will advise the crew that they are under laser scrutiny and from what direction, giving them a possible chance to avoid attack or at least be prepared for it.

LVT USA

Landing Vehicle, Tracked.

LVT(A) USA

Landing Vehicle, Tracked, Armoured.

LVTP USA

Landing Vehicle, Tracked, Personnel.

Mantlet

The moveable piece of armour surrounding the main gun in a turret. It is necessary to have a fairly large slot in the face of the turret to allow the gun to elevate and depress; the mantlet, which is attached to the moving mass (not to the gun itself), conceals the slot and prevents shot entering the turret. The mantlet also gives extra thickness of armour to the turret front

MBT

Main Battle Tank.

MICV

Mechanized Infantry Combat Vehicle.

Muzzle Reference System

A self-contained method of ensuring the the sights and gun of a tank both point at the same thing. In the past this could only be done by selecting a very distant object, or using a specially-made target board at a measured distance, fitting cross-wires across the gun muzzle, removing the firing mechanism to leave a hole in the breech-block, and then carefully laying the gun on to the target, using the hole and crosswires. The sights were then adjusted until they pointed at the same place. Obviously, this is not a system which can be used on the battlefield. The

Muzzle Reference System has a mirror permanently fitted on the gun muzzle and is used in conjunction with a fixed light source in the gun mounting. At a specified setting, the gunner's sight should see the mirror and the reflection of the pinpoint light source. If not, he can adjust until it does, without leaving his seat or unloading the gun.

NBC

Nuclear, Bacteriological and Chemical; in the context of armoured vehicles this usually relates to protection against contamination from such hazards.

PAK Germany

Panzer Abwehr Kanone: anti-tank gun.

Penetration

Armour penetration achieved by various anti-tank guns is given in the notation A/B/C where A is the thickness pierced, B is the range at which it is achieved, and C is the angle between the line of flight of the projectile and the face of the plate. This 100mm/1000m/30° means a hole 100mm deep, achieved at 1000m range, the projectile striking at a 30 degree angle. Note that until about 1960 British and US reports used a line at perfect right-angles to the plate as the reference plane for angle of attack, so that a shot arriving at right-angles was noted as 0°. The Continental method was to use the face of the plate as the reference plane, so that the right-angle shot was given as 90°, and this was selected as the NATO standard around 1960. All figures given in this book are in NATO standard terms, but bear in mind that a British or US wartime report will be in the earlier form: what is 30° to Us was 60° to Them. All penetration figures are based on the performance against homogeneous steel armour plate.

PWR

Power-to-Weight Ratio. An indication of the likely mobility of a tank, arrived at by dividing the engine horsepower by the weight of the vehicle. In other words, horse-power per ton. Hence the higher the figure, the more power the vehicle has available in relation to its weight and therefore one could expect it to be more nimble and have a greater range of operation. The figure itself is not very useful except as a rough guide; in the first place it depends upon what units the calculation is based upon – horsepower, kilowatts, Joules, metric tons, short tons, imperial tons – all of which give different answers. All PWR figures in this book are derived from imperial tons and brake horse-power. And in the second place there are other factors, such as transmission gearing or engine governors, which can upset one's assumptions. A more useful

indicator, in my view, is the maximum available torque, but this figure is rarely quoted.

PzBfW Germany

Panzerbefehlswagen: command tank.

PzKpfw Germany

Panzerkampfwagen; tank. (Literally 'armoured fighting vehicle').

Rpg/min

Rounds per gun per minute. Used to describe the rate of fire of a multiple gun installation.

SAM

Surface to Air Missile.

SAP/HE

Semi-Armour Piercing, High Explosive. An AP shell which is not capable of defeating its own calibre in armour thickness. In other words, a 3-inch SAP/HE shell would not penetrate three inches of armour plate.

Sd Kfz Germany

Sonder Kraftfahrzeug: special vehicle. Always followed by a number indicating the Ordnance Department nomenclature.

Skirting plates

Vertical armour plates outside the track, concealing the upper track run and much of the suspension. Their purpose is to intercept attacking projectiles before they strike the main structure. Capped AP shot will have the penetrating cap removed by the impact on the skirting plate; the shot will penetrate but it will have lost velocity and will probably not penetrate the hull. Shaped charges will be detonated but at such a distance from the hull that the piercing jet will have slowed considerably by the time it reaches the hull and, again, will be unlikely to penetrate. These impeded projectiles might do some damage to the suspension, but that is a secondary consideration to preserving the interior and the occupants. Skirting plates are no longer of much use, since modern APFSDS projectiles have such a surplus of energy they will go through a skirting plate like tissue paper and scarcely have their momentum checked before striking the hull. Similarly, modern shaped charges are so powerful that the skirting plate is no longer any deterrent.

SOMUA France

Société d'Outillage de Mécanique et d'Usinage d'Artillerie.

SP

Self-propelled.

SPAA

Self-propelled anti-aircraft.

SPAT
Self-propelled anti-tank.

TD
Tank destroyer.

Thermal Sleeve (or blanket)
Modern tank guns are long and thin, using high-grade steel in the interest of weight-saving. As a consequence, if a tank sits in the sun or in a cooling wind, one side of the gun barrel is at a different temperature to the other and there is a degree of differential expansion, which causes the gun barrel to bend. Not so much that you can detect it easily with the naked eye, but enough to cause you to miss the target at longer ranges. A thermal sleeve is simply an insulated blanket wrapped around the barrel which keeps all the barrel at the same temperature so that there is not differential expansion. Used in conjunction with a Muzzle Reference System (*qv*) it virtually guarantees first-round accuracy.

Trim vane (or plate)
A vertical plate erected at the nose of an amphibious vehicle in order to deflect water away from the glacis plate and thus prevent the nose from diving under the surface.

Turret basket
Early tank turrets were simply rotating structures on top of the hull; the occupants stood on the floor of the tank and shuffled round as they rotated the turret. A turret basket is a floor plate attached to the rotating turret, so that the occupants are rotated with the turret. This allowed them to be seated and also ensured that the various other fitments – radio, lights, periscopes and so forth – all rotated with them so that everything was in the same relative place.

VAB France
Véhicule d'Avant Blindé: armoured car.

VBC France
Véhicule Blindé de Combat: armoured fighting vehicle.

VBL France
Véhicule Blindé Léger: light armoured vehicle.

VCA France
Véhicule Chenille d'Accompagnement: tracked support vehicle.

VCG France
Véhicule Combat du Génie: armoured engineer vehicle.

VCI France
Véhicule Combat d'Infanterie: infantry fighting vehicle.

VCR France
Véhicule de Combat à Roules: wheeled fighting vehicle.

VCR/TT France
Véhicule de Combat à Roules, Transport de Troupes; wheeled armoured personnel carrier.

VCTP France
Véhicule de Combat Transport de Personnel: armoured personnel carrier.

Volute spring
An exceptionally stiff coil spring used for tank suspensions; takes the form of a coiled ribbon of steel with the centre pushed out to form the coil into a cone. May be arranged vertically or horizontally, the latter allowing a slightly lower profile.

List of Manufacturers

ACEC
Ateliers de Construction Électrique de Charleroi, Charleroi, Belgium.

ACF
American Car & Foundry Co., Berwick, Pennsylvania, USA.

ACMAT
Ateliers de Construction Mécanique de l'Atlantique, St Nazaire, France.

Adler
Adlerwerke, Frankfurt-am-Main, Germany.

AEC
Associated Equipment Company, Southall, Middlesex, England.

Alco
American Locomotive Company, Schenectady, New York, USA.

Alkett
Altmärkische Kettenwerke GmbH, Berlin-Tegel, Germany.

Allis-Chalmers
Allis-Chalmers Co., Milwaukee, Wisconsin, USA.

Allison
Allison Division of General Motors, Cleveland, Ohio, USA.

Alvis
Alvis Cars, Coventry, England.
Alvis Vehicles Ltd., Telford, Salop, England.

AMO
AMO Motor Factory, Moscow, USSR.

AMX
Atelier de Construction de Issy-les-Moulineaux, Paris, France.

Ansaldo
Ansaldo-Fossati, Genova-Sestri, Italy.

Aris
Aris SpA, Turin, Italy.

Armscor
Armaments Corporation of South Africa, Pretoria, South Africa.

Armstrong-Whitworth
Armstrong Whitworth & Co., Coventry, England.

ARTEC
ARTEC International, Munich, Germany.

Atlas-MaK
Atlas-MaK Maschinenbau GmbH, Kiel, Germany.

Austin
Austin Motor Co., Longbridge, Birmingham, England.

Austro-Daimler
Österreichisches Daimler Motoren AG, Wiener Neustadt, Austria.

Autocar
Autocar Co., Ardmore, Pennsylvania, USA.

Auto-Union
Auto-Union AG, Werk Audi, Zwickau, Germany.

Auverland
Auverland SA, Boulogne, France.

AV Technology
AV Technology Corp., Troy, Michigan, USA.

Aveling Barford
Aveling Barford, Ltd., Ashford, Kent, England.

Azamash
Azamash Zavodi, Gayanzha, Republic of Azerbaijan.

Baldwin
Baldwin Locomotive Co., Philadelphia, Pennsylvania, USA.

Becker
Gebr. Becker Maschinenfabrik, Wuppertal-Wichlinghausen, Germany.

Beherman Demoen
Beherman Demoen Engineering, Mechelen, Belgium.

Berliet
Automobiles Berliet Bourge, Courbevoie, France.

Bernardini
Bernardini SA Indústria e Comércio, São Paulo, Brazil.

Best
C.L. Best Tractor Co., Dayton, Ohio, USA.

Birmingham
Birmingham Railway Carriage & Wagon Works, Birmingham, England.

BMARC
British Manufacturing and Research Co., Grantham, Lincs, England.

BMKD
Böhmische-Mährische Kolben-Danek AG, Wysocany, Praque, Czechoslovakia.
The former CKD (*below*) taken over by the Germans in 1939–45.

BMY
BMY (Bowen-McLaughlin-York) Combat Systems, York, Pennsylvania, USA.

Bofors
Bofors AB, Karlskoga, Sweden.

Bolshevik
Bolshevik Machine Works, Leningrad, USSR.

Borgward
Carl F.W. Borgward, Bremen, Germany.

Bravia
Bravia SARL, Samora, Portugal.

British Leyland
British Leyland Motors, Longbridge, Birmingham, England.

Brotherhood
Brotherhood Engineering Co., Sheffield, England.

Brown Brothers
Brown Brothers, Edinburgh, Scotland.

Buick
Buick Division of General Motors, Flint, Michigan, USA.

Bumar-Labedy
Machinery Industrial Complex Bumar-Labedy, Czestochowa, Poland.

Büssing-NAG
Büssing-NAG Vereinigte Nutzkraftwagen AG, Brunswick, Germany.

Cadillac (1)
Cadillac Division of General Motors, Detroit, Michigan, USA.

Cadillac (2)
Cadillac Tank Factory, Southgate, California USA.

Cadillac Gage
Cadillac Gage Textron, Warren, Michigan, USA.
In 1998 became Textron Marine & Land Systems.

Carden-Loyd
Carden-Loyd Tractors, London, England.

Cardoen
Industrias Cardoen Chile Lda., Santiago, Chile.

CGV
Automobiles Charron, Griardot et Voigt, Puteaux, France.

Chelyabinsk
State Tank Factory, Chelyabinsk, USSR.

Chevrolet
Chevrolet Division, General Motors Corp., Detroit, Michigan, USA.

Chrysler
Chrysler Corporation, US Tank Arsenal, Warren, Michigan USA.

CKD
Ceskoslovensko-Kolben-Danek, Wysokany, Prague, Czechoslovakia.

Cleveland
Cleveland Tank Arsenal, Cleveland, Ohio, USA
Operated by Cadillac Div., General Motors.

Cockbridge
Cockbridge & Co., Ipswich, Suffolk, England.

Cockerill
Cockerill Mechanical Industries, Seraing, Belgium.

CPR
Canadian Pacific Railway, Montreal, Canada.

Creusot-Loire
Creusot-Loire, Chalon-sur-Saône, France.

Crossley
Crossley Motor Co., Manchester, England.

Cunningham
James Cunningham, Son & Co., Rochester, New York, USA.

Daewoo
Daewoo Heavy Industries Ltd., Seoul, South Korea.

DAF
DAF (Van Doorn Automobile Fabrik), Eindhoven, The Netherlands.
DAF Special Products BV, Eindhoven, The Netherlands.

Daimler
BSA Ltd (Daimler Car Co.), Coventry, England.

Daimler-Benz
Daimler-Benz AG, Berlin-Marienfeld, Germany.

Dassault Électronique
Dassault Électronique, St Cloud, Paris, France.

Delauney
Delauney-Belleville, St Denis, Seine, France.

Delco
Delco Defense Systems, Goleta, California, USA

Demag
Demag AG, Wetten, Ruhr, Germany.

Denel
Denel (Pty.) Ltd, Hennospmeer, South Africa.

Detroit
Detroit Tank Arsenal, Detroit, Michigan, USA.

Deutsche Eisenwerke
Deutsche Eisenwerke AG, Mühlheim, Ruhr, Germany.

Deutsche Werke
Deutsche Werke Kiel AG, Kiel, Germany.

Diamond-T
Diamond-T Motor Car Co., Chicago, Illinois, USA.

DIO
Defence Industries Organisation, Ministry of Defence, Teheran, Iran

Disston
Disston Tractor Co., Disston, Ohio, USA.

Dodge
Dodge Division of the Chrysler Corporation, Detroit, Michigan, USA.

Dorman Long
Dorman, Long Steel Co. of South Africa, Johannesburg, South Africa.

Edelstahl
Deutsche Edelstahlwerke AG, Linden-bei-Hannover, Germany.

East Indian Railways
East India Railway Co., Calcutta, India.

EFAB
Établissment d'Études et de Fabrications d'Armement de Bourges, Bourges, France.

ELBO
ELBO: Hellenic Vehicle Industry SA, Sindos Thessaloniki, Greece.

Engesa
Engenheiros Especializados SA, São Paulo, Brazil.

English Electric
English Electric Co., Stevenage, Herts., England.

FAMAE
Fabricaciónes Militares del Ejército, Santiago, Chile.

FAMH
Forges et Aciéries de la Marine et d'Homécourt, St Chamond, France.

FAMO
Fahrzeug und Motorenwerk GmbH, Breslau, Germany.

Fargo
Fargo Motor Co., Division of Chrysler Corp., Detroit, Michigan, USA.

FCM
Forges et Chantiers de la Méditerranée, Le Seyne, Toulon, France.

Federal Works
Federal Construction Works, Thun, Switzerland.

Federal Machine
Federal Machine & Welding Co., Chicago, Illinois, USA.

Fiat
Fiat-SpA, Turin, Italy.

Fisher Body
Grand Blanc Tank Arsenal, Grand Blanc, Michigan, USA.
Operated by Fisher Body Division of General Motors.

FMC
Foot Machinery Corp., San Jose, California, USA.
FMC Corp., Santa Clara, California, USA.

FN
Fabrique National des Armes de Guerre, Herstal, Liège, Belgium.
Now known as FN Herstal SA.

Ford
Ford Motor Co., Dearborn, Michigan, USA.

Ford Canada
Ford Motor Co. of Canada, Windsor, Ontario, Canada.

Ford Russia
Ford Motor Co. of Russia, Gorkii, USSR.

Ford St Paul
Ford Motor Co., St Paul, Minnesota, USA.

Ford South Africa
Ford Motor Co. of South Africa, Johannesburg, South Africa.

Ford UK
Ford Motor Co., Dagenham, Essex, England.

Foster
Wm. Foster & Co., Lincoln, England.

Front Drive
The Front Drive Motor Corp., Detroit, Michigan, USA.

FVRDE
Fighting Vehicles Research & Development Establishment, Chertsey, England.

Gar Wood Industries
Gar Wood Industries, Detroit, Michigan.
(A subsidiary of General American Transportation Co, Chicago, Illinois.)

GAZ
Gorkii Automobile Zavodi, Nizhni Novgorod, USSR.

General Dynamics
General Dynamics Amphibious Operations, Woodbridge, Virginia, USA.
General Dynamics Defense Systems, Pittsfield, Massachusetts, USA.
General Dynamics Land Systems, Warren, Michigan, USA.

General Electric (USA)
General Electric (Defense), Burlington, Vermont, USA.

GIAT
Groupement Industrièlle des Armements Terrestre, Velizy-Villacoublay, France.
Originally the French state organisation of ordnance factories, it was 'privatised' in the 1980s and became Giat Industries.

GKN
GKN, Smethwick, Birmingham, England.
GKN-Sankey Ltd., Wellington, Salop, England.
GKN Defence, Telford, England.

GM Canada
General Motors of Canada, London, Ontario, Canada.

GM NZ
General Motors of New Zealand, Auckland, NZ.

Graham-Paige
Graham-Paige Motor Corp., Detroit, Michigan, USA.

Guy
Guy Motors, Wolverhampton England.

Hagglund
Hagglund & Soner AB, Örnsköldsvik, Sweden.

Hanomag
Hannover Maschinenbau AG, formerly Georg Egestorff, Hannover-Linden, Germany.

Hansa-Loyd
Hansa-Loyd-Goliat-Werke, Bremen, Germany.

Harland & Wolff
Harland & Wolff Shipyard, Belfast, Northern Ireland.

Heinz
Heinz Manufacturing Co, Pittsburg, Pennsylvania, USA.

Henschel
Henschel & Sohn GmbH, Kassel, Germany.
Henschel Wehrtechnik GmbH, Kassel, Germany.
Henschel-Werke, Antwerp, Belgium.

Hispano-Suiza
Automobiles Hispano-Suiza SA, Bois-Colombes, France.

Holt
Holt Tractor Co., Stockton, California, USA.

Hotchkiss
SA des Anciens Établissments Hotchkiss et Cie., St Denis, Seine, France.

Hotchkiss-Brandt
Hochkiss-Brandt & Cie., Paris, France.

Humber
Rootes Group (Humber Motors), Ryton-on-Dunsmore, England.

Hyundai
Hyundai Precision & Industrial Company, Chongro-Ku, Seoul, South Korea.

IMI
Israel Military Industries, Ramat Ha Sharon, Israel.

Ingersoll
Ingersoll Division., Borg-Warner Corp, Kalamazoo, Michigan, USA.

International Harvester
International Harvester Co., Chicago, Illinois USA.

IOF
Indian Ordnance Factories, Medak Ordnance Factory, Medak, India.

Ishikawajima
Ishikawajima Motor Works, Ishikawa, Japan.

Isuzu
Isuzu Motor Company, Tokyo, Japan.

Iveco
Iveco-Fiat SpA, Defence Vehicles Division, Bolzano, Italy.

Jeffery
Thomas B. Jeffery Corp., Kenosha, Wisconsin, USA.

Kadr Factory
Kadr Factory for Developed Industries, Cairo, Egypt.

Karrier
Rootes Group (Karrier) Ltd., Luton, England.

Kharkov
Kharkov Locomotive Works, Kharkov, USSR.

Kirov
Kirov Tank Factory, Leningrad, USSR.

Klockner
Klockner-Humboldt-Deutz AG, Ulm/Donau, Germany.

Komatsu
Komatsu Seisakujyo, Minato-ku, Tokyo, Japan.

Komintern
Komintern Tank Factory, Kharkov, USSR.

Krasnoye-Sormovo
Krasnoye-Sormovo Tank Plant No. 112, Gorkii, USSR.

Krauss-Maffei
Lokomotivenfabrik Krauss & Cie., J.A. Maffei AG, Munich, Germany. (1936–45).
Krauss-Maffei Wehrtechnik GmbH, Munich, Germany. (post-1945).

Krupp
Fried. Krupp AG, Essen, Germany.

Krupp-Gruson
Fried. Krupp AG, Werk Gruson, Magdeburg, Germany.

Kurgan
Kurgan Machine Construction Plant, Kurgan, Russia.

Laffly
Établissments Laffly, Asnières, Seine, France.

La France
American La France Co., Elmira, New York, USA.
Ward La France Truck Co., Elmira, New York, USA.

Lanchester
Lanchester Motor Car Co., Coventry, England.

Lancia
Lancia & Co., Fabbrica Automobili, Turin, Italy.

Landsverk
Landsverk AB, Landskrona, Sweden.

Leyland
Leyland Motor Co., Leyland, Lancs, England.

Lima
Lima Locomotive Company, Lima, Ohio, USA.

Lima Tank
Lima Tank Arsenal, Lima, Ohio, USA.

LIW
LIW Division of Denel Pty., Lyttleton, South Africa.

LMS
London, Midland and Scottish Railway Co., Derby, England.

Lockheed
Lockheed Missile & Space Co., Sunnyvale, California, USA.

Lohr
Lohr Défense, Hangenbeiten, France.

Magirus
C.D. Magirus AG, Ulm/Donau, Germany.

Magyar
Magyat Allani Vosopor Gepgyar, Budapest, Hungary.

MaK
MaK Systems GmbH, Kiel, Germany.

Makina
Makina Lda., Santiago, Chile.

MAN
Maschinenfabrik Augsburg-Nürnberg, Augsburg, Germany.

Marmon-Herrington
The Marmon-Herrington Co., Indianapolis, Indiana, USA.

Marshall
William Marshall & Co., Gainsborough, Lincs. England.

Massey-Harris
Massey-Harris Corp., Racine, Wisconsin, USA.

Maxwell
Maxwell Motor Co., Dayton, Ohio, USA.

Metropolitan
Metropolitan Carriage & Wagon Works, London, England. (1916–17).
Metropolitan Carriage, Wagon & Finance Co., London, England. (1918).

MG
MG Motors Ltd., Abingdon, Oxon., England.

MIAG
Mühlenbau und Industrie AG, Werk Ammewerke, Brunswick, Germany.

Minerva
Minerva Motors SA, Mortsel, Belgium.

Mitsubishi
Mitsubishi Heavy Industries, Sagamihara, Japan.

MKEK
Makina ve Kimya Endüstrisi Kurumu, Tandogan, Ankara, Turkey.

Moelven
Moelven Brug SA, Moelve, Norway.

Montreal
Montreal Locomotive Works, Montreal, Canada.

Morris
Morris Motors, Cowley, Oxon, England.

Mors
Société Nouvelle des Autos Mors, Paris, France.

Moscow
Ordzhonikidze Tank Factory, Moscow, USSR.

Moto Peças
Moto Peças, Sorocaba SP, Brazil.

Mowag
Motorwagenfabrik AG, Kreuzlingen, Switzerland.

MPP Vozila
MPP Vozila Co., Ljubljana, Slovenia.

MTU
Motoren-Turbinen-Union GmbH, Friedrichshafen, Germany.

Neubrandenburg
Neubrandenburger Maschinenfabrik, Neubrandenburg, Germany.

Niebelungenwerke
Niebelungenwerke, Linz, Austria.

Niedersachsen
Maschinenfabrik Niedersachsen GmbH, Hannover-Wülfel, Germany.

Nizhni-Tagil
State Tank Factory, Nizhni-Tagil, USSR.

Norinco
China North Industries Co., Beijing, China.

North British
North British Locomotive Works, Edinburgh, Scotland.

NSWR
New South Wales Railway Co., Chullora, NSW, Australia.

Nuffield
Nuffield Aero & Mechanisation, Cowley, Oxford, England.

Nurol
Nurol Machinery & Industrial Co., Ankara, Turkey.

NZ Rail
New Zealand State Railways, Auckland, New Zealand.

Oerlikon-Contraves
Oerlikon-Contraves AG, Zurich, Switzerland.

OMC
OMC Engineering Pty. Ltd., Benoni, South Africa.

Osaka
Osaka Automobile Co., Osaka, Japan.

Ostbau
Ostbau GmbH, Sagan, Germany.

Otokar
Otokar Otobus Karoserim Sanay AS, Bahcelievier, Istanbul, Turkey.

OTO-Melara
OTO-Melara, La Spezia, Italy.

Pacific Car
Pacific Car & Foundry Co., Renton, Washington, USA.

Panhard et Levassor
Société Anonyme des Anciennes Établissements Panhard et Levassor, Marolles-en-Hurepoix, France.
Société des Constructions Mécaniques Panhard et Levassor, Paris, France.

Patria
Patria Vehicles Oy, Vammala, Finland.
Name adopted in 1998 for the firm hitherto known as SISU-Auto (*see below*).

Peerless
Peerless Motor Car Company, Cleveland, Ohio, USA.

Peugeot
Société Anonyme des Autos et Cycles Peugeot, Issy-les-Moulineaux., Seine, France.

Peugeot-Talbot
Peugeot-Talbot España SA, Madrid, Spain.

Pierce-Arrow
Pierce-Arrow Motor Car Co., Buffalo, New York, USA.

Pioneer
Pioneer Tractor Co., Winona, Minnesota, USA.

POF
Pakistan Ordnance Factories, Wah Cantoment,
Pakistan.

Pressed Steel Car
Pressed Steel Car Co., Pittsburgh, Pennsylvania,
USA.

Pullman-Standard
Pullman-Standard Car Co., Pittsburgh,
Pennsylvania, USA.

Putilov
Putilov Armaments Factory, St Petersburg, Russia.

Quad Cities
Quad Cities Tank Arsenal, Bettendorf, Iowa, USA.
Operated by International Harvester.

Ramta
Ramta Structures and Systems, Beersheba, Israel.

RATMIL
Ratmil, Reie Autonoma, Bucharest, Romania.

Renault
Renault Frères, Billancourt, Paris, France.
Renault SA, Billancourt, Paris, France.
Renault Véhicules Industrièlles, Paris, France.

Rheinmetall
Rheinmetall Defence Engineering, Düsseldorf,
Germany.

Rheinmetall-Borsig
Rheinmetall-Borsig AG, Düsseldorf, Germany.

Rheinstahl
Rheinstahl Sondefertigung, Düsseldorf, Germany.

Rheinstahl AG
Rheinstahl AG Transporttechnik, Kassel, Germany.

Roanne
Atelier de Construction de Roanne, France.

Rock Island
Rock Island Arsenal, Rock Island, Illinois, USA.

Roebling
Donald Roebling Co., Clearwater, Florida, USA.

ROF Leeds
Royal Ordnance Factory, Leeds, Yorkshire,
England.

Rolls-Royce
Rolls-Royce Ltd., Derby, England.

Romarm
Romarm, Bucharest, Romania.
Formerly known as Romtechnika.

Royal Ordnance
British Aerospace Ltd, Royal Ordnance Division,
Nottingham, England.

Rubcovskii
Rubcovskii Machinery Plant, Rubcovsk, Russia.

Ruston
Ruston & Hornsby Ltd, Grantham, Lincs,
England.

St Louis Car
St Louis Car Co., St Louis, Missouri, USA.

SAMM
Société des Applications des Machines Motrices,
Bièvres, France.

Samsung
Samsung Shipbuilding & Engineering Co., Pusan,
South Korea.

Sandcock-Austral
Sandcock-Austral Pty. Ltd., Boksburg, Transvaal,
South Africa.

Santa Barbara
Empresa Nacional Santa Barbara, Madrid, Spain.

Saurer
A. & E. Saurer, Le Lac Constance, Switzerland.

SAVA
SAVA, Antwerp, Belgium.

Scania-Vabis
Scania-Vabis, Södertälje, Sweden.

Schichau
F. Schichau GmbH, Elbing, Germany.

Schneider
Schneider et Cie., Lyons, France.

Schneider-Creusot
Schneider-Creusot SA, Le Creusot, France.

Sentinel
Sentinel Steam Wagon Co., Shrewsbury, Salop,
England.

Short Brothers
Short Brothers & Harland, Belfast, Northern
Ireland.

Singapore Technologies
Singapore Technologies, Jurong Town, Singapore.

SISU-Auto
Oy SISU-Auto AB, Sisu Defence, Hämeenlinna,
Finland.
Re-named Patria Vehicles in 1998.

Skoda
Skoda, Pilsen, Czechoslovakia.

SMG
Servicio de Material de Guerra, Guatemala City,
Guatemala.

Soltam
Soltam Ltd., Haifa, Israel.

Somua
Société d'Outillage de Mécanique et d'Usinage d'Artillerie, St Ouen, Seine, France.

South African Iron
South African Iron & Steel Industrial Corp., Johannesburg, South Africa.

Standard
Standard Motor Co., Coventry, England.

Steyr-Daimler-Puch
Steyr-Daimler-Puch AG, Steyr, Austria.

Strojarstva
Zavody Tazkeno Strojarstva, Povaske Strojarne, Czechoslovakia.

Talbot
Talbot Motor Co., Ladbroke Grove, London, England.

TAMSE
Tanque Argentino Mediano Sociedad del Estado, Buenos Aires, Argentina.

Tankograd
Tankograd Factory Combine, Chelyabinsk, USSR.

Tata
Tata Engineering & Locomotive Co., Jamshedpur, India.

Textron
Textron Marine & Land Systems, New Orleans, Louisiana, USA.

TGE
Tokyo Gas & Electric Co., Tokyo, Japan.

Thomson-CSF
Thomson-CSF, Bagneux, France.

Thornycroft
John I. Thornycroft & Co. Ltd, Basingstoke, Hants., England.

Timoney
Timoney Technology Ltd, Dublin, Eire

Thyssen-Henschel
Thyssen-Henschel, Kassel, Germany.

United Defense
United Defense LP, Ground Systems Division, Santa Clara, California, USA.

Uralmashzavod
Urals Machinery Works, Sverdlovsk, USSR.

Ursus
Fabrique des Automobiles Ursus, Katowice, Poland.

US Wheel & Track
US Wheel & Track-Layer Corp., Elizabeth, New Jersey, USA.

Van Dorn
Van Dorn Iron Works, Cleveland, Ohio, USA.

Vauxhall
Vauxhall Motors, Luton, England.

VEB
VEB Robur-Werke, Zittau, East Germany.

Vickers
Vickers-Armstrong, Newcastle-upon-Tyne, England.
Vickers Shipbuilding & Engineering Co., Barrow-in-Furness, Cumbria, England.
Vickers Ltd, Elswick Works, Newcastle-on-Tyne, England.
Vickers Ltd, Leeds, England. (Formerly ROF Leeds).

Volgograd
State Tank Factory, Volgograd, USSR.
Volgograd Tractor Plant, Joint Stock Company, Volgograd, Russia.

Vormag
Vormag-Betriebs AG, Plauen, Germany.

Vulcan
Vulcan Foundry (Tilling-Stevens Motors Ltd.), Warrington, Lancs. England.

Wegmann
Wegmann & Co., Waggonfabrik, Kassel, Germany.

Weiss
Manfred Weiss RT, Budapest, Hungary.

Weserhütte
Weserhütte AG, Bad Oyenhausen, Germany.

White
White Motor Co., Cleveland, Ohio, USA.

Woolwich
Royal Carriage Department, Woolwich Arsenal, Woolwich, England.

Yellow Truck
Yellow Truck & Coach Div., General Motors Corp. Pontiac, Michigan, USA.

Zacherts
A. Zacherts Karosserie und Fahrzeugfabrik, Freystadt N. Schl., Germany.

ZTS Dubnica
Zavody Tazkeno Strojarstva, Dubnica nad Vahom, Czech Republic.

Zundapp
Zundappwerke GmbH, Nürnberg, Germany.

TANKS

Unless specified otherwise, the following conventions apply to the entries in this and other sections:

Maker: The maker's name (where known) is given in short form at the beginning of each entry. The full name, location and any changes in the company's name or style of title will be found in the List of Manufacturers (see pages 15–22).

Dimensions: Are to the nearest inch/centimetre; there is no point in providing measurements to the millimetre unless you know how many coats of paint the vehicle has had in its lifetime.

Armament: Main armament, followed by machine guns.

Ammunition: Smaller (or only) figure is the number of main armament rounds carried; larger figure machine gun ammunition. These figures are not always available, especially for early and prototype tanks.

Armour: Maximum thickness, where known.

Crew: Number of men.

Weight: Imperial tons and kilogrammes, vehicle combat-loaded with crew, fuel, ammunition, rations and stores.

Hull length: Feet and metres, nose to tail without the gun overhang.

Width: Maximum – that is over side skirts and similar fittings.

Height: To turret roof or top of cupola, whatever is the highest part of the permanent structure, ignoring machine guns, searchlights and similar add-on devices.

Engine: Maker and model (if known), cylinders and their configuration, power in brake horsepower.

Road speed: Cross country may be about two-thirds of this.

Power/weight: Brake horsepower per imperial ton.

Range: Using hard roads, in-board fuel, no auxiliary tankage, and normally at cruising speed, about two-thirds of the maximum.

4TP Poland
State factories
1938. Two-man reconnaissance tank. Engine offset to the right, turret to the left. Two bogies each side, with torsion bar suspension; rear drive, front idler.

Armament: 1 × 7.92mm MG
Armour: 17mm
Crew: 2
Weight: 4 tons (4,064kg)
Hull length: 12ft 7in (3.84m)
Width: 6ft 10in (2.08m)
Height: 6ft 1in (1.85m)
Engine: 6-cylinder, petrol, 95bhp
Road speed: 34mph (55km/hr)
Power/weight: 23.75

7TP Poland
State factories
1934. Polish development of the Vickers Six-Ton, some of which had been bought in 1931. Originally with twin central turrets, two twin bogies each side, front sprocket, rear idler. Hull with low boxy superstructure carrying the turrets.

Armament: 2 × 7.92mm MG
Armour: 17mm
Crew: 3
Weight: 9.4 tons (9,550kg)
Hull length: 15ft 1in (4.60m)
Height: 7ft 0in (2.13m)
Width: 7ft 1in (2.16m)
Engine: Saurer diesel, 6-cylinder, 110bhp
Road speed: 20mph (32km/hr)

Power/weight: 11.70
Range: 100 miles (160km)

7TP-2 Poland
State factories

1937. After some experience with the twin-turret model, the design of the 7TP was changed by adopting a single Swedish turret mounting a 37mm Bofors anti-tank gun and coaxial machine gun. The turret was slightly offset to the left side of the hull. About 170 were built and became the mainstay of the Polish armoured force. Most were lost during the 1939 campaign, but a handful survived and were taken into German service.

7TP-3 Poland
State factories

1938. As for the 7TP-2 but with a new turret with bustle, thicker armour, new engine, stronger suspension and wider tracks. This generally improved version did not get into production until 1939 and very few had reached the hands of the army before the war began.

Data: generally as for 7TP, except
Weight: 11 tons (11,177kg)
Armour: 40mm

10TP Poland
State factories

1939. This was a wheel-and-track design based on a Christie original, with large roadwheels and spring suspension. The hull had a single turret slightly forward of centre, a boxy superstructure and a sloping tail. There were four roadwheels on each side with rear drive and front idler. A somewhat ambitious project, using a powerful American engine, development was abandoned on the outbreak of war.

Armament: 1 × 37mm; 2 × 7.92mm MG
Armour: 20mm
Crew: 4
Weight: 12.8 tons (13,005kg)
Hull length: 17ft 9in (5.41m)
Width: 8ft 5in (2.57m)
Height: 7ft 3in (2.16m)
Engine: La France V-12, petrol, 210bhp
Road speed: 31mph (50km/hr) on tracks; 46mph (74km/hr) on wheels
Power/weight: 16.40

A1E1 UK
See Independent

A2E1 UK
Woolwich

1924. Number applied to a Vickers Medium Mark 1 which had the suspension modified in Woolwich for test purposes.

A3E1 Light UK
Woolwich

1925. Light tank built as cheaply as possible by the use of commercial components wherever possible. Designed and built by Woolwich Arsenal, it had Vickers-type suspension and side plates with skirt and mud chutes, front turret offset to left of driver's cupola, second turret rear-facing at rear of flat hull.

Armament: 2 × .303in Vickers MG
Armour: 6mm
Crew: 3
Weight: 3 tons (3,048kg)
Hull length: 17ft 6in (5.33m)
Width: 9ft 0in (2.77m)
Height: 6ft 0in (1.83m)
Engine: AEC 4-cylinder, petrol, 40bhp
Power/weight: 13.33
Road speed: 16mph (26km/hr)

A4E1 UK
Vickers

1929. This was developed from the Carden-Loyd tankette and was a low boxy superstructure with a single sloped-top turret. The four roadwheels were connected by an outside girder, there were three return rollers, rear drive and front idlers. It was officially known as the **Light Tank Mark 7**, but none beyond the prototype was ever built and it never entered service.

Armament: 1 × Vickers MG
Armour: 6mm
Crew: 2
Weight: 2.5 tons (2,540kg)
Engine: Meadows 6-cylinder, petrol, 59bhp
Power/weight: 23.60
Road speed: 35mph (56km/hr)

A5E1 Light UK
Vickers

1930. Also known as the **Vickers Three-Man Tank**. The hull was based on that of the Light Tank Mark 2, with two four-wheeled bogies each side, three return rollers, rear drive and front idler. Sloped superstructure with single two-gun two-man turret, the guns being side-by-side. Only a single prototype model was built, which was scrapped in 1934.

Armament: 1 × .50in, 1 × .303in Vickers MG
Armour: 9mm
Crew: 3
Weight: 4.5 tons (4,572kg)
Engine: Meadows 6-cylinder, petrol, 85bhp
Power/weight: 18.88
Road speed: 30mph (48km/hr)

A6E1 Medium UK
Vickers

1928. Vickers 16-tonner; multi-turret design. Flat forward, rear sloped hill, central large turret with two smaller two-gun turrets in front and the driver positioned centrally, between the turrets. Multi-wheeled bogie suspension concealed by skirting plate with mud chutes. Low rear drive sprocket, high front idler. Prototype only.

Armament: 1 × 3-pdr + 1 × coaxial MG in main turret; 4 × MG in small turrets
Armour: 14mm
Crew: 7
Weight: 17.5 tons (17,780kg)
Hull length: 21ft 6in (6.55m)
Width: 8ft 9in (2.66m)
Height: 9ft 2in (2.79m)
Engine: Armstrong-Siddeley V-8, petrol, air-cooled, 180bhp
Power/weight: 10.28
Road speed: 30mph (48km/hr)

A6E2 Medium UK
Vickers

1929. As for the A6E1 but with Ricardo 180bhp diesel engine. Prototype only.

A6E3 Medium UK
Vickers

1930. As for the A6E1 but main turret with one cupola instead of two, smaller turrets now with one gun instead of two, bogie suspension replaced by Horstmann type. Prototype only; refitted with Thornycroft RY12 500bhp engine in 1937.

A7E1 Medium UK
Woolwich

1929. Woolwich Arsenal design. Low rectangular hull with single slope-sided turret. Small-wheel suspension with skirting plate and mud chutes. Rear drive, front idler.

Armament: 1 × 3-pdr gun, 1 × MG coaxial, 1 × MG in hull front
Armour: 14mm

Crew: 5
Weight: 14 tons (14,225kg)
Engine: Armstrong-Siddeley 6-cylinder, air-cooled, 120bhp
Power/weight: 8.57
Road speed: 25mph (40km/hr)

A7E2 Medium UK
Woolwich

As for the A7E1, but with different transmission and changes in the suspension.

A7E3 Medium UK
Woolwich

1937. A further advance on the A7E2 begun in 1933, which also incorporated ideas from other designs. In appearance very similar to the A7E2, with small-wheel suspension, six return rollers, and lozenge-shaped side armour on the superstructure sides. The last of the series, it was abandoned in 1937 due to unreliability of the engines and suspension.

Armament: 1 × 3-pdr; 2 × MG
Armour: 14mm maximum
Crew: 5
Weight: 18.2 tons (18,490kg)
Hull length: 22ft 6in (6.86m)
Width: 8ft 1in (2.72m)
Height: 9ft 1in (2.77m)
Engine: 2 × AEC 6-cylinder, diesel, nett 252bhp
Road speed: 25mph (40km/hr)
Power/weight: 13.84

A-7V Germany
Daimler-Benz

1918. Manufactured by Daimler and based on the tracked Holt tractor chassis; high-sided all-enveloping hull with pointed prow nose, cupola on top. Captured 57mm gun centrally-mounted in hull front. Single-compartment hull housed engine, crew and armament. 30 built.

Armament: 1 × 57mm; 6 or 7 × Maxim MG in hull
Armour: 15–30mm
Crew: 18
Weight: 29.43 tons (29,900kg)
Hull length: 24ft 1in (7.34m)
Width: 10ft 0in (3.05m)
Height: 10ft 10in (3.30m)
Engine: 2 × Daimler-Benz 4-cylinder, petrol, 200bhp at 1,600rpm
Power/weight: 6.96
Road speed: 8mph (13km/hr)
Range: 25 miles (40km)

A-7V/U Germany
Daimler-Benz
1918. An improved A7V with the tracks running round the hull in the same manner as the British tanks of the period. Central cupola, 57mm guns in sponsons on the sides. Prototype only.

Armament: 2 × 57mm; 4 × Maxim MG
Armour: 20mm–30mm
Crew: 7
Weight: 39 tons (39,625kg)
Hull length: 27ft 6in (8.38m)
Width: 15ft 10in (4.83m)
Height: 10ft 6in (2.67m)
Engine: 2 × Daimler-Benz 4-cylinder, petrol, 210bhp at 1,600rpm
Power/weight: 5.38
Road speed: 7.5mph (12km/hr)
Range: 25 miles (40km)

A8 UK
Vickers
1934. An experimental medium tank ordered by the War Office from Vickers. Little is known of it other than that it weighed 17.5 tons and was to be propelled by two Rolls-Royce 'Phantom' engines. The design was never completed and the project was abandoned in 1937.

A9 UK
See Cruiser Mark 1

A10 UK
See Cruiser Mark 2

A11 UK
See Matilda 1

A12 UK
See Matilda 2

A13 UK
A13 Mark 1: see Cruiser Mark 3
A13 Mark 2: see Cruiser Mark 4
A13 Mark 3: see Cruiser Mark 5

A14 UK
See Cruisers A14 and A16

A15 UK
See Crusader

A16 UK
See Cruisers A14 and A16

A17 UK
See Tetrarch

A18 UK
Vickers
A proposal for a cruiser tank based on the A17 pattern. Designs were drawn up but the idea was dropped in 1939. The design of the turret was later revived and used in later cruiser tank projects.

A19 UK
1939. A proposal by the Mechanisation Board for a heavy cruiser tank with auxiliary turrets on top of the main turret. The idea was abandoned.

A20 UK
The original pilot model for the 'shelled area infantry tank' which eventually became the Churchill.

A21 UK
Further development of the A20 design, which never got further than the drawing board.

A22 UK
See Churchill

A23 UK
A projected lighter version of A22. Never went beyond the sketch stage.

A24 UK
See Cavalier

A25 UK
See Harry Hopkins

A26 UK
A projected lighter and faster version of A22. Another which never got beyond the first sketches.

A27 UK
See Centaur and Cruiser Mark 8

A28 UK
Rolls-Royce
1941. A heavier version of Cromwell, with skirting plates and thicker armour, to weigh about 28 tons. Abandoned before drawings were completed.

A29 UK
Rolls-Royce
Proposal for a 'large cruiser' armed with the 17-pounder gun, to weigh about 43 tons and have double tracks. It was abandoned in favour of the A30 design.

A30 UK
See Avenger and Challenger

A31 UK
Rolls-Royce
Another proposal for up-armouring the Cromwell to weigh 32 tons. Abandoned.

A32 UK
Rolls-Royce
Yet another Cromwell improvement, this time to weigh 35 tons and have new suspension. Abandoned in the drawing stage.

A33 Heavy Assault Tank UK
English Electric
Known also as the **Excelsior**, designed as a tank for operating underneath artillery fire. Based on the A27 Cromwell but up-armoured and with wider tracks and stronger suspension. Two prototypes were built in 1943 but the design was then abandoned.

Armament: 1 × 75mm gun, 1 × MG
Armour: 114mm
Crew: 5
Weight: 45 tons (45,722kg)
Hull length: 22ft 8in (6.91m)
Width: 11ft 2in (2.88m)
Height: 7ft 11in (2.41m)
Engine: Rolls-Royce Meteor, V-12, 600bhp
Power/weight: 13.33
Road speed: 24mph (38km/hr)

A34 UK
See Comet

A35 UK
LMS, Rolls-Royce
Yet another proposal for a heavier Cromwell, with more armour and stronger suspension. This never even got into the drawing office.

A36 UK
Rolls-Royce
A proposal to up-armour the A30 Challenger to 41 tons. Abandoned before it got to the drawing stage.

A37 UK
English Electric
Proposal to make the A33 even heavier, add an extra roadwheel on each side, and give it the 17-pounder gun. Abandoned at the sketch stage.

A38 Infantry Tank UK
See Valiant

A39 Heavy Tank UK
See Tortoise (SP Guns)

A40 UK
Birmingham, Rolls-Royce
Another proposal to make the A30 heavier. Abandoned.

A41 Cruiser Tank UK
See Centurion

A42 UK
Leyland
The improved design which became the Churchill Mark 7.

A43 Infantry Tank UK
See Black Prince

Abrams M1 USA
Detroit, Lima
1983. Developed by the Chrysler Corporation, the M1 Abrams was the end result of another international effort which fell to pieces and left the Americans to go their own way and design their own tank. Long, wide, low, and powerful due to its gas turbine engine (the first successful tank application) the first model (**M1**) was armed with the NATO-standard 105mm gun. It rapidly acquired a reputation as a gas-guzzler, but this was gradually cured as experience with the new engine

was acquired and modifications made. In 1990 the **M1A1** appeared, armed with a 120mm smoothbore gun, and in 1992 the first pilot **M1A2** was built. The improvements which constitute the M1A2 are entirely internal and cover sighting, surveillance, communication and similar equipment. After 62 M1A2 had been built a programme to refurbish existing M1s up to M1A2 standard was launched, so that original 105mm M1 tanks are now uncommon.

M1A2
Armament: 1 × 120mm; 2 × MG
Ammunition: 55 + 12,400
Armour: not disclosed
Crew: 4
Weight: 62.09 tons (63,086kg)
Hull length: 31ft 0in (7.92m)
Width: 12ft 0in (3.66m)
Height: 7ft 9in (2.37m)
Engine: Lycoming AGT 1500, multi-fuel gas turbine, 1,500bhp
Road speed: 45mph (72km/hr)
Power/weight: 24.15
Range: 310 miles (500km)

AH-4 Czechoslovakia
CKD
1935. This began as a private commercial venture by the CKD company to produce two light tanks, this being the lighter of the two. Both had a four large roadwheel suspension using leaf springs, with raised front drive sprocket and rear idler. The slope-sided superstructure carried a one-man turret with a 15mm machine gun, and there was an additional 7.92mm machine gun mounted in the hull over the left track, alongside the driver.

Armament: 1 × 15mm MG, 1 × 7.92mm MG
Armour: 15mm
Crew: 2
Weight: 4 tons (4,065kg)
Hull length: 11ft 2in (3.40m)
Width: 6ft 2in (1.87m)
Height: 5ft 10in (1.78m)
Engine: Praga 6-cylinder, petrol, 50bhp
Power/weight: 12.5
Road speed: 25mph (40km/hr)

AH-4SV Czechoslovakia
See Strv m/37

Al-Khalid Pakistan
POF
1998. Also known as **MBT2000**, this tank was developed by Pakistan with assistance from China.

The layout of the vehicle is conventional, the armour is reinforced by a layer of composite armour on the front face, and the main armament is a 125mm smoothbore gun based upon the Russian pattern. An automatic loader, also based upon the Russian design, is fitted, so permitting the employment of a three-man crew. Sights and gun are fully stabilised and a modern computing fire control system is fitted.

Armament: 1 × 125mm; 2 × MG
Ammunition: 39
Armour: not disclosed
Crew: 3
Weight: 47.20 tons (48,000kg)
Hull length: 22ft 8in (6.90m)
Width: 11ft 1in (3.40m)
Height: 7ft 7in (2.30m)
Engine: diesel, 925bhp
Road speed: 34mph (55km/hr)
Power/weight: 19.59
Range: 310 miles (500km)

Alvis-Straussler Light Tank UK
Alvis
1937. Nicolas Straussler was a Hungarian engineer who produced a variety of designs for armoured vehicles and eventually worked for Alvis Ltd in Britain on some of them. The Alvis-Straussler light tank was nothing more than a metal box on tracks and was principally a demonstration vehicle for Straussler's suspension system. Each side had a long suspension arm pivoted at the centre of the tank; at each end was another arm, pivoted in its centre. At the outer ends of this arm were large roadwheels, at the inner end small idler bogie wheels, The track ran round the entire system, and the effect was that as the leading wheel dropped into a hole, the associated bogie would rise, so tending to keep the tank on an even keel. The British War Office watched a demonstration, were impressed, but not sufficiently to adopt it.

Crew: 3
Weight: 9 tons (9,144kg)
Hull length: 15ft 2in (4.62m)
Width: 8ft 3.5in (2.35m)
Height: 6ft 10in (2.09m)
Engine: 2 × Alvis SA
Road speed: 42mph (68km/hr)

Alvis Warrior LMT 105 UK
Alvis
1999. This vehicle is based upon the existing Warrior MICV with the addition of a South African turret and 105mm gun, the LMT 105, together with

the requisite fire control and sighting equipment. The design is currently under development, and the following specification is provisional.

Armament: 1 × 105mm; 1 × MG
Ammunition: 9 + 200
Armour: not disclosed
Crew: 4
Weight: 28.54 tons (29,000kg)
Hull length: 21ft 6in (6.55m)
Width: 10ft 1in (3.08m)
Height: 10ft 6in (3.19m)
Engine: Perkins V-8 diesel, 600bhp at 2,300rpm
Road speed: 47mph (75km/hr)
Power/weight: 21.02
Range: 372 miles (600km)

AMC-34 France
Renault
1934. Not one of the better French designs, this Renault tank was intended for the French mechanised cavalry divisions, and it was, in effect, an up-armoured version of the AMR-33. The first models actually had the turret of the Renault M1917 tank, but this anachronism was soon removed and replaced by a more modern design with a 25mm gun and a co-axial machine gun.

Armament: 1 × 25mm gun; 1 × MG
Armour: 20mm
Crew: 3
Weight: 10.8 tons (10,975kg)
Hull length: 13ft 2in (4.01m)
Width: 7ft 6in (2.29m)
Height: 6ft 9in (2.06m)
Engine: Renault, petrol, 4-cylinder, 120bhp
Power/weight: 11.11
Road speed: 25mph (40km/hr)

AMC-35 France
Renault
1935. Also called the **Renault 35 Medium**, the AMC-35 was an improved model of the AMC-34. The principal structural improvement was in the thicker armour and heavier suspension, a scissors-type arrangement of bogies, while the armament was upgraded to either a short 47mm or a long 25mm gun. The hull overhung the tracks on both sides and the turret was central. Several hundred of these were built and a number went to the Belgians, who fitted their own turret and gun.

Armament: 1 × 47mm or 1 × 25mm; 1 × co-axial MG
Armour: 25mm
Crew: 3
Weight: 14.5 tons (14,735kg)

Hull length: 14ft 7in (4.45m)
Width: 7ft 7in (2.31m)
Height: 6ft 10in (2.08m)
Engine: Renault, petrol, 4-cylinder, 180bhp
Power/weight: 12.41
Road speed: 25mph (40km/hr)

AMR-33 France
Renault
1933. A light and nimble vehicle for use by scouting and reconnaissance troops, this was a two-man machine with a good turn of speed on roads and quite reasonable cross-country performance due to a very compliant suspension. Hull with half-length superstructure, one-man turret with machine gun, four small roadwheels each side on bell-crank suspension, front drive, rear idler.

Armament: 1 × MG
Armour: 13mm
Crew: 2
Weight: 5 tons (5,080kg)
Hull length: 11ft 6in (3.51m)
Width: 5ft 8in (1.73m)
Height: 5ft 3in (1.60m)
Engine: Reinastella, petrol, 8-cylinder, 84bhp
Road speed: 37mph (60km/hr)
Power/weight: 16.8
Range: 85 miles (140km)

AMR-35 France
Renault
1935. Also known as the **Renault ZT** or **Renault 35 Light**, this was an improvement on the AMR-33. Although it was heavier and slower, it was more comfortable for the crew, easier to maintain, and easier to operate. The hull and turret were of riveted construction. There were four roadwheels on each side, with a peculiar Renault design of scissors-type suspension which proved very successful. 200 were built.

Armament: 1 × 25mm cannon or 1 × 13.2mm MG
Armour: 13mm
Crew: 2
Weight: 6.50 tons (6,605kg)
Hull length: 12ft 7in (3.84m)
Width: 5ft 4in (1.63m)
Height: 6ft 2in (1.88m)
Engine: Renault, petrol, 4-cylinder, 85bhp
Road speed: 34mph (55km/hr)
Power/weight: 13.08

AMX-13 France
Roanne, Creusot-Loire

1954. Many people have tried to design a light, airportable tank with a big gun, but few have succeeded so well as the designers of the AMX-13. Work on the design began in 1946 and production in 1954, after which about 4,500 were built, the chassis being used for a series of other vehicles and the tank itself being bought by some 25 countries. The hull and track are unremarkable, with five large roadwheels on each side. The unique feature of this tank was the oscillating turret; the upper portion of the turret was pivoted on trunnions so that it could elevate and depress with the gun. Thus the gun and turret were always at the same relative position and an automatic loader was built into the turret upper section and always moved with the gun. The autoloader had two revolving six-round drums and the gun could thus fire 12 fast shots, but then the crew had to dismount and refill them from the outside.

Armament: 1 x 90mm; 1 x MG
Ammunition: 32 + 3,600
Armour: 40mm
Crew: 3
Weight: 14.76 tons (15,000kg)
Hull length: 16ft 0in (4.88m)
Width: 8ft 3in (2.51m)
Height: 7ft 7in (2.30m)
Engine: SOFAM V-8, petrol, 250bhp at 3,200rpm
Road speed: 37mph (60km/hr)
Power/weight: 16.93
Range: 250 miles (400km)

AMX-30 France
Roanne

1967. The AMX-30 was originally intended to be a joint venture with Germany, but like most of these multi-national projects it fell apart and the Germans went on to build Leopard while the French produced this design. It was highly successful, several thousand having been built and sold abroad in several countries. Production of the chassis continued for some time, since it proved a useful platform for self-propelled guns, rocket launchers and other devices. The welded hull has five roadwheels on each side, with rear drive sprockets, and is topped by a cast turret mounting a powerful 105mm gun. The design has been improved in stages, with more modern fire control equipment, night vision equipment, NBC protection and similar features being added to or improved. In addition there have been bridge-layers, flail tanks and engineer tanks derived from the basic AMX-30.

Armament: 1 x 105mm; 1 x 20mm cannon; 1 x MG
Ammunition: 47 + 1,050 + 2,050
Armour: 81mm
Crew: 4
Weight: 35.43 tons (36,000kg)
Hull length: 21ft 7in (6.59m)
Width: 10ft 2in (3.1m)
Height: 9ft 2in (2.86m)
Engine: Hispano-Suiza, V-12, multi-fuel, supercharged, 720bhp at 2,000rpm
Road speed: 31mph (50km/hr)
Power/weight: 20.32
Range: 375 miles (600km)

AMX-32 France
Roanne

Development of this main battle tank began in 1975, and the first prototype was shown in 1979. Essentially, this was an AMX-30 for the export market. The first prototype was fitted with the same 105mm gun as the AMX-30, the second prototype, which appeared in 1983, had a 120mm gun, but this appears not to have been a very good choice and was not offered for sale. The fire control systems, sights and surveillance equipment were not the same as the standard French Army equipment, and the changes made throughout the vehicle made it heavier, so reducing the performance. Nobody appeared to be interested, and eventually the factory dropped it and concentrated on the AMX-40.

Armament: 1 x 105mm; 1 x 20mm cannon; 1 x MG
Ammunition: 47 + 480 + 2150
Armour: not disclosed
Crew: 4
Weight: 38.38 tons (39,000kg)
Hull length: 21ft 7in (6.59m)
Width: 10ft 7in (3.24m)
Height: 9ft 8in (2.96m)
Engine: Hispano-Suiza HS-110, V-12, multi-fuel, supercharged, 700bhp at 2,400rpm
Road speed: 40mph (65km/hr)
Power/weight: 18.24
Range: 330 miles (530km)

AMX-40 MBT France
AMX (design), Roanne (manufacture)

1983. This was designed purely for the export market, and was a completely new design bearing no relationship to the AMX-30. It was armed with a 120mm gun which had an assisted loading device which made the loader's life a little easier when the tank was moving over rough country. It also had a coaxial 20mm cannon, an idea which appears from time to time but never seems to succeed. The hull was slightly 'kicked up' over the engine compartment and carried on six roadwheels on each side, with rear drive and front idler. It was tested by several Middle Eastern countries in the late 1980s but no one was sufficiently impressed to buy it, and by the early 1990s it was history. But note that this nomenclature was also used for a self-propelled AA gun in the 1950s; *see* entry in the SP section.

Armament: I × 120mm; I × 20mm, I × MG
Ammunition: 40 + 580 + 2,150
Armour: not disclosed
Crew: 4
Weight: 43.00 tons (43,700kg)
Hull length: 22ft 4in (6.80m)
Width: I I ft 0in (3.35m)
Height: 7ft 10in (2.38m)
Engine: Poyayd V-12, diesel, 1300bhp at 2,500rpm
Road speed: 44mph (70km/hr)
Power/weight: 30.23
Range: 340 miles (550km)

Ariete CI Italy
Iveco, OTO-Melara

1990. Developed to meet a specification issued by the Italian Army in 1982, the Ariete ('Ram') is a main battle tank of conventional form, armed with a 120mm smoothbore gun. The hull and turret are of welded steel armour and have an additional layer of composite armour on the frontal surfaces. Gunner and commander both have stabilised sights, and both have access to the ballistic computer/laser rangefinder system of fire control which allows either man to select and engage targets. About 200 Ariete are in service with the Italian Army.

Armament: I × 120mm; 2 × MG
Ammunition: 42 + 2,500
Armour: not disclosed
Crew: 4
Weight: 51.18 tons (52,000kg)
Hull length: 24ft I I in (7.59m)
Width: I I ft 10in (3.60m)
Height: 8ft 3in (2.50m)
Engine: IVECO V-12 turbocharged diesel, 1,200bhp
Power/weight: 23.45
Road speed: 40mph (65km/hr)
Range: 340 miles (550km)

Arjun India
IOF

Development of this main battle tank began in the late 1970s; the first prototype was shown in 1985, but the designers bit off more than they could chew, specifying a 1,500bhp gas turbine engine, hydro-

pneumatic suspension and various other high-technology items, all of which gave problems. The engine specification was changed to an advanced variable-compression-ratio diesel, then fell to buying a ready-made engine and transmission from Germany to propel the first prototype. By 1990 about a dozen prototypes had been built with different engines. Financial constraints then entered the argument, and the most recent information is that production is proceeding slowly, as funds become available, with a view to having 125 tanks in service by 2003.

Armament: I × 120mm; I × MG
Armour: not disclosed
Crew: 4
Weight: 57.08 tons (58,000kg)
Length overall: 32ft 2in (9.80m)
Width: 10ft 5in (3.17m)
Height: 8ft 0in (2.43m)
Engine: MTU 636-Ka501 V-12, diesel, 1,400bhp
Road speed: 45mph (72km/hr)
Power/weight: 24.53
Range: 250 miles (400km)

ARL-44 France
FAMH, Renault, Schneider-Creusot

1945. The design of this tank was begun before war broke out and continued clandestinely whilst France was still under German occupation which, if nothing else, ensured that the design was well thought-out before it ever got to the hardware stage. It is an interesting blend of old and new: one can distinguish the pre-war Char B in the somewhat cumbersome track and suspension arrangements, but the hull is topped by a surprisingly modern three-man turret mounting a long 90mm gun and looking very much as if the designers had been studying an M26 Pershing. The result was one of the tallest tanks ever built and would have been a gift for any anti-tank gunner. Designed by the Atelier de Construction de Rueil, a prototype was built by Renault and St Chamond in co-operation, and was displayed in 1946. The intention was to build 300 of them, but only about 60 were completed, and even that was something of a strain on the postwar French industry.

Armament: I × 90mm; 2 × MG
Armour: not known
Crew: 5
Weight: 45 tons (45,729kg)
Hull length: 34ft 6in (10.52m)
Width: I I ft 2in (3.40m)
Height: 10ft 6in (3.20m)

Engine: Maybach HL230-P4, V-12, petrol, 700bhp at
3,000rpm
Road speed: 23mph (37km/hr)
Power/weight: 15.55
Range: 93 miles (150km)

Armored Gun System USA
See M8 Armored Gun System

Ascod 105 Light Tank Austria/Spain
Steyr-Daimler-Puch, Santa Barbara

1996. Developed by a Spanish/Austrian consortium,
this is the Spanish Ascod mechanised infantry
fighting vehicle which has been modified to accept
the turret and 105mm gun from the South African
Rooikat armoured car. The gun is accompanied by a
computerised fire control system and full day/night
sighting equipment. The resulting vehicle is a lively
and potent light tank which has been demonstrated
to a number of armies but is not yet in production.

Armament: 1 × 105mm; 2 × MG
Ammunition: 40 + 4,600
Armour: not disclosed
Crew: 4
Weight: 28.05 tons (28,500kg)
Hull length: 21ft 8in (6.61m)
Width: 10ft 4in (3.15m)
Height: 9ft 1in (2.76m)
Engine: MTU V-8 diesel, 600bhp at 2,300rpm
Road speed: 43mph (70km/hr)
Power/weight: 21.39
Range: 310 miles (500km)

Avenger A30 UK
Birmingham

1943–44. This was the second attempt at putting the
17-pounder gun into a lengthened Cromwell
chassis (the first having been the Challenger A30).
The turret was less tall but was open-topped,
although it had a cover held some distance above
the turret sides, so that the effect was rather like a
pill-box with vision slits all round. The result was
an effective vehicle and it was put into production as
a self-propelled anti-tank gun in late 1944. The war
ended before the first equipments were delivered,
and the original order for 500 was reduced to about
80, sufficient to equip two SP batteries and provide
for instructional units. They continued in service
until the Royal Artillery gave up the SP anti-tank
role in the early 1950s.

Armament: 1 × 17-pdr; 1 × MG
Ammunition: 55
Armour: 80mm maximum

Crew: 5
Weight: 30.75 tons (31,248kg)
Hull length: 26ft 4in (8.02m)
Width: 9ft 7in (2.90m)
Height: 7ft 3in (2.21m)
Engine: Rolls-Royce Meteor V-12, petrol, 570bhp at
2,500rpm
Road speed: 32mph (51km/hr)
Power/weight: 18.53
Range: 105 miles (170km)

Bernardini MB-3 Argentina
See Tamoyo

Beutepanzerwagen Germany

1918. The German word *beute* means 'booty' or
'loot', and the Beutenpanzerwagen were tanks
'looted' from the British, in other words, captured
or repaired after being found abandoned. There
were three versions; **Beutepanzerwagen 4** was
the British Mark 4 tank; **B-PzW 5** was the British
Mark 5 tank; and **B-PzW A** was the British
Medium A or Whippet. Most details will be found
under 'Tank Mark 4', 'Tank Mark 5' or 'Medium A'.
The only changes made were the substitution of an
ex-Russian 57mm gun for the British 6-pounder
(which was the same calibre and size) and the use of
Maxim machine guns instead of the British Vickers
or Hotchkiss weapons. They were identified as
German by large black crosses painted on the sides.

Black Prince UK
Vauxhall

1945. Black Prince was also called the **Super
Churchill**, which was a fair description since it was
simply the Churchill enlarged and improved and
armed with a 17-pounder gun. It used the same ten-
roadwheel suspension but had all the roadwheels on
the ground, instead of the first and last being on the
track slope, and the entire suspension system was
strengthened. The hull was wider, allowing a larger
turret ring and hence a more roomy turret. Only six
pilots were built, and they were not completed until
mid-1945, after the war in Europe had ended.

Armament: 1 × 17-pdr; 2 × MG
Armour: 150mm maximum
Crew: 5
Weight: 50 tons (50,802kg)
Hull length: 28ft 11in (8.81m)
Width: 11ft 3in (3.42m)
Height: 9ft 0in (2.74m)
Engine: Bedford, flat 12-cylinder, petrol, 350bhp at
2,200rpm

Road speed: 11mph (18km/hr)
Power/weight: 7
Range: 100 miles (160km)

Bob Semple New Zealand

1941. In 1940 New Zealanders had few illusions about Japanese territorial intentions, but not very much in the way of defences. Bob Semple, the Minister of Defence, proposed this 'mobile pillbox', and four were built in 1941. It consisted, quite simply, of a standard International Harvester tracked agricultural tractor enclosed in a box made of welded railway track. There was sufficient room for the driver and three machine-gunners, but the narrow track width and the high centre of gravity due to the additional weight of the steelwork and occupants meant that the vehicle was easily tipped on its side by any minor inequality of the ground. The design was promptly abandoned.

BT Series Medium Tanks Russia
State factories

The BT (*Bystrochodny Tankovy* – 'fast tank') series of Russian tanks were derived from a Christie specimen which the Russians bought in 1930. As with all Christie's tank designs, the only usable part was the suspension, which the Russians embraced with enthusiasm.

BT Variant Models

BT-1

1932. This was a direct copy of the Christie M1931, even to the Liberty engine, and it was therefore a wheel-and-track design A limited number were built, sufficient to give the basic design a thorough testing and indicate how it could be improved.

Armament: 2 x MG
Armour: 13mm maximum
Crew: 3
Weight: 10.0 tons (10,200kg)
Hull length: 18ft 0in (5.49m)
Width: 7ft 4in (2.23)
Height: 6ft 4in (1.92m)
Engine: Liberty-copy V-12, petrol, 350bhp
Road speed (tracks): 40mph (65km/hr)
Road speed (wheels): 65mph (105km/hr)
Power/weight: 34.89

BT-2

1933. This was the same hull as the BT-1 but with a new turret mounting a 37mm gun and one machine gun. This went into volume production and numbers were still in service in 1941.

Other data: as for BT-1, except
Weight: 10.82 tons (11,000kg)

BT-3

1934. This was a further improvement on the BT-1 by adopting solid disc roadwheels instead of spoked, and putting a 45mm gun into the turret instead of the 37mm. Production was limited, and most were later modified by removing the gun and converting the vehicle into a bridge-carrying tank. One or two were modified by fitting a flame-thrower in place of the gun, but that design was not adopted for service.

BT-4

1934. This was similar to BT-3 but had two machine gun turrets side by side instead of a single gun turret. One prototype was made and the idea was then abandoned.

BT-5

1935. This summed up all the lessons learned from the earlier models and went into mass production to form the backbone of the Red Army armoured force in the late 1930s. It had a larger turret with a 45mm gun and a coaxial machine gun, a new engine and improved vision devices.

Armament: 1 x 45mm; 1 x MG
Armour: 13mm
Crew: 3
Weight: 11.31 tons (11,500kg)
Hull length: 18ft 0in (5.49m)
Width: 7ft 4in (2.33m)
Height: 7ft 3in (2.21m)
Engine: V-12 petrol, 350bhp
Road speed (tracks): 40mph (65km/hr)
Road speed (wheels): 70mph (112km/hr)
Power/weight: 30.94

BT-6

1935. This was a commander's tank version of the BT-5, differing only in having a frame antenna around the turret and a radio in the turret bustle.

BT-7

1936. BT-7 was the next improvement, with conical turret, thicker armour, more fuel and ammunition capacity, a ball-mounted machine gun in the rear face of the turret, and a stronger transmission. This went into production to replace the BT-5 and was the major Soviet fighting tank in 1939.

Armament: 1 x 45mm; 2 x MG
Armour: 22mm
Crew: 3

Weight: 13.68 tons (13,900kg)
Hull length: 18ft 7in (5.66m)
Width: 7ft 6in (2.29m)
Height: 7ft 11in (2.42m)
Engine: M17-T V-12, petrol, 500bhp at 1,760rpm
Road speed: 45mph (72km/hr)
Power/weight: 36.55
Range: 265 miles (430km)

BT-7-V

BT-7-V was the commander's tank version of the BT-7, fitted with radio.

BT-7M

Also known as **BT-8** (reports vary), this was a considerably rebuilt BT-7 with a new diesel engine and a full-width sloping glacis plate at the front, instead of the pointed prow of the previous BT designs. It also reverted to the wheel-and-track option which had been dropped in the BT-7, but experience soon showed that beyond amusing the spectators at military exhibitions the system had no other advantages, and it was dropped again. The turret from a T-28 tank was installed, with a short 76.2mm gun and two machine guns. Not many were built as they were largely development pilots.

BT-IS

1939. This was the last of the BT series and was the BT-7M hull carried a step further by sloping the side armour similarly to the glacis plate. The BT-7 turret, with 45mm gun returned, though one gets the feeling that this was simply to fill the hole in the hull roof; what mattered in this design was the hull, engine and transmission, and only the one prototype was built to prove the concept. The whole thing was then transformed into the T-34.

Armament: 1 × 45mm; 2 × MG
Armour: 30mm
Crew: 3
Weight: 15.35 tons (15,600kg)
Hull length: 18ft 11in (5.76m)
Width: 7ft 6in (2.28m)
Height: 7ft 6in (2.28m)
Engine: M17-T V-12, diesel, 500bhp at 1,760rpm
Road speed: 40mph (65km/hr)
Power/weight: 32.57
Range: 250 miles (400km)

CA 32 Medium Tank Italy
Ansaldo

1933. CA = *Carro Armato* = armoured vehicle. The Model 32 was a purely experimental vehicle designed as a test bed for various ideas and mechanisms which Ansaldo put together in order to meet an Italian Army specification for a 'breakthrough tank'. By later standards it would be called an assault gun, since it had a rather tall superstructure with a sloping front, into which a 45mm howitzer and four machine guns fitted in ball mounts. The driver also sat in this central fighting compartment, access to which was by doors in the sides.

Armament: 1 × 45mm howitzer; 4 × MG
Crew: 3
Weight: 12 tons (12,192kg)
Hull length: 16ft 4in (4.98m)
Width: 6ft 0in (1.82m)
Height: 6ft 5in (1.96m)
Engine: 4-cylinder, petrol, 75bhp
Road speed: 14mph (23km/hr)
Power/weight: 6.25

CA 8-ton Light Tank Italy
Ansaldo

1935. Derived from the CA 32 this cut down the superstructure and placed a gun (normally a 37mm) in a fixed barbette mounting on the right front. A turret with two machine guns was then added, above and behind the barbette. A diesel engine replaced the petrol one, the whole vehicle was lightened, and the same articulated bogie suspension was used. It was never put into production but a number of prototypes were built, with small variations, for test purposes.

Armament: 1 × 37mm or 40mm; 2 × MG
Crew: 3
Weight: 8.5 tons (8,640kg)
Hull length: 16ft 4in (4.98m)
Width: 6ft 0in (1.82m)
Height: 6ft 5in (1.96m)
Engine: V-8, diesel, 105bhp
Road speed: 19mph (30km/hr)
Power/weight: 12.34

CA M11/39 Italy
Ansaldo, Fiat

1939. After seeing the vulnerability of their CA 8-ton light tanks during the Spanish Civil War, the Italian Army demanded something heavier and more resistant to enemy gunfire. The result was this M11/39 model, of which about 100 were built. It mounted a 37mm high velocity gun in the hull, to the right of the driver and firing only forward, and one or two machine guns in the small turret on top and to the left side of the superstructure. These tanks were used in the early days of the North African campaigns of 1940–41 but they proved no less vulnerable than their predecessor and were withdrawn by the summer of 1941.

Armament: 1 × 37mm; 2 × MG
Armour: 30mm
Crew: 3
Weight: 11 tons (11,176kg)
Hull length: 15ft 6in (4.72m)
Width: 7ft 1in (2.16m)
Height: 7ft 4in (2.23m)
Engine: V-8, diesel, 105bhp
Road speed: 21mph (34km/hr)
Power/weight: 9.54
Range: 125 miles (200km)

CA M13/40 Italy
Ansaldo, Fiat

1940. Intended to replace the 11/39 with a completely new design, this ended up as no more than an improved 11/39. Slightly bigger and better armoured, it moved the main gun into a larger turret and went from 37mm to 47mm calibre. The hull barbette was reduced in size and given two machine guns. The same articulated bogie suspension was used, and the same diesel engine. Almost 2,000 were built by Fiat and Ansaldo. Late models had a slightly more powerful (145bhp) engine.

Armament: 1 × 47mm; 2 × MG
Armour: 30mm
Crew: 4
Weight: 13.78 tons (14,000kg)
Hull length: 16ft 2in (4.92m)
Width: 7ft 3in (2.20m)
Height: 7ft 10in (2.4m)
Engine: SPA 8 TM40 V-8, diesel, 125bhp
Road speed: 20mph (32km/hr)
Power/weight: 9.07
Range: 125 miles (200km)

CA M15/42 Italy
Ansaldo

1942. The final product of the line of development begun with the 8-ton CA, the 15/42 was a great improvement on the 13/40, even though it retained the same general features. It had a more powerful engine, and a more powerful 47mm gun in a new power-operated turret. Production began in late 1942 but was stopped in March 1943, when only 82 had been made, in favour of assault gun production, using the same hull and running gear.

Armament: 1 × 47mm; 2 × MG
Armour: 30mm
Crew: 4
Weight: 14.37 tons (14,600kg)
Hull length: 16ft 2in (4.92m)
Width: 7ft 3in (2.20m)
Height: 7ft 10in (2.4m)
Engine: SPA 8 TM41 V-8, diesel, 145bhp at 1,900rpm
Road speed: 22mph (35km/hr)
Power/weight: 10.09
Range: 125 miles (200km)

CA P26/40 Heavy Tank Italy
Ansaldo

1943. P = *pesado* = heavy. Ordered in 1940 to fill the heavy tank gap in the Italian armoury, this was undertaken by Ansaldo, and thus the general hull and suspension design resemble those of the medium series. In its final form it had a well-faceted turret set forward on the hull mounting a 34-calibre 75mm gun. Production of 500 was ordered in mid-1942, soon doubled to 1,000, but work did not begin until early 1942 and only a handful had been built by the time of the Italian surrender in September 1943.

Armament: 1 × 75mm; 1 × MG
Armour: 50mm
Crew: 4
Weight: 26 tons (26,420kg)
Hull length: 19ft 1in (5.82m)
Width: 9ft 2in (2.80m)
Height: 8ft 3in (2.52m)
Engine: V-12 diesel, 275bhp
Road speed: 22mph (35km/hr)
Power/weight: 10.57
Range: 150 miles (240km)

CAC Sahariano Italy
Fiat

1942. CAC = *Carro armato celere* = fast armoured vehicle. This was designed after the Italian Army had encountered the British Crusader tank and was more or less copied from that. It had Christie suspension with four large roadwheels, a low profile and a well-sloped turret with a 47mm gun, though a 75mm gun was envisaged as the production standard. As the name implies it was begun with desert warfare in mind, and once the desert campaign was over, the project slowed down and was eventually terminated early in 1943. Full details are not available, but we know it weighed 18 tons, had a four-man crew, a 250bhp petrol engine and a claimed speed of 44mph (70km/hr).

Caernarvon UK
ROF Leeds
1954. Caernarvon was an experimental heavy tank, a step towards Conqueror, which never entered service but acted as a testbed for a number of projects, including a 183mm gun of fearsome power, and a gas turbine engine.

Carden-Loyd Tankettes UK
Carden-Loyd, Vickers
1925–29. The development of this series of vehicles occupied Sir John Carden (who became Vickers' chief tank designer) and Mr Loyd (a *garagiste*) for some years. None was ever adopted for British service, though many were given extended use trials; some were sold overseas and had some influence on foreign design; and some of their features were incorporated into later British light tank and weapon carrier designs. They were designed around the erroneous tactical theory, popular in the 1920s, of providing individual soldiers with armoured machine-gun vehicles; what they were supposed to do with them has never been satisfactorily explained.

The **Carden-Loyd One-Man Tankette** appeared in 1925 and was little more then an open-topped box on tracks, with sufficient room for a man and an engine. The large drive sprocket was at the front, small idler at the rear, and 14 small roadwheels on coil springs were attached to a side-girder. This was then improved into the **Carden-Loyd Mark 1**, which was much the same but with the addition of a small three-sided shield for the occupant, with a mounting for a Hotchkiss light machine gun.

The **Mark 1★** was an attempt at a wheel-and-track design, putting a large pneumatic-tyred road wheel on each side, with a third small wheel centrally at the rear; these could be lowered to save wear and tear on the track, and obtain a faster road speed. Apart from that it was the same as the Mark 1. The **Mark 2** changed the suspension from 14 wheels per side to four, while the **Mark 3** was the Mark 2 with the wheel-and-track conversion.

By 1926 the futility of the one-man design was apparent, and the **Carden-Loyd Two-Man Tankette** appeared; simply the One-Man widened to hold a driver and a machine-gunner side-by-side. It was soon followed by the **Carden-Loyd Mark 4**, which was the two-man fitted with the four-wheel suspension of the Mark 2 and mounting a Vickers machine gun. Then came the **Mark 5**, the inevitable three-wheel wheel-and-track conversion, but for two men and the Vickers gun. The British Army bought eight of these for comparative trials.

By this time some thought had been given to the tactical use of these light machines, and their role as armoured machine-gun carriers, to take a machine gun into position across bullet-swept ground, was envisaged. This led to the last model, the **Mark 6**, which was probably the most practical and workmanlike design of the lot. The body was the same open-topped box, but it now had armoured protection for the transmission, stowage for equipment, a better suspension, and the machine gun could be removed and emplaced upon its normal tripod once the vehicle had reached its destination. Several were sold to foreign countries and the British Army used a number for trials in various applications. Most were scrapped by 1935.

Mark 6
Armament: I × .303in Vickers MG
Armour: 9mm maximum
Crew: 2
Weight: I.5 tons (I,525kg)
Hull length: 8ft I in (2.46m)
Width: 5ft 7in (I.70m)
Height: 4ft 0in (I.22m)
Engine: Ford T, 4-cylinder, petrol, 40bhp
Road speed: 28mph (45km/hr)
Power/weight: 26.6
Range: 60 miles (96km)

Caterpillar G-9 USA
Holt
1917. One of the earliest US tank designs, this was one of several suggestions put forward by the Holt company and probably the only one which even got to the prototype stage. It consisted of the company's standard 10-ton agricultural tractor enclosed in a metal casing with several slots for vision and casual shooting of rifles, topped by a manually-operated revolving turret with a machine gun. The US Army tested it but did not adopt it.

Cavalier (Cruiser Mark 7) UK
Nuffield
1941. By 1941 British soldiers were getting tired of the procession of useless tanks being produced for them and demanded something better. It was to weigh about 24 tons, carry a 57mm gun and have 76mm of frontal armour. Nuffield produced this **A24** or Cavalier in response, generated by using as much of previous cruiser components as possible, stuffing them into a severely rectangular hull with Christie suspension and a very angular but roomy turret. Such was the desperation of the War Office that they gave an order for 500 tanks before a prototype had been built, a calculated gamble in

order to save development time. The gamble failed. Using previous cruiser tank components merely imported most of the defects of the existing designs. The 500 were built but served only as training tanks; some were given dummy guns and used as artillery observers' tanks by SP artillery regiments.

Armament: 1 × 6-pdr; 2 × MG
Armour: 76mm
Crew: 5
Weight: 26.5 tons (26,925kg)
Hull length: 20ft 10in (6.35m)
Width: 9ft 6in (2.88)
Height: 8ft 0in (2.44)
Engine: Nuffield-Liberty, V-12, petrol, 27 litres, 340bhp at 1,500rpm
Road speed: 24mph (39km/hr)
Power/weight: 12.83
Range: 185 miles (300km)

Centaur (Cruiser Mark 8) UK
Leyland

The Centaur, or **A27**, was developed by Leyland Motors to meet the same demand which had produced the Cavalier. It was hoped to use a Rolls-Royce aircraft engine, but at the time (mid-1941) these were desperately needed for aircraft and Leyland were told to use the Nuffield-Liberty as an interim measure. It looked very much like the Cavalier, with the same turret and Christie suspension, and carried a 6-pounder gun; later versions had the British 75mm gun. The **Mark 4** version mounted a 95mm howitzer as a close support tank, and was used by the Royal Marines in the 1944 invasion of France. There was also a **Centaur AA tank** armed with 20mm cannon and a **Centaur dozer**. Due to the shortcomings of the engine and transmission, the Centaur was never issued as a fighting tank, though many were later re-engined to become Cromwells.

Armament: 1 × 6-pdr; 2 × MG
Armour: 76mm
Crew: 5
Weight: 27 tons (27,940kg)
Hull length: 20ft 10in (6.35m)
Width: 9ft 6in (2.88m)
Height: 8ft 0in (2.44m)
Engine: Nuffield-Liberty, V-12, petrol, 27 litres, 340bhp at 1,500rpm
Road speed: 25mph (43km/hr)
Power/weight: 12.59
Range: 175 miles (300km)

Centurion (A41) UK
AEC, Leyland, ROF Leeds, Vickers

1945. This, the first British design of 'universal' tank, was begun in 1944 and the first production models arrived in Germany just in time for the surrender; they saw no action. The tank used Horstmann big-wheel suspension, a partly cast turret, a sloping glacis plate and was armed with a 17-pounder gun with a coaxial 20mm cannon. Later versions did away with the 20mm gun and replaced the 17-pounder with a 20-pounder which later gained a fume extractor.

It first saw combat in Korea, where it became obvious that it was a superb design. It was gradually improved by the adoption of the 105mm L7 gun, with advanced fire control equipment, night vision equipment and other technological advances. It was also widely bought by other countries and was used in combat by the Israeli and Indian Armies. A total of 4,423 were built before production ended in 1962.

Mark 7
Armament: 1 × 20-pdr or 1 × 105mm; 2 × MG
Ammunition: 64 + 4,250
Armour: 152mm
Crew: 4
Weight: 51.0 tons (51,820kg)
Hull length: 25ft 8in (7.82m)
Width: 11ft 2in (3.39m)
Height: 9ft 11in (3.01m)
Engine: Rolls-Royce Meteor 6b, V-12, petrol, 650bhp at 2,550rpm
Road speed: 22mph (35km/hr)
Power/weight: 12.75
Range: 120 miles (190km)

Centurion Variant Models

Mark 1
1945. 17-pounder and 20mm guns, partially cast turret.

Mark 2
1945. 17-pounder gun, MG instead of 20mm; no rear turret machine gun, completely cast turret.

Mark 3
1948. The 20-pounder (84mm) gun replaced the 17-pounder (76mm).

Mark 4
Intended to be close support tank with 95mm howitzer, but never approved for service.

Mark 5
1955. Redesigned turret, .30 Browning MG instead of Besa. AA machine gun added.

Mark 5/1
Mark 5 up-armoured.

Mark 5/2
Mark 5 refitted with 105mm gun.

Mark 6
Mark 5 up-armoured, additional fuel tanks, 105mm gun.

Mark 6/1
Mark 6 with infra-red night vision equipment.

Mark 6/2
Mark 6 with a ranging machine gun for the 105mm gun.

Mark 7
1954. Re-design by Leyland; 20-pounder gun with fume extractor.

Mark 7/1
Mark 7 up-armoured.

Mark 7/2
Mark 7 with 105mm gun.

Mark 8
1956. Mark 7 improved; new gun mantlet, no canvas cover; commander's cupola counter-rotates as turret turns.

Mark 8/1
Mark 8 up-armoured.

Mark 8/2
Mark 8/1 with 105mm gun.

Mark 9
1960. Mark 7 up-armoured and fitted with a 105mm gun.

Mark 9/1
Mark 9 with infra-red night vision equipment.

Mark 9/2
Mark 9 with ranging machine gun.

Mark 10
1960. Mark 8 up-armoured, fitted with 105mm gun, and with ammunition capacity of 70 rounds.

Mark 10
Mark 10 with infra-red night vision equipment.

Mark 10/2
Mark 10 with ranging machine gun.

Mark 11
Mark 6 with ranging machine gun and infra-red night vision sight.

Mark 12
Mark 9 with infra-red night vision equipment and ranging machine gun.

Mark 13
Mark 10 with infra-red night vision equipment and ranging machine gun.

Chaffee USA
See M24 Light Tank

Challenger (A30) UK
Birmingham
1943. The British fixation with giving their tanks names having the initial letter 'C' means that there is a danger of duplication, and this is one of these cases. There is no relationship between this Challenger and the tank developed by Vickers in the 1980s and currently used by the British Army.

Up to 1942 British tanks were generally notable for their unreliability and poor armament. The development of the Cromwell appeared to have conquered the reliability problem, and in 1942 the Birmingham Carriage & Wagon Company, who normally built railway rolling stock, were asked to build a tank armed with the 17-pounder gun on the Cromwell chassis. Challenger was the result. The Cromwell chassis was lengthened, adding one roadwheel to each side, and a new turret, large and tall to accommodate the big gun, went on top of the hull in place of the normal turret. It worked, but the height made it a vulnerable target and the additional weight degraded the performance. Nevertheless, 200 were built and it served for the rest of the war, usually acting as a tank destroyer to support other types of tank.

Armament: 1 × 17-pdr; 1 × MG
Armour: 100mm maximum
Crew: 5
Weight: 31.5 tons (32,000kg)
Hull length: 26ft 4in (8.02m)
Width: 9ft 7in (2.90m)
Height: 8ft 9in (2.66m)
Engine: Rolls-Royce Meteor V-12, petrol, 570bhp at 2,500rpm
Road speed: 31mph (40km/hr)
Power/weight: 18.1
Range: 135 miles (220km)

Challenger 1 UK
ROF Leeds, Vickers
1982. This tank is a representative of the best design thinking of the late 1970s. It is of conventional layout, with the driver in front, turret and fighting compartment central, and engine and transmission at the rear. The skirted suspension has six roadwheels, with the drive at the rear and idler at

the front. The turret is flat and ballistically shaped and carries a 120mm gun. The fire control equipment includes a laser rangefinder, thermal imaging equipment and a ballistic computer and is collectively known as TOGS (Thermal Observation and Gunnery System).

Armament: 1 × 120mm L11; 3 × MG
Ammunition: 64 + 4,000
Armour: not disclosed
Crew: 4
Weight: 61.02 tons (62,000kg)
Hull length: 26ft 3in (8.33m)
Width: 11ft 7in (3.52m)
Height: 8ft 3in (2.50m)
Engine: Perkins Condor V-12, diesel, 1,200bhp at 2,300rpm
Road speed: 35mph (57km/hr)
Power/weight: 19.66
Range: 240 miles (400km)

Challenger 2 UK
Vickers
1992. The Challenger 2 uses the same hull and running gear as the Challenger 1; the turret, though, is different, incorporating completely new fire control and imaging systems. It also incorporates Chobham Series 2 composite armour, and both turret and hull utilise 'stealth' technology to reduce the radar signature. The 120mm gun is of a new pattern, with chromed bore, and the coaxial machine gun is a mechanically-driven Chain Gun.

Armament: 1 × 120mm; 3 × MG
Ammunition: 50
Armour: not disclosed
Crew: 4
Weight: 61.51 tons (62,500kg)
Hull length: 27ft 4in (8.33m)
Width: 11 ft 6in (3.52m)
Height: 8ft 2in (2.49m)
Engine: Perkins Condor V-12 diesel, 1,200bhp
Road speed: 37mph (60km/hr)
Power/weight: 19.2
Range: 285 miles (450km)

Challenger 2E UK
Vickers
1997. Challenger 2E is essentially the same as Challenger 2 but has a more recent fire control system and has adopted a new engine. This saves space which has been used to fit an additional fuel tank, thus extending the operating range.

Armament: 1 × 120mm; 3 × MG
Ammunition: 50

Armour: not disclosed
Crew: 4
Weight: 61.51 tons (62,500kg)
Hull length: 27ft 4in (8.33m)
Width: 11 ft 6in (3.52m)
Height: 8ft 2in (2.49m)
Engine: MTU MT883 Ka501 diesel, 1,500bhp
Road speed: 45mph (72km/hr)
Power/weight: 24
Range: 340 miles (550km

Char 1A France
FCM
1917. In 1916 FCM were asked to develop a heavy 'break-through tank', and this was their first try. Long and low, it was among the first to break away from the all-round track pioneered by the British. It had a low hull with a turret set well forward and a secondary turret facing to the rear. It performed reasonably well on test but, due to the primitive steering and transmission technology of the day, manoeuvring it was difficult and further design work was abandoned.

Armament: 1 × 105mm; 2 × MG
Armour: 35mm
Crew: 7
Weight: 41 tons (41,660kg)
Hull length: 27ft 4in (8.33m)
Width: 9ft 4in (2.84m)
Height: 6ft 6in (1.98m)
Engine: Renault, V-12, petrol, 240bhp
Road speed: 4mph (6.5km/hr)
Power/weight: 5.85

Char 2C France
FCM
1918. This was FCM's second try, and here they used a petrol-electric transmission, driving the tracks independently and thus giving better steering. This had a much deeper hull than the 1A design, but retained the two turrets. Six of the ten built survived to be destroyed by German air attacks in 1940.

Armament: 1 × 75mm; 4 × MG
Armour: 45mm
Crew: 12
Weight: 68 tons (69,100kg)
Hull length: 33ft 8in (10.26m)
Width: 9ft 8in (2.94m)
Height: 13ft 2in (4.01m)
Engine: Mercedes-Benz (two) 180bhp each
Road speed: 10mph (16km/hr)
Power/weight: 5.29

Char 2C *bis* France
FCM
1926. A modified 2C, with heavier armour, wider tracks, new engines and a short 155mm fortress gun in the front turret. Only a few were made. Data as for the 2C except for the gun, two 250bhp engines, and unknown extra weight.

Char B France
FCM, Renault
1929. Three experimental tanks built by FCM and Renault in cooperation, as test-beds for a variety of ideas. They were extensively altered, revised and rebuilt until the result could serve as a production prototype. The design used a deep hull with all-round tracks and a small round turret/cupola on the hull top. Armament consisted of a short 75mm gun in the hull front, together with two machine guns, and a further two machine guns in the turret. No dimensions are given, since they varied from modification to modification.

Armament: 1 × 75mm; 4 × MG
Armour: 40mm maximum
Crew: 4
Weight: 25 tons (25,400kg)
Engine: Renault 5-cylinder, petrol, 180bhp
Road speed: 12mph (20km/hr)
Power/weight: 7.2

Char B-1 France
FCM
1931. This was the production model of the Char B and differed in several respects. The turret was now a cast unit with a commander's cupola, mounting a 47mm gun and a coaxial machine gun. The tracks still reached to the hull top but the ends were lowered to improve the driver's visibility and give the vehicle a lower ground pressure. The hull-mounted 75mm gun remained in the hull front, together with one machine gun. No more than 35 were made by 1935 when it was replaced by the improved **B-1 *bis*** model.

Armament: 1 × 75mm short; 1 × 47mm; 2 × MG
Armour: 40mm
Crew: 4
Weight: 30 tons (30,480kg)
Hull length: 20ft 11in (6.38m)
Width: 8ft 2in (2.49m)
Height: 9ft 3in (2.82m)
Engine: Renault, 6-cylinder, petrol, 180bhp
Road speed: 17mph (28km/hr)
Power/weight: 6
Range: 93 miles (150km)

Char B-1 *bis* France
AMX, FAMH, FCM, Renault, Schneider
1935. The B-1 *bis* was the B-1 improved, and it became the principal tank of the French Army, though only about 365 were built before France collapsed in 1940. Its appearance is very little changed from the B-1, since the improvements lay in up-armouring, a more powerful engine, and a new turret with a more powerful gun.

Armament: 1 × 75mm; 1 × 47mm; 2 × MG
Armour: 60mm maximum
Crew: 4
Weight: 32 tons (32,500kg)
Hull length: 21ft 5in (6.52m)
Width: 8ft 2in (2.50m)
Height: 9ft 2in (2.79m)
Engine: Renault, 6-cylinder, petrol, 307bhp at 1,900rpm
Road speed: 17mph (28km/hr)
Power/weight: 9.59
Range: 93 miles (150km)

Char B-1 ter France
FCM
1938. A further development from the Char B prototypes, this retained the same general layout, with the hull and turret guns, but put a great deal of protective armour around the tracks and suspension, with the side armour sloped, giving the appearance of mud chutes. A prototype was under test when war broke out and the design was forthwith abandoned, since it was obvious that the war would be over by Christmas and the tank could not be produced in that time.

Armament: 1 × 75mm; 1 × 47mm; 2 × MG
Armour: 70mm
Crew: 5
Weight: 36 tons (36,575kg)
Hull length: 20ft 10in (6.35m)
Width: 9ft 0in (2.74m)
Height: 9ft 6in (2.90m)
Engine: Renault, 6-cylinder, petrol, 310bhp
Road speed: 15mph (25km/hr)
Power/weight: 8.61
Range: 93 miles (150km)

Char D-1 France
Renault
1931. Designed as an infantry-accompanying tank, the D-1 had a skirted suspension system of 14 small wheels with coil springs, a rear drive and front idler. The hull was riveted, the turret cast, with the typical Renault 'mushroom' cupola. Armed with a short 47mm gun and provided with a radio, it was

underpowered and unreliable but remained in service until 1940.

Armament: 1 × 47mm; 2 × MG
Armour: 35mm
Crew: 3
Weight: 13 tons (13,200kg)
Hull length: 18ft 11in (5.76m)
Width: 7ft 1in (2.16m)
Height: 7ft 10in (2.39m)
Engine: Renault, 4-cylinder, petrol, 65bhp
Road speed: 11mph (18km/hr)
Power/weight: 5.0
Range: 60 miles (95km)

Char D-I/ST2 France
Renault
1935. Slightly improved D-1 with a new riveted turret. No change in data.

Char D-2 France
Renault
1934. This was the D-1 completely overhauled and given a new cast turret, a more powerful engine, improved suspension and a larger hull. Only 50 were built before production was stopped and the Somua 35 was adopted as its replacement.

Armament: 1 × 47mm gun; 2 × MG
Armour: 40mm
Crew: 3
Weight: 18.5 tons (18,800kg)
Hull length: 17ft 10in (5.43m)
Width: 8ft 9in (2.97m)
Height: 7ft 3in (2.21m)
Engine: Renault 6-cylinder, petrol, 150bhp
Road speed: 14mph (22km/hr)
Power/weight: 8.10
Range: 93 miles (150km)

Char NC-I France
Renault
1927. Although the resemblance is difficult to see, this was actually the Renault FT17 rebuilt in the light of ten years of experience. The hull was longer and better armoured, the track of a more even contour, suspension by three large coil springs with articulated bogies, rear drive and front idler, riveted hull and a cast turret with the usual Renault cupola. For its day, it was a very sound design, but the French Army were not interested and after selling a few to Japan and Yugoslavia, Renault stopped production and went on to develop its successor.

Armament: 1 × 37mm gun or 1 × MG
Armour: 30mm

Crew: 2
Weight: 8 tons (8,130kg)
Hull length: 14ft 6in (4.42m)
Width: 5ft 7in (1.70m)
Height: 7ft 0in (2.13m)
Engine: Renault 4-cylinder, petrol, 60bhp
Road speed: 11mph (18km/hr)
Power/weight: 7.50
Range: 45 miles (75km)

Char NC-2 France
Renault
1931. This was the improved design of NC-1, with a more powerful engine, improved cooling system, more robust tracks, and a new turret. Again the French Army were not interested, but the Greek Army bought several.

Armament: 1 × 37mm gun or 1 × MG
Armour: 35mm maximum
Crew: 2
Weight: 9.5 tons (9,659kg)
Hull length: 14ft 8in (4.47m)
Width: 5ft 2in (1.58m)
Height: 7ft 2in (2.19m)
Engine: Renault, 4-cylinder, petrol, 75bhp
Road speed: 13mph (20km/hr)
Power/weight: 7.89
Range: 50 miles (80km)

Chieftain UK
ROF Leeds, Vickers
1963. Chieftain replaced Centurion and might be said to have been built to the same general principles but with considerable improvements in detail and a completely innovative gun. The front of the hull and the entire turret were cast giving the turret a well-sloped and rounded profile to deflect shot, and the main armament was a 120mm gun using combustible charges and not the usual brass cartridge case. About 800 were built for the British Army and a further 450 or so for export to Iran, Iraq, Jordan, Kuwait and Oman.

Mark 3/3
Armament: 1 × 120mm; 2 × MG
Ammunition: 54 + 6,000
Armour: not disclosed
Crew: 4
Weight: 54.13 tons (55,000kg)
Hull length: 24ft 8in (7.52m)
Width: 11ft 6in (3.50m)
Height: 9ft 6in (2.90m)
Engine: Leyland, vertically-opposed 12-piston two-stroke, multi-fuel, 750bhp at 2,100rpm
Road speed: 30mph (48km/hr)

Power/weight: 13.85
Range: 310 miles (500km)

Chieftain Variant Models

Mark 1
1965. 585bhp engine.

Mark 1/2
Mark 1 brought up to Mark 2 standard.

Mark 1/3
Mark 1 with new power train.

Mark 1/4
Mark 1 with new power train and modified ranging machine gun.

Mark 2
1967. 650bhp engine. This was the first model issued for service, the earlier marks being for training only.

Mark 3
1969. Improvements to auxiliary generator, air cleaners, and cupola.

Mark 3/G
Prototype only; improved engine air supply.

Mark 3/2
Variation of Mark 3/G.

Mark 3/S
Production version of 3/G with addition of commander's firing switch.

Mark 3/3
Improved Mark 3 with extended range ranging machine gun, laser rangefinder, 720bhp engine, modified air cleaners, improved NBC equipment.

Mark 4
Increased fuel capacity, minor modifications. Only four built.

Mark 5
Improved Mark 3; stronger transmission, improved sights, improved exhaust system, greater ammunition capacity, new NBC pack.

Mark 5/2
Version of Mark 5 produced for Kuwait.

Mark 5/3P
Version of Mark 5 for Iranian Army.

Mark 6
Mark 2 with Mark 3/3 power train.

Mark 7
Mark 3 or 3/S with improved engine and ranging machine gun.

Mark 8
Mark 3/3 with improved engine and ranging machine gun.

Mark 9
Mark 6 with Integrated Fire Control System.

Mark 10
Mark 7 with Integrated Fire Control System.

Mark 11
Mark 8 with Integrated Fire Control System.

Mark 12
Mark 5 with Integrated Fire Control System.

Chi-Ha Japan
See Type 97 Medium

Christie M1919 USA
Front Drive

J. Walter Christie was either a brilliant designer or a certifiable lunatic; it depended upon who was describing him. An ordnance engineer, designer of heavy gun mountings for coast defence artillery, he was bitten by the automotive bug in the early 1900s. In about 1912 he set up the Front Drive Motor company to build trucks and fire engines, and when America entered the war he turned his attention to making tracked gun mountings for a 3-inch AA gun and an 8-inch howitzer. They worked, if not very well, and the US Army encouraged him to improve them. But Christie now demonstrated his most characteristic attitude: he was tired of self-propelled gun mountings, and went off to design tanks instead.

The first to appear was this M1919, based on a truck chassis but with a turret mounting a 57mm gun, surmounted by a cupola with a machine gun. The track could be removed and the vehicle could then run on its wheels, a feature which Christie retained on almost all his designs. The US Army was not impressed.

Armament: 1 × 57mm; 1 × MG
Armour: 25mm
Crew: 3
Weight: 13.5 tons (13,720kg)
Hull length: 18ft 2in (5.54m)
Width: 8ft 6in (2.59m)
Height: 8ft 9in (2.66m)
Engine: Christie 6-cylinder, petrol, 120bhp
Road speed: 7mph
Power/weight: 8.88

Christie M1921 USA
Front Drive

This was simply a re-arrangement of the M1919; the guns were fitted into a steeply-sloped front hull plate, with the driver and commander seated behind the gunner and having a raised superstructure to give them a higher vision line. The engine and transmission were at the rear, with rear drive, and the tracks could be removed for road travel. The US Army were still not impressed and Christie went off to design an amphibious vehicle for the Marine Corps.

Armament: 1 × 57mm, 1 × MG
Armour: 20mm
Crew: 3
Weight: 14 tons (14,225kg)
Hull length: 18ft 2in (5.53m)
Width: 7ft 6in (2.29m)
Height: 7ft 1in (2.16)
Engine: Christie, 6-cylinder, petrol, 120bhp
Road speed: 14mph (23km/hr)
Power/weight: 8.57

Christie M1928 USA
US Wheel & Track

1930. Christie now set up the US Wheel and Track-Layer Corporation and returned to AFV design with his one and only lasting contribution to tank design: the Christie suspension. This used large roadwheels (large enough to act as the return rollers for the top run of track) carried on coil spring suspension capable of a very large range of movement, so that the track could accommodate itself to any terrain, The vehicle had no turret, since it was merely a demonstrator of the mechanical aspects of the design, and not intended as a practical tank, although Christie sometimes stuck a machine gun on to remind his potential customers of the ultimate aim. This design achieved some success; the US Army ordered five, the Russians bought two, and the Poles ordered two but defaulted on the contract and these were later bought by the US Army.

Armament: none, see text
Armour: 13mm
Crew: 3
Weight: 8.6 tons (8,740kg)
Hull length: 17ft 0in (5.18m)
Width: 7ft 0in (2.13m)
Height: 6ft 0in (1.82m)
Engine: Liberty V-12, petrol, 338bhp
Road speed, wheels: 70mph (113km/hr)
Road speed, tracks: 42mph (68km/hr)
Power/weight: 39.30
Range: not known

Christie M1931 USA
US Wheel & Track

1931. These were actually the five M1928 tanks ordered by the US Army; by the time they were built and delivered, Christie had had a few more ideas and the design had changed in some respects. It now had a sharply-sloped and pointed glacis plate and a fully evolving turret mounting a 37mm M1916 Trench Cannon and a coaxial machine gun. Originally called the **T3 Medium Tank**, four were delivered to the US Cavalry and were re-christened the **Combat Car T1**, since by law only infantry could operate tanks. (For the subsequent Christie designs *see* T3E1 Medium Tank.)

Armament, Tank T3: 1 × 37mm; 1 × MG
Armament, CC T1: 1 × .50in MG, 1 × .30in MG
Armour: 13mm maximum
Crew: 3
Weight: 10.2 tons (10,360kg)
Hull length: 18ft 0in (5.49m)
Width: 7ft 4in (2.23m)
Height: 7ft 6in (2.29m)
Engine: Liberty V-12, petrol, 338bhp
Road speed, wheels: 46mph (75km/hr)
Road speed, tracks: 27mph (43km/hr)
Power/weight: 33.14

Churchill (A20/A22) UK
Vauxhall

1941. In 1939 there were many people in Britain who thought that the war would be a repetition of the 1914–18 affair and that a heavy, slow, infantry-accompanying tank would be needed. Harland and Wolff built a first A20 prototype to meet this demand, but it proved to be under-powered and was abandoned. Vauxhall Motors were then handed the specification for the A22 in mid-1940 and began by designing a suitable engine, after which they modified the A20 to fit. Easily recognisable from its all-round track and small-wheel suspension. First models had a 3-inch howitzer in the hull front, but this was soon dropped and a machine gun fitted. Turret armament began with a 2-pounder gun but was gradually increased to 6-pounder and then 75mm, and in the close support role a 95mm howitzer was fitted. After initial troubles, it became a reliable and well-liked machine which remained in service until the 1950s.

Mark 7 (Unless otherwise noted)
Armament: 1 × 2-pdr, or 6-pdr, or 75mm, or 95mm (see text); 2 × MG
Ammunition: 84 × 6-pdr; 2,700 × MG
Armour, Mks 7 & 8: 152mm
Crew: 5

Weight: 40 tons (40,645kg)
Hull length: 24ft 5in (7.44m)
Width: 11ft 4in (3.45m)
Height: 9ft 0in (2.74m)
Engine: Bedford 12-cylinder, petrol, 350bhp
Road speed: 15mph (24km/hr)
Power/weight: 8.75
Range: 88 miles (140km)

Churchill Variant Models

Mark 1
Tank, Infantry, Mark 4. 3-inch howitzer in hull, 2-pounder and Besa MG in turret.

Mark 2
Besa MG instead of 3-inch howitzer in hull.

Mark 2CS
3-inch howitzer in turret, 2-pounder in hull.

Mark 3
6-pounder gun in welded turret.

Mark 4
As for Mark 3, but with cast turret.

Mark NA75
Special conversion in North Africa, fitting the 75mm gun and coaxial Browning MG from a Sherman tank into the Churchill turret.

Mark 5
95mm howitzer in turret.

Mark 6
As for Mark 4 but British 75mm turret gun.

Mark 7
Complete re-design, heavier armour, 75mm gun.

Mark 8
As for 7 but with 95mm howitzer.

Mark 9
A Mark 3 or 4 rebuilt to Mark 7 standard of armour but retaining the original armament.

Mark 10
Mark 5 reworked as for Mark 8.

Mark 11
Mark 6 reworked as for Mark 8.

Close Combat Vehicle (Light) USA
See FMC CCV(L)

Clovis France/Germany
Thyssen-Henschel
1986. Described as a 'Multi-Role Combat Tank', this was little more than the German Marder MICV with a turret carrying a 105mm gun. It was put together as a cooperative effort by Thyssen-Henschel of Germany (the hull) and Fives-Cail-Babcock of France (the turret and gun). The conversion was done so that there was still a limited troop-carrying ability, five fully-equipped infantrymen having a troop compartment to themselves, with access via a rear door. It seemed a good idea at the time, but it failed to rouse any interest and was abandoned by 1990.

Armament: 1 × 105mm; 1 × 20mm coaxial; 3 × MG
Ammunition: 79 + 400 + 2,500
Armour: not disclosed
Crew: 3 + 5
Weight: 31.59 tons (32,100kg)
Hull length: 22ft 1in (6.73m)
Width: 10ft 8in (3.24m)
Height: 8ft 11in (2.72m)
Engine: MTU diesel, 750bhp
Road speed: 43mph (70km/hr)
Power/weight: 23.74
Range: 375 miles (600km)

Combat Cars USA
Rock Island
'Combat Car' was a euphemism forced upon the US Cavalry by the wording of the National Defense Act of 1920, which laid down that tanks would be operated only by infantry. As mechanisation began to take effect and tanks were allocated to cavalry for trial purposes, they were re-named 'Combat Cars' and the 37mm gun in the turret replaced by a .50-inch heavy machine gun.

Combat Car M1 USA
Rock Island
1937. This was the standardized version of the Combat Car T5E2. It had many of the features which became familiar on later US tanks, such as the vertical volute spring suspension, the sloping front plate and transmission cover, the star-like drive sprocket and the high superstructure necessitated by the radial engine. About 170 were manufactured and issued to mechanised cavalry regiments. In 1940, with the formation of the Armored Force, the restriction on nomenclature ended and this became the **Light Tank M1A2**.

Armament: 3 × MG
Armour: 16mm
Crew: 4
Weight: 9.7 tons (9,855kg)
Hull length: 13ft 7in (3.83m)
Width: 7ft 10in (2.39m)
Height: 7ft 5in (2.26m)

Engine: Continental 9-cylinder, radial, petrol, 250bhp
Road speed: 45mph (72km/hr)
Power/weight: 25.77

Combat Car M1E1 USA
Rock Island

1937. Combat Car M1 fitted with a Guiberson diesel engine, which was a conversion of the Continental radial to diesel operation. Only trials models made.

Combat Car M1E2 USA
Rock Island

1937. An improved M1; the rear part of the hull was re-contoured so as to permit easier access to the engine, the fuel capacity was increased, and the rear bogie was moved back about a foot in order to distribute the weight more evenly.

Armament: 4 × MG
Armour: 16mm
Crew: 4
Weight: 8.72 tons (8,858kg)
Hull length: 14ft 7in (4.44m)
Width: 7ft 10in (2.39m)
Height: 7ft 5in (2.26m)
Engine: Continental, 9-cylinder, radial, 250bhp
Road speed: 45mph (73km/hr)
Power/weight: 28.66

Combat Car M1E3 USA
Rock Island

1938. The E3 was purely a trials vehicle; it was a standard M1E2 but with various types of front drive sprocket and rear idler to suit a variety of experimental track designs, from rubber-backed to rubber-block types.

Combat Car M1A1 USA
Rock Island

1938. This was the M1E2 with new transmission, with the turret moved to the left side of centre, and with radio fitted.

Dimensions: as for the M1E2

Combat Car M1A1E1 USA
Rock Island

1938. The M1A1 fitted with the Guiberson diesel engine; made only in small numbers.

Combat Car M2 USA
Rock Island

1939. The last of the Combat Cars, this was simply the M1E2 with a few minor improvements to the turret and with the Guiberson diesel engine. As it began to enter service in 1940, so the restriction was lifted and it became the **Light Tank M1A1**.

Dimensions: as for the M1E2

Combat Cars, T series USA

The full series of developmental Combat Cars is as follows:

Combat Car T1
Was the Christie M1931 (*qv*).

Combat Car T2
1931. Convertible (wheel-and-track) design made by adding a front drive sprocket, rear idler and all-round tracks to a 6 x 6 armoured car.

Combat Car T2E1
1932. A T2 with rear transmission and drive sprocket, no front sprocket or idler.

Combat Car T3
1934. T5 (see below) fitted with a Guiberson diesel engine (a conversion of the Continental radial aircraft engine)

Combat Car T4
1933. Christie-type wheel-and-track tank designed and built by the Ordnance Department. Generally resembled Christie's designs but had the turret more centrally placed in the hull.

Combat Car T4E1
1935. A T4 but with a sloping front glacis, a built-up hull, and a two-machine gun turret. It is possible to see in this the germ of the wartime designs.

Armament: 6 × MG
Armour: 13mm
Crew: 3
Weight: 8.93 tons (9,070kg)
Hull length: 16ft 1in (4.90m)
Width: 7ft 7in (2.31m)
Height: not known
Engine: Continental 9-cylinder, radial, 264bhp
Speed, tracks: 25mph (40km/hr) tracks
Power/weight: 29.5

Combat Car T4E2
1934. The hull and running gear of the T2E1 but with the turret removed and replaced by an open-topped barbette mounting a .50-inch machine gun firing forward.

Combat Car T5

1935. Generally similar to the T2E1 Light Tank, this abandoned the Christie suspension for the volute spring type developed by Rock Island. Front drive sprocket, two two-wheel bogies and rear idler on each side. Sloped glacis plate, hull machine gun in front, twin machine gun turret.

Armament: 3 × MG
Armour: 16mm
Crew: 4
Weight: 9.70 tons (9,855kg)
Hull length: 13ft 4in (4.06m)
Width: 7ft 6in (2.29m)
Height: 6ft 8in (3.03m)
Engine: Continental 9-cylinder, radial, petrol, 264bhp
Road speed: 36mph (58km/hr)
Power/weight: 27.21

Combat Car T5E1

1935. As for the T5 but with the turrets removed and replaced by a fixed superstructure with a small commander's cupola.

Combat Car T5E2

1936. This more or less reverted to the T5 design but had a single turret with twin machine guns. It was standardised as the **Combat Car M1** in 1937.

Combat Car T7

1938. A wheel-and-track design arrived at by fitting the Combat Car T5 with three pneumatic-tyred roadwheels on each side (turning it into a six-wheeled armoured car) and then lengthening the hull and adding new front and rear sprockets and a removable track. The wheels were also fitted with large steel skeleton discs which were apparently needed to keep the track in its proper place.

Armament: 3 × MG
Armour: 16mm
Crew: 4
Weight: 10.7 tons (10,870kg)
Hull length: 16ft 8in (4.98m)
Width: 8ft 8in (2.64m)
Height: 8ft 1in (2.46m)
Engine: Continental, 9-cylinder radial, 250bhp
Road speed, wheels: 53mph (85km/hr)
Road speed, tracks: 24mph (38km/hr)
Power/weight: 23.36

Comet (A34) UK
Leyland

1945. Widely hailed as the first British tank with a reasonable chance of survival on the battlefield, the Comet was the perfection of the Cruiser/Cromwell line of development. It had the same flat-fronted driver's compartment and glacis plate sunk between the tracks, and the most sure way of telling it apart from a Cromwell is the presence of three return rollers on each side of the Comet, where the Cromwell and its other derivatives have none.

Armament: 1 × 77mm; 2 × MG
Ammunition: 61 + 5,175
Armour: 101mm
Crew: 5
Weight: 32.7 tons (33,223kg)
Hull length: 21ft 6in (6.55m)
Width: 10ft 1in (3.07m)
Height: 8ft 8in (2.67m)
Engine: Rolls-Royce Meteor, V-12, petrol, 600bhp at 2,550rpm
Road speed: 32mph (50km/hr)
Power/weight: 18.35
Range: 125 miles (200km)

Conqueror UK
ROF Leeds

1956. In many ways, the last of the wartime designs, since it was the last to preserve the distinction between cruiser and capital tanks. Modern technology had not yet arrived and the result was a huge and ponderous vehicle which demanded considerable logistic support. The gun was a 120mm, derived from the American 4.7-inch AA gun and using a large brass cartridge case, necessitating a very roomy turret. Suspension was by an eight-wheeled Horstmann array on each side, and the huge turret was a complex casting. It was never entirely reliable and the army got rid of them within seven years, replacing them with Chieftain.

Armament: 1 × 120mm gun L1; 1 × MG
Ammunition: 54
Armour: 200mm
Crew: 4
Weight: 65.0 tons (66,045kg)
Hull length: 38ft 0in (11.58m)
Width: 13ft 1in (3.98m)
Height: 11ft 0in (3.35m)
Engine: Rolls-Royce M120, V-12, petrol, 810bhp at 2,800rpm
Road speed: 21mph (34km/hr)
Power/weight: 12.46
Range: 95 miles (150km)

Covenanter UK
See Cruiser Mark 5 below

Crocodile UK

1942. Crocodile was the Churchill Mark 7 tank fitted with a flame gun in the hull front plate. The Crocodile equipment consisted of an armoured trailer in which were five nitrogen cylinders and 400 gallons (1,818 litres) of FTF (Flame Thrower Fluid – a thickened petrol mixture.) The flame gun was mounted in the hull front in place of the usual machine gun. Connection of trailer and tank was by a special link, which could be broken by remote control from inside the tank should the trailer sustain damage or when the flame fuel was expended; afterwards the tank could revert to normal operation since it still carried its normal turret armament. The trailer weighed 6 tons when loaded. A total of 800 Crocodile kits were built; production tanks were made with the various necessary attachment points, and any Churchill Mark 7 could be converted to a Crocodile tank in the field by fitting the components from the kit. The equipment remained in service after the war and some Crocodiles were used in Korea in 1951–52.

Specifications: generally as for Churchill Mk 7, and see text

Cromwell UK

See Cruiser Mark 8 below

Crossley-Martel UK
Crossley

1927. Another of the one-man 'Tankette' designs which proliferated in the middle 1920s, this was built by the Crossley Motor Company to a plan drawn up by Colonel G. le Q. Martel, a Tank Corps officer. It differed from earlier Martel designs in being a half-track with the steered wheels at the front, using the Crossley-Kégresse suspension unit, a small tracked assembly with three small roadwheels. It appears to have been bought by the British Army and used as a testbed for various types of track.

Armament: 1 × MG
Armour: 10mm
Crew: 1
Weight: 1.8 tons (1,930kg)
Hull length: 10ft 0in (3.05m)
Width: 4ft 9in (1.45m)
Height: 5ft 4in (1.62m)
Engine: Crossley, 4-cylinder, petrol, about 45bhp
Road speed: 20mph (32km/hr)
Power/weight: 25.0

Cruisers A14 and A16 UK
LMS (A14), Nuffield (A16)

1937. Whilst the Cruisers Marks 1–3 appeared to be satisfactory, the War Office were still apprehensive; they felt that more armour was required so that the cruisers could go in and mix it with the battleships, and they called for two more designs, the **A14** and **A16**. The A14 pioneered the Horstmann small-wheel suspension, later used on several designs, while the A16 was by Nuffield and used a Christie suspension with five large roadwheels.

A prototype of A14 was built and tipped the scales at 29 tons; with a 500bhp Thornycroft marine engine this had a power-weight ratio of 17.2, well down on the A13, and a top speed of less than 25mph, also a disappointment. The A16 promised to weigh about 22 tons, but it was obvious that it, too, would be no advance on the A13, and both projects were abandoned in 1939.

Cruiser Mark 1 UK
Vickers

1938. The armoured warfare theorists of the 1920s and 1930s were much taken with the naval analogy of 'fleets' of tanks, manoeuvring across open country like fleets of warships. It followed from this that the tanks could be compared to the ships; the heavy tank was the battleship, the light tank was the destroyer. Which left a gap in the middle, which simply had to be the cruiser.

In 1934 a design was called for to replace the ageing Vickers Medium tanks in British Army service, and the **A9** or Cruiser Mark 1 was the result, from the Vickers drawing office. A good design on paper, in real life the suspension was bad, the tracks came off and the crew were cramped. The suspension was gradually improved and the Cruiser Mark 1 performed creditably in the early part of the desert war in 1941. Principal recognition feature is the pair of subsidiary machine gun turrets on the front corners of the hull.

Armament: 1 × 2-pdr; 3 × MG
Armour: 14mm
Crew: 5
Weight: 12 tons (12,190kg)
Hull length: 19ft 3in (5.86m)
Width: 8ft 4in (2.53m)
Height: 8ft 4in (2.53m)
Engine: AEC, 6-cylinder, petrol, 150bhp
Road speed: 25mph (40km/hr)
Power/weight: 12.50
Range: 95 miles (150km)

Cruiser Mark 2 UK
Vickers

1938. This, called the **A10** during its gestation, was similar to the Mark 1 but did away with the subsidiary turrets and placed a machine gun in the hull alongside the driver. The armour was thicker, which increased the weight and decreased the performance. Like the Mark 1, the Mark 2 saw service in the early years of the war, but it was never entirely reliable.

Armament: 1 × 2-pdr; 2 × MG
Armour: 30mm maximum
Crew: 5
Weight: 13.75 tons (13,970kg)
Hull length: 18ft 1in (5.51m)
Width: 8ft 4in (2.52m)
Height: 8ft 6in (2.59)
Engine: AEC, 6-cylinder, petrol, 150bhp
Road speed: 20mph (32km/hr)
Power/weight: 10.91
Range: 93 miles (150km)

Cruiser Mark 3 UK
Nuffield

1938. The A9 and A10 turned out not to have sufficient speed across country to justify their description as 'cruisers', so a fresh design was called for from the Nuffield mechanisation company. This adopted the large-wheel suspension developed by Christie in the USA, which promised better cross-country performance. This, the **A13**, became the Cruiser Mark 3. It had an odd slab-sided and angular turret, four roadwheels on each side, with the rear pair closer set than the others, and rear drive. The design was good, and it had the desired speed, but the construction was faulty; the Nuffield organisation had a lot to learn about building tanks.

Armament: 1 × 2-pdr; 1 × MG
Armour: 14mm
Crew: 4
Weight: 14 tons (14,224kg)
Hull length: 19ft 9in (6.01m)
Width: 8ft 4in (2.53m)
Height: 8ft 6in (2.59m)
Engine: Liberty, V-12, petrol, 340bhp
Road speed: 31mph (50km/hr)
Power/weight: 24.28
Range: 108 miles (175km)

Cruiser Mark 4 UK
Nuffield

1938. This was a second version of the **A13**, with thicker armour to give the crew better protection.

Armament: 1 × 2-pdr; 1 × MG
Armour: 30mm
Crew: 4
Weight: 14.76 tons (15,000kg)
Hull length: 19ft 9in (6.01m)
Width: 8ft 4in (2.53m)
Height: 8ft 6in (2.59m)
Engine: Liberty, V-12, petrol, 340bhp
Road speed: 27mph (45km/hr)
Power/weight: 23.03
Range: 95 miles (150km)

Cruiser Mark 5 (Covenanter) UK
LMS

1940. The demand for a heavier cruiser persisted, and the London, Midland & Scottish Railway Company was invited to try its hand. The LMS produced a low-set Christie-suspended vehicle with a powerful purpose-built engine, and a 'squashed lozenge' turret with angled sides to deflect shot. Again, the design was good but the execution poor; the radiator was at the front, the engine at the rear, and the connecting pipes, in the words of one critic 'served the dual purpose of cooling the engine and roasting the crew.' The problems were intractable and the tank was never used in combat.

Armament: 1 × 2-pdr; 1 × MG
Armour: 40mm
Crew: 4
Weight: 18 tons (18,290kg)
Hull length: 19ft 0in (5.79m)
Width: 8ft 7in (2.61m)
Height: 7ft 4in (2.23m)
Engine: Meadows flat-12 cylinder, petrol, 300bhp
Road speed: 31mph (50km/hr)
Power/weight: 16.66
Range: 95 miles (150km)

Cruiser Mark 6 (Crusader) UK
Nuffield

1940. Nuffield, not having designed Covenanter, wanted nothing to do with manufacturing it, and set about developing their own design, which became **A15** or Crusader. It followed the same general lines as Covenanter, with a similar Christie suspension and angular turret. It added two machine gun cupolas at the front, one of which was the driver's station, and why he was provided with a gun when he presumably already had enough to do was never fully explained. It was removed in the **Mark 2** version, which also added more armour. The **Crusader Mark 3** put a 6-pounder gun into the turret. It was still far from perfect and still unreliable, but it was better than nothing; some 4,500 of all marks were built and many saw combat in North Africa.

Mark 2
Armament: 1 × 2-pdr or 1 × 6-pdr; 3 × MG, later reduced to 2 then 1 (variations according to Mark)
Ammunition: 110 (2-pdr) + 4,500
Armour: 50mm
Crew: 5
Weight: 19 tons (19,300kg)
Hull length: 19ft 8in (5.98m)
Width: 8ft 8in (2.64m)
Height: 7ft 4in (2.23m)
Engine: Nuffield-Liberty, V-12, petrol, 27 litres, 340bhp at 1,500rpm
Road speed: 28mph (45km/hr)
Power/weight: 17.89
Range: 200 miles (320km)

Cruiser Mark 7 UK
See Cavalier

Cruiser Mark 8 (Cromwell) UK
Leyland
1943. This is the design which Leyland Motors wanted to build in the first place; it is, essentially, the Centaur but with a Rolls-Royce Meteor engine (which was a de-rated version of the Merlin aircraft engine) and an improved transmission. A distinguishing feature of Cromwell was the turret, studded with large armour bolts and with an internal mantlet. Like the Centaur it began with a 6-pounder gun, but there was ample room for improvement and it was more usually seen with either the 75mm gun or the 95mm howitzer.

Cromwell was the last of the so-called cruiser tanks, and the only one which was anything like reliable enough for extended use in combat. But it was still seriously under-gunned and was at a severe disadvantage against the more powerful German machines in North-West Europe in 1944–45.

Armament: 1 × 6-pdr, or 1 × 75mm, or 1 × 95mm; 1 × MG
Ammunition: 64 + 4,950
Armour: 102mm
Crew: 5
Weight: 27.5 tons (27,945kg)
Hull length: 20ft 10in (6.34m)
Width: 10ft 0in (3.04m)
Height: 9ft 4in (2.83m)
Engine: Rolls-Royce Meteor V-12, petrol, 25 litres, 600bhp at 2,250rpm
Road speed: 40mph (65km/hr)

Power/weight: 21.82
Range: 170 miles (275km)

Crusader UK
See Cruiser Mark 6

CTL USA
See Marmon-Herrington

CV 29 Italy
Ansaldo
1929. CV = *Carro veloce* = fast vehicle. This was derived directly from the Carden-Loyd Mark 6 tankette, four of which were bought by Italy. The only significant change is the addition of overhead cover for the driver and gunner in the form of individual conical cupolas.

Armament: 1 × MG
Armour: 9mm maximum
Crew: 2
Weight: 1.7 tons (1,730kg)
Hull length: 8ft 2in (2.49m)
Width: 5ft 7in (1.70m)
Height: 4ft 0in (1.22m)
Engine: Ford T, 4-cylinder, petrol, 40bhp
Road speed: 25mph (40km/hr)
Power/weight: 23.5
Range: 50 miles (80km)

CV 33 Tankette Italy
Ansaldo, Fiat
1933. Probably the most produced of all Italian armoured vehicles, this was developed from the CV 29 and is more or less that vehicle but with the crew compartment roofed over and with one or two machine guns in the front face of the armour. About 2,000 were made, including a number of variant models such as a commander's vehicle (with radio but no weapons), flame-thrower, bridge-layer (*see below*), anti-tank rifle carrier, anti-aircraft machine gun carrier, and various types of improved or experimental suspension. It was also widely sold overseas.

Armament: 1 or 2 × MG
Armour: 15mm
Crew: 2
Weight: 3.15 tons (3,200kg)
Hull length: 10ft 5in (3.17m)
Width: 4ft 8in (1.42m)
Height: 4ft 3in (1.30m)
Engine: Fiat, 4-cylinder, petrol, 42bhp
Road speed: 26mph (42km/hr)

Power/weight: 13.33
Range: 78 miles (125km)

CV-90-120 Sweden
See Hagglund

CVR(T) Family UK
Alvis
1963. The Combat Vehicle, Reconnaissance (Tracked) family of vehicles comprises the Scorpion, Striker, Scimitar, Spartan, Stormer, Samson, Samaritan and Sultan, details of which will be found under those names.

DP-2 Amphibious Tank France
Schneider
1935. An amazingly advanced design for its day, this was a private venture which failed to interest the French Army, probably because the prototype sank on its first venture into water. The hull was boat-shaped, with a sharp prow and a large lozenge-shaped flotation sponson over each track. The track was kept low and there was a small turret carrying a heavy machine gun. Water propulsion was by a propeller at the stern.

Armament: 1 × MG
Armour: 16mm maximum
Crew: 3
Weight: 12 tons
Engine: Hispano-Suiza, V-12, petrol, 228bhp
Road speed: 25mph
Water speed: 4mph
Power/weight: 19

Disston Tractor Tank USA
Disston
1933. This was not a vehicle, rather a bolt-on kit of armour produced by the Disston Company, which was designed to fit around a standard commercial Caterpillar D-2 tracked tractor and convert it into a two-man tank. The 'body' was simply two rectangles enclosing the engine and cab, and above the latter portion was a small revolving turret with a machine gun mounting, into which a variety of weapons could be fitted. A second machine gun could be fitted into the cab front plate, presumably to be operated by the driver. A few of these kits appear to have been sold, and there is in existence a photograph of one in Afghanistan in the late 1930s, but none has survived and no details appear to have been recorded.

Duck UK
See Tank Mark 9, Amphibious

E-100 Germany
Adler
1943–45. The development of this super-heavy tank was carried on as a form of insurance against the failure of the Maus super-heavy tank project. Work almost stopped in late 1944 when Hitler ordered concentration of effort on assault guns, but the prototype chassis was almost completed when the war ended. Unlike Maus, it was a conventional German design, using interleaved roadwheels, front drive, rear engine and externally sprung suspension. No turret was ever built for this tank. The data given below are based upon the prototype chassis, captured in 1945, and examination of relevant documents; in view of the poor power/weight ratio, the road speed seems a trifle optimistic.

Armament: 1 × 17cm; 1 × MG
Ammunition: 200
Armour, hull front: 200mm
Armour, turret front: 240mm
Crew: 5
Weight: 137.8 tons (140,000kg)
Hull length: 33ft 8in (10.27m)
Width: 14ft 8in (4.48m)
Height: 10ft 10in (3.29m)
Engine: Maybach HL234 V-12, petrol, 800bhp at 3,000rpm
Road speed: 25mph (40km/hr)
Power/weight: 5.80
Range: 75 miles (120km)

English Workman Russia
State factories
1931. 'English Workman' was the name given by the Russians to a licensed copy of the **Vickers Medium Mark 2** which was built in Russia in the early 1930s. Some slight modifications were made to suit the Russian requirements, notably in the matter of withstanding the climatic conditions, but the design was still predominantly Vickers. It formed the starting point of the development which eventually produced the T-26 series. Dimensions and other data were essentially the same as those for the Vickers Medium Mark 2.

Excelsior UK
See A33

Experimental Heavy Tank Japan
Osaka Arsenal

1930. A period of practical testing with Experimental Tank No. 1 (*below*) led the Japanese Army to make a few changes and produce this model. It was generally the same as the earlier design but reduced the number of roadwheels to 17, built the hull of thinner armour to bring the weight down, and improved the firepower by adopting a short 70mm gun and adding a machine gun to the main turret. In the following year this design was further improved to become the Type 91 Heavy Tank (*qv*).

Armament: 1 × 70mm; 3 × MG
Armour: 12mm
Crew: 5
Weight: 18.0 tons (18,2880kg)
Engine: petrol, 140bhp
Power/weight: 7.78
Speed: 12mph (20km/hr)

Experimental Tank No. 1 Japan
Osaka Arsenal

1927. Having had a few years of experience with British Medium A Whippet, Vickers Medium, Carden-Loyd and Renault FT tanks, in 1926 the Japanese Army set about designing one to their own specification, and built it in 1927. The suspension had no less than 19 small roadwheels and five return rollers, a rear drive sprocket and a front idler. The tall superstructure overhung the tracks at each side and was surmounted by a main turret carrying a short 57mm gun and with a prominent round cupola. There were also two smaller auxiliary turrets, one at the left front and one at the right rear of the hull, carrying 6.5mm machine guns.

Armament: 1 × 57mm; 2 × MG
Armour: 15mm
Crew: 5
Weight: 20.0 tons (20,320kg)
Engine: petrol, 140bhp
Power/weight: 7
Speed: 12mph (20km/hr)

F-4-HE Czechoslovakia
CKD

1937. A light amphibious tank developed by CKD as a private venture. It was generally the same as the TNH/PS, with four large roadwheels on each side and a small turret, but with the addition of large buoyancy chambers along each side and concealing most of the suspension and upper run of track. It was tested and was apparently successful, but after the German occupation of Czechoslovakia the idea was abandoned.

Armament: 1 × MG
Armour: 15mm
Crew: 3
Weight: 6 tons (6,100kg)
Engine: Praga, 4-cylinder, petrol, 120bhp
Road speed: 28mph (46km/hr)
Water speed: 3.5mph (6km/hr)
Power/weight: 20.0

FAMH Light Tank France
FAMH

1924–26. Built by St Chamond as a speculative venture in the hope of attracting overseas sales. A light tank with the usual 75mm M1897 gun in the front of the hull, plus a small turret carrying a machine gun. Driver and hull gunner at the front, commander in the turret, and the engine and transmission in the rear of the boxy hull, with the exhaust and silencer prominently on top of the engine deck. No dimensions available; a prototype was built but the project got no further.

FCM-36 France
FCM

1936–40. This was built to the same specification which produced the Renault R-35 and Hotchkiss H-35 models. The hull and turret used welded construction, which later proved to be faulty. Nine roadwheels each side, in four pairs plus one adjusting wheel, covered by skirting armour with mud chutes. Peculiar octagonal turret which continued upwards to form a slab-sided cupola. 100 were built 1936–39; a subsequent order for another 100 was cancelled because of the extremely high price demanded by the manufacturers. Numbers were taken by the Germans and used as a basis for various self-propelled guns.

Armament: 1 × 37mm; 1 × MG
Armour: 40mm
Crew: 2
Weight: 12.60 tons (12,800kg)
Hull length: 14ft 7in (4.46m)
Width: 6ft 11in (2.13m)
Height: 7ft 7in (2.33m)
Engine: Berliet, diesel, 4-cylinder, 91bhp at 2,600rpm
Road speed: 15mph (24km/hr)
Power/weight: 7.22
Range: 140 miles (225km)

Fiat 2000 Heavy Tank Italy
Fiat

1918. Designed by Fiat as a private venture from 1916 onward; two prototypes appeared in 1918 but the perfected tank did not arrive until 1918. Six were built and it stayed in service until 1934. A large rectangular hull with spherical turret, prominent driver's housing on the sloped front, machine guns at each corner, in the middle of each side and in the middle of the vertical rear face. The turret carried a 65mm mountain gun, later supplemented by a heavy machine gun. The tracks were about half the hull height, the hull overhung them, and the suspension was concealed behind skirting plates.

Armament: 1 × 65mm; 6 or 7 MGs
Armour: 20mm
Crew: 10
Weight: 39.37 tons (40,000kg)
Hull length: 24ft 3in (7.40m)
Width: 10ft 2in (3.10m)
Height: 12ft 6in (3.81m)
Engine: Fiat 6-cylinder, petrol, 240bhp
Road speed: 4mph (6km/hr)
Power/weight: 6.09
Range: 47 miles (75km)

Fiat 3000 Light Tank Italy
Fiat

1923. This was really no more than an Italian copy, with variations, of the Renault FT17 two-man tank. It was, indeed, an improvement, being lighter, faster, and better armed with two machine guns in the turret. It was gradually improved, replacing one machine gun by a 37mm gun, and giving it a better engine, transmission and suspension. For most of the 1930s it was the backbone of the Italian tank force and some of them survived until 1943.

Armament: 2 × MG; or 1 × 37mm + 1 × MG
Armour: 16mm
Crew: 2
Weight: 5.41 tons (5,500kg)
Hull length: 11ft 9in (3.58m)
Width: 5ft 2in (1.66m)
Height: 7ft 0in (2.20m)
Engine: Fiat, 4-cylinder, petrol, 65bhp at 1,700rpm
Road speed: 15mph (24km/hr)
Power/weight: 12.0
Range: 60 miles (95km)

Fiat-Ansaldo 5-ton Italy
Ansaldo

1930–37. A progression of designs in an effort to develop a light tank. The first prototype had a fixed superstructure with a 37mm gun in it. Suspension was by double-wheel bogies sprung by torsion bars. The second design was the same vehicle but with a turret on top of the superstructure carrying a machine gun. The third and final model placed the 37mm gun in the turret and two machine guns in the hull. A handful of the third model were made, largely for test purposes, after which they were given to the army to use as training vehicles.

Armament: 1 × 37mm; 2 × MG
Armour: 12mm
Crew: 2
Weight: 4.75 tons (4,830kg)
Hull length: 11ft 6in (3.51m)
Width: 5ft 7in (1.70m)
Height: 6ft 6in (1.98m)
Engine: Fiat, 4-cylinder, petrol, 42bhp
Road speed: 20mph (32km/hr)
Power/weight: 8.84
Range: 50 miles (80km)

Fiat-Ansaldo Model L 6-40 Italy
Ansaldo

1941. This was the production version of the 5-ton series (*above*) and was based upon the lessons learned with that vehicle. The suspension was similar, but a cleaner design using double-wheel bogies and trailing suspension arms. Various types of turret armament were tried before settling on a 20mm Breda automatic cannon and a coaxial machine gun. Production continued throughout the war, though most of the later chassis were used for the Semovente 47/32 self-propelled gun.

Armament: 1 × 20mm; 1 × MG
Armour: 30mm
Crew: 3
Weight: 6.69 tons (6,800kg)
Hull length: 12ft 5in (3.81m)
Width: 6ft 4in (1.95m)
Height: 6ft 8in (2.0m)
Engine: Fiat 4-cylinder, petrol, 70bhp
Road speed: 25mph (40km/hr)
Power/weight: 10.46
Range: 125 miles (200km)

Firefly UK
Woolwich

1944. 'Firefly' was the British name for an M4 Sherman fitted with a British 17-pounder anti-tank gun in the turret. Provided with APDS ammunition, in 1944–45 it was the only Allied tank in Northwest Europe capable of taking on any German tank single-handed with a chance of survival. There were never enough of them. The only other modification was the removal of the hull machine gun position so as to provide more room for stowing ammunition. The dimensions were exactly the same as those of the standard M4A4 tank.

Flammpanzer 1 Germany
Field workshops
1941. Name applied to a field conversion carried out in North Africa; it consisted of fitting the standard man-portable infantry flame-thrower into the turret of the PzKpfw 1 tank, replacing the right-hand machine gun. The quantity of fuel carried was limited, as was the maximum range of 25 yards/metres, and the device saw very little combat use.

Flammpanzer 2 Germany
MAN
1940. Also known as **Flamingo** (the German and English words are the same). This was ordered early in 1939 and produced in 1940 and was a properly-designed and factory-assembled flame-throwing tank built on the PzKpfw 2, Ausf D chassis. 155 were built before production stopped in May 1942. Two flame guns were mounted on the front corners of the hull, and the normal turret was replaced by a smaller one with a single machine gun. The flame guns had a range of about 40–50 yards/metres. Due to the thin armour and the inevitable concentration of enemy fire which flamethrowers always attract, the casualties were high and the effects not worth the high price. The flamethrowing battalions were disbanded early in 1942 and the personnel re-assigned to normal tank units.

Armament: 2 × flame projectors; 1 × MG
Ammunition: 70 gallons (320 litres) FTF + 1,800
Armour: 30mm
Crew: 3
Weight: 11.81 tons (12,000kg)
Hull length: 16ft 1in (4.90m)
Width: 7ft 11in (2.40m)
Height: 6ft 1in (1.85m)
Engine: Maybach HL62TRM, 6-cylinder, petrol, 140bhp at 2,600rpm
Road speed: 34mph (55km/hr)
Power/weight: 11.85
Range: 155 miles (250km)

Flammpanzer 3 Germany
Wegmann
1942. Developed in 1942 as a close assault weapon, this was little more than the PzKpfw 3, Ausf M with

the turret gun removed and a flamethrower fitted in its place. The co-axial machine gun was retained and a second, portable, machine gun was stowed on board. Additional armour was welded on to the front surfaces of the hull, and the flame projector was capable of firing to a range of about 60 yards/metres. The flame projector was disguised by a light metal tube imitating a full-length gun. 100 were built in 1942 and all were used on the Eastern Front.

Armament: 1 × flame projector; 2 × MG
Ammunition: 220 gallons (1,000 litres) FTF + 3,750
Armour: 80mm
Crew: 3
Weight: 22.64 tons (23,000kg)
Hull length: 21ft 0in (6.41m)
Width: 9ft 8in (2.95m)
Height: 8ft 3in (2.50m)
Engine: Maybach HL120TRM, V-12, petrol, 300bhp at 3,000rpm
Road speed: 25mph (40km/hr)
Power/weight: 13.25
Range: 96 miles (155km)

Flammpanzer 38(t) Hetzer Germany
BMKD
1944. To meet a demand for a flamethrower tank for use in the Ardennes offensive in December 1944, 20 Hetzer assault guns were converted by having their main guns removed and replaced by a flame projector. The barrel of the projector was then covered with a light metal tube to resemble a conventional gun, so as not to draw attention to its armament until it fired. They were not notably effective and most were either captured or destroyed.

Armament: 1 × flame projector; 1 × MG
Ammunition: 154 gallons (700 litres) FTF + 1,200
Armour: 60mm
Crew: 4
Weight: 15.25 tons (15,500kg)
Hull length: 16ft 0in (4.87m)
Width: 8ft 8in (2.63m)
Height: 7ft 2in (2.17m)
Engine: Praga AC2, 6-cylinder, petrol, 160bhp at 2,800rpm
Road speed: 26mph (42km/hr)
Power/weight: 10.49
Range: 110 miles (177km)

Flying Elephant UK
Foster
1916. This was proposed in July 1916 as a heavy tank capable of withstanding direct attack by field

artillery – that is guns up to roughly 3-inch/75mm calibre firing high explosive shells. It was designed by Tritton, who had a good deal to do with the British Mark 1 tanks, and built by Fosters, who also built the first tanks. It was a massive, slab-sided vehicle with a rounded 'bay window' at the centre front of the hull in which a 6-pounder gun was mounted. It was to have twin engines, necessary to move the weight, and it had an additional pair of tracks, inside the normal tracks, to give extra propulsion power if the outer tracks sank into the mud. The prototype was nearing completion at Foster's factory in December 1916 when it was decided to concentrate on production of Mark 1 tanks. The Flying Elephant was abandoned and later scrapped.

Armament: 1 × 6-pdr; 6 × MG
Armour: 76mm
Crew: 8
Weight: about 100 tons (101,000kg)
Hull length: 26ft 9in 8.15m)
Width: 9ft 7in (2.92m)
Height: 10ft 0in (3.05m)
Engine: 2 × Daimler 6-cylinder, nett 210bhp
Road speed: 2mph (3km/hr)
Power/weight: 2.1

FMC CCV(L) USA
FMC

1983. The Close Combat Vehicle (Light) was developed by FMC as a private venture in order to be ready for a US Army demand for an 'Armored Gun System', or, in plain language, a light tank with good firepower. The hull was of aluminium armour with appliqué steel plates, carried on torsion bar suspension and six roadwheels per side. The multi-faceted turret carried a 105mm gun with an exceptionally high efficiency muzzle brake. It also contained an automatic loading system developed by FMC from their experience with the US Navy's 5-inch gun systems. The vehicle could be carried inside a C-130 Hercules aircraft. For the further history of this project *see* M8 Armored Gun System.

Armament: 1 × 105mm; 2 × MG
Ammunition: 43 + 5,999
Armour: not disclosed
Crew: 3
Weight: 19.11 tons (19,414kg)
Hull length: 20ft 4in (6.19m)
Width: 8ft 10in (2.69m)
Height: 7ft 9in (2.35m)
Engine: Detroit Diesel, V-6 turbocharged, 552bhp at 2,400rpm
Road speed: 43mph (70km/hr)

Power/weight: 28,88
Range: 300 miles (485km)

Ford Three-Man Mark I USA
Ford

1918. After testing the Ford Three-Ton tank, the US Army requested a three-man version, which would permit greater firepower. The Ordnance Department responded with this design, which was more or less the Ford 3-ton with a longer hull to allow space for a third man to operate a revolving turret with a 37mm gun in it. The two Ford engines were removed and replaced with a single Hudson engine, though separate transmissions for each track were retained. It was tried and rejected in 1919.

Armament: 1 × 37mm M1916; 1 × MG
Armour: 13mm
Crew: 3
Weight: 6.69 tons (6,800kg)
Hull length: 16ft 6in (5.03m)
Width: 6ft 6in (1.98m)
Height: 7ft 9in (2.36m)
Engine: Hudson, 6-cylinder, petrol, 60bhp
Road speed: 6mph (10km/hr)
Power/weight: 8.96

Ford Three-Ton USA
Ford

1918. Designed along similar lines to the Renault FT17, this was a two-man machine gun carrier. Driver and gunner sat side-by-side, the driver having a small round cupola and the machine gun appearing in an armoured box on the front face of the tank. The front idler wheel was as high as the tank itself, the rear drive sprocket small, so that there was a sharp taper to the track outline. It was driven by two Ford Model T engines, one for each track and each with its own gearbox. A total of 15,000 were ordered, but only 15 had been built when the Armistice put a stop to the contract. They were later tried as gun tractors, without much success, and one or two are still working, in the hands of collectors.

Armament: 1 × MG
Armour: 13mm
Crew: 2
Weight: 2.76 tons (2,805kg)
Hull length: 13ft 8in (4.16m)
Width: 5ft 6in (1.68m)
Height: 5ft 3in (1.60m)
Engine: 2 × Ford T, 4-cylinder, petrol, nett 45bhp
Road speed: 8mph (13km/hr)
Power/weight: 16.3

Grant USA
See M3 Medium

Grizzly Canada
Montreal
1943. The Grizzly was the Canadian name for the Sherman M4A1 manufactured in Canada. Production began in September 1943, but it soon became apparent that the several American plants producing the M4 tank could cope with any demand, and manufacture of the Grizzly ended in December 1943. Thereafter the Montreal factory was primarily concerned with building the Sexton SP gun.

Data: exactly the same as that for Sherman M4A1

Grosstraktor 1 Germany
Daimler-Benz
1928. Two heavy tank prototypes built secretly and shipped to the joint Russo-German test facility at Kazan, in Soviet Russia, for trials. Deep hull with all-round tracks, multiple small-wheel suspension mostly concealed by skirting plates with large mud-chutes. Small turret on top of hull, well forward. Armed with a 75mm gun and three machine guns, it weighed about 15 tons and had a 255bhp Daimler-Benz engine. No other details are known.

Grosstraktor 2 Germany
Rheinmetall
1928. Built at the same time as Grosstraktor 1 these were two very similar vehicles, with the same armament.

Armament: 1 × 75mm; 3 × MG
Armour: none; mild steel, for trials purposes only
Crew: 6
Weight: 19.32 tons (19,500kg)
Hull length: 21ft 8in (6.60m)
Width: 9ft 3in (2.81m)
Height: 7ft 6in (2.30m)
Engine: BMW Va, 6-cylinder, petrol, 250bhp
Road speed: 25mph (40km/hr)
Power/weight: 12.94
Range: 93 miles (150km)

Grosstraktor 3 Germany
Krupp
1929. Two more Grosstraktor prototypes were built by Krupp and sent to Russia for testing. The general appearance was the same, with all-round tracks and two turrets, and the dimensions were similar. All six Grosstrakotors were returned from Russia and were deployed in the 1935 German Army manoeuvres, after which they were distributed to Panzer regiments as gate guards and parade ornaments.

Hagglund CV 90-120 Sweden
Hagglund
1998. This is another case of an IFV being massaged into becoming a light tank; the basic vehicle is the CV-90 MICV, in service with the Swedish Army. Hagglund, who make it, have developed this light tank variant by grafting on a large turret carrying a Swiss 120mm Compact Tank Gun on to the MICV hull and equipping it with the necessary fire control and sighting equipment. This promises to be a very potent machine; it is still undergoing evaluation trials in Sweden.

Armament: 1 × 120mm; 1 × MG
Ammunition: 50 + 5000
Armour: not disclosed
Crew: 4
Weight: 24.60 tons (25,000kg)
Hull length: 21ft 3in (6.47m)
Width: 10ft 2in (3.10m)
Height: 9ft 6in (2.90m)
Engine: Scania 4-cylinder diesel, 600bhp at 2,200rpm
Road speed: 43mph (70km/hr)
Power/weight: 24.39
Range: 415 miles (670km)

Ha-Go Japan
See Type 95 Light

Harry Hopkins UK
Vickers
Harry Hopkins (1890–1946) was the confidential adviser to President Roosevelt and overseer of the Lend-Lease programme. He was probably the only civilian ever to have had a combat tank named after him. The **Light Tank Mark 8** was the successor to the Tetrarch and used similar four-wheel suspension with steering controlled by flexing the track. About 100 were built in 1943–44, even though the British Army no longer used light tanks and had no need of this one; it was never used in action. It has been suggested that the work was done simply to keep the workforce occupied until something more important turned up.

Armament: 1 × 2-pdr; 1 × MG
Ammunition: not known
Armour: 38mm maximum
Crew: 3
Weight: 8.5 tons (8,635kg)
Hull length: 14ft 3in (4.34m)

Width: 8ft 10in (2.65m)
Height: 6ft 11in (2.11m)
Engine: Meadows horizontally-opposed 12-piston, petrol, 165bhp at 2,700rpm
Road speed: 30mph (48km/hr)
Power/weight: 19.41
Range: 140 miles (225km)

Holt Gas-Electric USA
Holt, General Electric USA

1917. America was awash with tank proposals in 1917; this was one of the more practical ones. Based on standard Holt tractor tracks and suspension components, it was a boxy structure with a 2.95-inch pack howitzer in the hull front and a water-cooled machine gun on each side in a sponson. Propulsion was by Holt petrol engine driving a generator and supplying electrical power to an electric motor for each track. It worked, and was, for its day, a reasonable design, even though the tracks were somewhat vulnerable. But it never got past the prototype stage.

Armament: 1 × 2.95in howitzer; 3 × MG
Armour: 13mm
Crew: 6
Weight: 25 tons (25,400kg)
Hull length: 16ft 6in (5.03m)
Width: 9ft 1in (2.77m)
Height: 7ft 10in (2.39m)
Engine: Holt 4-cylinder, petrol, 90bhp, driving electric generator
Road speed: 6mph (10km/hr)
Power/weight: not known, since rating of electric motors is unknown

Holt Steam Tank USA
Holt

Holt's next attempt was not quite so practical, a three-wheeled machine (single trailing steered wheel) again mounting a 2.95-inch howitzer, but propelled by two steam engines, one to each of the two steel 7-foot driving wheels. As with the US Army's Steam Tank nobody seems to have considered what the inside of the vehicle would be like if an AP bullet pierced the boiler.

Armament: 1 × 2.95in howitzer. 2 × MG
Armour: 19mm
Crew: 6
Weight: 17 tons (17,275kg)
Hull length: 22ft 3in (6.78m)
Width: 10ft 1in (3.07m)
Height: 9ft 10in (3.0m)
Engine: 2 × Doble 2-cylinder, steam, 75bhp each

Road speed: 5mph (8km/hr)
Power/weight: 8.82

Hornet UK
See Medium C

Hotchkiss H-35 France
Hotchkiss

1935. The H-35 was a light reconnaissance tank built for the French cavalry, though the infantry tank battalions eventually adopted it as well. The hull was built up from castings welded together, and the superstructure tapered up to the turret which mounted a low-velocity 37mm gun. The suspension consisted of six roadwheels arranged in pairs in a scissors arrangement with a horizontal spring.

Armament: 1 × 37mm gun M1918; 1 × MG
Armour: 40mm
Crew: 2
Weight: 10.6 tons (10,770kg)
Hull length: 13ft 10in (4.22m)
Width: 6ft 1in (1.85m)
Height: 7ft 0in (2.13m)
Engine: Hotchkiss, 6-cylinder, petrol, 75bhp
Road speed: 17mph (27km/hr)
Power/weight: 7.07
Range: 93 miles (150km)

Hotchkiss H-38 France
Hotchkiss

1938. Recognising that the H-35 was underpowered, in 1938 Hotchkiss produced a new engine. This required some changes in the hull contours at the rear, in order to provide room for the new engine and its cooling system, but beyond that there was no change in the remainder of the vehicle.

Armament: 1 × 37mm gun M1918; 1 × MG
Armour: 40mm
Crew: 2
Weight: 12.0 tons (12,200kg)
Hull length: 13ft 10in (4.22m)
Width: 6ft 1in (1.85m)
Height: 7ft 0in (2.13m)
Engine: Hotchkiss, 6-cylinder, petrol, 120hp
Road speed: 22mph (35km/hr)
Power/weight: 10.0
Range: 93 miles (150km)

Hotchkiss H-39 France
Hotchkiss

1939. The final modification to the Hotchkiss design was to give it a more effective gun, the 37mm Modèle 36, which had a higher velocity and thus a better chance against other tanks. The armour was also thickened slightly, notably on the turret front. Numbers (over 100) of these were captured undamaged by the Germans and taken into their service, some as tanks, others as chassis for self-propelled guns and flamethrowers. Some even survived the war to be used by the Israeli Army until the early 1950s.

Armament: 1 × 37mm gun M36; 1 × MG
Armour: 45mm
Crew: 2
Weight: 12.2 tons (12,400kg)
Hull length: 13ft 10in (4.22m)
Width: 6ft 1in (1.85m)
Height: 7ft 0in (2.13m)
Engine: Hotchkiss, 6-cylinder, petrol, 120bhp
Road speed: 23mph (37km/hr)
Power/weight: 9.84
Range: 93 miles (150km)

Independent (A1E1) UK
Vickers

1925. In the 1920s the theorists were much taken with the idea of a powerfully armed tank roaming around on its own and dealing out death and destruction to whatever it found. In order to see if there was any validity in this notion the British Army asked Vickers to produce a multi-gun tank capable of independent operation – which is how the A1E1 got its name.

Although it never got beyond the prototype, it had an immense influence on later design, since it more or less laid down the optimum shape of tanks for all time: low tracks, hull between them, driver at the front, fighting compartment in the middle and engine at the rear. The suspension was a multi-wheel system covered by skirting plates, and the hull was crowned by five rotating turrets. The large central turret carried a 47mm 3-pounder gun, while the other four, at the corners of the fighting compartment, held single machine guns. The commander, in the main turret, communicated with his crew by means of an intercom system, and also by a mechanical indicator system.

It is generally said that lack of funds prevented further construction; the truth is more likely to be that trials with the tank showed the fallacy of the theory and the impossibility of the task for one man to direct the driver, give orders to the four machine gunners, control his own turret gun, read a map, select targets and assess the tactical situation minute by minute without going mad in the process, something which was discovered by every other army which tried multi-gun tanks.

Armament: 1 × 47mm; 4 × MG
Armour: 30mm
Crew: 8
Weight: 31.50 tons (32,000kg)
Hull length: 28ft 5in (7.74m)
Width: 10ft 6in (3.20m)
Height: 8ft 10in (2.69m)
Engine: Armstrong-Siddeley V-12, petrol, 398bhp
Road speed: 17mph (27km/hr)
Power/weight: 12.63
Range: 93 miles (150km)

JS-1 Russia
State factories

1944. The Josef Stalin (JS) series of heavy tanks began as an enlargement of the KV series in order to obtain a wider turret ring and thus be able to fit a bigger turret and bigger gun. The hull and suspension were similar to those of the KV but lowered so that the hull could extend over the tracks and thus obtain the desired width. The first models had an 85mm gun, but that was rapidly changed for a 100mm gun, and shortly after production had begun, in the autumn of 1944, it was halted and the gun changed for a 122mm fitted with a muzzle brake.

Armament: 1 × 122mm; 4 × MG
Armour: 120mm
Crew: 4
Weight: 44 tons (44,710kg)
Hull length: 27ft 4in (8.33m)
Width: 10ft 3in (3.12m)
Height: 8ft 11in (2.72m)
Engine: V-12 diesel, 510bhp
Road speed: 23mph (37km/hr)
Power/weight: 11.59
Range: 100 miles (160km)

JS-2 Russia
State factories

1945. The Josef Stalin 2 was simply a redesign of the JS-1 in an attempt to reduce the weight, improve the protection and simplify manufacture. The front glacis plate took on the streamlined slope that was to characterise all Russian tanks thereafter, and the hull shape was generally improved with several shell traps removed. Very few were built as it was rapidly superseded by the JS-3.

JS-3 Russia
Chelyabinsk, Kirov

1945. This was a complete re-design of the whole tank, based upon experience gained in action with the JS-1 and JS-2. An entirely new ballistically-shaped cast hull was topped by a 'frying-pan' turret of low profile and smoothly curved shape, carrying an improved 122mm gun. The suspension was generally similar though slightly lowered and mechanically improved. In later years the hull was used as a basis for SP guns and the tank itself was exported to various Communist-oriented countries.

Armament: 1 × 122mm D-25; 2 × MG
Armour: 132mm
Crew: 4
Weight: 45.52 tons (46,250kg)
Hull length: 22ft 4in (6.81m)
Width: 10ft 6in (3.44m)
Height: 8ft 11in (2.93m)
Engine: V-12 diesel, 520bhp at 2,000rpm
Road speed: 23mph (37km/hr)
Power/weight: 11.42
Range: 100 miles (160km)

KH50 Czechoslovakia
Skoda

1925. This, the first Czech tank, was a wheel-and-track machine designed by Vollmer, who had designed the German LK-1 tank during the war. It was a tall, boxy affair, with the hull overlapping the tracks, and with a sloping front plate which opened to give the driver a better view. A small turret with a commander's cupola sat on top, and four rubber-tyred roadwheels were mounted outside the tracks and could be lowered to lift the tracks clear of the ground. The Czech Army bought two for test but chose not to adopt it.

Armament: 1 × 37mm M1918, or 1 × MG
Armour: 13mm
Crew: 2
Weight: 6.8 tons (6,900kg)
Hull length: 14ft 9in (4.50m)
Width: 7ft 7in (2.31m)
Height: 7ft 10in (2.39)
Engine: Tatra, 4-cylinder, petrol, 50bhp
Road speed: 8mph (13km/hr) tracks; 22mph (35km/hr) tracks
Power/weight: 7.35

KH60, KH70 Czechoslovakia
Skoda

1929. 1930. These were simply the KH-50 (*above*) with 60bhp and 70bhp engines, giving them a little more speed. Four KH70 were bought by the Czech Army for evaluation in 1930. The design was not adopted but they were retained as driver training vehicles.

Khalid UK/Jordan
ROF Leeds

1981. This has been described as a Chieftain with the engine and transmission of the Challenger 1 tank, and that fairly sums it up. The hull has been raised over the engine compartment to provide room, which makes a difference to the silhouette, but the remainder of the vehicle is as Chieftain. The design was made at the request of the Jordanian Army, and 274 vehicles were built and delivered in the 1980s.

Armament: 1 × 120mm; 2 × MG
Ammunition: 54 + 6,000
Armour: not disclosed
Crew: 4
Weight: 57.08 tons (58,000kg)
Hull length: 21ft 0in (6.39m)
Width: 11ft 7in (3.52m)
Height: 9ft 11in (3.01m)
Engine: Rolls-Royce Condor V-12, diesel, 1,200bhp at 2,300rpm
Road speed: 30mph (48km/hr)
Power/weight: 21.02
Range: 310 miles (500km)

King Tiger Germany
Henschel

1944. Or **Royal Tiger**, or **Tiger 2**. No sooner was the Tiger 1 in production than there was a demand for a replacement having a turret large enough to take the big 71-calibre 88mm gun, a formidable weapon which could put a plain steel shot through seven inches of armour at at 1¼ miles range (185mm at 2,000m). Designs were canvassed from Henschel and Porsche; the latter were so confident that they began manufacturing turrets, but Henschel's design was simpler and they got the contract. Some of their first production used up the surplus Porsche turrets.

The prime feature of the King Tiger was the well-sloped armour, in contrast to the flat vertical surfaces of the Tiger 1; even the turret sides were sloped. So far as gun power and protection went, the King Tiger was the best tank of the war, but it paid for this in its lack of performance and lack of reliability due to the engine and transmission being over-stressed. Nevertheless, when properly handled, the King Tiger dominated the battlefield and was practically indestructible. It replaced the

Tiger 1 in production in August 1944 and 485 were built before the war ended.

Armament: 1 × 8.8cm gun L/71; 2 × MG
Ammunition: 72 + 5,850
Armour: 180mm
Crew: 5
Weight: 68.30 tons (69,400kg)
Hull length: 23ft 9in (7.23m)
Width: 12ft 3in (3.73m)
Height: 10ft 1in (3.07m)
Engine: Maybach, V-12 petrol, 700bhp at 3,000rpm
Road speed: 21mph (35km/hr)
Power/weight: 10.25
Range: 105 miles (170km)

Krupp LKA1 Germany
Krupp

1937. This was developed from the Krupp La S (*see below*) by decking over the open hull and adding a turret with two machine guns. The suspension was altered, removing the girder and leaf spring system and replacing it with coil springs. The design was offered for export sale but there do not appear to have been any buyers.

Armament: 2 × MG
Armour: 13mm
Crew: 2
Weight: 5 tons (5,100kg)
Hull length: 13ft 2in (4.02m)
Width: 6ft 9in (2.06)
Height: 6ft 1in (1.85m)
Engine: Krupp M305, flat-4, petrol, 57bhp at 2,500rpm
Road speed: 19mph (30km/hr)
Power/weight: 11.4
Range: 100 miles (160km)

Krupp LKA2 Germany
Krupp

1937. This was the LKA1 with a slightly larger turret to take a 20mm cannon, as specified by the Wehrmacht in their request for designs for the Panzer 2. It was submitted for consideration and turned down in favour of the MAN design.

Krupp MKA Germany
Krupp

In 1935 the Wehrmacht called for a design of 16-ton tank, which eventually became the Panzer 3. The MKA was Krupp's submission. It was generally similar to the production Panzer 3, but had six roadwheels on each side. The turret was rounded at the rear, wedge-shaped at the front and carried a 37mm gun. The design was turned down, though some of the minor features were incorporated into the final Panzer 3 design.

KS Light Russia
Krasnoye-Sormova

1920. This was simply a copy of the French Renault FT17, some of which had been captured from the Allied Intervention Force in 1918–19. Production did not commence until 1922, when it used Ford truck gearboxes and Fiat engines, from factories set up in Russia. Less than 50 were built.

Armament: 1 × 37mm gun or 2 × MG
Armour: 16mm
Crew: 2
Weight: 6.5 tons (6,600kg)
Hull length: 13ft 3in (4.04m)
Width: 5ft 8in (1.73m)
Height: 7ft 0in (2.13m)
Engine: Fiat, 4-cylinder, petrol, 45bhp
Road speed: 5mph (8km/hr)
Power/weight: 6.92
Range: 25 miles (40km)

KV-1 Heavy Russia
Kirov, Chelyabinsk

1940. Named KV after Klimenti Voroshilov, People's Commisar for Defence in 1940. This was designed as a breakthrough tank, to replace the multi-turret T-35, and its principal attraction was the adoption of a powerful 76.2mm gun. The armour was as thick as possible, the engine was that of the BT-7 but up-rated, and the multi-wheeled suspension with torsion bar springing came from the T-100 tank.

It saw action first in Finland in 1940, where it breached the Mannerheim Line, and it was in production in time for the German invasion on June 1941, though the numbers were not sufficient to make much difference. By 1945 over 13,000 had been built; they were constantly improved in detail and in 1943 the 76mm gun was replaced by an 85mm weapon. Unfortunately the principal weak spot – an unreliable transmission – was never really cured.

Armament: 1 × 76.2mm, or 1 × 85mm; 3 × MG
Armour: 77mm
Crew: 5
Weight: 42.23 tons (42,910kg)
Hull length: 20ft 7in (6.27m)
Width: 10ft 2in (3.10m)
Height: 7ft 11in (2.16m)
Engine: V-12 diesel, 600bhp
Road speed: 22mph (35km/hr)

Power/weight: 12.83
Range: 155 miles (250km)

KV-2 Heavy Russia
Kirov
1940. This was a variant of the KV-1 which was given a large, boxy turret mounting a 152mm howitzer. The intention was to make a close support tank, not a self-propelled howitzer; it worked against the Finns, but was found to be most cumbersome. Against the Germans it failed completely and the survivors were withdrawn.

Armament: 1 × 152mm D-10 howitzer; 2 × MG
Armour: 100mm
Crew: 6
Weight: 53 tons (53,850kg)
Hull length: 22ft 4in (6.81m)
Width: 10ft 11in (3.33m)
Height: 12ft 0in (3.66m)
Engine: V-12 diesel, 600bhp
Road speed: 16mph (26km/hr)
Power/weight: 11.32
Range: 125 miles (200km)

KV-85 Heavy Russia
Chelyabinsk
1943. The KV-85 was a re-design of the KV-1 with a new, larger, cast turret of more rounded contours, mounting the 85mm gun. Dimensions remained the same, though the weight was now 46 tons (46,740kg). Production was limited, since the Josef Stalin design was under way by this time and promised to be a considerable improvement.

K-Wagen Germany
Maker unknown
1918. First of several monster tank designs to emanate from Germany, the K-Wagen was designed by Josef Vollmer. It had a boxy hull with the tracks completely covered at the sides and top, exterior sponsons for four guns, was propelled by two aero-engines and featured an 'electro-magnetic' transmission, whatever that might have been. Two prototypes were begun in 1918 but were not completed before the Armistice and were thereafter destroyed by the Allied Disarmament Commission.

Armament: 4 × 77mm; 7 × MG
Armour: 30mm
Crew: 22
Weight: 148 tons (150,375kg)
Hull length: 42ft 7in (12.98m)
Width: 20ft 0in (6.10m)
Height: 9ft 5in (2.87m)

Engine: 2 × petrol-electric, each 650bhp
Road speed: not known
Power/weight: 8.78

Landsverk Sweden
See entries under 'Strv' for the various Landsverk tanks

La S Germany
Krupp
1933. In order to evade the provisions of the Versailles Treaty, when the German Army wanted to experiment with tracked vehicles, it ordered the La S (*Landwirtschaftlicher Schlepper* – 'Agricultural Carrier') from Krupp. In effect it was a tank chassis with the top of the hull left off and no turret. With no armament nor any apparent way of mounting armament, it was obviously not a tank, and thus legal. Some 15 were built and used in the early tank schools to teach driving and tactical manoeuvres.

Armament: none
Crew: 2
Weight: 3.5 tons (3560kg)
Hull length: 13ft 2in (4.02m)
Width: 6ft 9in (2.06)
Height: 3ft 9in (1.15m)
Engine: Krupp M305, flat-4, petrol, 57bhp as 2,500rpm
Road speed: 25mph (37km/hr)
Power/weight: 16.2
Range: 90 miles (145km)

Leclerc France
GIAT
1992. This design began in 1983 after the collapse of a Franco-German tank project; it was originally called the **EPC** – Engin Principal de Combat – but in 1986 was named Leclerc. It is in the contemporary form, wide, low, with a flat multi-faceted turret carrying a 120mm gun, and with the very latest sighting, surveillance and fire control equipment.

Armament: 1 × 120mm; 2 × MG
Ammunition: 40
Armour: not disclosed
Crew: 3
Weight: 53.64 tons (54,500kg)
Hull length: 22ft 7in (6.88m)
Width: 12ft 2in (3.71m)
Height: 8ft 4in (2.53m)
Engine: SACM V-8 XC79 diesel, 1,500bhp
Road speed: 44mph (71km/hr)
Power/weight: 27.96
Range: 340 miles (550km)

Leclerc Tropicalisé France
GIAT

1997. This is the same as the basic Leclerc but with air conditioning, air filtration, ventilation and other systems specifically developed for long service in hot climates.

Armament: 1× 120mm; 2 × MG
Ammunition: 40
Armour: not disclosed
Crew: 3
Weight: 54.13 tons (55,000kg)
Hull length: 22ft 7in (6.88m)
Width: 12ft 2in (3.71m)
Height: 8ft 4in (2.53m)
Engine: MTU MT883 Ka501 diesel, 1,500bhp
Road speed: 44mph (70km/hr)
Power/weight: 27.71
Range: 340 miles (550km)

Leopard 1 MBT Germany
Krauss-Maffei

1965. Design of this tank began in the late 1950s to replace the American tanks initially used by the Bundeswehr on its formation in 1954. Two competing designs were rigorously tested and the Krauss-Maffei model selected for production, after which more than 5,000 were built, many being sold to other countries. A thoroughly sound design, it represents the best thoughts of the pair, with a rounded and sloped turret, fume extractor, and large-wheel suspension with seven roadwheels. It was gradually improved during its life, with such items as night vision equipment and fire control computers being added from time to time as technology advanced.

Armament: 1 × 105mm L7; 2 × MG
Armour: 70mm maximum
Crew: 4
Weight: 39.37 tons (40,000kg)
Hull length: 23ft 3in (7.08m)
Width: 10ft 8in (3.25m)
Height: 8ft 8in (2.64m)
Engine: Mercedes-Benz, V-10, multi-fuel, supercharged, 830bhp at 2,200rpm
Road speed: 40mph (65km/hr)
Power/weight: 21.08
Range: 375 miles (600km)

Leopard 2 MBT Germany
Krauss-Maffei

1979. In 1963 the US and Germany agreed to develop a tank together, one which would outfit both armies and, due to economies of scale, be an attractive export package as well. As is the way with these co-operative efforts it soon fell apart, since the two armies had different ideas about what they wanted to see in a tank, so they went their own ways. The Americans developed the Abrams, the Germans the Leopard 2.

Leopard 2 was not simply an overhauled Leopard 1; it was entirely new, using a hull and turret made from cast composite armour, and armed with a new 120mm smoothbore gun. The engine was an improved version of that in Leopard 1, breathed-on to produce more power, and designed as a 'power pack' which could be removed in the field and replaced by a new pack in under 20 minutes. The turret contained all the latest electronic fire control and vision equipment, and, of course, the design has been constantly upgraded since its introduction. It has also been adopted by the Dutch and Swiss armies.

Armament: 1 × 120mm; 2 × MG
Ammunition: 42 + 4,750
Armour: not disclosed
Crew: 4
Weight: 54.28 tons (55,150kg)
Hull length: 25ft 4in (7.72m)
Width: 12ft 2in (3.70m)
Height: 9ft 2in (2.79m)
Engine: MTY MB873 Ka501 V-12 turbocharged diesel, 1,500bhp at 2,600rpm
Road speed: 45mph (72km/hr)
Power/weight: 27.63
Range: 340 miles (550km)

Leopard 2AV Germany
Krauss-Maffei

1976. This was a special 'Austere Vehicle' version of Leopard 2 prepared to try and interest the US Army and possibly provide a standard NATO tank. It used a new, larger turret with new fire control systems, laser rangefinding and other novelties, but the Americans were, by then, developing the XM-1 which eventually became the Abrams and the Leopard 2AV got no further.

Leopard Medium Reconnaissance Tank
Germany
Daimler-Benz (turret), MIAG (chassis)

1942. Experience in Russia suggested the need for a heavily armoured reconnaissance vehicle, one which could fight for its information, not merely observe – hence the German title of *Gefechts Aufklärer*, literally 'Fighting scout'. First suggested in March 1942 it was hoped that production would commence in April 1943. The vehicle resembled the PzKpfw 3, Ausf G, with sloped frontal armour and a turret carrying a 50mm gun. But before the first prototype could be completed, there was a change of tactical thought on the part of the General Staff and the project was cancelled. The turret was later adopted for the Puma 8 x 8 armoured car.

Armament: 1 × 5cm; 1 × MG
Ammunition: 50 + 2,400
Armour: 50mm
Crew: 4
Weight: 20.67 tons (21,900kg)
Hull length: 15ft 6in (4.74m)
Width: 10ft 2in (3.10m)
Height: 8ft 6in (2.60m)
Engine: Maybach HL157P, V-12, petrol, 550bhp at 3,500rpm
Road speed: 37mph (60km/hr)
Power/weight: 26.60
Range: not determined

Liberty USA

1918. This was actually the American title for the British Tank Mark 8, after the agreement to co-produce this in Britain, the USA and France in large numbers for the 1919 offensive. Due to delays in setting up factories, production had scarcely begun when the Armistice stopped it. However, the Americans had produced sufficient components to allow them to assemble 100 tanks in Rock Island Arsenal in the early 1920s. The only difference between these and the British Mark 8 was the use of Browning machine guns and a Liberty aero-engine. They remained in use until 1932, after which they were stored and eventually scrapped.

Light Infantry Tank UK
Woolwich

1921. This was based on the general shape of the Medium D but was lighter, and was intended to accompany advancing infantry to provide machine gun support. The fixed turret was set well forward on the hull, with the engine at the rear, and the multi-wheel suspension was fully skirted. It was fitted with 'Snake tracks' a novel form of track pioneered by Woolwich but never seriously taken up by anyone else. Shortly after this tank was designed the Woolwich design office was closed down and the Light Infantry Tank appears to have vanished.

Armament: 3 × MG
Armour: 10mm
Crew: 3
Weight: 17.5 tons (17,780kg)

Hull length: 22ft 3in (6.78m)
Engine: Hall & Scott, 6-cylinder, petrol, 100bhp
Road speed: 30mph (48km/hr)
Power/weight: 5.71

Light Tank Mark 1 UK
Vickers

This followed the A4E1 in 1930 and was the general name for a small batch of vehicles, all differing slightly, which were purchased by the British Army as their first light tanks. They stemmed from the Carden-Loyd tankette design, using similar, but stronger, suspension, had a shallow, rectangular superstructure and a round turret carrying a machine gun. The details of the suspension varied from vehicle to vehicle as different ideas were tried.

The **Light Tank Mark 1A** was a sub-species of the Mark 1, of similar dimensions but with more variations of engine, armament and suspension for trials purposes.

Mark 1

Armament: 1 × MG
Armour: 14mm
Crew: 2
Weight: 4.8 tons (48,775kg)
Hull length: 13ft 2in (4.02m)
Width: 6ft 1in (1.85m)
Height: 5ft 7in (1.78m)
Engine: Meadows, 6-cylinder, petrol, 58bhp
Road speed: 30mph (48km/hr)
Power/weight: 12.08
Range: 100 miles (160km)

Light Tank Mark 2 UK
Vickers

1931. A further development of the A4 family, of which 16 were built. The principal change was the general adoption of the Horstmann sprung bogie suspension, a rectangular turret and a Rolls-Royce engine.

Armament: 1 × MG
Armour: 10mm
Crew: 2
Weight: 4.25 tons (4,320kg)
Hull length: 11ft 9in (3.58m)
Width: 6ft 4in (1.93m)
Height: 6ft 8in (2.03m)
Engine: Rolls-Royce 6-cylinder, petrol, 66bhp
Road speed: 30mph (48km/hr)
Power/weight: 15.50
Range: 100 miles (160km)

Light Tank Mark 3 UK
Vickers

1933. Generally similar to the Mark 2 but with further changes to the Horstmann suspension, slightly thicker armour, and with the hull superstructure extended to the rear.

Armament: 1 × MG
Armour: 12mm
Crew: 2
Weight: 4.5 tons (4,575kg)
Hull length: 12ft 0in (3.6m)
Width: 6ft 4in (1.93m)
Height: 6ft 11in (2.11m)
Engine: Rolls-Royce, 6-cylinder, petrol, 66bhp
Road speed: 30mph (48km/hr)
Power/weight: 14.66
Range: 100 miles (160km)

Light Tank Mark 4 UK
Vickers

1934. This broke away from the A4 family and was based upon an experimental design by Vickers which had been tested in 1933. The principal change was in the suspension; while this was still basically Horstmann there was a single leading bogie with a return roller on top of it, then a single roadwheel, and finally the rear idler was lowered to act as the fourth roadwheel. This resulted in a distinctly triangular track path which became characteristic of the subsequent models of the series. The hull superstructure was higher and the rectangular turret had sloped sides.

Armament: 1 × MG
Armour: 12mm
Crew: 2
Weight: 4.6 tons (4,675kg)
Hull length: 11ft 2in (3.40m)
Width: 6ft 9in (2.06m)
Height: 7ft 0in (2.13m)
Engine: Meadows, 6-cylinder, petrol, 88bhp
Road speed: 35mph (56km/hr)
Power/weight: 19.13
Range: 125 miles (200km)

Light Tank Mark 5 UK
Vickers

1935. By now the British Army had realised that two-man tanks were of little use, and the Mark 5 introduced the two-man turret and three-man crew. The hull was slightly less deep than that of the Mark 4, but otherwise the vehicles were similar. The turret was, of course, larger but still of the same rectangular slope-sided form and had a circular cupola. The hull rear was also extended so as to make space for fuel tanks.

Armament: 1 × .50in MG, 1 × .303in MG
Armour: 12mm
Crew: 3
Weight: 4.15 tons (4,165kg)
Hull length: 12ft 1in (3.68m)
Width: 6ft 9in (2.06m)
Height: 7ft 3in (2.21m)
Engine: Meadows, 6-cylinder, petrol, 88bhp
Road speed: 32mph (51km/hr)
Power/weight: 21.46
Range: 125 miles (200km)

Light Tank Mark 6 UK
Vickers

1936. Generally similar to the Mark 5 but with thicker armour and with a new turret with sloped front and vertical sides, extended at the rear to form a bustle into which a radio set was fitted.

Armament: 1 × .50in MG, 1 × .303in MG
Armour: 15mm
Crew: 3
Weight: 4.8 tons (4,875kg)
Hull length: 13ft 2in (4.01m)
Width: 6ft 10in (2.08m)
Height: 7ft 5in (2.26m)
Engine: Meadows, 6-cylinder, petrol, 88bhp
Road speed: 35mph (56km/hr)
Power/weight: 18.33
Range: 125 miles (200km)

Light Tanks Marks 6A, 6B and 6C UK
Vickers

1937. These were developments of the Mark 6; they had a modified suspension, easily recognised by the return roller being between the second and third roadwheels. The **6A** had a new commander's cupola of rectangular form with prominent vision blocks at the front. The **6B**, which formed the majority of production, had the circular cupola, also with new vision blocks, and had only one square radiator air intake alongside the driver instead of the two which previous models had. The **6C** was similar to the 6B but carried a Besa machine gun instead of a Vickers.

Dimensions: as for Mark 6, except
Weight: 5.2 tons.

Light Tank Mark 7 UK
See Tetrarch

Light Tank Mark 8 UK
See Harry Hopkins

Little Willie UK
Foster
1915. Little Willie was not armoured, nor was it a fighting tank, but it was the first tracked potentially-armoured vehicle designed to meet a military specification laying down such things as width of trench to be crossed, gradient to be climbed and so forth. It also introduced the perfected track designed by Mr Tritton, managing director of Foster's, which became the standard for all wartime tanks. It also settled such points as steering, braking and gear-changing and was really no more than a mobile testbed for various ideas which were then incorporated into 'Mother' (*qv*)

Armament: none
Armour: none; 6mm mild steel plate
Crew: 6
Weight: 18 tons (18,290kg)
Hull length: 18ft 2in (6.53m)
Width: 9ft 4in (2.84m)
Height: 10ft 2in (3.09m)
Engine: Daimler, 6-cylinder, petrol, 105bhp at 1,000rpm
Road speed: 1.8mph (3km/hr)
Power/weight: 5.83

LK-1 Germany
Maker unknown
1918. A Josef Vollmer design, and a far more sensible one than his 148-ton K-Wagen monster. The LK-1 (*leicht Kampfwagen* – 'light combat car') was based on the contemporary Daimler car chassis, to the extent that the existing axles were used for the drive sprockets and idlers. The engine was in the front, with a louvred radiator, and a small fighting compartment for the driver, commander and gunner, who had a revolving turret for his machine gun. Only prototypes were built but it formed the basis of the later Swedish Strv m/21, in which many German officers learned to drive and handle tanks.

Armament: 1 × MG
Armour: 8mm
Crew: 3
Weight: 6.89 tons (7,000kg)
Hull length: 18ft 0in (5.49m)
Width: 6ft 7in (2.00m)
Height: 8ft 2in (2.48m)
Engine: 4-cylinder, sleeve-valve, petrol, 60bhp
Road speed: 8mph (13km/hr)
Power/weight: 8.70

LK-2 Germany
Maker unknown
1918. An improved version of the LK-1, this did away with the revolving turret and had a fixed superstructure with a 57mm gun facing forward over the engine. As with the LK-1 it was based directly upon the Daimler car chassis and layout, although the armour was thicker. Prototypes were tested successfully, and an order given for mass production, but the war ended before production could begin.

Armament: 1 × 57mm
Armour: 14mm
Crew: 3
Weight: 8.75 tons (8,900kg)
Hull length: 16ft 9in (5.10m)
Width: 6ft 6in (1.98m)
Height: 8ft 2in (2.49m)
Engine: Daimler, 4-cylinder, sleeve-valve, petrol, 60bhp
Road speed: 7.5mph (12km/hr)
Power/weight: 6.85

LMT-105 Warrior UK
See Alvis Warrior

LT-34 Czechoslovakia
CKD
1934. The first Czech tank to go into quantity production, 50 being ordered in 1934. Noisy and rough, it was improved slightly in 1938 by fitting it with the engine and transmission of the LT-38 (*below*), but when the Germans occupied the country they soon got rid of the LT-34s to Romania. Complex suspension with articulated bogies, exterior girders and leaf spring, rectangular superstructure and a small turret.

Armament: 1 × 37mm; 2 × MG
Armour: 15mm
Crew: 4
Weight: 7.5 tons (7,625kg)
Hull length: 13ft 3in (4.04m)
Width: 6ft 8in (2.03m)
Height: 6ft 0in (1.83m)
Engine: Praga, 4-cylinder, petrol, 62bhp
Road speed: 21mph (34km/hr)
Power/weight: 8.26

LT-35 Czechoslovakia
Skoda
1935. A very advanced design for its day, but like many very advanced designs initially unreliable. The defects were eventually cured and 424 were built, of which 219 were it adopted by the Germans

MIAI/MIA2 Light • Tanks

in 1939 as the **PzKpfw 35(*t*)** and used by them for about three years. The few which survived the early battles on the Russian front were converted into ammunition carriers. In original form it had a small-wheel suspension, broad tracks, and pneumatically-actuated steering and transmission. The small turret has a prominent commander's cupola.

Armament: I × 37mm; 2 × MG
Ammunition: 72 + 1,800
Armour: 25mm
Crew: 4
Weight: 10.5 tons (10,670kg)
Hull length: 16ft 1in (4.90m)
Width: 7ft 1in (2.16m)
Height: 7ft 3in (2.21m)
Engine: Skoda T-11, 6-cylinder, petrol, 120bhp
Road speed: 22mph (35km/hr)
Power/weight: 11.42
Range: 120 miles (190km)

LT-38 Czechoslovakia
See TNH/PS

LT-H Switzerland
Saurer
1938. This was actually the Czech TNH/PS made under licence in Switzerland and fitted with Swiss weapons, engine and transmission. It was designated **Panzer 39** by the Swiss Army and remained in use for several years.

Armament: I × 20mm Oerlikon cannon; 2 × MG
Armour: 32mm
Crew: 3
Weight: 7.5 tons (7,620kg)
Hull length: 14ft 2in (4.32m)
Width: 6ft 7in (2.00m)
Height: 6ft 3in (1.90m)
Engine: Saurer diesel, 4-cylinder, 125bhp
Road speed: 28mph (40km/hr)
Power/weight: 16.66
Range: 150 miles (240km)

LT-L Czechoslovakia
CKD
1938. Export version of the TNH for sale to Latvia.

LT-P Czechoslovakia
CKD
1938. Export version of the TNH built for sale to Peru.

Lobster UK
1945. An improved version of the Sherman Crab flail tank with automatic height control of the flail and a larger flail drum. The prototype was approved, but since the Crab with manual height control appeared to be adequate, the Lobster never went into production.

Locust USA
See M22 Light

Luchs Germany
MAN
1943. Luchs ('Lynx') was a variant model of the Panzer 2 light tank, the 'Ausf L, Sd Kfz 123', intended for use as a reconnaissance vehicle. It used the overlapping suspension developed for the later versions of the Panzer 2 and the hull was widened so as to extend over the tracks to allow for a larger turret ring and turret. The turret had no cupola or vision blocks, but had two revolving periscopes in the roof. 100 were built in 1943–44. Not to be confused with a Reconnaissance Vehicle of the same name from the 1970s, listed in that section.

Armament: I × 20mm cannon; I × MG
Ammunition: 330 + 2,250
Armour: 30mm
Crew: 4
Weight: 13.0 tons (13,210kg)
Hull length: 15ft 2in (4.63m)
Width: 8ft 2in (2.48m)
Height: 7ft 4in (2.231m)
Engine: Maybach HL66P, 6-cylinder, petrol, 180bhp at 2,600rpm
Road speed: 37mph (60km/hr)
Power/weight: 13.84
Range: 180 miles (290km)

MIAI/MIA2 Light USA
Rock Island
1940. These two vehicles had been developed by Rock Island in the mid-1930s under the title of **Combat Car M1** and **Combat Car M2** (*qv*). Both were full-tracked light tanks with a turret carrying two machine guns and a third machine gun alongside the driver. The sole difference as the the M1 was driven by a Continental radial petrol engine, and the M2 by a Guiberson radial diesel engine. However, since they had been developed for use by the US Cavalry, who were not permitted to operate tanks, they were called 'Combat Cars'. In 1940, when the US Armored Force was set up, this artificial restriction was removed, and the two

vehicles were promptly re-classified and standardised as the **Light Tank M1A1** (ex-CC M2) and the **Light Tank M1A2** (ex-CC M1). It was purely a bureaucratic formality, since no more were ever built.

M2 Light USA
Rock Island

1935. This began as the **T2E1**, and was the same hull as the Light T1 but with a new volute spring suspension by two bogies. It also had a better turret and a new track with rubber blocks. Nine pilots were built and it was then standardised as the **Light Tank M2**.

Armament: 3 × MG
Armour: 15mm
Crew: 4
Weight: 8.39 tons (8,528kg)
Hull length: 13ft 5in (4.08m)
Width: 7ft 5in (2.26m)
Height: 6ft 9in (2.06m)
Engine: Continental, 7-cylinder, radial, air-cooled, petrol, 260hp
Road speed: 46mph (74km/hr)
Power/weight: 30.98

M2 Variant Models

M2A1
New turret with large round cupola at rear.

M2A2
As for M2A1 but with Guiberson diesel engine 250bhp.

M2A2E2
Thicker armour, fixed superstructure, Continental engine.

M2A2E3
Similar to the E2 but lowered the rear idler to the ground so that it acted as a roadwheel; General Motors 165bhp diesel engine.

M2A3
E3 with twin turrets, longer hull, improved suspension, idler back up in the air.

M2A3E3
M2A3 with General Motors diesel engine.

M2A4 Light USA
ACF

Standardised in 1939, in production in 1940, this was the M2A3 but with a reversion to a single turret with 37mm gun. Armour on the hull sides and front was increased to 25mm, there were additional sponson-mounted machine guns on each side, and an anti-aircraft machine gun on the back of the turret. The Continental engine was retained, but a new synchromesh gearbox was adopted. This was the first US tank to go into mass production, 329 being ordered from American Car & Foundry in October 1939. Some were used in combat by US forces in the Philippines in 1942, and some were sent to Britain and used as training tanks.

Armament: 1 × 37mm; 4 × MG
Armour: 25mm
Crew: 4
Weight: 10.26 tons (10,435kg)
Hull length: 14ft 7in (4.44m)
Width: 8ft 4in (2.54m)
Height: 8ft 3in (2.51m)
Engine: Continental 7-cylinder, radial, petrol, 250bhp
Road speed: 25mph (40km/hr)
Power/weight: 24.38
Range: 70 miles (112km)

M2 Medium USA
Rock Island

1939. After the M1922 model, US medium tank design continued with the T1–T5 series and in 1939 the **T5** was standardised as the Medium M2. The design period had seen the adoption of the volute spring suspension system developed at Rock Island when they got tired of arguing with Christie, and the adoption of radial aircraft engines as the only way of obtaining the desired power. The M2 had a well-sloped front, an almost octagonal fighting compartment with barbette-mounted machine guns at the four corners, and a faceted, sloped plate turret. Manufacture of a first batch of 15 vehicles took plate at Rock island in the last months of 1939; further production never took place, since the war in Europe had begun to indicate where improvements could be made.

Armament: 1 × 37mm; 8 × MG
Armour: 25mm
Crew: 6
Weight: 16.96 tons (17,236kg)
Hull length: 17ft 8in (5.38m)
Width: 8ft 7in (2.62m)
Height: 9ft 5in (2.87m)
Engine: Wright Cyclone 9-cylinder, radial, petrol, 350bhp
Road speed: 28mph (45km/hr)
Power/weight: 20.63

M3 Light (Stuart) USA
ACF

1940. Even as the M2A4 Light Tank went into production the Ordnance Department were studying reports from Europe and deciding upon improvements to the design. The armour was increased to 37mm and the side vision ports were removed. This increased the weight and to distribute this better over the suspension the idler was brought down again to ground level and carried on a trailing arm. Engine covers were thickened to provide protection against air attack. A total of 5,811 were produced.

Armament: 1 × 37mm; 5 × MG
Ammunition: 103 + 8,270
Armour: 37mm
Crew: 4
Weight: 12.23 tons (12,430kg)
Hull length: 14ft 11in (4.54m)
Width: 7ft 4in (2.23m)
Height: 8ft 3in (2.51m)
Engine: Continental 7-cylinder, radial, petrol, 250bhp at 2,400rpm
Road speed: 36mph (57km/hr)
Power/weight: 20.44
Range: 70 miles (112km)

M3A1 Light USA
ACF

1941. This was similar to the M3 but with a power-operated turret and turret basket. There were also improvements in sights, vision equipment, radio and intercom equipment. A gyro-stabiliser was fitted to the 37mm gun, the first such equipment to go into service anywhere. The turret cupola was removed to try and make the vehicle less conspicuous and the sponson-mounted machine guns were taken out to increase ammunition space. After approval in August 1941, total production amounted to 4,621 before ending in January 1943.

Armament: 1 × 37mm; 3 × MG
Ammunition: 116 + 6,910
Armour: 37mm
Crew: 4
Weight: 12.72 tons (12,927kg)
Hull length: 14ft 11in (4.54m)
Width: 7ft 4in (2.23m)
Height: 7ft 7in (2.31m)
Engine: Continental 7-cylinder radial, petrol, 250bhp at 2,400rpm
Road speed: 36mph (57km/hr)
Power/weight: 19.65
Range: 70 miles (112km)

M3A3 Light USA
ACF

1942. The final and perfected M3, this embodied many lessons learned in combat. An all-welded hull with sloped sides speeded up production and improved protection; sand shields over the tracks were standard, better entrance and exit for the driver, extra fuel capacity obtained by removing the sponson machine guns, turret redesigned to take radio equipment in the bustle. 3,427 were manufactured.

Armament: 1 × 37mm; 3 × MG
Ammunition: 103 + 8,270
Armour: 37mm
Crew: 4
Weight: 14.17 tons (14,400kg)
Hull length: 16ft 6in (5.03m)
Width: 8ft 3in (2.51m)
Height: 7ft 7in (2.31m)
Engine: Continental 7-cylinder, radial, petrol, 250bhp at 2,400rpm; or Guiberson, 9-cylinder, radial, diesel, 220bhp at 2,200rpm
Road speed: 36mph (58km/hr)
Power/weight: 17.64
Range: 70 miles (125km)

M3 Medium (Lee) USA
Alco, Baldwin, Detroit, Pressed Steel Car, Pullman-Standard

1941. In June 1940 Chrysler engineers began planning Detroit Tank Arsenal and the production of the M2A1 Medium Tank. Before they got very far the Ordnance Department, reading reports from Europe, realised that the 37mm gun was no longer a viable armament and that a minimum of 75mm was required. Since the M2 would not take a 75mm gun, a hurried re-design was done to add a side sponson in the right front of the hull and insert a 75mm gun into this. Together with a few more modifications, this was accepted as the M3 Medium and the Chrysler engineers were told to tear up their M2 drawings and start again. The M3 was the first US medium tank to go into volume production. It used the Rock Island volute spring suspension, a Wright petrol or or Guiberson diesel radial engine, and had a cast turret with a smaller machine-gun cupola on top. The first tank left the production line in April 1941 and 6,258 were built before production ended in December 1942.

Armament: 1 × 75mm M2; 1 × 37mm M5; 3 × MG
Ammunition: 46 + 178 + 9,200
Armour: 57mm
Crew: 6
Weight: 26.79 tons (27,216kg)

Hull length: 18ft 6in (5.64m)
Width: 8ft 11in (2.72m)
Height: 10ft 3in (3.12m)
Engine: Continental R-975 9-cylinder, radial, petrol, 340bhp at 2,400rpm
Road speed: 26mph (42km/hr)
Power/weight: 12.69
Range: 120 miles (193km)

M3 Variant Models

There were a series of variant models, entirely for production convenience.

M3

Basic model, riveted hull, cast turret, Wright R-975 engine.

M3(D)

Basic model, but with Guiberson T-1020-4 diesel engine. 4,924 M3 and M3(D) were built.

M3A1

As M3 but with cast hull. 300 built.

M3A2

As M3 but with welded hull. 12 built.

M3A3

As for M3A2 but with twin General Motors 6046 Diesel engines giving 375bhp. 322 built.

M3A4

As M3, but with Chrysler A-57 multi-bank engines; 370bhp. 109 built.

M3A5

As M3, but with twin General Motors 6046 diesel engines. 375bhp. 591 built

M3 Medium (Grant) USA
Alco, Baldwin

1941. Grant was the name given to M3 Medium Tanks as supplied to the British. The design was generally as for the M3 Medium described above but with the machine gun cupola removed from the turret in an endeavour to reduce the silhouette, and with some changes to the turret to allow the fitting of British radio sets.

The M3 tanks were known as **Grant Mark 1** in British service; a further supply based on the M3A5 were known as **Grant Mark 2**. They arrived in North Africa in April 1942 and fought through the desert campaigns. After being replaced by M4 Shermans, they were then sent to Australia and served in the Pacific war until 1945.

M4 Medium (Sherman) USA
Alco, Baldwin, Detroit, Federal Machine, Fisher Body, Ford, Lima, Pacific Car, Pressed Steel Car, Pullman-Standard

1942. Developed from the M3 Lee by removing the side-mounted 75mm gun and placing it in the turret and making other improvements. Full-tracked, six paired roadwheels with volute spring suspension, rear engine, front drive, five-speed manual transmission. The Sherman became the standard battle tank of the Western Allies during WWII, being adopted by the British and other armies in the interest of standardisation, and was built in greater numbers than any other American tank. By 1944 it was outclassed by the German Tiger and Panther but by that time it was too late to contemplate changing it.

The data that follow are for the basic M4. There were minor differences in weight and dimensions between models. Differences in armament and engine are detailed below.

Armament: 1 × 75mm; 2 × .30in MG, 1 × .50in MG
Ammunition: 97 (90 M4A1) + 300 .50in + 4,750 .30in
Armour: 76mm
Crew: 5
Weight: 29.69 tons (30,164kg)
Hull length: 19ft 4in (5.89m)
Height: 9ft 0in (2.75m)
Width: 8ft 7in (2.62m)
Engine: various; see below
Road speed: 24mph (39km/hr)
Range: 120miles (193km)

M4 Variant Models

M4

Original design with welded hull. Continental 9-cylinder, radial petrol engine. Total production 6,748 with 75mm gun, 1,641 with 105mm howitzer.

M4A1

Cast hull, Continental engine. Production: 6,281 75mm, 3,396 76mm.

M4A2

Welded hull, General Motors 12-cylinder, 410bhp diesel engine. Production; 8,053 75mm, 3,230 76mm guns, Most were sent to Russia, though the US Marine Corps and British Army also used some of this model.

M4A3

Welded hull, Ford V-8 500bhp engine. Production 5,015 75mm, 3,370 76mm and 3,039 105mm howitzer. Principally used by the US Army.

M4A3E2

Heavy assault tank version with 12 inches of additional armour welded to frontal surfaces and six inches to the turret. 254 were built, converted from M4A3 models, in May-June 1944, armed with 75mm gun. Many had the 76mm gun fitted in the field. Weight 42 tons due to the extra armour.

M4A3E8

M4A3 with horizontal volute spring suspension, which made field maintenance and repair easier and quicker, and, with a wider track, gave better cross-country performance.

M4A4

Welded hull, Chrysler 30-cylinder, multi-bank engine, composed of five 6-cylinder, commercial truck engines arranged around a single crankcase. Production 7,499, all 75mm. This model was principally used by the British Army.

M4A5

US official designation for the Canadian **Grizzly** tank (*qv*).

M4A6

M4A4 with the Chrysler engine replaced by a Caterpillar diesel engine. Only 75 were made in 1943 before a decision was taken to standardise on the Ford and Continental engines, and production therefore ceased.

M5 Light (Stuart) USA
Cadillac (1), Cadillac (2)

1942. The supply of engines threatened to become a bottle-neck in the production of the M3 Light Tank (*above*) and in 1941 Cadillac suggested using two of their V-8 car engines coupled to their HydraMatic automatic transmissions. Ordnance were sceptical – the automatic transmission had only been on the market for a year or so – but Cadillac converted a tank and drove it 500 miles to a testing ground. That convinced Ordnance and it was approved for production. Slight changes in the hull were necessary to accommodate the two engines and transmission, but there were no significant changes in armament or equipment.

The **M5A1**, standardised in September 1942, had an improved turret with radio space, and also had a stowage box built on to the rear of the hull.

Armament: 1 × 37mm M6; 3 × MG
Ammunition: 123 + 6,250
Armour: 58mm
Crew: 4
Weight: 14.73 tons (14,970kg)
Hull length: 14ft 3in (4.34m)
Width: 7ft 4in (2.23mm)

Height: 7ft 7in (2.31m)
Engine: 2 × Cadillac V-8 Series 42, petrol; total 220bhp at 4,000rpm
Road speed: 36mph (58km/hr)
Power/weight: 14.93
Range: 100 miles (160km)

M6 Heavy USA
Baldwin, Fisher Body

1942. This was developed in response to a 1940 request for a heavy tank, and at the time of its standardisation was among the best tanks in the world. Unfortunately the political climate had changed and the Armored Board produced a series of infantile excuses for not adopting it until the Ordnance Department gave up. Thus, when the US Army really needed a heavy tank in 1944, it did not have one.

There were three models of the M6. The **M6** had a cast hull and turret; the **M6A1** had a welded hull and cast turret. Both used a Wright 9-cylinder, radial engine driving through a torque converted and automatic transmission to rear drive sprockets. Suspension was by horizontal volute springs, with four bogies on each side. These were dual-wheeled, and ran on two tracks, an inner and an outer. The main adjustable idler was at the front and beneath them were secondary fixed idlers which assisted the tank in climbing obstacles. Main armament was a 3-inch gun, with a 37mm gun mounted coaxially, and a bank of three fixed machine guns were in the bow. The third model was the **T1E1**, sometimes called the **M6A2**, which was the M6 but with a petrol-electric drive. In all, 40 were built: nine M6, 12 M6A1, 19 T1E1, and one experimental T1 with a GM HydraMatic transmission. The M6A1s were built by Fisher, the remainder by Baldwin.

Armament: 1 × 3in M7; 1 × 37mm M6; 2 × .30in MG; 2 × .50in MG
Ammunition: 75 + 202 + 7,500 + 5,700
Armour: 83mm
Crew: 6
Weight: 56.47 tons (57,380kg)
Hull length: 24ft 9in (7.54m)
Width: 10ft 3in (3.12m)
Height: 9ft 10in (3.00m)
Engine: Wright G-200, 9-cylinder, radial, petrol, 800bhp at 2,300rpm
Road speed: 22mph (35km/hr)
Power/weight: 14.17
Range: 100 miles (160km)

M7 Medium USA
Quad Cities
1942. This began life as the **T7E2** Light Tank, designed in early 1941 as a future replacement for the M3 Light. It had a cast hull with thicker armour, and a cast turret, with a much lower silhouette than the M3 series, partly achieved by using horizontal volute springing. But the 37mm gun was by then obsolescent, and fitting a 75mm gun lifted it out of the 'Light Tank' class and it was therefore re-designated as Medium Tank M7. It was standardised, and 3,000 were ordered, but on second thoughts it was decided to concentrate on production of the M4 and the orders were cancelled. Only 13 were ever made.

Armament: 1 × 75mm M3; 2 × MG
Armour: 38mm
Crew: 5
Weight: 22.77 tons (23,134kg)
Hull length: 17ft 7in (5.36m)
Width: 9ft 2in (2.79m)
Height: 7ft 4in (2.23m)
Engine: Continental R-975 9-cylinder, radial, petrol, 330bhp
Road speed: 35mph (56km/hr)
Power/weight: 14.49
Range: 125 miles (200km)

M8 Armored Gun System (AGS) USA
United Defense
This began life as the FMC Close Combat Vehicle (Light) (*qv*) in 1983 and was then entered into a US Army comparative trial from which it was selected for further development as a replacement for the M551 Sheridan. This led to the removal of the original 105mm gun and the fitting of a new and improved model, the changing of much of the surveillance, sighting and fire control equipment, and the fine-tuning of the design so as to use off-the-shelf components wherever possible. The development was completed and in 1992 it was adopted by the US Army as the M8 AGS, only to have the approval cancelled a few months later. The makers have continued to offer it on the market and there may yet be a future for it. The basic vehicle is a tracked tank with aluminium armour and a large turret carrying a 105mm gun. This version (**Level 1**) is capable of being air dropped. **Levels 2** and **3** see the addition of appliqué and explosive reactive armour so as to offer protection against higher threat levels.

Armament: 1 × 105mm; 2 × MG
Ammunition: 30 + 5,000
Armour: not disclosed

Crew: 3
Weight, Level 1: 17.76 tons (18,050kg)
     Level 2: 20.46 tons (20,825kg)
     Level 3: 23.21 tons (23,585kg)
Hull length: 19ft 11in (6.08m)
Width: 8ft 8in (2.64m)
Height: 8ft 6in (2.59m)
Engine: Detroit Diesel V-6, 550bhp at 2,400rpm
Road speed: 45mph (72km/hr)
Power/weight: 30.96 (Level 1)
Range: 300 miles (485km)

M22 Light (Locust) USA
Marmon-Herrington
In 1941 the US Airborne Command set about designing a tank to be carried into action by air, while the Air Force began designing an aeroplane to carry it. One is inclined to wonder whether they ever sat down together to discuss what they were doing. The **T9**, later M22, light tank resembled a miniature Sherman M4, with sloped front and cast turret, but it was armed only with a 37mm gun. The aircraft which appeared was the C-54 which could carry the tank slung beneath it – but only after the turret had been removed. Several hundred tanks were built and most were sent to Europe but the US Airborne never used them in action. The British 6the Airborne Division used a handful in the crossing of the Rhine in 1945, but that was their only combat. They were supposedly scrapped after the war but many found their way to the Middle East.

Armament: 1 × 37mm gun M6; 1 × MG
Ammunition: 50 + 2,500
Armour: 25mm
Crew: 3
Weight: 7.14 tons (7,257kg)
Hull length: 12ft 11in (3.93m)
Width: 7ft 4in (2.23m)
Height: 5ft 9in (1.75m)
Engine: Lycoming 6-cylinder, horizontally opposed, petrol, 162bhp at 2,800rpm
Road speed: 35mph (56km/hr)
Power/weight: 22.68
Range: 110 miles (177km)

M24 Light (Chaffee) USA
ACF, Cadillac (1), Massey-Harris
By 1943 it was obvious that the M3/M5 series of light tanks were no longer battlefield effectives, and a new light tank was needed with better armament. Named for General Adna Chaffee, 'Father of the Armored Force', it was a completely new departure and owed nothing to the M3/M5 design except the

twin Cadillac engines and automatic transmission. The hull was low and well shaped, and suspension was by five large roadwheels on torsion bars. A low and sloped, cast turret with a 75mm gun and coaxial machine gun completed the design. It arrived in Europe late in 1944 and saw some action, but really came into its own in Korea in 1951–52.

Armament: 1 × 75mm M6; 3 × MG
Ammunition: 48 + 440 (.50) + 3,750 (.30)
Armour: 38mm
Crew: 5
Weight: 18.08 tons (18,370kg)
Hull length: 16ft 4in (4.99m)
Width: 9ft 8in (2.94m)
Height: 8ft 2in (2.47m)
Engine: 2 × Cadillac Series 42 V-8 petrol, total 220bhp at 3,400rpm
Road speed: 30mph (48km/hr)
Power/weight: 12.17
Range: 100 miles (160km)

M26 Medium (Pershing) USA
Detroit, Fisher Body

1944. After the M6 Heavy tank had been dropped (*see above*) the US Ordnance Department continued working quietly away at a heavy tank design, the **T26**, on the assumption that one day somebody would need it. In June 1944 the design was perfected and submitted for standardisation but the Army Ground Forces and the Armored Board both argued against it. Ordnance, tired of this, went over their heads to the Chief of Staff and obtained permission to send 20 pilot models to Europe for troop testing. They were duly despatched, whereupon the AGF and Armored Board declared the T26 battleworthy. Although a further 200 were sent to Europe only the original 20 saw service.

The design was low-set and well-shaped, with six roadwheels and torsion bar suspension, a large turret and a powerful 90mm gun. The US Army in Europe finally had a tank which could fight the German Tiger.

Armament: 1 × 90mm M3; 3 × MG
Ammunition: 70 + 5,550
Armour: 102mm
Crew: 5
Weight: 41.07 tons (41,730kg)
Hull length: 22ft 4in (6.80m)
Width: 11ft 6in (3.50m)
Height: 9ft 1in (2.76m)
Engine: Ford V-8 petrol, 500bhp at 2,600rpm
Road speed: 30mph (48km/hr)
Power/weight: 12.17
Range: 110 miles (177km)

M41 Light (Walker Bulldog) USA
Cleveland

1951. Even before World War II ended, US Army designers were at work on the next generation of tanks, and the first of these to appear was this M41, named for General Walton W. Walker, killed in Korea in 1951. It was one of the first US tanks to be designed around a suitable engine, rather than being designed and then found an engine which would fit. It was conventional in form, driver in front, engine and transmission in rear, and a good-sized turret with a 76mm gun. Although called 'Light' it turned the scales at 23 tons and five years earlier would have been a medium.

Armament: 1 × 76mm gun M32; 2 × MG
Ammunition: 57 + 5,650
Armour: 40mm
Crew: 4
Weight: 23.12 tons (23,495kg)
Hull length: 19ft 1in (5.81m)
Width: 10ft 6in (3.19m)
Height: 10ft 1in (3.07m)
Engine: Continental, 6-cylinder, petrol, horizontally opposed, 500bhp at 2,800rpm
Road speed: 45mph (72km/hr)
Power/weight: 21.63
Range: 100 miles (160km)

M45 Medium USA
Cleveland

1952. An M26 Pershing medium tank with a 105mm howitzer in the turret, replacing the usual 90mm gun. Produced in limited numbers and was used in Korea, but did not remain in service for long. *And see T26E2.*

M46 Medium USA
Detroit

1947. The M46 was simply the M26 Pershing after an overhaul. At the end of World War II the US Ordnance decided upon a standard engine and transmission for future tanks; Continental would develop the engine, Ordnance and General Motors the transmission. The result, the Continental V-12 engine and the Allison 'cross-drive' transmission became standard on most American AFVs of the 1950s and 1960s, and were first installed into war-weary M26 tanks due for refurbishment, turning them into M46s. They were considered an interim measure until a new medium tank came along, but the Korean War led to them staying in service longer than intended. The type was unofficially named 'Patton', a name later officially adopted for the M47.

M47 Medium (Patton) USA
Alco, Detroit

1952. The outbreak of the Korean War caught the US Ordnance Department in the throes of redesigning their tanks, and their medium design, the T42, was not ready. The turret and gun, though, had been completed, and as an emergency measure these were grafted on to the hull of the M46 – which was, of course, the wartime M26 with a new engine. The result was better than might have been expected and the M47 not only served the US Army well but was widely exported. The new turret was sharply contoured and had a prominent bustle to carry its radio equipment. The 90mm gun was among the first to use a blast deflector and a fume extractor, and an optical rangefinder was built into the turret roof. Some even had an early ballistic computer installed.

Armament: 1 × 90mm gun M36; 3 × MG
Ammunition: 71 + 11,500
Armour: 100mm
Crew: 5
Weight: 45.44 tons (46,167kg)
Hull length: 23ft 3in (8.00m)
Width: 11ft 6in (3.50m)
Height: 10ft 11in (3.32m)
Engine: Continental AV-1790-5, V-12, petrol, 810bhp at 2,800rpm
Road speed: 37mph (60km/hr)
Power/weight: 17.82
Range: 100 miles (160km)

M48 Medium USA
Alco, Detroit, Ford, Fisher Body

1953. The M47 was an interim design; the M48 was the new medium tank which would sweep all before it. It was to have an entirely new hull, engine, transmission, tracks, suspension – everything would improve. It was also the first US medium tank to do away with the hull machine gun and co-driver/machine gunner. Production orders were given before trials were completed and the first tanks appeared in late 1953. Although all-new, the design was quite conventional, with an air-cooled petrol engine and torsion bar suspension, while the turret was, of course, that which had already appeared on the M47. It then went through a series of variations: the **M48A1** was a rarity, a tank made of mild steel for training purposes only; the **M48A2** brought fuel injection to the engine, while the **M48A3** got rid of the petrol engine and took a diesel instead. The **M48A4** was given the turret of the M60 tank, while the **M48A5** carried a 105mm gun and was practically a cut-price M60. The M48 was

widely exported and saw combat with the US in Vietnam and with the Israelis in the Middle East.

Armament: 1 × 90mm gun M41; 2 × MG
Ammunition: 60 + 6,400
Armour: 120mm
Crew: 4
Weight: 46.43 tons (47,173kg)
Hull length: 22ft 7in (6.88m)
Width: 11ft 11in (3.37m)
Height: 10ft 2in (3.09m)
Engine: Continental V-12 air-cooled diesel, 750bhp at 2,400rpm
Road speed: 38mph (48km/hr)
Power/weight: 16.15
Range: 290 miles (465km)

M-55 S1 Slovenia
State factories

1997. The M-55 S1 is an upgraded ex-Russian T-55, the principal features being the fitting of a western-type 105mm rifled gun; the addition of explosive reactive armour modules to the glacis plate, upper hull and turret; a new computerised fire control system; a new 850bhp diesel engine; and improved fire suppression and NBC equipment. No dimensions have been released, but apart from the longer gun there should be no significant changes from the T-55 apart from the weight, now 40,000kg.

M60 Medium USA
Detroit

1956. By 1956 the US Army had decided that the M48 was not quite as good as they had hoped; at much the same time they decided to adopt the British L7 105mm tank gun, making it in the USA as the M68. Adding this to the M48A3 tank produced a useful weapon, and this, with a few added refinements such as fire control instrumentation, became the M60. It was succeeded by the **M60A1**, which had a cast hull and turret; by the **M60A2**, which had a completely new turret mounting the 152mm gun-launcher developed for the M551 Sheridan; and by the **M60A3** which went back to the 105mm gun, added a thermal jacket to the barrel, added a new fire control computer with laser rangefinder, and added a large infra-red searchlight and night vision equipment. Various detail improvements have been added since, but the model number has not advanced.

M60A3
Armament: 1 × 105mm M68; 2 × MG
Ammunition: 63 + 6,900

Armour: 120mm
Crew: 4
Weight: 51.78 tons (52,617kg)
Hull length: 22ft 10in (6.95m)
Width: 11ft 11in (3.63m)
Height: 10ft 9in (3.27m)
Engine: Continental AVDS V-12 air-cooled diesel, 750bhp at 2,400rpm
Road speed: 30mph (48km/hr)
Power/weight: 14.48
Range: 300 miles (480km)

M-84 Yugoslavia
State factories
This is actually the Russian T-72 built under licence in Yugoslavia, and with a few modifications to suit the requirements of the Yugoslav Army. The fire control system with laser rangefinder and ballistic computer is of local manufacture, as is the night vision equipment, and the engine is a locally-built V-12 diesel giving better performance than the original Russian engine.

Armament: 125mm; 2 × MG
Ammunition: 42 + 2,300
Armour: not disclosed
Crew: 3
Weight: 41.33 tons (42,000kg)
Hull length: 22ft 6in (6.86m)
Width: 11ft 9in (3.59m)
Height: 7ft 2in (2.19m)
Engine: V-12 turbocharged diesel, 1,000bhp at 2,000rpm
Road speed: 40mph (65km/hr)
Power/weight: 24.15
Range: 435 miles (700km)

M103 Heavy USA
Detroit
1952. In spite of their wartime experiences with the M6 and M26 the US Ordnance Department continued playing with heavy tank designs. They over-cooked it with the T28 and then came up with the **T43**, which was more or less an enlarged M26. When the Korean War began the War Department demanded a new heavy tank and approved the T43 for production as the M103. It was armed with a 120mm gun derived from the wartime 4.7-inch heavy anti-aircraft gun, and had a fearsome anti-armour performance. Two hundred were built, but design had been hasty and numerous modifications had to be done before the tank was fit for battle. Its biggest defect was lack of performance due to being underpowered, and, like the contemporary British Conqueror which used the same gun, its size and

complexity demanded a special logistic support channel which was grossly uneconomic. It was removed from service in 1973.

Armament: 1 × 120mm gun M58; 2 × MG
Ammunition: 38 + 6,250
Armour: 178mm
Crew: 5
Weight: 55.80 tons (56,700kg)
Hull length: 22ft 11in (6.98m)
Width: 12ft 4in (3.75m)
Height: 9ft 5in (2.87m)
Engine: Continental AV-1790-5B V-12, petrol, 810bhp at 2,800rpm
Road speed: 21mph (34km/hr)
Power/weight: 14.52
Range: 80 miles (130km)

M551 (Sheridan) USA
Cleveland
1966. The Sheridan is a fine example of what happens when designers put all their technical eggs in one basket in the hopes of making a 'quantum leap' in technology. It was intended as an airborne vehicle with overwhelming gun power; it had aluminium armour and a 152mm weapon which would fire either conventional ammunition or a guided anti-tank missile. The vehicle was plagued with problems from day one, the first production batch having to be withdrawn from service and returned to the factory for rebuilding. Troubles with the missile, the combustible cartridge for the gun, and the transmission all took years to correct, though it eventually became reasonably reliable and saw much service in Vietnam. But its excessive cost, due to all the corrective engineering, made it unpopular and it ended its days disguised as a variety of Soviet tanks at the Desert Training Center.

Armament: 1 × 152mm gun/launcher; 2 × MG
Ammunition: 10 (missiles or conventional rounds) + 4,080
Armour: not disclosed
Crew: 4
Weight: 15.58 tons (15,830kg)
Hull length: 20ft 8in (6.30m)
Width: 9ft 3in (2.81m)
Height: 7ft 5in (2.27m)
Engine: Detroit Diesel 6-V 531, turbocharged, 300bhp at 2,800rpm
Road speed: 43mph (70km/hr)
Power/weight: 19.25
Range: 370 miles (600km)

M1917 Six-Ton USA
Van Dorn, Maxwell, Best

1918. This tank was the result of taking the French drawings of the Renault FT17 tank and converting them to US manufacturing standards. In the process various improvements, largely due to the easier availability of materials in the USA, were incorporated. A bulkhead was built to separate the engine compartment from the crew, an American engine with electric self-starter replaced the crank-started Renault engine, and a new gun mounting was designed to accept either a Browning machine gun or a 37mm trench gun. Over 4,000 were ordered, but only 64 had been built by the time of the Armistice and after a total of 950 had been constructed production was stopped. It remained the principal US tank until the early 1930s; it was then stored, and in 1940 329 were supplied to Canada as training vehicles.

Armament: 1 x MG or 1 x 37mm M1916 gun
Armour: 13mm
Crew: 2
Weight: 7.25 tons (7,385kg)
Hull length: 16ft 5in (5.0m)
Width: 5ft 11in (1.80m)
Height: 7ft 7in (2.31m)
Engine: Buda 4-cylinder, petrol, 42bhp
Road speed: 5.5mph (9km/hr)
Power/weight: 5.83
Range: 30 miles (48km)

M1917A1 Six-Ton USA

1929. This was the M1917 with the Buda engine and transmission removed, the engine compartment enlarged, and a Franklin air-cooled aircraft engine installed. This gave much more power but the rear of the hull had to be completely remodelled. Six were built but it was then decided to concentrate the available funds on the development of new tanks rather than patching up the old designs.

Armament: 1 x 37mm M1915 or 1 x MG
Armour: 13mm
Crew: 2
Weight: 7.1 tons (7,215kg)
Hull length: 17ft 4in (5.28m)
Width: 5ft 11in (1.80m)
Height: 7ft 7in (2.31m)
Engine: Franklin, 6-cylinder, petrol, 100bhp
Road speed: 10mph (16km/hr)
Power/weight: 14.08
Range: 30 miles (48km/hr)

M1921 Medium USA
Rock Island

1921. Like all the combatant armies, the US Army convened various Boards of Inquiry to look at various aspects of WWI and make recommendations for future equipment and tactics. One such board recommended a single 'medium' tank to replace both the Six-Ton M1917 Light and the ex-British Mark 7 Heavy. The shape was similar to the British mediums of the period, a low hull with all-round tracks and suspension covered by skirting, but the M1921 had a raised superstructure and a front-set turret with forward-firing gun, surmounted by a cupola with a rear-firing machine gun. One prototype was built.

Armament: 1 x 57mm; 2 x MG
Armour: 25mm
Crew: 4
Weight: 20.53 tons (20,860kg)
Hull length: 21ft 7in (6.58m)
Width: 8ft 0in (2.44m)
Height: 9ft 6in (2.90m)
Engine: Murray & Tregurtha marine, 6-cylinder, petrol, 250bhp
Road speed: 10mph (16km/hr)
Power/weight: 12.19

M1922 Medium USA
Rock Island

This followed the M1921 and was a revision of that design with some new ideas, notably the British 'snake track'. The shape was altered so as to raise the rear of the track in an endeavour to improve gap-crossing ability and climbing power.

Armament: 1 x 57mm; 1 x MG
Armour: 25mm
Crew: 4
Weight: 22.32 tons (22,6890kg)
Hull length: 25ft 11in (7.88m)
Width: 8ft 10in (2.69m)
Height: 10ft 0in (3.05m)
Engine: Murray & Tregurtha marine, 6-cylinder, petrol, 250bhp
Road speed: 15mph (24km/hr)
Power/weight: 11.20

M1985 North Korea
State factories

1985. This appears to be based upon the chassis of the North Korean VTT-323 APC, a copy of the Chinese YW-531, and is a tracked amphibian fitted with a small turret similar to that used on the PT-76 light tank but mounting a conventional 85mm gun.

Suspension is by six roadwheels on each side, with rear drive and front idlers.

Armament: I × 85mm; I × ATGW; 2 × MG
Ammunition: not disclosed
Armour: not disclosed
Crew: 3
Weight: 19.68 tons (20,000kg)
Hull length: 20ft 6in (6.25m)
Width: 10ft 2in (3.10m)
Height: 9ft 2in (2.80m)
Engine: diesel, 320bhp
Road speed: not disclosed
Power/weight: 16.26
Range: not disclosed

Marmon-Herrington CTL USA
Marmon-Herrington

1940. The Marmon-Herrington Company, from 1935 onwards, had built up a small trade in armoured vehicles for export to small countries. Their early models were turretless, but in 1940 they produced this design, with a turret, in response to a request from the US Marines. It generally resembled the Rock Island products of the period, with a similar form of volute spring bogie suspension, rectangular superstructure and small turret carrying a machine gun. In 1941 the company commenced building a version of this for the Netherlands East Indies, but before these machines could be delivered the East Indies fell to Japan and the balance of the order, a total of some 240 tanks, was taken by the US Army. Some were sent to Alaska for local defence, but the majority were used for training.

Armament: 3 × MG
Armour: 25mm
Crew: 3
Weight: 8.40 tons (8,535kg)
Hull length: 11ft 6in (3.50m)
Width: 6ft 10in (2.08m)
Height: 6ft 11in (2.10m)
Engine: Hercules, 6-cylinder, petrol, 124bhp at 2,200rpm
Road speed: 30mph (48km/hr)
Power/weight: 14.76
Range: 60 miles (100km)

Matilda 1 (A11) UK
Vickers

1936. As we have already observed, in the 1930s there were many soldiers who believed that the British Army needed a slow, heavily-armoured tank armed only with machine guns, to accompany the infantry as they advanced across no-man's-land. Matilda 1 was the result of this thinking, plus a demand to keep the price below £6,000. It was a poor design; a two-man tank, it was heavily armoured and under-powered, and was a very complicated and expensive method of getting one machine gun into battle. Only 136 were made.

Armament: I × MG
Armour: 60mm
Crew: 2
Weight: 10.98 tons (11,160kg)
Hull length: 15ft 11in (4.85m)
Width: 7ft 6in (2.28m)
Height: 6ft 2in (1.86m)
Engine: Ford V-8, petrol, 70bhp at 3,500rpm
Road speed: 8mph (12.8km/hr)
Power/weight: 6.38
Range: 78 miles (125km)

Matilda 2 (A12) UK
Harland & Wolff, LMS, North British, Ruston, Vulcan

1938. The soldiers soon voiced their dislike of a two-man tank and a fresh design of Infantry Tank, the A12, was put in hand. This was a far better vehicle, with heavier armour, more power, a 2-pounder gun and much improved suspension protected by an armoured skirting plate. Much of the hull was cast, and the turret was a one-piece casting and was rotated by hydraulic power. Matilda 2 was the only British tank to remain in service from 1939–45.

Armament: I × 2-pdr; or I × 3in howitzer; I × MG
Armour: 78mm
Crew: 4
Weight: 26.5 tons (26,925kg)
Hull length: 18ft 5in (5.61m)
Width: 8ft 6in (2.59m)
Height: 8ft 3in (2.51m)
Engine: 2 × AEC 6-cylinder, diesel, 174bhp
Road speed: 15mph (25km/hr)
Power/weight: 6.58
Range: 155 miles (250km)

Matilda 3 UK
Makers as Matilda 2

This was the same as Matilda 2 except that it was fitted with two Leyland diesel engines producing 190bhp. **Matilda 3CS** was the close support version, with 3-inch howitzer.

Matilda 4 and 5 UK
Makers as Matilda 2

These were as Matilda 2 with various minor production improvements; there was no significant change in data.

Matilda Frog Australia
Maker unknown

A Matilda 4 or 5 tank modified to accept a flamethrower in the turret instead of the 2-pounder gun. The fuel and propellant gas were stored inside the tank, using the old ammunition and other storage spaces. 25 tanks were converted in 1944–45.

Matilda Hedgehog Australia
Maker unknown

During the course of the Pacific campaign the Japanese bunker, a strongly built semi-underground strongpoint, became a major problem to the Allies since it was resistant to all but the heaviest forms of attack and usually impervious to anything the forward infantry were using. The Hedgehog was a naval anti-submarine spigot mortar, which fired a 63lb (28.5kg) bomb loaded with 37lb (17kg) of Torpex high explosive, and some unrecorded genius realised that such a bomb could demolish almost any bunker. The only problem was to get it into position, and from this idea the Matilda Hedgehog appeared. It was a standard Matilda 2 tank, with a platform of boiler-plate over the engine cover upon which seven spigots were mounted. The platform could be rotated or tilted by hydraulic rams so as to point the spigots and their bombs in the desired direction. Normal practice was to fire single bombs to adjust on to the target and then fire the remainder as a salvo, a performance which generally terminated any opposition.

Matilda Murray Australia
Maker unknown

A modification of a Matilda Frog from gas propulsion of the flame fluid to cordite propulsion, a measure which promised greater storage space for the flame thrower fluid. It is doubtful if more than one was ever made.

Maus Germany
Alkett

1942. In 1942 Porsche were ordered by Hitler to design a super-heavy tank with the maximum possible armour and a 128mm gun. Difficulties arose in the supply of components, substitutions and modifications had to be made, and it was not until December 1943 that the first chassis was tested. The complete tank, with turret and gun, was tested in June 1944. The second prototype suffered engine failure during its first tests in late 1944, and work was abandoned shortly afterwards. The tank was simply an enormous rectangle of armour on a multi-wheel volute spring suspension, Both prototypes were blown up at their proving ground in 1945 as the Allies approached.

Armament: 1 × 12.8cm KwK44; 1 × 75mm KwK33; 1 × MG
Ammunition: 32 × 12.8cm + 200 × 75mm
Armour: 240mm
Crew: 5
Weight: 188 tons (191,020kg)
Hull length: 33ft 1in (10.09m)
Width: 12ft 1in (3.67m)
Height: 12ft 0in (3.66m)
Engine: Mercedes-Benz V-12, petrol, 1,080bhp
Road speed: 12.5mph (20km/hr)
Power/weight: 5.75
Range: 120 miles (190km)

Medium A UK
Foster

1917. Also called the **Tritton Chaser** and **Whippet**. The first British lightweight tank, developed for cavalry use as a scout machine. Low tracks with the hull between them, sloped front engine compartment and small fighting compartment at rear with a fixed superstructure. Each track was driven by a separate engine and gearbox and steering was done by varying the engine speeds. Extensively used in combat during 1918.

Armament: 3 or 4 × MG
Armour: 14mm
Crew: 3
Weight: 14 tons (14,225kg)
Hull length: 20ft 0in (6.10m)
Width: 8ft 7in (2.62m)
Height: 9ft 0in (2.74m)
Engine: 2 × Tyler JB4, 6-cylinder, petrol, total 90bhp
Road speed: 8mph (12km/hr)
Power/weight: 6.43

Medium B UK
Metropolitan

1918. Designed by Major Wilson (who produced the Wilson epicyclic gearbox), this went back to the lozenge shape favoured by the early British designers, though in a smaller edition and with a large fixed rectangular turret on top of the hull. The engine was in a separate compartment, relieving the crew of the fumes, and what appear to be small sponsons are actually side entrance doors. An order for 450 was given, but only 45 were built before the Armistice stopped production. Several were sent to Russia with the Allied Intervention Force and left there. The rest were employed as training tanks until they fell to pieces. At least one had a revolving turret with a 2-pounder gun fitted experimentally.

Armament: 4 × MG
Armour: 14mm
Crew: 4
Weight: 18 tons (18,290kg)
Hull length: 22ft 9in (6.93m)
Width: 8ft 10in (2.69m)
Height: 8ft 6in (2.59m)
Engine: Ricardo, 6-cylinder, petrol, 100bhp
Road speed: 6mph (10km/hr)
Power/weight: 5.55

Medium C (Hornet) UK
Foster

1918. Designed by Fosters and probably the best tank of the WWI period, this resembled the Medium B in having all-round tracks and a large fixed turret on top of the hull mounting five machine guns in ball mounts. The engine was separated from the crew compartment, which was provided with forced ventilation, and several details such as communication were improved in line with suggestions made by service tank crews. 450 were ordered, but only 48 were built before production was stopped after the Armistice. These tanks formed the nucleus of the post-WWI Royal Tank Regiment.

Armament: 5 × MG
Armour: 12mm
Crew: 4
Weight: 20 tons (20,320kg)
Hull length: 26ft 0in (7.92m)
Width: 8ft 4in (2.54m)
Height: 9ft 6in (2.90m)
Engine: Ricardo 6-cylinder, petrol, 150bhp
Road speed: 8mph (12km/hr)
Power/weight: 7.5

Medium D UK
Woolwich

1920. This was designed in 1918 to be the tank which would crash through the German lines and harry their rear echelons during the 1919 Offensive. Indeed, it was the promise of this tank which prompted the famous 'Plan 1919' of Colonel J.F.C.

Fuller. In the event, it was perhaps just as well the war ended in 1918, since the Medium D would never have been ready for the spring of 1919, nor would it have been as reliable or effective as predicted. With low-set tracks, lower at the front so as to give better visibility, and a high forward fixed turret, it had the engine at the rear in a separate compartment. The prime novelty was the 'snake' track, a series of steel shoes suspended on a steel cable. This conformed to the ground well; and had some inherent springing, allowing the tank to reach a high speed (for its day). But it proved unreliable and prone to breakage and was too expensive. Only a handful were ever made, and they were soon replaced by the Vickers Medium.

Armament: 3 × MG
Armour: 10mm
Crew: 3
Weight: 20 tons (20,320kg)
Hull length: 30ft 0in (9.14m)
Width: 7ft 5in (2.26m)
Height: 9ft 3in (2.82m)
Engine: Armstrong-Siddeley Puma, 6-cylinder, 240bhp
Road speed: 23mph (37km/hr)
Power/weight: 12.0

Merkava Mark I Israel
IMI

1974. Experience showed Israel that armour and fire-power were more important than agility in their particular circumstances, and they set about designing a tank along those lines. The Merkava is low-set, well shaped to deflect shot from any direction, well-armoured and mounts a powerful 105mm gun. The layout is rather unusual, with the engine at the front, but this allows rear doors to be fitted in the hull giving access to the fighting compartment and allowing rapid restocking of ammunition, delivery of supplies or evacuation of casualties.

Armament: 1 × 105mm; 3 × MG
Ammunition: 62–85 + 10,000
Armour: not disclosed
Crew: 4
Weight: 59.05 tons (60,000kg)
Hull length: 24ft 5in (7.45m)
Width: 12ft 2in (3.70m)
Height: 8ft 8in (2.64m)
Engine: Teledyne Continental V-12 diesel, 900bhp at 2,400rpm
Road speed: 29mph (46km/hr)
Power/weight: 15.24
Range: 250 miles (400km)

Merkava Mark 2 Israel
IMI
1983. This was an improved Mark 1. Additional composite armour was fitted to the turret and frontal area, new fire control equipment installed, and a new transmission of local manufacture was adopted. No significant change in data.

Merkava Mark 3 Israel
IMI
1989. This constitutes a major re-design of the Merkava, with the installation of a 120mm smoothbore gun, a new engine, improved fire control systems, sights, vision equipment and turret controls, new NBC equipment, new suspension and the adoption of composite and explosive reactive armour in modular form on all surfaces of the tank.

Armament: 120mm; 3 × MG
Ammunition: 50 + 10,000
Armour: not disclosed
Crew: 4
Weight: 61.02 tons (62,000kg)
Hull length: 24ft 11in (7.60m)
Width: 12ft 2in (3.70m)
Height: 8ft 8in (2.64m)
Engine: Teledyne AVDS 1790-9Ar V-12, turbocharged diesel, 1,200bhp
Road speed: 34mph (55km/hr)
Power/weight: 19.67
Range: 310 miles (500km)

Merkava Mark 4 Israel
IMI
In 1992 it was disclosed that a Merkava Mark 4 was under development, and that the principal feature would be that it would be entirely designed and manufactured within Israel instead of, as the previous models, relying here and there on foreign suppliers for specialised component parts. No further details have been disclosed.

Morris-Martel UK
Morris
1925. In 1924, in an endeavour to convince the cavalry that they could have a useful mechanised role, Colonel G. le Q. Martel, who had served in the Tank Corps during World War I, designed and built at his own expense a one-man armoured 'tankette'. In 1925 he demonstrated it to the War Office, who were sufficiently impressed to order four to be built by Morris Motors. These performed well but showed that it was unreasonable to expect one man to drive and operate the machine gun, so the design was changed to a two-man vehicle. Six of these were built and employed as scouting vehicles by the British Army's Experimental Armoured Force in 1927, but subsequent development was left up to the inventors; Martel could not afford it, and Morris Motors were not interested in throwing their money down that particular hole, and the Morris-Martel tankette came to an end. They resembled half-tracks in reverse, having a tracked suspension beneath the front engine and the crew compartment, and dragging a pair of steerable wheels along behind them.

Armament: 1 × LMG
Armour: 8mm
Crew: 2
Weight: 2.75 tons (2,795kg)
Hull length: 9ft 2in (2.79m)
Width: 4ft 8in (1.22m)
Height: 5ft 7in (1.70m)
Engine: Morris 4-cylinder, petrol
Road speed: 15mph (24km/hr)

Mother UK
Foster
1915. The prototype of the first combat tank, and the first appearance of the traditional lozenge shape with all-round tracks. 'Mother' was built by Foster of Lincoln to a design by Lieutenant Wilson and the shape was due to a demand that it should be able to cross wide trenches and clamber over steep obstacles. Theoretically, a machine with 45-foot diameter wheels would meet the requirement, and the shape of the lower forward section of the track on Mother is virtually a quadrant of a 45-foot wheel. It first moved under its own power on 12 January 1916 and was later used to demonstrate the potential of the tank to the politicians and generals. It was decided that two types of tank would be built; 'Male' armed with two 6-pounder guns in sponsons, and 'Female' armed only with machine guns. 'Mother' was a Male.

Armament: 2 × 6-pdr; 2 × MG
Armour: none; prototype was of mild steel
Crew: 8
Weight: 31 tons (31,500kg)
Hull length: 31ft 3in (9.52m)
Width: 13ft 8in (4.16m)
Height: 8ft 1in (2.43m)
Engine: Daimler, 6-cylinder, petrol, 105bhp
Road speed: 3.7mph (6km/hr)
Power/weight: 3.38
Range: 23 miles (36km)

MS Light Russia
State factories

1923. This, the first purely Russian tank design, was based upon the Renault FT17 but made changes to the turret, adopted an entirely new transverse engine and transmission, re-shaped the hull, and introduced a new sprung suspension using seven small coil sprung roadwheels on each side. It also carried the usual Renault 'tail'; to improve trench-crossing ability. This became the **MS-1**; it was soon given a more powerful engine and became the **MS-2**. Finally, the **MS-3** appeared, with another new engine, the front re-designed to have a full-width sloping glacis plate and a second machine gun in the rear face of the turret. Numbers of these survived until the German invasion of 1941, when some were hurriedly fitted with a 45mm anti-tank gun, but proved useless against the more modern German tanks.

MS-3

Armament: 1 × 37mm M1916; 2 × MG
Armour: 16mm
Crew: 2
Weight: 5.41 tons (5,500kg)
Hull length: 11ft 6in (3.50m)
Width: 5ft 9in (1.76m)
Height: 6ft 11in (2.12m)
Engine: 6-cylinder, petrol, 65bhp
Road speed: 10mph (16km/hr)
Power/weight: 12.01
Range: 38 miles (60km)

Nbfz Germany
See PzKpfw 5 (Nbfz)

OF-40 Italy
OTO-Melara

1980. This was designed for the export market and a number were eventually purchased by Dubai. It is in the contemporary style with a low hull, sloped glacis, skirted tracks with seven roadwheels, and a large bustled turret carrying a 105mm gun. This has a thermal sleeve and fume extractor and is chambered to fire all 105mm NATO-standard tank ammunition. The fire control system appears to have been assembled from a variety of sources and includes laser rangefinding, day and night vision sights and full ballistic computation ability.

Armament: 1 × 105mm L/52; 2 × MG
Ammunition: 57 + 5,700
Armour: not disclosed
Crew: 4
Weight: 44.29 tons (45,500kg)

Hull length: 22ft 8in (6.89m)
Width: 11ft 6in (3.50m)
Height: 8ft 0in (2.45m)
Engine: MTU V-10 supercharged multi-fuel, 830bhp at 2,200rpm
Road speed: 37mph (60km/hr)
Power/weight: 18.06
Range: 375 miles (600km)

OF-40/120 Italy
OTO-Melara

1993. Another export venture from OTO-Melara, this is simply the OF-40 brought up to date and given a 120mm smoothbore gun. The hull and running gear are more or less the same as before but the turret is new and a more powerful engine is fitted. The gun is stabilised on both axes, has a thermal sleeve, fume extractor and muzzle reference system, and is chambered to fire the same ammunition as the Abrams, Leclerc and Leopard tank guns.

Armament: 1 × 120mm; 2 × MG
Ammunition: 40 + 2,500
Armour: not disclosed
Crew: 4
Weight: 48.22 tons (49,000kg)
Hull length: 23ft 0in (7.01m)
Width: 11ft 0in (3.35m)
Height: 7ft 11in (2.42m)
Engine: MTU V-10 supercharged multi-fuel, 1,000bhp
Road speed: 40mph (65km/hr)
Power/weight: 20.74
Range: 375 miles (600km)

Olifant Mark I/A South Africa
Armscor

1980. The Olifant ('Elephant') is a British Centurion (of which South Africa bought about 300) which has been modernised by the fitting of a 105mm L7-type gun and a new diesel engine, both made in South Africa. Various other improvements, in the sighting equipment, vision devices and other interior arrangements, were made, and the result became the Olifant Mark 1/A.

Armament: 1 × 105mm L7: 2 × MG
Ammunition: 73 + 5,600
Armour: not disclosed
Crew: 4
Weight: 55.12 tons (56,000kg)
Hull length: 25ft 7in (7.79m)
Width: 10ft 10in (3.30m)
Height: 9ft 10in (2.99m)
Engine: V-12 diesel, 750bhp at 2,300rpm
Road speed: 27mph (45km/hr)

Power/weight: 13.60
Range: 310 miles (500km)

Olifant Mark 1/B South Africa
OMC

1991. This is a complete rebuild of the Centurion (or Olifant Mark 1/A) to provide it with new torsion bar suspension set in a double floor; a new and more powerful engine with automatic transmission; additional armour on the front of the hull and turret; new track skirts intended to counter shaped charge attack; rebuilding of the turret to provide ammunition stowage in the bustle; new vision and sighting systems; new fire control computer; the addition of a fume extractor and thermal sleeve to the gun; a fire detection and suppression system in the crew compartment; and sundry minor changes intended to improve crew comfort and efficiency.

Armament: 1 × 105mm L7; 2 × MG
Ammunition: 68 + 5,500
Armour: not disclosed
Crew: 4
Weight: 57.08 tons (58,000kg)
Hull length: 27ft 2in (8.29m)
Width: 11ft 3in (3.43m)
Height: 8ft 4in (2.55m)
Engine: V-12 diesel, 940bhp
Road speed: 36mph (58km/hr)
Power/weight: 16.56
Range: 310 miles (500km)

Osorio EE-T1 Brazil
Engesa

1985. Designed in Brazil. The first prototype was fitted with a Vickers 105mm turret, the second with a GIAT 120mm gun turret. Both these have been extensively tested in several countries, but no major orders have yet been placed. Standard layout with three-man turret, six dual roadwheels on each side, hydro-pneumatic suspension, front idler, rear drive. Gyro-stabilised sights and gun, and various fire control options have been offered.

Prototype 1
Armament: 1 × 105mm (UK L7); 2 × MG
Ammunition: 45 + 5,000
Armour: not disclosed
Crew: 4
Weight: 40.25 tons (40,900kg)
Hull length: 23ft 5in (7.13m)
Width: 10ft 8in (3.26m)
Height: 7ft 9in (2.37m)
Engine: MWM TBD234 12-cylinder turbocharged diesel, 1,100bhp at 2,350rpm
Road speed: 43mph (70km/hr)

Power/weight: 27.32
Range: 340 miles (550km)

Prototype 2
Armament: 1 × 120mm; 2 × MG
Ammunition: 38 + 5,000
Armour: not disclosed
Crew: 4
Weight: 43 tons (43,700kg)
Hull length: 23ft 5in (7.13m)
Width: 10ft 8in (3.26m)
Height: 10ft 6in (3.20m)
Engine: MWM TBD234 12-cylinder turbocharged diesel, 1,100bhp at 2,350rpm
Road speed: 43mph (70km/hr)
Power/weight: 25.58
Range: 340 miles (550km)

Panther (Panzerkampfwagen 5), Ausf D
Germany
Daimler-Benz, Henschel, MAN, Niedersachsen

1942. The Panther tank originated with a demand for a tank capable of meeting the Soviet T-34 and beating it. It was developed by MAN and incorporated sloped armour and a 75mm gun twice as long as that of the PzKpfw 4. On Hitler's orders it was fitted with an even longer gun, and went into production in November 1942.

It was somewhat heavy for a medium tank but with its powerful gun, thick armour and a good turn of speed, it proved to be an excellent design. Its hurried development led to some teething troubles; of the first 300 made, those which survived their first battle went back to the factory for extensive modification. But after this setback it went on to become probably the best German tank of the war, superior to the Soviet T-34 in every respect. About 5,500 were built, a poor figure compared to the T-34 or M4 Sherman and indicative of Germany's inability to mobilize its full industrial potential.

Note that the Ausf D was the first production batch, followed by A, G and then F in that order.

Armament: 1 × 75mm L/70; 2 × MG
Ammunition: 79 + 5,100
Armour: 100mm
Crew: 5
Weight: 42.32 tons (43,000kg)
Hull length: 22ft 6in (6.85m)
Width: 11ft 2in (3.40m)
Height: 9ft 8in (2.95m)
Engine: Maybach HL230P30, V-12, petrol, 700bhp at 3,000rpm
Road speed: 28mph (46km/hr)
Power/weight: 16.54
Range: 125 miles (200km)

Panther Variant Models

Ausf A

August 1943. Stronger suspension, new commander's cupola, loader's escape hatch added, ammunition resupply hatch removed. Turret front armour increased to 110mm.

Ausf G

March 1944. Redesigned hull with thicker side armour, transmission oil cooler added, plus various minor improvements. Weight up to 44.29 tons (45,500kg).

Ausf F

March 1945. New turret with smaller frontal aspect and optical rangefinder (stereoscopic), hull roof thickened from 16mm to 25mm. Various other small changes but due to non-delivery of turrets, no Ausf F tanks were ever completed.

Panzer 39 Switzerland
See LT-H

Panzerbefehlswagen I Germany
Daimler-Benz

1935. This 'armoured command vehicle' was simply a conversion based upon the lengthened chassis of the PzKpfw 1B. The turret was removed and the hull built up to form a rigid superstructure with room inside for radio receivers and transmitters, maps and the other requirements of command. A single machine gun was in a ball mount on the right front of this office, with a commander's hatch above it. They could be found with the typical frame antenna of the period, or, in later years, with more modern whip antennas.

Armament: 1 × MG
Ammunition: 900
Armour: 13mm
Crew: 3
Weight: 5.80 tons (5,900kg)
Hull length: 14ft 6in (4.42m)
Width: 6ft 9in (2.06m)
Height: 6ft 6in (1.99m)
Engine: Maybach NL38TR, 6-cylinder, petrol, 100bhp at 3,000rpm
Road speed: 25mph (40km/hr)
Power/weight: 17.24
Range: 105 miles (170km)

Panzerkampfwagen I, Ausf A Germany
Daimler-Benz, Henschel, Krupp, MAN, Wegmann

1934. The PzKpfw 1 was an interim vehicle intended for rapid building and the training of the new armoured formations that were raised when the German Army openly rearmed from 1933 onwards. It was a small two-man tank very much in the style of the time, and like so many of its contemporaries, it shows evidence of deriving its layout from the Carden-Loyd carriers, although it improved on them by having a rotating turret. Driver and commander shared the same compartment, the driver on the left and the commander in the small turret on the right. The transmission train ran along the centre of the floor to a differential which drove the front sprockets. The suspension system used five roadwheels, the last three of which were held by an outside girder, a useful recognition feature.

Armament: 2 × MG
Ammunition: 2,250
Armour: 13mm
Crew: 2
Weight: 5.31 tons (5,400kg)
Hull length: 13ft 2in (4.02m)
Width: 6ft 9in (2.06m)
Height: 5ft 8in (1.72m)
Engine: Krupp M305, flat-4-cylinder, petrol, 57bhp at 2,500rpm
Road speed: 23mph (37km/hr)
Power/weight: 10.75
Range: 90 miles (145km)

PzKpfw I, Ausf B Germany
Daimler-Benz, Henschel, Krupp, MAN, Wegmann

1935. After 500 Ausf A had been built the Ausf B model was introduced with a larger engine, a slightly longer hull and better performance. Nearly 2,000 of the 1B were made and both types were tried out in the Spanish Civil War where they were found to be vulnerable to any form of anti-tank gun. However, there were not enough heavier tanks in 1939 and the 1A and 1B had to fight in Poland and France. A few were even taken to Russia in 1941, but the remainder were removed from front-line service and converted into SP anti-tank guns, gun tractors or command vehicles.

Armament: 2 × MG
Ammunition: 2,250
Armour: 13mm
Crew: 2
Weight: 5.71 tons (5,800kg)

Hull length: 14ft 6in (4.42m)
Width: 6ft 9in (2.06m)
Height: 5ft 8in (1.72m)
Engine: Maybach NL38TR, 6-cylinder, petrol, 100bhp at 3,000rpm
Road speed: 25mph (40km/hr)
Power/weight: 17.51
Range: 105 miles (170km)

PzKpfw 1, Ausf C Germany
Krauss-Maffei

1942. This was a totally different vehicle to the Ausf A and B types, and one is inclined to wonder why it never had a number of its own, since there is little resemblance between them. Development of this model was ordered in 1939 to produce a scouting tank for airborne troops but progress was slow and production did not commence until July 1942. The hull and turret were broadly similar to those of the Ausf A and B, but the suspension was by torsion bars to overlapping roadwheels, allowing it to develop a high speed. The driver and commander had new vision arrangements, the armour doubled in thickness, and the main armament was a 20mm cannon, with coaxial machine gun. Only 40 were made, and all went to the Eastern Front; and remained there.

Armament: 1 × 20mm cannon; 1 × MG
Armour: 30mm
Crew: 2
Weight: 7.87 tons (8,000kg)
Hull length: 13ft 9in (4.19m)
Width: 6ft 3in (1.92m)
Height: 6ft 4in (1.94m)
Engine: Maybach HL45P, 6-cylinder, petrol, 150bhp at 3,800rpm
Road speed: 50mph (80km/hr)
Power/weight: 19.05
Range: 185 miles (300km)

PzKpfw 1, Ausf F Germany
Krauss-Maffei

1942. This was another complete departure from the normal course of development. It resembled the Ausf C in having the interleaved roadwheels and torsion bar suspension, but its purpose was as an infantry assault tank, and it therefore had 80mm of armour all round and exceptionally wide tracks so as to spread the load in soft ground. Commander and driver were well protected and had only indirect vision devices, and the turret carried the usual two machine guns. The design had been ordered in 1939, but did not appear until April 1942; nevertheless it was small and just about impervious

to any Russian anti-tank gun of the time. Only 30 were built.

Armament: 2 × MG
Ammunition: 2,250
Armour: 80mm
Crew: 2
Weight: 20.66 tons (21,000kg)
Hull length: 14ft 4in (4.38m)
Width: 8ft 9in (2.64m)
Height: 6ft 9in (2.05m)
Engine: Maybach HL45P, 6-cylinder, petrol, 150bhp at 3,800rpm
Road speed: 25mph (40km/hr)
Power/weight: 7.26
Range: 93 miles (150km)

Panzerkampfwagen 2, Ausf a/ Germany
Daimler-Benz, MAN

1936. The new medium tanks which the German Army required in the 1930s proved slow to develop and produce, and another interim tank was necessary. The PzKpfw 2 was called for in 1935 and the first ones were issued in 1936. It was another light tank with a three-man crew and armed with a 20mm gun. This early model differed considerably from the production version in having a suspension of six small wheels linked by an external girder and a six-sided turret with a flat front.

Armament: 1 × 20mm; 1 × MG
Ammunition: 180 + 2,250
Armour: 13mm
Crew: 3
Weight: 7.48 tons (7,600kg)
Hull length: 14ft 4in (4.38m)
Width: 7ft 0in (2.14m)
Height: 6ft 5in (1.95m)
Engine: Maybach HL57TR, 6-cylinder, petrol, 130bhp at 2,600rpm
Road speed: 25mph (40km/hr)
Power/weight: 17.37
Range: 125 miles (200km)

PzKpfw 2, Ausf b/ Germany
Daimler-Benz

1937. After about 75 of the Ausf a/ tanks had been made, production stopped and large modifications were performed on the design to produce this Ausf b/ version. The general shape was the same but the turret was more smooth and with a prominent rounded mantlet, and there were several detail changes to the suspension, though it remained the same pattern. There were also improvements to the engine cooling and breathing systems.

Armament: 1 × 20mm; 1 × MG
Ammunition: 180 + 2,250
Armour: 13mm
Crew: 3
Weight: 7.77 tons (7,900kg)
Hull length: 15ft 7in (4.76m)
Width: 7ft 0in (2.14m)
Height: 6ft 5in (1.96m)
Engine: Maybach HL621TR, 6-cylinder, petrol, 140bhp
at 2,600rpm
Road speed: 25mph (40km/hr)
Power/weight: 18
Range: 125 miles (200km)

PzKpfw 2, Ausf c/A, B, C Germany
Alkett, Daimler-Benz, FAMO, Henschel, MAN, MIAG, Wegmann

March 1937. This became the first full production model of the Panzer 2, and was vastly different to the two pre-production types. The suspension was the greatest change, using five larger roadwheels on oblique leaf-spring suspension, with four return rollers. The hull was generally the same with a low superstructure just above track level, the turret was smoother and had a rounded mantlet, and there were improvements to the engine ventilation and cooling and to the steering and transmission systems. The differences between this Ausf A and the subsequent B and C were relatively minor and principally driven by production considerations.

Armament: 1 × 20mm; 1 × MG
Ammunition: 180 + 2,250
Armour: 16mm
Crew: 3
Weight: 8.75 tons (8,900kg)
Hull length: 15ft 9in (4.81m)
Width: 7ft 3in (2.22m)
Height: 6ft 6in (1.99m)
Engine: Maybach HL62TR, 6-cylinder, petrol, 140bhp
at 2,600rpm
Road speed: 25mph (40km/hr)
Power/weight: 16
Range: 125 miles (200km)

PzKpfw 2, Ausf D and E Germany
MAN

1938. These were entirely different to the other models in the Panzer 2 series, since they were intended as light cavalry reconnaissance vehicles and were thus geared to produce a higher speed. The hull superstructure was straight, and not curved back as in the earlier models, and the suspension was by torsion bars to four large roadwheels without return rollers. The track of the

Ausf D was dry-pin; that of the Ausf E was fully lubricated and this led to new designs of drive sprockets and idlers. Only 48 of these were built; they saw action in Poland but revision of tactical theories led to their withdrawal and conversion into flamethrowers in March 1940.

Armament: 1 × 20mm; 1 × MG
Ammunition: 180 + 2,250
Armour: 30mm
Crew: 3
Weight: 9.84 tons (10,000kg)
Hull length: 15ft 3in (4.65m)
Width: 7ft 6in (2.30m)
Height: 6ft 9in (2.06m)
Engine: Maybach HL62TRM, 6-cylinder, petrol, 140bhp
at 2,600rpm
Road speed: 34mph (55km/hr)
Power/weight: 14.22
Range: 125 miles (200km)

PzKpfw 2, Ausf F Germany
FAMO

1941. This version of the Panzer 2 series differed in having the nose of the hull made of flat plates instead of a single rounded plate. It also had the front of the superstructure as a straight plate the width of the hull. Armour thickness was increased all round. The suspension was the same five-sheet leaf-spring system as before, but with a new convex idler wheel.

Armament: 1 × 20mm; 1 × MG
Ammunition: 180 + 2,250
Armour: 35mm
Crew: 3
Weight: 9.35 tons (9,500kg)
Hull length: 15ft 9in (4.81m)
Width: 7ft 6in (2.28m)
Height: 7ft 1in (2.15m)
Engine: Maybach HL521TR, 6-cylinder, petrol, 140bhp
at 2,600rpm
Road speed: 25mph (40km/hr)
Power/weight: 14.97
Range: 125 miles (200km)

PzKpfw 2, Ausf G Germany
MAN

1941. Also known as the **PzKpfw 2 *nA*** (*neuer Art* – new pattern) or **VK901**, this was developed in the quest for a faster tank. The specification was issued in 1939 but the design was not perfected until 1941. The prime innovation was the introduction of the system of overlapping roadwheels sprung by torsion bars, which was gradually adopted by almost all subsequent German tanks. The hull was similar to previous PzKpfw 2 versions, as was the turret, but direct vision ports were removed from the turret and the commander had only periscopes. No more than a dozen were made and there is apparently no record of their ever being issued to service units.

Armament: 1 × 20mm cannon; 1 × MG
Ammunition: 180 + 2,250
Armour: 30mm
Crew: 3
Weight: 10.33 tons (10,500kg)
Hull length: 13ft 11in (4.24m)
Width: 7ft 10in (2.38m)
Height: 6ft 9in (2.05m)
Engine: Maybach HL66, 6-cylinder, petrol, 180bhp at 2,800rpm
Road speed: 31mph (50km/hr)
Power/weight: 17.42
Range: 125 miles (200km)

PzKpfw 2, Ausf J Germany
MAN

1942. Also called the **PzKpfw 2 *nA* Verstärkt** ('strengthened') or **VK1601**. This was called for in 1939, the object being to provide as much armour protection as possible. Development appears to have been at a low priority and production did not begin until mid-1942. The armour was thickened to 80mm and the hull and superstructure were in one welded unit, making a much smoother contour than earlier models. The driver and radio operator had heavier vision blocks, and they now entered their seats via round hatches on the hull side. The commander entered the turret by means of a small cupola hatch. The interleaved torsion bar suspension was adopted, suitably strengthened to take the weight. A new engine was fitted, but the benefit of this was more than cancelled out by the doubling of the weight. No more than 22 were made.

Armament: 1 × 20mm cannon; 1 × MG
Ammunition: 180 + 2,250
Armour: 80mm
Crew: 3
Weight: 18.20 tons (18,500kg)
Hull length: 13ft 11in (4.24m)
Width: 8ft 6in (2.59m)
Height: 6ft 10in (2.08m)
Engine: Maybach HL45P, 6-cylinder, petrol, 150bhp at 3,800rpm
Road speed: 19mph (31km/hr)
Power/weight: 8.24
Range: 125 miles (200km)

PzKpfw 2 *nA*, Ausf H Germany
MAN

1942. Also known as **VK903**, this was to have rather more armour than the basic Panzer 2 models, and different gearing in order to produce more speed; in the event, and due to indecision about which transmission to adopt, production plans slipped further and further back, and by the time it was decided to use the PzKpfw 38(t) gearbox, nobody was interested, Four were built and the project was then cancelled.

PzKpfw 2, Ausf L Germany
See Luchs

PzKpfw 2, Ausf M Germany
MAN

1943. Also called VK1301 this was an off-shoot from the Ausf H above; when that failed, the remains were suggested as a basis for a heavily-armoured reconnaissance tank. Although a photograph purporting to be of this vehicle exists, one suspects it to be a mock up since there is no record of production ever commencing nor any reliable data.

Panzerkampfwagen 3, Ausf A Germany
Daimler-Benz

1939. The PzKpfw 3 was one of the two tanks specifically designed for the new armoured formations of the Wehrmacht and it was based on the experience gained with the two small interim designs. It was intended to be the 'anti-tank' tank, and to be armed with a high-velocity armour-piercing gun, but when it first appeared it was armed with a not very adequate version of the infantry 37mm anti-tank gun. However, it did have a large turret ring which enabled bigger guns to be fitted later. Only ten of this first pre-production model were built; the armour was too thin and the suspension, using five coil-sprung roadwheels, proved unsatisfactory.

Armament: 1 × 37mm L/46; 3 × MG
Ammunition: 150 + 4,500
Armour: 15mm
Crew: 5
Weight: 15.15 tons (15,400kg)
Hull length: 17ft 8in (5.69m)
Width: 9ft 3in (2.81m)
Height: 7ft 8in (2.34m)
Engine: Maybach HL108TR, V-12, petrol, 250bhp at 3,000rpm
Road speed: 21mph (34km/hr)

Power/weight: 16.50
Range: 100 miles (165km)

PzKpfw 3, Ausf B Germany
Daimler-Benz

1937. This model introduced a completely new suspension using eight small roadwheels set in pairs on leaf springs, with three return rollers. There were also some small alterations to the turret and engine deck, but only 15 were built since the suspension still wasn't right. Except for being slightly heavier, the dimensions and performance were the same as for the Ausf A.

PzKpfw 3, Ausf C Germany
Daimler-Benz

1937. This was still part of the development phase of the Panzer 3 design and was an attempt to improve the riding qualities. It still had eight roadwheels on each side but the springing was a combination of leaf and coil springs on different wheel stations. There were also improvements to the final drive gearing and the brake steering and a servo-assisted clutch. Only 17 were built; they went into service and saw action in Poland in 1939, after which they were withdrawn and scrapped.

Armament: 1 × 37mm; 3 × MG
Ammunition: 121 + 4,500
Armour: 15mm
Crew: 5
Weight: 15.75 tons (16,000kg)
Hull length: 19ft 2in (5.85m)
Width: 9ft 3in (2.82m)
Height: 7ft 11in (2.42m)
Engine: Maybach HL108TR, V-12, petrol, 250bhp at 3,000rpm
Road speed: 25mph (40km/hr)
Power/weight: 15.87
Range: 100 miles (165km)

PzKpfw 3, Ausf D Germany
Daimler-Benz

1938. The 'D' series represented another step towards the final design, and another design of suspension; this time it was leaf springs all round with those springing the first and last roadwheels canted at an angle so as to improve the weight distribution. There were also changes to the driving sprocket and idler, a new cupola and new engine covers designed to improve protection for the engine and transmission. This turned out to improve the protection at the expense of ventilation, and as a rule the tanks travelled with the engine

covers wedged open. A total of 30 were built in the first half of 1938, all of which saw action in Poland. Most were withdrawn early in 1940 though a handful appeared in Norway later in that year.

Dimensions and data: exactly the same as Ausf C

PzKpfw 3, Ausf E Germany
Daimler-Benz, Henschel, MAN

1938. The second half of 1938 was spent in doing a complete re-design of the suspension system, after which the Ausf E became the standard and went into series production in December. The suspension had finalised on six dual wheels carried on torsion bars, with three return rollers. This also allowed the weight to be increased and more armour was added. Escape hatches were placed on both sides of the hull, the engine was more powerful, and a new transmission was introduced.

Armament: 1 × 37mm; 3 × MG
Ammunition: 131 + 4,500
Armour: 30mm
Crew: 5
Weight: 19.19 tons (19,500kg)
Hull length: 17ft 9in (5.38m)
Width: 9ft 6in (2.91m)
Height: 8ft 0in (2.44m)
Engine: Maybach HL120TR, V-12, petrol, 300bhp at 3,000rpm
Road speed: 25mph (40km/hr)
Power/weight: 15.63
Range: 100 miles (165km)

PzKpfw 3, Ausf F Germany
Alkett, Daimler-Benz, FAMO, Henschel, MAN

1939. This was the second major production run and the change was principally to the engine ignition system, though some minor improvements were thrown in. First models had the usual 37mm gun, but the final 100 or so, built in the spring of 1940, were given the first of several armament changes, the 50mm KwK L/42 gun. A total of 432 Ausf F were built and they remained in service until 1944.

Data: as for Ausf E above

PzKpfw 3, Ausf G Germany
Alkett, Daimler-Benz, FAMO, Henschel, MAN, Niedersachsen, Wegmann

This model, of which 600 were built between April 1940 and February 1941, saw the first major changes in the basic design. Armour thickness was increased all round, turret ventilation improved, the 50mm L/42 gun became standard (although some early examples were built with the 37mm gun, they were later recalled and up-gunned) and a new commander's cupola was introduced.

Armament: 1 × 50mm L/42; 2 × MG
Ammunition: 99 + 2,700
Armour: 37mm
Crew: 5
Weight: 20.17 tons (20,500kg)
Hull length: 17ft 9in (5.41m)
Width: 9ft 8in (2.95m)
Height: 8ft 0in (2.44m)
Engine: Maybach HL120TR, V-12, petrol, 300bhp at 3,000rpm
Road speed: 25mph (40km/hr)
Power/weight: 14.87
Range: 100 miles (165km)

PzKpfw 3, Ausf H Germany
Alkett, Henschel, MAN, MIAG, Niedersachsen, Wegmann

1940. The Ausf H was the first Panzer 3 to be designed to take the 5cm L/42 gun (all the earlier ones had it fitted as a retrospective modification) and hence the turret differed slightly in shape and had the rear formed from a single sheet of armour steel. At the same time the hull was given additional 30mm plates, thus doubling the armour thickness. This model also introduced the turret basket for the first time in a German tank. It also had new transmission and drive sprockets, probably necessitated by the increase in weight. A total of 300 Ausf H were built 1940–44.

Armament: 1 × 50mm L/42; 2 × MG
Ammunition: 99 + 2,700
Armour: 60mm
Crew: 5
Weight: 21.46 tons (21,800kg)
Hull length: 17ft 9in (5.41m)
Width: 9ft 8in (2.95m)
Height: 8ft 0in (2.44m)
Engine: Maybach HL120TR, V-12, petrol, 300bhp at 3,000rpm
Road speed: 25mph (40km/hr)
Power/weight: 13.97
Range: 100 miles (165km)

PzKpfw 3, Ausf J Germany
Alkett, Daimler-Benz, Henschel, MAN, MIAG, Niedersachsen, Wegmann

1941. This model thickened the basic hull armour to 50mm, which meant re-designing most of the hull fittings and hatches. Some 1,549 were built with the 50mm L/42 gun, followed by a separate

series, still Ausf J, of 1,061 fitted with the longer 50mm L/60 gun.

Data: as for Ausf H, except
Hull length: 20ft 7in (6.28m)
Weight: slightly less due to the removal of the appliqué armour

PzKpfw 3, Ausf L Germany
Makers, as for Ausf J

1942. This was the Ausf J with the 50mm gun L/60 and with 20mm spaced armour plate added to the front of the hull, superstructure and gun mantlet. 653 were built in 1942.

Armament: 1 × 50mm L/60; 2 × MG
Ammunition: 92 + 4,950
Armour: 57mm
Crew: 5
Weight: 22.34 tons (22,700kg)
Hull length: 20ft 7in (6.28m)
Width: 9ft 8in (2.95m)
Height: 8ft 2in (2.50m)
Engine: Maybach HL120TRM, V-12 petrol, 300bhp at 3,000rpm
Road speed: 25mph (40km/hr)
Power/weight: 13.43
Range: 96 miles (155km)

PzKpfw 3, Ausf M Germany
Henschel, MAG, MAN, Niedersachsen, Wegmann

1942. This was the same as the Ausf L but fitted with deep fording equipment, extensions to the exhaust, hull seals and other modifications to permit driving through deep Russian rivers. Armed with the L/60 50mm gun, it weighed 22,700kg and 250 were built. Many were later fitted with large skirting plates over the suspension and tracks and with wider tracks for operations in snow and mud.

PzKpfw 3, Ausf N Germany
Makers, as for Ausf M

1942. This is the same as the J, L or M models except that the turret was modified to carry a short 75mm gun of the same type as used in the PzKpfw 4. The additional weight and size of the gun meant the removal of the 20mm spaced armour plate from the mantlet. Most were also fitted with skirting plates and a spaced plate around the turret sides.

Armament: 1 × 75mm L/24; 2 × MG
Ammunition: 64 + 3,750
Armour: 50mm base + 20mm
Crew: 5
Weight: 22.64 tons (23,000kg)

Hull length: 18ft 6in (5.65m)
Width: 9ft 8in (2.95m)
Height: 8ft 3in (2.50m)
Engine: Maybach ML 120TR, V-12, petrol, 300bhp at 3,000rpm
Road speed: 25mph (40km/hr)
Power/weight: 13.25
Range: 100 miles (160km)

PzKpfw 3 Tauchpanzer Germany
Daimler-Benz
1940. *Tauchpanzer* = 'Submersible tank'. This was a standard Ausf J tank modified by the sealing of apertures and hatches, the addition of a one-way valve in the exhaust system and the provision of a large air tube from the turret to a float. It was intended that landing craft with ramps would launch these tanks into depths of up 50ft/15m of water for the invasion of England in 1940. When this fixture was cancelled they were modified, by having fixed breathing tubes attached to the turret, and were used in the first wave of the attack on Russia in 1941, crossing the River Bug from Poland into Russian territory.

Panzerkampfwagen 4
Krupp-Gruson
1939. The PzKpfw 4 was to be the close support tank to match the 'anti-tank' Panzer 3 tank, and was therefore a similar design, though with a bigger turret and a short-barrelled 75mm gun. It soon proved itself in the Polish campaign and again in France. Production got under way slowly as it was originally envisioned that fewer would be needed than the Panzer 3. When it was seen to be successful and capable of standing up to the best of the Allied and Soviet vehicles, there was an urgent call for more. In the end, about 9,000 Panzer 4 were built between 1939 and 1945 and it was the only German tank to be in continuous production throughout the war.

The hull was made up of welded plates with a large bolted superstructure on top carrying the turret ring. The turret was also welded and well sloped. It held three crew members and was big enough to permit the mounting of larger guns, though with modifications to the mantlet. The engine was the same Maybach which also powered the Panzer 3. The suspension used four twin bogies on each side and four return rollers, a sure recognition feature.

Ausf A
Armament: 1 × 75mm L/24; 2 × MG
Ammunition: 122 + 3,000

Armour: 15mm
Crew: 5
Weight: 18.11 tons (18,400kg)
Hull length: 18ft 4in (5.60m)
Width: 9ft 6in (2.90m)
Height: 8ft 7in (2.65m)
Engine: Maybach HL108TR, V-12, petrol, 250bhp at 3,000rpm
Road speed: 19mph (31km/hr)
Power/weight: 13.80
Range: 93 miles (150km)

PzKpfw 4 Variant Models, early
Ausf B
Larger engine (300bhp), six-speed transmission, frontal armour increased to 30mm, hull machine gun removed. 42 built in 1938. Data as above.

Ausf C
Minor changes to Ausf B pattern; new carburettor and other modifications. 134 built 1938–39.

Ausf D
Increase in side armour from 15mm to 20mm, new gun mantlet. Late production had 30mm plates welded to hull and 20mm to turret to thicken armour. 229 built.

Ausf E
Hull front armour thickened to 50mm, improved turret, 20mm plates welded to side armour. 223 built 1940–41.

Ausf F
General increase in armour thickness. 462 built 1941–42.

Ausf F2
Fitted with long 75mm L/43 gun, with consequent modifications. 200 built 1942.

PzKpfw 4, Ausf G Germany
Krupp-Gruson, Niebelungenwerke, Vormag
1942. Ausf A to F were basically tinkering with the original design, but Ausf G was the first major production model, 1,687 being built between May 1942 and June 1943. It was much the same as the F2 model but with improved armour and the elimination of various vision ports and other apertures in the plates. Skirting plates to defeat shaped charge attack were fitted to the turret sides and over the tracks.

Armament: 1 × 75mm L/43 or L/48; 2 × MG
Ammunition: 87 + 3,000
Armour: 50mm + 30mm
Crew: 5
Weight: 23.13 tons (23,500kg)

Hull length: 19ft 6in (5.95m)
Width: 9ft 5in (2.88m)
Height: 8ft 9in (2.68m)
Engine: Maybach HL120TR, V-12, petrol, 300bhp at
  3,000rpm
Road speed: 25mph (40km/hr)
Power/weight: 12.97
Range: 130 miles (210km)

PzKpfw 4 Variant Models, later

Ausf H

As for Ausf G but with new transmission; frontal armour increased from 50mm basic to 80mm basic. 3,664 built between April 1943 and July 1944.

Ausf J

Final production model, 1,758 being built June 1944 to March 1945. The electric turret traverse was dropped and a two-speed manual traverse replaced it. Various minor detail changes, mostly for easier and quicker production, for example three return rollers instead of four. Built only by the Niebelungenwerke.

Panzerkampfwagen 5 Germany
See Panther

PzKpfw 5 (*Neubaufahrzug*) Germany
Rheinmetall-Borsig

1935. The first Panzer 5 was this heavy tank design, which was developed from the Grosstraktor. It was a multi-turret type, with one large turret mounting a 75mm and a 37mm gun side by side, and smaller machine gun turrets in front and behind. A small-wheel suspension, mud chutes and a distinctly triangular track layout with high front idler and low rear drive sprocket make it readily recognisable. Only three were built, and these were sent to Norway in 1940, where photographs were taken; the subsequent publication of these set the Allies in a turmoil for the remainder of the war, wondering when these monsters would appear again. In fact one was destroyed in Norway and the other two returned to Germany to become parade ornaments at the Panzer school.

Armament: 1 × 75mm L/24; 1 × 37mm L/45; 3 × MG
Ammunition: 80 + 50 + 6,000
Armour: 20mm
Crew: 6
Weight: 23.04 tons (23,410kg)
Hull length: 21ft 8in (6.60m)
Width: 7ft 2in (2.19m)
Height: 9ft 9in (2.98m)
Engine: BMW, 6-cylinder, petrol, 250bhp

Road speed: 18mph (30km/hr)
Power/weight: 10.85
Range: 75 miles (120km)

Panzerkampfwagen 6 Germany
See Tiger

Panzerkampfwagen 7 (VK6501) Germany
Henschel

1941. This stemmed from the VK3001 project, and was the final pre-war attempt by the German Army to obtain a heavy tank. Ordered in 1939, a mild steel prototype was built in 1941. It was conventional in its layout, using one large and two small frontal turrets in a similar manner to the British cruisers of the same era. The final design was so heavy that it became necessary to arrange for it to be dismantled into three major assemblies for transport by rail over long distances, and the company even went to the length of designing a mobile crane to accompany each troop. The design was found impractical and abandoned.

Armament: 1 × 75mm L/24; 2 × MG
Ammunition: not determined
Armour: 100mm proposed
Crew: 5
Weight: 63.97 tons (65,000kg)
Hull length: 23ft 0in (7.00m)
Width: 10ft 6in (3.20m)
Height: 9ft 7in (2.92m)
Engine: Maybach HL224, V-12, petrol, 600bhp at
  3,000rpm
Road speed: 12mph (20km/hr)
Power/weight: 9.37
Range: not determined

Panzerkampfwagen 35(t) Germany
See LT-35

Panzerkampfwagen 38(t) Germany
See TNH/PS

PzKpfw 38(t) Ausf S Germany
See TNH/SV

Patrol Tank Marks 1 and 2 UK
Carden-Loyd

1932. This was a Carden-Loyd Mark 4 machine gun carrier with the hull built up into a covered superstructure and with a hand-rotated turret carrying a machine gun. The suspension was the usual small wheels with outside girder of the period, and the Mark 1 tank used coil springs, while the Mark 2 used leaf springs. Small numbers appear to have been sold to various countries.

Armament: 1 × MG
Armour: 11mm
Crew: 2
Weight: 2 tons (2,035kg)
Hull length: 8ft 6in (2.59m)
Width: 5ft 5in (1.65m)
Height: 5ft 9in (1.75m)
Engine: Meadows, 6-cylinder, petrol, 40bhp
Road speed: 30mph (48km/hr)
Power/weight: 20

Patton USA
See M47/M48 Medium

Pershing USA
See M26 Heavy

Peugeot Char Léger France
Peugeot
1918. This resembled the Renault FT17 in its general appearance, a stubby body between two tracks, with a larger driving sprocket at the front and a small idler at the rear, but the layout was different in that the engine was at the front of the hull and the fighting compartment at the rear. The hull was crowned by a fixed cast steel superstructure with a 37mm trench cannon and a machine gun both firing forward. Only a prototype was built.

Armament: 1 × 37mm M1916; 1 × MG
Armour: not known
Crew: 2
Weight: 6 tons
Engine: Peugeot 4-cylinder, petrol
Road speed: 3mph (5km/hr)

PT-76 Russia
State factories
1952. The PT-76 is perhaps the longest-lived AFV still in regular service with many armies, since it fills a highly specialised niche, that of a light reconnaissance tank capable of swimming. The squat, two-man turret carries a 76mm gun, the armour is well sloped, and the glacis plate is particularly effective. It can swim without any preparation and carries a snorkel tube on the back of the turret and trim plate on the nose. Propulsion is by water jets in the back of the hull. The engine is powerful and there is adequate performance under all conditions. The chassis has been used for an

entire family of variants and the tank and many variants have been exported to more than 20 Communist-inclined countries.

Armament: 1 × 76mm; 1 × MG
Ammunition: 40 + 1,000
Armour: 14mm
Crew: 3
Weight: 13.78 tons (14,000kg)
Hull length: 22ft 8in (6.94m)
Width: 10ft 4in (3.16m)
Height: 7ft 2in (2.22m)
Engine: V-6 diesel, 240bhp at 1,800rpm
Road speed: 27mph (45km/hr)
Power/weight: 17.42
Range: 160 miles (260km)

PT-91 Poland
Bumar-Labedy
1993. This is a further improvement of the Polish-built T-72M1 MBT. It incorporates all the improvements noted for the T-72, such as the explosive reactive armour (ERA), and adds a new computerised fire control system, new steel track skirts with ERA on the forward sections, a laser detection and warning system, computerised engine management, improved night vision systems, uprated engine, improved fire detection and suppression system and new tracks with replaceable rubber pads.

Armament: 1 × 125mm; 2 × MG
Ammunition: 44
Armour: not disclosed
Crew: 3
Weight: 45.27 tons (46,000kg)
Hull length: 22ft 10in (6.95m)
Width: 11ft 9in (3.59m)
Height: 7ft 2in (2.19m)
Engine: S-120 V-12 supercharged diesel, 850bhp
Road speed: 43mph (70km/hr)
Power/weight: 18.77
Range: 405 miles 650km)

PZ-61 Switzerland
Federal Works
1961. This was a Swiss-designed and built main battle tank which, good though it was, showed the Swiss that it would be cheaper to buy abroad in the future. It was generally similar to the American M48/M60 tanks of the same era, Belleville-sprung with six roadwheels per side, front idler and rear drive. The driver was front and centre, with the fighting compartment and turret behind him and the engine and transmission at the rear in a power

pack which could be removed and replaced in an hour. The gun was the British 105mm L7, but made in Switzerland and firing non-NATO-standard ammunition.

Armament: 1 × 105mm L7; 2 × MG
Ammunition: 52 + 5,400
Armour: 120mm
Crew: 4
Weight: 37.40 tons (38,000kg)
Hull length: 22ft 3in (6.78m)
Width: 10ft 1in (3.08m)
Height: 8ft 11in (2.72m)
Engine: MTU MB-837 V-8, diesel, 630bhp at 2,200rpm
Road speed: 34mph (55km/hr)
Power/weight: 16.84
Range: 185 miles (300km)

PZ-68 Switzerland
Federal Works

1971. This was a further improvement to the PZ-61 design, the principal features being the addition of gyro-stabilisation to the gun, a more powerful engine and improved transmission, wider tracks with replaceable rubber pads and with a greater length of track in ground contact, and the addition of the Swedish 'Lyran' illuminating rocket to the turret roof to allow the silhouetting of targets at night. This became the **PZ-68 Mark 1**. The **Mark 2** was the same but with the addition of a thermal sleeve to the gun and a fume extraction system in the turret. **Mark 3** had a larger turret, and **Mark 4** was a Mark 3 with several minor improvements.

Armament: 1 × 105mm L7; 2 × MG
Ammunition: 56 + 5,200
Armour: 120mm
Crew: 4
Weight: 39.07 tons (39,700kg)
Hull length: 22ft 7in (6.88m)
Width: 10ft 4in (3.14m)
Height: 9ft 0in (2.75m)
Engine: MTU MB-837 V-8, diesel, 660bhp at 2,200rpm
Road speed: 34mph (55km/hr)
Power/weight: 16.89
Range: 215 miles (350km)

Ram 1 Canada
Montreal

1942. When the British adopted the American M3 Medium they requested some changes; the US would only countenance changing the turret slightly to accommodate radios. The idea then occurred of building the M3 Medium in Canada, but incorporating all the modifications that the US

had refused to include. This became the Ram. The principal change was the removal of the sponson-mounted 75mm gun and the fitting of a 6-pounder into the turret. Unfortunately, the Ram was classed as a cruiser, and it was an immutable law of nature that cruiser tanks carried 2-pounder guns, not 6-pounders. So the first 50 Rams were fitted with 2-pounder guns and became the Ram 1.

Armament: 1 × 2-pdr; 3 × MG
Ammunition: not known
Armour: 88mm maximum
Crew: 5
Weight: 28.57 tons (29,030kg)
Hull length: 19ft 0in (5.79m)
Width: 9ft 5in (2.87m)
Height: 8ft 9in (2.66m)
Engine: Continental R975 9-cylinder radial, petrol, 400bhp at 2,400rpm
Road speed: 25mph (40km/hr)
Power/weight: 14.0
Range: 125 miles (200km)

Ram 2 Canada
Montreal

1942. After the 50 Ram 1 tanks had been built, common sense prevailed and the turret gun was changed to a 6-pounder. This was achieved relatively easily, the turret having been designed with that gun in mind. A total of 1,899 Ram 2 were then built before production ceased in September 1943. Almost all were shipped to Britain and used for training by Canadian forces, but for the sake of standardisation and logistic simplicity, they were withdrawn and replaced by M4 Shermans before D-Day. After production of the Ram ceased, the chassis and hull continued to be made as the foundation of the Sexton self-propelled gun.

Armament: 1 × 6-pdr; 3 × MG
Ammunition: 92 + 2,500
Armour: 88mm maximum
Crew: 5
Weight: 29.02 tons (29,485kg)
Hull length: 19ft 0in (5.79m)
Width: 9ft 6in (2.90m)
Height: 8ft 9in (2.66m)
Engine: Continental R975 9-cylinder radial, petrol, 400bhp at 2,400rpm
Road speed: 25mph (40km/hr)
Power/weight: 13.78
Range: 125 miles (200km)

Ram Command/OP Tank Canada
Montreal

1943. Self-propelled artillery supporting armoured formations require specialised Observation Post tanks for their forward observers, and the final 84 Ram 2 tanks were equipped with dummy gun barrels, thus leaving space inside the turret for additional radio equipment and specialist observing instruments and other artillery equipment. Apart from being slightly lighter, the data are the same as those of the standard Ram 2 tank.

Renault BS France
Renault

1918. This was an off-shoot from the FT17 (*below*) and was the FT17 body with an enlarged turret carrying a short 75mm gun. The turret was the first to have a 'bustle' at the rear, in this case simply an empty box to provide space for the gun to recoil. A contract for 970 was issued in 1918 but before production could begin the war ended. A handful were made and shipped off to North Africa, where they survived to re-appear in 1942 when the Allies invaded Algeria.

Armament: 1 × 75mm gun Modèle 06/09; 1 × MG
Armour: 22mm
Crew: 2
Weight: 7.08 tons (7,200kg)
Hull length: 16ft 5in (5.00m)
Width: 5ft 9in (1.75m)
Height: 6ft 7in (2.00m)
Engine: Renault, 4-cylinder, petrol, 35bhp at 1,500rpm
Road speed: 5mph (8km/hr)
Power/weight: 4.94
Range: 22 miles (35km)

Renault FT17 France
Renault

1917. This little Renault, which became the most common tank in the world between the wars, appearing in every sort of conflict, was developed as an alternative to the huge and heavy gun tanks which formed the initial British and French tank forces. Over 3,500 were built on wartime contracts and in postwar years they changed hands frequently. The machine was very basic: a metal box with the driver at the front, the commander/machine gunner in the middle, and the engine at the rear. The gunner had a rotating turret and was originally provided with a Hotchkiss machine gun. This was later changed to a 37mm Modèle 1916 'Trench Cannon', and there were also models specially adapted for radio communications.

Over 1,500 of them survived in French service

until 1940, by which time they were a liability on the battlefield.

Armament: 1 × 37mm gun or 1 × MG
Armour: 22mm
Crew: 2
Weight: 6.88 tons (7,000kg)
Hull length: 16ft 5in (5.02m)
Width: 5ft 9in (1.74m)
Height: 6ft 7in (2.14m)
Engine: Renault 4-cylinder, petrol, 35bhp at 1,500rpm
Road speed: 5mph (8km/hr)
Power/weight: 5.08
Range: 22 miles (35km)

Renault FT Kégresse-Hinstin M24/25
France
Renault

1924. Alphonse Kégresse, financially backed by M. Hinstin, developed a very useful half-track unit which could be used to replace the rear wheels on a truck, and much work was done on this during the 1920s. This, however, was an attempt to apply his system to a tank in the interests of quietness (rubber tracks instead of steel) and speed. It was the standard FT17 body with the tracks replaced by a special assembly designed by Kégresse. The suspension was by eight small wheels, and the rear sprocket and front idler were almost the same size and were on the ground. There were also rollers on outriggers front and rear to improve the trench-crossing capability. The French Army purchased a number and used them in Morocco, and other armies bought them for evaluation.

Armament: 1 × 37mm M1916; or 1 × MG
Armour: 22mm
Crew: 2
Weight: 6.5 tons (6,600kg)
Hull length: 16ft 5in (5.00m)
Width: 5ft 11in (1.80m)
Height: 6ft 0in (1.83m)
Engine: Renault 4-cylinder, petrol, 35bhp at 1,500rpm
Road speed: 7.5mph (12km/hr)
Power/weight: 5.38

Renault FT Kégresse-Hinstin M26/27
France
Renault

1925. This was an improved version of the 1924 design, dispensing with the forward trench rollers but retaining the rear rollers in place of the usual Renault 'tail', The sprocket and idler were off the ground and there was a single return roller for the track. It does not appear to have found any buyers.

Armament: 1 × 37mm M1916; or 1 × MG
Armour: 22mm
Crew: 2
Weight: 6.4 tons (6,500kg)
Hull length: 15ft 9in (4.80m)
Width: 8ft 6in (2.59m)
Height: 5ft 11in (1.89m)
Engine: Renault 4-cylinder, petrol, 35bhp at 1,500rpm
Road speed: 10mph (16km/hr)
Power/weight: 5.38

Renault R-35 France
Renault

1936. This was developed in response to a French infantry demand for a light, but well armoured support tank. It was conventionally laid out with the driver at the front, commander in the middle and engine at the rear. The commander had a turret carrying a 37mm Modèle 1916 gun and a coaxial machine gun. The hull and turret were of cast armour and well-shaped to deflect shot. About 2,000 were built, and it was perhaps the most numerous of the various French tanks in 1939. It failed to distinguish itself in 1940 and most of the survivors were taken by the Germans and used as ammunition carriers or as chassis for SP anti-tank guns.

Armament: 1 × 37mm; 1 × MG
Armour: 45mm maximum
Crew: 2
Weight: 9.84 tons (10,000kg)
Hull length: 13ft 10in (4.20m)
Width: 6ft 1in (1.85m)
Height: 7ft 9in (2.40m)
Engine: Renault, 4-cylinder, petrol, 82bhp at 2,200rpm
Road speed: 12mph (20km/hr)
Power/weight: 8.33
Range: 88 miles (140km)

Renault TSF France

A variant model of the Renault FT17 designed to carry radio (TSF – *téléphone sans fil*) equipment.

Rhinoceros; or the Culin Hedgerow Device USA
Field workshops

1944. The *bocage* country of Normandy proved to be a formidable obstacle to tank operations in 1944, due to the thick hedges planted on small banks alongside the roads. This confined the tank to the road, or else exposed its thin belly to anti-tank fire as it climbed over the hedges. The solution was devised by Sergeant Curtis D. Culin of the 102nd US Cavalry Reconnaissance Regiment, and it is pleasing to be able to record that he was awarded the Legion of Merit for his invention.

The Culin Hedgerow Device or, as it was known to British troops, the Sherman Prong, was a set of steel plates formed like plough shares and welded to the front plate of the tank. There were numerous minor variations of the basic design, depending upon which field workshop or unit mechanic made it, but they all worked in the same way. As the tank came up to the hedge, the prongs bit into the embankment and prevented the tracks pulling the tank over the hedge. Instead, a whole section of the embankment, complete with hedge, was chopped out and pushed ahead of the tank, sometimes conveniently burying an enemy machine-gunner or anti-tank rocket launcher on the other side.

The Culin device was used on American, British and Canadian tanks in considerable numbers, but once the Allies broke clear of Normandy there was no longer any requirement and they were removed almost as fast as they had been installed.

Royal Tiger Germany
See King Tiger

S-Tank (Stridsvagn 103) Sweden
Bofors

1966. The Strv 103 was unique in its day for having a crew of three and no turret. The intention behind this unusual design was to reduce the overall height, and thus make it easier to conceal in battle; to simplify the manufacture by having no turret with its complicated rotating mechanism and power linkages; and to reduce the number of trained men required by having a three-man crew and fitting an automatic loader.

The tank also bristled with other novelties. There were two engines, a diesel for normal running and a gas turbine as a 'booster' when extra power was needed. The driver was also the gunner. The commander also manned the anti-aircraft machine gun, and the radio operator sat facing backwards: he had the basic controls duplicated and was able to drive the tank backwards when a rapid departure was the only option.

The gun was laid by the driver pointing the entire vehicle at the target and the suspension was hydro-pneumatic with a large degree of vertical movement, so that the whole tank could be canted up or down to give the desired elevation to the gun. There were very fine servo motors to make the final movements for aiming, but it meant that the engine had to run all the time the tank was in action in order to provide the power. It was also a little slower to aim than a conventional turret gun. Despite the advantages of the idea, it was probably no cheaper to build than any other tank and it is noticeable that no other country ever bought any or developed the idea any further.

Armament: 1 × 105mm; 3 × MG
Ammunition: 50 + 2,750
Armour: not disclosed
Crew: 3
Weight: 39.07 tons (39,700kg)
Hull length: 27ft 7in (8.42m)
Width: 11ft 10in (3.62m)
Height: 8ft 3in (2.50m)
Engines: Rolls-Royce K60, multi-fuel, 240bhp at 3,750rpm + Boeing 553 gas turbine, 490shp at 38,000rpm
Road speed: 31mph (50km/hr)
Power/weight: 18.68
Range: 242 miles (390km)

Sabra MBT Israel
IMI

1998. This tank, developed privately by Israel Military Industries, is a comprehensive upgrading of the American M60A3 which, it is hoped, will prove attractive to the several armies still operating M60s. The standard 105mm M68 gun is replaced by an Israeli 120mm smoothbore gun as used on the Merkava 3, and the existing fire control, sighting and observation equipment is replaced by a complete new package. This is reinforced by a new electro-hydraulic turret and gun control system which permits the gun to be laid and fired by either the commander or the gunner. The armour protection has been improved and a threat warning system is installed. A more powerful engine is installed and the suspension has been fitted with new shock dampers and torsion bars.

Armament: 1 × 120mm; 2 × MG
Ammunition: 44
Armour: not disclosed
Crew: 4
Weight: 54.13 tons (55,000kg)
Hull length: 27ft 1in (8.26m)
Width: 11ft 11in (3.63m)
Height: 10ft 0in (3.05m)
Engine: General Dynamics V-12 turbocharged diesel, 908bhp at 2,400rpm
Road speed: 30mph (48km/hr)
Power/weight: 16.77
Range: 280 miles (450km)

Sahariano Italy
See CAC Sahariano

Saint Chamond France
FAMH

1917. This was designed by the French Army and built by St Chamond, using a Holt tractor as the foundation. Easily identified by its large pointed bow and enormous frontal overhang, it mounted a St Chamond 75mm gun in the hull front, had a flat roof and two round cupolas at the front end of the hull. Propulsion was petrol-electric, using a Panhard motor to drive a dynamo which then fed to electric motors driving each track. A second version had a slightly peaked roof and no cupolas, and replaced the St Chamond gun with the more powerful Modèle 1897 gun. In 1918 a third version was built, with the front underside of the hull raised to give better cross-country performance, and with thicker armour. About 550 of all three types were built, but the short track and long overhangs made them poor at crossing rough country.

Version 1
Armament: 1 × 75mm; 4 × MG
Armour: 17mm
Crew: 8
Weight: 21.65 tons (22,000kg)
Hull length: 28ft 6in (8.68m)
Width: 8ft 9in (2.66m)
Height: 7ft 9in (2.36m)
Engine: Panhard, 4-cylinder, petrol, 90bhp
Road speed: 5mph (8km/hr)
Power/weight: 4.16
Range: 27 miles (60km)

Schneider CA-1 France
Schneider

1917. This, the first French tank (CA = *Char d'Assaut*) was planned by Colonel Estienne and built by Schneider, and like most of the early designs was built on a Holt tractor chassis. It mounted a short 75mm gun in a sponson on the right front corner of the hull, had sprung suspension, the bow was shaped to cut wire, it had forced ventilation and double doors at the rear, altogether a quite well thought-out design. But, like the St Chamond, the short track length and large overhang of the hull made it a difficult vehicle over rough country and a poor trench crosser. About 400 were built.

Armament: 1 × 75mm; 2 × MG
Armour: 12mm
Crew: 3
Weight: 14.36 tons (14,600kg)

Hull length: 19ft 10in (6.04m)
Width: 6ft 7in (2.00m)
Height: 6ft 11in (2.11m)
Engine: Schneider, 4-cylinder, petrol, 55bhp
Road speed: 3mph (5km/hr)
Power/weight: 3.83
Range: 30 miles (48km)

Schneider CA-2 and CA-3 France
Schneider

1918. These were improved versions of the Schneider CA-1 *above*. The **CA-2** had a 37mm gun in a revolving turret, while the **CA-3** had twin roof cupolas and a longer hull. A prototype of the CA-2 was built, but the end of the war saw both projects cancelled.

Schneider-Laurent Amphibious Tank
France
Schneider

1928. Looking like a fugitive from a Jules Verne novel, this was a private venture by Schneider which failed to attract any practical interest. Not only did it swim, it was also a wheel-and-track design, so ensuring the maximum of complication. The hull was expanded into a turtle-shell upper section allied to a v-shaped lower section, at the sides of which were the track units (fully skirted) and the four wheels, which could be raised or lowered. There was a small cupola with a searchlight and provision for the usual combination of a 37mm trench cannon and a machine gun.

Armament: 1 × 37mm M1916; 1 × MG
Armour: 15mm
Crew: 3
Weight: 10 tons (10,160kg)
Hull length: 19ft 8in (6.00m)
Width: 7ft 2in (2.18m)
Height: 8ft 0in (2.43m)
Engine: V-8, petrol, 100bhp
Road speed, wheels: 28mph (45km/hr)
Power/weight: 10

Schofield New Zealand
Maker unknown

1942. A 'home-made' wheel-and-track tank assembled from parts of commercial Chevrolet trucks, Bren gun carriers and other odds and ends. Boxy hull with flat front, open-topped turret, Bren carrier suspension, plus four pneumatic-tyred wheels which were carried on brackets on the hull and could be assembled to hubs when required to run on roads. It worked, but it was neither practical nor battleworthy. Only the prototype was made.

Armament: 1 × 2-pdr; 1 × MG
Armour: 10mm
Crew: 3
Weight: 5.21 tons (5,300kg)
Hull length: 13ft 1in (3.99m)
Width: 6ft 7in (2.00m)
Height: 6ft 8in (2.02m)
Engine: Chevrolet 6-cylinder, petrol, 30bhp
Road speed, tracks: 25mph (40km/hr)
Road speed, wheels: 45mph (72km/hr)
Power/weight: 5.76

Sentinel AC1 Australia
NSWR

1940. Appreciating that Britain could scarcely spare tanks, the Australians decided to build their own, and made a remarkably good job of it. The **AC1** (Australian Cruiser Mark 1) adopted the mechanical layout of the US M3 Medium, with a suspension which resembled the contemporary Renault 'scissors' type. The hull and turret were cast and of good ballistic shape, and a 2-pounder gun was carried. Motive power was from three Cadillac engines strapped together, though with manual gearbox, and this gearbox proved to be a bottleneck, delaying production until suitable gear-cutting machinery could be obtained and imported.

In the interim, work began on a simplified model, the **AC2**, but as soon as the machinery for the AC1 arrived, this was dropped. Production began in August 1942 and 66 were built. By 1943 American tanks were arriving in Australia in large numbers, and production of the Sentinel therefore stopped, and they were all used as training vehicles.

The **AC3** was a proposal for a support tank mounting a 25-pounder gun in the turret; a prototype was built. The **AC4** was another variant with a 17-pounder gun in the turret, and again only a prototype was built.

Armament: 1 × 2-pdr gun: 2 × MG
Ammunition: 130 + 4,250
Armour: 65mm
Crew: 5
Weight: 28 tons (28,450kg)
Hull length: 20ft 9in (6.32m)
Width: 9ft 11in (3.02m)
Height: 8ft 4in (2.54m)
Engine: 3 × Cadillac V-8 Model 75, each 110bhp at 3,050rpm
Road speed: 30mph (48km/hr)
Power/weight: 11.78
Range: 200 miles (320km)

Sheridan USA
See M551

Sherman USA
See M4 Medium

Six-Ton Tank USA
See M1917

Skeleton Tank USA
Pioneer
1918. Early tanks were big in order to cross big trenches and negotiate big craters, but big tanks were unfortunately usually very heavy. The Skeleton Tank was a fine example of lateral thinking; keep it big but reduce the weight by making a skeleton framework to carry the tracks, and concentrate the crew and engine into a small box suspended inside the framework. It also made it a harder target.

The result was a lozenge-shaped construction of steel tubing holding a rectangular hull with a machine gun turret. Rear sprockets propelled the tracks and were driven by a shaft and differential system encased in parts of the tubing. It worked, but like so many other early tanks, it was a terribly complicated way to get one machine gun into the battle.

Armament: 1 × MG
Armour: 13mm
Crew: 2
Weight: 8.03 tons (8,165kg)
Hull length: 25ft 0in (7.62m)
Width: 8ft 0in (2.43m)
Height: 9ft 6in (2.89m)
Engine: 2 × Beaver 4-cylinder, petrol, total 100bhp
Road speed: 5mph (8km/hr)
Power/weight: 12.45

Skink AA Tank Canada
Montreal
1944. This was an adaptation of the Grizzly (which was in turn the Canadian-built version of the M4A1 Sherman) into an anti-aircraft tank by replacing the turret with a new turret carrying four 20mm Polsten cannons. These were aimed by a joystick-controlled electro-hydraulic power system using a reflecting sight mounted in the turret roof. The tank was designed to give air defence to troops after the invasion of Europe, but the invasion took place before the design was completed, and it became apparent that the Allied air forces had complete air superiority and that the Skink was not needed.

Three were completed for evaluation and the contract cancelled.

Dimensions: as for the Sherman M4A1

Skoda S-1 Czechoslovakia
Skoda
1936. A two-man 'tankette' on Carden-Loyd lines, this had an all-welded hull with a raised superstructure which overhung the tracks at each side. The driver sat on the left, the gunner on the right, and there were two machine guns, one on either side of the gunner. A neat design, but it failed to interest the Czech or Polish Armies or attract any overseas buyers.

Armament: 2 × MG
Armour: 6mm
Crew: 2
Weight: 2.3 tons
Engine: Skoda 4-cylinder, petrol, 40bhp
Road speed: 28mph
Power/weight: 17.4

Skoda S-1d Czechoslovakia
Skoda
1938. Another two-man design, but although derived from the S-1, bearing little resemblance to it. This looks more like a miniature tank, with a raised superstructure and a large observation cupola with vision blocks, and it had far better armour and a more powerful engine. Driver and gunner were side-by-side as before but with only one machine gun. Suspension was by two double bogies and a single trailing roadwheel, rear drive sprocket and front idler. The type was purchased by Yugoslavia and Romania.

Armament: 1 × MG
Armour: 15mm
Crew: 2
Weight: 4.5 tons (4.575kg)
Hull length: 8ft 6in (2.59m)
Width: 6ft 0in (1.83m)
Height: 4ft 6in (1.37m)
Engine: 6-cylinder, petrol, 60bhp
Road speed: 28mph (45km/hr)
Power/weight: 13.33
Range: 125 miles (200km)

Skoda S-2a Light Tank Czechoslovakia
See LT-35

Skoda S-2b Medium Tank Czechoslovakia
Skoda

1938. This was a medium tank obtained by simply scaling up the Light S-2a. Trials proved it to be totally worthless and unreliable, and the design was abandoned forthwith.

Skoda S-2r Medium Tank Czechoslovakia
See Turan

SMK Heavy Russia
Kirov

1938. Sergei Mironovitch Kirov produced this in competition with the T-100 as a possible replacement for the T-35 heavy tank. Like the T-100 it clung desperately to the multiple turret idea but went for a naval style with two turrets, one at the front of the hull with a 45mm gun, and one, larger, behind it on top of a plinth, mounting a 76mm gun. The front turret had limited traverse, while the upper turret had all-round traverse. The hull was long and rectangular with eight roadwheels and four track return rollers and rear drive sprockets. Like the T-100 the first prototypes were sent to Finland in the 1939–40 Winter War; like the T-100 they turned out to be unwieldy and cumbersome, and the design was abandoned.

Armament: 1 × 45mm; 1 × 76mm; 3 × MG
Armour: 60mm
Crew: 6
Weight: 45 tons (45,720kg)
Hull length: 31ft 6in (9.60m)
Width: 10ft 6in (3.20m)
Height: 10ft 6in (3.20m)
Engine: 400bhp, petrol
Road speed: 20mph (32km/hr)
Power/weight: 8.88
Range: not known

Somua S-35 France
Somua

1935. Designed as a cavalry medium tank, this was the first production tank to have an all-cast hull and turret. Nine small roadwheels each side, covered by skirting plates. Turret with 47mm gun and electric power traverse. Well built, and an impressive specification but, like most French tanks of the time, the one-man turret reduced its potential. About 500 were built, of which many were captured and later put to use by the German and Italian Armies.

Armament: 1 × 47mm; 1 × MG
Armour: 40mm

Crew: 3
Weight: 19.73 tons (20,048kg)
Hull length: 17ft 11in (5.50m)
Width: 6ft 11in (2.10m)
Height: 8ft 10in (2.70m)
Engine: Somua V-8 petrol, 190bhp at 2,000rpm
Road speed: 23mph (37km/hr)
Power/weight: 9.63
Range: 160 miles (255km)

SR-1 Amphibious Tank Japan
Maker unknown

1933. This first attempt at an amphibious design never got past the prototype stage; the hull resembled the Type 92 Light but with the addition of metal buoyancy chambers on each side above the tracks and a suspension system using four double bogies and leaf springs on each side. Propelled by a water jet and using a Mitsubishi diesel engine, it no doubt taught the designers a few useful lessons.

Data: none available

SR-2 Amphibious Tank Japan
Maker unknown

1936. Having studied the shortcomings of the SR-1 the designers tried again. The suspension now had two larger-wheeled twin bogies on bell-crank and coil spring suspension, with the rear wheel of the rear bogie acting as the track idler The buoyancy tanks were above the tracks and around the front to make a prow-shaped nose which had a retractable trim vane. Propulsion in the water was by two propeller units in tunnels under the hull. There was a one-man turret and a driver and hull machine gunner.

Armament: 2 × MG
Armour: 10mm
Crew: 3
Weight: 4 tons (4,065kg)
Hull length: 16ft 8in (5.98m)
Width: 6ft 2in (1.88m)
Height: 7ft 10in (2.39m)
Engine: Mitsubishi, 6-cylinder, petrol, air-cooled
Road speed: 25mph (40km/hr)

SR-3 Amphibious Tank Japan
Maker unknown

1939. The Japanese Army's final amphibious design, this was a refined version of the SR-2. It was approved for production, but since there did not appear to be any requirement for such a vehicle the approval was cancelled and the project ended.

Armament: I × MG
Armour: 10mm
Crew: 2
Weight: 3.8 tons (3,860kg)
Hull length: 13ft 9in (4.19m)
Width: 5ft 9in (1.75m)
Height: 6ft 3in (1.91m)
Engine: 4-cylinder, petrol, 72bhp
Road speed: 30mph
Power/weight: 18.95

ST-39 Medium Tank Czechoslovakia
CKD

1938. This was developed by CKD and accepted by the Czech Army, a contract for 300 being signed. Then the Germans invaded Czechoslovakia and the whole project collapsed, only the prototypes ever being built. Conventional for its day, with driver and hull gunner and a two-man turret, it had a suspension system using two four-wheeled bogies on each side and an unusual track tensioner wheel between the front drive sprocket and the first roadwheel.

Armament: I × 47mm; 2 × MG
Armour: 50mm
Crew: 4
Weight: 16.5 tons (16,765kg)
Hull length: 17ft 3in (5.26m)
Width: 7ft 5in (2.26m)
Height: 7ft 7in (2.36m)
Engine: Praga V-8, petrol, 240bhp
Road speed: 28mph (45km/hr)
Power/weight: 14.54

Steam Tank USA
US Army

1918. Built by the US Corps of Engineers, this was generally to the same size and shape as a British Tank Mark 4 but was driven by steam engines. This was arrived at as a by-product of its armament; it was intended as a carrier for a powerful flame-thrower, and high pressure steam was the method of delivering the flame fuel. Since this was available, it was decided to use it for motive power as well. In the event, it was found that steam was not suitable for the flame device and a petrol engine with compressor was adopted. The steam propulsion remained, however, using two twin-cylinder engines each with its own kerosene-fuelled boiler and each driving one track. It worked, but by the time it was working properly the war was over.

Armament: I × flame-thrower; 4 × MG
Armour: 13mm
Crew: 8

Weight: 44.64 tons (45,360kg)
Hull length: 38ft 9in (10.59m)
Width: 12ft 6in (3.81m)
Height: 10ft 5in (3.17m)
Engine: 2 × 2-cylinder steam; total 500bhp
Road speed: 4mph (6.5km/hr)
Power/weight: 11.20

Stingray 1 Light Tank USA
Cadillac Gage

Development of this tank began in the later 1970s as a private venture. Of conventional layout it is lightly armoured but carries a Royal Ordnance Low Recoil Force 105mm gun in the two-man turret, together with an automatic loader. The gun is fully stabilised in both axes and provided with a modern computerised fire control system with laser rangefinder and night vision capabilities. The running gear uses torsion-bar suspension and six roadwheels per side and is generally based on that of the M109 SP 155mm howitzer. In 1988–90 106 Stingrays were built and delivered to the Thai Army.

Armament: I × 105mm; 2 × MG
Ammunition: 36 + 3,500
Armour: not disclosed
Crew: 4
Weight: 18.97 tons (19,278kg)
Hull length: 22ft 0in (6.72m)
Width: 8ft 11in (2.71m)
Height: 8ft 4in (2.55m)
Engine: Detroit Diesel 8V-92 TA, 535bhp at 2,300rpm
Road speed: 40mph (65km/hr)
Power/weight: 28.20
Range: 310 miles (500km)

Stingray 2 Light Tank USA
Textron

1996. The Stingray 2 is an improved and developed version of the Stingray 1, the improvements generally being in the field of fire control, sighting and night vision equipment. The same 105mm LRF gun is fitted, the armour has been slightly improved and an appliqué armour uprating kit is available for those demanding a higher level of protection.

Armament: I × 105mm; 2 × MG
Ammunition: 32 + 3,500
Armour: not disclosed
Crew: 4
Weight: 21.87 tons (22,220kg)
Hull length: 21ft 2in (6.44m)
Width: 8ft 11in (2.71m)
Height: 8ft 4in (2.55m)
Engine: Detroit Diesel V-8, 550bhp at 2,300rpm

Road speed: 41mph (66km/hr)
Power/weight: 25.15
Range: 300 miles (480km)

Stridsvagn (Strv) 103 Sweden
See S-tank

Strv L-30 Sweden
Landsverk

1931. This was one of the better wheel-and-track designs. It was based on the m/31 tank, being developed in parallel with it, and was more or less an m/31 with four large pneumatic-tyred wheels on swinging arms outside the tracks. These could be lowered hydraulically so as to lift the tracks off the ground and take up the drive on hard surfaces. It was one of the very few designs of this type which could transfer from tracks to wheels or back again whilst on the move. It was tested by the Swedish Army but turned down.

Armament: 1 × 37mm; 1 × MG
Armour: 14mm
Crew: 3
Weight: 11.5 tons (11,685kg)
Hull length: 17ft 0in (5.18m)
Width: 8ft 0in (2.44m)
Height: 7ft 4in (2.23m)
Engine: Maybach V-12 150bhp
Power/weight: 13.04

Strv L-60 Light Sweden
Landsverk

1934. Another advanced design from Landsverk, this one had torsion bar suspension and a 20mm cannon as the main armament. A number of variant models with differing armament were proposed, but only this basic model became a success, being licence-built in Hungary as the **Toldi 38M**.

Armament: 1 × 20mm cannon 1 × MG
Armour: 13mm
Crew: 3
Weight: 6.8 tons (6,900kg)
Hull length: 15ft 1in (4.60m)
Width: 6ft 7in (2.00m)
Height: 6ft 10in (2.08m)
Engine: Büssing-NAG V-8, petrol, 160bhp
Road speed: 28mph (45km/hr)
Power/weight: 23.52

Strv L-80 Sweden
Landsverk

1933. Landsverk's final throw in the wheel-and-

track stakes, this was smaller and lighter than the L-30 design and hence more agile, but there was no great difference in shape, the same system of exterior wheels being used. It had no more success that had the previous design, probably because people were beginning to realise the vulnerability of all that machinery outside the tank. After this, Landsverk abandoned the duplex idea and concentrated on full-track tanks.

Armament: 1 × 20mm cannon; 1 × MG
Armour: 13mm
Crew: 2
Weight: 6.5 tons (6,600kg)
Hull length: 12ft 2in (2.743m)
Width: 9ft 0in (2.74m)
Height: 6ft 11in (2.11m) on tracks
Engine: Scania-Vabis, 6-cylinder, petrol, 100bhp
Power/weight: 15.38
Road speed, tracks: 21mph (35km/hr)
Road speed, wheels: 46mph (75km/hr)

Strv L-100 Sweden
Landsverk

1934. This was virtually a scaled-down L-60 intended to be an ultra-light, ultra-fast machine carrying either a machine gun or a 20mm cannon. It appears to have carried things too far, since no army was interested.

Armament: 1 × 20mm cannon or 1 × MG
Armour: 9mm
Crew: 2
Weight: 4.5 tons (4,675kg)
Hull length: 13ft 5in (4.09m)
Width: 5ft 5in (1.65m)
Height: 6ft 1in (1.85m)
Engine: Scania-Vabis 6-cylinder, petrol, 130bhp
Road speed: 30mph (49km/hr)
Power/weight: 28.88
Range: 100 miles (165km)

Strv m/21 Sweden
Maker unknown

1920. At the end of World War I the German designer Vollmer went to Sweden, where he designed this tank, very similar to the LK-1 he had designed in Germany. It followed contemporary vehicle practice in having the engine in front under a long armoured hood, with a 'cab' behind it acting as the fighting compartment with a simple round turret and a machine gun. The fully-skirted suspension had mud chutes. Ten were built, plus a command tank with radio transmitter. They were upgraded in 1929 by fitting a Scania-Vabis 85bhp engine and thicker armour, being known thereafter as the **m/21/29**.

Armament: 1 × MG
Armour: 14mm
Crew: 4
Weight: 9.7 tons (9,850kg)
Hull length: 18ft 9in (5.71m)
Width: 6ft 9in (2.06m)
Height: 8ft 3in (2.51m)
Engine: Daimler sleeve-valve, 4-cylinder, petrol, 56bhp
Road speed: 10mph (16km/hr)
Power/weight: 5.77

Strv m/31 Sweden
Landsverk

1931. Also known as the **Landsverk L-10**, this was generally considered to be among the best of pre-war designs. Hull and turret were welded armour and suspension was by two twin bogies with large wheels and a combination of leaf and coil springing. The turret was equipped with radio, and in 1934 a number were purchased by the Swedish Army.

Armament: 1 × 37mm; 2 × MG
Armour: 9mm
Crew: 4
Weight: 11.31 tons (11,500kg)
Hull length: 17ft 0in (5.18m)
Width: 7ft 0in (2.13m)
Height: 7ft 4in (2.23m)
Engine: Büssing V6, petrol, air-cooled 140bhp at 2,500rpm
Road speed: 25mph (40km/hr)
Power/weight: 12.37
Range: 125 miles (200km)

Strv m/37 Sweden
CKD

1937. This was the Czech **AH-4SV** assembled in Sweden from components shipped from Czechoslovakia. It had a well-sloped hull with a turret offset to the left and carrying two machine guns. It was also unusual for its day in carrying a radio set. Suspension was the usual CKD bell-crank bogies. Fifty were built and fitted with Swedish engines.

Armament: 2 × 8mm MG
Armour: 15mm
Crew: 2
Weight: 4.5 tons (4,572kg)
Hull length: 11ft 2in (3.40m)
Width: 6ft 2in (1.88m)
Height: 5ft 10in (1.78m)
Engine: Volvo 6 cylinder, petrol, 80bhp

Power/weight: 17.77
Road speed: 30mph (48km/hr)

Strv m/38 Sweden
Landsverk

1939. The m/38 was an improved version of the L-60 and was taken into Swedish service, but only in small numbers. A Swedish engine was adopted, and it was unusual in using a steering wheel instead of the usual tiller levers.

Armament: 1 × 37mm; 1 × MG
Armour: 13mm
Crew: 3
Weight: 8.5 tons (8,835kg)
Hull length: 15ft 4in (4.67m)
Width: 6ft 0in (2.06m)
Height: 6ft 10in (2.09m)
Engine: Scania-Vabis 6 cylinder, petrol, 142bhp
Power/weight: 16.70
Road speed: 28mph (45km/hr)
Range: not known

Strv m/39 Sweden
Landsverk

1940. This was simply the m/38 with a new gun mantlet so as to carry the main gun and two coaxial machine guns. The weight went up by half a ton (500kg) but beyond that there was no change in the dimensions. It also reverted to using tiller levers and dropped the steering wheel; some ideas are just too revolutionary.

Strv m/40 Sweden
Landsverk

1941. The Strv m/40 was developed from the series of light armoured vehicles built by Landsverk in the mid-1930s and which were native designs, though they may have owed a good deal to existing vehicles in other countries. The m/40 was the first tank to be built in quantity for the Swedish Army. It was fairly conventional in design, with a built-up riveted and welded hull. The driver was in the front of the hull with the transmission beside him and there was a low two-man turret mounting a 37mm gun and two coaxial machine guns. The turret shape was advanced for its time and bore a resemblance to some of the German types. The engine compartment was behind a firewall at the rear. Cross-country performance and reliability were good, though it must be remembered that these tanks were only ever used on exercises and never saw action. The 37mm gun was quickly outdated, but was not replaced, and the vehicle remained in service long after it was technically obsolete. A few were sold to Dominica in the 1950s for use as internal security vehicles.

Armament: 1 × 37mm; 2 × MG
Armour: 24mm
Crew: 3
Weight: 9.35 tons (9,500kg)
Hull length: 16ft 1in (4.9m)
Width: 6ft 11in (2.10m)
Height: 6ft 11in (2.10m)
Engine: Scania-Vabis, 6-cylinder, petrol, 142bhp
Road speed: 30mph (48km/hr)
Power/weight: 15.19
Range: 125 miles (200km)

Strv m/41 Sweden
Scania-Vabis

1942. The Strv m/41 is the Czechoslovakian **TNH/SV** built under licence in Sweden and fitted with a more powerful Swedish engine. These tanks were obviously a good investment for Sweden, since they continued to serve until the 1950s and were then totally rebuilt and their components used in making the Pbv 301 armoured personnel carrier, the first tracked carrier to be built for the Swedish Army. There were two versions of the m/41, the second one having a more powerful 160hp engine, but otherwise being unchanged.

Armament: 1 × 37mm; 2 × MG
Armour: 25mm
Crew: 3
Weight: 10.33 tons (10,500kg)
Hull length: 15ft 0in (4.57m)
Width: 7ft 0in (2.13m)
Height: 7ft 9in (2.37m)
Engine: Scania-Vabis, 6-cylinder, petrol, 145bhp
Road speed: 27mph (45km/hr)
Power/weight: 14.03
Range: 125 miles (200km)

Strv m/42 Sweden
Landsverk

1942. The Strv m/42 was developed from the m/40: the hull and chassis of the m/40 were lengthened by adding two more roadwheels and on to this enlarged hull a new turret was fitted. It had a small overhang at the back and a larger mantlet projecting forward so that there was room for a 75mm gun. This was a substantial step forward in armament, even though it was only a low-velocity gun. A distinction of the turret was that it carried two spare roadwheels on the back, one on either side. In 1958 these tanks were rebuilt and fitted with a larger

turret and a high-velocity 75mm gun, bringing their specification more up-to-date, and they were then known as the **Strv m/74**.

Armament: 1 × 75mm; 3 × MG
Armour: 80mm
Crew: 4
Weight: 22.14 tons (22,500kg)
Hull length: 16ft 1in (4.90m)
Width: 7ft 4in (2.20m)
Height: 5ft 3in (1.61m)
Engine: Scania-Vabis, 320bhp
Road speed: 27mph (45km/hr)
Power/weight: 14.45
Range: 125 miles (200km)

Stuart USA
See M3 and M5 Light Tanks

T1 Light USA
Cunningham

1927. This well illustrates the 'agricultural tractor' line of approach often used by early experimenters. The engine and transmission were at the front of the hull with a fighting/ driving compartment at the rear, surmounted by a small revolving turret carrying a 37mm trench cannon and a coaxial .30-inch machine gun. Full-diameter rear drive and front idler, small-wheel suspension system covered by skirting plate with mud chutes.

Armament: 1 × 37mm M1916; 1 × MG
Armour: 10mm
Crew: 2
Weight: 6.69 tons (6,805kg)
Hull length: 12ft 6in (3.81m)
Width: 5ft 11in (1.80m)
Height: 7ft 2in (2.18m)
Engine: Cunningham V-8, water-cooled, petrol 105bhp
Road speed: 20mph (32km/hr)
Power/weight: 15.89

T1E1 Light USA
Cunningham

1929. An improved T1, with various small modifications, notably the shortening of the nose. Four were built for trials; it was recommended for standardisation as the **Light Tank M1**, but the decision was later cancelled.

Armament: 1 × 37mm M1916; 1 × MG
Armour: 10mm
Crew: 2
Weight: 6.69 tons (6,805kg)
Hull length: 12ft 9in (3.89m)
Width: 5ft 11in (1.80m)

Height: 7ft 2in (2.18m)
Engine: Cunningham V-8, water-cooled, petrol, 110bhp
Road speed: 20mph (32km/hr)
Power/weight: 16.44

T1E2 Light USA
Cunningham

1929. Although to the same front-engined form as the earlier T1s, this began to resemble a tank more than a tractor. The nose was more curved, with the radiator grille in the glacis plate; the hull overhung the tracks. The turret was fitted with a high velocity 37mm gun and a coaxial machine gun. Thicker armour and more engine power completed the package.

Armament: 1 x 37mm; 1 x MG
Armour: 16mm
Crew: 2
Weight: 7.95 tons (8,075kg)
Hull length: 12ft 10in (3.91m)
Width: 6ft 3in (1.91m)
Height: 7ft 7in (2.31m)
Engine: Cunningham V-8, water-cooled, petrol, 132bhp
Road speed: 18mph (28km/hr)
Power/weight: 16.60

T1E3 Light USA
Rock Island

1931. A T1E1 modified by fitting a high-velocity 37mm gun in the turret, improving the suspension and fitting a more powerful Cunningham engine.

T1E4 Light USA
Rock Island

1932. This introduced a new suspension system based on leaf-sprung bogies, which leaned sufficiently heavily upon the current Vickers designs to raise questions of patent infringement. The entire mechanical train was reversed, placing the engine at the rear and driving front sprockets, and the front was rounded and had a well-sloped glacis plate. The fighting compartment overhung the tracks and the turret was now midway down the length of the hull and carried a short 37mm gun and a machine gun.

Armament: 1 x 37mm; 1 x MG
Armour: 16mm
Crew: 3
Weight: 7.68 tons (7,800kg)
Hull length: 15ft 5in (4.69m)
Width: 7ft 3in (2.20m)
Height: 6ft 7in (2.00m)
Engine: Cunningham V-8 water-cooled, petrol, 140bhp

Road speed: 20mph (32km/hr)
Power/weight: 19.22

T1E5 Light USA
Rock Island

1932. Until this time all US tanks had used clutch-and-brake steering. The T1E5 introduced the controlled differential system and was simply a one-off test-bed, being a T1E1 suitably modified.

T1E6 Light USA
Rock Island

1933. Generally as the T1E4, but with the hull dimensions changed so as to fit an American La France engine instead of the Cunningham engine.

Armament: 1 x 37mm; 1 x MG
Armour: 16mm
Crew: 3
Weight: 8.88 tons (9,027kg)
Hull length: 15ft 0in (4.57m)
Width: 6ft 8in (2.03m)
Height: 6ft 6in (1.98m)
Engine: American La France, water-cooled, petrol, 240bhp
Road speed: 20mph (32km/hr)
Power/weight: 27.00

T1 Medium USA
Rock Island

1925. Broadly based on the earlier M1921 Medium this had deep tracks with skirting plates, a hull raised above the upper track, slope-roofed turret with large commander's cupola and a short-barrelled 57mm gun. It was recommended for standardisation in 1928 and was approved by the War Department, but this approval was later withdrawn in favour of continued development.

Armament: 1 x 57mm; 2 x MG
Armour: 25mm
Crew: 4
Weight: 19.64 tons (19,960kg)
Hull length: 25ft 11in (7.90m)
Width: 8ft 0in (2.44m)
Height: 9ft 5in (2.86m)
Engine: Packard, 8 cylinder, petrol, 200bhp
Road speed: 14mph
Power/weight: 10.18

T1E1 Medium USA
Rock Island

1929. The T1 Medium but with a 338bhp Liberty engine in place of the original Packard engine.

T2 Light USA
Rock Island

1934. The T1 light tank series had shown that a more powerful engine was needed. Nothing short enough could be found commercially, and an entirely new design was financially impossible. Someone suggested an aircraft engine, and the only one short enough was a Continental seven-cylinder radial. The T2 was thus designed around this engine, and proved to be the turning point in US tank design, the precursor of almost all the World War Two combat tanks. Vickers-type suspension by very small four-double-wheel bogies and leaf springs, high-set rear hull, round turret, front drive, two return rollers.

Armament: 3 × MG
Armour: 15mm
Crew: 4
Weight: not known
Hull length: 13ft 5in (4.08m)
Width: 7ft 10in (2.31m)
Height: 6ft 9in (2.06m)
Engine: Continental, 7-cylinder, radial, air-cooled, petrol, 260bhp
Road speed: 27mph (43km/hr)
Power/weight: not known

T2E1 Light USA
Rock Island

1934. This was the T2 fitted with vertical volute spring suspension by two two-wheeled bogies on each side and a slightly improved turret. This was standardised as the **Light Tank M2A1** in 1938, a total of nine having been built in 1934–35.

Armament: 3 × MG
Armour: 16mm
Crew: 4
Weight: 8.39 tons (8,528kg)
Hull length: 13ft 5in (4.09m)
Width: 7ft 5in (2.26)
Height: 6ft 9in (2.06m)
Engine: Continental, 7-cylinder radial, petrol, air-cooled, 260bhp
Road speed: 45mph (72km/hr)
Power/weight: 30.98

T2E2 Light USA
Rock Island

1932. As for the T2E1 but had two turrets side-by-side, each with a single machine gun.

T2 Medium USA
Cunningham

1930. Much different to the T1 Medium, this had a lowered track line so that the hull could overhang the track, and a flat front set back between the front idlers. It had a 47mm gun and a .50-inch machine gun in the turret, and a 37mm gun and .30-inch machine gun in the right front of the superstructure. The turret had the usual mushroom-style cupola of the period. Multi-small-wheel suspension with skirting plate but exposed four return rollers. Only the prototype was built.

Armament: 1 × 47mm; 1 × 37mm; 2 × MG
Armour: 25mm
Crew: 4
Weight: 13.92 tons (14,152kg)
Hull length: 16ft 0in (4.88m)
Width: 8ft 0in (2.44m)
Height: 9ft 1in (2.77m)
Engine: Liberty V-12, petrol, 312bhp
Road speed: 25mph (40km/hr)
Power/weight: 22.41

T3 Light USA
Rock Island

1936. An odd little vehicle which seems to have been built more as a test-bed than as a serious combat machine. Small hull, level with the track upper run; two-bogie modified volute spring suspension. Two small fixed cupolas, one for the driver, one for a machine gunner. Rear engine, front drive. Extensive use of aluminium alloys in non-stressed parts.

Armament: 1 × MG
Armour: 16mm
Crew: 2
Weight: 6.32 tons (6,422kg)
Hull length: 11ft 3in (3.43m)
Width: 6ft 10in (2.08m)
Height: 4ft 6in (1.37m)
Engine: Ford V-8, water-cooled, petrol, 83bhp
Road speed: 35mph (56km/hr)
Power/weight: 13.13

T3 Medium USA
See Christie M1931

T3E1 Medium USA
US Wheel & Track

1932. Nomenclature given to two Christie M1928 tanks ordered by the Polish government in 1930 but not purchased. The two were then bought by the US Army and called the T3E1. They differed from the T3 in having the drive to the wheels by gears rather than by chain.

See Christie M1931 for further details

T3E2 Medium Tank USA
La France

1932. The T3E2 designation covers five additional tanks ordered from Christie and his US Wheel & Track Layer company by the US Army. Certain modifications to the T3/M1931 design were requested, but Christie refused to listen to the army's request, telling them to wait for his latest design. By this time the army were tiring of J. Walter and his tantrums, so with the several patents they had bought from Christie, and some ideas of their own, they went to the La France company to have the tanks built to their specification. This model was generally similar to the T3 but with a wider hull to allow a machine gunner to sit alongside the driver, a wider, octagonal, turret to hold two crew members, three additional machine guns pointing to the sides and rear and various minor refinements.

Armament: 1 × 37mm gun, 5 × MG
Armour: 13mm
Crew: 4
Weight: 11.5 tons (11,685kg)
Hull length: 18ft 9in (5.72m)
Width: 8ft 0in (2.44m)
Height: 7ft 8in (2.33m)
Engine: Curtiss V-12, petrol, 435bhp
Road speed, wheels: 30mph (48km/hr)
Road speed, tracks: 20mph (32km/hr)
Power/weight: 37.82

T3E3 Medium USA
La France

1936. Wheel-and-track tank which was simply the T3E2 with some minor modifications but with controlled differential steering and transmission. Only one built and principally intended as a testbed for the transmission and steering system.

T4 Medium USA
Rock Island

1936. Wheel-and-track design, using Christie-type suspension as improved by Rock Island. Basically the Combat Car T4, lengthened and strengthened. Four rubber-tyred roadwheels each side, with raised front idler and rear drive sprocket. Sloped glacis plate, low superstructure with sloped-down rear end, small turret with two machine guns. A total of 15 were built.

Armament: 3 × MG
Armour: 16mm
Crew: 4
Weight: 12.05 tons (12,248kg)
Hull length: 16ft 1in (4.90m)
Width: 8ft 2in (2.49m)
Height: 7ft 3in (2.21m)
Engine: Continental 7-cylinder radial, air-cooled, 268bhp
Road speed, wheels: 35mph (56km/hr)
Road speed, tracks: 20mph (32km/hr)
Power/weight: 22.24

T4E1 Medium USA
Rock Island

1936. As for the T4 Medium but with a fixed barbette structure in place of a turret, mounting six machine guns, and with a central commander's cupola. Together with the T4 it was given Limited Standard approval as the **Tank, Medium, M1, Convertible**, in early 1937, but very few were built.

Armament: 6 × MG
Armour: 16mm
Crew: 4
Weight: 13.39 tons (13,808kg)
Hull length: 16ft 1in (4.90m)
Width: 8ft 2in (2.49m)
Height: 7ft 4in (2.23m)
Engine: Continental 7-cylinder radial, air-cooled, 268bhp
Road speed, wheels: 35mph (56km/hr)
Road speed, tracks: 25mph (40km/hr)
Power/weight: 20.01

T5 Medium (T5 Phase 1) USA
Rock Island

1938. This tank established the general pattern and major mechanicals of the American wartime medium tanks. The Christie suspension was abandoned for the vertical volute spring suspension using three two-wheeled bogies on each side, with front drive and rear idler. It had a sloped glacis plate, the hull overhung the tracks, there was a short superstructure bristling with six machine guns surmounted by a turret carrying a 37mm gun.

Armament: 1 × 37mm; 6 × MG
Armour: 25mm
Crew: 5
Weight: 13.39 tons (13,810kg)
Hull length: 17ft 3in (5.26m)
Width: 8ft 2in (2.49m)
Height: 9ft 0in (2.74m)
Engine: Continental 7-cylinder radial, air-cooled, 250bhp

Road speed: 20mph (32km/hr)
Power/weight: 18.67

T5 Medium (T5 Phase 2) USA
Rock Island

The T5 Phase 1 proved to be sadly underpowered when it was submitted for trials in 1938, and after some debate it was proposed to fit a Guiberson diesel engine in place of the 7-cylinder Continental. This, though it improved the torque, produced little or no more power, and the idea – which was provisionally entitled T5 Phase 2 – was abandoned in favour of fitting a 9-cylinder Wright Continental which promised 350 horse-power and which then became Phase 3, *below*.

T5 Medium (T5 Phase 3) USA
Rock Island

1938. As for the T5 Phase 1 above, but fitted with a Wright 9-cylinder radial air-cooled engine developing 345bhp The power-to-weight ratio was now 25.2 and performance increase proportionately. It was also fitted with wider tracks in order to improve flotation on soft ground, and the return rollers had supporting brackets which sat outside the tracks.

T5E1 Medium USA
Rock Island

1938. As for T5 Phase 1 above, but with two 37mm guns in the turret and a Guiberson-converted diesel radial engine. It also moved the supporting brackets for the bogies inside the track instead of, as in earlier designs, spanning the upper run of the track.

T5E2 Medium USA
Rock Island

1939. This was the T5 Phase 3 rebuilt to provide heavier firepower. The right-hand hull machine gun position was removed and the hull built up into a sponson into which a 75mm pack howitzer was mounted. There were two fixed machine guns in the glacis plate, three machine guns on the other three corners of the hull, and one in the turret. The object in view was to explore the practicality of a self-propelled artillery piece mounted on a tank chassis; the pilot was built but the idea was not pursued further, although it was later to provide the inspiration for the M3 Medium.

Armament: 1 × 75mm howitzer M1; 6 × MG
Armour: 32mm
Crew: 5
Weight: not known

Hull length: 18ft 0in (5.49m)
Width: 8ft 7in (2.62m)
Height: 9ft 3in (2.82m)
Engine: Wright, 9-cylinder air-cooled radial, petrol, 346bhp

T6 Light USA
Rock Island

1939. Another test-bed vehicle, this was without a turret, having an open-topped hull, and was driven by two straight-eight Buick engines coupled together. Suspension was by two twin bogies with volute springs, coupled by a girder. In order to reduce the pitching movement, the rear idler wheel was lowered to the ground on a training arm.

Armament: none
Armour: 25mm
Crew: 3
Hull length: 12ft 6in (3.81m)
Width: 7ft 11in (2.41m)
Height: 5ft 3in (1.60m)
Engine: 2 × Buick 8-cylinder OHV, petrol, each 140bhp
Road speed: 30mph (48km/hr)

T9 Light (Locust) USA
See M22 Light

T-10 Heavy Russia
State factories

1957. The T-10 was the ultimate design of the Josef Stalin series and was more or less an enlarged JS-3, with a longer hull, an extra roadwheel on each side, uprated gun with fume extractor, larger turret, thicker armour and a more powerful engine. Numbers were sold to Syria and Egypt, as well as to Warsaw Pact armies, but by the middle 1960s they were seen to be overweight and a logistic burden on their formations. Improved armament on medium tanks meant that the same results could be achieved in a more agile, lighter and more economical package, and the heavy tank's day was over.

Armament: 1 × 122mm; 2 × MG
Armour: 250mm
Crew: 4
Weight: 51.18 tons (52,000kg)
Hull length: 24ft 4in (7.41m)
Width: 11ft 8in (3.56m)
Height: 8ft 0in (2.43m)
Engine: V2-IS V-12 diesel, 39 litres, 700bhp at 2,000rpm
Road speed: 26mph (42km/hr)
Power/weight: 13.68
Range: 155 miles (250km)

T-12 Medium Russia
State factories
Ca 1925. Developed from the MS series, which had been developed from the Renault FT17. A simple hull structure between two tracks with small-bogie suspension, Cylindrical turret with a rounded commander's cupola. Apart from the fact that it weighed about 19 tons, had a 45mm gun in the turret, and was mechanically unreliable, nothing is known of the details. The design was abandoned.

T14 Assault Tank USA
Rock Island
1943. This was the result of an Anglo-American agreement for each to develop a heavy assault tank for the anticipated invasion of Europe. It was, in effect, an up-armoured M4 Sherman with the addition of skirting plates over the suspension (which was taken from the M6 heavy tank). It was a lot of tank for only a 75mm gun, and the idea was abandoned in 1944.

Armament: 1 × 75mm; 3 × MG
Armour: 76mm
Crew: 5
Weight: 41.93 tons (42,606kg)
Hull length: 20ft 10in (6.35m)
Width: 10ft 3in (3.12m)
Height: 8ft 2in (2.48m)
Engine: Ford GAXZ V-8, petrol, 470bhp
Road speed: 24mph (38km/hr)
Power/weight: 11.20

T-17 Tankette Russia
State factories
Ca 1926. Another design with its roots in the Renault two-man tank, this stemmed from the MS series and had a fixed superstructure with a forward-firing machine gun and a two-man crew. The tracks had three two-wheeled bogies on each side, idlers at the front and rear drive. This must have been one of the last designs to use the upswept 'Renault Tail' appendage. No details known, other than that it had a two-cylinder air-cooled engine, which could have done nothing for the power-to-weight ratio.

T20 Medium USA
Fisher Body
1942. A potential replacement for the M4 Sherman. Generally similar to the Sherman but with an early form of horizontal volute spring suspension with exterior support brackets, large cast turret with bustle, mounting a 76mm gun, and a Ford engine with the Torquematic automatic transmission. Trials were stopped because of the unreliability of this transmission and the design was then abandoned.

Armament: 1 × 76mm; 3 × MG
Armour: 64mm
Crew: 5
Weight: 29.35 tons (29,828kg)
Hull length: 18ft 10in (5.74m)
Width: 9ft 10in (3.00m)
Height: 8ft 0in (2.44m)
Engine: Ford GAN, V-8, petrol, 470bhp
Road speed: 25mph (40km/hr)
Power/weight: 16.01

T20E3 Medium USA
Fisher Body
1942. The same tank as the T20 but with a large-wheel torsion-bar suspension system developed by Buick. It had the same engine and transmission as the T20 and inherited the same mechanical problems, plus a few more due to the newly-developed suspension. One prototype built, standardisation as the **M27B1** proposed but later rescinded and the design abandoned.

Armament: 1 × 76mm; 3 × MG
Armour: 64mm
Crew: 5
Weight: 30.13 tons (40,820kg)
Hull length: 18ft 10in (5.74m)
Width: 9ft 10in (3.00m)
Height: 8ft 0in (2.44m)
Engine: Ford GAN, V-8 petrol, 470bhp
Road speed: 25mph (40km/hr)
Power/weight: 15.60

T22 Medium USA
Chrysler
1942. Generally similar to the T20, and using the same horizontal volute spring suspension with external support brackets. Fitted with a five-speed manual gearbox instead of an automatic transmission. The manual gearbox also gave problems, and the general transmission difficulties, together with a demand from the European Theater of Operations for a more effective gun than the 76mm, led to the termination of the entire T20/22 project in December 1944.

T22E1 Medium USA
Rock Island
A T22 tank fitted with a new turret mounting a 75mm gun with auto-loading mechanism, adapted

from the airborne 75mm system. It, too, was terminated in December 1944.

T23 Medium USA
Fisher Body
1943. This was broadly the same as the T20 series, intended to be an improved M4, but differed in having a petrol-electric transmission system developed by General Electric. There were a number of test versions, with various guns, suspensions and so forth, but the final version had a 76mm gun, horizontal volute spring suspension and various minor improvements. Production of 250 was authorised, though the design was never standardised, but since the Armored Board doubted the reliability of the petrol-electric drive it was never used in combat.

Armament: 1 × 76mm; 3 × MG
Ammunition: 64
Armour: 64mm maximum
Crew: 5
Weight: 32.80 tons (33,334kg)
Hull length: 19ft 9in (6.02m)
Width: 9ft 11in (3.02m)
Height: 8ft 4in (2.54m)
Engine: Ford GAN, V-8, petrol, 470bhp
Road speed: 35mph (56km/hr)
Power/weight: 14.32

T23E3 Medium USA
Chrysler
1944. The Armored Board considered the T23 to be too heavy, with its weight badly distributed, and attributed this to the cumbersome petrol-electric system. They therefore ordered some test vehicles built to try various re-arrangements The **T23E3** had Buick torsion-bar suspension taken from a T25 tank, with large roadwheels; the **T23E4** was to have horizontal volute springs and 23-inch wide tracks but this was cancelled before it began. It was proposed to standardise the T23E3 as the **Medium Tank M27**, and the T20E3 as the **Medium Tank M27B1**, but nothing came of this and the whole project was dropped in the late summer of 1945.

Armament: 1 × 76mm; 3 × MG
Ammunition: 84
Armour: 65mm
Crew: 5
Weight: 33.48 tons (34,020kg)
Hull length: 19ft 2in (5.84m)
Width: 10ft 4in (3.15m)
Height: 8ft 5in (2.58m)
Engine: Ford GAN V-8, petrol, 470bhp

Road speed: 35mph (56km/hr)
Power/weight: 14.05

T-24 Medium Russia
State factories
Ca 1930. Descended from the failed T-12 Medium this was a good design let down by poor mechanicals. The hull was widened to overlap the tracks, and the superstructure was given a V-shaped front with the driver at the point. The turret was roomy and had a cupola, and the vehicle was well armoured. After 25 had been built, the drive-train and suspension problems caused the design to be cancelled.

Armament: 1 × 45mm; 3 × MG
Armour: 25mm
Crew: 3
Weight: 18.20 tons (18,500kg)
Dimensions: not known
Engine: 8-cylinder, petrol, 300bhp
Road speed: 15mph (24km/hr)
Power/weight: 16.48
Range: 125 miles (200km)

T24E1 Light USA
Rock Island
1944. This was a standard M24 Light modified by removing the Cadillac engines and inserting a Continental R-975-C4 radial engine and a stepless torque converter Torquematic transmission, the object being a comparison with the standard Cadillac system. In order to fit the air-cooled engine the rear of the hull had to be lifted and ventilating louvres added.

Armament: 1 × 75mm; 3 × MG
Armour: 25mm
Crew: 3
Weight: 18.5 tons (18,800kg)
Engine: Continental R-975-C1 9-cylinder radial, air-cooled, petrol, 400bhp at 2,400rpm
Road speed: 35mph (55km/hr)
Power/weight: 21.6

T25 Medium USA
Chrysler
1943. This was developed to meet an Ordnance Department demand for a tank carrying a 90mm gun, and it was basically the T23 beefed up and with a new, larger turret. It had horizontal volute spring suspension and a track 23 inches wide. It was originally intended to have petrol-electric transmission, but by the time the hull was ready, Army Ground Forces had decided that the petrol-

electric system was of no use, and the Torquematic transmission would be used, since this had now been developed to a reasonable level of reliability. Plans were made for production, but in the event only two pilots were built.

Armament: 1 × 90mm; 3 × MG
Armour: 90mm
Crew: 5
Weight: 36.80 tons (37,195kg)
Hull length: 18ft 7in (5.66m)
Width: 10ft 11in (3.32m)
Height: 8ft 11in (2.71m)
Engine: Ford GAF V-8, petrol, 470bhp
Road speed: 30mph (48km/hr)
Power/weight: 12.77

T-26 Light Russia
Kirov, and other state factories
1932. This was a licence-built version of the Vickers Six-Ton tank, specimens of which were purchased by Russia in 1930. The original **T-10A** version was a two-turret model, with the usual spindly multiple-bogie Vickers suspension; the **A-1** was the Vickers-built article, the **A-2** the Russian-built version. The only significant difference was that the A-1 had Vickers .303-inch machine guns in the turrets, while the A-2 had Degtyarev 7.62mm DT guns. A number of variations have been reported, but must be treated with some caution; the **A-4**, for example, is said to have had a 27mm gun in the right turret, but there is no record of any such calibre in Russian service.

Armament: 2 × MG (see text)
Armour: 15mm
Crew: 3
Weight: 8.5 tons (8,635kg)
Hull length: 15ft 9in (4.80m)
Width: 7ft 10in (2.38m)
Height: 6ft 9in (2.06m)
Engine: 4-cylinder, petrol, 91bhp at 2,200rpm
Road speed: 22mph (35km/hr)
Power/weight: 10.70
Range: 140 miles (225km)

T-26B, T-26S Light Russia
State factories
1935. These were advances on the original T-26; the 'B' series used the same hull but with a single turret with a 37mm or, later, a 45mm gun with coaxial machine gun. There were also commander's tanks (with radio frame antenna surrounding the turret) and flamethrower tanks. The 'S' series was the final production T-26 design, with heavier armour, larger

turret, and a welded hull with 'rounded-off' corners.

T-26S
Armament: 1 × 45mm; 2 × MG
Armour: 25mm
Crew: 3
Weight: 10.30 tons (10,465kg)
Hull length: 15ft 9in (4.80m)
Width: 7ft 10in (2.39m)
Height: 7ft 8in (2.33m)
Engine: 4-cylinder, petrol, 91bhp at 2,200rpm
Road speed: 17mph (28km/hr)
Power/weight: 8.8
Range: 125 miles (200km)

T26 Medium USA
Chrysler
1943. This was another stage in the T20/23/25 progression and was originally designed with an eye to a petrol-electric transmission system. It was based on the T25 but with an additional 25mm of armour all round, which led to a stronger suspension, 24-inch (600mm) wide tracks and five return rollers over six roadwheels per side. The weight now put electric transmission out of court, and power was instead supplied by a Ford GAF engine with Torquematic automatic transmission. After trials more modifications were made which put the weight up so far that in June 1944 it became the **Heavy Tank T26E1**.

Armament: 1 × 90mm Gun; 3 × MG
Armour: 101mm
Crew: 5
Weight: 38.61 tons (39,235kg)
Hull length: 22ft 5in (6.83m)
Width: 11ft 2in (3.41m)
Height: 9ft 2in (2.80)
Engine: Ford GAF V-8 petrol, 470bhp
Road speed: 25mph (40km/hr)
Power/weight: 12.17

T26E1 Heavy USA
Chrysler
1944. As related above, this began life as the T26 Medium but became overweight in the course of development and was reclassified. Ten pilots were built for developmental testing and at the conclusion of this modifications were made to the design. This modified tank became the **T26E3**, and this was standardised as the **M26 Heavy (General Pershing)** in January 1945.

T26E2 Heavy USA
Chrysler
1945. This was the culmination of a line of development aimed at putting a 105mm howitzer into the turret of the T23 Medium tank. As the T23 progressed, so did the howitzer idea, until it finally came to rest with the standardisation of the T26 tank as the M26. At that point final designs were drawn up for fitting the 105mm howitzer into a modified Pershing turret, The frontal armour of the turret had to be increased to maintain the balance with the lighter gun barrel. It was type-classified Limited Standard in July 1945 and went into production. It was later reclassified Standard as the **M45 Medium Tank**.

Armament: 1 x 105mm howitzer; 3 x MG
Armour: 127mm
Crew: 5
Weight: 41.52 tons (42,185kg)
Hull length: 20ft 9in (6.32m)
Width: 11ft 6in (3.50m)
Height: 9ft 1in (2.76m)
Engine: Ford GAF V-8 petrol, 470bhp
Road speed: 20mph (32km/hr)
Power/weight: 11.32

T26E4 Heavy USA
Chrysler
1945. This was to be an M26 Heavy Tank with the turret, gun mount and recoil mechanism modified to take a 90mm T15E2 gun. This was a high-velocity (3,200ft/sec; 975m/sec) gun designed to fire separate-loading ammunition, since storing fixed ammunition made with this extra-long cartridge case was almost impossible. The pilot gun was fitted and fired successfully in December 1944, and procurement of 1,000 guns and 500,000 rounds of ammunition were authorised in April 1945, with standardisation imminent. In June it was pointed out that production of guns and ammunition had been halted because it had been discovered that nobody had ordered any tanks to fit. The end of the war came and went, and in February 1946 the whole project was cancelled and the 90mm HV gun reverted to the research and development stage once more.

T26E5 Heavy USA
Chrysler
1945. A project to convert 27 M26 tanks into heavy assault tanks by increasing the armour thickness. The resultant vehicle was as for the M26 except that hull armour was 152mm thick, turret front 190mm, and gun mantlet 280mm. This increased the vehicle weight to 44.08 tons (44,795kg) and the tracks were given an outer extension, bringing them to 28 inches (711mm) wide in order to reduce the ground pressure.

T-27 Light Russia
State factories
1931. Another Vickers design licensed to the Soviets, this was the Vickers-Carden Loyd tankette, recognisable by the truncated cone superstructure, panniers over the tracks, and the large front driving sprockets. It was of no more practical use in Russia than it had been in Britain, but about 2,500 were built and they were doubtless useful training machines for both drivers and commanders. Many were later put to use as towing tractors for anti-tank guns and light field artillery.

Armament: 1 x MG
Armour: 10mm
Crew: 2
Weight: 2.65 tons (2,700kg)
Hull length: 8ft 6in (2.59m)
Width: 6ft 0in (1.83m)
Height: 4ft 9in (1.45m)
Engine: Ford 4-cylinder, petrol, 40bhp at 2,200rpm
Road speed: 26mph (42km/hr)
Power/weight: 15.09
Range: 75 miles (120km)

T-28 Medium Russia
State factories
1933. Another of the multiple-turret designs so popular in the 1930s, this was based upon the British A6 Medium, with some additions from the German NbFz design. One main turret and two auxiliary turrets at the front corners of the hull, multi-wheel suspension with three return rollers, front idler and rear drive. Much of the suspension was covered by skirting with mud chutes. The main turret originally held a 45mm gun but this was soon changed to a low-velocity 76mm type; in some late production models the right front auxiliary turret mounted a 45mm gun instead of a machine gun. Used in the 1940 Winter War and in the first weeks of the German invasion in 1941.

Armament: 1 x 45mm or 1 x 76.2mm (see text);
    3 x MG
Armour: 80mm
Crew: 6
Weight: 31.50 tons (32,000kg)
Hull length: 24ft 5in (7.44m)
Width: 9ft 3in (2.86m)
Height: 9ft 3in (2.86m)

Engine: M-17L V-12, petrol, 500bhp at 1,400rpm
Road speed: 22mph (37km/hr)
Power/weight: 15.87
Range: 135 miles (220km)

T28 Super Heavy USA
Pacific Car

1945. This was the American equivalent of the British Tortoise or the German Jagdtiger SP guns, a massive and impervious vehicle mounting the biggest possible gun in a limited-traverse mounting. And like the others, it proved to be too big to be manageable. The T28 was intended as an assault tank for dealing with heavily protected obstacles with a high velocity 105mm gun. The suspension was by horizontal volute spring bogies with two complete sets of tracks and suspension on each side; one set could be detached to reduce the weight and width for transport. The gun was set in a ball mount on the front face of the turtle-backed cast hull structure, limited to 20° of traverse. As a result it was reclassified as the **T95 Gun Motor Carriage** in March 1945. Two pilot models were completed in late 1945. They were subsequently tested, for the record, and then the design was abandoned.

Armament: 1 × 105mm gun T5E1; 1 × MG
Ammunition: 63 + 4,920
Armour: 305mm
Crew: 8
Weight: 84.82 tons (86,178kg)
Overall length: 36ft 6in (11.12m)
Width: 14ft 5in (4.39m)
Height: 9ft 4in (2.84m)
Engine: Ford GAF, V-8, petrol, 410bhp at 2,600rpm
Road speed: 8mph (13km/hr)
Power/weight: 4.83
Range: 100 miles (160km)

T29 Heavy Tank USA
Chrysler, Pressed Steel Car

1944. This was another proposal for a powerful tank to make frontal assaults on fortified positions. It was of conventional form, differing only in being enormous. There were eight roadwheels on each side, sprung by torsion bars, and a massive cast steel turret carrying a 105mm T5E2 gun, a slightly different weapon to that used on the T28. The turret held four men, the commander being in the bustle, and there was an optical rangefinder and a separate engine for driving the turret traverse machinery. Three were built for test in the late 1940s, but by then it had become obvious that these enormous tanks brought logistic problems with them, and the design was not pursued.

Armament: 1 × 105mm T5E1; 4 × MG
Armour: 105mm
Crew: 6
Weight: 62.05 tons (63,050kg)
Hull length: 25ft 0in (7.72m)
Width: 12ft 6in (3.81m)
Height: 10ft 7in (3.22m)
Engine: Ford GAC, V-12, petrol, 770bhp
Road speed: 22mph (35km/hr)
Power/weight: 12.40

T30 Heavy USA
Chrysler, Pressed Steel Car

1944. This was developed in parallel with the T29 and was the same hull, running gear and turret but with a Continental engine instead of a Ford, and with a 155mm gun instead of the 105mm weapon. The 155mm Gun T7 was a 40-calibre weapon with muzzle brake, firing a 95lb (43kg) shell at 2,300ft/sec (700m/sec). Procurement of 504 guns was authorised in August 1945 but in view of the war ending a few days later that was rapidly rescinded. Twelve tanks were authorised, two were built and tested, after which the program was closed down. As with most of these supertanks, as fighting weapons they were nonsense, but as research tools they were well worth the trouble.

Armament: 1 × 155mm gun T7; 3 × MG
Ammunition: 34 + 4,770
Armour: 105mm
Crew: 6
Weight: 64.74 tons (65,772kg)
Hull length: 24ft 2in (7.37m)
Width: 12ft 6in (3.81m)
Height: 10ft 7in (3.22m)
Engine: Continental AV-1790-3, V-12, petrol air-cooled, 819bhp at 2,800rpm
Road speed: 22mph (35km/hr)
Power/weight: 12.51

T32 Heavy USA
Chrysler

1945. This began as an attempt to improve the armour protection of the M26/T26E3 without impairing the performance. The chassis was lengthened by an extra set of roadwheels, the armour was thickened all round, the 90mm Gun T15E2 was installed and the engine was breathed upon to boost the power. The Torquematic transmission was dropped in favour of a new cross-drive transmission by Allison. Four were ordered in 1945; two of them appeared with cast noses instead of welded and thus became the **T32E1**. They were tested, reported on, and that was the end of them.

Armament: 1 × 90mm T15E2; 3 × MG
Ammunition: 54 + 5,550
Armour: 203mm
Crew: 5
Weight: 55.80 tons (58,700kg)
Hull length: 23ft 3in (7.16m)
Width: 12ft 5in (3.78m)
Height: 9ft 8in (2.94m)
Engine: Ford GAC V-12, petrol, 770bhp at 2,800rpm
Road speed: 22mph (35km/hr)
Power/weight: 13.80
Range: 75 miles (120km) (at 3.5 US gallons per mile!)

T-32 Heavy Russia
State factories
1932. Yet another multi-turret design, this time based upon the British Vickers Independent and boasting five turrets. The main turret carried a 76mm gun, two smaller turrets carried 37mm guns, and two had a 7.62mm machine gun each. The suspension was by six large roadwheels on each side, concealed by heavy skirting plates, with front idlers and rear sprockets. A limited number were built before it was replaced by the T-35.

Armament: 1 × 76.2mm; 2 × 37mm; 6 × MG
Armour: 25mm
Crew: 10
Weight: 44.8 tons (43,520kg)
Hull length: 30ft 6in (9.30m)
Width: 10ft 6in (3.20m)
Height: 10ft 0in (3.05m)
Engine: V-8, petrol, 345bhp
Road speed: 18mph (30km/hr)
Power/weight: 7.70
Range: 75 miles (120km)

T-33 Tankette Czechoslovakia
CKD
1933. A two-man machine, probably influenced by the Carden-Loyd and other tankettes which were being hawked around Europe in the late 1920s, this was simply a rectangular box on tracks, sloped edges to the superstructure roof, a single hatch and a stepped front with vision slots for the two crew members. There was a prominent differential cover on the front plate, and an equally prominent radiator air intake between the two vision slots. The Czech Army didn't like it, but they got 70 of them because they were cheap. They remained in use by Border Guards until the German occupation in 1939.

Armament: 2 × MG
Armour: 12mm
Crew: 2

Weight: 2.46 tons (2,500kg)
Engine: Praga 4-cylinder, petrol, 31bhp
Road speed: 20mph (32km/hr)
Power/weight: 12.60
Range: 125 miles (200km)

T34 Heavy USA
Pressed Steel Car, Chrysler
1945. The T34 was the T30 Heavy with a different gun; instead of the 155mm gun, this had a 120mm gun which was actually the 4.7-inch M1 anti-aircraft gun in disguise. This used separate-loading ammunition with a massive brass cartridge case, and in its air defence form used mechanical ramming and loading. It was a more practical proposition than the 155mm T7 gun, and after testing and tinkering, which turned it into the **T34E1**, it was eventually standardised as the **M103 Heavy Tank** (*qv*) in December 1953.

Armament: 1 × 120mm T53; 4 × MG
Armour: 105mm
Crew: 6
Weight: 62.95 tons (63,960kg)
Hull length: 24ft 3in (7.39m)
Width: 12ft 6in (3.81m)
Height: 10ft 7in (3.22m)
Engine: Continental AV-1790-3, V-12, petrol, 810bhp at 2,800rpm
Road speed: 22mph (35km/hr)
Power/weight: 12.87
Range: 80 miles (128km)

T-34/76 Medium Russia
Komintern, Uralmashzavod, and others
1940. The tank which won the war for Russia and is considered, by many critics, as the best tank design to come out of the war years. Low, with well-sloped armour, wide tracks for good flotation on snow, a powerful 3-inch gun and a reliable and powerful engine were its good points, which far outweighed the cramped interior and spartan standard of fitments. Based on the earlier BT tanks using Christie suspension, with five roadwheels per side, front idler and rear drive, it set the mechanical pattern which the Soviets followed for years. And although almost agricultural in its simplicity of design, the T-34 nevertheless had the earliest form of gun stabilisation to be used in combat, which greatly improved the chance of hitting when firing on the move.

The design was perfected, and the prototypes built, by the Kharkov Locomotive Works in 1939–40 and in March 1940 they were sent to the Finnish front for practical trials, though that war was over by the time they got there. Manufacture began in September 1940 at the Komintern tank plant at Kharkov; it was also scheduled to take place at the Stalingrad Tractor Plant, but initial problems with setting up production delayed this until the summer of 1941, by which time just over 1,000 had been built. The German invasion caused considerable disruption of manufacturing plans, as factories had to be dismantled and moved bodily eastwards out of range of the Germans and then set up and brought back into production. Including the T-34/85 (*below*) which used the same hull and chassis, over 53,000 T-34 were built by July 1945, plus another 5,000 chassis which were used for assault guns. Several thousand more were built in Poland after the war, and they have been widely distributed around the world.

Armament: 1 × 76mm; 2 × MG
Armour: 80mm
Crew: 5
Weight: 26.30 tons (26,720kg)
Hull length: 20ft 3in (6.19m)
Width: 9ft 7in (2.92m)
Height: 7ft 10in (2.39m)
Engine: V-2-34 V-12, diesel, 500bhp at 1,800rpm
Road speed: 31mph (50km/hr)
Power/weight: 19.00
Range: 190 miles (300km)

T-34/85 Medium Russia
State factories

1943. This used the same hull and track assembly as the T-34/76 but with thicker frontal armour and a larger cast steel turret with a thick frontal mantlet and a prominent bustle. There was a single commander's cupola. The gun was improved to an 85mm model, but no changes were made to the engine or transmission. Like the T-34/76, it was widely distributed to pro-Communist nations after the war. The basic hull was also used for AA tanks, bridge-layers, engineer and flamethrower tanks.

Armament: 1 × 85mm; 2 × MG
Ammunition: 56 + 2,395
Armour: 90mm
Crew: 5
Weight: 31.50 tons (32,000kg)
Hull length: 20ft 3in (6.19m)
Width: 9ft 7in (2.99m)
Height: 9ft 0in (2.74m)
Engine: V-2-34M V-12, diesel, 500bhp at 1,800rpm
Road speed: 31mph (50km/hr)
Power/weight: 15.87
Range: 190 miles (300km)

T-35 Heavy Russia
State factories

1933. The T-35 was one of several 1930s designs which was influenced by the Vickers Independent and which featured a rash of subsidiary turrets. It had a large central turret mounting a short 3-inch gun, and four smaller turrets, two of which mounted a 37mm gun and a machine gun, while the other two carried only a machine gun. There was also a hull-mounted machine gun alongside the driver, all of which added up to 11 crew. The size was such that armour had to be skimped to keep the weight within reasonable bounds. About 600 were built, and there were numerous variations as different ideas were tried out, but the improvement in anti-tank guns in the later 1930s sealed their fate. A few were used in the Winter War in 1940.

Armament: 1 × 76.2mm; 2 × 37mm; 5 × MG
Armour: 30mm
Crew: 11
Weight: 49.20 tons (49,985kg)
Hull length: 31ft 10in (9.72m)
Width: 10ft 6in (3.23m)
Height: 11ft 3in (3.44m)
Engine: M-17T V-12, petrol, 500bhp at 2,000rpm
Road speed: 19mph (30km/h)
Power/weight: 10.16
Range: 93 miles (150km)

T-37 Light Russia
State factories

1934. A light, amphibious, reconnaissance tank which appears to have been based upon the Vickers Carden-Loyd light tank of the day. The hull and suspension are obviously Vickers, though the tall and round turret is of local design. A small propeller provided the water propulsion. About 1,200 made, and many minor variations appeared during series production. As well as being amphibian they were also air-lifted on one or two operations, slung beneath TB-3 bombers.

Armament: 1 × 7.62mm MG
Armour: 10mm
Crew: 2
Weight: 3.15 tons (3,200kg)
Hull length: 12ft 4in (3.75m)
Width: 6ft 7in (2.07m)
Height: 5ft 11in (1.82m)
Engine: GAZ-AA, 4-cylinder, petrol, 40bhp at 3,000rpm
Road speed: 21mph (35km/hr)
Power/weight: 12.70
Range: 115 miles (185km)

T-38 Light Russia
State factories

1936. Another amphibian, an improved version of the T-37 above. The improvement lay mainly in the engine, transmission and suspension, though the hull was also lowered. The performance was slightly improved, the reliability considerably improved, and it stayed in service until 1942.

Armament: 1 × 7.62mm MG
Armour: 10mm
Crew: 2
Weight: 3.28 tons (3,332kg)
Hull length: 12ft 4in (3.76m)
Width: 6ft 5in (1.95m)
Height: 5ft 4in (1.62m)
Engine: GAZ-55, 4-cylinder, 50bhp at 3,000rpm
Road speed: 25mph (40km/hr)
Power/weight: 15.24
Range: 93 miles (150km)

T-40 Light Amphibian Russia
State factories

1941. This was the successor to the T-37 and T-38, though it actually had its roots further back in the T-30 tank and was a considerably different design to the -37 and -38. The hull contained buoyancy tanks, had an upswept bow front like the later PT-76, a stepped deck with driver's vision cupola, a small slope-sided turret and a swept-down tail. Four roadwheels each side were suspended by torsion bars, there was a rear idler and front driver, and three track return rollers. Water propulsion was by a propeller. The **T-40A** had a more pointed nose and introduced the trim vane for the first time, while the **T-40S** had thicker armour and did away with the amphibian feature to become simply a light tank.

T40A
Armament: 1 × 12.7mm MG and 1 × 7.62mm MG;
  or 1 × 20mm cannon and 1 × 7.62mm MG;
  both options coaxially mounted in the turret
Armour: 13mm
Crew: 2
Weight: 5.50 tons (5,590kg)
Hull length: 13ft 6in (4.43m)
Width: 8ft 3in (2.51m)
Height: 6ft 11in (2.12m)
Engine: GAZ-202, 6-cylinder, petrol, 85bhp at 3,600rpm
Road speed: 28mph (45km/hr)
Power/weight: 15.45
Range: 215 miles (350km)

T-41 Light Russia
State factories

This was developed *ca* 1940 to replace the T-37/T-38 designs, and was simply the same design with slight improvements. It was not sufficient of an improvement to warrant being put into production and never got beyond the prototype stage.

T-43 Medium Russia
State factories

1942. This was an improved T34/76, with thicker armour, five-speed gearbox and various other detail mechanical changes. Very few were built because it was realised that the prime requirement was to improve the gun, and the T-34/85 was therefore developed and the T-43 abandoned.

Armament: 1 × 76mm; 2 × MG
Armour: 110mm
Crew: 5
Weight: 31.50 tons (32,000kg)
Hull length: 22ft 6in (6.86m)
Width: 9ft 7in (2.92m)
Height: 7ft 10in (2.39m)
Engine: V-2-34 V-12, diesel, 500bhp at 1,800rpm
Road speed: 31mph (50km/hr)
Power/weight: 15.87
Range: 190 miles (300km)

T-44 Medium Russia
State factories

1944. This was a total re-design of the T-34/85 tank, taking in all the lessons learned during the war and setting the pattern for future designs. Like the contemporary Centurion, it saw the end of the distinction between heavy and medium and the dawn of the Main Battle Tank or all-purpose tank. Longer and lower, it had a larger turret, thicker armour, torsion bar suspension, did away with the hull machine gun (and the machine gunner), and mounted the engine transversely. Initial production was with an 85mm gun, later changed to a 100mm gun. Limited production, replaced by the T-54.

Armament: 1 × 85mm or 1 × 100mm; 2 × MG
Armour: 120mm
Crew: 4
Weight (with 100mm gun): 34 tons (34,545kg)
Hull length: 21ft 4in (6.50m)
Width: 10ft 9in (3.28m)
Height: 8ft 2in (2.49m)
Engine: V-12 diesel, 512bhp
Road speed: 32mph (50km/hr)
Power/weight: 15.06
Range: 155 miles (250km)

T-50 Light Russia
State factories
1940. This was intended to replace the T-26 Light and it resembles a scaled-down T-34 Medium in appearance, having six roadwheels each side on torsion bars, a sloped front and a turret well forward on the hull. Armed with a 45mm gun, it went into production, but proved to be a very difficult manufacturing proposition. By 1941, moreover, the light tank's day was over, and the Russians decided to concentrate on the medium for future production. After just over 50 had been made, the T-50 was cancelled.

Armament: I × 45mm; 2 × MG
Armour: 37mm
Crew: 4
Weight: 13.5 tons (13,715kg)
Hull length: 17ft 0in (5.18m)
Width: 8ft 1in (2.48m)
Height: 6ft 8in (2.00m)
Engine: diesel, 300bhp
Road speed: 31mph (50km/hr)
Power/weight: 22.22

T-54 Russia
State factories
1948. An improved version of the T-44, with the same characteristic gap between the first two roadwheels. It had a longer hull, larger and better-shaped turret, improved tracks, a simplified design of hull and an improved 100mm gun. Suspension was by torsion bars, and the engine was transversely mounted at the rear of the hull. It was usually provided with a snorkel to allow submerged fording. Strangely, the bow machine gun reappeared, but no gunner; it was now the driver's responsibility. Some 35 countries adopted this tank as their standard.

Armament: I × 100mm; 3 × MG
Ammunition: 34 + 3,500
Armour: 203mm
Crew: 4
Weight: 35.43 tons (36,000kg)
Hull length: 21ft 2in (6.45m)
Width: 10ft 9in (3.27m)
Height: 7ft 10in (2.40m)
Engine: V-12 diesel, 39 litres, 520bhp at 2,000rpm
Road speed: 30mph (48km/hr)
Power/weight: 14.67
Range: 250 miles (400km)

T-55 Russia
State factories
1960. This is simply an improved T-54; it had a more powerful engine, no AA machine gun on the turret (though this was frequently added later), improved transmission, the gun stabilised in both azimuth and elevation, a revolving turret floor and improved ammunition stowage. The **T-55A** was a further improvement, adding infra-red night vision equipment, an NBC protection system and sundry other refinements.

Armament: I × 100mm; I × MG
Ammunition: 42 + 3,500
Armour: 203mm
Crew: 4
Weight: 35.43 tons (36,000kg)
Hull length: 21ft 1in (6.45m)
Width: 10ft 9in (3.27m)
Height: 7ft 11in (2.40m)
Engine: V-12 diesel, 580bhp at 2,000rpm
Road speed: 31mph (50km/hr)
Power/weight: 16.37
Range: 310 miles (500km)

T-60 Light Russia
State factories
1941. This was the replacement for the T-40 amphibious tank. The drawbacks of the light amphibians had been discovered: the thin armour necessary for flotation was no sort of protection against anti-tank guns, and so the amphibian function was completely discarded in this design. An unusual layout, a legacy of the amphibians, had the offset turret with the engine alongside it in the centre of the hull. It was a useful design as long as the light tank was able to survive on the battlefield, and when they were finally retired many went on to serve as gun tractors and rocket carriers.

Armament: I × 20mm cannon; I × MG
Ammunition: not known
Armour: 20mm
Crew: 2
Weight: 5.07 tons (5,150kg)
Hull length: 14ft 1in (4.29m)
Width: 8ft 1in (2.46m)
Height: 6ft 2in (1.89m)
Engine: GAZ-202, 6-cylinder, petrol, 70bhp at 2,800rpm
Road speed: 38mph (45km/hr)
Power/weight: 13.81
Range: 380 miles (615km)

T-62 MBT Russia
State factories

1961. This was the successor to the T-54/55 and closely resembles it. The principal visible differences lie in the longer and wider hull, the spacing of the roadwheels – instead of the gap between the first and second wheels there are gaps between three/four and four/five. The gun barrel is longer and thicker and has a fume extractor close to the muzzle, and the turret is more rounded and lower at the front. The engine is more powerful, the armour thicker and more sloped on various faces. The gun was a smoothbore 115mm weapon which failed to live up to its promises and had to be partially rifled to give it a reasonable degree of accuracy. It was, of course, fully stabilised. The T-62 also had full NBC protection, night vision and snorkel equipment. The Soviets are estimated to have built some 20,000 of them and they were also built in large numbers in Czechoslovakia and North Korea.

Armament: 1 × 115mm smoothbore; 2 × MG
Ammunition: 40 + 3,000
Armour: 242mm
Crew: 4
Weight: 39.37 tons (40,000kg)
Hull length: 21ft 9in (6.63m)
Width: 10ft 10in (3.30m)
Height: 7ft 10in (2.39m)
Engine: V-12 diesel, 580bhp at 2000rpm
Road speed: 31mph (50km/hr)
Power/weight: 14.73
Range: 280 miles (450km)

T-64 MBT Russia
State factories

1966. The successor to the T-62 was solicited from two different design offices, and the T-64 was the first to appear. It is an example of the profligate system of provision in the Soviet Union, since although it is universally agreed to have been a bad design, nevertheless almost 14,000 were built over a period of several years. It was completely new; though generally resembling the T-62 in the turret area, it abandoned the Christie suspension for a system with six roadwheels on each side, smaller than those on previous tanks, with the upper track run concealed by skirting plates. The gun was a smoothbore 125mm, a better weapon than the previous 115mm and one which was later adapted to fire the AT-8 'Songster' missile as well as conventional ammunition. However, for all its paper attractions, the T-64 suffered from problems with its engine, transmission, fire control system and automatic loader. Much retrospective modification has been done and there are a variety of sub-models, each marking a solved problem.

Armament: 1 × 125mm smoothbore; 2 × MG
Ammunition: 40 + 3,500
Armour: not disclosed
Crew: 3
Weight: 41.34 tons (42,000kg)
Hull length: 24ft 3in (7.40m)
Width: 11ft 11in (3.64m)
Height: 7ft 3in (2.20m)
Engine: 5DTF 5-cylinder opposed-piston diesel, 750bhp
Road speed: 47mph (75km/hr)
Power/weight: 18.14
Range: 250 miles (400km)

T-70 Light Russia
GAZ

1942. This was the last Soviet light tank to be built in quantity, and was built by the Gorki car factory so as not to interfere with medium tank production which had been severely disrupted by the German invasion. So the T-70 was produced in large numbers simply to give the hard-pressed Russian infantry some support until the T-34 and other heavier tanks arrived on the scene. The basic hull and chassis are those of the T-60 but with five roadwheels on each side and with the drive sprockets at the front. The armour was thicker, the turret somewhat larger, and twin engines gave it a considerable boost in power.

Armament: 1 × 45mm; 1 × MG
Armour: 60mm
Crew: 2
Weight: 9.79 tons (9,950kg)
Hull length: 15ft 2in (4.66m)
Width: 7ft 8in (2.52m)
Height: 6ft 9in (2.10m)
Engine: 2 × ZIS-202, 6-cylinder, petrol, 70bhp at 2,800rpm
Road speed: 31mph (50km/hr)
Power/weight: 14.30
Range: 280 miles (450km)

T-72 MBT Russia
Chelyabinsk, Nizhni-Tagil, Kirov

1971. The T-72 was the second contender to replace the T-62; the designers took their time, so that the T-64 went into production first, as described above, but the T-72 appeared in 1971 and proved to be the better design. Even though designed by a different team, the T-72 can be difficult to distinguish from the T-64, since they both use the same gun and the suspension and track are similar. The roadwheels on the T-72 are closer together, and that is about the only external recognition point.

Armament: 1 × 125mm; 2 × MG
Ammunition: 39 + 3,500
Armour: 280mm
Crew: 3
Weight: 44.78 tons (45,500kg)
Hull length: 22ft 10in (6.95m)
Width: 12ft 9in (3.59m)
Height: 7ft 3in (2.22m)
Engine: W-46 V-12 diesel, 780bhp at 2,000rpm
Road speed: 40mph (65km/hr)
Power/weight: 17.42
Range: 250 miles (400km)

T-64/T-72 Variant Models

The list of variant models of the T-64 and T-72 is, quite honestly, ridiculous, and it represents frantic efforts on the part of present-day Russia and Ukraine to sell the tank on the export market by producing whatever modification or variation looks likely to attract buyers. For the record, the brief differences between the principal variants of these two tanks are as follows:

T-64A
Improved sights, improved suspension, added smoke dischargers on turret.

T-64B
Improved 125mm gun/missile launcher.

T-64K
Command tank version with additional radio equipment.

T-72A
Original production model.

T-72B
Improved gun and automatic loader; infra-red searchlight.

T-72K
Command tank version with additional radios.

T-72G
Export model; licence-built in Czechoslovakia and Poland; laser rangefinder.

T-72M
Improved Soviet model; laminated armour, plastic armour side skirts, laser rangefinder. (*And see below* for Polish version)

T-72M1
Improved engine cooling system, additional layer of armour on front.

T-72M2
Additional armour on upper surfaces to defeat top attack missiles; later models may also have explosive reactive armour on glacis plate and turret.

T-72MS
New suspension, new engine, attachments for adding explosive reactive armour. Gun reputed to fire a laser guided projectile.

T-72S
This is a Russian production, using a new 825bhp multi-fuel engine.

T-72M1 MBT Poland
State factories
1992. This is the standard Soviet T-72 which has been modified by the Poles with the intention of improving it; whether they have succeeded is an open question. These improvements include Polish-designed explosive reactive armour added to the hull and turret fronts, new computing power for the ballistic computer and sighting system, new night vision equipment, stabilisation of the 125mm gun in both axes with a new electro-hydraulic system, and several minor adjustments.

Armament: 1 × 125mm; 2 × MG
Ammunition: 44
Armour: not disclosed
Crew: 3
Weight: 40.84 tons (41,500kg)
Hull length: 22ft 10in (6.95m)
Width: 11ft 9in (3.59m)
Height: 7ft 2in (2.19m)
Engine: V-12 supercharged multi-fuel, 770bhp at 2,000rpm
Road speed: 37mph (60km/hr)
Power/weight: 18.85
Range: 285 miles (460km)

T-80 Light Russia
State factories
1943. This was little more than a T-70 with additional armour plates welded on, but relatively few were ever built as by the time it was entering production the T-34 and others were in service and by the end of 1943 the light tanks were completely replaced. Most of those which had survived were converted into gun tractors. Except for the additional armour, and consequently greater weight, data and dimensions were generally as for the T-70 Light.

T-80 MBT Russia
Kirov

1976. This is really an improved T-64, having laminated armour, plus the necessary fitments for the attachment of explosive reactive armour,. It carries the 125mm smoothbore gun from the T-72, firing conventional ammunition or the AT-8 gun-launched anti-tank missile, together with an improved fire control, sighting and surveillance package. There are several minor variant models, with changes in fire control, or communications, or some other detail fitment, but the basic vehicle remains the same.

The T-80 introduced the gas turbine engine into Soviet service; but at 1.2 gallons per mile, and a range of no more than 208 miles on a clear day with the wind behind it, scarcely an economic proposition.

Armament: 1 × 125mm smoothbore; 2 × MG
Ammunition: 36 + 1,750
Armour: not disclosed
Crew: 3
Weight: 41.83 tons (42,500kg)
Hull length: 24ft 3in (7.40m)
Width: 11ft 2in (3.40m)
Height: 7ft 3in (2.20m)
Engine: gas turbine, 1,000bhp
Road speed: 43mph (70km/hr)
Power/weight: 23.90
Range: 208 miles (335km)

T-90 Russia
State factories

1990. Designed for the export market, this is actually no more than an improved T-72M incorporating several features of the T-80. It had explosive reactive armour on the turret and hull front, stabilised day/night sights for both commander and gunner, a new ballistic computer and fire control system, and a fully-stabilised 125mm gun which can fire conventional fin-stabilised ammunition or a laser-beam-riding guided anti-tank missile.

Armament: 1 × 125mm smoothbore; 2 × MG
Ammunition: 43
Armour: not disclosed
Crew: 3
Weight: 45.76 tons (46,500kg)
Hull length: 22ft 6in (6.86m)
Width: 11ft 1in (3.37m)
Height: 7ft 4in (2.23m)
Engine: V-84-2 V-12 turbocharged diesel, 770bhp at 2,000rpm
Road speed: 37mph (60km/hr)
Power/weight: 16.82
Range: 400 miles (650km)

Tadpole UK
Field workshops

1917–18. 'Tadpole' tanks were standard British Mark 4 or 5 tanks which had the tail lengthened by fitting triangular brackets to the rear of the tank so as to lengthen the track base by about nine feet. The extensions were braced by struts in the space between the rear 'horns' and some had platforms built on these braces to carry stores, men or even a trench mortar. The whole purpose of this was to improve trench-crossing ability since, after seeing the first tanks in action, the Germans had begun widening their trenches to make them impassable.

Length: see text
Other data: as for Mks 4 or 5

TAM Argentina
TAMSE

1978. TAM = *Tanque Argentino Mediano*. Medium tank based on the chassis of the German Marder APC, fitted with a 105mm gun in a turret derived from the French AMX-13. The gun is stabilised, the turret low, well sloped and with a pronounced bustle. Armour thickness is less than might be expected, having been sacrificed in order to save weight, necessary for crossing country bridges in South America. About 350 in service with Argentina; others were ordered by Peru, Panama and Ecuador, but all the orders were cancelled for financial reasons before manufacture could commence.

Armament: 1 × 105mm; 2 × MG
Ammunition: 50 + 6,000
Armour: not disclosed
Crew: 4
Weight: 29.52 tons (30,000kg)
Hull length: 22ft 2in (6.75m)
Width: 10ft 9in (3.29m)
Height: 8ft 9in (2.66m)
Engine: MTU MB 833 Ka500 6-cylinder, diesel, 720bhp at 2,200rpm
Road speed: 47mph (75km/hr)
Power/weight: 24.39
Range: 373 miles (600km)

Tamoyo Brazil
Bernardini

1982. This was developed as a private venture, using an American M41 as the starting point. The Bernardini company had refurbished and rebuilt

M41s for the Brazilian Army and their idea was to fit a new turret with a 90mm or 105mm gun and turn the M41 from a light tank into an MBT. The layout is conventional, with a three-man turret carrying a 90mm gun, six dual roadwheels on each side, torsion bar suspension, front idler and rear drive. Prototypes have been built but no further progress is likely until a firm order is forthcoming.

Armament: 1 × 90mm; 2 × MG
Ammunition: 68
Armour: not disclosed
Crew: 4
Weight: 29.52 tons (30,000kg)
Hull length: 21ft 4in (6.50m)
Width: 10ft 7in (3.22m)
Height: 8ft 3in (2.50m)
Engine: Saab-Scania DSI-14 diesel, 500bhp at 2,100rpm
Road speed: 40mph (65km/hr)
Power/weight: 16.94
Range: 340 miles (550km)

Tank Mark 1 UK
Foster
1916. The original and first tank to see combat. Derived from 'Mother' (*qv*), designed by Tritton and others, built by Foster's of Lincoln, and first used in action on 15 September 1916 on the Somme front, the tank being 'D-1' commanded by Lieutenant H.W. Mortimore. It was rhomboid or lozenge-shaped, with all-round tracks and steered by braking one or other of the tracks, or, for more gentle turns, by operating a two-wheeled trailer or 'hydraulic compensator' by a wheel and wire cable. 'Male' versions were armed with two 6-pounder ex-naval guns in side sponsons, plus four Hotchkiss machine guns – one between driver and commander, one in the rear face, and one in each sponson, behind the 6-pounders. The crew consisted of nine men – commander, driver, two 'gearsmen' operating the transmission, two 6-pounder gunners and three machine gunners. 'Female' tanks had no 6-pounders, but two more machine guns in their place.

Armament: 2 × 6-pdr + 4 × MG (Male); or 6 × MG (Female)
Armour: 12mm
Crew: 8
Weight: 28 tons (28,450kg)
Hull length: 32ft 6in (9.90m)
Width: 13ft 9in (4.19m)
Height: 8ft 0in (2.43m)
Engine: Daimler, 6-cylinder, petrol, 105bhp
Road speed: 3.75mph (9km/hr)

Power/weight: 3.75
Range: 22 miles (45km)

Tank Mark 2 UK
Foster
1917. Tank Mark 2 was practically identical to the Mark 1 design but incorporated a number of detail improvements which experience had shown to be desirable. The tracks were improved and the roof of the vehicle was given a raised 'manhole' hatch. Fifty were built.

Data: as for Mark 1

Tank Mark 3 UK
Metropolitan
1917. This appeared more or less at the same time as Mark 2 and was a Mark 2 with slightly thicker armour in parts, and some Female versions had a smaller sponson of the type later more commonly seen on the Mark 4 tank. Fifty were built.

Data: as for Mark 1

Tank Mark 4 UK
Foster, Metropolitan, North British
1917. To the same general design as the Marks 1–3 tanks, but with considerable improvement. The gun sponsons were smaller and were hinged so as to fold into the inside of the tank, so reducing the width when loaded on railway wagons; sponsons on Female tanks were smaller still. A shorter, monobloc gun, specially designed for tank use, was adopted, and the machine guns were standardised on the Lewis pattern. Improved steel was used for the armour, in an endeavour to resist the German AP bullet. The fire hazard was reduced by moving the petrol tank to the outside of the hull and protecting it in an armoured casing. Most important, from the crews' point of view, was the improvement in cooling and ventilating the interior of the tank.

Armament: 2 × 6-pdr + 4 × MG; or 6 × MG
Armour: 15mm
Crew: 8
Weight: 28 tons (28,450kg)
Hull length: 26ft 4in (8.02m)
Width: 12ft 10in (3.91m)
Height: 8ft 2in (2.49m)
Engine: Daimler, 6-cylinder, petrol, 105bhp
Road speed: 3.75mph (6km/hr)
Power/weight: 3.75
Range: 22 miles (35km)

Tank Mark 4 Hermaphrodite UK
Foster
1918. A Mark 4 Female tank with the right side machine gun sponson removed and replaced by a 6-pounder gun sponson as used by Male tanks. The object was to provide Female tanks with the means of defending themselves if attacked by German tanks. Few were built as the threat never materialised.

Tank Mark 5 UK
Metropolitan
1918. This version showed considerable improvements, primarily the adoption of a new epicyclic transmission which gave the driver full control of the gears and did away with the two 'gearsmen'. It also had a new and more powerful engine, better armour, a rear turret, rear door and better vision arrangements.

Armament: 2 × 6-pdr + 4 × MG; or 6 × MG
Armour: 15mm
Crew: 8
Weight: 29 tons (29,465kg)
Hull length: 26ft 5in (8.04m)
Width: 13ft 6in (4.11m)
Height: 8ft 8in (2.64m)
Engine: Ricardo, 6-cylinder, petrol, 150bhp
Road speed: 5mph (8km/hr)
Power/weight: 5.17
Range: 25 miles (40km)

Tank Mark 5* UK
Metropolitan
1918. This was a Mark 5 tank lengthened so as to provide space to carry supplies or up to 25 soldiers. The design, developed by the tank units in France, proved more stable and more versatile than the 'Tadpole' (*qv*) conversions and went into production in May 1918.

Armament: 2 × 6-pdr + 4 × MG; or 6 × MG
Armour: 15mm
Crew: 8
Weight: 33 tons (33,530kg)
Hull length: 32ft 5in (9.88m)
Width: 13ft 6in (4.11m)
Height: 8ft 8in (2.64m)
Engine: Ricardo, 6-cylinder, petrol, 150bhp
Road speed: 4mph (6.5km/hr)
Power/weight: 4.55
Range: 20 miles (32km)

Tank Mark 5** UK
Metropolitan
1918. This was similar in principle to the Mark 5★ but built from new rather than being a lengthened Mark 5. The commander's cupola was enlarged and moved to behind the driver and a more powerful engine was fitted. The first production model did not appear until December 1918 and only a few were made.

Armament: 2 × 6-pdr + 4 × MG; or 6 × MG
Armour: 15mm
Crew: 8
Weight: 35 tons (35,560kg)
Hull length: 32ft 5in (9.88m)
Width: 13ft 6in (4.11m)
Height: 9ft 0in (2.74m)
Engine: Ricardo, 6-cylinder, petrol, 225bhp
Road speed: 6mph (10km/hr)
Power/weight: 6.42
Range: 25 miles (40km)

Tank Mark 6 UK
North British
1917. Although retaining the all-round track system, this was an entirely fresh design which did away with the sponsons and mounted a 6-pounder gun facing forward, alongside the driver. A fixed turret carried four MGs and two further MGs were mounted in the sides. The US Army were greatly taken by this design and plans were made for mass-production, but the design was then abandoned.

Tank Mark 7 UK
Brown Brothers
1917. This replaced the Mark 6, and was more or less a Mark 5 with the tail lengthened to improve its trench-crossing performance. It was given an hydraulic drive system, and the Ricardo engine was actually fitted with an electric starter, making life a little easier for the crew. One was built and then design was then abandoned, doubtless due to problems with the hydraulic drive.

Data: as for Mark 5, except
Weight: 33 tons
Length: 29ft 5in
Height: 8ft 7in

Tank Mark 8 UK
North British
1918. This was the ultimate wartime design, incorporating virtually everything which experience had shown was necessary. A more powerful engine was housed in a separate compartment, with a

ventilating system to keep fumes and hot air out of the crew space. The sponsons were mounted on roller bearings so that they could be easily swung into the tank for transportation and the commander had a separate cupola on top of the main turret. The US Army transferred its allegiance to this design after the Mark 6 went down, christened it the **Liberty Tank** (*qv*) and began making arrangements for mass production for the 1919 offensive, but before very much could be done the war ended.

Armament: 2 × 6-pdr + 7 × MG
Armour: 16mm
Crew: 12
Weight: 37 tons (37,595kg)
Hull length: 34ft 2in (10.41m)
Width: 12ft 4in (3.76m)
Height: 10ft 3in (3.12m)
Engine: Ricardo or Liberty, 6-cylinder, petrol, 300bhp
Road speed: 7mph (11km/hr)
Power/weight: 8.11
Range: 30 miles (48km)

Tank Mark 9 UK
Marshall

1918. Design as an 'infantry supply tank' this was simply a large and roomy hull with all-round tracks and with doors in the sides, which could carry 50 fully-equipped soldiers or 10 tons of supplies. The engine and transmission were moved well back in the hull to leave a large clear space, and the adoption of the new epicyclic gearbox placed control entirely under the driver and allowed the crew to be reduced to only four men. A machine gun was carried for defensive purposes. Easily recognised by its length and the prominent oval doors in the sides. Only 23 were built.

Armament: 1 × MG
Armour: 10mm
Crew: 4
Weight: 33 tons (33,525kg)
Hull length: 31ft 10in (9.78m)
Width: 8ft 3in (4.11m)
Height: 8ft 8in (2.64m)
Engine: Ricardo, 6-cylinder, petrol, 150bhp
Road speed: 3.5mph (6km/hr)
Power/weight: 4.55
Range: 20 miles (32km)

Tank Mark 9 Amphibious UK
Conversion by Dept. of Tank Design

1919. Also called the **Duck** and not to be confused with the later 'Duck' or DUKW of World War II, which was an amphibious truck, this was a swimming version of the Mark 9 supply tank. The driving cab was enlarged and raised, the exhausts extended vertically, and cylindrical buoyancy tanks were fitted along each side. Propulsion was by means of the existing tracks, to which hinged flaps were added at intervals so as to act like paddles. Steering was achieved by speeding up one track and slowing down the other. It floated, but was not particularly successful and the idea was not pursued.

Tankette

Term popular in the 1930s and applied indiscriminately to any lightweight, lightly armed, lightly armoured, one- or two-man armoured vehicle or to some light tanks. There appears never to have been any formal definition of the term, and it fell into disuse during World War II.

Tank Tender Mark 1 UK
Conversions in army workshops

1917. Mark 1 tanks, when superseded by later models, were converted into cargo-carrying vehicles by removing the sponsons and replacing them with steel boxes so as to increase the internal storage space. They were also fitted with a towing connection and could pull up to three sledges loaded with stores. Their purpose was, initially, to accompany a tank attack and provide a ready source of munitions, rations and so forth, but in practice they became general-duties tractors, shifting stores around behind the line, and rarely accompanied an attack; this role was taken over by the Mark 9 tank.

Tetrarch UK
Vickers

1940. Privately developed by Vickers from 1937, this was accepted for service as the **Light Tank Mark 7** in 1938. It used a modified Christie suspension in which the front wheels could be steered so as to bend the track for gentle turns; further movement of the steering controls then braked one track in the usual manner for tighter turns. It entered production in 1940, just as the army decided the light tank was no longer of any use, and production was halted. But shortly afterwards the airborne forces began forming and the Tetrarch was adopted as an air-portable tank for their use. Production recommenced in 1941 and 177 were built. Carried in Hamilcar gliders they were used in the invasion of Normandy in 1944 and remained in service until 1950.

Armament: 1 × 2-pdr; 1 × MG
Armour: 16mm
Crew: 3
Weight: 7.5 tons (7,620kg)
Hull length: 13ft 6in (4.11m)
Width: 7ft 7in (2.31m)
Height: 6ft 11in (2.10m)
Engine: Meadows flat-12, petrol, 165bhp at 2,700rpm
Road speed: 40mph (65km/hr)
Power/weight: 22.0
Range: 140 miles (225km)

Tetrarch CS UK
Vickers
1942. A modified version of the Tetrarch to turn it into a Close Support tank. The 2-pounder gun was removed and replaced by a 3-inch tank howitzer. The dimensions and performance remained the same. Only a small number were so converted.

TG Heavy Russia
State factories
Ca 1926. Experimental design; very low hull, large low, flat turret with large cupola. Main armament 75mm gun. Five large roadwheels each side, partly shielded by side skirt, at the top of which were the four track return rollers. Details are scant, and the only known picture has no tracks, so this may be an early wheel/track experimental model based on Christie's contemporary designs but not, apparently, with Christie suspension. Weight about 25 tons, crew 5, petrol engine delivering 300bhp and giving the vehicle a speed of 25mph.

THE301 Medium Tank Germany
Thyssen-Henschel
Developed as a private venture in 1978, this was a slight variant of the TAM tank supplied to Argentina. Externally it was almost identical; internally it was fitted with a Rheinmetall 105mm gun, and with the fire control and sighting systems used in the Leopard 1A4 tank. The engine was also uprated to provide more power. The project was dropped in the early 1980s.

Armament: 1 × 105mm; 2 × MG
Ammunition: 50 + 6,000
Armour: not disclosed
Crew: 4
Weight: 30.51 tons (31,000kg)
Hull length: 22ft 3in (6.78m)
Width: 10ft 10in (3.31m)
Height: 8ft 0in (2.44m)

Engine: MTU MB 833 turbocharged 6-cylinder, diesel, 750bhp at 2,400rpm
Road speed: 45mph (72km/hr)
Power/weight: 24.58
Range: 310 miles (500km)

Tiger Germany
Henschel
Also called the **PzKpfw 6**. The German Army's desire for a heavy tank was ignored until the invasion of Russia introduced them to the T-34. Two prototype heavy tanks were produced, one by Porsche and one by Henschel. The Henschel was selected, being easier to build, and production began in August 1942. It was the most formidable tank of its day, with thick frontal armour and a powerful gun, but uninspiring performance due to the great weight. One notable design defect was that if the engine was not running, the turret could only be operated by hand.

Armament: 1 × 88mm L/56; 2 × MG
Ammunition: 92 + 4,800
Armour: 110mm
Crew: 5
Weight: 56.10 tons (57,000kg)
Hull length: 20ft 7in (6.27m)
Width: 12ft 3in (3.73m)
Height: 9ft 4in (2.84m)
Engine: Maybach HL210P45 V-12, petrol, 700bhp at 3,000rpm
Road speed: 24mph (38km/hr)
Power/weight: 12.48
Range: 62 miles (100km)

TK1 and TK2 Poland
State factories
1929. An open-topped, two-man 'tankette' derived from the British Carden-Loyd machine gun carrier. TK1 was the prototype, TK2 was the production model. About 300 TK2 were built in 1929/30 but it was soon realised that it was not a practical design.

Armament: 1 × MG
Armour: 7mm
Crew: 2
Weight: 1.75 tons (1,780kg)
Hull length: 7ft 9in (2.36m)
Width: 5ft 10in (1.77m)
Height: 3ft 5in (1.04m)
Engine: Ford A, 4-cylinder, petrol, 40bhp at 2,300rpm
Road speed: 30mph (48km/hr)
Power/weight: 22.8
Range: 155 miles (250km)

TK3 Poland
State factories

1931. The shortcomings of the TK2 being quickly realised, the TK3 was designed to replace it. The same double-bogie suspension with an outer supporting girder was used, though strengthened and improved, the superstructure was totally enclosed in armour and the armour was slightly thicker. About 390 were built and in 1938 a number were upgraded by being fitted with a 20mm gun. Almost all were destroyed in attempting to resist the German attack in 1939.

Armament: 1 × MG; or 1 × 20mm gun
Armour: 8mm
Crew: 2
Weight: 2.46 tons (2,500kg)
Hull length: 8ft 6in (2.65m)
Width: 5ft 10in (1.55m)
Height: 4ft 4in (1.35m)
Engine: Ford A, 4-cylinder, petrol, 40bhp at 2,300rpm
Road speed: 28mph (45km/hr)
Power/weight: 16.26
Range: 125 miles (200km)

TKF Poland
State factories

1937. This was the final Polish try at making something useful out of the Carden-Loyd-derived TK series, and it was even more ridiculous than those which had gone before. In this case the superstructure was fitted with a combination mount which carried a 7.92mm machine gun and a 9mm submachine gun, side by side. The mount could reach an extreme elevation, and the theory apparently was that the 9mm weapon should be used for personnel while the 7.92mm machine gun could be fired against aircraft.

Armament: 1 × MG; 1 × SMG
Armour: 10mm
Crew: 2
Weight: 2.55 tons (2,600kg)
Hull length: 8ft 9in (2.67m)
Width: 5ft 10in (1.78m)
Height: 4ft 5in (1.34m)
Engine: Fiat 4-cylinder, petrol, 46bhp
Road speed: 26mph (41km/hr)
Power/weight: 18.03
Range: 125 miles (200km)

TKS Poland
State factories

1933. A further development of the TK3 design, this used the same suspension and had a similar superstructure built up from flat armour plates. The right side of this had a large ball-type machine gun mount, while the right front was lowered to form a driver's hatch. The suspension was stronger, a Polish-built engine was fitted, and the armour was thickened. A few survived the 1939 campaign to be used by the Germans as artillery tractors and internal security vehicles.

Armament: 1 × MG
Armour: 10mm
Crew: 2
Weight: 2.56 tons (2,600kg)
Hull length: 8ft 9in (2.67m)
Width: 5ft 10in (1.78m)
Height: 4ft 5in (1.36m)
Engine: Fiat, 4-cylinder, petrol, 40bhp
Road speed: 25mph (40km/hr)
Power/weight: 15.62
Range: 125 miles (200km)

TKS-D Poland
State factories

1936. An experimental variation of the TKS in which the right rear of the superstructure was opened up and a 37mm Bofors anti-tank gun was fitted on a pedestal mounting, with shield, behind the driver. The hull machine gun mounting was removed. The result was cumbersome, the gun had a limited field of fire, and the one man trying to lay, load, fire and observe the fall of shot was overworked.

TKW Poland
State factories

1934. Another experimental variation of the basic TK design, this was a revolving turret on top the superstructure and carrying a heavy machine gun. Only a prototype was built, which was sufficient to show that the design was a poor one.

TM-800 MBT Romania
State factories

1994. This is generally similar to the TR-580 (*below*) and appears to be a slightly improved version, possibly for commercial sale.

Armament: 1 × 100mm; 2 × MG
Ammunition: 43 + 4,000
Armour: not disclosed
Crew: 4
Weight: 44.29 tons (45,000kg)
Hull length: 22ft 2in (6.74m)
Width: 10ft 10in (3.30m)
Height: 7ft 8in (2.35m)

Engine: diesel, 830bhp
Road speed: 40mph (65km/hr)
Power/weight: 18.74
Range: 310 miles (500km)

TNH/PS Czechoslovakia
CKD

1937. Also known as the **LT 38**, **vz/38** and, in German service, the **PzKpfw 38(*t*)**, this was one of the better pre-war designs and, first as a tank and then as the chassis for various anti-tank guns, it managed to survive until the 1950s. Developed for the Czech Army, the eventual production was all taken by the German Army, and a sizeable proportion of their Panzer troops were equipped with this in the first two years of the war. Recognisable by its four large roadwheels, square-front superstructure and turret with a small bustle and a cupola. The Czech design called for a three-man crew, but the Germans preferred four men, relieving the commander of the task of loading the main gun. Space was found for the extra man by reducing the ammunition carried. German models originally had a frame antenna along the left side of the hull.

Armament: 1 × 37mm; 2 × MG
Ammunition: 72 + 2,400
Armour: 25mm
Crew: 4
Weight: 9.25 tons (9,400kg)
Hull length: 15ft 1in (4.60m)
Width: 6ft 11in (2.12m)
Height: 7ft 10in (2.40m)
Engine: Praga EPA, 6-cylinder, petrol, 140bhp at 2,500rpm
Road speed: 26mph (42km/hr)
Power/weight: 15.14
Range: 155 miles (250km)

TNH-SV Czechoslovakia
CKD

1938. This was a slight variant of the TNH/PS which was prepared for supply to Sweden. Before deliveries could begin, the Germans occupied Bohemia and took over the CKD factory, commandeering the tanks for use by the German Army. The Swedes were later given a licence to build the tanks in Sweden, where it became the **Strv m/41** (*qv*). Similar to the TNH/PS but without the frame antenna. In German service this tank was known as the **PzKpfw 38(*t*), Ausf S**.

Armament: 1 × 37mm; 2 × MG
Ammunition: 72 + 2,400
Armour: 25mm

Crew: 4
Weight: 9.35 tons (9,500kg)
Hull length: 15ft 2in (4.61m)
Width: 7ft 0in (2.14m)
Height: 7ft 10in (2.40m)
Engine: Praga EPA, 6-cylinder, petrol, 140bhp at 2,500rpm
Road speed: 26mph (42km/hr)
Power/weight: 14.97
Range: 155 miles (250km)

TOG 1 UK
Foster

1940. When the British Ministry of Supply was formed to take over the duties of designing and providing munitions, it set up numerous committees. One of these, composed of men who had been responsible for tank design and production during World War I, considered that a heavy tank was necessary, and produced TOG. The initials stand for 'The Old Gang', that is the designers. It was really a Tank Mark 8 brought up to date; it had the all-round tracks, but mounted a revolving turret (that of the Valentine tank) on top of the hull. Transmission was initially petrol-electric, later changed to hydraulic; neither of them worked well. A prototype was built and showed that it could no nothing that could not be done better by the Churchill, and TOG 1 was abandoned and scrapped.

Armament: 1 × 2-pdr gun in turret; 1 × 3-in howitzer in nose; 1 × MG
Armour: 62mm
Crew: 6
Weight: 80 tons (81,280kg)
Hull length: 33ft 3in (10.13m)
Width: 10ft 3in (3.12m)
Height: 10ft 0in (3.05m)
Engine: Paxman-Ricardo diesel, 600bhp
Road speed: 8.5mph (14km/hr)
Power/weight: 7.5

TOG 2 UK
Foster

This was to the same general pattern as TOG 1 but with the track lowered and the upper run covered by the hull and skirting plate. A large, rectangular turret at the front of the hull mounted a 6-pounder gun, which was later changed to a 17-pounder. It was not considered practical as a combat tank and spent its life as a trials machine. This preserved it until the war ended, after which it was sent to the Tank Museum.

Toldi 38M Hungary
Weiss
1937. This was the Swedish Landsverk L-60 tank built under licence in Hungary/
See Strv L-60

TR-85 Romania
State factories
1987. This, like the TR-580, *below*, (which appears to have acted as a development prototype for this design) is another locally-manufactured copy of the Russian T-55, but with a new German power pack, new suspension, and a new and rather more angular turret. It is distinguishable by the six solid roadwheels, rather than the T-55's five, with a skirting plate concealing the upper part of the wheels. The 100mm gun carries the usual fume extractor close to the muzzle but also carries a thermal blanket, and there is a prominent laser rangefinder housing on the turret above the mantlet. The engine compartment is larger and with entirely different exhaust and air intake arrangements due to the new and larger engine, which is reputed to deliver 600bhp. The turret is provided with day and night vision and sighting apparatus and there is also a deep fording snorkel apparatus on the rear of the hull. Weight is said to be 42.6 tons (43,300kg) but no other figures have been released.

TR-125 Romania
State factories
1989. This is a Romanian-built version of the Russian T-72, with some modifications. What little knowledge we have suggests that it has better armour and better performance than the original; externally the principal feature is the seven roadwheels on each side.

Armament: 1 × 125mm; 2 × MG
Ammunition: 39 + 3,500
Armour: not disclosed
Crew: 3
Weight: 47.24 tons (48,000kg)
Hull length: 22ft 10in (6.95m)
Width: 10ft 10in (3.60m)
Height: 7ft 9in (2.37m)
Engine: V-12 diesel, 880bhp at 2,000rpm
Road speed: 37mph (60km/hr)
Power/weight: 18.62
Range: 335 miles (540km)

TR-580 Romania
State factories
1985. This was a locally-manufactured medium tank which appears to have been a copy of the Russian T-55, with a similar curved turret and smoothbore gun with fume extractor near the muzzle. It was unusual in having six spoked roadwheels rather than the five solid wheels of the T-55, but the engine compartment and exhaust arrangements appear to be pure T-55. Beyond a reported weight of 38,200kg (37.6 tons) no reliable data have emerged.

Tritton Chaser UK
An early name for the light tank designed by Mr Tritton of Foster's, which later became the Medium A (*qv*) or Whippet.

Turan 40M Medium Tank Hungary
Weiss
1941. This actually began life as the **Skoda S-2r Medium** tank in 1937 and was based upon the general design of their S-2 Light tank, using a modified Vickers bogie suspension with eight roadwheels in four pairs on each side, with bellcranks and coil springs. A licence was bought by Hungarians, who then modified it to their own taste, enlarging the turret to take three men and giving it a more powerful engine. Originally with a 47mm gun in the turret, the **Turan 2** had a short 75mm with a prominent armoured jacket over the recoil system. Manufacture ceased in 1943 when the Hungarian Army adopted German Panzer 3 and 4 tanks.

Armament: 1 × 47mm or 1 × 75mm; 2 × MG
Armour: 20mm
Crew: 5
Weight: 16 tons (16,256kg)
Engine: V-8, petrol, 260bhp
Power/weight: 16.25

Type 1 Medium Japan
State factories
1941. This was a much-improved Type 97 Medium, with thicker armour, a more powerful gun and a better engine. The general shape, suspension and layout was the same, but the Type 1 was a little larger and heavier, and had a new type of superstructure with a vertical front plate and sloping glacis.

Armament: 1 × 47mm Type 1 anti-tank; 2 × MG
Armour: 50mm
Crew: 5

Weight: 17 tons (17,275kg)
Hull length: 18ft 9in (5.71m)
Width: 7ft 8in (2.33m)
Height: 7ft 10in (2.39m)
Engine: Type 100 V-12, diesel, 240bhp
Road speed: 27mph (43km/hr)
Power/weight: 14.12

Type 2 Amphibious Tank Japan
Naval arsenals

1942. Developed by the Japanese Navy for use by their Marine force, this was based on a Type 95 light tank with special buoyancy chambers at both ends of the hull, and with the hull built up and carefully sealed against the ingress of water. The hull was fitted with twin propellers and rudders, the former being driven by a power take-off from the tank's engine. The tank was designed to be launched from a landing craft some distance from the shore, swim ashore, driving across any intermediate reefs, and, after reaching the shore, discard its buoyancy tanks and operate as a normal tank.

Armament: 1 x 37mm; 2 x MG
Armour: 12mm maximum
Crew: 3
Weight: 11.07 tons (11,255kg)
Hull length: 24ft 4in (7.41m) with buoyancy tanks
Width: 9ft 2in (2.79m)
Height: 7ft 8in (2.33m)
Engine: Mitsubishi 6-cylinder, diesel, 110bhp at 1,400rpm
Road speed: 25mph (40km/hr)
Power/weight: 9.94
Range: 125 miles (200km)

Type 2 Gun Tank Japan
State factories

1942. Some authorities claim that this was a self-propelled gun, others that it was a close support tank, and on the whole the evidence favours the latter. Derived from the Type 1 Medium (*above*) it carried a 75mm Type 99 gun which appears to be a shortened version of the Model 94 field gun. The gun was in a closed turret. with limited elevation, which rules it out for most normal indirect fire tasks and strengthens the close support theory. Although approved for service in 1942 only a limited number were manufactured.

Armament: 1 x 75mm Type 99; 1 x MG
Armour: 50mm maximum
Crew: 5
Weight: 16.7 tons (16,970kg)
Hull length: 18ft 9in (5.71m)
Width: 7ft 8in (2.33m)

Height: 8ft 5in (2.56m)
Engine: Type 100 V-12 diesel, 240bhp
Road speed: 27mph (43km/hr)
Power/weight: 14.37

Type 2 Light Japan
State factories

1944. This was a further development of the Type 98A design, using the same three-bogie six-wheel suspension system and centrally-positioned driver. The principal difference was the adoption of the 37mm anti-tank gun Type 00 as the turret gun in place of the usual low-velocity tank gun. As with the Type 98A, production was delayed since the Army were content with their existing tanks and saw no need to change. This was probably because most of their tank formations were operating in China, against the Chinese Army, which provided negligible opposition.

Armament: 1 x 37mm high velocity; 1 x MG
Armour: 16mm maximum
Crew: 3
Weight: 7.2 tons (7,320kg)
Hull length: 13ft 6in (4.11m)
Width: 7ft 0in (2.13m)
Height: 6ft 0in (1.83m)
Engine: diesel, 6-cylinder, supercharged, 150bhp
Road speed: 31mph (50km/hr)
Power/weight: 20.83

Type 3 Amphibious Japan
Naval arsenals

1943. This was similar in general design to the Type 2 Amphibious, but heavier and longer. It used the same method of flotation, buoyancy pontoons fore and aft which could be rapidly discarded once the tank had reached land. An interesting (and suggestive) innovation was a submarine-type escape hatch on top of the turret which would allow the crew, provided with breathing apparatus, to leave the tank in the event of it sinking.

Armament: 1 x 47mm; 2 x MG
Armour: 50mm
Crew: 7
Weight: 28.8 tons (29,260kg)
Hull length: 33ft 9in (10.28m)
Width: 9ft 10in (2.99m)
Height: 12ft 7in (3.83m)
Engine: V-12 diesel, air-cooled, 240bhp
Speed, land: 20mph (32km/hr)
Speed, water: 7mph (11km/hr)
Power/weight: 8.33

Type 3 Light Japan
State factories

Combat experience led to attempts to improve the effectiveness of the Type 95 Light by fitting larger guns. Type 3 was a Type 95 with a 57mm gun mounted in the turret, and the idea was very quickly abandoned when the prototype was built, since the gun was simply too big for the turret.

Armament: 1 × 57mm; 1 × MG
Armour: 16mm maximum
Crew: 3
Weight: 7.4 tons (7,520kg)
Hull length: 13ft 6in (4.11m)
Width: 7ft 0in (2.13m)
Height: 6ft 0in (1.83m)
Engine: diesel, 6-cylinder, 110bhp
Road speed: 31mph (50km/hr)
Power/weight: 20.83

Type 3 Medium Japan
State factories

1943. This was little more than the hull and running gear of the Type 1 Medium with a new turret carrying a 75mm gun adapted from the Type 90 field gun and complete with the field gun's cradle and recoil system. The angular turret had side and rear doors, and a commander's cupola. Relatively few were built in 1944, since by that time the Japanese industrial base was over-stretched.

Armament: 1 × 75mm; 1 × MG
Armour: 50mm
Crew: 5
Weight: 18.5 tons (18,795kg)
Hull length: 18ft 6in (5.63m)
Width: 7ft 8in (2.33m)
Height: 8ft 7in (2.62m)
Engine: Type 100 V-12 air-cooled diesel, 240bhp
Road speed: 24mph (38km/hr)
Power/weight: 12.97

Type 4 Light Japan
State factories

A further attempt to improve the firepower of the Type 95 Light series, this was a combination of the Type 95 hull married to the turret and 57mm gun from the Type 97 Medium tank. The idea appears to have been successful, but since the modification of the Type 95 meant cutting a larger hole in the hull and fitting a larger turret ring, few were actually built.

Armament: 1 × 57mm; 2 × MG
Armour: 25mm
Crew: 3

Weight: 8.4 tons (8,535kg)
Hull length: 14ft 2in (4.31m)
Width: 6ft 10in (2.08m)
Height: 7ft 5in (2.26m)
Engine: 6-cylinder, diesel, air-cooled, 100bhp
Road speed: 25mph (40km/hr)
Power/weight: 13.10

Type 4 Medium Japan
State factories

1944, This was a further progression from the Type 1 in an attempt to improve the firepower. The general design was the same as the Types 2 and 3, but the hull was lengthened and an extra roadwheel added on each side. The gun was changed, from the 75mm field Type 90 to the 75mm Type 4 which was an adapted Type 88 anti-aircraft gun. Only a handful were built, all pre-production models which were still on test and undergoing adjustment and modification when the war ended.

Armament: 1 × 75mm Type 4; 2 × MG
Armour: 75mm
Crew: 5
Weight: 30 tons (30,480kg)
Hull length: 20ft 9in (5.32m)
Width: 9ft 5in (2.87m)
Height: 9ft 5in (2.87m)
Engine: V-12 diesel, 400bhp
Road speed: 28mph (45km/hr)
Power/weight: 13.33

Type 5 Amphibious Japan
Naval arsenals

1945. The last amphibian to be developed by Japan was this, simply an improved Type 4. The most unusual point was the placing of a 47mm gun and a machine gun in the front face of the hull superstructure, where they were masked by the buoyancy pontoons until these were discarded. In addition, though, there was a 25mm automatic cannon and a machine gun in the turret. The escape tower had been done away with, probably because the depths of water involved did not really justify such a device on a tank. The war ended before the Type 5 was ready for production.

Armament: 1 × 47mm; 1 × 25mm; 2 × MG
Armour: 50mm
Crew: 7
Weight: 29 tons (29,465kg)
Hull length: 35ft 5in (10.80m)
Width: 9ft 10in (2.99m)
Height: 11ft 1in (3.38m)
Engine: Type 100 V-12 air-cooled diesel, 240bhp
Speed, land: 20mph (32km/hr)

Speed, water: 7mph (11km/hr)
Power/weight: 8.27

Type 5 Light Japan
State factories
1945. This was designed in 1941 and tested in 1942, after which nothing happened until the decision to manufacture it was taken, too late, in 1945. None were built, as might be expected. The chassis was completely redesigned, but few details of the construction have survived. The turret carried the 47mm anti-tank gun Type 1 and a new supercharged engine was adopted.

Armament: 1 × 47mm; 2 × MG
Armour: 20mm
Crew: 4
Weight: 10 tons (10,160kg)
Hull length: 14ft 5in (4.39m)
Width: 7ft 4in (2.23m)
Height: 7ft 3in (2.20m)
Engine: 6-cylinder supercharged diesel, 150bhp
Road speed: 31mph (50km/hr)
Power/weight: 15

Type 5 Medium Japan
State factories
1945. Another roadwheel was added to the undercarriage of the Type 4 Medium and the hull lengthened to suit; a 37mm tank gun went into the hull front, and the 75mm Type 4 ex-AA gun was in the turret. It was intended to have a new V-12 diesel engine, but this was still under development and the prototype was given a V-12 BMW petrol engine which happened to be available. The end of the war put an end to development while it was still in prototype form.

Armament: 1 × 75mm; 1 × 37mm; 2 × MG
Armour: 75mm
Crew: 5
Weight: 37 tons (37,590kg)
Hull length: 24ft 0in (7.31m)
Width: 10ft 0in (3.05m)
Height: 10ft 0in (3.05m)
Engine: BMW V-12, petrol, 550bhp
Road speed: 28mph (45km/hr)
Power/weight: 14.88

Type 59 China
State factories
The Type 59 was the first tank to be built in China and is little more than a Soviet T-54 with a few minor modifications added from time to time. These included a fume extractor on the gun barrel,

night vision equipment based upon a turret mounted infra-red searchlight, and laser rangefinding. Numbers were supplied to Albania, Bangladesh, Congo, North Korea, Pakistan, Tanzania, Vietnam and Zimbabwe. Many of these have been upgraded by Western companies, with passive night vision equipment and improved fire control systems.

Armament: 1 × 100mm smoothbore; 2 × MG
Ammunition: 34 + 3,700
Armour: 203mm
Crew: 4
Weight: 35.43 tons (36,000kg)
Hull length: 19ft 10in (6.04m)
Width: 10ft 9in (3.27m)
Height: 8ft 6in (2.59m)
Engine: V-12 diesel, 520bhp at 2,000rpm
Road speed: 31mph (50km/hr)
Power/weight: 14.68
Range: 260 miles (420km)

Type 61 MBT Japan
Mitsubishi
1961. This was the first postwar Japanese-designed tank, produced in order to replace the various American vehicles with which the Japanese Self-Defence Force was first equipped. It seems fairly safe to say that the designers followed the general lines of the American M47 but made it more compact. The gun was also Japanese, though ballistically similar to the American gun on the M47, but the engine was a diesel. Suspension was by torsion bars, with six roadwheels on each side.

Armament: 1 × 90mm; 2 × MG
Armour: 64mm
Crew: 4
Weight: 34.45 tons (35,000kg)
Hull length: 20ft 8in (6.30m)
Width: 9ft 8in (2.95m)
Height: 8ft 2in (2.49m)
Engine: Mitsubishi V-12 turbocharged diesel, 600bhp at 2,100rpm
Road speed: 28mph (45km/hr)
Power/weight: 17.41
Range: 125 miles (200km)

Type 62 Light China
State factories
1970. This is a small-scale Type 59, apparently reduced in size in order to operate in mountainous terrain where the Type 59 finds it difficult. The shape and layout are exactly the same as the 59, though the main armament is a conventionally

rifled 85mm gun. There are five roadwheels each side, with torsion bar suspension, rear drive, front idler. In addition to use by the Chinese Army and marines, numbers were sold to Zaire, Tanzania and other African countries.

Armament: 1 × 85mm; 2 × MG
Ammunition: 41 + 3,000
Armour: not disclosed
Crew: 4
Weight: 20.66 tons (21,000kg)
Hull length: 18ft 3in (5.55m)
Width: 9ft 5in (2.86m)
Height: 8ft 4in (2.55m)
Engine: diesel, 380bhp at 1,800rpm
Road speed: 37mph (60km/hr)
Power/weight: 18.54
Range: 310 miles (500km)

Type 63 Light Amphibious China
State factories

1966. This is an improved copy of the Russian PT-76 amphibious tank, numbers of which were taken into service by the Chinese in the late 1950s. The Type 63 has a more powerful engine and a heavier gun than the PT-76, and there are some minor differences in shape, notably the slope of the hull front. It is used by North Korea and Vietnam in addition to China.

Armament: 1 × 85mm; 2 × MG
Ammunition: 47 + 1,500
Armour: 14mm maximum
Crew: 4
Weight: 18.40 tons (18,700kg)
Hull length: 23ft 6in (7.15m)
Width: 10ft 6in (3.20m)
Height: 8ft 3in (2.52m)
Engine: V-12 diesel, 400bhp at 2,000rpm
Road speed: 40mph (64km/hr)
Power/weight: 21.74
Range: 230 miles (370km)

Type 64 Taiwan
ROC Army

1975. This is 'based upon' the US M41 light tank, so firmly based indeed that the earliest models were little more than rebuilt M41s, but gradually locally-manufactured components replaced the original until the entire vehicle was made in Taiwan. The protection has been improved by the addition of laminated add-on plates, and the gun is a Taiwan design claimed to be more powerful than the original US pattern. The dimensions and interior arrangements have been subtly changed so as to fit

in better with the smaller stature of the average Chinese crewman.

Armament: 1 × 76mm; 2 × MG
Ammunition: 57 + 5,000
Armour: not disclosed
Crew: 4
Weight (estimated): 28.04 tons (28,500kg)
Hull length: 19ft 2in (5.83m)
Width: 10ft 6in (3.20m)
Height: 8ft 11in (2.72m)
Engine: Detroit Diesel V-8
Road speed: not disclosed
Power/weight: not disclosed
Range: 280 miles (450km)

Type 69 China
State factories

1980. This was an improved Type 59, using the same basic hull and chassis arrangement, with five irregularly-spaced roadwheels on each side. It began by using the same 100mm smoothbore gun as the Type 59, but very soon the Chinese realised that a rifled gun delivers better accuracy and the majority of Type 69s were given a rifled 100mm weapon. Fire control was improved, with better night vision equipment, and there was a slight increase in power. The basic chassis was also used for a variety of specialist vehicles – anti-aircraft tanks, bridgelayers and engineer tanks.

Armament: 1 × 100mm; 2 × MG
Ammunition: 34 + 3,900
Armour: not disclosed
Crew: 4
Weight: 36.41 tons (37,000kg)
Hull length: 20ft 6in (6.24m)
Width: 10ft 9in (3.29m)
Height: 9ft 2in (2.80m)
Engine: V-12 diesel, 580bhp at 2,000rpm
Road speed: 31mph (50km/hr)
Power/weight: 15.92
Range: 260 miles (420km)

Type 72Z MBT Iran
DIO

1996. This is a Russian T-54 or T-55, or a Chinese Type 59 which has been upgraded in Iran. The original 100mm gun has been replaced by a 105mm L7 type; a computerised fire control system developed in Slovenia is installed, and a new V-12 diesel engine and automatic transmission package is fitted. There have also been improvements to the tracks and suspension. The appearance remains that of the original T-54 pattern.

Armament: I × 105mm; 2 × MG
Ammunition: 38 + 7,000
Armour: not disclosed
Crew: 4
Weight: 35.43 tons (36,000kg)
Hull length: 21ft 5in (6.54m)
Width: 11ft 0in (3.35m)
Height: 7ft 9in (2.37m)
Engine: V-12 diesel, 780bhp at 2,000rpm
Road speed: 40mph (65km/hr)
Power/weight: 22.02
Range: not disclosed

Type 74 MBT Japan
Mitsubishi

1974. After getting their Type 61 into service, the Japanese set about designing the next generation, which appeared in 1973. The result was a competent and conventional design, with five large roadwheels on each side and a turret with pronounced sloping sides for better deflection of shot. The 105mm L7 type gun has a fume extractor about half-way along the barrel and there is a remote-controlled AA machine gun on top of the turret which can be operated from inside the turret. As might be expected, a sophisticated electronic fire control system was installed, and infra-red night vision equipment was also standard.

Armament: I × 105mm gun, 2 × MG
Ammunition: 55 + 5,160
Armour: not disclosed
Crew: 4
Weight: 37.40 tons (38,000kg)
Hull length: 22ft 0in (6.70m)
Width: 10ft 5in (3.17m)
Height: 8ft 10in (2.69m)
Engine: Mitsubishi V-10 turbocharged, air-cooled diesel, 720bhp at 2,200rpm
Road speed: 33mph (53km/hr)
Power/weight: 19.25
Range: 310 miles (500km)

Type 79 China
State factories

This model is something of a mystery, having only been seen in small numbers. It appears to be an upgraded Type 69, improved by removing the 100mm gun and replacing it with a 105mm gun capable of firing either Chinese or Western ammunition. The experiment proving successful, the gun was then used as the main armament on the Type 80 tank (*below*) and the Type 79, having served its purpose, was allowed to waste out. No dimensions are available, but it would seem probable that, except for the gun calibre and therefore the overall weight, the principal dimensions will be the same as those of the Type 69.

Type 80 China
State factories

1985. A further progression from the Type 69 which broke new ground by lengthening the wheelbase, improving the fire control system, adopting a new 105mm gun with the chamber based on NATO dimensions so as to be able to fire Chinese or Western ammunition, and inserting a more powerful engine. Six irregularly-spaced roadwheels on each side, front idler, rear drive; upper part of tracks covered by skirt with zig-zag indentations on the lower edge. Formed the basis for the later Types 85 and 90.

Armament: I × 105mm; 2 × MG
Ammunition: 44 + 2,750
Armour: not disclosed
Crew: 4
Weight: 37.40 tons (38,000kg)
Hull length: 20ft 9in (6.32m)
Width: 11ft 0in (3.35m)
Height: 7ft 5in (2.29m)
Engine: V-12 diesel, 730bhp
Road speed: 37mph (60km/hr)
Power/weight: 19.52
Range: 265 miles (430km)

Type 85-2M China
State factories

1990. This is an improved Type 80 and is generally of the same appearance, but differs in having a welded turret of compound armour. It is also said to be equipped with a greatly improved fire control system incorporating a fully stabilised gunner's sight. The first improvement on the Type 80 was simply the **Type 85-2**, which was armed with the standard 105mm rifled gun; the **2M** has a 125mm rifled gun of considerably better performance.

Armament: 125mm; 2 × MG
Ammunition: 46 + 2,750
Armour: not disclosed
Crew: 3
Weight: 40.39 tons (41,000kg)
Hull length: 20ft 9in (6.32m)
Width: 11ft 4in (3.45m)
Height: 7ft 6in (2.30m)
Engine: diesel, 730bhp
Road speed: 35mph (57km/hr)
Power/weight: 18.07
Range: not disclosed

Above: Where it all began. A British Tank Mark 1 at Thiepval, 25 September 1916, during the Battle of the Somme. This is a 'Male' with 6-pounder guns in the side sponsons; it has the 'Hydraulic Equaliser' steering tail wheels, and the netting on top is to prevent hand grenades being thrown on to the roof. This is the classic 'lozenge' shape with all-round tracks.

Below: Another World War I classic was the Renault FT17. This one is being marshalled into position before the Battle of Tardenoi, July 1918. Note the 'Renault Tail', the curved framework just visible at the rear. This prevented the tail end of the tank falling back into a trench after it had crossed it.

Left: The American wheel-and-track exponent was Walter Christie, and this is his M1931 tank. Changing over to wheeled operations was supposedly simple: just break the track and drive off it – the roadwheels had rubber tyres. Putting the track back on again might have been a little more difficult.

Below: Another attempt to relieve the stresses on the tracks when running on roads was the Vickers Medium Mark 1 Wheel & Track. This example is seen with the wheel units lowered and the tracks just clear of the ground.

Above: What happens when you build tanks down to a price rather than up to a standard: the British Matilda I Infantry Tank.

Below: All wheels and rivets. The Vickers Medium Mark I which equipped the British Army's tank regiments 1924–38. The high-set body, squared-off superstructure and sloped roof to the turret made the Vickers product immediately recognisable.

Above: Lots of wheels and leaf springs. The Italian CA M13/40 illustrates yet another way of spreading the load and giving the occupants a more comfortable cross-country ride.

Below: The French Renault R-35 with its 'scissors' suspension system, with a central coil spring acting between each pair of bogie wheels. This tank was captured by British troops in Syria and is here being examined by two American officers.

Above right: The Soviets bought the Christie suspension system and perfected it in the BT series of fast tanks. This is a BT-7 seen during the fighting with the Japanese in Manchuria in 1939. Note the frame antenna for the radio, the set of rails around the turret. The radio frequencies in use in those days demanded a fairly long aerial and this was the only way to fit

it to a tank. As frequencies became higher, aerials became shorter and the whip type eventually took over.

Below right: An American M3 light tank. Points of note are the side-mounted forward-firing machine guns, a common feature of 1930s tanks, but one which was soon seen to be totally useless in war. This picture also gives an excellent view of the vertical volute springs over the bogies which were the Rock Island Arsenal's greatest contribution to tank design. The name Banning appears because this tank was paid for by War Bond purchases made in Banning, California.

Britain also embraced the Christie suspension with a series of cruiser tanks. This was the Covenanter, with its odd sloped-sided turret which was supposed to deflect shot. It did, but some of it went downward into the turret joint.

Above left: This is Matilda 2, looking a good deal more business-like than her predecessor. The slots in the skirting are mud chutes, with sloping plates at the bottom, which collect the mud that drops off the upper track run and keeps it off the suspension below.

Left: The Churchill came in a variety of guises; this is the Mark 7 with 75mm gun (and muzzle brake). This also gives a good view of the multi-wheel suspension.

Right: Maid of all work. The Soviet BA-64 armoured car, a simple enough device but one which had a remarkably high survival rate being small fast and manoeuvrable.

The Russian attitude to firepower was simple: get a bigger gun. Hence the T-34 had a 76mm (3-inch) gun in 1941, while most of the rest of the world was fooling around with 37mm or 50mm weapons. Note also the well sloped armour, wide tracks, Christie suspension and cast turret.

Above far right: Ferdinand, also called the Hunting Tiger or Elefant. The 88mm gun was fitted in a limited traverse mount in the superstructure. Most armies tried this idea but they all had weak close range defence against infantry attack.

Right: The King Tiger with sloped armour, cast turret, even wider tracks and an even longer and more potent 88mm gun. Notice that the surface of the armour is covered with 'Zimmerit', a sort of plastic coating which prevented magnetic bombs sticking to the armour.

Far right: The Marder 2, a 75mm anti-tank gun mounted into an open-topped superstructure built on the chassis of the Panzer 3 tank.

Top left: Early self-propelled guns tended to the primitive; this was Bishop, a large square box on top of a Valentine tank chassis, containing a 25-pounder gun.

Above left: As World War II progressed, so the designs improved; the US M37 105mm SP gun has the appearance of being designed, not just assembled from handy parts.

Left: The Oxford Carrier; like its ancestors the Bren and the Universal, a peculiarly British device and one which a lot of soldiers still wish they had. A sort of Jeep on tracks, with armour.

Above: The American M12 155mm SP gun introduced a feature which became universal — a bulldozer blade behind the hull to act as a recoil spade.

Right: Designs usually start by being simple and uncluttered, and then take off. This is the first Roebling amphibian, the LVT-1, a cargo or personnel-carrying hull, paddle-wheel tracks, and a cab. After that they started to get complicated.

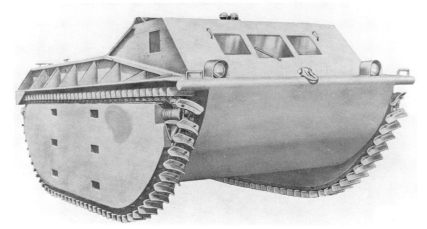

Above left: This is T92 King Kong, a 240mm (9.45-inch) howitzer on the modified chassis of the M26 heavy tank. The size of the recoil spade speaks volumes for the power of the gun.

Left: These are some of the 20,000-plus T-62 tanks which were built. Note the fume extractor on the gun barrel, and the 'inverted frying pan' shape of the turret, very characteristic of Soviet tank designs from 1945 to the 1980s.

Above: The German Gepard anti-aircraft tank, with two 35mm Oerlikon guns, a surveillance radar at the back of the turret and a tracking and gun control radar on the turret front.

Below: This is the AMX-13 tank with its oscillating turret. The gun and the top half of the turret move in elevation, so that the automatic loader (in the bustle at the back of the turret) is always lined up ready for reloading. This one is non-standard – it has a 90mm instead of the usual 75mm gun.

Left: Armour for the infantry comes in all shapes. This is the Saxon armoured personnel carrier (APC) which was derived from a truck chassis, and looks that way.

Far left: Infantry with British armoured formations get to ride in the Warrior Infantry Fighting Vehicle (IFV).

Centre left: The Soviets were particularly keen on Mechanised Infantry Combat Vehicles (MICV) from the early days of the idea. These are BMP-2s, mounting a turret gun and a wire-guided missile as well. There are some drawbacks in firing a wire-guided missile from something which depends on mobility to survive.

Below left: An elegant though expensive design is the French AMX-10RC. Like a traditional armoured car this is more of a cavalry scouting and reconnaissance vehicle, prepared to fight to get its information.

Right: Widely used and widely copied, the Renault VAB 6 × 6 comes in a variety of guises; this is the basic APC.

Below: The daddy of all IFVs was this German Marder, here seen fresh from the builder in 1969, complete with a remote-controlled machine gun mount at the rear of the hull and a remote-controlled 20mm cannon over the main turret.

Above: Soviet T-72 tanks approaching a river with their snorkel tubes up and hatches sealed.

Below: The modern demand is for 'survivability', by using composite armour, angling surfaces to deflect not only shot but radar signals, and making the silhouette as low as possible. The British Challenger tries all these in one package. Note, too, that the gun has a thermal blanket and a muzzle reference system.

Type 85-3 China
State factories
1988. Developed from the Type 80, using the same basic chassis but with a welded turret using composite armour and a heavier gun using automatic loading. They are not easy to tell apart, the most distinctive point being the longer fume extractor on the 125mm gun barrel. Layout is conventional with a two-man turret with automatic loader, six dual roadwheels on each side with torsion bar suspension, front idler, rear drive, and a zig-zag-hemmed skirt over the upper part of the tracks.

Armament: I × 125mm; 2 × MG
Armour: not disclosed
Crew: 3
Weight: 40.04 tons (41,700kg)
Hull length: 23ft 0in (7.0m)
Width: 11ft 4in (3.45m)
Height: 7ft 6in (2.30m)
Engine: V-12 turbocharged diesel, 770bhp
Road speed: 35mph (57km/hr)
Power/weight: 19.23
Range: not disclosed

Type 88 MBT South Korea
Hyundai
1986. This was actually designed by Chrysler in the USA to a specification drawn up by the South Korean government in 1980. The first two prototypes were known as the **XK-1** and were submitted to tests in 1983–84. Production facilities were organised in South Korea and the first Korean-built XK-1 was completed in 1985. It was then standardised as the Type 88, though it was not made public until late 1987 by which time several regiments had been equipped. A total of just over 800 were manufactured.

The Type 88 is of conventional form, with a low and multi-faceted turret mounting a 105mm gun with fume extractor. The fire control system has been put together from components from several different countries but appears to work efficiently. The suspension uses six dual roadwheels each side and is partly by torsion bars and partly by a controlled hydro-pneumatic system which allows the tank's attitude to be varied, allowing it to fire at a lower angle of depression than most other tanks. Given South Korea's mountainous terrain, this is a very sensible refinement.

A design mounting a 120mm smoothbore gun has been drawn up but no further details on this, provisionally called the **Improved Type 88** have been divulged. A bridgelayer and a recovery tank have also been developed on the Type 88 hull and chassis.

Armament: I × 105mm; 3 × MG
Ammunition: 47 + 10,600
Armour: not disclosed
Crew: 4
Weight: 50.19 tons (51,000kg)
Hull length: 24ft 7in (7.48m)
Width: 11ft 9in (3.59m)
Height: 7ft 5in (2.25m)
Engine: MTU V-12 diesel, 1,200bhp at 2,600rpm
Road speed: 40mph (65km/hr)
Power/weight: 23.91
Range: 310 miles (500km)

Type 89 Medium Japan
Mitsubishi
Although design began in 1929 (hence the number) issues of this tank did not start until 1934. A series of pilot models were built and submitted to long trials in the hands of troops in the field before the final decision was taken. The principal result of these trials, some of which took place in Manchuria in winter, was the adoption of air-cooled diesel engines as standard for Japanese tanks. Bodily, the Type 89 introduced the 'bevelled' form of superstructure, with sloping edges, which became another universal Japanese feature in the early 1930s. Suspension was by leaf springs with nine small roadwheels on each side. The body had a flat sloping front with driver's hatch and a hull machine gun, and there was a small turret mounted well forwards.

Armament: I × 57mm gun, 2 × MG
Armour: 17mm maximum
Crew: 4
Weight: 11.32 tons (11,500kg)
Hull length: 14ft 1in (4.29m)
Width: 7ft 0in (2.13m)
Height: 7ft 2in (2.18m)
Engine: Mitsubishi, 6-cylinder, diesel, 120bhp at 1,800rpm
Road speed: 18mph
Power/weight: 10.6
Range: 100 miles (160km)

Type 90 MBT Japan
Mitsubishi
1990. Developed entirely in Japan, this vehicle has some resemblance to the German Leopard 2, especially in the turret; the use of a licence-built copy of the Rheinmetall 120mm smoothbore gun may have some bearing on that. Much of the turret

and hull are of composite armour developed by the Mitsubishi company. The turret bustle contains an auto-loader holding 16 rounds, and which requires that the gun return to a loading angle of 10° after each shot. The day/night sights are fully stabilised and the fire control computer takes its range from a laser rangefinder and incorporates an unusual automatic tracking facility based upon the thermal imaging element of the sight.

Armament: 1 × 120mm smoothbore; 2 × MG
Ammunition: 16 in auto-loader
Armour: not disclosed
Crew: 3
Weight: 49.21 tons (50,000kg)
Hull length: 24ft 7in (7.50m)
Width: 11ft 3in (3.43m)
Height: 7ft 8in (2.34m)
Engine: Mitsubishi 10-cylinder, diesel, 1,500bhp at 2,400rpm
Road speed: 43mph (70km/hr)
Power/weight: 30.48
Range: 217 miles (350km)

Type 90-2 China
State factories
Developed *ca* 1988–90. Developed from the Type 85 with improved armour and engine. Conventional layout for Soviet-derived tanks, using a two-man turret with automatic loader. Additional laminated armour plating over the frontal arc. Six dual roadwheels with torsion bar suspension on each side, front idler, rear drive. Three track return rollers but these are covered by skirting with a zig-zag lower edge. The type is also licensed to Pakistan in a highly modified form, where it is known as the **Al-Khalid** (*qv*).

Armament: 1 × 125mm; 2 × MG
Armour: not disclosed
Crew: 3
Weight: 47.24 tons (48,000kg)
Hull length: 23ft 0in (7.00m)
Width: 11ft 2in (3.40m)
Height: 6ft 7in (2.00m)
Engine: 8-cylinder turbocharged diesel, 1,200bhp
Road speed: 37mph (60km/hr)
Power/weight: 25.00
Range: 248 miles (400km)

Type 91 Heavy Japan
State factories
1931. Experimental design with 17 roadwheels on each side, and a massive superstructure with a slope-sided roof and a small turret set well forward,

a main turret on the superstructure roof, and a third turret at the rear. It was the follow-on to an **Experimental Tank No. 1** begun in 1927 and of very similar design but with two turrets. The main turret carried a 70mm howitzer and a machine gun, and the smaller turrets each had one machine gun. It had a five man crew, weighed about 18 tons and had a top speed of about 15mph.

Type 92 Amphibious Japan
Naval arsenals
1932. The was simply a modified Type 92 Light tank (*below*) with seams welded watertight, additional buoyancy tanks added, and the dimensions slightly increased in order to provide more interior volume to assist the buoyancy. A screw propeller, driven from the main engine, was fitted. The idea does not appear to have been successful, since it never passed the prototype stage.

Type 92 Light Japan
State factories
1932. Also referred to in reports as the **Combat Car Type 92**, this more or less laid down the pattern for Japanese light tanks thereafter; sloped glacis, superstructure with driver on one side and a set-forward machine gun position on the other, the superstructure being surmounted by a one-man turret with another machine gun. Double-bogie, small wheel suspension with four return rollers and leaf springs, replaced in late production models by double-bogies with large spoked wheels and coil springs.

Armament: 2 × MG
Armour: 6mm maximum
Crew: 3
Weight: 3.5 tons (3,555kg)
Hull length: 12ft 10in (3.92m)
Width: 5ft 4in (1.62m)
Height: 6ft 0in (1.83m)
Engine: Ishikawa, 6-cylinder, petrol, 45bhp
Road speed: 21mph (34km/hr)
Power/weight: 12.85

Type 94 Tankette Japan
TGE
1934. This started out to be a tracked artillery and cargo tractor with some means of self-defence, but it finished up as quite a useful light tank. It had a two-bogie bell-crank suspension system and a sloped-front hull surmounted by a turret offset to the right and carrying a single machine gun. The original request for a cargo carrier was met by

having a rear door in the hull and a small cargo space. A useful reconnaissance vehicle, its principal fault was a tendency to throw its tracks if driven with too much verve.

Armament: 1 × MG
Armour: 12mm maximum
Crew: 2
Weight: 3.34 tons (3,400kg)
Hull length: 10ft 1in (3.07m)
Width: 5ft 4in (1.62m)
Height: 5ft 4in (1.62m)
Engine: Type 94 4-cylinder, petrol, 32bhp
Road speed: 25mph (40km/hr)
Power/weight: 9.58
Range: 130 miles (210km)

Type 94 Modified Tankette Japan
State factories

1936. This was an improved model of the Type 94; the suspension was changed by lowering the rear idler until it became a roadwheel and lowering the front drive sprocket, so that the end result was to increase the contact length of track. A number of small changes were made, and the turret was given asbestos insulation against the sun's heat.

Armament: 1 × MG
Armour: 12mm
Crew: 2
Weight: 3.5 tons (3,556kg)
Hull length: 11ft 1in (3.38m)
Width: 5ft 4in (1.62m)
Height: 5ft 10in (1.78m)
Engine: Type 94 4-cylinder, petrol, 32bhp
Road speed: 25mph (40km/hr)
Power/weight: 9.14
Range: 125 miles (240km)

Type 95 Light Japan
Mitsubishi

1935. Also known as **Ha-Go**. One of the better Japanese designs, it was adequate for sparring with Chinese warlords in Manchuria but totally outclassed when it encountered American tanks in the Pacific theatre. Recognisable by the double-bogie suspension and the hull machine gun bay pushed forward on the left front. Small one-man turret with low velocity 37mm gun and a rearward-facing machine gun. Later versions had a better 45mm gun fitted. About 1,350 built 1935–43.

Armament: 1 × 37mm or 1 × 45mm; 2 × MG
Armour: 30mm
Crew: 3
Weight: 7.28 tons (7,400kg)

Hull length: 14ft 4in (4.37m)
Width: 6ft 9in (2.06m)
Height: 7ft 2in (2.19m)
Engine: Mitsubishi NVD 6-cylinder, air-cooled, diesel, 120bhp at 1,800rpm
Road speed: 29mph (45km/hr)
Power/weight: 16.48
Range: 155 miles (250km)

Type 95 Heavy Japan
Mitsubishi

1935. This succeeded the Type 91 Heavy and was the final Japanese attempt at a multi-turret design. The front sub-turret now had a 37mm anti-tank gun, while the main and rear turrets retained their 70mm howitzer and two machine guns. The suspension had been simplified to nine roadwheels on each side, carried on leaf springs. One prototype was built in 1935, and after thorough trials the Japanese Army decided they had no requirement for such a vehicle.

Armament: 1 × 70mm; 1 × 37mm; 2 × MG
Armour: 30mm
Crew: 5
Weight: 24 tons (24,385kg)
Hull length: 21ft 3in (6.48m)
Width: 8ft 9in (2.67m)
Height: 9ft 6in (2.90m)
Engine: aircraft, 6-cylinder, petrol, 290bhp
Road speed: 13mph (20km/hr)
Power/weight: 12.08

Type 97 Medium Japan
Mitsubishi

Medium tank, also known as the **Chi-Ha**, introduced 1937. Six paired rubber-tyred wheels each side, helical spring suspension, rear engine, front drive. Probably the best Japanese design of the war years.

Armament: 1 × 57mm; 2 × 7.7mm MG
Ammunition: 50 + 2,000
Armour: 8–25mm
Crew: 4
Weight: 14.76 tons (15,000kg)
Hull length: 18ft 1in (5.51m)
Height: 7ft 4in (2.23m)
Width: 7ft 8in (2.33m)
Engine: Mitsubishi V-12 diesel, air-cooled, 170bhp
Road speed: 25mph (38km/hr)
Power/weight: 11.52
Range: 130 miles (210km)

Type 97 Tankette Japan
TGE

1937. The last tankette design to be taken into use by the Japanese Army, this replaced the unreliable Type 94. Well-sloped frontal armour, rear engine and drive, small turret with 37mm gun. This design moved away from the cargo-carrying rear-door aspect of earlier tankettes, but the Army demanded the cargo facility and much of later production had no turret and the engine moved forward to provide a protected cargo space in the rear.

Armament: 1 × 37mm
Armour: 12mm
Crew: 2
Weight: 4.68 tons (4,750kg)
Hull length: 12ft 1in (3.68m)
Width: 5ft 11in (1.90m)
Height: 5ft 10in (1.77m)
Engine: Ikega 4-cylinder, air-cooled, diesel, 65bhp at 2,300rpm
Road speed: 26mph (42km/hr)
Power/weight: 13.08
Range: 155 miles (250km)

Type 98A Light Japan
State factories

This was an improved version of the Type 95 Light using three-bogie suspension with interior springing. More welded construction then hitherto, the driver moved to a central position and no hull machine gun. Supercharged engine gave greatly improved performance. Production began in 1942 but no more than about 200 were made.

Armament: 1 × 37mm; 2 × MG
Armour: 12mm
Crew: 3
Weight: 7.2 tons (7,315kg)
Hull length: 13ft 6in (4.11m)
Width: 7ft 0in (2.13m)
Height: 6ft 0in (1.83m)
Engine: diesel, supercharged, 6-cylinder, 150bhp
Road speed: 31mph (50km/hr)
Power/weight: 20.83
Range: not known

Type 98B Light Japan
State factories

An replacement design for the Type 95 Light, this was the same hull and power train as the Type 98A *above*, but with a four roadwheel Christie-type suspension. It never got past the prototype stage.

Data: generally as for the Type A

Valentine UK
Vickers-Armstrong, CPR

1940. This was developed by Vickers after they saw the Matilda 1 and realised that something better would inevitably be demanded. An 'infantry' tank originally, it was also adopted in place of defective cruiser tanks, since it proved to be a strong and reliable tank at a time when such things were scarce in Britain. It was the only pre-war design of tank to remain in production until the war ended. Always recognisable by the rear drive sprocket, the centre of which revolved backwards at high speed. It was originally armed with the usual 2-pounder gun but later versions carried the 6-pounder or British 75mm guns. Over 8,000 built in Britain and Canada, of which about 1,400 went to Russia.

Armament: 1× 2-pdr, or 6-pdr, or 75mm; 1 × MG
Ammunition: 79 × 2-pdr; or 53 × 6-pdr; or 50 × 75mm
Armour: 65mm maximum
Crew: 3 or 4
Weight: 17.0 tons (17,272kg)
Hull length: 19ft 4in (5.89m)
Width: 8ft 8in (2.63m)
Height: 7ft 6in (2.27m)
Engine: AEC 6-cylinder, petrol, 135bhp; or AEC 6-cylinder, diesel 131bhp; or GMC 6- cylinder, diesel, 138bhp
Road speed: 15mph (24km/hr)
Power/weight: 7.94 (AEC engine)
Range: 90 miles (115km)

Valiant (A38) UK
Vickers, Ruston

1943–45. Together with the Black Prince, Valiant was the last design of 'infantry tank' to be built. A Vickers design, later taken over by Ruston & Hornsby, it was largely based on the Valentine and used several Valentine components. The hull nose had the same shape, but the hull and turret were castings and the tracks much wider. The turret could take a 6-pounder or 75mm gun and coaxial machine gun. Two pilot models were built in mid-1944: **Valiant 1** had a GM diesel engine with an AEC transmission, while **Valiant 2** had a Rolls-Royce Meteorite engine and Rolls-Royce transmission. They were tested successfully, but by the end of 1944 the infantry tank concept was dead, and the design was abandoned early in 1945.

Armament: 1 × 6-pdr or 1 × 75mm; 1 × MG
Armour: 114mm maximum
Crew: 4
Weight: 27 tons (27,435kg)
Hull length: 17ft 7in (5.40m)

Width: 9ft 3in (2.82m)
Height: 7ft 0in (2.13m)
Engine: GMC diesel, 210bhp
Road speed: 12mph (20km/hr)
Power/weight: 7.77
Range: 60 miles (95km)

Vickers-Carden-Loyd T-15 Belgium
Vickers

1934. This was a two-man design with the driver at the left front. The engine was to his right, and the turret was offset to the left of the fighting compartment and carried a heavy machine gun. Suspension was by the Horstmann coil-sprung bogie system with front drive and rear idler. About 40 of these were bought by the Belgian Army in 1934–35.

A similar design, produced as the **Model 1936**, was bought by the Dutch in 1936–37 for their East Indies Army.

Armament: 1 × HMG (2 × MG on Dutch)
Armour: 9mm
Crew: 2
Weight: 3.8 tons (3,860kg)
Hull length: 11ft 11in (3.63m)
Width: 6ft 2in (1.88m)
Height: 6ft 4in (1.93m)
Engine: Meadows 6-cylinder, petrol, 90bhp
Road speed: 40mph (65km/hr)
Power/weight: 23.68
Range: 150 miles (240km)

Vickers D3E1 UK
Vickers

1928. This was Vickers' third attempt at a wheel-and-track design. As before, the wheels were fixed and the track unit could be raised and lowered, and in this attempt the wheel track was narrower than the tracks and the rear wheels were concealed under the overhang of the hull. The front wheels were complete with mudguards and looked incongruous when compared to the stark outlines of the hull and turret behind. Having got the idea out of their system with this design, Vickers wisely left it alone thereafter and devoted their attention to better things.

Armament: 2 × MG
Armour: 10mm
Crew: 3
Weight: 8.4 tons (8,535kg)
Hull length: 18ft 0in (5.49m)
Width: 8ft 0in (2.44m)
Height: 9ft 0in (2.74m)

Engine: Armstrong-Siddeley, 6-cylinder, air-cooled, 90bhp
Road speed, tracks: 15mph (24km/hr)
Road speed, wheels: 45mph (72km/hr)
Power/weight: 10.71

Vickers Light 1933 UK
Vickers

1933. This was the first of a series of light tanks, very similar to the British Army light tanks then being developed and built by Vickers, but for export sale. This first member of the series generally resembled the British Light Mark 4 but had outside leaf-spring suspension on its two bogies and a cylindrical turret armed with a standard water-cooled Vickers machine gun in an armoured casing. It was sold to the Baltic states in some numbers.

Armament: 1 × MG
Armour: 9mm
Crew: 2
Weight: 3.8 tons (3,860kg)
Hull length: 11ft 10in (3.60m)
Width: 6ft 3in (1.90m)
Height: 6ft 2in (1.88m)
Engine: Meadows, 6-cylinder, petrol, 90bhp
Road speed: 40mph (65km/hr)
Power/weight: 23.66

Vickers Light 1934 UK
Vickers

1934. Similar to the 1933 but with coil-spring and bell-crank suspension. Numbers were sold to the Argentine, Belgium and Switzerland.

Armament: 1 × MG
Armour: 9mm
Crew: 2
Weight: 3.8 tons (3,860kg)
Hull length: 11ft 11in (3.63m)
Width: 6ft 2in (1.88m)
Height: 6ft 4in (1.93m)
Engine: Meadows 6-cylinder, petrol, 90bhp
Road speed: 40mph (65km/hr)
Power/weight: 23.68

Vickers Light 1936 UK
Vickers

1936. The 1936 model was the 1934 model with a six-sided turret and some minor changes to the hull structure and the suspension, which was still a two-bogie design with coil springs and bell-cranks. This model was sold to China, the Netherlands, and the Netherlands East Indies, and as the war clouds gathered over Europe a number were acquired by the British Army to augment their own stock of light tanks.

Data: as for the Light 1934

Vickers Light 1937 UK
Vickers

1937. This was a radical step forward; it was the hull of the 1936 Light tank with a new turret mounting a version of the then-new 2-pounder 40mm anti-tank gun, fitted with a muzzle brake to keep the recoil to manageable proportions, or a 20mm Oerlikon cannon. It does not appear to have sold.

Armament: 1 × 2-pdr 40mm; or 1 × 20mm cannon
Armour: 9mm
Crew: 2
Weight: 4 tons (4,085kg)
Hull length: 11ft 10in (3.60m)
Width: 6ft 2in (1.88m)
Height: 7ft 4in (2.23m)
Engine: Meadows, 6-cylinder, petrol, 90bhp
Road speed: 30mph (48km/hr)
Power/weight: 22.5

Vickers Light Amphibious UK
Vickers

1931. This was developed privately by Vickers and submitted to the War Office for trial; to conform with various regulations they were given military nomenclature as the **A4E11** and **A4E12**, although they bore no resemblance to the official A4 tanks. The hull was that of the contemporary light tank, with a small turret and single machine gun, and the suspension was by double bogies, with the rear bogie wheel acting as the track idler. Around the hull, like a lifebelt, was a buoyancy float of balsa wood inside a thin metal casing, and at the rear was a steerable rudder and propeller unit. They were not adopted by the British but sold briskly overseas, notably to China and the USSR.

Armament: 1 × MG
Armour: 11mm
Crew: 2
Weight: 2.17 tons (2,205kg)
Hull length: 13ft 4in (4.06m)
Width: 6ft 9in (2.06m)
Height: 6ft 2in (1.88m)
Engine: Meadows, 6-cylinder, petrol, 90bhp
Speed, land: 25mph (40km/hr)
Speed, water: 4mph (6/5km/hr)
Power/weight: 41.47

Vickers Light Command Tank UK
Vickers

1938. Convinced they were on the right path, Vickers now improved the Light 1937, giving it a new double-bogie suspension, a new smaller turret, and a new front to the hull with a well sloped glacis plate. Armament could be one or two medium machine guns, or one heavy or a 40mm, or anything else which would fit into the turret. Some were bought by the Belgian Army.

Armament: 1 or 2 MGs; or 1 × 40mm gun
Armour: 11mm
Crew: 3
Weight: 5 tons (5,080kg)
Hull length: 13ft 8in (4.16m)
Width: 6ft 9in (2.06m)
Height: 6ft 7in (2.01m)
Engine: Meadows, 6-cylinder, petrol, 90bhp
Road speed: 31mph (50km/hr)
Power/weight: 18
Range: not known

Vickers MBT Mark I UK
Vickers

1964. This was an 'economy' tank, designed to sell to countries which wanted a tank with modern attributes but without having to pay enormous amounts of money for it. In essence, it has the engine, transmission, steering and fire control systems of the Chieftain tank, allied to a 105mm gun, and all inserted into a new lightweight hull and chassis. Suspension is by torsion bars and six roadwheels on each side, and the layout is conventional, with the driver at the front and engine at the rear, separated by the fighting compartment. The design was licensed to India and built there as the **Vijayanta**, some 1500 being made before production ended in the mid-1980s.

Armament: 1 × 105mm; 3 × MG
Ammunition: 44 + 3,600
Armour: 80mm
Crew: 4
Weight: 37.99 tons (38,600kg)
Hull length: 26ft 0in (7.92m)
Width: 10ft 5in (3.17m)
Height: 8ft 0in (2.44m)
Engine: Leyland L60 6-cylinder multi-fuel, 650bhp at 2,670rpm
Road speed: 30mph (48km/hr)
Power/weight: 17.11
Range: 300 miles (480km)

Vickers MBT Mark 2 UK
Vickers

The Mark 2 never got past the project stage; it was a proposal to place two Swingfire anti-tank missile launchers on each side of the turret.

Vickers MBT Mark 3 UK
Vickers

1977. This was an improved model, the principal changes being in the engine and fire control systems. This period was one of rapid advances in computerised fire control technology, and new systems were appearing every month. This particular one was the Marconi SFC, allied to a Marconi gun control and stabilising system. The Mark 3 was sold to Kenya and Nigeria.

Armament: 1 × 105mm; 3 × MG
Ammunition: 50 + 3,300
Armour: 80mm
Crew: 4
Weight: 36.90 tons (37,500kg)
Hull length: 24ft 10in (7.56m)
Width: 10ft 5in (3.17m)
Height: 8ft 2in (2.48m)
Engine: Detroit Diesel V-12 turbocharged, 720bhp at 2,500rpm
Road speed: 31mph (50km/hr)
Power/weight: 19.51
Range: 330 miles (530km)

Vickers MBT Mark 3 (I) UK
Vickers

1985. 'I' is for Improved, and this was the result of a complete overhaul of the Vickers Mark 3 MBT, to improve speed, agility, cross-country performance and general appearance. The hull was a combination of welded and cast sections and was more smoothly streamlined, with the skirt indented for the roadwheels. The turret was that of the previous Mark 3, complete with the same gun, fire control and sighting systems. The engine and transmission were completely new, delivering greater power. Suspension was improved to give greater wheel movement and better shock damping. For all its improvements and virtues, it found no market and was discontinued in 1992.

Armament: 1 × 105mm L7; 3 × MG
Ammunition: 50 + 6,000
Armour: not disclosed
Crew: 4
Weight: 40.35 tons (41,000kg)
Hull length: 23ft 11in (7.29m)
Width: 10ft 8in (3.24m)

Height: 8ft 0in (2.44m)
Engine: Rolls-Royce V-12 turbocharged diesel, 850bhp at 2,300rpm
Road speed: 31mph (50km/hr)
Power/weight: 21.08
Range: 340 miles (550km)

Vickers MBT Mark 7 UK
Vickers

1985. In 1982 Vickers displayed a short-lived technology demonstrator called **Valiant**, principally to show their mastery of composite armour. In 1985 they allied the turret of that design to the running gear of the German Leopard 2 to develop the Mark 7. The turret is large, angular, made of composite armour and carries the British 120mm rifled gun, though a French or German smoothbore could easily be fitted in its place. The turret is fitted with the Marconi Centaur integrated gun and fire control system.

Armament: 1 × 120mm; 2 × MG
Ammunition: 40 + 2,000
Armour: not disclosed
Crew: 4
Weight: 53.77 tons (54,640kg)
Hull length: 25ft 4in (7.72m)
Width: 11ft 3in (3.42m)
Height: 8ft 4in (2.54m)
Engine: MTU MB873 V-12 turbocharged diesel, 1,500bhp at 2,600rpm
Road speed: 45mph (72km/hr)
Power/weight: 27.90
Range: 340 miles (550km)

Vickers Medium Mark I UK
Vickers

1924. After Vickers dropped their **Tank Number 1** they took a clean sheet of paper and came up with a design which became recognisable as theirs, and which, into the bargain, more or less laid down the 'conventional' shape and layout of tanks for evermore. The tracks no longer went around the entire hull but were alongside it, the suspension being skirted and with mud chutes. The front was vertical and flat, with a sloping glacis plate running up to the driver's position in the superstructure. Finally came the turret with a curved front and peculiarly slope-sided roof. Today the whole thing looks narrow-gutted, tall and top-heavy, but in fact its cross-country performance was quite good. Also unusual to our eyes was the placement of the engine alongside the driver and the consequent provision of a rear door to the fighting compartment. It may not have been precisely at the cutting edge of technology, but it was cheap, simple and, above all, reliable, and in the 1920s those were the things that counted.

Armament: 1 × 3-pdr; 6 × MG
Armour: 6.5mm
Crew: 5
Weight: 11.7 tons (11,885kg)
Hull length: 17ft 6in (5.33m)
Width: 9ft 2in (2.79m)
Height: 9ft 3in (2.82m)
Engine: Armstrong-Siddeley V-8, petrol, air-cooled, 90bhp
Road speed: 15mph (24km/hr)
Power/weight: 7.69
Range: 100 miles (160km)

Vickers Medium Mark 1A UK
Vickers

1924. Like the Mark 1 this actually entered service under the designation **Light Tank** which, compared to the 1916–18 vehicles, it was. It was later re-classified Medium. The Mark 1A was similar to the Mark 1 but with various minor improvements, and a machine gun mounting in the rear face of the turret.

The **Mark 1A★** was a 1A with a Vickers coaxial machine gun instead of a Hotchkiss, and with a small cupola for the commander in the turret. The **Mark 1 CS** was a close support tank with a 15-pounder (3-inch) howitzer in the turret instead of the 3-pounder gun.

Armament: 1 × 3-pdr; 6 × MG
Armour: 6.5mm
Crew: 5
Weight: 11.9 tons (12,090kg)
Hull length: 17ft 6in (5.33m)
Width: 9ft 2in (2.79m)
Height: 8ft 11in (2.72m)
Engine: Armstrong-Siddeley V-8, petrol, 90bhp
Road speed: 15mph (24km/hr)
Power/weight: 7.56
Range: 100 miles (160km)

Vickers Medium Mark 1 Wheel/Track UK
Vickers

1926. The wheel-and-track idea was attractive because of the rapid rate of wear of the early tracks when running on hard roads. This was simply a Mark 1 Medium tank with a retractable wheel assembly at each end. These could be lowered, using engine power, to lift the tracks clear of the ground. The system worked, but the ride was nauseating due to excessive pitching fore-and-aft

on the springs, and the idea was dropped. For a while.

Armament: 1 × 3-pdr; 1 × MG
Armour: 8mm
Crew: 5
Weight: 13.7 tons (13,920kg)
Hull length: 21ft 0in (6.40m)
Width: 9ft 2in (2.79m)
Height: 9ft 6in (2.90m) on wheels
Engine: Armstrong-Siddeley V-8 petrol, 90bhp
Road speed, tracks: 10mph (16km/hr)
Road speed, wheels: 20mph (32km/hr)
Power/weight: 6.57
Range: 85 miles

Vickers Medium Mark 2 UK
Vickers

1925. This improved on the Mark 1 by having thicker armour, a more elevated position for the driver, and armoured skirts which completely concealed the suspension. This and its variant models became the principal British tank between the wars; about 200 were built and they survived to become training tanks during World War II; indeed a handful in Egypt actually went into battle against the Italian Army in 1940–41.

The **Mark 2★** had a Vickers coaxial gun instead of a Hotchkiss; **Mark 2★★** (1932) had a new twin mounting for the main gun and the coaxial gun, a commander's cupola and an armoured turret bustle containing a radio set. **Mark 2A** (1930) had various improvements to the suspension, ventilation and other details.

Armament: 1 × 3-pdr; 6 × MG
Armour: 8.25mm
Crew: 5
Weight: 13.2 tons (13,410kg)
Hull length: 17ft 6in (5.33m)
Width: 9ft 2in (2.79m)
Height: 8ft 10in (2.69m)
Engine: Armstrong-Siddeley, V-8, petrol, 90bhp
Road speed: 15mph (24km/hr)
Power/weight: 6.82
Range: 125 miles (200km)

Vickers Medium Mark 2A CS UK
Vickers

1928. This was a Mark 2A adapted to the close support (CS) role by removing the 3-pounder gun from the turret and replacing it with a short 3.7-inch howitzer (which was always called a mortar to distinguish it from the existing 3.7-inch mountain howitzer). Only a small number built.

Armament: I × 3.7in mortar; 3 × MG
Armour: 8mm
Crew: 5
Weight: 14 tons (14,225kg)
Hull length: 17ft 6in (5.33m)
Width: 9ft 2in (2.79m)
Height: 10ft 0in (3.05m)
Engine: Armstrong-Siddeley, V-8, petrol, 90bhp
Road speed: 15mph (24km/hr)
Power/weight: 6.43
Range: 125 miles (200km)

Vickers Medium Mark C UK
Vickers

1926. The Mark C was a commercial variant of the Medium Mark 1 which incorporated a number of ideas that had occurred to the Vickers engineers in the course of development. The hull superstructure was taller and carried well forward, with a steeply sloped glacis over the central driver's position, while the turret face was swept back so as to deflect shot. The multi-wheel suspension was just visible under the side skirts. Specimens were bought by the Japanese, who used them to guide the development of their Type 89.

Armament: I × 6-pdr; 4 × MG
Armour: 6mm
Crew: 5
Weight: 11.5 tons (11,885kg)
Hull length: 17ft 4in (5.28m)
Width: 8ft 4in (2.54m)
Height: 7ft 11in (2.42m)
Engine: Sunbeam, 6-cylinder, petrol, 132bhp
Road speed: 20mph (32km/hr)
Power/weight: 11.48
Range: 125 miles (200km)

Vickers Number I & Number 2 UK
Vickers

1921. These were Vickers' first private venture into tank building, and resembled the standard lozenge-shaped British tank of World War I with a hemispherical revolving turret at the forward end of the hull, **No. 1** had three Hotchkiss machine guns in the turret, while **No. 2** had a 3-pounder gun plus mountings for three Hotchkiss guns. On trial they proved to be unreliable due to mechanical defects, and Vickers decided to abandon them and set about a completely fresh approach to the tank.

Armament: I × 3-pdr and/or 3 × MG
Armour: 13mm
Crew: 5
Weight: 8.75 tons (8,900kg)
Engine: 6-cylinder, petrol, 85bhp

Road speed: 15mph
Power/weight: 9.71

Vickers Six-Ton UK
Vickers

1928. Undoubtedly Vickers' greatest commercial success in the pre-war tank business was this light tank; it was sold widely throughout the world, it was copied with or without licence in several more countries, and it influenced design in every country which was attempting to make tanks. The suspension was by double bogies with leaf springs, and the track had four return rollers. The hull had a vertical-sided superstructure; the **Type A** had two turrets, side by side, each with a single machine gun; the **Type B** had a single two-man turret with a 47mm gun and a coaxial machine gun. Other innovations included a firewall between the engine and crew compartments, and the 'Laryngophone' inter-communication system between the crew members. The only unanswered question is why a vehicle weighing seven tons has gone into history as the Six-Tonner.

Armament: I × 47mm + I × MG; or 2 × MG
Armour: 14mm
Crew: 3
Weight: 7 tons (7,115kg)
Hull length: 15ft 0in (4.57m)
Width: 7ft 11in (2.42m)
Height: 6ft 10in (2.08m)
Engine: Armstrong-Siddeley, 4-cylinder, petrol, air-cooled, 80bhp
Road speed: 22mph (35km/hr)
Power/weight: 11.43
Range: 125 miles (200km)

Vickers Three-Man UK
See A5E1

Vickers VFM 5 Battle Tank UK/USA
Vickers, FMC

1986. This is the result of a cooperative venture by Vickers and FMC Inc of the USA, to produce a modified version of the FMC Close Combat Vehicle (Light) (CCV(L)) which would be suitable for the export market. The design is conventional in layout, but uses a welded aluminium armour hull with very rounded contours and a railed tail similar to that of the US Abrams. The turret is 'modern angular' with a sharp-wedged front and mantlet, and it carries the 105mm Gun L7 with fume extractor, thermal sleeve and muzzle reference system. The engine compartment is unusual in having a drop-down ramp door at the hull rear; this allows the entire power pack to be slid out from the hull for maintenance or repair.

Armament: 1 × 105mm L7; 2 × MG
Ammunition: 41 + 3,100
Armour: not disclosed
Crew: 4
Weight: 19.44 tons (19,750kg)
Hull length: 20ft 4in (6.20m)
Width: 8ft 10in (2.69m)
Height: 8ft 7in (2.62m)
Engine: Detroit Diesel V-6, turbocharged, 552bhp at 2,300rpm
Road speed: 43mph (70km/hr)
Power/weight: 28.40
Range: 300 miles (480km)

Vickers-Wolseley Wheel and Track UK
Vickers

1927. This was the company's second try at the convertible tank idea, and this time Vickers took a standard commercial Wolseley truck chassis, armoured it and arranged for the tracked suspension unit to be moved up and down. When down, it raised the wheels from the ground; on reaching a firm surface it was then retracted so that the wheels came into contact with the road. It worked, but in spite of the token hemispherical turret on top of the body, it was scarcely a practical combat vehicle.

Armament: 3 × MG
Armour: 6.5mm
Crew: 4
Weight: 7.5 tons (7,625kg)
Hull length: 16ft 8in (5.08m)
Width: 7ft 3in (2.21m)
Height: 7ft 0in (2.13m)
Engine: Wolseley, 6-cylinder, petrol, 120bhp
Road speed, tracks: 15mph (24km/hr)
Road speed, wheels: 25mph (40km/hr)
Power/weight: 16

Vijayanta India
See Vickers MBT Mark 1

VK Numbers Germany

VK (*versuchs Kraftfahrzeug* – 'experimental fighting vehicle') numbers were allocated to various tank projects by the German Army Weapons Office in the 1933–45 period. There seems to have been little system to their allocation. The same number appeared on different projects at various times.

VK 302 Germany
Borgward

1941. Development number for the **Gepanzerte Munitionsschlepper** (armoured ammunition carrier). This was requested in 1937 as an ammunition carrier for supplying tanks in the field; 20 were built, after which a production order for 100 was issued. But other things had a greater priority, and nothing appeared until late in 1941, when production finally commenced. It was halted after 26 vehicles had been built, and the contract annulled. Experience had shown that it was rare for tanks to need resupply in the middle of a battle, and other, less complicated vehicles were suggested as more general carriers. Borgward made the best of a bad job and adapted the chassis to their B4 demolition vehicle.

VK 601

Development number for PzKpfw 1, Ausf C with dry-pin tracks.

VK602

Development number for PzKpfw 1, Ausf C with lubricated tracks.

VK 901

Development number for the PzKpfw 2 *nA*, Ausf G.

VK 903

Development number for the PzKpfw 2 *nA*, Ausf H.

VK 1301

Development number for the PzKpfw 2 *nA*, Ausf M.

VK 1303

Development number for the PzKpfw 2, Ausf L.

VK 1601

Development number for the PzKpfw 2, Ausf J; it was later used again for the development of a competing design to VK 1602 by Porsche and Skoda, which never materialised.

VK 1602

Development number for the Leopard Medium Reconnaissance Tank.

VK 1801

Development number for the PzKpfw 1, Ausf F.

VK 2001

Development number for the PzKpfw 4 prototypes: by Rheinmetall – VK 2001(Rh), by Krupp – VK 20001(K) and by Daimler – VK 2001(D).

VK 2002

Development number for the PzKpfw 4 prototype by MAN.

VK 30001 (H)
Development number for the first PzKpfw 6 Tiger tank pilot by Henschel.

VK 3001 (P) Germany
Niebelungenwerke
1939–41. Development number for a medium tank by the Porsche design bureau of Stuttgart, ordered from them in 1939, two pilot models being built by Niebelungenwerke. It featured several novelties, including longitudinal torsion bar suspension, an air-cooled engine and a petrol-electric transmission. Tested in 1941, the general features of the design were acceptable but the engines were unreliable. The pilot was simply a hull with suspension (six roadwheels each side), superstructure and a plain cylindrical turret. The project was cancelled in the latter half of 1941 and Porsche then concentrated on the Tiger. The data given here are based partly upon the pilots and partly upon the proposals.

Armament: 1 × 75mm; 2 × MG
Ammunition: not determined
Armour: 80mm
Crew: 5
Weight: 29.52 tons (30,000kg)
Hull length: 21ft 7in (6.58m)
Width: 12ft 6in (3.80m)
Height: 8ft 0in (3.05m)
Engine: 2 × Porsche Type 100 V-10, petrol, 210bhp each at 2,500rpm
Road speed: 37mph (60km/hr)
Power/weight: 14.23
Range: not determined

VK 3002
Development number for the PzKpfw 5 Panther pilot by MAN.

VK 3002 (DB)
Development number for the PzKpfw 5 Panther pilot by Daimler-Benz.

VK 3601(H)
Development number for the second PzKpfw 6 Tiger tank pilot by Henschel.

VK 4501(H)
Development number for the third PzKpfw 6 Tiger pilot by Henschel.

VK 4501(P)
Development number for the Porsche pilot of the Tiger tank.

VK 4503
Development number for the PzKpfw 6, Ausf B, King Tiger.

VK 6501
See PzKpfw 7.

VK 7001
Development number for the 'Löwe' or 'Tiger-Maus', a Krupp project to replace the King Tiger. This never got far beyond the back-of-an-envelope and wooden model stage.

Walker Bulldog USA
See M41 Light

Warrior LMT 105 UK
See Alvis Warrior

Whippet UK
See Medium A

Wireless Tank Mark 1 UK
Foster
1917. A standard British Mark 1 Female tank with the armament removed from the side sponsons and the space used to install radio and office equipment, to be employed as a command tank. A tall mast was mounted on the roof and used to suspend a number of radio antennae. These vehicles were first used at the Battle of Cambrai in November 1917, reporting the course of the battle back to GHQ, after which they saw occasional use until the open warfare of autumn 1918 outstripped the design.

Dimensions: as for Tank Mark 1

X1 Brazil
Bernardini
1975. This is simply the American-built M3A1 Stuart tank rebuilt in Brazil and given a new engine, new suspension and a new turret with a French 90mm gun. A total of 100 were so converted for the Brazilian Army in the late 1970s.

Armament: 1 × 90mm; 2 × MG
Ammunition: not known
Armour: 37mm
Crew: 4
Weight: 14.76 tons (15,000kg)
Hull length: 14ft 11in (4.54m)
Width: 7ft 4in (2.23m)
Height: 8ft 3in (2.51m)
Engine: Saab-Scania V-6 diesel, 280bhp
Road speed: 40mph (65km/hr)
Power/weight: 18.97
Range: 280 miles (450km)

X1A1 Brazil
Bernardini
1977. The X1 having been accepted, the manufacturers decided to improve it by stretching the hull and suspension, adding a further roadwheel set on each side. Although it performed reasonably well, the Brazilian Army were not sufficiently impressed to order any. The company kept it on their sales brochures for a few years but attracted no export orders and finally abandoned the design. By that time, however, they had progressed to the X1A2.

Armament: 1 × 90mm; 2 × MG
Armour: 58mm
Crew: 4
Weight: 16.73 tons (17,000kg)
Hull length: 17ft 5in (5.30m)
Width: 7ft 10in (2.40m)
Height: 8ft 0in (2.45m)
Engine: Saab 6-cylinder, diesel, 280bhp
Road speed: 37mph (60km/hr)
Power/weight: 16.73
Range: 325 miles (520km)

X1A2 Brazil
The X1A2 can hardly be called a development of the X1A1, since it involved a completely new design of hull and chassis, and was no longer simply a made-over Stuart. The hull was longer and used three double bogies on each side, with high-set rear idler and front drive. The turret was a modern design, similar to that on the X1A1, and carried the same 90mm gun, with a coaxial machine gun. The Brazilian Army accepted this design and purchased 50 tanks, all of which were delivered by 1983. The makers then fitted one with an automatic transmission, calling it the **X1A3**, but the idea was not followed up.

Armament: 1 × 90mm; 2 × MG
Ammunition: 60 + 3,250
Armour: not disclosed
Crew: 3
Weight: 18.70 tons (19,000kg)
Hull length: 21ft 4in (6.50m)
Width: 8ft 6in (2.60m)
Height: 8ft 0in (2.45m)
Engine: Saab DS-11, 6-cylinder, turbocharged diesel, 300bhp at 2,200rpm
Road speed: 34mph (55km/hr)
Power/weight: 16.04
Range: 310 miles (500km)

XK-1 South Korea
1985. Development nomenclature for the prototypes of what became the Type 88 main battle tank (*qv*).

Zulfiqar MBT Iran
DIO
1994. Little information has been released about this tank, which appears to have been locally developed and designed to use a number of components from T-72 tanks supplied to Iran by Russia. The suspension uses six roadwheels on each side and is probably by torsion bars; the engine is probably a diesel. The gun is known to be the usual Russian 125mm smoothbore, and is undoubtedly backed up by a computerised fire control system and laser rangefinding.

Data: none available

COMPARATIVE TABLES

CONVENTIONS

The following conventions are used in the comparative tables in each chapter:

An asterisk * indicates that the particular figure has not been publicly revealed; **a question mark ?** shows that the figure is not known; **a dash –** that no equipment in the particular category was fitted to the vehicle concerned (light tanks armed only with a machine gun have a dash in the main armament column, for example).

Weight: is in Imperial tons.

Armour: is in millimetres and is the greatest thickness – usually the front face of the hull and turret.

Crew: Two figures separated by a + indicate the vehicle's actual crew and the passenger space available.

Armament: This is divided in two columns; the first is the main armament calibre in mm. Where two major-calibre weapons are installed they will be shown by a + sign – thus 75 + 37 indicates both a 75mm gun and a 37mm gun. Two calibres separated by an oblique stroke – 75/90 – means that the vehicle started out with a 75mm gun but was upgraded during its lifetime to a 90mm gun. The letters HMG indicate the use of a heavy machine gun (.50-inch/12.7mm or larger) as the main armament. The letters GW indicate an anti-tank guided missile or similar. The second column lists the number of rifle-calibre machine guns installed.

Engine: P = petrol, D = diesel, M = multi-fuel. V = cylinders arranged in a V-formation, R = radial, HO = horizontally-opposed; VO = vertically opposed, F = flat. GT = gas turbine. No distinguishing letter means an in-line engine. The number indicates the number of cylinders. T = turbocharged, S = supercharged, L = liquid cooled, A = air cooled. Thus P/V/10/L means a V-10 petrol engine, liquid-cooled. The prefix 2 × indicates dual engines.

Power: The rated brake horsepower of the engine; not all of these may appear at the wheels or tracks. In the case of multiple engines this is the total power available; an exception to this is the Swedish S-Tank where the power of the two engines is shown separately but the PWR is calculated on both engines in use at once.

PWR: Power-to-weight ratio; bhp per ton, rounded to one decimal place.

Speed & Range: In miles and miles per hour. These are the official figures, usually the manufacturer's, and are often optimistic. Range figures for early vehicles are frequently not available; it seems that it was not considered of particular importance until the 1940s. In the case of wheel-and-track designs the tracked speed is given.

IN ASCENDING ORDER OF WEIGHT

Name	Weight	Length	Crew	Armour	Armament		Engine	Power	PWR	Speed	Range	Country
Crossley-Martel	1.8	10.0	1	10	–	1	P/4/L	45	25.0	20	?	UK
Carden-Loyd	1.5	8.08	2	9	–	1	P/4/L	40	26.6	28	60	UK
CV 29	1.7	8.17	2	9	–	1	P/4/L	40	23.5	25	50	Italy
TK1, TK2	1.75	7.75	2	7	–	1	P/4/L	40	22.8	30	155	Poland
Patrol Tanks Mks 1, 2	2.0	8.5	2	11	–	1	P/6/L	40	20.0	30	?	UK
Vickers Light Amphib	2.17	13.33	2	11	–	1	P/6/L	90	41.5	25	?	UK
Skoda S-1	2.30	?	2	6	–	2	P/4/L	40	17.4	28	?	Czech
T-33 Tankette	2.46	?	2	12	–	2	P/4/L	31	12.6	20	125	Czech
TK3	2.46	8.5	2	8	20 or	1	P/4/L	40	16.3	28	125	Poland
A4E1	2.5	?	2	6	–	1	P/6/L	59	23.6	35	?	UK

Name	Weight	Length	Crew	Armour	Armament		Engine	Power	PWR	Speed	Range	Country
TKF	2.55	8.75	2	10	–	1	P/4/L	46	18.0	26	125	Poland
TKS	2.56	8.75	2	10	–	1	P/4/L	40	15.6	25	125	Poland
T-27 Light	2.65	8.5	2	10	–	1	P/4/L	40	15.1	26	75	Russia
Morris-Martel	2.75	9.17	2	8	–	1	P/4/L	?	?	15	?	UK
Ford Three-Ton	2.76	13.67	2	13	–	1	2 × P/4/L	45	16.3	8	?	USA
A3E1	3.0	17.5	3	6	–	2	P/4/L	40	13.3	16	?	UK
CV 33	3.15	10.42	2	15	–	1	P/4/L	42	13.3	26	78	Italy
T-37 Light	3.15	12.33	2	10	–	1	P/4/L	40	12.7	21	115	Russia
T-38 Light	3.28	12.33	2	10	–	1	P/4/L	50	15.2	25	93	Russia
Type 94 Tankette	3.34	10.08	2	12	–	1	P/4/L	32	9.6	25	130	Japan
La S	3.5	13.17	2	–	–	–	P/F/4/L	57	16.2	25	90	Germany
Type 92 Light	3.5	12.83	3	6	–	2	P/6/L	45	12.9	21	?	Japan
Type 94 (M) Tankette	3.5	11.08	2	12	–	1	P/4/L	32	9.1	25	125	Japan
SR-3 Amphibious	3.8	13.75	2	10	–	1	P/4/A	72	18.9	30	?	Japan
Vickers Carden-Loyd	3.8	11.92	2	9	HMG or	2	P/6/L	90	23.7	40	150	Belgium
Vickers Light 1933	3.8	11.83	2	9	–	1	P/6/L	90	23.7	40	?	UK
Vickers Light 1934	3.8	11.92	2	9	–	1	P/6/L	90	23.7	40	?	UK
AH-4	4.0	11.17	2	15	HMG	1	P/6/L	50	12.5	25	?	Czech
4TP	4.0	12.58	2	17	–	1	P/6/L	95	23.7	34	?	Poland
SR-2 Amphibious	4.0	16.67	3	10	–	2	P/6/A	?	?	25	?	Japan
Vickers Light 1936	4.0	11.92	2	9	20/40	–	P/6/L	90	22.5	30	?	UK
Light Tank Mk 5	4.15	12.08	3	12	HMG	1	P/6/L	88	21.5	32	125	UK
Light Tank Mk 2	4.25	11.75	2	10	–	1	P/6/L	66	15.5	30	199	UK
A5E1	4.5	?	3	9	HMG	1	P/6/L	85	18.9	30	?	UK
Light Tank Mk 3	4.5	12.0	2	12	–	1	P/6/L	66	14.7	30	100	UK
Skoda S-1d	4.5	8.50	2	15	–	1	P/6/L	60	13.3	28	125	Czech
Strv L-100	4.5	13.42	2	9	20 or	1	P/6/L	130	28.9	30	100	Sweden
Strv m/37	4.5	11.17	2	15	–	2	P/6/L	80	17.8	30	?	Sweden
Light Tank Mk 4	4.6	11.17	2	12	–	1	P/6/L	88	19.1	35	125	UK
Type 97 Tankette	4.68	12.08	2	12	37	–	D/4/A	65	13.1	26	155	Japan
Fiat-Ansaldo 5-ton	4.75	11.5	2	12	37	1	P/4/L	42	8.8	20	50	Italy
Light Tank Mk 1	4.8	13.17	2	14	–	1	P/6/L	58	12.1	30	100	UK
Light Tank Mk 6	4.8	13.17	3	15	HMG	1	P/6/L	88	18.3	35	125	UK
AMR-33	5.0	11.5	2	13	–	1	P/V/8/L	84	16.8	37	85	France
Krupp LKA1	5.0	13.17	2	13	–	2	P/F/4/L	57	11.4	19	100	Germany
Vickers Light Cmnd	5.0	13.67	3	11	40 or	2	P/6/L	90	18.0	31	?	UK
T-60 Light	5.07	14.08	2	20	20	1	P/6/L	70	13.8	38	380	Russia
Schofield	5.21	13.08	3	10	40	1	P/6/L	30	5.8	25	?	N Zealand
PzKpfw 1, Ausf A	5.31	13.17	2	13	–	2	P/F/4/L	57	10.8	23	90	Germany
Fiat 3000	5.41	11.75	2	16	37	1	P/4/L	65	12.0	15	60	Italy
MS Light	5.41	11.5	2	16	37	2	P/6/L	65	12.0	10	38	Russia
T-40 Light Amphibian	5.5	13.5	2	13	HMG/20	1	P/6/L	85	15.5	28	215	Russia
PzKpfw 1, Ausf B	5.71	14.5	2	13	–	2	P/6/L	100	17.5	25	105	Germany
Pz.befehlswagen 1	5.8	14.42	3	13	–	1	P/6/L	100	17.2	25	105	Germany
F-4-HE	6.0	?	3	15	–	1	P/4/L	120	20.0	28	?	Czech
Peugeot Char Léger	6.0	?	2	?	37	1	P/4/L	?	?	3	?	France
T3 Light	6.32	11.25	2	16	–	1	P/V/8/L	83	13.1	35	?	USA
Renault FT K-H M26/27	6.4	15.75	2	22	37 or	1	P/4/L	35	5.4	10	?	France
AMR-35	6.5	12.58	2	13	25	–	P/4/L	85	13.0	34	?	France
KS Light	6.5	13.25	2	16	37 or	2	P/F/4/L	45	6.9	5	25	Russia
Renault FT K-H M24/25	6.5	16.42	2	22	37 or	1	P/4/L	35	5.4	7.5	?	France

Name	Weight	Length	Crew	Armour	Armament		Engine	Power	PWR	Speed	Range	Country
Strv L-80	6.5	12.17	2	13	20	1	P/6/L	100	15.4	21	?	Sweden
Fiat-Ansaldo L 6-40	6.69	12.42	3	30	20	1	P/4/L	70	10.5	25	125	Italy
Ford Three-Man	6.69	16.5	3	13	37	1	P/6/L	60	9.0	6	?	USA
T1 Light	6.69	12.5	2	10	37	1	P/V/8/L	105	15.9	20	?	USA
T1E1 Light	6.69	12.75	2	10	37	1	P/V/8/L	110	16.4	20	?	USA
KH50	6.8	14.75	2	13	37 or	1	P/4/L	50	7.4	8	?	Czech
Strv L-60	6.8	15.08	3	13	20	1	P/V/8/L	160	23.5	28	?	Sweden
Renault FT17	6.88	16.42	2	22	37 or	1	P/4/L	35	5.1	5	22	France
LK-1	6.89	18.0	3	8	–	1	P/4/L	60	8.7	8	?	Germany
Renault BS	7.00	16.42	2	22	75	1	P/4/L	35	4.9	5	22	France
Vickers 6-ton	7.0	15.0	3	14	47	1	P/4/A	80	11.4	22	125	UK
M1917A1 Six-ton	7.1	17.33	2	13	37 or	1	P/6/A	100	4.1	10	30	USA
M22 Light	7.14	12.92	3	25	37	1	P/HO/6/A	162	22.7	35	110	USA
Type 2 Light	7.2	13.5	3	16	37	1	D/6/S/L	150	20.8	31	?	Japan
Type 98A Light	7.2	13.5	3	12	37	2	D/6/S/L	150	20.1	31	?	Japan
M1917 Six-ton	7.25	16.42	2	13	37 or	1	P/4/L	42	5.8	5.5	30	USA
Type 95 Light	7.28	14.33	3	30	37/45	2	D/6/A	120	16.5	29	155	Japan
Type 3 Light	7.4	13.5	3	16	57	1	D/6/L	110	20.9	31	?	Japan
PzKpfw 2, Ausf a/	7.48	14.33	3	13	20	1	P/6/L	130	17.4	25	125	Germany
LT-34	7.5	13.25	4	15	37	2	P/4/L	62	8.3	21	?	Czech
LT-H	7.5	14.17	3	32	20	2	D/4/L	125	16.7	28	150	Switzerland
Tetrarch	7.5	13.5	3	16	40	1	P/F/12/L	165	22.0	40	140	UK
Vickers-Wolseley	7.5	16.67	4	6.5	–	3	P/6/L	120	16.0	15	?	UK
T1E4 Light	7.68	15.42	3	16	37	1	P/V/8/L	140	19.2	20	?	USA
PzKpfw 2, Ausf b/	7.77	15.58	3	13	20	1	P/6/L	140	18.0	25	125	Germany
PzKpfw 1, Ausf C	7.87	13.75	2	30	20	1	P/6/L	150	19.1	50	185	Germany
T1E2 Light	7.95	12.83	2	16	37	1	P/V/8/L	132	16.6	18	?	USA
Char NC-1	8.0	14.5	2	30	37	1	P/4/L/	60	7.5	11	45	France
Skeleton Tank	8.03	25.0	2	13	–	1	2 x P/4/L	100	12.5	5	?	USA
M2 Light	8.39	13.42	4	15	?	3	P/R/7/A	260	31.0	46	?	USA
T2E1 Light	8.39	13.42	4	16	–	3	P/R/7/A	260	31.0	45	?	USA
Marmon-Herrington	8.4	11.5	3	25	–	3	P/6/L	124	14.8	30	60	USA
Type 4 Light	8.4	14.17	3	25	57	2	D/6/A	100	13.1	25	?	Japan
Vickers D3E1	8.4	18.0	3	10	–	2	P/6/A	90	10.7	15	?	UK
CA 8-ton	8.5	16.33	3	?	37	2	D/V/8/L	105	12.3	19	?	Italy
Harry Hopkins	8.5	14.25	3	38	40	1	P/HO/12/L	165	19.4	30	140	UK
T-26 Light	8.5	15.75	3	15	–	2	P/4/L	91	10.7	22	140	Russia
Strv m/38	8.5	15.33	3	13	37	1	P/6/L	142	16.7	28	?	Sweden
Christie M1928	8.6	17.0	3	13	–	–	P/V/12/L	338	39.3	42	?	USA
Combat Car M1E2	8.72	14.58	4	16	–	4	P/R/9/A	250	28.7	45	?	USA
LK-2	8.75	16.75	3	14	57	–	P/4/L	60	6.9	7.5	?	Germany
Vickers Nos 1, 2	8.75	?	5	13	47	3	P/6/L	85	9.7	15	?	UK
PzKpfw 2, Ausf c/	8.75	15.75	3	16	20	1	P/6/L	140	16.0	25	125	Germany
T1E6 Light	8.88	15.0	3	16	37	1	P/4/L	240	27.0	20	?	USA
Combat Car T4E1	8.93	16.08	3	13	–	6	P/R/9/A	264	29.5	25	?	USA
Alvis-Straussler	9.0	15.17	3	–	–	–	2 x P	?	?	42	?	UK
TNH/PS	9.25	15.08	4	25	37	2	P/6/L	140	15.1	26	155	Czech
TNH/SV	9.35	15.17	4	25	37	2	P/6/L	140	15.0	26	155	Czech
PzKpfw 2, Ausf F	9.35	15.75	3	35	29	1	P/6/L	140	15.0	25	125	Germany
Strv m/40	9.35	16.08	3	24	37	2	P/6/L	142	15.2	30	125	Sweden
7TP	9.4	15.08	3	17	–	2	D/6/L	110	11.7	20	100	Poland

Name	Weight	Length	Crew	Armour	Armament		Engine	Power	PWR	Speed	Range	Country
Char NC-2	9.5	14.67	2	35	37	1	P/4/L	75	7.0	13	50	France
Combat Car T5	9.7	13.33	4	16	–	3	P/R/9/A	264	27.2	36	?	USA
Combat Car M1	9.7	13.58	4	16	–	3	P/R/9/A	250	25.8	45	?	USA
Strv m/21	9.7	18.75	4	14	–	1	P/4/L	56	5.8	10	?	Sweden
T-70 Light	9.79	15.17	2	60	45	1	P/6/L	70	14.3	31	280	Russia
PzKpfw 2, Ausf D ,E	9.84	15.25	3	30	20	1	P/6/L	140	14.2	34	125	Germany
Renault R-35 Light	9.84	13.83	2	45	37	1	P/4/L	82	8.3	12	88	France
BT-1	10.0	18.0	3	13	–	2	P/V/12/L	350	34.9	40	?	Russia
Schneider-Laurent	10.0	19.67	3	15	37	1	P/V/8/L	100	10.0	28	?	France
Type 5 Light	10.0	14.42	4	20	47	2	D/6/S/L	150	15.0	31	?	Japan
Christie M1931	10.2	18.0	3	13	37	1	P/V/12/L	338	33.1	27	?	USA
M2A4 Light	10.26	14.58	4	25	37	4	P/R/7/A	250	24.4	25	70	USA
T-26S Light	10.3	15.75	3	25	45	2	P/4/L	91	8.8	17	125	Russia
PzKpfw 2m, Ausf G	10.33	13.92	3	30	20	1	P/6/L	180	17.4	31	125	Germany
Strv m/41	10.33	15.0	3	25	37	1	P/6/L	145	14.0	27	125	Sweden
LT-35	10.5	16.08	4	25	37	2	P/6/L	129	11.4	22	120	Czech
Hotchkiss H-35	10.6	13.83	2	40	37	1	P/6/L	75	7.1	17	93	France
Combat Car T7	10.7	16.67	4	16	–	3	P/4/L	250	23.4	24	?	USA
AMC-34	10.8	13.17	3	20	25	1	P/4/L	120	11.1	25	?	France
Matilda I	10.98	15.92	2	60	–	1	P/V/8/L	70	6.4	8	78	UK
CA M11/39	11.0	15.5	3	30	37	2	D/V/8/L	105	9.5	21	125	Italy
Type 2 Amphibious	11.07	24.33	3	12	37	2	D/6/L	110	9.9	25	125	Japan
BT-5	11.31	18.0	3	13	45	1	P/V/12/L	350	30.9	40	?	Russia
Strv m/31	11.31	17.0	4	9	37	2	P/V/6/A	140	12.4	25	125	Sweden
Type 89 Medium	11.32	14.08	4	17	57	2	D/6/L	120	10.6	18	100	Japan
Strv L-30	11.5	17.0	3	14	37	1	P/V/12/L	150	13.0	?	?	Sweden
T3E2 Medium	11.5	18.75	4	13	37	5	P/V/12/A	435	37.8	20	?	USA
Vickers Med Mk C	11.5	17.33	5	6	57	4	P/6/L	132	11.5	20	125	UK
Vickers Med Mk 1	11.71	17.5	5	6.5	47	6	P/V/8/L	90	7.7	15	100	UK
Flammpanzer 2	11.81	16.08	3	30	2 flame	1	P/6/L	140	11.9	34	155	Germany
Vickers Med Mk 1A	11.9	17.5	5	6.5	47	6	P/V/8/L	90	7.6	15	100	UK
CA-32	12.0	16.33	3	?	45	4	P/4/L	75	6.3	14	?	Italy
Cruiser Mk 1	12.0	19.25	5	14	40	3	P/6/L	150	12.5	25	95	UK
DP-2 Amphibious	12.0	?	3	15	–	1	P/V/12/L	228	19.0	?	?	France
Hotchkiss H-38	12.0	13.83	2	40	37	1	P/6/L	120	10.0	22	93	France
T4 Medium	12.05	16.08	4	16	–	3	P/R/7/A	268	22.2	20	?	USA
Hotchkiss H-39	12.2	13.83	2	45	37	1	P/6/L	120	9.8	23	93	France
M3 Light	12.23	14.92	4	37	37	5	P/R/7/A	250	20.4	36	70	USA
FCM-36	12.6	14.58	2	40	37	1	D/4/L	91	7.2	15	140	France
M3A1 Light	12.72	14.92	4	37	37	3	P/R/7/A	250	19.7	36	70	USA
10TP	12.8	17.75	4	20	37	2	P/V/12/L	210	16.4	31	?	Poland
Char D-1	13.0	18.92	3	35	47	2	P/4/L	65	5.0	11	60	France
Luchs	13.0	15.17	4	30	20	1	P/6/L	180	13.8	37	180	Germany
Vickers Med Mk 2	13.2	17.50	5	8.25	47	6	P/V/8/L	90	6.8	15	125	UK
T4E1 Medium	13.39	16.08	4	16	–	6	P/R/7/A	268	20.0	20	?	USA
T5 Medium	13.39	17.25	5	25	37	6	P/R/7/A	250	18.7	20	?	USA
Christie M1919	13.5	18.17	3	25	57	1	P/6/L	120	8.9	7	?	USA
T50 Light	13.5	17.0	4	37	45	2	D	300	22.2	31	?	Russia
BT-7	13.68	17.58	3	22	45	2	P/V/12/L	500	36.6	45	265	Russia
Cruiser Mk 2	13.7	18.08	5	30	40	2	P/6/L	150	10.9	20	93	UK
Vickers Med Mk 1 W&T	13.7	21.0	5	8	47	1	P/V/8/L	90	6.6	10	85	UK

Name	Weight	Length	Crew	Armour	Armament		Engine	Power	PWR	Speed	Range	Country
CA M13/40	13.78	16.17	4	30	47	2	D/V/8/L	125	9.1	20	125	Italy
PT-76	13.78	22.67	3	14	76	1	D/V/6/L	240	17.4	27	160	Russia
T2 Medium	13.92	16.0	4	25	47 + 37	2	P/V/12/L	312	22.4	25	?	USA
A7E1	14.0	?	5	14	47	2	P/6/A	120	8.5	25	?	UK
Christie M1921	14.0	18.17	3	20	57	1	P/6/L	120	8.6	14	?	USA
Cruiser Mk 3	14.0	19.75	4	14	40	1	P/V/12/L	340	24.3	31	108	UK
Medium A	14.0	20.0	3	14	–	3	2 × P/6	90	6.4	8	?	UK
Vickers Med Mk 2A CS	14.0	17.5	5	8	94	3	P/V/8/L	90	6.4	15	125	UK
M3A3 Light	14.17	16.5	4	37	37	3	P/R/7/A	250	17.6	36	70	USA
Schneider CA-1	14.36	19.83	6	12	75	2	P/4/L	55	3.8	3	30	France
CA M15/42	14.37	16.17	4	30	47	2	D/V/8/L	145	10.1	22	125	Italy
AMC-35	14.5	14.58	3	25	47	1	P/4/L	180	12.4	25	?	France
M5 Light	14.73	14.25	4	58	37	3	2 × P/V/8/L	220	14.9	36	100	USA
AMX-13	14.76	16.0	3	40	90	1	P/V/8/L	250	16.9	37	250	France
Cruiser Mk 4	14.76	19.75	4	30	40	1	P/V/12/L	340	23.0	27	95	UK
Type 97 Medium	14.76	18.08	4	25	57	2	D/V/12/L	170	11.5	25	130	Japan
X-1	14.76	14.92	4	37	90	2	D/V/6/L	280	19	40	280	Brazil
PzKpfw 3, Ausf A	15.15	17.67	5	15	37	3	P/V/12/L	250	16.5	21	100	Germany
Flammpanzer 38(t)	15.25	16.0	4	60	1 flame	1	P/6/L	160	10.5	26	110	Germany
BT-IS	15.35	18.92	3	30	45	2	D/V/12/L	500	32.6	40	250	Russia
M551 Sheridan	15.58	20.67	4	*	152	2	D/V/6/T/L	300	19.3	43	370	USA
PzKpfw 3, Ausf C	15.75	19.17	5	15	37	3	P/V/12/L	250	15.9	25	100	Germany
Turan 40M	16.0	?	5	20	47/75	2	P/V/8	260	16.2	?	?	Hungary
ST-39	16.5	17.25	4	50	47	2	P/V/8/L	240	14.5	28	?	Czech
Type 2 Gun Tank	16.7	18.75	5	50	75	1	D/V/12/L	240	14.4	27	?	Japan
X1A1	16.73	17.42	4	58	90	2	D/V/8/L	280	16.7	37	325	Brazil
M2 Medium	16.96	17.67	6	25	37	8	P/R/9/A	350	20.6	28	?	USA
Holt Steam	17.0	22.25	6	19	75	2	2 steam	150	8.8	5	?	USA
Type 1 Medium	17.0	18.75	5	50	47	2	D/V/12/L	240	14.1	27	?	Japan
Valentine	17.0	19.33	4	65	40/57/75	1	P/6/L	135	7.9	15	90	UK
A6E1	17.5	21.5	7	14	47	5	P/V/8/A	180	10.3	30	?	UK
Light Infantry Tank	17.5	22.25	3	10	–	3	P/6/L	100	5.7	30	?	UK
M8 AGS	17.76	19.92	3	*	105	2	D/V/6/L	550	31.0	45	300	USA
Cruiser Mk 5	18.0	19.0	4	40	40	1	P/F/12/L	300	16.7	31	95	UK
Experimental Heavy	18.0	?	5	12	70	3	P	140	7.8	12	?	Japan
Little Willie	18.0	18.17	6	–	–	–	P/6/L	105	5.8	2	?	UK
Medium B	18.0	22.75	4	14	–	4	P/6/L	100	5.6	6	?	UK
M24 Light	18.08	16.33	5	38	75	3	2 × P/V/8/L	220	12.2	30	100	USA
T-24 Medium	18.2	?	3	25	45	3	P/V/8/L	300	16.5	15	125	Russia
PzKpfw 4	18.11	18.33	5	15	75	2	P/V/12/L	250	13.8	19	93	Germany
A7E3	18.2	22.5	5	14	47	2	2 × D/6/L	252	13.8	25	?	UK
PzKpfw 2m, Ausf J	18.2	13.92	3	80	20	1	P/6/L	150	8.2	19	125	Germany
Type 63 Light Amphib	18.4	23.50	4	14	85	2	D/V/12/L	400	21.7	40	230	China
Char D-2	18.5	17.83	3	40	47	2	P/6/L	150	8.1	14	93	France
T24E1 Light	18.5	?	3	25	75	3	P/R/9/A	400	21.6	35	?	USA
Type 3 Medium	18.5	18.5	5	50	75	1	D/V/12/A	240	13.0	24	?	Japan
X1A2	18.7	21.33	3	*	90	2	D/V/6/T/L	300	16.0	34	310	Brazil
Stingray 1	18.97	22.0	4	*	105	2	D/V/8/L	535	28.2	40	310	USA
Cruiser Mk 6	19.0	19.67	5	50	40/57	3	P/V/12/L	340	17.9	28	200	UK
FMC CCV(L)	19.11	20.33	3	*	105	2	D/V/6/T/L	552	28.9	43	300	USA
PzKpfw 3, Ausf E	19.19	17.75	5	30	37	3	P/V/12/L	300	15.6	25	100	Germany

Name	Weight	Length	Crew	Armour	Armament		Engine	Power	PWR	Speed	Range	Country
Grosstraktor 2	19.32	21.67	6	–	75	3	P/6/L	250	12.9	25	93	Germany
Vickers VFM 5	19.44	20.34	4	*	105	2	D/V/6/T/L	552	28.4	43	300	UK/USA
T1 Medium	19.64	25.92	4	25	57	2	P/8/L	200	10.2	14	?	USA
M1985 Light	19.68	20.5	3	*	85 + GW	2	D	320	16.3	?	?	N Korea
Somua S-35	19.73	17.92	3	40	47	1	P/V/8/L	190	9.6	23	160	France
Experimental No. 1	20.0	?	5	15	57	2	P	140	7.0	12	?	Japan
Medium C	20.0	26.0	4	12	–	5	P/6/L	150	7.5	8	?	UK
Medium D	20.0	30.0	3	10	–	3	P/6	240	12.0	23	?	UK
PzKpfw 3, Ausf G	20.17	17.75	5	37	50	2	P/V/12/L	300	14.9	25	100	Germany
M1921 Medium	20.53	21.58	4	25	57	2	P/6/L	250	12.2	10	?	USA
PzKpfw 1, Ausf F	20.66	14.33	2	80	–	2	P/6/L	150	7.3	25	93	Germany
Type 62 Light	20.66	18.25	4	*	85	2	D	380	18.5	37	310	China
Leopard Recon	20.67	15.50	4	50	50	1	P/V/12/L	550	26.6	37	?	Germany
PzKpfw 3, Ausf H	21.46	17.75	5	60	50	2	P/V/12/L	300	14.0	25	100	Germany
St Chamond	21.63	28.5	8	17	75	4	P/4/L	90	4.2	5	27	France
Stingray 2	21.87	21.17	4	*	105	2	D/V/8/L	550	25.1	41	300	USA
Strv m/42	22.14	16.08	4	80	75	3	P/6/L	320	14.5	27	125	Sweden
M1922 Medium	22.32	25.92	4	25	57	1	P/6/L	250	11.2	15	?	USA
PzKpfw 3, Ausf L	22.34	20.58	5	57	50	2	P/V/12/L	300	13.4	25	96	Germany
Flammpanzer 3	22.64	21.0	3	80	1 flame	2	P/V/12/L	300	13.3	25	96	Germany
PzKpfw 3, Ausf J	22.64	18.5	5	70	50	2	P/V/12/L	300	13.3	25	100	Germany
PzKpfw 3, Ausf N	22.64	18.5	5	70	75	2	P/V/12/L	300	13.3	25	100	Germany
M7 Medium	22.77	17.58	5	38	75	2	P/R/9/A	330	14.5	35	125	USA
PzKpfw 5 (*Nbfz*)	23.04	21.67	6	20	75 + 37	3	P/6	250	10.9	18	75	Germany
M41 Light	23.12	19.08	4	40	76	2	P/HO/6/S/A	500	21.6	45	100	USA
PzKpfw 4, Ausf G	23.13	19.5	5	80	75	2	P/V/12/L	300	13.0	25	130	Germany
Type 95 Heavy	24.0	21.25	5	30	70 + 37	2	P/6/A	290	12.1	13	?	Japan
Hagglund CV 90-120	24.6	21.25	4	*	120	1	D/4/L	600	24.4	43	415	Sweden
Char B	25.0	see text	4	40	75	4	P/6/L	180	7.2	12	?	France
Holt Gas-Electric	25.0	16.5	6	13	75	3	P/4/L	90	?	6	?	USA
CA P 26/40	26.0	19.07	4	50	75	1	D/V/12/L	275	10.6	22	150	Italy
T-34/76 Medium	26.3	20.25	5	80	76	2	D/V/12/L	500	19.0	31	190	Russia
Cavalier	26.5	20.83	5	76	57	2	P/V/12/L	340	12.8	24	185	UK
Matilda 2	26.5	18.42	4	78	40	1	D/6/L	174	6.6	15	155	UK
M3 Medium	26.79	18.5	6	57	75 + 37	3	P/R/9/A	340	12.7	26	120	USA
Centaur	27.0	20.83	5	76	57	2	P/V/12/L	340	12.6	25	175	UK
Valiant (A38)	27.0	17.58	4	114	57/75	1	D/6/L	210	7.8	12	60	UK
Cruiser Mk 8	27.5	20.83	5	102	57/75/95	1	P/V/12/L	600	21.8	40	170	UK
Sentinel AC-1	28.0	20.75	5	65	40	2	3 × P/V/8/L	330	11.8	30	200	Australia
Tank, Marks 1, 2, 3	28.0	32.5	8	12	2 × 57	4	P/6/L	105	3.8	3.8	22	UK
Tank Mark 4	28.0	26.33	8	15	2 × 57	4	P/6/L	105	3.8	3.8	22	UK
Type 64	28.04	19.17	4	*	76	2	D/V/8/L	?	?	?	280	Taiwan
ASCOD 105	28.05	21.67	4	*	105	2	D/V/8/L	600	21.4	43	310	Spn/Austria
Alvis Warrior	28.54	21.5	4	*	105	1	D/V/8/L	600	21.0	47	372	UK
Ram 1	28.57	19.0	5	88	40	3	P/R/9/A	400	14.0	25	125	Canada
Type 3 Amphibious	28.8	33.75	7	50	47	2	D/V/12/A	240	8.3	20	?	Japan
Tank Mark 5	29.0	26.42	8	15	2 × 57	4	P/6/L	150	5.2	5	25	UK
Type 5 Amphibious	29.0	35.42	7	50	47 + 25	2	D/V/12/A	240	8.3	20	?	Japan
Ram 2	29.02	19.0	5	88	57	3	P/R/9/A	400	13.8	25	125	Canada
T20 Medium	29.35	18.83	5	64	76	3	P/V/8/L	470	16.0	25	?	USA
A-7V	29.4	24.08	18	30	57	7	2 × P/4/L	200	7.0	8	25	Germany

Name	Weight	Length	Crew	Armour	Armament		Engine	Power	PWR	Speed	Range	Country
TAM Medium	29.52	22.17	4	*	105	2	D/6/L	720	24.4	47	373	Argentina
Tamoya	29.52	21.33	4	*	90	2	D/6/L	500	16.9	42	340	Brazil
VK 3001 (P)	29.52	21.58	5	80	75	2	2 × P/V/10/L	420	14.2	37	?	Germany
M4 Medium	29.69	19.33	5	76	75	3	P/R/9/A	400	13.5	24	120	USA
Char B-1	30.0	20.92	4	40	75 + 47	2	P/6/L	180	6.0	17	93	France
Type 4 Medium	30.0	20.75	5	75	75	2	D/V/12/L	400	13.3	28	?	Japan
T20E3 Medium	30.13	18.83	5	64	76	3	P/V/8/L	470	15.6	25	?	USA
THE30 Medium	30.51	22.25	4	*	105	2	D/V/6/T/L	750	24.6	45	310	Germany
Avenger A30	30.75	26.33	5	80	76	1	P/V/12/L	570	18.5	32	105	UK
Mother	31.0	31.25	8	–	2 × 57	2	P/6/L	105	3.4	3.7	23	UK
Type 61 MBT	31.45	20.67	4	64	90	2	D/V/12/T/L	600	17.4	28	125	Japan
Challenger	31.5	26.33	5	100	76	1	P/V/12/L	570	18.1	31	135	UK
Independent A1E1	31.5	28.42	8	30	47	4	P/V/12/A	398	12.6	17	93	UK
T-28 Medium	31.5	24.42	6	80	76	3	P/V/12/L	500	15.9	22	135	Russia
T-34/85 Medium	31.5	20.25	5	90	85	2	D/V/12/L	500	15.9	31	190	Russia
T-43 Medium	31.5	22.5	5	110	76	2	D/V/12/L	500	15.9	31	190	Russia
Clovis	31.59	22.27	3	*	105 + 20	3	D/6/L	750	23.7	43	375	France/Ger
Char B-1 *bis*	32.0	21.42	4	60	75 + 47	2	P/6/L	307	9.6	17	93	France
T23 Medium	32.8	19.75	5	64	76	3	P/V/8/L	470	14.3	35	?	USA
Comet	32.7	21.5	5	101	77	2	P/V/12/L	600	18.4	32	125	UK
Tank Mark 5*	33.0	32.42	8	15	2 × 57	4	P/6/L	150	4.6	4	20	UK
Tank Mark 9	33.0	31.83	4	10	–	1	P/6/L	150	3.5	3.5	20	UK
T23E3 Medium	33.48	19.17	5	64	76	3	P/V/8/L	470	14.0	35	?	USA
T-44 Medium	34.0	21.33	4	120	85/100	2	D/V/12/L	512	15.1	32	155	Russia
Type 61 MBT	31.45	20.67	4	64	90	2	D/V/12/T/L	600	17.4	28	125	Japan
Tank Mark 5**	35.0	32.42	8	15	2 × 57	4	P/6/L	225	6.4	6	25	UK
AMX-30	35.43	21.58	4	81	105 + 20	1	M/S/V/12/L	720	20.3	31	375	France
T-54 MBT	35.43	21.17	4	203	100	3	D/V/12/L	520	14.7	30	250	Russia
T-55 MBT	35.43	21.08	4	203	100	1	D/V/12/L	580	16.4	31	310	Russia
Type 59 MBT	35.43	19.83	4	203	100	2	D/V/12/L	520	14.7	31	260	China
Type 72Z MBT	35.43	21.42	4	*	105	2	D/V/12/L	780	22.0	40	*	Iran
Char B-1 *ter*	36.0	20.83	5	70	75 + 47	2	P/6/L	310	8.6	15	93	France
Type 69 MBT	36.4	20.5	4	*	100	2	D/V/12/L	580	15.9	31	250	China
T25 Medium	36.8	18.58	5	90	90	3	P/V/8/L	470	12.8	30	?	USA
Vickers MBT Mk 3	36.9	24.83	4	80	105	3	D/V/12/T/L	720	19.5	31	330	UK
Tank Mark 8	37.0	34.17	12	16	2 × 57	7	P/6/L	300	8.1	7	30	UK/USA
Type 5 Medium	37.0	24.0	5	76	75 + 37	2	P/V/12/L	550	14.9	28	?	Japan
PZ-61	37.4	22.25	4	120	105	2	D/V/8/L	630	16.8	34	185	Switzerland
Type 74 MBT	37.4	22.0	4	*	105	2	D/V/10/T/A	720	19.3	33	310	Japan
Type 80 MBT	37.4	20.75	4	*	105	2	D/V/12/L	730	19.5	37	265	China
Vickers MBT Mk 1	37.99	26.0	4	80	105	3	M/6/L	650	17.1	30	300	UK
AMX-32	38.38	21.58	4	*	105 + 20	1	M/S/V/12/L	700	18.2	40	330	France
T26 Medium	38.61	22.42	5	101	90	3	P/V/8/L	470	12.2	25	?	USA
A-7V/U	39.0	27.5	7	30	2 × 57	4	2 × P/4/L	210	5.4	7.5	25	Germany
PZ-68	39.07	22.58	4	120	105	2	D/V/8/L	660	16.9	34	215	Switzerland
S-Tank	39.07	27.58	3	*	105	3	M/V/8/L	249					Sweden
							M/GT	490	18.7	31	242	
Fiat 2000	39.37	24.25	10	20	65	6	P/6/L	240	6.0	4	47	Italy
Leopard 1 MBT	39.37	23.25	4	70	105	2	M/V/10/S/L	830	21.1	40	375	Germany
T-62 MBT	39.37	21.75	4	242	115	2	D/V/12/L	580	14.7	31	280	Russia
Churchill	40.0	24.42	5	152	40/57/75	2	P/HO/12/L	350	8.8	15	88	UK

Name	Weight	Length	Crew	Armour	Armament		Engine	Power	PWR	Speed	Range	Country
Type 85-3	40.04	23.0	3	*	125	2	D/V/12/T/L	770	19.2	35	*	China
Osorio EE-T1	40.25	23.42	4	*	105	2	C/V/12/T/L	1100	27.3	43	340	Brazil
Vickers MBT Mk 3(I)	40.35	23.92	4	*	105	3	D/V/12T/L	850	21.1	31	340	UK
Type 85-2M	40.39	20.75	3	*	125	2	D	730	18.1	35	*	China
T-72M1 MBT	40.84	22.83	3	*	125	2	M/V/12/T/L	770	18.9	37	285	Poland
Char 1A	41.0	27.33	7	35	105	2	P/V/12/L	240	5.9	4	?	France
M26 Pershing	41.07	22.25	5	102	90	3	P/V/8/L	500	12.2	30	110	USA
M-84 MBT	41.33	22.5	3	*	125	2	D/V/12/T/L	1000	24.2	40	435	Yugoslavia
T-64 MBT	41.34	24.25	3	*	125	2	D/HO/5/L	750	18.1	47	250	Russia
T26E2 Heavy	41.52	20.75	5	127	105	3	P/V/8/L	470	11.3	20	?	USA
T-80 MBT	41.83	24.25	3	*	125	2	GT	1000	23.9	43	208	Russia
T14 Assault	41.93	20.83	5	76	75	3	P/V/8/L	470	11.2	24	?	USA
KV-1	42.23	20.58	5	77	76/85	3	D/V/12/L	600	12.8	22	155	Russia
Panther, Ausf D	42.32	22.5	5	100	75	2	P/V/12/L	700	16.5	28	125	Germany
AMX-40	43.0	22.33	4	*	120 + 20	1	D/V/12/L	1300	30.2	44	340	France
JS-1	44.0	27.33	4	120	122	4	D/V/12/L	510	11.6	23	100	Russia
OF-40	44.29	22.67	4	*	105	2	M/V/10/S/L	830	18.1	37	375	Italy
TM-800 MBT	44.29	22.17	4	*	100	2	D	830	18.8	40	310	Romania
Steam Tank	44.64	38.75	8	13	1 flame	4	2 steam	500	11.2	4	?	USA
T-72 MBT	44.78	22.83	3	280	125	2	D/V/12/L	780	17.4	40	250	Russia
T-32 Heavy	44.8	30.5	10	25	76 + 2 × 37	6	P/V/8/L	345	7.7	18	75	Russia
A33 Excelsior	45.0	22.67	5	114	75	1	P/V/12/L	600	13.3	24	?	UK
ARL-44	45.0	34.5	5	?	90	2	P/V/12/L	700	15.6	23	93	France
SMK Heavy	45.0	31.5	6	60	76 + 45	3	P	400	8.9	20	?	Russia
PT-91	45.27	22.83	3	*	125	2	D/V/12/S/L	850	18.8	43	405	Poland
M47 Medium	45.44	23.25	5	100	90	3	P/V/12/A	810	17.8	37	100	USA
JS-3	45.52	22.33	4	132	122	2	D/V/12/L	520	11.4	23	100	Russia
T-90 MBT	45.76	22.5	3	*	125	2	D/V/12/T/L	770	16.8	37	400	Russia
M48 Medium	46.43	22.58	4	120	90	2	D/V/12/A	750	16.2	38	290	USA
Al-Khalid	47.2	22.67	3	*	125	2	D	925	19.6	34	310	Pakistan
TR-125	47.24	22.83	3	*	125	2	D/V/12/L	880	18.6	37	335	Romania
Type 90-2 MBT	47.24	23.0	3	*	125	2	D/V/8/T/L	1200	25.0	37	248	China
T-35 Heavy	49.2	31.83	11	30	76 + 2 × 37	5	P/V/12/L	500	10.2	19	93	Russia
Type 90 MBT	49.21	24.58	3	*	120	2	D/V/10/T/L	1500	30.5	43	217	Japan
OF-40/120	48.22	28.0	4	*	120	2	M/S/V/10/L	1000	20.7	40	375	Italy
Black Prince	50.0	28.92	5	150	76	2	P/F/12/L	350	7.0	11	100	UK
Type 88 MBT	50.19	24.58	4	*	105	3	D/V/12/L	1200	23.9	40	310	S Korea
Centurion	51.0	25.67	4	152	76/84/105	2	P/V/12/L	650	12.7	22	120	UK
Ariete C1	51.18	24.83	4	*	120	2	D/V/12/T/L	1200	23.5	40	340	Italy
T-10 Heavy	51.18	24.33	4	250	122	2	D/V/12/L	700	13.7	28	155	Russia
M60A3 Medium	51.78	22.83	4	120	105	2	D/V/12/A	750	14.5	30	300	USA
KV-2	53.0	22.33	6	100	152	2	D/V/12/L	600	11.3	16	125	Russia
Leclerc	53.64	22.58	3	*	120	2	D/V/8/T/L	1500	28.0	44	340	France
Vickers MBT Mark 7	53.77	23.33	4	*	120	2	D/V/12/T/L	1500	27.9	45	340	UK
Chieftain	54.1	24.67	4	*	120	2	M/VO/12/L	750	13.9	30	310	UK
Leclerc Tropicalisé	54.13	22.58	3	*	120	2	D/V/8/T/L	1500	27.7	44	340	France
Sabra	54.13	27.08	4	*	120	2	D/V/12/T/L	908	16.8	30	280	Israel
Leopard 2 MBT	54.28	25.33	4	*	120	2	D/V/12/T/L	1500	27.6	45	340	Germany
Olifant 1/A	55.12	25.58	4	*	105	2	D/V/12/L	750	13.6	27	310	S Africa
M103 Heavy	55.8	22.92	5	178	120	2	P/V/12/A	810	14.5	21	80	USA
T32 Heavy	55.8	23.25	5	203	90	3	P/V/12/L	770	13.8	22	75	USA

Name	Weight	Length	Crew	Armour	Armament		Engine	Power	PWR	Speed	Range	Country
Tiger	56.1	20.58	5	110	88	2	P/V/12/L	700	12.5	24	62	Germany
M6 Heavy	56.47	24.75	6	83	76 + 37	2	P/R/9/A	800	14.2	22	100	USA
Khalid	57.0	21.0	4	*	120	2	D/V/12/L	1200	21.0	30	310	UK/Jordan
Arjun	57.08	32.17	4	*	120	1	D/V/12/T/L	1400	24.5	45	250	India
Olifant 1/B	57.08	27.17	4	*	105	2	D/V/12/L	940	16.6	36	310	S Africa
Merkava 1	59.05	24.42	4	*	105	3	D/V/12/L	900	15.2	29	250	Israel
Challenger 1	61.0	26.25	4	*	120	3	D/V/12/L	1200	19.7	35	240	UK
Merkava 3	61.02	24.92	4	*	120	3	D/V/12/T/L	1200	19.7	34	310	Israel
Challenger 2	61.5	27.33	4	*	120	3	D/V/12/L	1200	19.2	36	285	UK
Challenger 2E	61.5	27.33	4	*	120	3	D/V/12/T/L	1500	24	45	340	UK
T29 Heavy	62.05	25.0	6	105	105	4	P/V/12/L	770	12.4	22	?	USA
Abrams M1A2	62.09	31.0	4	*	120	2	M/GT	1500	24.2	45	310	USA
T34 Heavy	62.95	24.25	6	105	129	4	P/V/12/L	810	12.9	22	80	USA
PzKpfw 7 (VK6501)	63.97	23.0	5	100	75	2	P/V/12/L	600	9.4	12	?	Germany
T30 Heavy	64.74	24.17	6	105	155	3	P/V/12/A	819	12.5	22	?	USA
Conqueror	65.0	38.0	4	200	120	1	P/V/12/L	810	12.5	21	95	UK
Char 2C	68.0	33.67	12	45	75	4	2 × P/L	360	5.3	10	?	France
King Tiger	68.3	23.75	5	180	88	2	P/V/12/L	700	10.3	21	105	Germany
TOG 1	80.0	33.25	6	62	76 + 40	1	D	600	7.5	8.5	?	UK
T28 Super Heavy	84.82	36.5	8	305	105	1	P/V/8/L	410	4.8	8	100	USA
Flying Elephant	100.0	26.75	8	76	57	6	2 × P/6/L	210	2.1	2	?	UK
E-100	137.8	33.67	5	200	170	1	P/V/12/L	800	5.8	25	75	Germany
K-Wagen	148.0	42.58	22	30	4 × 77	7	2 × P/6/L	1300	8.8	?	?	Germany
Maus	188.0	33.08	5	240	128 + 75	1	P/V/12/L	1080	5.8	12	120	Germany

SPECIAL PURPOSE VEHICLES

This category includes vehicles specifically designed for bridging, recovery, repair, mine clearing and similar tasks.

4K 7FA SB20 Greif ARV Austria
Steyr-Daimler-Puch

1976. The Grief ARV is a variant of the Panzerjäger SK105 tank destroyer and as a result it is a fairly light ARV. However, it is able to cope with both the tank destroyer and the Saurer APC (*qv*), which is all that the Austrian Army needs. It is well equipped and has a full range of tools and welding equipment as a standard load. The crane is hydraulic and has a telescoping jib with a lift of 14,300lb (6,500kg). The main winch is in the lower front hull, with the cable leading out through an opening in the front plate. There is 328ft (100m) of cable with a pull of 44,000lb (20,000kg). A small bulldozer blade on the front steadies the vehicle when it is winching or lifting. There are floodlights for night work, but no night-driving aids.

Armament: 1 × MG
Armour: 12mm
Crew: 4
Weight: 19.48 tons (19,800kg)
Length: 20ft 8in (6.30m)
Width: 8ft 2in (2.50m)
Height: 7ft 9in (2.37m)
Engine: Steyr Type 7FA, 6-cylinder, diesel, 320bhp at 2,300rpm
Speed: 40mph (63km/hr)
Range: 280 miles (450km)

4KH 7FA-Pi Pioneer and Engineer Vehicle Austria
Steyr-Daimler-Puch

This is the same basic vehicle as the armoured recovery vehicle described above, but with special equipment for the pioneer and combat engineer role, It carries a much larger bulldozer blade at the front of the hull, has a more powerful winch, and instead of the ARV's crane there is a hydraulic excavator arm.

Data: as for the ARV, except
Weight: 18.7 tons (19,000kg)

AMX-10 ECH Armoured Repair Vehicle France
Creusot-Loire

1977. The ECH is a variant of the AMX-10P MICV and it is intended to be the repair vehicle of a unit using this type. It has insufficient power to recover dead vehicles and it is foreseen as limiting its activities to changing engines and similar components while in the field and without additional workshop help. In construction it is virtually an armoured personnel carrier, with the same turret and armament, but with a crane mounted at the rear. This crane is operated by a driver who has to stand with his head out of a hatch. It is hydraulic and has an extending jib, which will lift 13,200lb (6,000kg).

Armament: 1 × 20mm cannon; 1 × coaxial MG
Armour: 30mm estimated
Crew: 5
Weight: 13.58 tons (13,500kg)
Length: 18ft 1in (5.82m)
Width: 9ft 2in (2.78m)
Height: 8ft 7in (2.62m)
Engine: Hispano-Suiza HS115, V-8, supercharged diesel, 276bhp at 3,000rpm
Speed: 40mph (65km/hr)
Range: 370 miles (600km)

AMX-13 Bridgelayer France
Creusot-Loire

1958. This vehicle is the standard AMX-13 with a folding bridge on the superstructure in place of the turret. There is an hydraulic motor driven off the engine to provide the power for the bridgelaying operation, and two steadying spades are driven into the ground to support the vehicle while lowering the bridge. The vehicle was adopted in several countries other than France.

Armament: none
Crew: 3
Weight: 19.39 tons (19,700kg) with bridge
Length: 25ft 5in (7.75m)
Length of bridge: 45ft 10in (14m)
Width: 10ft 0in (3.05m)
Width of bridge: 10ft 0in (3.05m)
Height: 14ft 2in (4.3m) with bridge
Other details: as for the AMX-13 tank

AMX-13 ARV France
Roanne

1952. This vehicle is a variant of the AMX-13 tank. In place of the turret there is a small box-like structure for the commander and winch operator. An A-frame jib is carried on the rear deck and swings forward for lifting; it can lift a maximum of 11,000lb (5,000kg). There are two winches, the main one with 164ft (50m) of cable and a pull of 35,273lb (16,000kg) and a secondary one which has 393ft (120m) of cable and can pull 3,500lb (2,000kg). Four spades steady the hull. A large number of these ARVs has been built and they are in service in several countries.

Armament: 1 × MG
Armour: 40mm
Crew: 3
Weight: 13.9 tons (14,125kg)
Length: 18ft 1in (5.51m)
Width: 8ft 6in (2.62m)
Height: 8ft 8in (2.68m)
Other details: as for the AMX-13 tank

AMX-30 Bridgelayer France
Roanne

1978. The AMX-30 bridgelayer took some time to be accepted into French Army service, the principal stumbling-block being the enormous cost of using a main battle tank as the carrier vehicle. It is the basic tank chassis with a folding bridge on top controlled by an hydraulic motor operating rams to provide the power. It can be laid inside ten minutes and when opened fully will span a 72-foot (22m)

gap. The tank is identical to the AMX-30, the only difference being that the turret is removed and the flat top of the hull is prepared for carrying and erecting the bridge. There is an extra hydraulic motor in the engine compartment, but all major features are unchanged.

Armament: none
Armour: not disclosed
Crew: 3
Weight: 42.32 tons (43,000kg)
Length: 37ft 6in (11.43m) with bridge
Width: 12ft 11in (3.95m)
Height: 14ft 1in (4.29m) with bridge
Engine: Hispano-Suiza HS-110, V-12, multi-fuel, 700bhp at 2,400rpm
Speed: 31mph (50km/hr)
Range: 375 miles (600km)

AMX-30 ARV France
Roanne

1975. This vehicle is a modified AMX-30 tank with the turret removed and another superstructure fitted. It carries a substantial crane on the right side of this superstructure and has a large bulldozer blade on the front. When using the crane the blade is lowered to provide stability, and the lift of the crane is between 4 and 15 tons depending on the angle of the jib. There are two winches, a main one with 295ft (90m) of cable and a pull of 77,000lb (35,000kg) and a secondary one with 393ft (120m) of cable and a pull of 8,800lb (4,000kg). The vehicle can be used for lifting engines out of other tanks, and there is provision on the decking for carrying a spare AMX-30 engine.

Armament: 1 × MG
Crew: 3
Weight: 39.37 tons (40,000kg)
Length: 23ft 6in (7.18m)
Height: 8ft 6in (2.65m)
Speed: 37mph (60km/hr)
Range: 375 miles (600km)
Other details: as for the AMX-30 tank

AMX-30 Combat Engineer Tractor France
Roanne

Like the companion ARV, this is based upon the AMX-30 tank chassis, with considerable modification to fit its combat role. The normal turret is replace by a smaller turret with large cupola, in which are mounted a demolition mortar and a machine gun. There is a bulldozer blade at the front and a powerful winch at the rear, a folding jib for light lifting, and various items of equipment for mine-laying and clearing, obstacle construction and other battlefield tasks.

Armament: 1 × 142mm mortar; 1 × MG
Armour: 80mm
Crew: 3
Weight: 37.40 tons (38,000kg)
Length: 25ft 11in (7.90m)
Width: 11ft 6in (3.50m)
Height: 9ft 8in (2.94m)
Power: Hispano-Suiza MS110-2, V-12, multi-fuel, 700bhp at 2000rpm
Speed: 40mph (65km/hr)
Range: 310 miles (500km)

Bargnningstrabdvagn 82 ARV Sweden
Hagglund

1973. The Bgbv 82 is a variant of the Pvb 302 armoured personnel carrier, but it is larger, heavier and more powerful. It is one of the very few recovery vehicles not derived from a tank and the reason is that the Swedish S-Tank was comparatively light by modern standards and, moreover, it made no economic sense to adapt such a complex and expensive vehicle for the relatively simple role of a recovery vehicle. The resulting vehicle is perfectly adequate for its role, apart from its light armour, and it is amphibious with minimal preparation, an advantage in Sweden. It protects itself with a turret of the same type as is carried on the APC, and the crew compartment is also similar to the 302. There is a bulldozer blade on the front for moving small obstacles and steadying the vehicle when winching or using the crane. The crane will lift 12,000lb (5,500kg) and the winch will pull 44,000lb (20,000kg) on 475ft (145m) of rope. All equipment can be operated from inside the vehicle with the crew under protection.

Armament: 1 × 20mm cannon
Armour: not disclosed
Crew: 4
Weight: 22.93 tons (23,300kg)
Length: 23ft 9in (7.23m)
Width: 10ft 10in (3.25m)
Height: 8ft 0in (2.45m)
Engine: Volvo-Penta THD-100C, 6-cylinder, diesel, turbocharged, 310bhp at 2,200rpm
Speed: 35mph (56km/hr)
Range: 250 miles (400km)

Bergepanther ARV Germany
MAN, Henschel, Demag

1943. The German Army had long relied on wheeled or semi-tracked wreckers to salvage tanks in the field, but as tanks became larger and heavier these no longer sufficed, and in late 1942 development of a tracked recovery vehicle was begun. The first dozen were provided in June 1943 by simply taking a Panther chassis and hull, without turret, from the production line as it stood. After this, however, the basic hull was improved by the addition of a bulldozer-type spade, which could be dropped to form a ground anchor, a 40-ton winch and a 1.5-ton hoist for changing engines and transmissions. The winch and hoist were in the central compartment, and the hull top was opened up and surrounded by a rectangular open-topped box for the crew. For local protection the Bergepanther was usually provided with two machine guns and some also carried a 20mm anti-aircraft cannon. A total of 447 were made, some being converted from battle-weary tanks sent in for refurbishing.

Armament: 2 × MG or 1 × 20mm automatic cannon
Armour: 80mm
Crew: 5
Weight: 42.32 tons (43,000kg)
Length: 28ft 11in (8.82mm)
Width: 10ft 9in (3.27m)
Height: 9ft 0in (2.74m)
Power: Maybach HL250 P30, V-12, petrol, 700bhp at 3,000rpm
Speed: 28mph (45km/hr)
Range: 200 miles (320km)

Bergepanzer 3 ARV Germany
Conversion by military workshops

By late 1943 it was apparent that the PzKpfw 3 tank was obsolescent, and at the same time more recovery tanks were needed. The obvious course was followed, that of taking PzKpfw 3s that were sent back for overhaul and converting them into Bergepanzer. The tank had its turret removed and a wooden superstructure built up on the hull. Attachment points for a jib crane were fitted at the front and rear of the hull and the crane was carried dismantled on the tank. A heavy-duty winch was fitted, driven from the main engine, and the tank was then provided with an enormous wheeled earth anchor. This could be towed until required, whereupon the wheels were thrown out of alignment and the anchor hook dropped to the ground. The tank then pulled the hook into firm anchorage, after which it could use its winch to pull ditched vehicles out of their predicament. Special wide tracks were fitted, to improve traction in Russian snow, and some 150 were converted throughout 1944.

Armament: 2 × MG
Armour: 50mm
Crew: 3
Weight: 19.0 tons (19,300kg)
Length: 20ft 7in (6.28m)
Width: 9ft 8in (2.95m)
Height: 8ft 0in (2.45m)
Power: Maybach HL120TRM V-12 petrol, 300bhp at 3,000rpm
Speed: 25mph (40km/hr)
Range: 125 miles (200km)

Bergepanzer 4 ARV Germany
Conversion by military workshops

These were conversions of PzKpfw 4 gun tanks by removal of the turret and armament and construction of a wooden superstructure on top of the hull. An A-frame crane jib and winch were installed on the rear engine deck, and a variety of timber baulks and towing cables were stowed on the hull. No dimensions are available, but they would be essentially those of the PzKpfw 4, Ausf D or E except for a reduction in weight due to the absence of the turret.

Bergepanzer 38(t) ARV Germany
BMKD

1944. This was developed to accompany the Hetzer tank destroyer units and carry out battlefield recovery. It was simply the hull and running gear of the Panzer 38(t) tank, with the hull top removed to leave an open crew compartment into which a winch was mounted. A light A-frame crane was carried dismounted and could be assembled to anchorage points on the hull when required. A total of 170 were built, of which 106 were new and the remainder converted from Hetzer tank destroyers.

Armament: 1 × MG
Armour: 60mm
Crew: 4
Weight: 14.27 tons (14,500kg)
Length: 16ft 0in (4.87m)
Width: 7ft 7in (2.63m)
Height: 5ft 7in (1.71m)
Power: Praga AC/2, 6-cylinder petrol, 160bhp at 2,800rpm
Speed: 26mph (42km/hr)
Range: 110 miles (177km)

Biber Bridgelaying Tank Germany
Atlas-MaK

1973. Biber ('Beaver') is based on a modified Leopard 1 tank chassis and hull, the turret being omitted and the hull completely roofed in. At the rear of the hull is the mounting for a cantilever arm, which supports the bridge unit. The bridge is in two sections, carried one above the other, and is made of aluminium alloy. To lay the bridge the tank is driven forward to the gap and then lowers a bulldozer blade at the front to act as a support. The lower section of the bridge is then slid forward, beneath the upper section, until the ends align, whereupon the upper section is lowered and locked to form a solid unit. This is now extended, by means of the cantilever arm, across the gap and then lowered into place. The tank can then disconnect and retire, leaving the bridge in place, and it can return later to recover the bridge by a reversal of the laying process. The bridge will span a 65-foot (20m) gap and will support a maximum weight of 60 tonnes.

Armament: none
Armour: 40mm
Crew: 2
Weight: 44.29 tons (45,000kg) with bridge
Length: 38ft 3in (11.65m) with bridge
Width: 13ft 1in (4.00m) with bridge
Height: 11ft 6in (3.50m) with bridge
Engine: MTU, V-10, multi-fuel, 830bhp at 2,200rpm
Speed: 40mph (65km/hr)
Range: 340 miles (550km)

BLG-60 Bridgelayer East Germany/Poland
State factories

A variant of the Russian T-55 tank, this was built as a cooperative venture by the East German and Polish authorities. The bridge folds in two halves across the top of the tank and is unfolded by an hydraulic ram and laid to the front of the tank. The tank itself is the usual turret-less T-55 conversion, with the crew compartment covered over.

Armament: 1 × MG
Armour: 100mm
Crew: 3
Weight: 36.41 tons (37,000kg) with bridge
Length: 34ft 8in (10.57m)
Length of bridge: 70ft 10in (21.60m)
Gap spanned: 65ft 7in (20m)
Bridge capacity: 49.21 tons (50,000kg)
Other details: as for the T-55

Borgward B4 Demolition Robots
Germany
Hansa-Loyd, Borgward

1941. This originated in 1939 as the **B1**, a small, cheap, remote-controlled tractor which would tow a mine-clearing roller into a minefield so as to detonate mines. Being cheap, it would be expendable should it perish in the blast. But the device proved to be more expensive than anticipated and the idea was dropped. By this time Goliath (*below*) was being criticised because it could not carry a sufficiently heavy charge to deal with some of the more formidable obstacles found in Russia and the B1 was revived as the B4.

B4 was basically a small tracked vehicle to the front of which a large explosive charge container was hooked. The hull hatch could be opened and a driver then got in and drove the vehicle in the normal way as far as he could safely go; he then dismounted, closed the hatch, and the remainder of the mission was completed by radio remote control. Once the vehicle arrived at the target, the charge was released and the vehicle backed away. Dropping the charge activated a delay device which detonated the explosive after a short interval. This allowed the vehicle to be taken clear of the blast, turned and driven back to be used again. In practice, however, it was found that the delay mechanism usually failed and the vehicle was destroyed by the detonation of the charge as soon as it was released.

Payload: 1 × 1,100lb (500kg) explosive charge
Armour: 10mm
Crew: 1
Weight: 3.60 tons (3,660kg)
Length: 12ft 0in (3.65m)
Width: 5ft 11in (1.80m)
Height: 3ft 10in (1.19m)
Engine: Borgward, 6-cylinder, petrol, 49bhp at 3,3000rpm
Speed: 24mph (38km/hr)

Brobandvagn 941 Armoured Bridgelayer Sweden
Hagglund

1973. This was a variant of Pbv 302 APC and without its bridge the hull looks much like an APC without its cupolas and armament. The bridge weighed seven tons and could carry vehicles up to 50 tons in weight across a 49 foot (15m) gap. It was a single span and was laid by an original method devised by Hagglund. In outline it amounts to first pushing a telescopic rail across the gap, sliding the one-piece bridge over the rail and then withdrawing the rail leaving the bridge in place. This is a much less conspicuous way of laying a bridge than the more usual type of folding span, but it does restrict the length that can be carried on the vehicle. Recovering the bridge is the reverse of this operation, and both take no more than five minutes.

Armament: none
Crew: 4
Weight: 28.93 tons (29,400kg) with bridge
Length: 55ft 9in (17.00m) with bridge
Width: 13ft 2in (4.02m) with bridge
Height: 10ft 6in (3.23m) with bridge
Other details: as for the Pbv 302

Bruckenleger 4 Bridgelayer Germany
Krupp, Magirus

1940. The German Army began experiments with armoured bridgelayers as early as 1938 and in 1939 work was started on a design using the PzKpfw 4 tank. Two types were developed, one by Krupp, which used a pivoted A-frame to swing the bridge span from the top of the tank across the gap (rather like a present-day skip or dumpster truck), and one by Magirus which used hydraulic rams and a tipping frame to slide the bridge span across the gap. Although 60 were ordered, only 20 were built before the contract was cancelled. Four bridgelayers were attached to each of five of the ten Panzer divisions used in France in 1940, but they saw little use, and as a result the remainder of the order was stopped. The Germans realised that tactical surprise was worth any number of bridgelaying tanks, and by 1941 almost all the bridgelayers had been converted back into combat tanks.

Armament: 1 × MG
Armour: 30mm
Crew: 2
Weight: 28 tons (28,450kg) with bridge
Length: 36ft 1in (11.00m) with bridge
Width: 9ft 10in (3.00m) with bridge
Height: 11ft 7in (3.54m) with bridge
Bridge span: 29ft 6in (9m)
Bridge capacity: 29.52 tons (30,000kg)
Engine: Maybach, V-12, petrol, 300bhp at 3,000rpm
Speed: 25mph (40km/hr)
Range: 125 miles (200km)

Bruckenlegerpanzer 68 Switzerland
Federal Works

1984. This is based on the chassis and hull of the PZ-68 tank, the turret being removed and the hull roofed over. The bridge is a solid span and is laid in a manner similar to the Swedish system described in the Brobandvagn 941 entry above. The vehicle stops short of the obstacle, a beam is extended across to the far bank, the bridge is then slid across the beam and into position, and the beam is then withdrawn.

Armament: none
Crew: 3

Weight: 43.90 tons (44,600kg) with bridge
Length: 59ft 9in (18.23m) with bridge
Width: 9ft 11in (3.00m) with bridge
Bridge length: 59ft 9in (18.2m)
Bridge capacity: 59 tons (60,000kg)
Engine: MTU 8-cylinder, diesel, 630bhp at 2,200rpm
Speed: 20mph (32km/hr)
Range: 125 miles (200km)

BTS Series ARVs Russia
State factories

The BTS series shows a steady progression of improvement as experience was gained with ARVs. They were based upon the T-54/55 tank chassis and the first model, **BTS-1**, which appeared in the mid-1950s, was simply a T-54 without a turret. It was followed by **BTS-2** in 1959, which was the same vehicle, but now with a winch, a rear spade to act as an earth anchor when winching, and racking and storage space for various tools.

1963 saw the **BTS-3** in service. This added an hydraulic crane for engine changing, a bulldozer blade at the front in addition to the rear spade, and saw some changes in the ancillary equipment and tool stowage. Finally the **BTS-4** moved the crane from the left front of the hull to a position roughly midway along the left side of the tank

Büffel ARV Germany
MaK, Krauss-Maffei

1991. Büffel ('Buffalo') is the recovery vehicle version of the Leopard 2 MBT, a total of 100 being built in the early 1990s. As with the later Leopard conversions, the turret was removed and an armoured superstructure built above the driver's position and extending back to the crew compartment. On the right side of this structure is a traversing crane, and the vehicle also carries a powerful winch and a bulldozer blade which can act as a ground anchor when winching and as a stabilizer when using the crane.

Carrot UK

Also called **Light Carrot**, this was simply a charge of explosive in a rectangular box carried in a boom about 6 feet/2 metres in front of any convenient tank (usually a Churchill). The idea was to defeat minor obstacles by driving the tank up until the explosive charge was pressed against the obstacle, and then detonating it. The subsequent blast would remove or damage the obstacle without causing damage to the tank or crew. The maximum charge which could be detonated in safety was 25lb (11kg); since this could only remove small obstacles which

the tank could probably climb over anyway, the idea was abandoned.

Centurion ARV UK
ROF Leeds

1947. The Centurion armoured recovery vehicle was developed from the Centurion battle tank. and the first version, the **Mark 1**, was simply a standard Centurion fitted with towing equipment. This was soon abandoned in favour of a more purpose-built version. The **Mark 2** had a superstructure of 30mm armour plate built up over the hull in place of the turret, a rear-mounted spade to act as a ground anchor, and a 30-ton winch. A jib crane capable of lifting 1 ton was carried unshipped and could be rapidly assembled when required. A cupola on top of the superstructure was armed with a machine gun for local defence, and smoke dischargers were also fitted.

Mark 2

Armament: 1 × MG
Armour: 76mm
Crew: 4
Length: 29ft 5in (8.97m)
Width: 11ft 1in (3.37m)
Height: 9ft 6in (2.90m)
Weight: 49.50 tons (50,292kg)
Engine: Rolls-Royce Meteor, 650bhp at 2,550rpm
Speed: 21mph (34km/hr)
Range: 62 miles (100km)

Centurion AVRE UK
ROF Leeds

This was a Centurion Mark 5 with the turret gun removed and replaced by a 165mm demolition gun and with an hydraulically-operated bulldozer blade mounted on the hull front. Various attachment points for specialist equipment were provided and there was a towing connection for the Giant Viper mine-clearing rocket apparatus trailer.

Armament: 1 × 165mm gun; 2 × MG
Armour: 118mm
Crew: 5
Weight: 51 tons (51,810kg)
Length: 28ft 6in (8.69m)
Width: 13ft 0in (3.96m)
Height: 9ft 10in (3.0m)
Power: Rolls-Royce V-12 petrol, 650bhp at 2,550rpm
Speed: 21mph (34km/hr)
Range: 110 miles (175km)

Centurion BARV (Beach ARV) UK
ROF Leeds
A variant of the Centurion tank. The turret was removed and the hull built up into a superstructure with a shaped prow, and the entire vehicle was waterproofed, with air induction and exhaust above the superstructure level. The resulting vehicle could operate in 9ft 6in (2.90m) of water and was intended to be landed early in an amphibious operation so as to be able to rescue tanks and other vehicles which, launched from landing craft into too deep water, might 'drown' their engines and require towing out before they drowned their crews as well. Weight 40 tons (40,643kg). Only 12 were built.

Centurion Bridgelayer UK
ROF Leeds
1954. This vehicle appeared in the early 1950s to replace the Churchill bridgelayer, which had remained in service since the war. The standard hull and chassis were used, without turret, and the single-span bridge was pivoted about a girder extension at the front of the tank so that in the travelling position it lay along the hull top, upside down. When the bridge was to be used the vehicle was driven to the edge of the gap and, with hydraulic rams, the entire spanning unit was turned about its pivot through 180° so that it was lowered across the gap. Once the bridge was in place the tank could be disconnected and backed away. The span could be used immediately by tracked vehicles; for use by wheeled vehicles a centre deck between the treadways had to be laid by hand. Laying the bridge took only two minutes, and it could be recovered in four minutes by the tank reconnecting and lifting it back into the travelling position.

Armament: 1 × MG
Crew: 3
Weight: 49.69 tons (50,485kg) with bridge
Length: 53ft 6in (16.30m) with bridge
Width: 14ft 0in (4.26m) with bridge
Height: 12ft 9in (3.88m) with bridge
Bridge span: 45ft (13.72m)
Engine: Rolls-Royce, 12-cylinder, petrol, 650bhp at 2,550rpm

Chieftain ARV UK
Vickers
1974. Introduction of this vehicle to replace the Centurion ARV, began in 1974. It uses the Chieftain Mark 5 hull, which is considerably modified by removing the turret and converting the interior into two compartments, of which one carries the crew

and the other two independent winches, one with 30-ton and one with 3-ton capacity. These winches are driven by hydraulic motors and a power take-off from the main engine. An hydraulically actuated earth spade is fitted, and also a bulldozer blade at the front of the vehicle. A cupola on top of the hull carries a machine gun for local defence.

Armament: 1 × MG
Armour: not disclosed
Crew: 4
Weight: 51.18 tons (52,000kg)
Length: 27ft 1in (8.25m)
Width: 11ft 7in (3.52m)
Height: 9ft 0in (2.74m)
Engine: Leyland 12-cylinder, vertically-opposed, 2-stroke, multi-fuel, 720bhp at 2,250rpm
Speed: 26mph (42km/hr)
Range: 200 miles (325km)

Chieftain AVRE UK
Vickers
1986. Although a Chieftain AVRE was designed together with the MBT, it was never adopted, and eventually, in desperation, the British Army converted a dozen Chieftain gun tanks into home-made AVREs for use by the armoured corps in Germany. The conversion consisted of little more than removing the turret and fitting a set of rails to carry fascines. This appears to have spurred the Treasury to find some money, and in 1989 Vickers were instructed to built 48 new AVRE tanks. These were built on standard Chieftain hull and chassis units provided by the army, and involved replacing the turret with a raised superstructure and commander's cupola and installing a winch, crane and various racks for the carriage of engineer stores. There are also fitments to which a variety of specialised equipment can be attached, such as a bulldozer blade, mine-clearing rollers or ploughs, fascines and trackways.

Armament: 1 × MG
Armour: not disclosed
Crew: 3
Weight: 51 tons (51,810kg)
Length: 24ft 8in (7.52m)
Width: 12ft 0in (3.66m)
Height: 9ft 6in (2.89m)
Power: Leyland L60, 12-cylinder, horizontally opposed, multi-fuel, 730bhp at 2,100rpm
Speed: 30mph (48km/hr)
Range: 310 miles (500km)

Chieftain Bridgelayer UK
ROF Leeds

1974. This consists of a standard Chieftain hull and running gear, without turret, and with a folded bridge (Bridge, Tank, No. 8) on top, the front end of which is carried on an extended girder structure. Hydraulic pumps driven from the engine actuate five rams, which, applied to various parts of the bridge, cause it to pivot at its forward end and then unfold so as to stretch out in front of the tank and span a gap of up to 75 feet (22.9m) in width. It takes between three and five minutes to unfold the bridge, after which the tank casts itself clear and backs away. When necessary, the tank can return, hook on to the bridge, and recover it in about ten minutes. The bridge span is made of light alloy and weighs only 26,900lb (12,200kg). A shorter bridge (Bridge, Tank, No. 9), capable of carrying heavier loads, is also available; this is carried on the tank in one single unit and pivoted through 180° to be laid in front.

Armament: none
Crew: 3
Weight: 52.46 tons (53,300kg) with bridge
Length: 45ft 1in (13.74m) with bridge
Width: 13ft 9in (4.16m) with bridge
Height: 12ft 9in (3.88m) with bridge
Bridge span: 75ft (22.86m)
Engine: Leyland, 12-cylinder, multi-fuel, 720bhp at 2,250rpm

Churchill ARK UK

ARK was an acronym for Armoured Ramp Karrier, and the purpose of this specialized vehicle was to land on a beach and then, by means of ramps folded on top of the hull, provide a means for other vehicles to overcome beach walls and esplanades. The basic vehicle is the Churchill tank hull and running gear, the turret being absent. The flat deck had timber trackways bolted to it with folding ramps at each end. The tactic was to drive the tank up to the wall, lower the front ramp on to the top of the wall and the rear ramp on to the beach, after which other tanks and vehicles could drive up the rear ramp, along the hull and up the forward ramp to gain the top of the wall and the usual roadway which edged the beach. It was also used to cross ditches by driving into the ditch and unfolding the ramps, and in extremis a second ARK could be driven on top to reduce the slope of the ramps in a deep ditch.

Armament: none
Armour: 88mm
Crew: 4

Weight: 37.77 tons (38,385kg)
Length: 24ft 5in (7.44m)
Width: 8ft 0in (2.43m)
Height: 7ft 0in (2.13m)
Power: Bedford 12-cylinder, petrol, 350bhp at 2,200rpm
Speed: 8mph (12km/hr)
Range: 90 miles (145km)

Churchill AVRE UK
Cockbridge (conversion kits), MG (actual conversion of tanks)

1943. The Dieppe Raid in 1942 indicated that a specialized armoured vehicle was needed for use by combat engineers clearing obstacles from beaches. After considering various tanks, the Churchill was selected since it offered maximum protection and ample space for stowage of the various items of engineer equipment. In order to provide the vehicle with the capability of smashing concrete or other obstacles, a special spigot mortar was mounted on the turret. This fired a fin-stabilized bomb carrying 40lb (18kg) of high explosive, capable of breaching most types of obstacle at short range, and from its shape and low velocity it gained the nickname of the Flying Dustbin.

The interior of the tank was stripped of the usual ammunition racks and converted for engineer stores, demolition equipment, tools and similar items. After extensive trials the design was accepted and in 1943 work began on converting Churchill tanks into AVREs (Armoured Vehicles, Royal Engineers). The first 108 were converted by army workshops, the remainder by the MG Car Company. AVRE tanks were frequently used as a basis for attaching other special devices and could be found with a wide variety of brackets and attachments on the outside. They proved to be invaluable in the invasion of Europe and in the subsequent advance into Germany, and remained in use for several years after the war.

Armament: 1 × 'Petard' spigot mortar with 26 bombs; 1 × MG
Armour: 88mm
Crew: 6
Weight: 38 tons (38,610kg)
Length: 25ft 2in (7.67m)
Width: 10ft 8in (3.25m)
Height: 8ft 2in (2.48m)
Engine: Bedford, 12-cylinder, petrol, 350bhp at 2,200rpm
Speed: 15mph (24km/hr)
Range: 120 miles (200km)

Churchill Assault Bridge AVRE UK

1944. Whilst a proper bridge-carrying tank had been developed on the Churchill chassis, it was designed for crossing major obstacles, and the Canadian Army, in training for the invasion of Europe, felt that something smaller was needed to cope with anti-tank ditches, parapets and the lesser obstacles which might be met on the beachheads. Their solution was to mount a 34-foot (10.40m) SBG (Small Box Girder) bridge on the front of a Churchill AVRE. It was carried in an elevated position, the weight taken by a winch cable from the rear of the tank, and by simply releasing the winch brake the bridge could be rapidly dropped ahead of the tank across the obstacle. It could bear a weight of 40 tons, and as well as bridging gaps it could be used to surmount walls; the bridge was dropped against the wall, after which a second AVRE, could drive up the bridge and drop fascines (bundles of brushwood) over the wall so as to cushion its landing as it drove over.

Churchill Bridgelayer UK
Military workshops

1942. After trying various expedients for crossing ditches, this design really introduced the concept of a bridgelaying tank as it is known today. It consisted of a turretless Churchill tank carrying a 30-foot (9.14m) bridge span on its deck, complete with a hydraulic system which would lift the bridge on a pivoting arm and lay it horizontally in front of the vehicle. It was then disconnected and the vehicle withdrawn, leaving the bridge in position for the advancing combat tanks to use. It could support a 60-ton weight. The carrier was a Churchill Mark 3 or Mark 4 with the fighting compartment largely filled with the hydraulic machinery. The vehicle, with bridge weighed 40.8 tons (41,450kg).

Churchill Carpet Obstacle Crosser UK

1944. During World War II, when the British and their allies were preparing for the invasion of Europe, gapping wire on landing beaches was seen as a major potential problem, and the gaps had to be capable of being passed not only by foot soldiers but also by wheeled vehicles. As a result, the Carpet tank was developed. The Carpet Churchill was a standard Churchill tank complete with armament, which carried on its front two arms supporting a drum. On this drum was wound a length of reinforced hessian matting, the free end of which was weighted. Hydraulic arms, or winches in some models, lifted the drum well into the air so that the driver could see where he was going. Once landed

and approaching the wire, the drum was lowered and the weighted end of the matting allowed to fall free on the ground, where it was run over by the tank's tracks. This held the mat down, and as the tank went forward the remainder unwound from the drum. As the tank crossed the wire obstacle, so the carpet unrolled beneath it and was laid on top of the crushed wire, providing a smooth path for troops and vehicles. Several minor variants existed, each showing some small improvement on its predecessor.

Combat Engineer Tractor UK
ROF Leeds

1971. There are times when a versatile engineer vehicle is required in the combat zone, and for this purpose the British Army developed the 'Combat Engineer Tractor' in the early 1970s. The CET consists of an aluminium armoured hull on a torsion-bar tracked suspension. The two-man crew is seated at the front, and the controls are arranged so that either can drive the vehicle. Their seats can be reversed to give them command of the rear when operating some of the equipment. At the rear end is an excavator bucket of light alloy with steel cutting edges, which kit can be used for digging or bulldozing, or as an earth anchor when winching. A crane can be attached to the bucket and used in conjunction with the vehicle winch. On top of the hull a rocket-propelled ground anchor is carried; this can be fired from the vehicle to a distance of just over 100 yards (90m), where it digs into the ground and gives purchase to allow the winch to pull the vehicle out of soft ground, water or up otherwise insuperable obstacles. The CET can also tow a trailer with Giant Viper mine-clearing rocket equipment. The vehicle is amphibious, being propelled in water by two water jet units; additional buoyancy is provided by a plastic foam block carried in the bucket when swimming. Full night-vision aids are carried and the vehicle is proofed against all forms of NBC attack.

Armament: 1 × MG
Armour: not disclosed
Crew: 2
Weight: 16.8 tons (17,100kg)
Length: 24ft 9in (7.50m)
Width: 9ft 6in (2.90m)
Height: 8ft 6in (2.60m)
Engine: Rolls-Royce, 6-cylinder, turbocharged diesel, 320bhp at 2,100rpm
Speed: 37mph (60km/hr)
Range: 300 miles (480km)

Crab UK

1944. Also called **Sherman Crab**. A mine-clearing 'flail' tank which carried a revolving drum on arms, ahead of the vehicle, to which were attached lengths of chain. The drum was driven by a separate engine, mounted on an armoured box on the side of the tank hull. When running, the drum revolved and the chains thrashed the ground ahead of the tank in an entirely random manner, so that any buried mine would be detonated. The chains, being flexible, suffered little damage from the blast and in any case could be easily replaced. In this respect the flail was superior to ploughs and rollers, which were more seriously damaged when they detonated a mine.

Data: as for the M4A3 Sherman, except
Speed when flailing: 2–3mph (3–5km/hr)

CV 33 Bridgelayer Italy
Maker unknown

1936. A small number of CV 33 tankettes were fitted with a bridge which could be laid in front of the vehicle. The bridge was in one piece and was a little longer than the CV 33 itself. It was carried on a lightweight tubular structure which winched it forward and down to the ground, motive power being provided by the crew. It seems likely that the bridge treadways were similar to the ramps that were used for running these small tanks up into their transporter trucks, and the span covered by the bridge was short. Recovering the bridge almost certainly involved the crew in having to get out and attach the lifting links by hand.

Engineer Armored Vehicle USA
See T1 Demolition Tank

Entpannungspanzer 65 ARV Switzerland
Federal Works

1970. The Entp PZ 65 is the standard ARV of the Swiss Army and three of them are on the establishment of every tank battalion The chassis is derived from the PZ 68 tank; the turret and ring are removed and the hull is built up into a square box-like superstructure with a small armoured cupola at the front. There is a bulldozer blade on the front and a substantial winch, which has a pull of 55,000lb (25,000kg) on 400ft (120m) of cable. The lifting gear is an A-frame attached at the front.which can lift 33,000lb (15,000kg), which is sufficient to take a turret off one of the tanks or to replace an engine. There is also the usual range of tools and welding gear for the crew. The vehicle is in service only with the Swiss Army.

Armament: 1 × MG
Armour: not disclosed
Crew: 5
Weight: 38.38 tons (39,000kg)
Length: 24ft 1in (7.34m)
Width: 10ft 4in (3.15m)
Height: 10ft 7in (3.25m)
Engine: MTU MB837, 8-cylinder, horizontally-opposed diesel, 705bhp at 2,200rpm
Speed: 34mph (55km/hr)
Range: 186 miles (300km)

Goat UK

1943. Goat was from the same stable as Carrot and Onion, a demolition charge carried on the front of a tank for dealing with obstacles. This was the most powerful of the three, with 1,800lb (816kg) of explosive fitted to a frame 10ft 6in by 6ft 6in (3.2m x 1.98m) which lay across the front hull of a Churchill AVRE tank. Side arms, hydraulically actuated, could erect the frame to the vertical and then thrust it forward, clear of the tank nose. The tank was then driven forward to place the frame in contact with the obstacle, the frame disconnected, and the tank then backed off to a safe distance and fired the charge by remote control. Several were employed in the D-Day landings in Normandy to demolish beach obstacles and minor strongpoints.

Goliath Demolition Robot Germany
Makers, see below

1940. In 1940 the German Army requested a remote-controlled vehicle that could carry a demolition charge up to an obstacle and there be detonated; it was also to have a secondary purpose as a mine-clearance vehicle, to be driven into a minefield and there detonated so as to set off the mines by blast over-pressure. The result was Goliath, a small tracked unit propelled by electric motors and carrying a 132lb (60kg) charge of explosive. The construction was of simple pressed metal and the electric motors were powered by batteries carried in sponsons, around which ran the tracks. A drum at the rear of the vehicle carried about 1 mile (1.5km) of cable, two strands of which were used to transmit steering signals and the third for the firing signal.

Over 2,500 of these were made and they were extensively used in both demolition and mine-clearing tasks, but it was found that the electric motors and battery power limited the range and power of the vehicles, particularly in cold weather. A second version was therefore developed, powered by a 703cc (42.9 cu in) twin-cylinder, motorcycle engine. The first of these carried a 165lb (75kg) charge, but it was soon replaced by a larger model carrying a 220lb (100kg) charge. Over 4,500 were built.

Goliath E (electric)
Maker: Borgward, Zundapp
Payload: 132lb (60kg) explosive charge
Armour: 5mm
Weight: 828lb (375kg)
Length: 4ft 11in (1.50m)
Width: 2ft 9in (0.85m)
Height: 1ft 10in (56cm)
Engine: 2 × Bosch MM/RQL 2.5kW electric motors
Speed: 6mph (10km/hr)

Goliath V (petrol)
Maker: Zacherts, Zundapp
Payload: 100kg (220lb) explosive charge
Armour: 10mm
Weight: 960lb (435kg)
Length: 5ft 4in (1.63m)
Width: 3ft 0in (0.91m)
Height: 2ft 0in (0.62m)
Engine: Zundapp, 2-cylinder, 703cc, 12.5bhp at 4,500rpm
Speed: 7.5mph (12km/hr)
Range: 7.5 miles (12km)

Grant CDL Tank UK
Vulcan

1942. During World War I a Commander Oscar de Thoren, RN, proposed mounting a powerful light on tanks or other vehicles so as to blind an enemy during a night attack. The idea was not pursued, but he continued to develop it in post-war years. In 1933 several demonstrations were made, and in 1940 the War Office accepted the idea, giving orders for some 300 special turrets to be built. These turrets, designed in the first place for fitting to the Matilda 2 tank, contained a 13 million candlepower arc light and a special reflector, together with a stroboscopic shutter. The effect of this was to emit a dazzling light which temporarily blinded any onlooker and allowed tanks to manoeuvre and concealed bodies of troops at night.

First installations were made on Matilda and Churchill tanks, but it was then found that the turrets could be fitted to M3 Grant tanks, and these became the usual vehicle. The term CDL stands for **Canal Defence Light**, a misleading term adopted as a security measure. A similar conversion was carried out by US units, who called their versions the **Shop Tractor**. In spite of its virtues, the CDL saw very little use; it was deployed at the crossing of the Rhine by both British and US forces, but

functioned principally as a floodlight and not in the manner envisaged by its inventor. It is generally understood that the lack of use was due to excessive secrecy, which concealed the device's ability from commanders, and the lack of troops trained to accompany the CDL tanks in battle. In post-war years the concept was refined and became known as the Xenon Searchlight, but advances in night vision technology have more or less consigned the idea to history.

IMR Combat Engineer Vehicle Russia
State factories

1975. This is a variant of the T-54/55 tank and it appears to be specifically designed for the removal of obstacles and also the building of new ones. In place of the turret there is a small cupola in which the crane operator is seated. He has a large hydraulically operated crane with a telescopic jib and large pincer-like grabs, which can pick up trees and similar objects. There is a bulldozing blade on the front of the hull and an unditching beam at the back. The vehicle was used by Russia and various Warsaw Pact armies.

Armament: none
Armour: 200mm
Crew: 2
Weight: 33.46 tons (34,000kg)
Length: 34ft 5in (10.60m)
Width: 11ft 5in (3.48m)
Height: 11ft 1in (3.37m) to top of crane
Power: Type V5 V-12 diesel, 520bhp at 2,000rpm
Speed: 30mph (48km/hr)
Range: 250 miles (400km)

Infanterie Sturmsteg auf PzKpfw 4
Germany
Magirus

Whichever way the German Army chose to advance in 1939 it would run into permanent fortifications, and much energy and ingenuity was deployed in measures to defeat them. One of the oldest ideas in the attack of a fortified place is the use of scaling ladders to surmount walls and obstacles, and the Stürmsteg ('Assault ladder') was designed as a modern mechanised scaling ladder. Basically it was a Panzer 4 tank chassis and hull carrying a modified fire-engine telescoping ladder. It was only capable of limited elevation, and two machines were built, the theory being that they would go into action side by side in front of the work, extend their ladders to the top of the wall or obstacle, and the two ladders would then be joined by cross-pieces so as to form a wide walk-way up which assault infantry could run. The assumption seems to have been that the defenders would be so astonished by this piece of mechanical ingenuity that they would forebear to shoot at it. This assumption was wrong, and the machines did not survive their first deployment in the French campaign of 1940. No dimensions are available.

It is perhaps worth noting that a similar device was produce by the British in 1943. This was a standard turntable fire-engine ladder mounted on an unarmoured 3-ton truck, and the object was to drive it ashore from a landing craft and erect it so as to scale cliffs, thus permitting troops to land in places which the defenders might be expected to have neglected on the grounds that the cliff was not climbable. A handful were built but the idea was never put to the test of combat.

JS ARVs Russia
State factories

1950. The JS assault gun chassis as used in the SU-122 and SU-152 was also used as the basis of an ARV. Like the ones based on the T-54 there were several types all differing in some slight degree, and all of them more lightly equipped than would be the case in a western army. The nomenclature is confusing, but it can be assumed that all are so similar as to defy recognition except by experts. No data are quoted, but they can be taken to be almost the same as for the SU guns, the only exception being that the height of the ARV will be slightly greater due to the cranes stowed on top.

The **JS-2-T** is simply a JS-2 tank with no turret and a small cupola. There is no equipment at all, and all that the vehicle can do is tow or push. The **JSU-T** is an SU without gun and fitted with a winch. The **JSU-T Model B** has the winch and a crane in addition. The lift of this crane is about 3 tons (3,000kg). The **JSU-T Model C** has no crane but does have a spade at the rear for winching. The **Models D** and **E** differ only in the provision of spades and an A-frame lifting crane. All of them were in service in the Warsaw Pact countries and with their allies until the late 1970s.

Leopard ARV (Bergepanzer 2) Germany
Atlas-MaK

1966. While the Leopard 1 main battle tank was being developed, work also began on an armoured recovery vehicle on the same chassis, and production of these commenced in 1966. The vehicle was designed so as to be able to perform a variety of functions: recover damaged tanks, tow disabled tanks, act as a crane in performing engine changes and, if necessary, lift smaller vehicles; carry a spare engine so as to be able to perform an engine change at any time in the field; bulldoze; and act as a refueller.

The vehicle consists of a basic Leopard 1 hull and chassis without turret. The hull is extended upwards by an armoured superstructure surmounted by a commander's cupola with machine gun. At the side front, next to the driver, is a rotatable crane boom capable of lifting 20 tonnes, and on the front of the hull is a bulldozer blade which can be used for earth-moving or as a support for the tank when the crane or winch is being used. The main hauling winch is inside the hull and can provide a straight pull of 35 tonnes; this can, of course, be increased by judicious use of pulley-blocks.

A platform at the rear of the hull is specially fitted to carry a complete Leopard power pack and an engine/transmission change can be performed in the field in 30 minutes.

Armament: 2 × MG
Armour: 40mm
Crew: 4
Weight: 39.17 tons (39,800kg)
Length: 24ft 10in (7.56m)
Width: 10ft 11in (3.32m)
Height: 8ft 10in (2.69m)
Engine: MTU, V-10, multi-fuel, 830bhp at 2,200rpm
Speed: 40mph (65km/hr)
Range: 530 miles (850km)

Leopard Armoured Engineer Vehicle
Germany

This is the same vehicle as the ARV described above but has provision for carrying explosives in an insulated compartment and also carries an earth auger on the rear platform in place of the spare power pack. A bulldozer blade is available and can be fitted when required, and it is provided with a scarifier to rip up road surfaces and build obstacles.

Dimensions: as for the ARV

Leopard Bridgelayer Germany
See Biber

Lulu UK

1944. An experimental mine detecting apparatus carried on a Sherman tank. It consisted of three large wooden rollers, suspended by telescoping arms, one in front of and two alongside the tank. These contained magnetic anomaly detection equipment which detected the presence of a mine as they passed over it. What happened next has never been made very clear; presumably the tank stopped and called up somebody to remove the mine before proceeding. Which is probably why the idea was abandoned.

M31 ARV USA
Baldwin

In 1942, with heavier tanks entering service, the need for a heavier recovery vehicle than the previous wheeled wrecker became apparent to the US Army, and the first such model was produced by modifying the M3 (Grant/Lee) tank chassis. Major armament was removed, leaving only two machine guns, one in the turret and one in the bow, and the side sponson was closed by a door upon which a dummy gun was mounted. The turret was turned through 180° and a plate fitted in place of the 37mm gun mount to act as the anchorage for a crane arm, which extended over the rear of the hull. This arm was fitted with two support jacks, which could either be pinned into attachments on the vehicle hull or rested on the ground to provide support for lifting heavier loads. A winch in the crew compartment could have its cable fed beneath the hull to front or rear for direct hauling or over a pulley and to the crane arm for hoisting. Stowage boxes were added to the hull in order to carry spare parts and tools. Just over 800 of these vehicles were built before the end of the war and they remained in service until the early 1950s.

Armament: 1 × MG
Armour: 50mm
Crew: 6
Weight: 26.78 tons (27,215kg)
Length: 26ft 5in (8.05m)
Width: 8ft 4in (2.54m)
Height: 9ft 9in (2.97m)
Engine: depending upon original tank converted;
   GMC diesel, V-12, 410bhp at 2,900rpm; or
   Continental petrol, 9-cylinder, radial, 400bhp at
   2,400rpm
Speed: 25mph (40km/hr)
Range: 110 miles (180km)

M32 ARV USA
Lima, Pressed Steel Car, Baldwin, Federal Machine, International Harvester

1943. As the manufacture of M3 tanks ceased, it became necessary to develop a fresh tank recovery vehicle based on the M4 Sherman, and work on this began in April 1943. The turret was removed and replaced by a fixed superstructure with a rounded front made from flat plate; brackets were attached

to the hull sides to which an A-frame jib was pivoted. This could be laid back alongside the turret when not required, or erected over the front of the vehicle to act as a crane. A winch was mounted inside the hull, behind the driver's seat, and could be used for pulling or, in conjunction with the crane, for lifting. The tank's bow machine gun was retained and augmented by a .50-inch machine gun on the turret top, and an 81mm mortar was carried on the left side of the hull and could be brought into action to fire screening smoke bombs to conceal a recovery from enemy observation. Various other detail improvements were made as production continued.

The actual model number of the tank varied according to which version of the M4 was used as the starting point. Thus the M4 tank became the **M32**, the M4A1 the **M32B1**, and so on. First vehicles used the resting boom of the crane as a towbar, but a stronger towbar and hook were later fitted at the rear. The suspension was designed so as to have the springs locked out of action and thus give a more stable platform for winching and lifting. In 1945 the horizontal volute-spring suspension was adopted, adding **A1** to the nomenclature, so that, for example, the M32B1 became the **M32A1B1**. Of the various models of M32 1,599 were built, and they continued to serve for many years after the war.

Armament: 1 × MG
Armour: 50mm
Crew: 4
Weight: 27.68 tons (28,123kg)
Length: 19ft 1in (5.82m)
Width: 8ft 7in (2.62m)
Height: 8ft 9in (2.87m)
Engine: dependent on model of M4 tank converted
Speed: 24mph (39km/hr)
Range: 120 miles (193km)

M47E2 Engineer Tank Spain
Peugeot-Talbot

1980. The Spanish army operated a number of American M47 and M48 medium tanks, and when these were replaced by more modern designs numbers were refurbished by fitting new engines, while others were converted to other roles, and one of these conversions resulted in this engineer tank. The standard M47 tank was given a completely new power pack, a bulldozer blade was fitted on the front, a heavy-duty winch was fitted, and a hydraulic crane, convertible into an earth auger, was mounted on the right hull front.

Armament: 2 × MG
Armour: 100mm
Crew: 4
Weight: 45.96 tons (46,700kg)
Length: 20ft 10in (6.36m)
Width: 11ft 2in (3.39m)
Height: 11ft 0in (3.35m)
Power: Continental 1790-2D, V-12 diesel, 760bhp at
 2,400rpm
Speed: 35mph (56km/hr)
Range: 370 miles (600km)

M48 AVLB USA
Alco
This is a stock M48 tank with the turret removed, the hull decked over, and a scissors bridge attached to the front of the hull and folded back across the hull top. Hydraulically operated, the bridge can be launched to the front of the tank in about three minutes. The carrier tank is then disconnected and withdrawn; it can return and will take about six minutes to recover the bridge and prepare it for travelling.

Armament: 1 × MG
Armour: 100mm
Crew: 2
Weight: 41.0 tons (41,685kg)
Length of bridge: 63ft (19.2m)
Gap spanned: 60ft (18m)
Bridge capacity: 5.90 tons (6,000kg)
Weight: 55.84 tons (55,746kg) with bridge
Other details: as for M48 tank

M60 AVLB USA
Chrysler
1963. This is basically an M60 battle tank with the turret removed and the hull covered over. On top is carried a scissors bridge unit, hinged to the front of the hull and extended by hydraulic rams. As the bridge is hinged forward the upper section unfolds, and as the bridge reaches the horizontal, so the two units lock securely to form a single rigid span. The bridge will span a gap of 60 feet (18.29m) and can be emplaced in three minutes; it takes about 15 minutes to recover it.

Armament: none
Armour: not disclosed
Crew: 2
Weight: 54.87 tons (55,746kg) with bridge
Length: 31ft 6in (9.60m) with bridge
Width: 13ft 11in (4.24m) with bridge
Height: 13ft 3in (4.03m) with bridge
Engine: Continental, 12-cylinder, diesel, 750bhp at
 2,400rpm

Speed: 25mph (40km/hr)
Range: 310 miles (500km)

M74 ARV USA
BMY, Rock Island
1953. With the addition of even heavier tanks to the American armoury, by the early 1950s a more powerful recovery tank was needed, and in 1952 it was decided to see if a fresh design could be developed, but still using the M4 tank as a basis – since there were still large numbers available for conversion. After some trials and modifications, the M74 was standardized in 1953 and remained in service until the 1970s.

The M74 was basically an M4A3E8 hull and chassis, with horizontal volute springs and wide tracks. The turret was replaced by a fixed structure, which carried a winch on its front. A second winch was inside the hull, feeding its cable through a fairlead in the front glacis plate. The same type of jib crane was provided as was used on the M32 (*qv*), but it was hydraulically erected, which allowed it to be used as a travelling jib. A bulldozer blade was added at the front of the hull for use as a stabilizer when winching or lifting, and a special towing mount and bars were provided at the rear. As with most ARVs the outline of the tank tended to disappear under stowage bins and spare parts hung on every available surface.

Armament: 2 × MG
Armour: 50mm
Crew: 4
Weight: 41.85 tons (42,524kg)
Length: 25ft 1in (7.95m)
Width: 10ft 2in (3.10m)
Height: 10ft 2in (3.10m)
Engine: Ford GAA, V-8 petrol, 450bhp at 2,600rpm
Speed: 21mph (34km/hr)
Range: 100 miles (160km)

M728 Combat Engineer Vehicle USA
Chrysler
1968. This entered service in 1968 and is based on the chassis of the M60A1 battle tank. The hull is fitted with a front-mounted bulldozer blade, hydraulically operated, and an A-frame crane is hinged to the hull front and usually carried folded down around the turret. A two-speed winch with an 11-tonne capacity is mounted behind the turret. The turret is armed with a 165mm low-velocity demolition gun M135, an American copy of the British AVRE 6.5-inch gun L9A1.

Armament: 1 × 165mm; 2 × MG
Armour: not disclosed

Crew: 4
Weight: 51.34 tons (52,163kg)
Length: 25ft 10in (7.88m)
Width: 12ft 2in (3.70m)
Height: 10ft 6in (3.20m)
Engine: Continental, 12-cylinder, diesel, 750bhp at 2,400rpm
Road speed: 30mph (48km/hr)
Range: 310 miles (500km)

Matilda Scorpion UK
1942. A Matilda 2 tank fitted with a flail-type mine clearing device, driven by an auxiliary Ford engine mounted on the side of the hull.

MT-34 Armoured Bridgelayer
Czechoslovakia
State factories
1960. The chassis of this vehicle is that of the Czech ARV based on the T-34 tank (see T-34-T, *below*). It is one of the older types of bridgelayer in which the unfolding process is carried out by a combination of hydraulic rams, winches and cables. This takes a little longer than an all-hydraulic operation. The bridge is 55.7 feet (17m) long when unfolded and will span a 49-foot (15m) gap, carrying a load of up to 49 tons (50,000kg)

Armament: 1 × MG
Armour: 75mm
Crew: 4
Weight: 31.5 tons (32,000kg) with bridge
Length: 27ft 9in (8.50m) with bridge
Width: 10ft 6in (3.23m) with bridge
Height: 12ft 2in (3.71m) with bridge
Engine: V-2-34M V-12 diesel, 500bhp at 1,800rpm
Speed: 25mph (40km/hr)
Range: 125 miles (200km)

MT-55 Armoured Bridgelayer
Czechoslovakia
State factories
1970. The MT-55 was the replacement for the MT-34 bridgelayer and was based on the T-55 tank chassis. It used a conventional scissors bridge carried folded on top of the tank, which was unfolded and laid by hydraulic power provided by a pump driven from the main engine. The equipment was also adopted by the Soviet Army, who used it for several years. The bridge weighs 6.4 tons (6,500kg) and opens out to 59 feet (18m) long and will span a 52-foot (16m) gap.

Armament: 1 × MG
Armour: 203mm

Crew: 2
Weight: 35.43 tons (36,000kg) with bridge
Length: 32ft 2in (9.81m) with bridge
Width: 11ft 2in (3.41m) with bridge
Height: 12ft 2in (3.71m) with bridge
Engine: V-12 diesel, 580bhp at 2,000rpm
Road speed: 25mph (40km/hr)
Range: 185 miles (300km)

MTU-1 Bridgelayer Russia
State factories
1958. The MTU-1 is the usual sort of conversion, in this case of the T-54 tank, by removal of the turret and gun, plating over the turret ring, and mounting the necessary apparatus for carrying and launching a 40-foot (12.3m) bridge.

Armament: 1 × MG
Crew: 2
Weight: 33.40 tons (34,000kg) with bridge
Length of bridge: 40ft 4in (12.3m)
Gap spanned: 35ft 0in (11m)
Bridge capacity: 49.2 tons (50,000kg)
Other details: as for the T-54 tank

MTU-20 Bridgelayer Russia
State factories
1968. This is very similar in general concept to the MTU-1 described above, but based on the T-55 tank chassis. The principal improvement is that the bridge span is longer, though when carried on the tank the ends are hinged up and back so that the overall length is little more than the MTU-1. Prior to launching the bridge ends are folded down and locked.

Armament: 1 × MG
Crew: 2
Weight: 36.4 tons (37,000kg) with bridge
Length: 38ft 2in (11.64m)
Length of bridge: 65ft 7in (20m)
Gap spanned: 59ft 1in (18m)
Bridge capacity: 59.05 tons (60,000kg)
Other details: as for the T-55 tank

NM-130 ARV Norway
Moelven
1978. Designed and built in Norway, this is simply an ex-USA M24 Chaffee light tank with the turret removed and an hydraulic crane and winch fitted. A relatively lightweight machine it was perfectly adequate for M24 tanks which Norway employed and has still in reserve.

Armament: 1 × MG
Armour: 38mm

Crew: 3
Weight: 16.24 tons (16,500kg)
Length: 16ft 4in (4.99m)
Width: 9ft 8in (2.94m)
Height: 7ft 7in (2.31m)
Power: Detroit Diesel 6v-53T, V-6 diesel
  turbocharged, 300bhp at 2,800rpm
Speed: 37mph (60km/hr)
Range: 280 miles (450km)

OF-40 ARV Italy
OTO-Melara
1992. The ARV version of the OF-40 main battle tank is in the usual style, removing the turret and adding a small superstructure to give more headroom for the crew, fitting a winch, a crane and a stabilizer-cum-bulldozer blade at the front, and making a platform on the engine deck, with suitable fastenings, to carry a complete replacement power pack. A small number were built for the Italian Army in the 1990s.

Armament: 1 × MG
Armour: not disclosed
Crew: 4
Weight: 44.25 tons (45,000kg)
Length: 25ft 2in (7.68m)
Width: 11ft 6in (3.51m)
Height: 7ft 9in (2.35m)
Power: MTU90 V-10, multi-fuel, supercharged, 830bhp
  at 2,200rpm
Speed: 37mph (60km/hr)
Range: 370 miles (600km)

Onion UK
1944. A relative of Carrot and Goat, this was a demolition charge carrier fitted to a Churchill tank. The basis was a vertical framework, 9ft wide by 4ft 6in high (2.74m x 1.37m) to which explosive charges could be attached according to the nature of the target. The frame was held vertically by support arms on the tank, which was driven up to the obstacle. The frame was then released and was designed so that the top fell forward and the entire frame rested against the target. The tank then backed away, fired the charge electrically, cast off the supports, which were no longer needed, and became a normal combat tank.

Panzerfähre Germany
Magirus
1942. The Germany Army had a variety of unarmoured amphibian vehicles which were exceptionally useful for crossing the many unbridged rivers on the Eastern Front, and in 1941 decided that an armoured amphibian might be useful in cases where the crossing was opposed. Magirus were given a development contract and produced two prototypes in 1942. The vehicle used the chassis, lower hull and running gear of the Panzer 4 tank, on top of which was a wide hull (overhanging the tracks) with a blunt prow somewhat similar to the much later Soviet PT-76 hull. It does not appear to have had much load-carrying capacity, and after trials the idea was abandoned.

No further data available

Raumer-S Mine-Clearing Vehicle Germany
Krupp
1945. In 1944, the German Army asked Krupp to develop a suitable vehicle for clearing minefields. Krupp chose to develop a massive vehicle impervious to mines, it would simply roll over them and detonate them harmlessly. This approach was also tried by the British and Americans, but without much success – manufacturing a massive and impervious vehicle is one thing, driving it another. The Raumer-S consisted of two huge steel boxes each containing an engine and carried on two extremely heavy steel wheels about 9 feet (2.75m) in diameter. These two boxes were connected together by an articulated joint, which allowed each unit to roll independently and allowed the whole machine to be steered by hydraulic rams which 'bent' the assembly in its centre. The front of the forward unit carried the driver's cab, from which both motors were controlled. The total weight was in the region of 130 tonnes, and one vehicle had been completed and was undergoing trials at the end of the war.

No further data available

Royal Engineer Tank UK
Metropolitan
1918. One of the prime design features of the original tanks was that they had to be able to cross trenches, and even though their ability to do this was greater than most tanks designed since then, there were still some wide ditches they found impassable. In 1918 this RE Tank was designed in order to overcome this problem, and it consisted of a Mark 5★★ battle tank with a 20-foot (6.1m) bridge slung from the front. A jib unit on the hull top was connected by cables to the bridge and could be operated by a combination of winch and hydraulic ram either to raise the bridge to allow the tank to move forward or lower the bridge across the ditch

to be crossed. Once lowered it could be detached from the tank, which then withdrew. It was intended to equip special bridging companies with these tanks towards the end of 1918, but the end of of the war cancelled this plan. A small number of vehicles were built and were retained for training purposes for some years after the war.

Armament: 2 × MG
Armour: 12mm
Crew: 10
Weight: 34.5 tons (35,050kg) without bridge
Length: 32ft 5in (9.88m) without bridge
Width: 10ft 6in (3.20m)
Height: 16ft 6in (5.02m) with jib
Engine: Ricardo, 6-cylinder, petrol, 225bhp
Speed: 4mph (6.5km/hr)
Range: 90 miles (145km)

Samson ARV UK
Alvis

1978. Samson is a light armoured recovery vehicle constructed on the chassis of the Scorpion CVR(T). It uses the same hull as the Spartan APC, a turretless box which offers more space than the tank hull, and is equipped with a power winch capable of hauling 12 tons. At the rear of the hull are two ground anchor spades, which can be lowered to stabilize the Samson when using the winch or when acting as a holdfast to permit another vehicle to winch itself out of difficulty by hauling against the Samson. The three-man crew have hatches with periscopes, and whilst no armament is permanently mounted, personal weapons and a light machine gun can be carried inside the vehicle.

Armament: none, see text
Armour: not disclosed
Crew: 3
Weight: 7.87 tons (8,000kg)
Length: 16ft 2in (4.93m)
Width: 7ft 2in (2.18m)
Height: 6ft 7in (2.02m)
Engine: Jaguar, 6-cylinder, petrol, 195bhp at 4,750rpm
Speed: 55mph (88km/hr)
Range: 400 miles (645km)

Scorpion (Flail) UK
See Matilda Scorpion

SU-85 and SU-100 ARVs Russia
State factories

1950. These two ARVs were so similar that they can be considered together. They were the SU-85 and SU-100 self-propelled gun chassis with the gun removed and a plate bolted over the hole in the mantlet. They had neither winch nor crane and could only push or tow stalled vehicles. The crew carried the usual range of tools to undertake field repairs, but with so little heavy gear they were handicapped and it was an expensive way to carry a repair crew on to the battlefield. They were in service throughout the Warsaw Pact countries until the later 1970s. Data generally are as for the relevant SP gun.

T1 Mine Exploder USA
Gar Wood Industries

1944–45. Whilst the British Army concentrated on developing flail devices to explode mines in the path of tanks (*see* Matilda Scorpion and Sherman Crab), the Americans concentrated on roller devices. The first of these appeared in 1943 as the Mine Exploder T1 and consisted of two large rollers, each made of heavy steel discs 40 inches (101cm) in diameter, pushed ahead of the tank so that each roller cleared space for the tracks. A third set of rollers was towed behind the tank in a central position, so that the effect of the three was to clear a path as wide as the tank.

The T1 had some defects and was replaced by the **T1E1**, in which the third set of rollers was brought round to the front of the tank and placed ahead of the side rollers. A jib crane was mounted on the front of the vehicle, a Recovery Tank M32 (*above*), to lift the rollers out of the craters resulting from the detonation of mines. Although a cumbersome device, it was accepted for use and 75 were built.

The T1E1 proved effective in the field but cumbersome to operate, and to try and make things better for the driver the **T1E2** was designed. This dispensed with the central roller and widened the two outer rollers, but the principal complaint was that it was still built on to a recovery tank which carried no armament, and a mine-clearing tank usually operated in the very front of an advance, where armament was a comforting thing to have. This led to the **T1E3**, a Sherman M4A1 tank, complete with armament, and twin rollers chain-driven from the tank's front driving sprocket so as to assist manoeuvre, mounted ahead of it. In 1944 two of these were sent to Britain and two to Italy; named **Aunt Jemima** they were well received, and more were dispatched to Europe shortly after the June 1944 invasion.

The final roller-type exploder was the **T1E5**, which used serrated edges on the roller discs to provide additional traction. Each roller consisted of six discs each 2 inches (63mm) thick and 6 feet

(1.83m) in diameter, and covered a 40-inch (102cm) strip with 36 inches (91cm) between the two rollers. A completely cleared strip was made by positioning two or more tanks so that their roller paths overlapped. The total weight of the roller unit attached to the front of the tank was 41,000lb (18,600kg). An attempt to improve the manoeuvrability of mine-exploding devices was the **T1E4**, developed by the Chrysler Corporation. This used a wide sheepsfoot roller made up of 16 serrated discs of 4 feet (1.2m) diameter, suspended from an A-frame at the front of the tank. It improved mobility and cleared a 9ft 7in (2.92m) path at a speed of 5mph (8km/hr). A wider version, the **T1E6** cleared a 11ft 5in (3.49m) path and was designed to protect later model tanks with wider tracks.

The total production of all these various models of mine exploder was small, probably no more than 300 of all types. Their effect was good, but they were so slow and cumbersome that they were rarely used, troops preferring to push ahead and take their chances.

T31 Demolition Tank USA
Heinz

1945. When the British Army began developing the Churchill AVRE the Americans were informed and, in response to a Corps of Engineers request, development of a similar vehicle was begun in the USA. The resulting machine was the **Engineer Armored Vehicle**, a Sherman M4A3 converted by removing the gun from the turret, removing the ammunition racks from inside the hull to leave space for explosives and other engineer stores, and installing a multiple rocket launcher, with 18 7.2-inch rockets, above the turret. Attachments were fitted to mount a bulldozer blade on the front, and an armoured sledge was provided for carrying additional stores. Finally an 81mm mortar was issued, which could be fired from the turret to provide smoke cover.

While the EAV was a good interim solution, there was no official organization in which it would fit, and the US Army refused to adopt the British solution and assemble a specialized armour unit, with the result that only two vehicles were built and they were still awaiting shipment when the war ended.

Recognizing the defects of the EAV, in November 1944 a new proposal was put up, for a Demolition Tank T31 to replace it. This was to be a late-model Sherman with belly armour strengthened against mines, a bulldozer blade, a mine excavator, a flamethrower, two automatic 7.2-inch rocket launchers on the turret sides, and twin machine guns in the turret front. The vehicle was built and sent for test late in 1945; the revolver-type automatic rocket launchers failed to perform properly and rather than spend more money it was decided to abandon the whole thing.

T-34-T ARVs Russia
State factories

1948. There were at least six distinct ARVs built on the T-34 tank chassis, the earliest ones being unsophisticated machines in which the only modification was the removal of the turret so as to provide room for a repair crew to be carried. These vehicles did no more than tow a damaged tank off the battlefield and attempt to repair it with hand tools. Later versions fitted cranes, winches and the usual extras.

T-34-T

This is the earliest and simplest version in which only the turret was removed and nothing added.

T-34-T, Model B

In this version a crane and winch were fitted and a cargo platform was built over the engine decking.

T-34-T, Model B East Germany

This was a Model B with a pushbar on the front.

WPT-34 Poland

This was the Polish version and was a much better ARV than the others. It had a large superstructure at the front of the hull for the crew and a powerful winch in the hull. At the rear there were spades, and extra tools were carried on the outside of the hull.

SKP-5

This was another half-equipped ARV which had a crane but no winch, bulldozer blade or spades.

T-34 ARV Czechoslovakia

The designation of this vehicle is uncertain, but it was a T-34 chassis with a heavy-duty crane on top. Once again there was neither a bulldozer blade nor spades and its chief use seems to have been more for lifting heavy items from tanks and in placing bridge components for the engineers rather than in actual recovery of dead vehicles.

For all the foregoing vehicles the basic data of the T-34 tank apply. The only variable dimension is the height.

T41 Armored Utility Vehicle USA
Buick

1944. This was an unusual vehicle insofar as it was designed to be an armoured crew-carrier and tractor for the 3-inch M6 towed anti-tank gun, and it was based upon the chassis and hull of the M18 76mm Gun Motor Carriage so that the towed guns of an anti-tank battalion could keep up with the self-propelled weapons when moving across country. It was a praiseworthy idea and one which appears to have worked, but it has never been properly exploited since then, probably because of the expense involved. It would probably have been cheaper to outfit the entire unit with SP guns.

The modification merely involved leaving off the turret and ring so as to provide a large open-topped crew compartment to accommodate the driver and co-driver and the seven-man gun detachment. Various components had their positions changed in order to facilitate the stowage of equipment and ammunition. Driver and co-driver had hatches with periscopes which they could close down, but the gunners merely had a canvas cover over their compartment to keep the rain out. Armament was a single .50-inch machine gun on a ring mount over the front centre of the troop compartment. The vehicle was approved as Limited Standard in June 1944 and did not survive for long after the war ended.

Armament: I × MG
Armour: 16mm
Crew: 2 + 7
Weight: 15.62 tons (15,870kg)
Length: 17ft 4in (5.28m)
Width: 9ft 1in (2.77m)
Height: 5ft 11in (1.80m)
Power: Continental R975-C1, 9-cylinder radial, petrol, 400bhp at 2,400rpm
Speed: 50mph (80km/hr)
Range: 150 miles (240km)

T-54/55 ARV Russia
State factories
There were at least four models of the recovery version of the T-54/55 built either in the USSR or in East Germany. the first of which was a T-54 tank without a turret and the chassis fitted with a loading platform and a crane. A dozer blade was mounted at the back of the hull. There appears to have been no winch and the value of the vehicle was undoubtedly limited to some extent by the light equipment. The second was an East German model known as a **T-54A** ARV, which again had what seemed to be fairly light gear. There was a pushbar instead of a winch, and a 2,200lb (1,000kg) jib crane. This vehicle could be fitted with mine-clearing ploughs. The third was the **T-54B**, another East German vehicle identical in all respects to the T-54A except

for the addition of a generator on the back of the hull. Both of these ARVs would appear to have been used more as engineer vehicles rather than ARVs in the sense that this is understood in NATO. The fourth model was again East German, the **T-54C**, and it can best be described as a Model A fitted with steadying spades. The crane was stronger, but there was still no winch nor was there a bulldozer blade.

Weight: 33.46 tons (34,000kg)
Crew: 3
Other details: as for the T-54 tank

TOPAS ARV Poland
State factories
1976. The WPT-TOPAS was a variant of the Czechoslovak OT-62 armoured personnel carrier as used by the Polish Army. There are not many details available on this vehicle, but it would appear to have been more of an engineer support vehicle than a true ARV, as, it seems, were so many of the Warsaw Pact ARVS. It had a hand-operated crane with a lift of only one ton (1,000kg) and a winch with a pull of 2.5 tons (2,500kg). The crew of four carried a full set of tools and welding gear for field repairs. All data are presumed to be the same as for the OT-62A since there are no apparent structural modifications.

Type 67 Armoured Bridgelayer Japan
Mitsubishi
1971. The Type 67 is a variant on the basic chassis of the Type 61 MBT. The turret is removed and a flat decking substituted. On top of this is a folding bridge from the United States M48 AVLB. This bridge folds forward to open out in front.

Armament: I × MG
Armour: 46mm
Crew: 4
Weight: 34.45 tons (35,000kg)
Overall length: 23ft 9in (7.27m)
Width: 11ft 6in (3.53m) with bridge
Height: 11ft 6in (3.53m) with bridge
Engine: Mitsubishi V-12 turbocharged diesel, 600bhp at 2,100rpm
Road speed: 28mph (45km/hr)
Power/weight: 17.41
Range: 125 miles (200km)

Type 67 Armoured Engineer Vehicle
Japan
Mitsubishi
1967. This vehicle is something like an ARV and is designed to carry a repair crew on the battlefield. It does not have the lifting or towing capacity of a

proper ARV, but it does have a selection of special tools together with welding equipment and a range of spare parts. It is a turretless Type 61 tank fitted with an armoured superstructure for the crew and their equipment.

Armament: 2 × MG
Armour: 46mm
Crew: 4
Weight: 34.45 tons (35,000kg)
Length: 24ft 6in (7.46m)
Width: 10ft 6in (3.23m)
Height: 7ft 4in (2.23m)
Engine: Mitsubishi V-12 turbocharged diesel, 600bhp at 2,100rpm
Road speed: 27mph (45km/hr)
Range: 125 miles (200km)

Type 70 ARV Japan

1971. This is another variant of the Type 61 tank. It is fitted with a bulldozer blade on the front of the hull and a small flat-sided superstructure replaces the turret. There is a winch on the rear of the hull and an A-frame lifting jib on the front.

Armament: 1 × MG
Length: 27ft 6in (8.41m)
Other details: as for the Type 67 AEV

Type 88 AVLB South Korea
Hyundai, Vickers

This is a conversion of the Type 88 MBT by removal of the turret and adding the necessary fittings to carry a bridge. Rather than waste time and energy re-inventing the wheel, Hyundai very sensibly contracted the bridge part of the conversion to Vickers in Britain, who produced a design more or less based upon the scissors bridge used with the Chieftain AVLB. The bridge folds in half to lie on top of the tank hull, and is unfolded and extended to the front by means of hydraulic rams. Launching can be completed in three minutes; recovering the bridge takes about ten minutes.

Armament: 1 × MG
Armour: not disclosed
Crew: 2
Weight: 52.16 tons (53,000kg) with bridge
Length: 41ft 0in (12.5m)
Length of bridge: 72ft 2in (22m)
Gap spanned: 67ft 3in (20.5m)
Width: 13ft 2in (4.0m)
Height: 13ft 2in (4.0m) with bridge
Power: MTU Ka502 V-12 diesel, 1,200bhp at 2,600rpm

Speed: 34mph (55km/hr)
Range: 310 miles (500km)

Type 97 'Se-Ri' ARV Japan
Mitsubishi

1937. The Type 97 Se-Ri was a variant of the Type 97 Chi-Ha medium tank and was at the time described as an engineering vehicle. In place of the main turret was a low, conical cupola and on the back of the decking was a small A-frame crane, though some versions seem to have carried a jib crane. There were several versions of this engineering vehicle, and some were fitted with flamethrowers, though there was no apparent attempt to build a specific flamethrower tank. The main use of the Se-Ri was to tow tanks that had broken down on the line of march and to effect field repairs at the first halt. Not many of the type were made. At least one version had two cranes, mounted fore and aft with the driver in the middle. These cranes could be fitted with earth-moving buckets and they were worked by winches and drums of wire rope.

Armament: 2 × MG
Length: 18ft 1in (5.51m)
Width: 7ft 6in (2.31m)
Height: 7ft 11in (2.16m)
Crew: 3
Other details: as for Type 97 tank

Vickers Armoured Bridgelayer UK
Vickers

1981. This was an off-shoot of the Vickers Mark 3 MBT and is the usual turret-less conversion. The one-piece bridge span is supported, upside-down, above the hull, with a prominent launching structure at the front of the vehicle. Hydraulic rams force the bridge up and over the front and once in position it is released from the launching structure. It can be recovered in a reverse sequence.

Vickers ARV UK
Vickers

1980. This is also based upon the Vickers Mark 3 tank. The turret is absent and the sides built up into a low superstructure. There is a winch under armour alongside the driver at the front of the vehicle, and an anchoring spade under the front of the hull. The remaining three crew members have a compartment in the centre of the vehicle. A crane may or may not be fitted: ARVs with and without have been produced. Those so equipped are specifically designed for lifting the Vickers power pack in and out of a tank, a spare power pack being carried on a platform on the engine deck.

Armament: I × MG
Armour: 80mm
Crew: 4
Weight: 35.42 tons (36,000kg)
Length: 24ft 10in (7.56m)
Width: 10ft 5in (3.17m)
Height: 8ft 0in (2.45m)
Engine: GMC V-12 turbocharged diesel, 720bhp at 2,500rpm
Speed: 34mph (55km/hr)
Range: 372 miles (600km)

VT-72B ARV Czechoslovakia
State factories
Although designed and built in Czechoslovakia, this is actually based on the Russian T-72 tank chassis and hull. There is a short and simple superstructure over the crew compartment and driver's position, with a cupola for the commander, and the vehicle is fitted with the usual winch, hydraulic crane and bulldozer blade. Like most East European ARVs it seems to combine the functions of recovery, repair and field engineering.

Armament: I × MG
Armour: not disclosed
Crew: 3
Weight: 41.33 tons (42,000kg)
Length: 22ft 10in (6.95m)
Width: 11ft 9in (3.59m)
Height: 5ft 5in (1.65m)
Engine: V-12 multi-fuel, 840bhp at 2,000rpm
Speed: 37mph (60km/hr)
Range: 310 miles (500km)

COMPARATIVE TABLES

CONVENTIONS

This table follows the pattern used in the previous chapter. Bridge lengths are the gap spanned, rounded to a whole number of feet.

IN ALPHABETICAL ORDER

Name	Weight imp ton	Length ft	Crew	Engine	Power bhp	Speed mph	Range miles	Dozer	Winch	Crane	Bridge feet	Country
4K 7FA Greif ARV	19.48	29.67	4	D/6/L	320	40	280	Yes	Yes	Yes	No	Austria
AMX-10 ECH	13.58	18.08	5	D/V/8/S/L	276	40	370	No	No	Yes	No	France
AMX-13 Bridgelayer	19.39	25.42	3	P/V/8/L	250	31	375	No	No	No	46	France
AMX-13 ARV	13.90	18.08	3	P/V/8/L	250	37	265	No	2	Yes	No	France
AMX-30 Bridgelayer	42.30	37.50	3	M/V/12/L	700	31	375	No	No	No	72	France
AMX-30 ARV	39.37	23.50	3	M/V/12/L	700	31	375	Yes	2	Yes	No	France
AMX-30 CET	37.40	25.92	3	M/V/2/L	700	40	310	Yes	Yes	Yes	No	France
Bgbv 82 ARC	22.93	23.75	4	D/6/T/L	310	35	250	Yes	Yes	Yes	No	Sweden
Bergepanther ARV	42.32	28.92	5	P/V/12/L	700	28	200	Yes	Yes	No	No	Germany
Bergepanzer 3 ARV	19.00	20.58	3	P/V/12/L	300	25	125	No	Yes	Yes	No	Germany
Bergepanzer 38(t) ARV	14.27	16.0	4	P/6/L	160	26	110	No	Yes	A-frame	No	Germany
Biber Bridgelayer	44.29	38.25	2	M/V/10/L	830	40	340	No	No	No	65	Germany
BLG-60 Bridgelayer	36.41	34.67	3	D/V/12/L	520	20	150	No	No	No	71	Germany
Brbv 941 Bridgelayer	28.93	55.75	4	D/6/T/L	280	30	155	No	No	No	45	Sweden
Bruckenleger 4	28.0	36.08	2	P/V/12/L	300	25	125	No	No	No	30	Germany
Bruckenleger Pz 68	43.90	59.75	3	D/V/8/L	630	20	125	No	No	No	60	Switz
Centurion ARV	49.50	29.42	4	P/V/12/L	650	21	62	No	Yes	Yes	No	UK
Centurion AVRE	51.0	28.50	5	P/V/12/L	650	21	110	Yes	No	No	No	UK
Centurion Bridgelayer	49.69	53.50	3	P/V/12/L	650	21	125	No	No	No	45	UK
Chieftain ARV	51.18	27.08	4	M/12/L	720	26	200	Yes	2	No	No	UK
Chieftain AVRE	51.10	24.67	3	M/12/L	730	30	310	Option	Yes	Yes	No	UK
Chieftain Bridgelayer	52.46	45.08	3	M/12/L	720	20	130	No	No	No	75	UK
Churchill ARK	37.77	24.42	4	P/12/L	350	8	90	No	No	No	Ramps	UK
Churchill AVRE	38.0	25.17	6	P/12/L	350	15	120	No	No	No	No	UK
Combat Engr Tractor	16.8	24.75	2	D/6/T/L	320	37	300	Yes	Yes	Yes	No	UK
Entpannungspanzer 65	38.38	24.08	5	D/8/L	705	34	186	Yes	Yes	Yes	No	Switz
IMR CEV	33.46	34.42	2	D/V/12	520	30	250	Yes	No	Yes	No	Russia
Leopard ARV	39.17	24.83	4	M/V/10/L	830	40	530	Yes	Yes	Yes	No	Germany
M21 ARV	26.78	26.42	6	P/9/R/A	400	25	110	No	Yes	Yes	No	USA
M32 ARV	27.68	19.08	4	various		24	120	No	Yes	Yes	No	USA
M47E2 Engineer Tank	45.96	20.83	4	D/12/A	760	35	370	Yes	Yes	Yes	No	Spain
M48 Bridgelayer	55.84	37.0	2	P/12/A	810	23	100	No	No	No	60	USA
M60 Bridgelayer	54.87	31.50	2	D/12/L	750	25	310	No	No	No	60	USA
M74 ARV	41.85	25.08	4	P/V8/L	450	21	100	Yes	2	Yes	No	USA
M728 CEV	51.34	25.83	4	D/12/L	750	30	310	Yes	Yes	A-frame	No	USA
MT-34 Bridgelayer	31.50	27.75	4	D/V/12/L	500	25	125	No	No	No	49	Czech

Name	Weight imp ton	Length ft	Crew	Engine	Power bhp	Speed mph	Range miles	Dozer	Winch	Crane	Bridge feet	Country
MT-55 Bridgelayer	35.43	32.17	2	D/V/12/L	580	25	185	No	No	No	52	Czech
MTU-1 Bridgelayer	33.40	40.33	2	D/V/12/L	520	20	150	No	No	No	35	Russia
MTU-20 Bridgelayer	36.40	38.17	2	D/V/12/L	520	20	150	No	No	No	59	Russia
NM-130 ARV	16.24	16.33	3	D/V/6/T/L	300	37	280	No	Yes	Yes	No	Norway
OF-40 ARV	44.25	25.17	4	M/V/10/S/L	830	37	370	Yes	Yes	Yes	No	Italy
RE Tank	34.50	32.42	10	P/6/L	225	4	90	No	No	No	20	UK
Samson ARV	7.87	16.17	3	P/6/L	195	55	400	No	Yes	No	No	UK
T41 AUV	15.62	17.33	2 + 7	P/9/R/A	400	50	150	No	No	No	No	USA
T-54/55 ARV	33.46	21.25	3	D/V/12/L	520	20	150	Yes	Yes	Yes	No	Russia
Type 67 Bridgelayer	34.45	23.75	4	D/V/12/T/L	600	28	125	No	No	No	60	Japan
Type 67 AEV	34.45	24.50	4	D/V/12/T/L	600	27	125	No	No	No	No	Japan
Type 70 ARV	34.45	27.50	4	D/V/12/T/L	600	27	125	Yes	Yes	A-frame	No	Japan
Type 88 Bridgelayer	52.16	41.0	2	D/V/12/L	1200	34	310	No	No	No	67	S Korea
Type 97 ARV	15.40	18.08	3	D/V/12/A	240	20	100	No	Yes	A-frame	No	Japan
Vickers ARV	35.42	24.83	4	D/V/12/T/L	720	34	372	No	Yes	Option	No	UK
VT-72B ARV	41.33	22.83	3	M/V/12/L	840	37	310	Yes	Yes	Yes	No	Czech

RECONNAISSANCE VEHICLES

This category includes armoured cars, scout cars and similar types.

ABI Armoured Car Romania
RATMIL
1994. The ABI is a light 4 x 4 armoured car intended for internal security roles and border patrolling. The basis is a standard 4 x 4 light military chassis, on to which goes a boxy steel body with 8–10mm armour. The layout is conventional, with the engine at the front, driver and commander in the cab, and a rear troop compartment with two rear doors. Firing ports and vision blocks are provided, and the roof can have a simple hatch or a light turret with one or two machine guns. Numbers are in use by Romanian military and security forces, and a version with a more powerful engine has been sold to Algeria.

Armament: 1 or 2 x MG
Armour: 10mm
Crew: 2 + 4
Weight: 2.19 tons (2,225kg)
Length: 13ft 10in (4.22m)
Width: 7ft 4in (2.23m)
Height: 6ft 11in (2.12m) (turret version)
Engine: D-12 diesel, 68bhp at 3,200rpm
Speed: 55mph (90km/hr)
Range: 370 miles (600km)

AC30 Armoured Car Czechoslovakia
Maker not known
1930. The AC30 does not have a clearly defined history. It apparently came into service with the Czechoslovak forces in late 1930 as a scout car and may, or may not, have survived until the German takeover in 1938. It had a long chassis with 4 x 4 drive and a sloping rear deck running back to cover the rear wheels. The stubby turret was mounted directly behind the driver and co-driver and carried two machine guns, The bonnet was heavily louvered. General mobility was bad and protection was inadequate, since the armour was hardly sloped at all.

Data: none available

ADKZ Armoured Car Austria
Austro-Daimler
1938. Said to be an advanced design for its time, the Austro-Daimler KZ gives the appearance of being half-finished, since everything is packed into a short length behind the bonnet and the rest of the hull is flat. In fact, the rear of the vehicle is the engine compartment, the driver is well up to the front, and the rest of it is all fighting compartment and turret. Armament is frequently said to have been a 15mm machine gun, though no confirmation of this can be found; an 8mm machine gun appears to be the normal.

Armament: 1 x 8mm or 15mm MG in turret;
1 x 7.92mm MG coaxial
Crew: 4
Length: 15ft 7in (4.74m)
Width: 7ft 10in (2.38m)
Height: 7ft 11in (2.41m)
Engine: Daimler, 6-cylinder, petrol

Adler Kfz 13 Light Armoured Car
Germany
Adler (chassis), Edelstahl (body)
1932. German Army reconnaissance vehicle which also acted as an interim vehicle for armoured formations until more specialized cars and tanks became available. To keep it cheap and as quick to produce as possible, a standard Adler commercial

car chassis was adopted and a welded steel hull built around it. This open body carried a two-man crew and a machine gun. Mechanically the vehicle was purely commercial, with a front engine driving the rear wheels only, rigid axles and semi-elliptic springs. As a result, its cross-country performance was relatively poor. Nevertheless, as training vehicles they were useful and they continued to serve until 1944. Some were used in the 1940 campaigns and some even saw active service in Russia in 1941. A companion vehicle was the Adler Kfz 14, which was the same car but with provision for radio and without armament.

Armament: 1 × MG
Armour: 8mm
Crew: 2
Weight: 2.16 tons (2,200kg)
Length: 13ft 9in (4.20m)
Width: 5ft 7in (1.70m)
Height: 4ft 11in (1.50m)
Engine: Adler, 6-cylinder, petrol, 60bhp at 3,200rpm
Speed: 43mph (70km/hr)
Range: 185 miles (300km)

AEC Armoured Car UK
AEC
1942. In 1941 the Associated Equipment Company, makers of heavy trucks and buses, took one of their Matador medium gun tractor chassis and built a mock-up armoured car on it, arming it with a 2-pounder gun. It was then inserted into an exhibition of military vehicles, where it attracted official attention, and an order for 150 was given. The design was an ingenious adaptation of the original truck chassis. The engine was placed at the rear and tilted so as to lie alongside the rear differential and thus reduce the height. Normally, only the front wheels were driven, the rear wheels being engaged only for cross-country work. The body was of flat armour plate, tapering from the centre to each end, and surmounted by a turret.

The basic **Mark 1** design used a Valentine tank turret with 2-pounder gun, though some cars were later modified to take the 6-pounder gun. A **Mark 2** was then devised, with a larger, three-man, turret and 6-pounder gun, larger engine and other improvements, and finally a **Mark 3** appeared in which the main armament was a 75mm gun. A total of 629 of all marks was built.

Armament: 1 × 2-pdr, or 1 × 6-pdr, or 1 × 75mm;
   1 × MG
Armour: 57mm
Crew: 3 or 4
Weight: 11 tons (11,175kg)

Length: 17ft 0in (5.18m)
Width: 9ft 0in (2.74m)
Height: 8ft 4in (2.55m)
Engine: AEC, 6-cylinder, diesel, 105 or 158bhp at 2,000rpm
Speed: 40mph (65km/hr)
Range: 250 miles (400km)

Alvis Reconnaissance Vehicle UK
Alvis
1998. Development of this vehicle began with the GKN company and was continued after their merger with Alvis. The basis is the Warrior IFV hull and chassis, but there have been some subtle changes in order to reduce the thermal, acoustic and radar signature and give the vehicle better survivability on the battlefield. The most noticeable of these is the provision of a deep skirt with flexible flaps to cover most of the suspension and thus reduce or confuse the very distinctive 'tracked vehicle' signal common to almost all ground surveillance radars. There is a roof-mounted turret with a 25mm Chain Gun, a coaxial 7.62mm Chain Gun and two anti-tank TOW missiles, and at the rear is a telescopic mast carrying a radar and electro-optical surveillance package. The vehicle is currently being evaluated.

Armament: 1 × 25mm cannon; 1 × MG; 2 × ATGW
Armour: not disclosed
Crew: 4
Weight: 26.57 tons (27,000kg)
Length: 21ft 1in (6.43m)
Width: 12ft 0in (3.66m)
Height: 9ft 0in (2.73m)
Engine: Perkins V-8 diesel, 650bhp at 2,300rpm
Speed: 56mph (90km/hr)
Range: 435 miles (700km)

AMX-10RC Armoured Car France
Roanne
1978. The AMX-10RC replaced the Panhard EBR series. It is a large, heavy and sophisticated vehicle, heavily armed and with much expensive equipment. The hull is all-welded and well sloped, particularly on the glacis plate. The driver sits on the left side and behind him is the fighting compartment with the large turret. The loader is on the left and the commander and gunner on the right. They have full night-vision equipment. The engine and transmission are at the rear. The six wheels do not steer, and the vehicle changes direction in the same way as a tank, that is to say each side can be slowed or skidded. The suspension can be adjusted to alter the ground clearance, and

the vehicle is fully amphibious, requiring only a trim vane to be erected by the crew before entering the water, where propulsion is effected by built-in hydro-jets.

Armament: 1 × 105mm; 1 × coaxial MG
Armour: not disclosed
Crew: 4
Weight: 15.63 tons (15,880kg)
Length: 20ft 10in (6.36m)
Width: 9ft 8in (2.95m)
Height: 8ft 10in (2.68m)
Engine: Hispano-Suiza 8-cylinder, horizontally-opposed supercharged diesel, 260bhp at 3,000rpm
Speed: 53mph (85km/hr)
Range: 620 miles (1000km)

Austin Armoured Car UK
Austin

1918. Austin were kept busy supplying armoured cars to Russia (*see* Austin-Putilov below) until the 1917 Revolution, whereupon their manufacturing capability was available for the British Army, and they modified the Russian pattern lowering the cab roof so that both guns had a wider arc of fire and making a few other changes which experience had shown were desirable, but which the Russians had refused. The general appearance remained much the same with two turrets above round side sponsons, a machine gun in each turret, rear wheel drive and pneumatic tyres.

Armament: 2 × MG
Armour: 8 mm
Crew: 4
Weight: 4.14 tons (4,210kg)
Length: 16ft 0in (4.88m)
Width: 6ft 8in (2.03m)
Height: 9ft 4in (2.84m)
Engine: Austin, 4-cylinder, petrol, 50bhp
Speed: 35mph (56km/hr)
Range: 125 miles (200km)

Austin-Putilov Armoured Car Russia
Austin, Putilov

In early 1915 the Russian government arranged for a supply of armoured cars from the Austin company in Britain. They were designed by Austin and their principal recognition feature was the use of two turrets, side-by-side, on top of semi-cylindrical 'sponsons' on each side of the body. Each turret carried a Maxim machine gun, and the roof of the driving cab was of such a height that it prevented the two guns from pointing inwards across the roof. Drive was, of course, to the rear wheels only, and

pneumatic tyres were fitted, although the Russians performed many later trials with solid tyres or pneumatic tyre covers filled with rubber and other expedients. As the pressure on Austins for other products increased, the contract was changed to the supply of chassis to Russia, where the Putilov works would build and fit the armoured body. These Putilov cars were to the same general design but differed in having the two turrets arranged diagonally, allowing them wider arcs of fire.

Armament: 2 × MG
Armour: 8mm
Crew: 5
Weight: 5.71 tons (5,800kg)
Length: 22ft 2in (6.75m)
Width: 7ft 10in (2.39m)
Height: 8ft 10in (2.69m)
Engine: Austin, 4-cylinder, petrol, 50bhp
Speed: 18mph (25km/hr)
Range: 50 miles (80km)

Austin-Putilov-Kegresse Armoured Car Russia
Putilov

1916. In 1915 the Putilov company was ordered to build armoured cars using the Kegresse light track system instead of rear wheels, and these cars were founded on Austin chassis imported from Britain. Sixty were built and were successful. The layout was the familiar one for the time: a front engine, box body with vertical sides, and turret above the rear tracks. Thirty of the cars had single guns in the turret, but the other 30 were given two guns, in two small turrets. The light rubber track gave these cars good mobility, and they were used well up at the front, very much in the manner of tanks. Most survived the war and were employed by the Bolsheviks in the subsequent civil war. In winter, skis could be fitted to the front wheels and there was a rather clumsy form of extra roller that could be fitted for crossing wide trenches

Data: none available

Austro-Daimler Armoured Car Austria
Austro-Daimler

1904. Although this vehicle never went into production nor ever saw military service, it earns its place here by virtue of being the first armoured vehicle to have four-wheel drive. Developed as a private venture by Austro-Daimler, it was based upon one of their standard touring car chassis and conformed to the usual layout with the engine in front and the crew on seats alongside and behind the driver. The hemispherical turret was carried on a cylindrical portion of the body, behind the driving position, and was armed with a single Maxim gun; a second (1905) model was given two Schwarzlose machine guns. The driver could see through a slot in his armoured cab, but if conditions were favourable he could open his hatch and lift his seat by about a foot to allow his head to be in the open and thus gain better visibility. All wheels were driven and the cross-country performance appears to have been impressive for its day. But the armies of Europe evinced no interest and the idea was dropped. Nobody knows what happened to the car.

Armament: 1 × Maxim or 2 × Schwarzlose MG
Armour: 4mm
Crew: 4
Weight: 2.95 tons (3,000kg)
Length: 15ft 11in (4.86m)
Width: 5ft 9in (1.76m)
Height: 9ft 0in (2.74m)
Engine: Daimler, 4-cylinder, petrol, 40bhp
Speed: 28mph (45km/hr)
Range: 155 miles (250km)

Autoblinda 40 Armoured Car Italy
Ansaldo
A remarkably advanced design, this had a rear-mounted engine driving to a five-speed and overdrive gearbox, which in turn drove a distribution box with four propeller shafts, one to each wheel. There were two driving positions and the vehicle could proceed in reverse using the four lower gears in the box. Suspension was all-independent by coil springs, and the two free-mounted spare wheels, one on each side, were slung low so that they could act as a support in rough country and prevent the vehicle bellying. Armed with a 20mm cannon, these were very practical vehicles, and the British put several of them into use after capturing them in North Africa.

Armament: 1 × 20mm; 2 × MG
Armour: 9mm
Crew: 4
Weight: 6.74 tons (6,850kg)
Length: 17ft 1in (5.20m)
Width: 6ft 4in (1.93m)
Height: 7ft 8in (2.33m)
Engine: Ansaldo, 6-cylinder, petrol, 80bhp
Speed: 47mph (75km/hr)
Range: 250 miles (400km)

BA-7 Armoured Car Russia
Ford Russia
1934. Commonly called the **Bronieford** ('armoured Ford'), this was based upon the Ford V-8 engine and chassis, surmounted by a simple armoured body. The armouring was confined to the engine and crew compartment, so that the result is an incongruous mixture of flat armour plate and rounded commercial wings, running boards, bumpers and hub-caps. A small hand-operated turret was on the rear of the boxy body and was fitted with a machine gun. Some vehicles carried radio and used the contemporary style of tubular rail antenna surrounding the roof.

Armament: 1 × MG
Armour: 10mm
Crew: 3
Weight: 3.5 tons (3,556kg)
Length: 12ft 2in (3.71m)
Width: 5ft 7in (1.70m)
Height: 6ft 4in (1.93m)
Engine: Ford V-8 petrol, 60bhp at 3,200rpm
Speed: 45mph (72km/hr)
Range: 155 miles (250km)

BA-10 Armoured Car Russia
State factories
1938. Throughout the 1930s the Soviet Army developed a number of armoured cars, the best ones being a series of six-wheelers starting with the BA-1 in 1932. The final one, which went into mass-production in 1938, was the BA-10 and it became the standard vehicle of reconnaissance and independent armoured units. It was not a particularly innovative design, being a slab-sided body riveted together and built on to a military truck chassis. However, it was robust and reliable and, despite the limitations of 6 x 4 drive, it served well in several different variants until the German invasion. After 1941 there were few armoured cars left in service, most having been lost in the first few months of the war, and such was the need for tanks that no effort was put into making more cars. One prewar version of the BA-10 was built for railway running with flanged wheels and was used in that way in quite substantial numbers.

Armament: 1 × 45mm; 1 × coaxial MG; 1 × hull mounted MG
Armour: 15mm
Crew: 4
Weight: 5.06 tons (5,140kg)
Length: 15ft 3in (4.64m)
Width: 6ft 9in (2.05m)
Height: 7ft 3in (2.20m)

Engine: GAZ-MI, 4-cylinder, petrol, 50bhp at 2,800rpm
Speed: 35mph (55km/hr)
Range: 190 miles (300km)

BA-27 Armoured Car Russia
AMO

1927. The BA-27 was the first armoured car to be built since the Putilov designs of 1916 and was intended to provide fire support for infantry on the march as well as ranging ahead in the reconnaissance role. With a 37mm gun in the turret it was looked upon in much the same way as the contemporary close support tank but it was a good deal cheaper. The BA series of cars were not particularly distinguished in appearance or performance, but the BA-27 had the same turret as the MS Light tank (*qv*) and could be maintained much more easily than a tracked vehicle. When it was phased out of first-line service it continued in use for internal security duties.

Armament: 1 × 37mm; 1 × hull MG
Armour: 8mm
Crew: 4
Weight: 4.43 tons (4,500kg)
Length: 15ft 2in (4.63m)
Width: 5ft 11in (1.81m)
Height: 8ft 3in (2.51m)
Engine: Model AMO, 4-cylinder, petrol, 36bhp at 1,700rpm
Speed: 30mph (45km/hr)
Range: 250 miles (400km)

BA-64 Armoured Car Russia
GAZ

1942. The BA-64 was put into production to fill a need for a light armoured car for commanders and their staffs, for light reconnaissance and for liaison duties. The general layout came from the soft-skinned GAZ-64 light cross-country vehicle but the angled armour was heavily influenced by contemporary German designs. The usual version carried a single machine gun in the open-topped turret, but there were innumerable variants, the most common being a command car with radio. One version copied the Austin-Putilov-Kegresse and had a half-track at the rear. Production took second place to tanks, and was erratic until it ended in 1945. Nevertheless, the little car survived in service until 1956 in the Soviet Union, and even later in some minor Communist armies.

Armament: 1 × 7.62mm MG
Armour: 10mm
Crew: 2

Weight: 2.36 tons (2,400kg)
Length: 12ft 0in (3.65m)
Width: 5ft 0in (1.52m)
Height: 6ft 3in (1.90m)
Engine: GAZ, 4-cylinder, petrol, 54bhp at 2,800rpm
Speed: 50mph (80km/h)
Range: 375 miles (600km)

Beaverette Light Reconnaissance Car UK
Standard

1940. The summer of 1940 saw an orgy of armoured car building in Britain as almost every Home Guard company, and many regular army units, bolted boiler plate on to any available civilian car and stuck a Lewis gun on top. Beyond boosting morale and giving people something to do, they had very little purpose, and there would no point in cataloguing these vehicles, even if it were possible. However, out of all this activity came one or two officially-sponsored designs which, even if they were of little more practical value than the home-made creations, were nevertheless given formal approval and went into mass production. Beaverette was perhaps the most prolific of these; it was an armoured body mounted on top of the chassis of the Standard 14 saloon car. Slab-sided and open-topped, with the sides built up to head height and given slots for vision and a machine gun, the body overloaded the springs so that they always had a distinct tail-down attitude. Named after Lord Beaverbrook, Minister of Aircraft Production, who demanded then for the protection of aircraft factories and airfields.

Armament: 1 × MG
Armour: 11mm of mild steel; later, 10mm armour
Crew: 3
Weight: 2 tons (2,040kg)
Length: 12ft 6in (3.81m)
Width: 5ft 3in (1.60m)
Height: 5ft 0in (1.52m)
Engine: Standard 14, 4-cylinder, petrol, 45bhp
Speed: 40mph (65km/hr)
Range: not known

Boarhound USA
See T18E2

BRDM-1 Russia
See BTR-40P

BRDM-2 Amphibious Reconnaissance Vehicle Russia
State factories

1963. The BRDM-2 was the successor to the BTR-40P, the main differences between the two being that the later vehicle has a more powerful engine, a greater range, and a small turret. Like the BRDM-1 this vehicle was fitted with a single water jet for propulsion in the water, but it also had an NBC outfit. For night movement there was a complete set of infra-red lights and vision equipment. There were roughly the same variants on this chassis as on the earlier one, except that it has occasionally been seen carrying anti-aircraft missiles. Manufacture ceased in the later 1980s, but they can still be found in service with many armies around the world.

Armament: 1 × 14mm MG in turret; 1 × coaxial 7.62mm MG
Armour: 10mm
Crew: 4
Weight: 6.88 tons (7,000kg)
Length: 18ft 9in (5.71m)
Width: 7ft 6in (2.28m)
Height: 7ft 6in (2.28m)
Engine: GAZ-41, V-8, petrol, 140bhp
Speed: 62mph (100km/hr)
Range: 465 miles (750km)

BRM (BMP-3K) Reconnaissance Vehicle Russia
Kurgan

1993. This is a specialised variation of the full-tracked BMP-3 MICV (described in the Infantry Armour section) which is equipped for the reconnaissance and target acquisition role. The principal changes are the removal of the 100mm gun and its replacement by a collection of electro-optical and other surveillance and target finding devices, position-finding equipment and other apparatus for the specified role. The troop compartment and turret space now hold the electronics with their operators and there are additional firing and vision ports for their use when required. A 30mm cannon is carried, in a small turret, together with the usual machine gun.

Armament: 1 × 30mm cannon; 1 × MG
Armour: not disclosed
Crew: 6
Weight: 18.70 tons (19,000kg)
Length: 23ft 0in (7.0m)
Width: 10ft 4in (3.15m)
Height: 7ft 9in (2.37m)
Engine: UTD V-10 diesel, 500bhp

Speed: 43mph (70km/hr)
Range: 370 miles (600km)

BRM-23 Reconnaissance Vehicle Bulgaria
State factories

This is a variant of the BMP-23 MICV described in the Infantry Armour section and is derived from the Russian MT-LB multi-purpose carrier chassis. Full-tracked and amphibious, it carries a turret armed with a 23mm cannon, a coaxial machine gun and an anti-tank missile launcher. It has a five-man crew and is liberally equipped with observation, surveillance, viewing and measuring equipment to cover virtually any type of reconnaissance mission.

Armament: 1 × 23mm cannon; 1 × coaxial MG; 1 × ATGW
Armour: not disclosed
Crew: 5
Weight: 13.28 tons (14,800kg)
Length: 22ft 2in (7.29m)
Width: 9ft 8in (3.05m)
Height: 7ft 1in (2.53m)
Engine: Model V-6, 6-cylinder, diesel, 310bhp at 3,000rpm
Speed: 40mph (65km/hr)
Range: 310 miles (500km)

Bronieford Russia
See BA-7

BTR-40P/BRDM-1 Amphibious Reconnaissance Vehicle Russia
State factories

1957. The BTR-40P was later known as the **BRDM-1** and it followed the earlier BTR-40 APC. Although it is now fairly old, it is still in service with many Communist-supplied countries. The hull is roughly boat-shaped, with four well-spaced wheels, and on each side, between the wheels, are two auxiliary wheels which can be raised, for good going, or lowered on rough ground so as to prevent bellying. The engine is at the front, with the crew compartment behind. There is no turret, a machine gun being carried on an external pedestal mount. In the original version the roof of the crew compartment could be opened to allow the occupants to stand up and fire, using the roof plates as shields. In 1959 the design was changed to a solid roof with two hatches, and this remained the subsequent standard pattern. There is a single water-jet propulsion unit at the rear, and apart from erecting a trim plate at the front, the vehicle requires no preparation before taking to the water. There are three standard variant models: a command version with extra communications equipment, a CBW reconnaissance vehicle, and an anti-tank missile carrier

Armament: 1 × MG
Armour: 10mm
Crew: 5
Weight: 5.51 tons (5,600kg)
Length: 18ft 8in (5.71m)
Width: 7ft 3in (2.25m)
Height: 6ft 3in (1.92m)
Engine: GAZ-40P, 6-cylinder, petrol, 90bhp at 3,400rpm
Speed: 50mph (80km/hr)
Range: 310 miles (500km)

Cadillac Gage Commando V-150 Armoured Car USA
Cadillac Gage

1964. This was developed as a private venture, was offered to the US Army and accepted by them, and was then sold widely overseas. It was also adopted by the Portuguese Army in a locally-made licensed version called the **Chaimite**

The hull is of welded construction and well-sloped, carrying a turret which can be fitted with a variety of armament. The driver is seated in the front, with the engine and transmission at the rear. All wheels are driven, but the wheels are carried on modified truck axles and are not independently sprung. The vehicle is fully amphibious, being propelled in water by the paddle-action of the wheels. The Model **V-100** was the first to appear; it was followed by the **V-200**, which was simply an enlarged model with more powerful engine and capable of carrying heavier armament, up to a 90mm gun. In 1971 the **V-150** was produced, which is to the same dimensions as the V-100 but with better performance and various engineering improvements, and this became the production standard.

Armament: to customer's requirements
Armour: not disclosed
Crew: 2 + 10
Weight: 9.40 tons (9,550kg)
Length: 19ft 8in (5.68m)
Width: 7ft 5in (2.26m)
Height: 8ft 0in (2.43m)
Engine: Chrysler, V-8, diesel, 202bhp
Speed: 55mph (88km/hr)
Range: 600 miles (950km)

Cadillac Gage Commando V-300 USA
Cadillac Gage

1983. This was another private venture, virtually an enlarged V-150. It uses a similarly-sloped hull but has six wheels instead of four and is consequently larger and heavier and carries heavier armament. The driver and engine are side-by-side at the front of the welded hull, with the large troop compartment behind, surmounted by a turret. The turret can carry any desired armament up to the Cockerill 90mm gun and the crew compartment has room for up to 9 fully-equipped infantrymen. They enter and leave via two doors at the rear of the hull, and when inside they each have a vision block and firing port. No preparation is required for swimming, and the vehicle is propelled in the water by its wheels.

Armament: to customer's choice
Armour: not disclosed
Crew: 3 + 9
Weight: 14.73 tons (14,970kg)
Length: 21ft 0in (6.40m)
Width: 8ft 4in (2.54m)
Height: 8ft 10in (2.69m)
Engine: 6CTA 6-cylinder turbocharged diesel, 275bhp at 2,500rpm
Speed: 62mph (100km/hr)
Range: 435 miles (700km)

Cadillac Gage V-600 Armoured Car USA
Cadillac Gage

This is really an improved V-300, having originally been known (until 1989) as the **V-300A1**. A 6 x 6 with recognisably Cadillac Gage family shape, it is distinguished by carrying the Cadillac Gage Low Recoil Turret as fitted to the Stingray tank, complete with 105mm gun and a large multi-baffle muzzle brake. A prototype was built but there does not appear to have been any subsequent production.

Armament: 1 × 105mm; 2 × MG
Armour: not disclosed
Crew: 4
Weight: 18.20 tons (18,500kg)
Length: 20ft 8in (6.30m)
Width: 8ft 9in (2.68m)
Height: 9ft 0in (2.74m)
Engine: Cummins turbocharged 6-cylinder diesel, 275bhp at 2,500rpm
Speed: 63mph (100km/hr)
Range: 370 miles (600km)

Cadillac Gage Commando Scout USA
Cadillac Gage

1977. This is the smallest car in the Cadillac Gage family and is recognisable by the distinct wedge shape, the hull rising from the pointed nose for almost two-thirds of the length before flattening into the hull top and supporting a small turret. The vehicle is a 4 x 4 and both axles have locking differentials; it is not amphibious, but can negotiate water up to 3ft 10in (1.16m) deep. Normally armed with a single machine gun, there are various options offered, including twin machine guns, a 40mm grenade launcher or a TOW anti-tank missile launcher. About 200 have been purchased by various countries.

Armament: 1 x MG; other options
Armour: not disclosed
Crew: 2 or 3
Weight: 7.12 tons (7,240kg)
Length: 16ft 5in (5.00m)
Width: 6ft 9in (2.06m)
Height: 7ft 1in (2.16m)
Engine: Cummins V-6 diesel, 149bhp at 2,300rpm
Speed: 60mph (96km/hr)
Range: 800 miles (1,290km)

Cadillac Gage LAV Series USA
Cadillac Gage

1998. The Cadillac Gage series of vehicles hitherto known (and described above) as the V-150, V-300 etc., are now known under the nomenclature **LAV-150**, **LAV-300** etc. Cadillac Gage itself is now Textron Marine and Land Systems.

Cascavel Brazil
See Engesa EE-9

Chaimite Portugal
See Cadillac Gage Commando V-150

Charron Armoured Car France
CGV

1902. This was the first armoured car ever built, and probably counts as the first armoured fighting vehicle, if we ignore the various chariots and war carts in previous centuries. Charron, Griardot and Voigt were three ex-racing drivers who, after selling Panhard cars to their considerable profit, set up their own car factory to make CGV cars in 1900. In 1901 the French Army were showing interest in motor cars, and CGV clad one of their touring cars in steel plate, put a Hotchkiss machine gun on a pintle mounting in the rear seat area, put a shield

around it and sold it to the French Army. They sent it to Algeria, where it vanished into obscurity.

In 1904 CGV were approached by the Russian Army who produced a specification of what they wanted and asked for 36 to be built. The result was a boxy structure of steel with holes for windows. On the roof was a revolving turret with a Maxim machine gun, and on the sides were channel-shaped steel girders for unditching the vehicle if it got stuck. It was, for its time, a reasonably practical design and the first example was duly delivered to Russia. It appears to have been used in St Petersburg for quelling riots, but the Russians then repudiated the remainder of the contract. The second car, which was ready for delivery, was sold to the French Army and CGV decided to get out of the armoured vehicle business while they still had a whole skin.

Armament: 1 x Hotchkiss 8mm MG
Armour: 5mm
Crew: 4
Engine: Charron, 4-cylinder, petrol, 30bhp

Coventry Armoured Car UK
Karrier, Daimler

1945. By the middle of the WWII the British Army was equipped with four marks of Humber and two of Daimler armoured car. Both types had their advantages, and so, in order to rationalize manufacture, it was decided to combine forces and develop one car incorporating the best of both designs and then put it into production in both BSA and Rootes factories. Design work was undertaken by Humber of Coventry, from which the name of the new car was derived; Commer (a Rootes subsidiary) worked on the transmission, and Daimler developed the suspension and steering. An American engine was selected for use, and the first pilot models were put under test late in 1944.

The Coventry car was based largely on the Daimler design, but with a more roomy hull. The prototype **Mark 1** carried a 2-pounder gun in the turret, but a **Mark 2** with a 75mm gun was also built. Independent suspension by swinging axles was used, with the drive taken by two shafts from a central transmission unit. About 1,600 vehicles were ordered, but the war ended and the orders were cancelled. Only a few were produced, and most of them were sold to France shortly afterwards, to be used in Indo-China.

Armament: 1 x 2-pdr or 75mm gun; 1 x MG
Armour: 14mm
Crew: 4
Weight: 11.50 tons (11,685kg)
Length: 15ft 6in (4.72m)

Width: 8ft 9in (2.66m)
Height: 7ft 9in (2.36m)
Engine: Hercules RXLD, 6-cylinder, petrol, 175bhp at 2,600rpm
Speed: 40mph (65km/hr)
Range: 250 miles (400km)

Crossley-Chevrolet Armoured Car UK

This name is loosely applied to a number of Crossley Indian Pattern cars which, in 1939, were refurbished by removing the bodies, scrapping the Crossley chassis and mechanicals, and replacing the bodies on to Chevrolet truck chassis. Except for the pressed-steel wheels with balloon tyres and the necessarily-altered front mudguards, the resulting vehicle was virtually indistinguishable from the original; it had, though, a higher road speed and a better ride for the crew. A small number – fewer than 20 – were used in Palestine and Syria in 1940–41 and were eventually given to the Persian Army in 1942.

Crossley Indian Pattern Armoured Car
UK
Crossley

1923/25. A 4 x 2 car developed for service on the Indian frontiers, this was based on a Crossley truck chassis and was of the usual 'car' shape but with a dome-shaped turret on top of the fighting compartment. This had four ball-pattern machine gun mountings at 90° spacing around it, into which two machine guns could be placed in whatever combination best suited the day's task. A small rotating observation cupola was on top of the turret, and some had a spotlight on top of the cupola. The footbrake acted on the propeller-shaft, which made the vehicle somewhat skittish on slippery surfaces.

Armament: 2 x MG
Armour: 8mm
Crew: 4
Weight: 5 tons (5,080kg)
Length: 16ft 6in (5.03m)
Width: 6ft 0in (1.83m)
Height: 7ft 1in (2.16)
Engine: Crossley, 6-cylinder petrol, 50bhp
Speed: 40mph (65km/hr)
Range: 125 miles (200km)

Crossley Mark I Armoured Car UK
Woolwich

1931. This design was developed in Woolwich Arsenal from 1928 onward, the finally-approved model being built as the Mark 1 in 1931. The body

was mounted on a Crossley light six-wheeled truck chassis to produce a 6 x 4 machine. The design was the usual 'car' shape of the period, a long bonnet followed by a short cab for driver and machine gunner, then a small fighting compartment carrying the revolving turret, and finally a flat cargo space over the rear pair of wheels. The turret originally was that of the contemporary Lanchester car, but this appears to have been removed and replaced by one from the contemporary Vickers Light Tank at some later stage. Armament was a single machine gun in the turret and another in the hull alongside the driver.

Armament: 2 x MG
Armour: 8mm
Crew: 4
Weight: 5.43 tons (5,516kg)
Length: 15ft 3in (4.64m)
Width: 6ft 2in (1.87m)
Height: 8ft 7in (2.62m)
Engine: Crossley, 6-cylinder petrol, 50bhp
Speed: 45mph (72km/hr)
Range: not known

Crossley RAF Pattern Armoured Car UK
Vickers

1928/30. This title covers a number of designs of 6 x 4 car developed in the period. The first was built by Vickers on the 30/70 Crossley truck chassis. It followed the usual 'car' shape of the time but with rather larger fighting compartment and with the domed turret with four gun mounts first used on the Indian pattern cars. It was also notable for having the spare wheels slung on the side so as to be capable of revolving, and somewhat lower than the chassis, so that they prevented the vehicle bellying on rough ground. Many were fitted with ground/air radio, using a large frame antenna suspended on four poles.

A second version, built in 1930, used the Crossley 38/110 truck chassis, which differed principally in using a more powerful 110bhp engine; the dimensions remained the same.

A third version, which was also placed on the export market by Vickers, was a lighter vehicle built on the Crossley 20/60 light 6 x 4 chassis using a 4-cylinder 60bhp engine and with a turret similar to that on the current Vickers light tank.

First version
Armament: 2 x MG
Armour: 8mm
Crew: 4
Weight: 7.12 tons (7,235kg)
Length: 20ft 7in (6.27m)

Width: 7ft 10in (2.40m)
Height: 9ft 5in (2.56m)
Engine: Crossley, 6-cylinder petrol, 70bhp
Speed: 50mph 80km/hr)
Range: not known

Csaba 39 Armoured Car Hungary
Magyar

1939. The Csaba was a small car with simple lines and sloped armour. In many ways it resembled the British Daimler Dingo, though it carried a rotating turret and heavier armament. The driver sat in the stubby bow with the two turret crew directly behind him. The engine was immediately behind them, housed in a compartment which sloped under at the back plate. The commander had a radio and the antenna ran around the turret in the contemporary manner. Only a small number of these cars were built, and it is doubtful if they ever saw active service.

Armament: 1 x 37mm; 1 x MG
Armour: 10mm
Crew: 3
Length: 14ft 9in (4.49m)
Width: 6ft 10in (2.08m)
Height: 7ft 5in (2.27m)
Weight: 5.80 tons (5,900kg)

Daimler Armoured Car UK
Daimler

1941. The success of the Daimler Dingo Scout Car led to the suggestion that it might be scaled-up to become a full-sized armoured car. Work began in April 1939 but due to initial troubles with transmission and other components, it was not until April 1941 that the Daimler Armoured Car **Mark 1** entered service. It had many unusual technical features for its time; the vehicle used no chassis, the wheels and mechanical components being attached directly to the lower hull. Drive was via a fluid flywheel torque converter and pre-selector gearbox, and disc brakes were used some 20 years before they were accepted for use on commercial vehicles. The turret was that of the Tetrarch light tank and carried a 2-pounder gun, the first time that an armoured car was armed as well as the contemporary tanks. Duplicate steering was provided so that the vehicle could be driven backwards at speed to escape ambush.

In 1943 a **Mark 2** Daimler was developed; this differed in its gun mounting, radiator and radiator protection, and added an escape hatch for the driver, but was otherwise the same as the Mark 1. The Daimler was used extensively in the North African and European campaigns and remained in service for some years after the war.

Armament: 1 x 2-pdr gun
Armour: 16mm
Crew: 3
Weight: 7.5 tons (7,620kg)
Length: 13ft 0in (3.96m)
Width: 8ft 0in (2.43m)
Height: 7ft 4in (2.23m)
Engine: Daimler, 6-cylinder, petrol, 95bhp at 3,600rpm
Speed: 50mph (80km/hr)
Range: 205 miles (330km)

Daimler Dingo Scout Car UK
Daimler

1938. When the British Army began thinking seriously about armoured formations, a small and nimble reconnaissance vehicle was among the first demands. Three designs were submitted and that by the BSA company was chosen. The BSA organisation produced a front-wheel drive car, and also owned the Daimler company, and since they chose to build the armoured car in the Daimler works it took the Daimler name. A small vehicle with a central crew compartment and rear engine, it relied on speed and agility to survive, since its sole armament was a machine gun and its armour thin. Early models had four-wheel steering and a folding roof, but these were soon abandoned as being of no practical value. It was a highly successful design, remained in production throughout the war, some 6,600 being built, and numbers remained in service until the 1950s. It was universally known to the troops as the 'Dingo' although that name originally belonged to an Alvis design which was not adopted.

Armament: 1 x MG
Armour: 30mm
Crew: 2
Weight: 2.95 tons (3,000kg)
Length: 10ft 5in (3.23m)
Width: 5ft 8in (1.72m)
Height: 4ft 11in (1.50m)
Engine: Daimler 6-cylinder, petrol, 55bhp at 2,800rpm
Speed: 55mph (88km/hr)
Range: 200 miles (325km)

Delaunay-Belleville Armoured Car UK
Delaunay

The Delaunay-Belleville was a luxurious and expensive car considered (by the French at least) to be superior to the Rolls-Royce. As with most cars of that class, chassis were manufactured for supply to specialist coachbuilders, and thus a small number of chassis were in Britain in 1914 and were acquired by the Admiralty and provided with armoured bodies. In general terms the D-B models were similar in layout to the Rolls-Royce, though rather larger and with a flat-topped circular turret. Only a small number were built.

Eland Armoured Car South Africa
Sandcock-Austral

1962. The Eland is actually the Panhard AML adopted by the South African Army. The Eland **Mark 1** was the original French-manufactured vehicle; the **Mark 2** was a copy made in South Africa, but apart from improved steering is the same as the Mark 1, and uses the same French engine. The **Mark 3** was as for the Mark 2 but with improved brakes, and the **Mark 4** had improvements to the fuel system and introduced a locally-made hydraulic clutch mechanism. The **Mark 5**, in 1972, adopted a South African engine, improved suspension and runflat tyres, and the **Mark 6** was any earlier Mark brought up to Mark 5 standard. Finally, the **Mark 7** of 1979 had new brakes, a more comfortable driving compartment and a host of minor improvements. Armament varies; some are fitted with a 60mm gun-mortar, others with a 90mm gun, still others with a 20mm cannon; all have a 7.62mm coaxial machine gun. Although nominally the same size as the original Panhard, over the period of development the dimensions have changed and, of course, depend upon the armament and equipment.

Eland Mark 7DT/60
Armament: 1 × 60mm gun-mortar; 2 × MG
Armour: not disclosed
Crew: 3
Weight: 5.22 tons (5,300kg)
Length: 13ft 3in (4.05m)
Width: 6ft 8in (2.02m)
Height: 6ft 2in (1.88m)
Engine: diesel, 4-cylinder, turbocharged, 103bhp at 4,000rpm
Speed: 53mph (85km/hr)
Range: 280 miles (450km)

Engesa EE-3 Jararaca Scout Car Brazil
Engesa

1979. The Jararaca is the smallest member of the Engesa family. It is scarcely larger than a Jeep, but carries three men with armoured protection. The hull is made from standard Engesa double plate, welded at all joints, and has three top hatches and two side doors for the crew. All plating is sloped, and the silhouette is kept low. The Jararaca can carry

a variety of light weapons, including a Milan missile launcher or a 20mm cannon, but all have to be on external mounts without armour protection. The rear-mounted engine drives all four wheels, which have run-flat tyres. The vehicle has been adopted by Cyprus, Gabon, Jordan and Uruguay.

Armament: 1 × MG
Armour: not disclosed
Crew: 3
Weight: 5.70 tons (5,800kg)
Length: 13ft 8in (4.16m)
Width: 7ft 4in (2.23m)
Height: 5ft 6in (1.56m)
Engine: Mercedes-Benz 4-cylinder, turbocharged diesel, 120bhp at 2,800rpm
Speed: 62mph (100km/hr)
Range: 435 miles (700km)

Engesa EE-9 Cascavel Armoured Car
Brazil
Engesa

1973. The Cascavel was built in Brazil by the Engesa Company. It used some of the components and techniques of the EE-11 APC (*qv*) and as many commercially available parts as possible. The result was a simple and reliable 6 x 6 vehicle at a reasonable price. The hull was made of spaced armour welded at the joints; the outer plate was harder than the inner one to improve the protection and all were sloped. The turret was the same as on the Panhard AML armoured car. It also carried the same 90mm gun, licensed from the Belgian firm of Cockerill and made in Brazil. The suspension was unique to the Engesa range of military vehicles and included the firm's Boomerang double-axle rear-drive. The hull was divided into three sections: driving compartment, fighting compartment and engine/transmission. The entire hull was air-conditioned, which made it impervious to the fumes of Molotov cocktails or smoke grenades. The vehicle was also sold to Libya and Qatar.

The **Mark 1** Cascavel was the first (1975) production model; armed with a 37mm gun it used a Mercedes engine. **Mark 2** was the first export model, had a Mercedes engine and a Hispano-Suiza turret with 90mm gun. **Mark 3** (1977) used a turret and 90mm gun manufactured by Engesa, a Mercedes engine and an automatic transmission. **Mark 4** used a Detroit Diesel engine with Engesa turret and gun, while **Mark 5** reverted to using a Mercedes engine.

Mark 5
Armament: 1 × 90mm; 1 × coaxial MG
Armour: 16mm

Crew: 3
Weight: 13.19 tons (13,400kg)
Length: 17ft 1in (5.20m)
Width: 8ft 8in (2.64m)
Height: 9ft 9in (2.68m)
Engine: Detroit Diesel 6v-63N, V-6 diesel, 212bhp at
  2,800rpm
Speed: 62mph (100km/hr)
Range: 545 miles (880km)

Engesa EE-17 Sucuri Armoured Car Brazil
Engesa
1977. The Sucuri was a large armoured car based on
the experience gained with the Cascavel (*above*) and
the EE-11 APC (*qv*). It was described by the firm as
fulfilling the role of a wheeled tank, and was a large
and well-armed 6 x 6 car. The turret was that used
on the French AMX-13 light tank, and it gave the
Sucuri a considerable offensive capability. As with
all the Engesa vehicles, the Sucuri was designed to
use as many commercial components as possible
and had the Boomerang rear axle with an extra drive
to the front wheels. However, it appears to have
found no takers, and had vanished by 1980, to
reappear some years later as the EE-18 (*below*).

Armament: 1 × 105mm; 1 × coaxial MG
Armour: not disclosed
Crew: 3
Weight: 18.20 tons (18,500kg)
Length: 20ft 9in (6.32m)
Width: 8ft 2in (2.49m)
Height: 9ft 2in (2.80m)
Engine: Detroit Diesel 6V 53T V-6, turbocharged
  diesel, 300bhp at 2,800rpm
Speed: 68mph (110km/hr)
Range: 372 miles (600km)

Engesa EE-18 Sucuri Tank Destroyer
Brazil
Engesa
1987. Engesa continued to develop their Sucuri
idea, and in 1987 came round for a second bite at
the cherry. This model used a new hydro-
pneumatic suspension system and adopted the
OTO-Melara 105mm gun with thermal sleeve and
muzzle brake, though it was also said that other
105mm guns could be mounted if required. A
modern electronic fire control system allowed
engagement of moving or stationary targets, and full
night vision equipment was provided. The 6 x 6
vehicle was built from face-hardened armour and
had the engine at the front, alongside the driver,
leaving the rear of the hull for the fighting
compartment and turret. However, it again failed to

arouse any military interest and was finally
abandoned in about 1993.

Armament: 1 × 105mm; 1 coaxial MG
Armour: not disclosed
Crew: 4
Weight: 18.20 tons (18,500kg)
Length: 19ft 2in (5.84m)
Width: 9ft 2in (2.80m)
Height: 8ft 6in (2.59m)
Engine: Scania DSI-11, 6-cylinder, turbocharged diesel,
  380bhp at 2,100rpm
Speed: 65mph (105km/hr)
Range: 435 miles (700km)

Fennek Multi-Purpose Reconnaissance
  Vehicle Netherlands
See DAF MPC in the Infantry Armour section

Ferret UK
Daimler
1953. This was developed in the late 1940s to
replace the wartime Daimler Dingo, and it
resembles it to the extent that it has a central crew
compartment, four wheels and a rear engine. But
the crew compartment was deeper, giving better
protection to the occupants, and so arranged that
the driver was seated towards the front of the
vehicle, leaving space for two crewmen behind him.
Several variants were developed; perhaps the most
common had a small machine gun turret on top of
the roofed-over crew compartment. Others had
flotation screens for swimming or anti-tank missile
launchers attached. It proved to be a popular vehicle
and was sold to some 35 other countries beside
Britain.

Armament: 1 × MG
Armour: 16mm
Crew: 3
Weight: 3.42 tons (3,485kg)
Length: 11ft 1in (3.37m)
Width: 6ft 3in (1.90m)
Height: 6ft 2in (1.87m)
Engine: Rolls-Royce, 6-cylinder petrol, 129bhp at
  3,750rpm
Speed: 58mph (93km/hr)
Range: 185 miles (300km)

Fiat 611 Armoured Car Italy
Fiat
1935. In 1934 Fiat began production of an armoured
car based on a 6 x 4 military truck chassis. When
completed, the car looked very much like a larger
version of the current Lancia 1Z. It had the same

general shape of body, with a small turret on top mounting two machine guns firing forward, and one in the rear face. In the hull was another machine gun facing rearwards. An alternative version mounted a 37mm gun in the turret. The hull was fairly large and it was well suited to internal security duties and frontier patrolling. It was used in Ethiopia, East Africa, and in Italy by the Public Security Corps.

Armament: 4 × MG; or 1 × 37mm + 2 × MG
Armour: 15mm
Crew: 5
Weight: 6.79 tons (6,900kg)
Length: 18ft 7in (5.68m)
Width: 6ft 2in (1.88m)
Height: 8ft 8in (2.65m)
Engine: Fiat, 6-cylinder, petrol, 45bhp
Speed: 17mph (28km/hr)
Range: 347 miles (560km)

FIAT-OTO 6616 Armoured Car Italy
Iveco

1976. This is built by Iveco-Fiat in conjunction with the armaments firm of OTO-Melara and is a light 4 x 4 vehicle intended for frontier patrols, convoy escorts, internal security and reconnaissance. It is amphibious, propelling itself in the water by its wheels, and there is an NBC system, air-conditioning, a built-in fire-extinguishing system and a powered winch. The turret has powered traverse and is normally fitted with a 20mm cannon, but guns of up to 90mm calibre can be accommodated. It is in service in Italy, Peru, Somalia and other undisclosed countries.

Armament: 1 × 20mm; 1 × MG coaxial
Armour: 8mm
Crew: 3
Weight: 7.87 tons (8,000kg)
Length: 17ft 7in (5.37m)
Width: 8ft 3in (2.50m)
Height: 6ft 8in (2.04m)
Engine: Model 8062, 6-cylinder, turbocharged, diesel, 160bhp at 3,200rpm
Speed: 62mph (100km/hr)
Range: 435 miles (700km)

FN 4RM/62F AB Light Armoured Car
Belgium
FN

1971. This was the last armoured vehicle to be built by Fabrique Nationale of Liège, who have since confined their activities to the manufacture of weapons and training equipment. It was developed for the Belgian Gendarmerie and was based on the

chassis of a military truck which the company had produced. The hull was of armour steel, with the driver seated centrally, a crew compartment behind him and the engine in the rear. The turret housed the commander and gunner. Two machine guns were standard but the armament could be selected by the buyer. At the top end of the scale came a 90mm gun and coaxial machine gun; alternatively, one 60mm gun-mortar and two machine guns could be fitted, or simply a single machine gun. In addition to the Gendarmerie, a number were sold to Uruguay.

Armament: 2 × MG in turret
Armour: 6.5–13mm
Crew: 3
Weight: 8.86 tons (8,800kg)
Length: 14ft 8in (4.49m)
Width: 7ft 5in (2.26m)
Height: 7ft 9in (2.36m)
Engine: FN Model 652, 6-cylinder, petrol, 130bhp at 3,500rpm
Speed: 68mph (110km/h)
Range: 372 miles (600km)

Ford Lynx Scout Car Canada
Ford Canada

1941. This is best described as being the Daimler scout car built in Canada and using Canadian components. It followed the same general design, a central two-man compartment, open-topped 4 x 4 car with a short nose and rear engine, armed with a single light machine gun. Built by Ford of Canada, it used Ford commercial components to the greatest extent possible. The **Mark 2** was an improved model which dispensed with the (rarely used) folding roof, improved the cooling system and made various changes to stowage and other details.

Mark 1
Armament: 1 × MG
Armour: 30mm
Crew: 2
Weight: 4.01 tons (4,075kg)
Length: 12ft 2in (3.71m)
Width: 6ft 1in (1.85m)
Height: 5ft 10in (1.77m)
Engine: Ford V-8 petrol, 95bhp at 3,600rpm
Speed: 57mph (92km/hr)
Range: 200 miles (320km)

Mark 2
Armament: 1 × MG
Armour: 30mm
Crew: 2
Weight: 4.20 tons (4,270kg)
Length: 12ft 8in (3.86m)

Width: 6ft 4in (1.93m)
Height: 5ft 9in (1.75m
Engine: Ford V-8 petrol, 95bhp at 3,600rpm
Speed: 57mph (92km/hr)
Range: 200 miles (320km)

Fordson Armoured Car UK
Army workshops, Cairo

1940. These vehicles were built by removing the bodies from Rolls-Royce armoured cars which had been in service since the early 1920s with the Royal Air Force in the Middle East, and installing them on to Fordson truck chassis. The Fordson wheelbase was rather longer than that of the Rolls, so some modification was done by extending the armour of the body slightly, but otherwise their appearance was that of the Rolls-Royce, except for the perforated steel truck wheels.

Fox Armoured Car Canada
GM Canada

1941. Just as the Ford Lynx was a Daimler scout car made of Canadian parts, so the Fox was more or less the Humber Mark 3 armoured car made by General Motors of Canada, using their own commercial components wherever possible.

Armament: 1 x HMG; 1 x MG
Armour: 15mm
Crew: 4
Weight: 7.37 tons (7,490kg)
Length: 14ft 9in (4.50m)
Width: 7ft 6in (2.27m)
Height: 8ft 1in (2.46m)
Engine: GMC 6-cylinder, petrol, 104bhp at 3,000rpm
Speed: 44mph (70km/hr)
Range: 210 miles (336km)

Fox CVR(W) UK
ROF Leeds

Fox was designed in the late 1960s by a military research establishment, developed by Daimler, who built the first prototypes, and then manufactured by the ROF organisation. CVR(W) = Combat Vehicle, Reconnaissance, (Wheeled). Its purpose was to replace Ferret with a car carrying more firepower, and Fox has a larger turret armed with a Rarden 30mm semi-automatic gun. Apart from this the general outline is very similar to that of Ferret, a simple four-wheeled car with the driver at the front and engine at the rear, though the hull is of aluminium armour rather than steel. The new gun is accompanied by modern fire control equipment, night vision aids, and surveillance radar if required.

As well as being used by the British Army it has also been supplied to Malawi and Nigeria.

Armament: 1 x 30mm Rarden cannon; 1 x MG
Armour: not disclosed
Crew: 3
Weight: 6.02 tons (6,120kg)
Length: 7ft 4in (2.24m)
Width: 7ft 1in (2.13m)
Height: 6ft 6in (1.98m)
Engine: Jaguar XK, 6-cylinder petrol,190bhp at 4,500rpm
Speed: 65mph (105km/hr)
Range: 270 miles (435km)

FUG-65 Amphibious Reconnaissance Car Hungary
State factories

1963. The FUG (Feldcrito Uszo Gepkocsi) is the Hungarian equivalent of the Soviet BTR-40 but it has a number of differences.It is fully amphibious and NBC protected and the driver has infra-red vision for night driving. Armament is light but with a five-man crew, space inside must be restricted. Variant models include a light armoured ambulance and an NBC reconnaissance vehicle, both in Hungarian service, and a version known as the **OF-65A** (*qv*) which is in Czech service.

Armament: 1 x MG
Armour: 13mm
Crew: 5
Weight: 6.89 tons (7,000kg)
Length: 19ft 0in (5.79m)
Width: 8ft 3in (2.50m)
Height: 6ft 3in (1.91m)
Engine: Csepel D-414, 4-cylinder, diesel, 100bhp at 2,300rpm
Speed: 54mph (87km/hr)
Range: 375 miles (600km)

FUG-70 Light Armoured Car Hungary
State factories

1970. The FUG-70 is a derivative of the FUG-65. It is very similar but has no superstructure and has a small turret mounted on the hull. It is fully amphibious, propelled by two water jets, is fully protected against NBC and carries infra-red driving aids. The small turret normally carries a heavy machine gun and a rifle-calibre gun. It appears to have been made only in small numbers.

Armament: 1 x 14.5mm MG; 1 x 7.62mm MG
Armour: 13mm
Crew: 3
Weight: 6.89 tons (7,000kg)

Length: 19ft 1in (5.82m)
Width: 7ft 6in (2.30m)
Height: 8ft 3in (2.50m)
Engine: Csepel, 6-cylinder, diesel, 160bhp
Speed: 62mph (100km/hr)
Range: 310 miles (600km)

Guy 4 x 4 Armoured Car UK
Guy

1938. In 1938 the War Office ran a long competitive trial to select a suitable armoured car, and at the end a contract was given to Guy Motors of Wolverhampton to produce what was then officially called a Light Tank (Wheeled). It was, in fact, a four-wheeled armoured car which Guy had based on components of their successful Quad Ant artillery tractor chassis. The vehicle had four-wheel drive, though without independent suspension, a simple armoured body and a turret mounting the new 15mm Besa heavy machine gun. Although the pilot models used riveted construction, Guy devised a method of welding which speeded up production.

After building 101 Guy cars, the company became more involved in mass-production of other vehicles and had no more space to make armoured cars, but they continued to produce armoured hulls and turrets which were furnished to the Karrier company for building into the Humber armoured car, based on the Guy design. A small number of Guy cars were in use in France in 1940, but after that they were used solely as training vehicles.

Armament: 1 × .50in or 15mm MG + 1 × .303in or 7.92mm MG
Armour: 15mm
Crew: 3
Weight: 5.20 tons (5,285kg)
Length: 13ft 6in (4.11m)
Width: 6ft 9in (2.05m)
Height: 7ft 6in (2.28m)
Engine: Meadows, 4-cylinder, petrol, 53bhp at 2,200rpm
Speed: 40mph (65km/hr)
Range: 210 miles (340km)

Guy 6 x 4 Armoured Car, Indian Pattern UK
Guy

1927. Also called the **Vickers-Guy**, since Vickers built the bodywork and Guy the chassis. The usual contemporary shape of long bonnet and short crew compartment, with a domed turret with four ball-mounts into which two machine guns could be fitted as required. The turret was topped by an observation cupola, and this had a searchlight on top

of it. A 6 x 4 arranged as two-and-four, the rear wheels could have tracks fitted to improve flotation in soft ground. The vehicle was produced to meet a requirement for patrolling on the North-West Frontier of India, but proved to be too big and heavy for that environment and all were withdrawn by 1934.

Armament: 2 × MG
Armour: 6mm
Crew: 4
Weight: 9 tons (9,145kg)
Length: 20ft 4in (6.20m)
Width: 7ft 7in (2.31m)
Height: 9ft 4in (2.84m)
Engine: Guy 6-cylinder petrol, 120bhp
Speed: 40mph (65km/hr)
Range: 150 miles (240km)

Harimau 2000 Scout Car UK
GKN

1986. This was essentially the old Daimler Ferret rebuilt with new automotive and other components so as to extend its life for another 15–20 years or so. It could be produced either by rebuilding existing Ferrets or it could be built from new. The most prominent difference was a larger and taller central crew compartment and a larger turret with vision blocks, periscopes, infra-red searchlight and smoke dischargers. The remainder of the vehicle was much the same, though with the headlights on the front mudguards rather than on the glacis plate. In spite of its apparent attractions, it failed to make an impression in the market and was discontinued by the early 1990s.

Harimau is the Malay word for 'tiger'; the vehicle was designed with a Malaysian Army contract in mind.

Armament: 1 × .50in MG
Armour: 16mm
Crew: 2
Weight: 4.72 tons (4,800kg)
Length: 12ft 8in (3.85m)
Width: 6ft 8in (2.03m)
Height: 6ft 10in (2.07m)
Engine: KHD V-8 air-cooled diesel, 140bhp at 3,600rpm
Speed: 62mph (100km/hr)
Range: 250 miles (400km)

Humber Armoured Car UK
Karrier

1941. In 1939 the existing British facilities for building armoured cars were fully committed, yet more were still needed, so the Rootes Group of motor manufacturers was asked to design and produce a car. To save time, Rootes adopted the existing Guy armoured car design and built it on the Karrier KT4 chassis produced by one of their subsidiaries as an artillery tractor for the Indian Army. This was modified by moving the engine to the rear and strengthening the suspension, after which a Guy-type of body was placed on top. Due to this employment of well-tried components, the design gave little difficulty, and production began in early 1941. Although built by Karrier Ltd., the name Humber (another Rootes company) was adopted so as to avoid confusion with other military vehicles known as carriers. The design was uncomplicated; solid axles were carried on semi-elliptic springs, and the turret carried a 15mm Besa heavy machine gun and a 7.92mm Besa machine gun.

The design was gradually improved. The **Mark 2** had the same chassis but an altered hull, with the driver's position better protected and a better arrangement of armour around the rear radiator. **Mark 3** had the Mark 2 hull but with a larger and more spacious turret, a raised roof line and a four-man crew and the **Mark 4** was as the Mark 3 but armed with an American 37mm gun in place of the 15mm Besa.

Armament: 1 × 15mm (1 × 37mm Mark 4); 1 × 7.92mm MG
Armour: 30mm
Crew: 3 (Marks 1 & 2) or (4 Marks 3 & 4)
Weight: 6.85 tons (6,960kg)
Length: 15ft 0in (4.57m)
Width: 7ft 2in (2.18m)
Height: 7ft 10in (2.38m)
Engine: Rootes, 6-cylinder, petrol, 90bhp at 3,200rpm
Speed: 45mph (72km/hr)
Range: 250 miles (400km)

Humberette UK
Humber
1940. This was generally similar to the Beaverette described above, a thinly armoured body placed on the chassis of the Humber Super Snipe saloon car. Few were made, since it was very quickly transformed into the **Humber Mark 1 Reconnaissance Car**, a somewhat more serviceable design. No dimensions available.

Humber Light Reconnaissance Car UK
Humber
1940. As soon as the Humberette was built, it was realised that the Super Snipe chassis was strong enough to support something rather better than the hastily-conceived boiler-plate body first drawn up. The body was improved in thickness and quality, the wheels were to the military pattern with run-flat tyres and the shock absorbing and springing more carefully matched to the weight. This became the **Ironside Mark 1**. The **Mark 2** added roof covering and a small manually-operated machine gun turret; while the **Mark 3** was given four-wheel drive. This final version was sufficiently good to be used in combat in Italy and Northwest Europe in 1944–45.

Mark 3
Armament: 2 × MG
Armour: 10mm
Crew: 3
Weight: 3.8 tons (3,860kg)
Length: 14ft 4in (4.37m)
Width: 6ft 2in (1.88m)
Height: 7ft 1in (2.16m)
Engine: Humber, 6-cylinder petrol, 87bhp
Speed: 50mph (80km/hr)
Range: not known

Ironside UK
Name given to the Humber Light Reconnaissance Car of 1940. It was something of a play on words; it represented the metal skin of the vehicle, and also alluded to Field Marshal Sir Edmund Ironside, C-in-C Home Forces at the time of its design.

Jeffery Quad Armoured Car UK
Jeffery
1917. These were built on Jeffery four-wheel drive truck chassis imported from the USA and were intended for use in India, where it was hoped that the all-wheel drive would improve performance in the difficult terrain. Somewhat higher than usual, the body had a recessed roof line into which the revolving turret fitted, with its single machine gun just clearing the roof. It had electric starting and dual controls allowing it to be driven from either end. It failed to live up to its promise, due to the combination of weight and narrow solid-tyred wheels, which caused it to sink into most types of ground. Nevertheless, they remained in use until the mid-1920s.

Armament: 1 × MG
Armour: 8mm
Crew: 3
Weight: 6.51 tons (6,615kg)
Length: 18ft 0in (5.49m)
Width: 6ft 4in (1.93m)
Height: 8ft 0in (2.44m)

Engine: Buda, 4-cylinder, petrol, 40bhp
Speed: 20mph (32km/hr)
Range: 100 miles (160km)

Kfz-13 Adler Germany
See Adler

Lanchester Armoured Car UK
Lanchester

1915. The Lanchester Sporting Forty touring car of 1914 was of advanced design and highly regarded, and it was adopted as a basis for an armoured car by the Royal Naval Air Service in 1915. The driver sat alongside the engine, a configuration which allowed the front of the car to be well shaped to deflect bullets, while the transmission was via a pre-selective epicyclic gearbox. The rear suspension was improved by using dual wheels, and the body was surmounted by a turret carrying a Vickers machine gun. The Lanchester car was used in Belgium by the RNAS, but after the naval units were disbanded, the Army standardized on Rolls-Royce and the Lanchesters were phased out. The only cars to survive for any length of time were those which accompanied No. 1 Squadron to Russia in 1916–17.

Armament: 1 × Vickers .303in MG
Armour: 8mm
Crew: 4
Weight: 4.80 tons (4,877kg)
Length: 16ft 0in (4.87m)
Width: 6ft 4in (1.93m)
Height: 7ft 6in (2.28m)
Engine: Lanchester, 6-cylinder, petrol, 60bhp
Speed: 50mph (80km/hr)
Range: 180 miles (290km)

Lanchester Armoured Car Mark 1 UK
Lanchester

1927. A completely different design to the 1915 model, the **Mark 1** had the usual car-type layout of the period, with front engine, driver in a cab behind it, and then a short fighting compartment with turret and a short flat cargo bed at the rear. Two front wheels, eight wheels in four doubles beneath the fighting compartment, all wheels driven. The turret carried two machine guns and was manually rotated, and the transmission was epicyclic. This was the first British armoured car to have any pretensions towards cross-country performance. The **Mark 2** version had a different cupola and single instead of dual rear wheels; the **Marks 1A** and **2A** had the hull machine gun removed to make space for radio equipment and an operator.

Armament: 3 × MG
Armour: 8mm
Crew: 3
Weight: 7.5 tons (7,820kg)
Length: 16ft 1in (4.90m)
Width: 6ft 4in (1.93m)
Height: 9ft 10in (2.99m)
Engine: Lanchester, 6-cylinder, petrol, 86bhp
Speed: 55mph (88km/hr)
Range: 200 miles (320km)

Lancia 1Z Armoured Car Italy
Lancia

1915. The Lancia became the standard Italian armoured car of World War I and was still in service in the Italian colonies when World War II started. In many ways it resembled the Rolls-Royce of the same era, built on a high-quality large touring car chassis, using a big engine and a robust chassis frame. In fact the chassis for most of them was a Lancia truck's, but it differed little from the large car's. The conversion work was done by the Ansaldo factory in Turin, which has led to some confusion over the correct name. The original turret mounted three machine guns, two in the main turret and a single one in a small cupola on the roof. Later this was removed and the third gun placed in a ball mounting at the rear of the hull. The driver was well protected by sloped armour and there were twin wire-cutting rails running over the front.

Armament: 3 × MG
Armour: 6mm
Crew: 6
Weight: 4.12 tons (4,190kg)
Length: 18ft 9in (5.73m)
Width: 6ft 5in (1.94m)
Height: 7ft 10in (2.37m)
Engine: Lancia, 4-cylinder, petrol, 70bhp at 2,200rpm
Speed: 37mph (60km/hr)
Range: 248 miles (400km)

Landsverk 180 Armoured Car Sweden
Landsverk

1935. The Landsverk company made armoured cars in some numbers in the 1930s both for the Swedish forces and for export. The 180 is typical of their general series of large cars; although there were several minor variants, they all retained the same general body shape and size. The 180 was built on to a Scania-Vabis truck chassis with 6 x 4 wheel drive and twin wheels on both rear axles, making ten wheels in all. The engine was in front, with the usual louvred armoured bonnet. The driver had a gunner sitting beside him, and the turret was forward of the rear wheels. It was fairly large for its time and carried a Madsen 20mm cannon with a coaxial machine gun. There was another machine gun in the hull, firing over the rear decking, and this gunner had a second steering wheel so that he could drive the car backwards.

The **Landsverk 182** was a similar vehicle, but slightly smaller and with a smaller engine. At least three survived in reserve service in Eire until the early 1970s, though their engines had been replaced by Leylands. Finland and Hungary also bought this model.

Armament: 1 × 20mm cannon;1 × coaxial MG;
  1 × hull MG
Armour: 8.5mm
Crew: 5
Weight: 7.70 tons (7,825kg)
Length: 18ft 10in (5.60m)
Width: 7ft 2in (2.18m)
Height: 6ft 11in (2.09m)
Engine: Scania-Vabis, 6-cylinder, 80bhp
Speed: 50mph (80km/hr)
Range: 180 miles (288km)

Leyland Armoured Car UK
Leyland

1915. Four heavy armoured cars were manufactured by Leyland Motors in 1915 for service in East Africa. The basis was the firm's standard lorry chassis, with an armoured body constructed by Messrs. Beardmore. This followed the usual 'car' shape, but was exceptionally tall, with a rotating turret on top of the fighting compartment; the turret carried a medium machine gun, and another machine gun was installed in the rear face of the fighting compartment. Solid axles and solid tyres of a somewhat narrow section must have been something of a trial in the roadless terrain of East Africa, and it has been said that the cars had very little effect upon the course of the campaign there.

Armament: 2 × MG
Armour: 7mm
Crew: 6
Dimensions: no reliable information available
Engine: Leyland, 4-cylinder petrol, 40bhp
Speed: 20mph (32km/hr)
Range: not known

Lohr RPX 90 Armoured Car France
Lohr

1983. This was a 4 x 4 car of the usual slope-sided, sharp-prowed form with recessed wheels very similar to the 6000 and 3000 models but carrying a

turret with a 90mm gun. As with other Lohr designs the driver sat front and centre with good vision through bullet-proof screens, which could be covered with armoured shutters when necessary. Entrance to the crew compartment was by two-piece doors in each side of the vehicle, and the engine compartment was at the rear. So far as can be ascertained, no production of this model ever took place beyond the prototype.

Armament: 1 × 90mm; 2 × MG
Armour: not disclosed
Crew: 3
Weight: 10.82 tons (11,000kg)
Length: 17ft 1in (5.20m)
Width: 8ft 8in (2.65m)
Height: 8ft 4in (2.54m)
Engine: 6-cylinder turbocharged diesel, 310bhp
Speed: 68mph (110km/hr)
Range: 620 miles (1,000km)

Lohr RPX 6000 Scout Car France
Lohr

1981. The Lohr RPX 6000 is a 4 x 4 wheeled scout vehicle developed as a private venture and not in response to any military demand. It is of conventional form, with prow-like front, sloped sides, recessed wheels and a flat roof with a one-man turret carrying a machine gun. The driver has excellent vision through bullet-proof glass wind-and side-screens with armour shutters. The three-man crew compartment is central, and the engine is at the rear of the hull. Several variations have been proposed, mounting small mortars or anti-tank or air defence missiles, but apart from a few prototypes, the design appears to have made little progress.

Armament: 1 × MG
Armour: not disclosed
Crew: 3
Weight: 6.69 tons (6,800kg)
Length: 15ft 0in (4.58m)
Width: 7ft 1in (2.16m)
Height: 5ft 5in (1.65m)
Engine: BMW, 6-cylinder petrol, 180bhp
Speed: 68mph (110km/hr)
Range: 375 miles (600km)

Luchs Reconnaissance Vehicle Germany
Rheinstahl AG

1975. Luchs ('Lynx') is an eight-wheeled amphibious car with all wheels driven and steerable, though in normal use only the front four wheels steer. The armoured steel hull is surmounted by a two-man turret carrying a 20mm cannon and a machine gun, together with infra-red sighting and vision equipment and a white-light searchlight. The driver sits at the front, while the radio operator sits at the rear where he can also drive the vehicle in reverse if needed. The interior is fully air-conditioned and protected against chemical, nuclear and biological weapons, while the fuel system is bullet-proof and the interior fully protected by automatic firefighting equipment. A total of 408 were built between 1975 and 1978, whereupon production ceased; it is used only by the German Army and was never exported.

Armament: 1 × 20mm; 1 × MG
Armour: not disclosed
Crew: 4
Weight: 19.19 tons (19,500kg)
Length: 25ft 5in (7.74m)
Width: 9ft 9in (2.98m)
Height: 9ft 6in (2.90m)
Engine: Daimler-Benz, V-10-cylinder, turbocharged, multi-fuel, 390bhp (diesel) or 320bhp (petrol), both at 2,500rpm
Speed: 56mph (90km/hr)
Range: 455 miles (730km)

Lynx Command and Reconnaissance Vehicle USA
FMC

1965. The Lynx Command and Reconnaissance Vehicle was developed as a private venture by FMC in the early 1960s, using many components of the M113A1 APC which they were then making. Development of the prototype was completed in 1963, but the US Army did not accept it for service and it was placed on the open market. It was subsequently adopted by the Netherlands Army (1966) and the Canadian Army (1968)

Lynx resembled the M113 APC in having a box-like body carried on full tracks; the hull was of aluminium armour, and the engine and transmission were at the rear. On top of the hull was a shallow turret carrying periscopes, on top of which was a .50-inch Browning machine gun in a remote-control mounting which could be operated from within the vehicle. The driver was at the left front; the commander occupied the turret, and a third crewman sat at the rear of the crew compartment to man the radio and also a machine gun in his open roof hatch. The Dutch version differed slightly in seating the radio operator alongside the driver. In 1974 the Dutch Army modified 266 of their vehicles by removing the turrets and replacing them with turrets mounting 25mm Oerlikon cannon which can be used in ground or anti-aircraft roles.

Armament: 2 × MG standard
Armour: not disclosed
Crew: 3
Weight: 8.63 tons (8,775kg)
Length: 15ft 1in (4.59m)
Width: 7ft 11in (2.41m)
Height: 7ft 2in (2.17m)
Engine: Detroit Diesel, V-6-cylinder, 215bhp at 2,800rpm
Speed: 45mph (70km/hr)
Range: 325 miles (525km)

M3A1 Scout Car USA
White

1939. During the 1930s the US Army experimented with a variety of armoured cars to be used by armoured cavalry for scouting missions, and in June 1939 the M3A1 scout car was standardized. It was subsequently widely used by all branches of the US Army and also by the British and other Allied armies. In view of its makers, it was invariably known as the **White Scout Car**.

The M3A1 consisted of a specially designed and strengthened chassis with all-wheel drive, surmounted by an open-topped armoured body. Seats in the cab held the driver and vehicle commander, while seats in the rear compartment were provided for an additional six passengers. A 'skate rail' ran around the rear compartment, upon which a .50-inch and a .30-inch machine gun could be mounted, while tripods carried in the vehicle allowed the guns to be dismounted for ground action. The windscreen was of shatter-proof glass and could be further protected by a hinged steel plate with vision slots. A detachable canvas top was provided for non-combat use.

Armament: 1 × .50in, 1 × .30in MG
Armour: 7mm
Crew: 2 + 6
Weight: 5.53 tons (5,625kg)
Length: 18ft 5in (5.62m)
Width: 6ft 8in (2.03m)
Height: 6ft 6in (1.99m)
Engine: Hercules JXD, 6-cylinder, petrol, 87bhp at 2,400rpm
Speed: 50mph (80km/hr)
Range: 250 miles (400km)

M8 Greyhound Armoured Car USA
Ford St Paul

1943. This vehicle started life as a design for a wheeled tank destroyer mounting a 37mm gun, but early in 1942 it became apparent that there was no point in such a device and the designation was changed to armoured car. It was standardized as the M8 in June 1942 and went into immediate production; by the end of the war some 8,523 had been built.

The M8 was a six-wheeled car with welded body, on top of which was an open-topped turret mounting a 37mm gun. Driver and bow gunner sat in the front of the hull, while the turret was occupied by the gunner and vehicle commander. The engine and transmission were at the rear of the hull.

The M8 was the most widely-used American armoured car, and it was accompanied in service by the **Armoured Utility Car M20**, which was simply the M8 without the turret but with a ring-mounted machine gun above the hull. This was used as a command vehicle and personnel carrier. In post-war years the US and British Armies disposed of all their M8s, but many are still in use throughout the world, notably in some African countries.

Armament: 1 × 37mm M6; 2 × MG
Armour: 20mm
Crew: 4
Weight: 7.76 tons (7,892kg)
Length: 16ft 5in (5.00m)
Width: 8ft 4in (2.54m)
Height: 7ft 4in (2.33m)
Engine: Hercules JXD, 6-cylinder, petrol, 110bhp at 3,000rpm
Speed: 55mph (88km/hr)
Range: 350 miles (560km)

M38 Wolfhound Armoured Car USA
Chevrolet

1945. While the M8 armoured car was an excellent road vehicle, it was less successful at cross-country work, largely because of the conventional 'two and four' layout of its six wheels, which prevented it crossing any sort of trench. To overcome this, and also to improve the vehicle in many other respects, Chevrolet developed the M38, standardised in March 1945. This was a six-wheeled vehicle with evenly-spaced wheels; this configuration improved the trench-crossing ability and also, improved the ride over all surfaces. The body was ballistically well-shaped, and carried a turret with a 37mm gun. All wheels were driven, and the front four were steerable.

Excellent though the M38 design was, it came to an abrupt end; as soon as it had been standardized, the Armored Board stated that they had no requirement for any further armoured cars and that the existing M8 would satisfy their immediate

needs. As a result, only the prototypes of the M38 were ever built.

Armament: 1 × 37mm; 1 × coaxial MG
Armour: 10mm
Crew: 4
Weight: 6.83 tons (6,940kg)
Length: 16ft 9in (5.10m)
Width: 8ft 0in (2.43m)
Height: 6ft 6in (1.98m)
Engine: Cadillac, V-8, petrol, 148bhp at 3,200rpm
Speed: 60mph (96km/hr)
Range: 300 miles (480km)

M39 Armoured Car Netherlands
DAF

1939 The M39 was based on a DAF commercial truck chassis. The hull was well shaped and carefully sloped, though rather bulky. The driver had a hull-gunner beside him, armed with a machine gun in a ball mounting. The small turret mounted a 37mm gun and a coaxial machine gun. The engine was at the rear and drove the four rear wheels. Cross-country mobility was reasonably good, and to improve the vehicle's ability to cross wide gaps there were two small idler wheels at the bottom of the glacis plate. When the Germans invaded in May 1940 there was only one squadron of these cars and they saw no action. They were taken over by the Wehrmacht and employed in internal security duties until the end of the war.

Armament: 1 × 37mm; 2 × MG
Armour: 10mm
Crew: 6
Weight: 6.90 tons (6,000kg)
Length: 15ft 2in (4.63m)
Width: 6ft 7in (2.00m)
Height: 6ft 7in (2.00m
Engine: Ford, V-8, petrol, 95bhp
Speed: 37mph (60km/hr)
Range: 180 miles (300km)

m/39 Armoured Car Sweden
Landsverk

1939. The m/39 was one of many designs produced by the Landsverk company, but it differed from the majority in not being just a truck chassis with a box body built on top. This was a purpose-built armoured car with a proper 4 x 4 chassis and well-sloped armour. The turret was typical of other Landsverk products in being carefully shaped and fitted with a rounded mantlet. The first models were given solid tyres, but it was soon found that these inhibited road speeds too much and all subsequent production used large pneumatic tyres. Two features which indicated contemporary thought were the size of the crew and the fact that there were separate machine guns to fire forwards and backwards, the rear gunner also having a steering wheel for backwards driving. In Swedish service the car was known as the **Lynx** and it stayed in service until the 1950s.

Armament: I × 20mm cannon; 2 × MG
Armour: 18mm
Crew: 6
Weight: 7.67 tons 7,800kg)
Length: 16ft 9in (5.10m)
Width: 7ft 6in (2.28m)
Height: 7ft 3in (2.20m)
Engine: Volvo, 6-cylinder, petrol, 135bhp
Speed: 45mph (70km/hr)
Range: 153 miles (250km)

M114 Command & Reconnaissance Vehicle USA
Cleveland

1962. The M114 command and reconnaissance carrier was developed in the late 1950s, the first issues taking place in 196. It was developed to meet a US Army requirement for a protected scouting vehicle, and some 3,710 were built. It was used in Vietnam but was found to have poor cross-country performance there and was removed from service in the early 1980s.

The M114 had a boxy bull of aluminium armour and torsion-bar suspension for its tracked running gear. The engine and transmission were in the right front of the hull, with the driver on the left side. The commander and radio operator occupied the crew compartment, and there was room for an additional man to serve as gunner if required. On the first models the commander was provided with a .50-inch machine gun, and the additional crewman with a 7.62mm machine gun, both of which had to be fired from the open hatch; the later models provided the commander with a rotatable cupola carrying a remote-controlled .50-inch machine gun. In 1969 a number were converted by fitting the cupola with a remote-controlled 20mm Hispano-Suiza cannon.

Armament: 2 × MG; or I × 20mm and I × MG
Armour: 37mm
Crew: 3 or 4
Weight: 6.82 tons (6,928kg)
Length: 14ft 8in (4.46m)
Width: 7ft 8in (2.33m)
Height: 7ft 1in (2.15m)
Engine: Chevrolet, V-8, petrol, 160bhp at 3,600rpm

Speed: 36mph (58km/hr)
Range: 300 miles (480km)

Marmon-Herrington Armoured Cars
South Africa
Marmon-Herrington (4 x 4 conversion kit), Ford Canada (chassis), South African Iron (armoured bodies, turrets etc), Ford South Africa (assembly), Dorman Long (assembly)

During the 1930s the Marmon-Herrington Company developed a kit of parts for transforming commercial truck chassis into all-wheel-drive vehicles, on to which chassis they then built a variety of armoured cars. Small numbers of these were bought by the US National Guard as scout cars, while others were sold to various small nations around the world, armed to their purchaser's choice.

In 1939 the South African government selected a Marmon-Herrington conversion as the basis for a new armoured car, the conversion being applied to a standard Ford 3-ton truck chassis. The four-wheel-drive kits were supplied from the United States, the chassis from Canada, and the armoured bodies were built in South Africa. In order to speed things up, the first 113 **Mark 1** cars were actually built on to the standard chassis without the all-wheel drive suspension.

The **Mark 2** cars were 4 x 4, and in their original form were provided with a hull-mounted machine gun and a second machine gun in the turret; once these cars went into action in the Western Desert this armament was often changed according to the fancies of the individual units, and cars were variously armed with .55-inch Boys anti-tank rifles, captured Italian 20mm cannon, or German 37mm and Italian 47mm anti-tank guns.

The **Mark 3** next appeared, with a shorter wheelbase and with several improvements due to combat experience; the rear doors of the earlier models were abandoned, the transmission and suspension strengthened and the hull machine gun omitted.

This was followed, late in 1941, by the **Mark 4** in which the chassis layout was radically altered by moving the engine to the rear. A much heavier turret, mounting a 2-pounder tank gun and coaxial machine gun, was mounted. This was the most successful of the various design.

In 1942 two further models, the **Marks 5** and **6**, were mooted; the 5 appears to have been an improved Mark 3, though there are few records of it, while the Mark 6 was to be a powerful eight-wheeled vehicle mounting either a 2-pounder or 6-pounder gun and propelled by twin Ford engines.

In the event, it was appreciated that the North African campaign would be over before the Mark 6 could be put into production, and after two prototypes had been built the design was abandoned.

Mark 4
Armament: 1 × 2-pdr; 1 × MG
Armour: 12mm
Crew: 4
Weight: 6.19 tons (6,290kg)
Length: 16ft 0in (4.87m)
Width: 6ft 6in (1.98m)
Height: 7ft 7in (2.31m)
Engine: Ford, V-8, petrol, 85bhp at 3,000rpm
Speed: 50mph (80km/hr)
Range: 200 miles (325km)

Minerva Armoured Car Belgium
Minerva
1914. During the brief period of mobile warfare in the autumn of 1914 the Belgians used motor cars to harass the German invaders. They quickly developed armour protection and the Minerva touring car formed the basis for a more or less standard pattern of armoured car. The engine and cab were covered with armour plate in place of the normal metal cladding, and at the back a crew compartment was constructed in the simplest manner using two straight plates and one rounded one for the back. A single Hotchkiss machine gun was mounted on a pedestal. Against ordinary small-arms fire these cars were quite effective, and a few were given a 37mm trench cannon instead of the machine gun. Some stayed in Belgian service until the 1930s.

Armament: 1 × MG
Armour: 5mm
Crew: 3
Weight: 3.44 tons (3,500kg)
Length: 14ft 5in (4.40m)
Engine: Minerva, 4-cylinder, sleeve-valve, petrol, 40bhp at 2,000rpm
Speed: 30mph (48km/hr)
Range: 150 miles (240km)

Morris Armoured Reconnaissance Car UK
Morris
This vehicle was put together somewhat hastily in 1935 as an interim measure to give the expanding British Army some vehicles of warlike shape until the properly-designed 4 x 4 cars came along. It was built on the C9 15cwt 4 x 2 military truck chassis, with a slab-sided hull and a boxy open-topped turret behind the driver's cab. 100 were built in 1936–37. Some of these went to the Middle East and others accompanied the British Expeditionary Force to France in 1939. In spite of being a 'second best' design, they served well in both places and continued in use until 1943.

Armament: 1 × .55in AT rifle; 1 × MG
Armour: 7mm
Crew: 4
Weight: 4.2 tons (4268kg)
Length: 15ft 8in (4.77m)
Width: 6ft 9in (2.05m)
Height: 7ft 0in (2.13m)
Engine: Morris, 6-cylinder, 96bhp
Speed: 45mph (73km/hr)
Range: 240 miles (385km)

Morris Light Reconnaissance Car UK
Morris
1941. One of the better designs of light car to come out of the 1940-41 rash of manufacture, this had a monocoque body of welded armour steel, solid rear axle, independent suspension at the front but only two-wheel drive. The engine was at the rear, with a compact crew compartment behind a short nose. The driver sat centrally, with a turret and gunner to his right and a hatch, capable of being used for an anti-tank rifle or a second machine gun, on his left. In 1942 a **Mark 2** was produced, which had four-wheel drive and all-round independent suspension. This proved to be a very serviceable vehicle and over 2,200 were built.

Armament: 2 × MG
Armour: 14mm
Crew: 3
Weight: 3.70 tons (3,760kg)
Length: 13ft 4in (4.06m)
Width: 6ft 8in (2.03m)
Height: 6ft 2in (1.88m)
Engine: Morris, 4-cylinder petrol, 72bhp
Speed: 45mph (72km/hr)
Range: not known

Mors Armoured Car Belgium
Mors
1915. This was a French vehicle with a Belgian engine, used by the Belgian Army. A few were bought to supplement the Minerva cars, but when the German Army captured the Minerva factory in late 1914, the Mors suddenly became a vital commodity. They were armoured in similar fashion to the Minerva, the engine and drive being

completely covered-in, but with an open-topped crew compartment at the rear. This had high sides and no doors, and carried a machine gun or a 37mm trench gun on a pivot mount protected by a semi-circular shield. The crew compartment stopped in front of the rear axle, and there was a large tool and accessory chest over the axle, leaving the differential exposed to gunfire.

Armament: 1 x MG or 1 x 37mm M1916
Armour: 5mm
Crew: 4
Engine: Minerva 4-cylinder sleeve-valve, petrol, 4,392cc, 40bhp at 2,000rpm
Speed: 30mph (48km/hr)
Range: 150 miles (240km)

Mowag Eagle Switzerland
Mowag
1995. This is a 4 x 4 wheeled armoured vehicle developed to meet a Swiss Army demand for a reconnaissance vehicle, and it has since been supplied to the Danish, Egyptian and other forces. It is based upon the chassis of the US HMMWV (Humm-Vee) High Mobility Vehicle to which a lightly armoured body with bullet-proof glass screen and side windows is fitted in Switzerland. There is a roof hatch over the commander's seat (alongside the driver) and a one-man observation cupola behind the driver. This carries a range of electro-optical surveillance devices and also smoke dischargers and a machine gun.

Armament: 1 x MG
Armour: not disclosed
Crew: 4
Weight: 5.02 tons (5,100kg)
Length: 16ft 1in (4.90m)
Width: 7ft 6in (2.28m)
Height: 5ft 9in (1.75m)
Engine: GMC V-8 diesel, 160bhp at 1700rpm
Speed: 78mph (125km/hr)
Range: 280 miles (450km)

OT-65A Czechoslovakia
State factories
This amphibious scout vehicle was actually the Hungarian FUG-65 fitted with the turret of the Czech OT-62B APC. This mounted a 7.62mm machine gun and also carried, on external brackets, an 82mm recoilless gun, which could be aimed and fired from inside the turret but which had to be loaded externally. There was a roof hatch behind the turret through which the crew entered and left the vehicle. Entered service in 1966.

Armament: 1 x MG, 1 x 82mm recoilless
Armour: 13mm
Crew: 5
Weight: 7.28 tons (7,400kg)
Length: 19ft 0in (5.79m)
Width: 8ft 3in (2.50m)
Height: 7ft 2in (2.20m)
Engine: Csepel D-414, 4-cylinder, diesel, 100bhp at 2,300rpm
Speed: 54mph (87km/hr)
Range: 375 miles (600km)

Osaka Model 2592 Armoured Car Japan
Osaka
1932. The Osaka was introduced into Japanese service in 1932, the year 2592 in the old Japanese calendar. It was a design largely based on the armoured cars used in World War I and was virtually obsolete on the day it was built. The chassis was a commercial 4 x 2 truck fitted with twin rear wheels. On this was built a conventional box body of thin armour plate, fitted with a small hand-powered turret, mounting one machine gun. In the first versions the driver had another machine gun mounted so that it fired forwards on a fixed line. Although suitable for internal security duties the Osaka was of very limited value in mobile warfare.

Armament: 1 or 2 x MG
Armour: 6mm
Crew: 3
Weight: 5.71 tons (5,805kg)
Length: 16ft 4in (5.00m)
Width: 6ft 1in (1.85m)
Height: 8ft 7in (2.63m)
Engine: Commercial, 4-cylinder, petrol, 85bhp
Speed: 37mph (60km/hr)
Range: 150 miles (240km)

Otter Light Reconnaissance Car Canada
GM Canada
1942. As with other Canadian designs, this was actually a Canadian-built version of a British vehicle, made using Canadian parts. In this case the model was the Humber Light Reconnaissance Car Mark 3, though the Otter turned out a good ton heavier and almost a foot taller. Front engine, slope-sided boxy body, with a small conical turret carrying a light machine gun.

Armament: 1 x MG
Armour: 12mm
Crew: 3
Weight: 4.80 tons (4,880kg)
Length: 14ft 9in (4.50m)
Width: 7ft 0in (2.13m)

Height: 8ft 0in (2.44m)
Engine: GMC 6-cylinder, petrol, 104bhp at 3,000rpm
Speed: 45mph (72km/hr)
Range: 225 miles (360km)

PA-4/27 Scout Car Czechoslovakia
Skoda
1927. This 4 x 4 car was extremely advanced for its day and was among the first armoured vehicles to employ sloped and ballistically shaped armour to deflect shot rather than merely relying upon thickness to stop it. A relatively simple design, it had a central forward-firing machine gun alongside the driver, and a second machine gun in a hand-operated turret. All four wheels were driven and entrance was by means of doors in the flat sides.

Armament: 2 × MG
Armour: 6mm
Crew: 4
Weight: 7.70 tons (7,825kg)
Length: 19ft 8in (5.99m)
Width: 6ft 10in (2.08m)
Height: 8ft 10in (2.69m)
Engine: Skoda, petrol, 100bhp
Speed: 38mph (60km/hr)
Range: 150 miles (240km)

PA-4/35 Scout Car Czechoslovakia
Skoda
1935. The new PA-4 was an entirely different model from the /27, and reverted to the conventional 'two and four' six-wheel arrangement, with a long engine hood and a boxy crew compartment with an open-topped machine gun turret. Only the rear wheels were driven, which made its cross-country performance poor. There was a forward-firing hull machine gun in addition to the turret gun, and a self-sealing petrol tank was fitted. Most were taken over by the German Army in 1939 and later given to the Italians.

Armament: 2 × MG
Armour: 13mm
Crew: 4
Weight: 6.50 tons (6,605kg)
Length: 17ft 6in (5.33m)
Width: 6ft 5in (1.95m)
Height: 7ft 4in (2.23m)
Engine: Skoda, petrol, 100bhp
Speed: 45mph (72km/hr)
Range: 150 miles (240km)

Panhard AMD 178 Armoured Car France
Panhard et Levassor
1935. The AMD (*Automitrailleuse de Découverte*) was the successor to the wartime White-Laffly which by 1930 was well out of date. The prototype 178 appeared in 1933 and entered service with the French Army in 1935. It was a good design, with a simple, clean outline and the interior divided into fighting and engine compartments. The armour was sloped, though the construction used rivets, and the performance was good. Armament usually consisted of a 25mm gun with a coaxial machine gun, but some had twin machine guns. Many of these cars were taken over by the Germans in 1940 and were used for internal security duties, but a sufficient number survived the war to be taken back by the French Army in 1945. Production was then resumed by Panhard, so that the 178 once again became the standard armoured car of the French Army and remained so until replaced by the Panhard EBR.

Armament: 1 × 25mm and 1 × MG; or 2 × MG; or (post-1945) 1 × 47mm and 1 × MG
Armour: 18mm maximum
Crew: 3
Weight: 14.27 tons (14,500kg)
Length: 15ft 0in (4.57m)
Width: 7ft 4in (2.23m)
Height: 7ft 8in (2.33m)
Engine: Renault, 4-cylinder, petrol, 180bhp
Speed: 45mph (72km/hr)
Range: 145 miles (300km)

Panhard AML Armoured Car France
Panhard et Levassor
1960. The AML was developed in the late 1950s to meet a French Army requirement for a lighter vehicle than the EBR. The first production models were delivered in 1960, after which about 3,000 were built and exported to many countries throughout the world. It was built under licence in South Africa (as the Eland) and became standard equipment in armies from the Far East to South America. One reason for its success was that it was a relatively simple vehicle which was capable of adaptation to many different roles. The hull was a welded steel box with the driver in front, a fighting compartment in the middle and the engine at the rear. There were doors on each side for the crew, and two more in the back for access to the engine. The most usual version was fitted with a 90mm gun which was housed in a large, low turret which took up most of the top deck; however there were many different armament fits and different turrets to

accommodate them. Another option offered by Panhard was a flotation kit consisting of bolt-on boxes filled with plastic foam and a bow screen. Propellers could also be fitted to improve the speed through the water.

Armament: 1 × 90mm; 1 × coaxial MG; 1 × MG on roof of turret
Armour: 12mm
Crew: 3
Weight: 5.41 tons (5,500kg)
Length: 12ft 5in (3.79m)
Width: 6ft 6in (1.98m)
Height: 6ft 10in (2.07m)
Engine: Panhard Model 4 HD, 4-cylinder, petrol, 90bhp at 4,700rpm
Speed: 62mph (100km/hr)
Range: 370 miles (600km)

Panhard EBR-75 Armoured Car France
Panhard et Levassor
1950. The EBR (*Engin Blindé de Reconnaissance* – armoured reconnaissance vehicle) appeared in 1948 and production started in 1950. Manufacture ceased in 1960, about 1,200 having been made. It was a large vehicle with eight wheels. It normally ran on the outer four, and could steer with either two or four of them. The centre four were lowered for cross-country movement, and were then driven, giving the car excellent mobility with low ground pressure. The engine was in the centre, below the floor, and the transmission could drive the vehicle in either direction at the same speed. There were two drivers, one at each end, and in normal running the rear driver acted as the radio operator. The EBR was armed with the 75mm gun and oscillating turret from the AMX-13 tank, though without the automatic loader. Later versions had a conventional turret with a 90mm gun. Both versions had a single machine gun in the floor of each driving compartment, firing forwards and controlled by the drivers. Although large, heavy, and fairly complicated, the EBR proved to be most effective and remained in service for almost thirty years before being being replaced by the AMX-10RC.

Armament: 1 × 75mm; 1 × coaxial MG; 2 × MG in drivers' compartments
Armour: 15mm
Crew: 4
Weight: 13.28 tons (13,500kg)
Length: 20ft 2in (6.15m)
Width: 7ft 11in (2.42m)
Height: 7ft 7in (2.34m)
Engine: Panhard, flat-12-cylinder, petrol, 200bhp at 3,700rpm

Speed: 65mph (105km/hr)
Range: 400 miles (650km)

Panhard ERC-90-F4 Sagaie France
Panhard et Levassor
1978. (ERC = *Engin de Reconnaissance Canon* – reconnaissance gun-carrier). The purpose of this vehicle is 'the search for intelligence over large areas and the destruction of enemy tanks' according to the French Army, and it seems well suited to the task. A medium-sized 6 × 6 wheeled vehicle mounting a 90mm gun, it has been adopted by the French and, in variant forms, by several African countries and Mexico. The layout is fairly standard, with the driver at the left front, fighting compartment and turret behind him and engine at the rear of the hull. The gun is a high-velocity weapon, not the usual low-pressure 90mm used on lighter armoured cars, and has a formidable performance against tanks. The car is amphibious, being propelled by swivelling water jets.

Armament: 1 × 90mm; 2 × MG
Armour: not disclosed
Crew: 3
Weight: 8.16 tons (8,300kg)
Length: 17ft 3in (5.27m)
Width: 8ft 3in (2.50m)
Height: 7ft 7in (2.32m)
Engine: Peugeot V-6, petrol, 145bhp at 3,000rpm
Speed: 60mph (95km/hr)
Range: 435 miles (700km)

Panhard VBL Armoured Car France
Panhard et Levassor
1985. This was developed by Panhard to meet a French Army requirement for a vehicle weighing under 3,500kg and capable of reconnaissance and missile launching roles. A simple 4 × 4 design, with a three-man crew, the VBL (*Véhicule Blindé Léger* – light armoured vehicle) has a conventional layout, with the engine in front, driver and commander in the cab and the third member of the crew manning a roof-top machine gun through a hatch. The design was later modified and absorbed into a complete family of vehicles all based upon the same chassis and collectively known as the **Ultrav M11** (Ultrav for Ultra-Light Armoured Vehicle). The APC and other versions will be found under the Ultrav name in the Infantry Armour section.

Armament: 1 × MG
Armour: not disclosed
Crew: 3
Weight: 3.53 tons (3,590kg)
Length: 12ft 2in (3.70m)

Width: 6ft 8in (2.02m)
Height: 5ft 7in (1.70m)
Engine: Peugeot XD 3T 4-cylinder turbocharged diesel, 95bhp at 2,250rpm
Speed: 60mph (85km/hr)
Range: 375 miles (600km)

Peerless Armoured Car UK
Peerless
1915. This was developed in order to provide the Royal Naval Air Service armoured cars with some supporting firepower heavier than their machine guns, and was simply a standard 4 x 2 Peerless truck chassis with a high-sided, open-topped body. The driver and commander had overhead protection, and behind them in the fighting compartment, was a 1-pounder Vickers Pom-Pom automatic gun and a medium machine gun. The vehicle used chain drive and solid tyres, and 16 were assembled by the Wolseley Motor Company in 1915; by the time they were completed the RNAS no longer needed them and they were taken by the British Army.

Armament: 1 × 1-pdr QF; 1 × MG
Armour: 8mm
Crew: 5
Weight: 5.8 tons (5,890kg)
Length: 20ft 6in (6.25m)
Width: 7ft 8in (2.34m)
Height: 8ft 10in (2.69m)
Engine: Peerless, 4-cylinder petrol, 40bhp
Speed: 20mph (32km/hr)
Range: 90 miles (145km)

Peerless Armoured Car UK
Peerless
1919. The second Peerless design was a 4 x 2 car built on a 3-ton truck chassis, strengthened to carry the extra weight. Chain driven, with solid tyres. The body was to a similar design to the Austin, using the standard 'car' shape and with twin turrets over sponsons.

Armament: 2 × MG
Armour: 8mm
Crew: 4
Weight: 6.8 tons (6,900kg)
Length: 20ft 1in (6.12m)
Width: 7ft 4in (2.23m)
Height: 9ft 1in (2.77m)
Engine: Peerless 4-cylinder, petrol, 40bhp
Speed: 18mph (30km/hr)
Range: not known

Peugeot Armoured Cars France
Peugeot
1916–18. The Peugeot company built armoured cars from the start of the war, using the then normal practice of mounting a machine gun on a pedestal and surrounding it with an armoured shield. In 1916 they took their 18hp standard touring-car chassis and fitted twin rear wheels. On to this was built a square box-like structure with a gun above the level of the sides. This gun was either a Hotchkiss machine gun or a 37mm trench cannon, and both were given a shield. The cars continued in service until 1918 when there were less than 20 left and it is presumed that they were gradually wasted out over the following years.

Armament: 1 × MG or 1 × 37mm gun
Armour: not known
Crew: 4
Weight: 4.82 tons (4,900kg)
Length: 15ft 9in (4.80m)
Width: 5ft 11in (1.80m)
Height: 9ft 3in (2.82m)
Engine: Peugeot 4-cylinder petrol, 40bhp
Speed: 25mph (40km/hr)
Range: 85miles (1400km)

Pierce-Arrow Armoured Cars UK
Pierce-Arrow
Pierce-Arrow chassis were imported from the USA in pre-WWI days for bodies to be fitted in Britain; the practice continued in 1914–15 and several were used to build armoured cars. The first models might more properly have been called self-propelled guns, had the term been invented, since they were fitted with Vickers 2-pounder automatic guns for anti-aircraft use by the Royal Marine Artillery. The bodywork was the usual 8mm armour of the day, with a covered cab for the driver, and a circular armoured barbette with the gun behind the driving compartment.

The second version was designed as a support vehicle for the RNAS squadron which was operating in Russia and was shipped there in pieces to be assembled at the RNAS depot in Archangel. The chassis was the standard Pierce-Arrow type and the engine, bonnet and cab were the same as those of the earlier model, but behind the cab was a rotating armoured turret carrying a 3-pounder Nordenfelt gun in an 'elastic mounting', a form of pedestal built up from steel strip so as to have some degree of shock-absorbing ability in the absence of any more elaborate form of recoil mechanism. Experience soon showed that the vehicle was grossly overloaded in this form, and the turret was discarded and the gun merely given a flat shield to protect the gunners.

PRP-4 Reconnaissance Vehicle Russia
Rubcovskii

1995. This is a variant of the BMP-1 MICV, described in the Infantry Armour section, which is equipped specifically for the target acquisition and surveillance roles and is normally organic to air defence and other artillery formations. A full-tracked amphibian, it differs from the MICV in having a small turret with a single machine gun, and a different arrangement of hatches through which various types of surveillance equipment can be exposed and operated, notably a surveillance radar which can be retracted under armour when not in use.

Armament: 1 × MG
Armour: not disclosed
Crew: 5
Weight: 13.0 tons (13,200kg)
Length: 22ft 1in (6.73mm)
Width: 9ft 8in (2.94m)
Height: 7ft 0in (2.14m)
Engine: UTD-20 diesel, 300bhp
Speed: 49mph (65km/hr)
Range: 370 miles (600km)

Puma Armoured Car Germany
See Sd Kfz 234/2

Ramta RBY Armoured Reconnaissance Vehicle Israel
Ramta

1975. The RBY was an interesting attempt to produce a light, cheap vehicle suitable for reconnaissance and general armoured-car work. It was built from standard commercial components wherever possible and incorporated some unusual ideas. It was open-topped, since the Israelis have found that it is essential to see clearly in battle and periscopes and vision blocks are just not good enough. The wheels are set well out from the body to the front and rear to minimize the effects of blast from mines. The engine is at the back, behind the crew compartment, so that the personnel are as far away as possible from the point of a mine explosion, which usually occurs under the wheels with the heaviest loading. There is no fixed armament and the crew are meant to fire with their personal weapons from the fighting compartment.

Armament: none, see text
Armour: 8mm

Crew: 2 + up to 6
Weight: 3.54 tons (3,600kg)
Length: 16ft 5in (5.01m)
Width: 6ft 7in (2.02m)
Height: 5ft 3in (1.60m)
Engine: Dodge Model 225, 6-cylinder, petrol, 120bhp
Speed: 62mph (100km/hr)
Range: 340 miles (550km)

RAM V-1 Israel
Ramta

1979. The RAM family of vehicles were derived from the earlier Ramta RBY (*above*) and follow the same philosophy. The V-1 comes in two wheel-base lengths; both are open-topped and are more or less the same as the RBY, but the engine is now diesel, giving a longer radius of action; the wheels and tyres are larger, giving better ground clearance; the manual transmission has been replaced by an automatic; and the interior is slightly more comfortable for the occupants.

V-1 Short
Armament: personal weapons or 3 × MG
Armour: 8mm
Crew: 2 + 4
Weight: 5.31 tons (5,400kg)
Length: 16ft 5in (5.02m)
Width: 6ft 8in (2.03m)
Height: 5ft 8in (1.72m)
Engine: Deutz 6-cylinder air-cooled diesel, 132bhp
Speed: 60mph (95km/hr)
Range: 372 miles (600km)

V-1 Long
Armament: personal weapons or 3 × MG
Armour: 8mm
Crew: 2 + 7
Weight: 5.64 tons (5,750kg)
Length: 18ft 2in (5.52m)
Width: 6ft 8in (2.03m)
Height: 5ft 8in (1.72m)
Engine: Deutz 6-cylinder air-cooled diesel, 132bhp
Speed: 60mph (95km/hr)
Range: 500 miles (800km)

RAM V-2 Light Armoured Vehicle Israel
Ramta

1979. The V-2 RAM vehicles are similar to the V-1, in short and long wheelbase forms, but have the troop compartment roofed over and provided with hatches. Except for being 200kg heavier, their dimensions are the same as those of the two V-1 models.

Renault Armoured Car France
Renault

1914. By November 1914 the Renault factory had standardized on an armoured car, using a truck chassis fitted with twin rear wheels. The body was built up from flat plate and was simple in its construction, with an open top and a single machine gun mounted on a pedestal at the rear. After the introduction of the 37mm Trench Cannon M1916 many cars had this fitted in place of the machine gun. The attrition rate must have been high as very few were still in service when the war ended, and were then quickly disposed of.

Armament: 1 × Hotchkiss 8mm MG, or 1 × 37mm
Crew: 3 or 4
Engine: Renault, 4-cylinder, petrol, 4,600cc, 38bhp

Renault VBC-90 Armoured Car France
Renault

1979. This was developed as a private venture by Renault, using their successful VAB 6 x 6 APC as the basis and fitting it with a GIAT TS90 turret carrying a 90mm gun. The interior arrangements differ from the VAB in that the engine is at the rear, instead of the troop compartment, and the fighting compartment and turret are central, behind the driver. The turret also carries a searchlight and is provided with a comprehensive electronic fire control system with laser rangefinder, night vision and sighting equipment and ballistic computer. The vehicle was purchased initially by the Gendarmerie Nationale, after which a small number were sold to Oman.

Armament: 1 × 90mm; 1 × coaxial MG
Armour: not disclosed
Crew: 3
Weight: 13.28 tons (13,500kg)
Length: 18ft 6in (5.63m)
Width: 8ft 3in (2.50m)
Height: 8ft 5in (2.55m)
Engine: Renault 6-cylinder turbocharged diesel, 220bhp at 2,200rpm
Speed: 56mph (90km/hr)
Range: 620 miles (1,000km)

Rolls-Royce Armoured Car UK
Rolls-Royce

1915. In 1914 the Royal Naval Air Service set up an advanced airbase in Belgium and required armoured cars in order to go forward and rescue downed aviators. After making their own vehicles from boiler-plate and miscellaneous civilian touring car chassis, an official design was produced in December 1914 which became the standard British armoured car. The Rolls-Royce Silver Ghost touring chassis was adopted, strengthened by adding leaves to the springs, and fitted with a steel body. The rear of the body was left as a load-carrying deck, and the cab position was surmounted by an open-topped turret mounting a machine gun; after some experience, these turrets were given armoured tops.

In 1920 a further batch was built, much the same as the original 1914 model, but with some small improvements to the engine and with louvres on the armoured doors in front of the radiator. Finally, in 1924, a further consignment was made in which the turret was built up and given a commander's cupola on top. In the post-war models disc wheels were used instead of the original wire-spoked pattern, and the 1924 model had wider wheels in order to support the weight better. These cars were extensively used throughout the Empire between the wars and the last of them saw action in the Western Desert as late as 1940.

1914 Model
Armament: 1 × MG
Armour: 9mm
Crew: 4
Weight: 3.5 tons (3,555kg)
Length: 16ft 9in (5.10m)
Width: 6ft 3in (1.91m)
Height: 7ft 7in (2.31m)
Engine: Rolls-Royce 6-cylinder petrol, 50bhp
Speed: 60mph (95km/hr)
Range: 150 miles (240km)

1920 Model
Armament: 1 × MG
Armour: 9mm
Crew: 4
Weight: 3.79 tons (3,860kg)
Length: 17ft 0in (5.18m)
Width: 6ft 3in (1.90m)
Height: 7ft 5in (2.33m)
Engine: Rolls-Royce, 6-cylinder, petrol, 80bhp at 2,000rpm
Speed: 50mph (80km/hr)
Range: 150 miles (240km)

Rooikat Armoured Car South Africa
Sandcock-Austral, LIW (turret)

1990. Development of this 8 x 8 vehicle began in 1978 with the construction of an 8 x 8 chassis to prove the concept was workable. Prototypes with various wheel arrangements followed, but the 8 x 8 was selected for further development, resulting in its issue to service in 1990.

The layout of the Rooikat ('Lynx') is conventional: driver at the front, three-man crew compartment and turret in the centre and engine compartment at the rear. The eight wheels are in two pairs, the front four being steerable, and the driver can select all wheels powered or only the rear four, according to the driving conditions. The engine drives through an automatic transmission. The main armament is a 76mm gun developed in South Africa but which has the same chamber contours as the Italian OTO-Melara naval gun. It is fully stabilized and provided with HE and APFSDS ammunition; with the latter it is quite capable of killing a main battle tank at 2,000 yards range.

Variant models mounting 35mm anti-aircraft guns and missiles, and a tank destroyer mounting a 105mm gun have also been developed.

Armament: 1 × 76mm; 1 × coaxial MG; 1 × air defence MG
Armour: not disclosed
Crew: 4
Weight: 27.55 tons (28,000kg)
Length: 23ft 3in (7.09m)
Width: 9ft 6in (2.90m)
Height: 9ft 2in (2.80m)
Engine: V-10 diesel, 563bhp
Speed: 75mph (120km/hr)
Range: 560 miles (900km)

Saladin Armoured Car UK
Alvis

1959. The British Army used armoured cars with some success during World War II, and immediately afterwards requested an improved design to incorporate all the lessons learned in combat. A prime requirement was better cross-country mobility, and for this the six equally-spaced wheel configuration pioneered by the American M38 car was adopted.

Originally intended to have a crew of four and a 2-pounder gun, production was delayed to allow Saracen APCs (*qv*) to be given first priority, and during this time an improved 76mm gun was developed, reducing the crew to three men. Saladin had the driver seated centrally at the front of the hull, with the turreted fighting compartment behind him and the engine and transmission at the rear. All wheels were driven, and the front four were steered. The car could continue to function after the loss of any one wheel on a mine. The 76mm gun was provided with anti-personnel and anti-tank ammunition.

The Saladin entered service with the British Army in 1959 and many were subsequently purchased by other countries. Although no longer employed by the British Army, numbers are still in use in various Middle Eastern and African countries, and in the early 1990s Alvis prepared a 're-powering kit', for replacing old engines with modern Perkins diesel engines.

Armament: 1 × 76mm; 1 × coaxial MG; 1 × AA MG
Armour: 32mm
Crew: 3
Weight: 11.4 tons (11,590kg)
Length: 16ft 2in (4.92m)
Width: 8ft 4in (2.53m)
Height: 8ft 7in (2.92m)
Engine: Rolls-Royce, 8-cylinder, petrol, 170bhp at 3,750rpm
Speed: 45mph (72km/hr)
Range: 250 miles (400km)

Saurer Armoured Car France
Saurer

1930–36. Several of these large armoured cars were made by the Saurer company especially for the convoying of lorries across the Sahara. They were bought by the Compagnie Africaine des Transports and spent their lives driving up and down the rough tracks across the northern Sahara Desert region. The chassis was that of a conventional lorry with a faceted armoured box on top and a small turret above the box. There were one or two of these vehicles to each convoy and reliability was of more importance than fighting ability. The armour only needed to be sufficient to stop a rifle bullet. Crew comfort was of prime importance in the desert climate, and there was ample room in the hull and plenty of ventilation.

Length: 19ft 7in (5.96m)
Width: 6ft 5in (1.98m)
Height: 8ft 7in (2.6m)
Crew: 4

SAVA Armoured Car Belgium
SAVA

1914. The SAVA was another of the several armoured cars that were hurriedly built in Belgium when the war started. SAVA built large touring cars, and they fitted the chassis of these with an armoured body mounting the conventional single Hotchkiss machine gun at the rear. Some thought was given to sloping the frontal armour and all the weight was between the axles. After a few engagements with the German advance guards a rotating barbette was fitted for the machine gun so that the crew had some protection. Although successful, this type of armoured car did not survive the static warfare which appeared after 1915.

Armament: 1 × Hotchkiss 8mm MG
Crew: 4

Scimitar UK
See Scorpion

Scorpion, Scimitar, Striker Reconnaissance Vehicles UK
Alvis
1973. Although officially termed the **Combat Vehicle, Reconnaissance, Tracked (CVR(T))**, Scorpion is, by any standards, a light tank. It is a tracked vehicle using welded aluminium armour for the hull and mounting a turret which carries a 76mm gun, a lighter version of that used in the Saladin armoured car. The engine is mounted at the right front of the hull, and the driver sits alongside on the left. The standard engine is a detuned version of the Jaguar car engine, but a GMC diesel can be fitted as an alternative. The hull carries a flotation screen and Scorpion is propelled in the water by its tracks, though an auxiliary propeller kit is available to give better speed in water. Development of Scorpion began in the middle 1960s and first orders were placed in 1970. Since adoption by the British Army, it has also been taken into service by 12 other countries Those used by the Belgian Army are assembled in Belgium, using some Belgian-made components.

In addition to Scorpion, a family of specialist vehicles was developed around the basic chassis. Most of these are dealt with elsewhere but relevant to this section are the Scimitar and Striker. **Scimitar** is the same as Scorpion, except that the turret armament is the 30mm Rarden cannon. **Striker** is a turretless vehicle with the hull built up and mounting a launcher unit for the Swingfire anti-tank guided missile at the rear of the hull. This unit carries five missiles ready for firing, and a further five are carried inside the hull but have to be reloaded into the launcher from outside.

Another member of the 'family' is **Sultan** (*qv*).

Scorpion
Armament: 1 × 76mm; 1 × MG
Armour: not disclosed
Crew: 3
Weight: 7.94 tons (8,073kg)
Length: 14ft 5in (4.38m)
Width: 7ft 2in (2.18m)
Height: 6ft 10in (2.09m)
Engine: Jaguar 6-cylinder, petrol, 195bhp at 4,750rpm

Speed: 55mph (88km/hr)
Range: 400 miles (645km)

Scimitar
Armament: 30mm Rarden cannon; 1 × MG
Weight: 7.67 tons (7,800kg)
Other details: as for Scorpion

Striker
Armament: Swingfire missile launcher; 1 × MG
Armour: not disclosed
Crew: 3
Weight: 8.21 tons (8,346kg)
Length: 15ft 10in (4.83m)
Width: 7ft 6in (2.28m)
Height: 7ft 6in (2.28m)
Engine: Jaguar, 6-cylinder, petrol, 195bhp at 4,750rpm
Other details: as for Scorpion

Sd Kfz Series Germany
See Sonder Kraftfahrzeug below

Seabrook Armoured Car UK
Admiralty workshops
1915. The British Royal Navy cars in Belgium required some heavier support than could be provided by their machine guns, and the Seabrook was designed by the Admiralty Air Department to provide it. It was a truck chassis with armoured sides, mounting a 3-pounder Hotchkiss QF gun and two heavy machine guns. The upper sections of the sides were hinged so that they could be dropped to permit the three guns to fire to one side or the other. The intention was good but the chassis was overloaded and the vehicles gave constant trouble from broken springs and axles.

Armament: 1 × 3-pdr QF; 2 × MG
Armour: 8mm
Crew: 7
Weight: 10 tons (10,160kg)
Length: 24ft 0in (7.32m)
Width: 7ft 0in (2.13m)
Height: 6ft 0in (1.83m)
Engine: Continental 4-cylinder petrol, 33bhp
Speed: 20mph (32km/hr)
Range: 100 miles (160km)

Sheffield Simplex Armoured Car UK
Brotherhood
1916. The Brotherhood company were well-known in naval circles for their high-speed torpedo engines, and when the Admiralty wanted more armoured cars they looked to this firm, who had set up a separate factory in 1908 to build cars. As usual, the result was simply their standard heavy touring

chassis with an armoured body built by Vickers (who were almost next door to the Simplex factory). It was remarkable for its period in having electric starting, by means of a flywheel dynamotor.

Shorland Light Scout Car UK
Short Brothers
1965. The Shorland car was originally developed as an internal security vehicle for use by the Royal Ulster Constabulary; it has since been adopted by the British Army and by several other countries as a light scout car. Development began in 1965, using the chassis of the well-known Land-Rover as the basis. The armoured body follows the lines of the Land-Rover in several respects, but is built up and carries a small hand-operated turret armed with a machine gun. Smoke or riot-gas dischargers can also be fitted. An armoured trunk at the rear holds the petrol tank and spare wheel. An experimental version mounting the Vigilant anti-tank missile was produced but was not taken into military service.

Armament: 1 × MG
Armour: 11mm
Crew: 3
Weight: 3.30 tons (3,360kg)
Length: 15ft 1in (4.59m)
Width: 5ft 10in (1.77m)
Height: 7ft 6in (2.28m)
Engine: Rover, 6-cylinder, petrol, 91bhp at 1,750rpm
Speed: 55mph (88km/hr)
Range: 320 miles (515km)

SK-1 Armoured Car East Germany
VEB
1954. This vehicle was developed by the East German authorities in the middle 1950s solely for use as an internal security vehicle. It consisted of a commercial Robur truck chassis with the wheelbase shortened and a steel body built on top. Dual rear wheels support the extra weight. The layout was quite conventional, with the engine at the front, and a hand operated machine gun turret on top of the hull.

The SK-1 was partnered by another vehicle, the **SK-2** water cannon, which was a standard six-wheeled truck with an armoured cab surmounted by a high-pressure water cannon. The rear of the truck carried an unarmoured 4,000-litre (880-gallon) water tank.

Armament: 1 × MG
Armour: 8mm
Crew: 5
Weight: 5.31 tons (5,400kg)

Length: 13ft 1in (4.00m)
Width: 6ft 6in (2.00m)
Height: 9ft 2in (2.80m)
Engine: Robur, 4-cylinder, diesel, 55bhp at 2,800rpm
Speed: 50mph (80km/hr)
Range: 215 miles (350km)

Snezka Reconnaissance Vehicle Czech Republic
State factories
1995. This is a somewhat specialized tracked vehicle for the acquisition and engagement of targets for various fire support systems. Based on a lengthened version of the Russian BMP-1 MICV, with seven roadwheels on each side, its principal feature is a large 'cherry-picker' articulated arm which lies along the centreline of the hull when folded and can be extended upwards to a height of about 15m. At the end of this arm is a sensor pack carrying a rotating radar antenna, a thermal imaging camera, day-night low-light-level TV camera, laser rangefinder and wind direction and velocity sensor. There is a cupola on the left of the hull, carrying a heavy machine gun, and the vehicle is, of course, fully amphibious.

Armament: 1 × HMG
Armour: not disclosed
Crew: 4
Weight: 17.16 tons (17,440kg)
Length: 24ft 9in (7.53m)
Width: 10ft 4in (3.15m)
Height: 11ft 5in (3.47m)
Engine: UTO-20 6-cylinder diesel, 300bhp at 2,600rpm
Speed: 35mph (55km/hr)
Range: 372 miles (600km)

Sonder Kraftfahrzeug (Sd Kfz) Germany
German vehicles of the Nazi era built to military specifications were given an identification number preceded by the letters Sd Kfz for *Sonder Kraftfahrzeug* or 'Special Motor Vehicle'. Tanks and other vehicles rarely use these numbers, but they are the standard method of referring to armoured cars and APCs. A complete listing of Sd Kfz numbers appears in the Appendices, pages 354–8.

Sonder Kraftfahrzeug (Sd Kfz) 221 and 222 Light Armoured Cars Germany
Auto-Union (engine & chassis), Weserhütte (body), Schichau & Niedersachsen (assembly)
1935. The smallest in the German Army series of specialised and standardized chassis was this four-

wheel type developed by Auto-Union/Horch. It used a rear engine, four-wheel drive, self-locking differentials, all-independent suspension, and low-range gears for cross-country work. On this chassis the **Sd Kfz 221** armoured car was developed, to replace the early Adler cars. The body had well-sloped sides and carried a shallow open-topped turret mounting a single machine gun, though some were seen with anti-tank rifles in the early days of the war. The standard car was not fitted with radio, but a special *Funkwagen* version was built to carry long-range radio equipment.

In 1938 the engine was improved to develop more power and the turret armed with a 20mm cannon in addition to the machine gun. There were also minor changes in the hull construction, and the model thus became the **Sd Kfz 222**.

Armament: 1 × MG; or 1 × 20mm plus 1 × MG
Armour: 15mm
Crew: 2
Weight: 3.93 tons (4,000kg)
Length: 15ft 9in (4.80m)
Width: 6ft 5in (1.95m)
Height: 5ft 7in (1.70m)
Engine: Auto-Union V-8, petrol, 75bhp at 3,600rpm; later 81bhp at 3,600rpm
Speed: 50mph (80km/hr)
Range: 200 miles (320km)

Sd Kfz 223 Armoured Car Germany
Weserhütte, Niedersachsen, Bussing-NAG
1935. This was the Sd Kfz 221 car (*above*) slightly modified for fitting a long-range radio. The most obvious change was the adoption of a large flat frame antenna on four legs which could hinge down so as to lay the frame flat on the car hull or up to raise the antenna into a working position. The hull was open-topped and a machine gun was carried. The dimensions were the same as those of the 221, the weight being slightly less.

Sd Kfz 231 (6 rad) Armoured Car
Germany
Daimler-Benz, Büssing-NAG, Klockner
1933. In the late 1920s development of a six-wheeled armoured car was begun by three major German automobile manufacturers. The first design to be accepted for service was that by Daimler-Benz, 37 being delivered in 1932. In the following year the Bussing-NAG model appeared, and in 1934 the Magirus version. About 1,000 of the various models were built up to 1936, when manufacture was stopped in favour of an eight-wheeled car. The six-wheeled cars remained in use,

numbers seeing combat in Poland and France, but thereafter they were restricted to training and internal security tasks.

Apart from differences in detail, all three versions were similar, having been built to the same specification. Structurally, they were all based on their maker's commercial truck chassis, suitably strengthened. The engines were at the front, and the transmission included a forward-reverse selector which, coupled with a secondary driving position at the rear, allowed the car to be driven at top speed in either direction. The rear wheels were dual, and all wheels had bullet-proof tyres. The body was surmounted by a hand operated turret which mounted either a 7.92mm machine gun or a 20mm cannon. Minor variants included a *Funkwagen* equipped with long-range radio and recognizable by the tubular horizontal-frame aerial above the turret and rear hull.

Armament: 1 × 7.92mm MG or 1 × 20mm cannon
Armour: 15mm
Crew: 4
Weight: 5.41 tons (5,500kg)
Length: 19ft 0in (5.80m)
Width: 5ft 11in (1.82m)
Height: 7ft 5in (2.25m)
Engine: Daimler-Benz, 6-cylinder, petrol, 3,460cc, 60bhp at 2,800rpm
Speed: 38mph (60km/hr)
Range: 250 miles (400km)

Sd Kfz 231 (8 rad) Armoured Car
Germany
Deutsche Werke
Although the Sd Kfz number was the same, this eight-wheeled car was an entirely different vehicle to the six-wheeler. The body was larger and the turret was mounted more centrally, with sloping sections to front and rear, and two groups of four wheels. All wheels drove and steered, and controls were duplicated so that the vehicle could be driven in either direction with equal facility. Armour was originally 15mm maximum, but after 1940 additional plates were often attached to the front, and from 1943 onwards the turret and frontal armour were increased to 30mm thickness and the additional plates were no longer used.

Armament: 1 × 20mm cannon + 1 × 7.92mm MG
Armour: 15–30mm (see text)
Crew: 4
Weight: 8.30 tons (8,435kg)
Length: 19ft 2in (5.85m)
Width: 7ft 3in (2.20m)
Height: 7ft 8in (2.33m)

Engine: Bussing-NAG L8V, petrol, 160bhp at 3,000rpm
Speed: 52mph (85km/hr)
Range: 185 miles (300km)

Sd Kfz 232 (6 rad) Armoured Car
Germany
Bussing-NAG, Daimler-Benz, Magirus

The 232 (6 rad) was simply the radio-carrying command car version of the 231 (6 rad) armoured car. It can easily be recognised by the large frame antenna erected over the turret. The dimensions are the same as those of the combat car version.

Sd Kfz 232 (8 rad) Germany
Deutsche Werke

This 232 (8 rad) was the same as the 8-wheeled 231 armoured car but was fitted with long range radio and had the usual frame antenna mounted over the top of the turret. The dimensions and performance were the same as those on the parent vehicle.

Sd Kfz 233 Germany
Deutsche Werke

The 233 was the 232 8-wheeled armoured car with the turret removed, the roof left open, and a short 75mm tank gun mounted behind a low shield. The object was to provide armoured car units with a support vehicle capable of dealing with enemy armour and 115 were built in 1943. The survivors remained in service throughout the remainder of the war.

Data: as for the standard Sd Kfz 231 (8 rad), except
Armament: 1 × 75mm gun and 1 × MG.

Sd Kfz 234/1 Germany
Bussing-NAG

In production 1944. In spite of the numbering, this vehicle was an adaptation of the 234/2 (*below*) whose design began some two years later. It was the same hull and running gear but with a low open-topped turret carrying a 20mm cannon. 200 were produced in the second half of 1944.

Sd Kfz 234/2 Germany
Bussing-NAG

Design of this vehicle, also known as the **Puma**, began in 1940, the object being an improved 8-wheel vehicle. Instead of being built in the traditional chassis-and-hull mode, it was a monocoque design in which the hull was the basic structure and everything was attached to it. Whilst of the same general shape as the earlier

Sd Kfz 231 (8 rad) model, there are some very obvious differences, prominent among them being the long one-piece mudguards running the whole length of the vehicle and echoing the hull shape in the rise below the turret. The slope of the long rear engine compartment is not so pronounced as on the earlier model. The most significant change was the well-designed and armoured turret mounting a 50mm L/60 tank gun. It also had a new air-cooled engine so that it would operate in any climate. Had the development been quicker, this could have been a very formidable wheeled tank; as it was, production did not begin until late in 1943 and just over 100 were built before it was halted in favour of the simple 234/1 (*above*).

Armament: 1 × 50mm KwK 39/1 L/60; 1 × MG
Armour: 30mm
Crew: 4
Weight: 11.74 tons (11,925kg)
Length: 22ft 4in (6.80m)
Width: 7ft 10in (2.4m)
Height: 7ft 6in (2.28m)
Engine: Tatra 103, V-12 air-cooled diesel, 220bhp at 2,250rpm
Speed: 50mph (80km/hr)
Range: 560 miles (900km)

Sd Kfz 234/3 Germany
Bussing-NAG

1943. This was the Sd Kfz 234/2 (*above*) modified to mount a short (KwK 51 L/24) 75mm gun in an open-topped superstructure which replaced the turret. A total of 88 were built between June and December 1944, when production was switched to the 234/4 (*below*). Dimensions the same as the 234/2 except for slightly less weight.

Sd Kfz 234/4 Germany
Bussing-NAG

In November 1944 Hitler ordered the fitting of the long 75mm (PaK 40 L/46) tank gun to the Sd Kfz 234 series, resulting in this 234/4 model. It replaced the 234/3 on the production line in December 1944 and 89 were built by March 1945 when the factory finally stopped operating. The hull of the vehicle was topped by a long open-topped superstructure with the shielded gun mounted to fire forwards.

Data: as for the 234/2, except for the armament

Sd Kfz 263 (6 rad) Germany
Magirus

This was a variant of the Sd Kfz 231/232 (6 rad) family. It resembled the 232, since it was a communications vehicle and had the usual frame antenna, but the turret was fixed and the armament only a single machine gun.

Dimensions: as for the parent Sd Kfz 231 (6 rad)

Sd Kfz 263 (8 rad) Germany
Deutsche Werke

A communications variant similar to the 263 (6 rad) in having a fixed, turret-like superstructure with a single machine gun, and a massive frame antenna almost the length of the vehicle.

Dimensions: as for the 231 (8 rad), except
Weight: 8.1 tons (8,230kg)

Stormer 30 Reconnaissance Vehicle UK
Alvis

1997. This is a tracked vehicle, based upon the Alvis Stormer APC (described in the Infantry Armour section) and intended as a light reconnaissance tank. It has been developed as a private venture and uses an Italian turret mounting the American 30mm Bushmaster cannon. There are rear doors and ample room inside for a variety of surveillance and target acquisition equipment as required.

Armament: 1 × 30mm cannon; 1 × MG; 2 × ATGW
Armour: not disclosed
Crew: 3
Weight: 12.79 tons (13,000kg)
Length: 17ft 3in (5.25m)
Width: 8ft 10in (2.69m)
Height: 8ft 3in (2.50m)
Engine: Cummins 6-cylinder diesel, 250bhp at 2,600rpm
Speed: 50mph (80km/hr)
Range: 250 miles (400km)

Striker UK
See Scorpion

Sultan Command Vehicle UK
Alvis

This is another member of the Scorpion (*qv*) family of light tracked vehicles, and was designed to permit a commander to have a command post close up to his forward elements. The boxy body is built up so as to give reasonable headroom to the interior, which is provided with desks, mapboards, radios, computers and all the other apparatus now considered vital to commanders. There is also the usual extendable tent structure which can be attached at the rear so as to increase the working space, albeit without protection from much more

than rain. A machine gun is provided for local defence.

Armament: 1 × MG
Armour: not disclosed
Crew: 3
Weight: 8.04 tons (8,172kg)
Length: 16ft 9in (5.12m)
Width: 7ft 4in (2.45m)
Height: 8ft 6in (2.60m)
Engine: Jaguar, 6-cylinder, petrol, 190bhp
Speed: 50mph (80km/hr)
Range: 300 miles (480km)

Sumida Type 2593 Armoured Car Japan
Ishikawajima

1933. Also known as the **Type 93**. The Sumida was designed by Japanese military engineers with the particular intention that it should be equally adaptable to running on railway lines or roads. It was a 6 x 4 commercial chassis with some novel modifications. The wheels could be easily removed and replaced with railway wheels, carried on the sides in special racks. There were built-in jacks to speed the wheel changing and for different rail gauges the track could be altered. On the road the wheels were solid-tyred, so speed and cross-country mobility were not good, but in China where the car had most operational use, its rail-running ability was more useful and it appears that it was quite effective. The layout was the usual one for the time, a front engine and a large body with a small machine gun turret on top.

Armament: 1 × MG
Armour: 10mm
Crew: 6
Weight: 6.88 tons (7,000kg)
Length: 21ft 6in (6.55m)
Width: 6ft 3in (1.90m)
Height: 9ft 8in (2.97m)
Engine: Commercial, 4-cylinder, petrol, 45bhp
Speed: 37mph (60km/hr)
Range: 150 miles (240km)

T17E1 Armoured Car USA
Chevrolet

1942. In mid-1941 the British Amy staff in Washington and the US Armored Force combined to draw up specifications for an armoured car. As a result, the T17 was produced by the Chevrolet company and 3,500 were ordered. Shortly after this, the confused state of American armoured car development led to a Board of Review which first cut back the order for the T17E1 to 250 cars and then cancelled it altogether. The British, however, managed to keep it in production and eventually 2,844 were made, all of which were shipped to Britain. A further 1,000 **T17E2** models were also built; these differed in being designed for anti-aircraft protection and carried a Frazer-Nash turret with twin .50-inch Browning machine guns.

The standard T17E1, named **Staghound** by the British, was a 4 x 4 car with a turret carrying a 37mm gun. Once in Britain numbers were modified to become **Staghound 2** by taking out the 37mm gun and substituting a 3-inch tank howitzer, so that the cars had a close support capability. Others, **Staghound 3**, were modified by removing the turret and replacing it with that of the Cruiser Mark 6 (Crusader) tank, but fitted with a 75mm gun.

Armament: 1 x 37mm; 1 x coaxial MG; 1 x hull MG
Armour: 45mm
Crew: 5
Weight: 13.70 tons (13,925kg)
Length: 18ft 0in (5.48m)
Width: 8ft 10in (2.69m)
Height: 7ft 9in (2.36m)
Engine: two GMC 6-cylinder, petrol, each 97bhp at 3,000rpm
Speed: 56mph (90km/hr)
Range: 450 miles (725km)

T18E2 Boarhound Armoured Car USA
Yellow Truck

1943. Impressed by the German eight-wheel armoured car and its activities in the Western Desert, the British Army asked the US Armored Force to co-operate in the design of a similar vehicle early in 1942. An eight-wheeled car, the **T18**, was designed, and, as an alternative, a six-wheeled car the **T18E1** was also developed. Both these vehicles used the turret of the M3 series light tank, complete with a 37mm gun, but the British then requested a heavier weapon and a fresh eight-wheel car mounting a 6-pounder (57mm) gun, the **T18E2**, was developed. By that time the Board of Review had ruled that no car over 14,000lb (6,350kg) weight was to be perpetuated; moreover, the US Army were studying another design (the **T19**, which eventually came to nothing) which they considered superior to the T18 series. As a result, the T18 programme was closed down, but 30 T18E2 cars already under construction were completed for supply to Britain. By the time they had been shipped, the desert campaign was over and the reason for their existence had gone. Apart from being used for a variety of tests and trials in Britain

the Boarhound armoured car had come to the end of its career.

Armament: 1 x 57mm; 2 x MG
Armour: 30mm
Crew: 5
Weight: 23.68 tons (24,040kg)
Length: 20ft 6in (6.24m)
Width: 10ft 1in (3.07m)
Height: 8ft 7in (2.61m)
Engine: two GMC 6-cylinder, petrol, each 97bhp at 3,000rpm
Speed: 50mph (80km/hr)
Range: 250 miles (400km)

Talbot Armoured Car UK
Talbot

1914. Known as the **Admiralty Talbots**, these were, like most of the 1914 crop of vehicles procured by the Royal Naval Air Service, a standard commercial heavy touring car chassis with an armoured body. The Talbot car of the period was actually a British-made Belgian Clement with some minor variations. The resulting armoured car was generally similar to the Rolls-Royce type, with a bevelled turret over a short fighting compartment, and a flat cargo space above the dual rear wheels. It is quickly distinguished from the Rolls by having artillery-spoked wheels instead of wire-spoked. No more than three were built before it was discovered that the weight was too much for the transmission, and manufacture was halted, the design changed to an unarmoured 'tender' or logistics vehicle, and about 40 were completed and issued to armoured car squadrons.

THE200 Armoured Car Germany
Thyssen-Henschel

This was the junior member of a family of armoured vehicles proposed by Thyssen-Henschel in the 1980s. The THE200 was a 4 x 4 broadly resembling the Renault 4 x 4 VAB design or the Cadillac Gage vehicles with sloped sides and recessed wheels, Suspension was by a new system developed by Thyssen-Henschel involving double trailing arms to provide independent suspension on all wheels, which, coupled with low-pressure tyres, was claimed to give a remarkably smooth ride. A variety of turrets, armed with virtually anything up to 90mm calibre, were offered, as well as a pure APC version, but the design appears to have made no impact on the market.

Armament: to choice, up to 90mm gun
Armour: not disclosed

Crew: 4 + 7 troops in the APC role
Length: 19ft 0in (5.80m)
Width: 9ft 2in (2.79m)
Height: 5ft 9in (1.75m) to hull roof
Weight: 9.10 tons (9,250kg)
Engine: MTU diesel, 225bhp
Speed: 68mph (110km/hr)
Range: 500 miles (800km)

THE400 Armoured Car Germany
Thyssen-Henschel

This, the middle member of the T-H family, was a 6 x 6 with the same general appearance as the smaller car, with rear engine, sloped sides and recessed wheels. It used the same independent suspension system and carried a three-man turret mounting a 105mm L7-type gun; it was claimed that it could equally well be armed with a 120mm smoothbore gun if that was what took your fancy. Development was completed but no orders ensued.

Armament: 1 x 105mm; other options available
Armour: not disclosed
Crew: 4
Weight: 24.11 tons (24,500kg)
Length: 20ft 4in (6.20m)
Width: 9ft 9in (2.98m)
Height: 6ft 1in (1.85m) to hull roof
Engine: MTU diesel, 465bhp
Speed: 68mph (110km/hr)
Range: 620 miles (1,000km)

THE800 Armoured Car Germany
Thyssen-Henschel

This was the senior member of the T-H group and was similar in shape to the others but with an 8 x 8 wheel arrangement. No armament was specified but it was said that the vehicle could carry any turret and gun arrangement up to a gross weight of 13 tons, and proposed weapon fits ranged from twin 35mm AA guns through various missiles and direct-fire weapons to a 155mm howitzer. However, there appear to have been no takers for the designs and no production for sale has taken place.

Armament: to choice
Armour: not disclosed
Crew: 6
Weight: 34.45 tons (35,000kg)
Length: 23ft 3in (7.10m)
Width: 9ft 9in (2.98m)
Height: 6ft 3in (1.90m) to hull roof
Engine: MTU diesel, 650bhp
Speed: 75mph (120km/hr)
Range: 620 miles (1,000km)

Type 1 'Ho-Ha' Half-Track Armoured Car Japan
Isuzu

1938. The Type 1, or **Type 98** as it is sometimes confusingly known, was the one attempt of the Japanese to produce an up-to-date armoured car before World War II started. The design was heavily influenced by German ideas and in fact the vehicle was much nearer to being a three-quarter-track. The basis was an Isuzu truck fitted with suspension components, tracks and roadwheels from a light tank in place of the rear wheels. The sides were armoured, but there was an open roof and protection was barely adequate. Only a few were made, since the construction was more than the over-loaded Japanese industry could manage.

Length: 20ft 2in (6.12m)
Width: 6ft 11in (2.09m)
Height: 6ft 6in (1.99m)
Crew: 2 + up to 12

Type 87 Reconnaissance/Patrol Vehicle Japan
Komatsu

1980. This shares most of its hull and running gear with the Type 82 Command Vehicle (*qv*), though the hull shape and layout differs. The driver is at the left front and the radio operator is alongside him. Behind them is the fighting compartment, with a power-operated turret manned by the commander and gunner and carrying a 25mm Oerlikon KBA cannon and a coaxial machine gun. The fifth man is the observer who has rearward and side-facing periscopes. The engine and transmission compartment take up the rear of the vehicle.

Armament: 1 x 25mm cannon; 2 x MG
Armour: not disclosed
Crew: 5
Weight: 13.77 tons (14,000kg)
Length: 19ft 8in (5.99m)
Width: 8ft 2in (2.48m)
Height: 9ft 2in (2.80m)
Engine: Isuzu V-10 diesel, 308bhp at 2,700rpm
Speed: 62mph (100km/hr)
Range: 310 miles (500km)

Type 92 Armoured Car Japan
See Osaka

Type 93 Armoured Car Japan
See Sumida

Type 98 Armoured Car Japan
See Type 1

UR416 Internal Security Vehicle Germany
Thyssen-Henschel
1965. This was a private-venture design originally by Rheinstahl (who were absorbed into Thyssen Henschel) and consists basically of the commercial Mercedes-Benz Unimog truck chassis fitted with an armoured body. Its primary role is internal security, though the makers have put forward a selection of suggested variants. Numbers have been bought by countries throughout the world.

The vehicle hull is of welded steel with sloped surfaces; the engine and transmission are at the front, with the driver behind them, and the remainder of the vehicle is available for the crew and occupants. Access is by doors in both sides and the rear of the hull. There are two hatches in the roof, one of which can be fitted with various armament options. Five firing ports are provided in each side of the hull and two in the rear. The basic model is provided with a machine gun, protected by a small shield. Other armament packages developed include a 20mm cannon, a 90mm recoilless rifle, or anti-tank missiles. Other versions of the basic vehicle can be adapted for use as ambulances, repair trucks, observation and command vehicles or obstacle clearing vehicles for internal security units.

Armament: optional, see text
Armour: 9mm
Crew: 2 + 8
Weight: 7.48 tons (7,600kg)
Length: 16ft 9in (5.10m)
Width: 7ft 5in (2.26m)
Height: 7ft 4in (2.24m)
Engine: Daimler-Benz, 6-cylinder, diesel, 120bhp at 2,800rpm
Speed: 50mph (80km/hr)
Range: 435 miles (700km)

Ursus wz/29 Armoured Car Poland
Ursus
1926. The Ursus was a conventional armoured car built on a truck chassis with the usual high body, though some attempt was made to slope the armour slightly. The construction was by the usual method of bolting plates to a frame, and the rear of the hull was made of short sections of straight plate to prevent having to roll the armour into curves. The octagonal turret carried a 37mm M1916 French trench cannon firing forward and a machine gun which faced to the left and could only be used at right angles to the 37mm. There was another

machine gun in the rear of the hull. These cars were under cavalry control and were used in conjunction with the horsed units, but all were swept away in 1939 and there is no record of any surviving the German invasion.

Armament: 1 × 37mm Puteaux; 2 × MG
Armour: 9mm
Crew: 5 or 6
Weight: 5.90 tons (6,000kg) estimated
Length: 15ft 9in (4.80m)
Width: 5ft 11in (1.79m)
Height: 9ft 1in (2.76m)
Engine: 4-cylinder, petrol, 60bhp
Speed: 35mph (56km/hr)
Range: 120 miles (195km)

VEC Cavalry Scout Vehicle Spain
Santa Barbara
1980. This is a 6 x 6 wheeled vehicle which uses the same basic structure as the BMR-600 APC), the principal visible difference being the presence of a large turret with a 25mm cannon; this is actually an Italian design built under licence in Spain. Internally the main difference is that the engine is at the rear of the vehicle so as to leave a relatively roomy central fighting compartment under the turret. The vehicle is fully amphibious, using water-jet propulsion.

Armament: 1 × 25mm M242 cannon; 1 × coaxial MG
Armour: not disclosed
Crew: 5
Weight: 13.53 tons (13,750kg)
Length: 20ft 0in (6.10m)
Width: 8ft 3in (2.50m)
Height: 6ft 6in (2.0m) to hull roof
Engine: Pegaso 6-cylinder turbocharged diesel, 310bhp at 2,200rpm
Speed: 65mph (105km/hr)
Range: 500 miles (800km)

VEXTRA 105 Armoured Car France
GIAT
1994. This is a heavy and powerful 8 x 8 wheeled car with a turret mounting a 105mm gun. When first displayed it was armed with a 25mm gun turret, but this was followed in 1997 with the adoption of an unstabilized 105mm gun and in 1998 by a fully stabilized weapon. The gun is, of course, backed up by the most modern fire control, sighting and surveillance equipment. The vehicle is of simple form, using aluminium armour with an added layer of steel armour in parts, wedge-shaped in the front and with the eight wheels set well into the hull. In

addition to its normal crew it is capable of carrying eight fully-equipped infantrymen in a passenger compartment.

Armament: 1 x 105mm; 1 x MG
Armour: not disclosed
Crew: 4 + 8
Weight: 27.56 tons (28,000kg)
Length: 24ft 3in (7.40m)
Width: 11ft 2in (3.40m)
Height: 6ft 7in (2.00m) to top of hull
Engine: Scania diesel, 700bhp
Speed: 75mph (120km/hr)
Range: 500 miles (800km)

White-Laffly Auto-Mitrailleuse France
White, Laffly

1915. In 1915 France imported the White truck from the United States, for which an armoured body was then constructed. The resulting vehicle was heavy, but practical and it proved to be the best and most useful of all the French cars of World War I. The layout was conventional, with a front engine driving twin rear wheels, and a turret mounted on the load-carrying platform at the rear. Driver and co-driver were in an armoured tub, and the turret was enclosed. Armament was usually a 37mm gun and a single machine gun, mounted on opposite sides of the turret; some had two machine guns, mounted in the same manner. There were over 200 of these cars in service in 1918 and they remained in dwindling numbers until 1940.

Armament: 1 x 37mm gun and 1 x MG; or 2 x MG
Armour: 8mm
Crew: 4
Weight: 5.9 tons (6,000kg)
Length: 18ft 4in (5.57m)
Width: 6ft 10in (2.24m)
Height: 8ft 11in (2.92m)
Engine: White, 4-cylinder, petrol, 35bhp
Speed: 28mph (45km/hr)
Range: 150 miles (240km)

Wolseley Model CP Armoured Car UK
Wolseley

1915. A tall, slab-sided and rectangular-looking car, using solid tyres in 4 x 2 configuration, the rear wheels being twins. A roomy vehicle, with a turret by Vickers and carrying two machine guns, it was, though, sadly underpowered. Only three or four were made.

Armament: 2 x MG
Armour: 5mm
Crew: 4

Weight: approx 6 tons (6,100kg)
Wheelbase: 12ft 0in (3.65m)
Engine: Wolseley, 4-cylinder petrol, 45bhp
Speed: 30mph (48km/hr)

wz/34 Armoured Car Poland
State factory

A simple machine in basic 'motor-car' style, with a long engine hood in front of a short crew compartment topped by a small turret carrying the usual 37mm trench cannon or a light machine gun. Although of 4 x 2 configuration, the rear wheels were dual. Springing was by half-elliptics all round and the ground clearance was surprisingly large for its day. Built on a commercial chassis, these were small and nimble vehicles for reconnaissance but their protection was poor and most were destroyed in the first few days of combat in 1939.

Armament: 1 x 37mm cannon or 1 x MG
Armour: 6mm
Crew: 2
Weight: 2.2 tons (2,235kg)
Length: 11ft 10in (3.61m)
Width: 6ft 3in (1.91m)
Height: 7ft 3in (2.21m)
Engine: Citroën 6-cylinder petrol 20bhp; or Fiat 6-cylinder petrol 25bhp
Speed: 25mph (40km/hr)
Range: 160 miles (260km)

XM800 Armoured Reconnaissance Vehicle USA
FMC, Lockheed

1974. In 1971 the US Army canvassed a number of companies for a suitable light scouting vehicle. Of the various designs submitted, two were selected and orders were given for the construction of four prototypes of each. One was by the FMC Corporation and was a tracked vehicle, the other was by the Lockheed Company and was wheeled. In 1974–75 these prototypes were extensively tested in competition with various similar vehicles from other countries, but complaints were voiced that the vehicle had no anti-aircraft protection other than a light machine gun, could not be operated for 24 hours continuously, and could not carry the requisite amount of equipment. Modification and further tests were discussed but nothing came of it and the two companies abandoned their projects and proceeded to other things.

The **FMC Tracked Scout** resembled a light tank; it had an aluminium armour hull with the driver seated centrally at the front. The two-man turret was in the centre of the body and mounted a

20mm cannon. The turret was fully powered and the gun was stabilized; fire control was based on a complex image-intensifying sight. The vehicle was fully amphibious, being propelled in the water by the paddle-wheel action of the tracks.

The **Lockheed Wheeled Scou**t resembled a conventional six-wheeled armoured car at first sight, but the two forward wheels, together with the suspension, steering, front drive and fuel tank, were enclosed in a distinct unit which was roll-articulated to the rest of the vehicle so that the range of movement of the front wheels was far greater than that possible with any normal means of suspension. The remainder of the body held the crew, engine and turret, and was made of aluminium with an additional thickness of steel armour. The turret was of cast aluminium armour and mounted a 20mm cannon with full stabilisation, power control and image-intensifying sights. The engine and transmission were at the rear of the vehicle.

FMC Tracked Scout
Armament: 1 x 20mm cannon, 1 x MG
Armour: not disclosed
Crew: 3
Weight: 8.48 tons (8,618kg)
Length: 15ft 4in (4.67m)
Width: 8ft 0in (2.43m)
Height: 7ft 10in (2.39m)
Engine: GMC diesel, 6-cylinder, 280bhp at 2,900rpm
Speed: 55mph (88km/hr)
Range: 450 miles (725km)

Lockheed Wheeled Scout
Armament: 1 x 20mm cannon; 1 x MG
Armour: not disclosed
Crew: 3
Weight: 7.57 tons (7,697kg)
Length: 16ft 1in (4.91m)
Width: 8ft 0in (2.43m)
Height: 8ft 2in (2.48m)
Engine: GMC diesel, 6-cylinder, 300bhp at 2,100rpm
Speed: 65mph (105km/hr)
Range: 450 miles (725km)

COMPARATIVE TABLES

CONVENTIONS

The conventions used in these tables are as for Tanks (see page 157) with the addition of the following:

Wheels: The first figure is the number of wheels, the second the number of those wheels which are driven. In the case of the four-wheelers with an additional pair of wheels in the centre which can be raised or lowered, these are noted as 4 x 4s – the middle wheels were not always driven, and a shorthand form of sorting them out was not feasible. In early designs, using narrow high pressure tyres, double rear wheels were often used to distribute the weight and improve cross-country traction. The development of large-section, deep-tread low-pressure tyres ended this practice. Double wheels, where used, are mentioned in the text entries; there is no special notation in the data tables. The letters FT in this column indicate 'full tracked; and 'HT' indicate 'half tracked'.

IN ASCENDING ORDER OF WEIGHT

Name	Wheels	Weight	Length	Crew	Armour	Armament		Engine	Power	Speed	Range	Country
Beaverette	4 × 2	2.0	12.5	3	10	–	1	P/4/L	45	40	?	UK
Adler Kfz 13	4 × 4	2.16	13.75	2	8	–	1	P/6/L	60	43	185	Germany
ABI	4 × 4	2.19	13.83	2 + 4	10	–	1	D	68	55	370	Romania
wz/34	4 × 2	2.20	11.92	2	6	37 or	1	P/6/L	20	25	160	Poland
BA-64	4 × 4	2.36	12.0	2	10	–	1	P/4/L	54	50	375	Russia
Austro-Daimler	4 × 4	2.95	15.93	4	4	–	1	P/4/L	40	28	155	Austria
Daimler Dingo	4 × 4	2.95	10.42	2	30	–	1	P/6/L	55	55	200	UK
Shorland	4 × 4	3.30	15.08	3	11	–	1	P/6/L	91	55	320	UK
Ferret	4 × 4	3.42	11.08	3	16	–	1	P/6/L	129	58	185	UK
Minerva	4 × 2	3.44	14.42	3	5	–	1	P/4/L	40	30	150	Belgium
BA-7	4 × 4	3.50	12.16	3	10	–	1	P/V/8/L	60	45	155	Russia
Rolls-Royce 1914	4 × 2	3.50	16.75	4	9	–	1	P/6/L	50	60	150	UK
Panhard VBL	4 × 4	3.53	12.17	3	*	–	1	D/4/T/L	95	60	375	France
Ramta RBY	4 × 4	3.54	16.43	2 + 6	8	–	–	P/6/L	120	62	340	Israel
Morris Light Recon	4 × 4	3.70	13.33	3	14	–	2	P/4/L	72	45	?	UK
Rolls Royce 1920	4 × 2	3.79	17.0	4	9	–	1	P/6/L	80	50	150	UK
Humber Light Recon	4 × 4	3.80	14.33	3	10	–	2	P/6/L	87	50	?	UK
Sd Kfz 221/222	4 × 4	3.93	15.75	2	15	20	1	P/V/8/L	75/81	50	200	Germany
Ford Lynx Mk 1	4 × 4	4.01	12.17	2	30	–	1	P/V/8/L	95	57	200	Canada
Lancia 1Z	4 × 2	4.12	18.75	6	6	–	3	P/4/L	70	37	248	Italy
Austin	4 × 2	4.14	16.0	4	8	–	2	P/4/L	50	35	125	UK
Morris Arm'd Recon	4 × 2	4.20	15.67	4	7	.55	1	P/6/L	96	45	240	UK
BA-27	6 × 4	4.43	15.17	4	8	37	1	P/4/L	36	30	250	Russia
Harimau 2000	4 × 4	4.72	12.67	2	16	HMG	–	D/V/8/A	140	62	250	UK
Lanchester (1915)	4 × 4	4.80	16.0	4	8	–	1	P/6/L	60	50	180	UK
Otter Light Recon	4 × 4	4.80	14.75	3	12	–	1	P/6/L	104	45	225	Canada
Peugeot	4 × 2	4.82	15.75	4	*	37 or	1	P/4/L	40	25	85	France

Name	Wheels	Weight	Length	Crew	Armour	Armament		Engine	Power	Speed	Range	Country
Crossley Indian Pattern	4 × 2	5.0	16.5	4	8	—	2	P/6/L	50	40	125	UK
Mowag Eagle	4 × 4	5.02	16.08	4	*	—	1	D/V/8/L	160	78	280	Switzerland
BA-10	6 × 6	5.06	15.25	4	15	45	2	P/4/L	50	35	190	Russia
Guy	4 × 4	5.20	13.5	3	15	HMG	1	P/4/L	53	40	210	UK
Eland	4 × 4	5.22	13.25	3	*	60	2	D/4/T/L	103	53	280	S Africa
RAM V-1 (Short)	4 × 4	5.31	16.43	2 + 4	8	—	3	D/6/A	132	60	372	Israel
SK-1	4 × 2	5.31	13.08	5	8	—	1	D/4/L	55	50	215	E Germany
Panhard AML	4 × 4	5.41	12.42	3	12	90	2	P/4/A	90	62	370	France
Sd Kfz 231 (6 rad)	6 × 6	5.41	19.0	4	15	20 or	1	P/6/L	60	38	250	Germany
Crossley Mark 1	6 × 4	5.43	15.25	4	8	—	2	P/6/L	50	45	?	UK
BTR-40P/BRDM-1	6 × 6	5.51	18.67	5	10	—	1	P/6/L	90	50	310	Russia
M3A1 Scout Car	4 × 4	5.53	18.42	2	7	HMG	1	P/6/L	87	50	250	USA
RAM V-1 (Long)	4 × 4	5.64	18.17	2 + 7	8	—	3	D/6/A	132	60	500	Israel
Engesa EE-3	4 × 4	5.70	13.67	3	*	—	1	D/4/T/L	120	62	435	Brazil
Austin-Putilov	4 × 2	5.71	22.17	5	8	—	2	P4/L	50	18	50	Russia
Osaka (Type 92)	6 × 4	5.71	16.33	3	6	—	2	P/4/L	85	37	150	Japan
Csaba 39	4 × 4	5.80	14.75	3	10	37	1	?	?	?	?	Hungary
Peerless 1915	4 × 2	5.80	20.5	5	8	1-pdr	1	P/4/L	40	20	90	UK
Ursus wz/29	4 × 2	5.90	15.75	5	9	37	2	P/4/L	60	35	120	Poland
White-Laffly	4 × 2	5.90	18.33	4	8	37	1	P/4/L	35	28	150	France
Fox (UK)	4 × 4	6.02	7.33	3	*	30	1	P/6/L	190	65	270	UK
Wolseley CP	4 × 2	6.0	12.0	4	5	—	2	P/4/L	45	30	?	UK
Marmon-Herrington	6 × 6	6.19	16.0	4	12	40	1	P/V/8/L	85	50	200	S Africa
PA-4/35	6 × 4	6.50	17.5	4	13	—	2	P/4/L	100	45	150	Czech
Jeffery Armd C	4 × 4	6.51	18.0	3	8	—	1	P/4/L	40	20	100	USA/UK
Lohr RPX 6000	4 × 4	6.69	15.0	3	*	—	1	P/6/L	180	68	375	France
Autoblinda 40	4 × 4	6.74	17.08	4	9	20	2	P/6/L	80	47	250	Italy
Fiat 611	6 × 4	6.79	18.58	5	15	37	2	P/6/L	45	17	347	Italy
Peerless 1919	4 × 2	6.80	20.08	4	8	—	2	P/4/L	40	18	?	UK
M114 C & R	FT	6.82	14.67	4	37	20	1	P/V/8/L	160	36	300	USA
M38 Wolfhound	6 × 6	6.83	16.75	4	10	37	1	P/V/8/L	148	60	300	USA
Humber Arm'd Car	4 × 4	6.85	15.0	3/4	30	HMG/37	1	P/6/L	90	45	250	UK
BRDM-2	4 × 4	6.88	18.75	4	10	HMG	1	P/V/8/L	140	62	465	Russia
Sumida	6 × 4	6.88	21.5	6	10	—	1	P/4/L	45	37	150	Japan
FUG-65	4 × 4	6.89	19.0	5	13		1	D/4/L	100	54	375	Hungary
FUG-70	4 × 4	6.89	19.08	3	13	HMG	1	D/6/L	160	62	310	Hungary
M39 (DAF)	6 × 6	6.90	15.17	6	10	37	2	P/V/8/L	95	37	180	Neth'lands
Cad Gage C'do Scout	4 × 4	7.12	16.42	3	*	—	1	D/V/6/L	149	60	800	USA
Crossley RAF Pattern	6 × 4	7.12	20.58	4	8	—	2	P/6/L	70	50	?	UK
OF-65A	4 × 4	7.28	19.0	5	13	82	1	D/4/L	100	54	375	Czech
Fox (Canada)	4 × 4	7.37	14.75	4	15	HMG	1	P/6/L	104	44	210	Canada
UR416	4 × 4	7.48	16.75	2 + 8	9	options		D/6/L	120	50	435	Germany
Daimler	4 × 4	7.50	13.0	3	16	40	1	P/6/L	95	50	205	UK
Lanchester Mk 1	4 × 4	7.50	16.08	3	8	—	3	P/6/L	86	55	200	UK
XM-800 Wheeled Scout	6 × 6	7.57	16.08	3	*	20	1	D/6/L	300	65	450	USA
m/39 (Landsverk)	4 × 4	7.67	16.75	6	18	20	2	P/6/L	135	45	155	Sweden
Scimitar	FT	7.67	14.42	3	*	30	1	P/6/L	195	55	400	UK
Landsverk 180	6 × 4	7.70	18.83	5	8.5	20	2	P/6/L	80	50	180	Sweden
PA-4/27	4 × 4	7.70	19.67	4	6	—	2	P/4/L	100	38	150	Czech
M8 Greyhound	6 × 6	7.76	16.42	4	20	37	2	P/6/L	110	55	350	USA
Fiat-OTO 6616	4 × 4	7.87	17.58	3	8	20	1	D/6/T/L	160	62	435	Italy

Name	Wheels	Weight	Length	Crew	Armour	Armament		Engine	Power	Speed	Range	Country
Scorpion	FT	7.94	14.42	3	*	76	1	P/6/L	195	55	400	UK
Sultan	FT	8.04	16.75	3	*	–	1	P/6/L	190	50	300	UK
Panhard ERC-90 F4	6 × 6	8.16	17.25	3	*	90	2	P/V/6/L	145	60	435	France
Striker	FT	8.21	15.82	3	*	GW	1	P/6/L	195	55	400	UK
Sd Kfz 231 (8 rad)	8 × 8	8.30	19.17	4	30	20	1	P/V/8/L	160	52	135	Germany
XM-800 Tracked Scout	FT	8.48	15.33	3	*	20	1	D/6/L	280	55	450	USA
Lynx C&RV	FT	8.63	15.08	3	*	–	2	D/V/6/L	215	45	325	USA
FN 4RM/62F AB	4 × 4	8.86	14.67	3	13	–	2	P/6/L	130	68	372	Belgium
Guy, Indian Pattern	6 × 4	9.0	20.33	4	6	–	2	P/6/L	120	40	150	UK
Cad Gage C'do V-150	4 × 4	9.40	19.67	2 + 10	*	as desired		D/V/8/L	202	55	600	USA
Seabrook Armd C	4 × 2	10.0	24.0	7	8	3-pdr	2	P/4/L	33	20	100	UK
Lohr RPX 90	4 × 4	10.82	17.08	3	*	90	2	D/6/T	310	68	620	France
AEC	4 × 4	11.0	17.0	4	57	40/57/75	1	D/6/L	105	40	250	UK
Saladin	6 × 6	11.4	16.17	3	32	76	2	P/V/8/L	170	45	250	UK
Coventry	4 × 4	11.50	15.50	4	14	40/75	1	P/6/L	175	40	250	UK
Sd Kfz 234/2	8 × 8	11.74	22.33	4	30	50	1	D/V/12/A	220	50	560	Germany
Stormer Recon	FT	12.79	17.25	3	*	30 + 2 × GW	1	D/6/L	250	50	250	UK
PRP-4 Recon	FT	13.0	22.08	5	*	–	1	D	300	49	370	Russia
Engesa EE-9	4 × 4	13.19	17.08	3	16	90	1	D/V/6/L	212	62	545	Brazil
BRM-23	FT	13.28	22.17	5	*	23 + GW	1	D/V/6/L	310	40	310	Russia
Panhard EBR-75	8 × 8	13.28	20.17	4	15	75	3	P/F/12/L	200	65	400	France
Renault VBC-90	6 × 6	13.28	18.5	3	*	90	1	D/6/T/L	220	56	620	France
VEC Cavalry Scout	6 × 6	13.53	20.0	5	*	25	1	D/6/T/L	310	65	500	Spain
T17E1 Staghound	6 × 6	13.70	18.0	5	45	37	2	2 × P/6/L	194	56	450	USA
Type 87 R/PV	6 × 6	13.77	19.67	5	*	25	2	D/V/10/L	308	62	310	Japan
Panhard AMD 178	4 × 4	14.27	15.0	3	18	25	1	P/4/L	180	45	145	France
Cad Gage C'do V-300	6 × 6	14.73	21.0	3 + 9	*	as desired		D/V/6/T/L	275	62	435	USA
AMX-10RC	6 × 6	15.63	20.83	4	*	105	1	D/HO/8/S/L	260	53	620	France
Snezka	FT	17.16	24.75	4	*	HMG	–	D/6/L	300	35	372	Czech
Cadillac Gage V-600	6 × 6	18.20	20.67	4	*	105	2	D/6/T/L	275	63	370	USA
Engesa EE-17	6 × 6	18.20	20.75	3	*	105	1	D/V/6/T/L	300	68	372	Brazil
Engesa EE-18	6 × 6	18.20	19.17	4	*	105	1	D/6/T/L	380	65	435	Brazil
BRM	FT	18.70	23.0	6	*	30	1	D/V/10/L	500	43	370	Russia
THE200 Armd C	4 × 4	19.10	19.0	4 + 7	*	options		D	225	68	500	Germany
Luchs RV	8 × 8	19.19	25.42	4	*	20	1	M/V/10/T/L	390	56	455	Germany
T18E2 Boarhound	8 × 8	23.68	20.5	5	30	57	2	2 × P/6/L	194	50	250	USA
THE400 Armd C	6 × 6	24.11	20.33	4	*	options		D	465	68	620	Germany
Alvis Recon Vehicle	FT	26.57	21.08	4	*	25 + 2 × GW	1	D/V/8/L	650	56	435	UK
Rooikat	8 × 8	27.55	23.25	4	*	76	2	D/V/10/L	563	75	550	S Africa
VEXTRA 105	8 × 8	27.55	24.25	4 + 8	*	105	1	D	700	75	500	France
THE800 Armd C	8 × 8	34.45	23.25	6	*	options		D	650	75	620	Germany

No Weight Available

Name	Wheels	Weight	Length	Crew	Armour	Armament		Engine	Power	Speed	Range	Country
ADKZ	6 × 6	?	15.58	4	?	HMG	1	P/6	?	?	?	Austria
Leyland Armd C	4 × 2	?	?	6	7	–	2	P/4/L	40	20	?	UK
Mors	4 × 2	?	?	4	5	37 or	1	P/4	40	30	150	Belgium

INFANTRY ARMOUR

Armoured Personnel Carriers (APC), Infantry Fighting Vehicles (IFV), Mechanized Infantry Combat Vehicles (MICV) and such.

Achzarit IFV Israel
Israeli Defence Force Workshops
1988. Most IFVs are lightly armoured and intended to deposit their cargo short of its objective so that they may fight on foot. The Israelis have other ideas and demanded an IFV which was tough enough to go into battle alongside their main battle tanks. Consequently, this vehicle is based upon a redundant Russian T-55 tank chassis and hull, which is entirely dismantled and then rebuilt with additional armour to give protection far superior to any other infantry armoured vehicle in the world. Its firepower is also impressive, there being a remote-controlled machine gun mounted above the front of the crew compartment and controlled from inside, and three additional machine guns mounted on roof hatches. Driver, commander and machine gunner sit alongside each other in the front, and seven infantrymen occupy the rear of the hull compartment. The original Russian engine and transmission are replaced by a Detroit Diesel 850bhp powerplant coupled to an Allison automatic transmission, and the unit is designed so as to leave a passageway down one side, leading to a rear door for the use of the infantrymen.

Armament: see text
Engine: see text
Other data: none disclosed

ACMAT TPK 4.20 APC France
ACMAT
1980. ACMAT has long been a maker of rugged military trucks, particularly well-suited to North African conditions. Taking the chassis of their VLRA 4 x 4 2.5-tonne truck, and putting an armoured body on it, has resulted in this economical but practical APC which was promptly bought by several African armies. The layout is simple and conventional, with the engine at the front, driver and commander in the cab, and the rear of the vehicle forming a troop compartment with seats down both sides. What happens after that is more or less up to the purchaser: the troop compartment can be open-topped, or roofed over, with firing ports or without, with a turret or not. When closed-in and turreted it is sold as the **Light Armoured Car.**

Armament: 1 x MG upwards, to customer's choice
Armour: 8mm
Crew: 2 + 10
Weight: 7.18 tons (7,300kg)
Length: 19ft 7in (5.98m)
Width: 6ft 11in (2.10m)
Height: 7ft 3in (2.20m)
Engine: Perkins 6-cylinder diesel, 135bhp at 2,800rpm
Speed: 60mph (95km/hr)
Range: 1,000 miles (1,600km)

AIFV USA
See Armored Infantry Fighting Vehicle

Alacran Chile
See Cardoen BMS-1

AMX-10P MICV France
Roanne
1973. The AMX-10P was one of the earliest MICVs and was a very advanced concept for its day. The hull was made of a light alloy armour, well sloped at

231

the front. Behind this glacis plate were the driver and the engine. The engine drove a hydraulic torque converter and preselector gearbox to the rear sprocket. Behind the driver was the fighting compartment with a powered turret mounted above it, and at the rear was the troop compartment. There were roof hatches but no firing ports, and there was an electrically operated ramp at the rear instead of doors. Night-vision driving equipment was standard, as was NBC protection. The tracks were carried on five roadwheels, which were sprung by torsion bars, and there were two water jets at the back for propulsion when swimming. There were at least 18 variants of the AMX-10, and the design is capable of further modification and improvement. It has been supplied to Greece, Indonesia, Singapore and several Middle Eastern countries, and is still in service with the French Army.

Armament: 1 × 20mm cannon; 1 × coaxial MG
Armour: 6–30mm estimated
Crew: 2 + 9
Weight: 13.58 tons (13,500kg)
Length: 18ft 1in (5.82m)
Width: 9ft 2in (2.78m)
Height: 8ft 4in (2.54m)
Engine: Hispano-Suiza HS115, V-8, supercharged diesel, 276bhp at 3,000rpm
Speed: 40mph (65km/hr)
Range: 370 miles (600km)

AMX-VCI MICV France
Creusot-Loire

1956. The first tracked APC to enter French service, the VCI was a variant of the highly successful AMX-13 light tank and it used several common components. The forward section was almost identical with that of the tank, the driver sitting alongside the engine and the commander and gunner behind him. The troop compartment was at the rear and the hull was built up to give sufficient headroom for the infantry. They sat in the middle of the hull, facing outwards, and had firing ports in the sides and the rear doors. On the original vehicle the gunner had a simple pintle mount for one machine gun, but in later models almost any weapon or missile could be fitted, There were over a dozen variants, including an engineer version with lifting tackle, a mortar carrier and an ambulance. The vehicle has been in use for over 40 years and it is still in service with at least eight armies outside France and complete vehicles have been assembled in Argentina.

It should be noted that this was originally known as the **AMX-VTP** (*Véhicule Transport de Personnel*) and classed as an APC; it later became VCI (*Véhicule Combat d'Infanterie*) and is now classed as an MICV.

Armament: 1 × MG
Armour: 30mm
Crew: 1 + 12
Weight: 13.77 tons (14,000kg)
Length: 18ft 2in (5.54m)
Width: 8ft 3in (2.51m)
Height: 7ft 7in (2.32m)
Engine: SOFAM 8 GXB, 8-cylinder, petrol, 8,250cc, 250bhp at 3,200rpm
Speed: 40mph (65km/hr)
Range: 250 miles (400km)

Arisgator APC Italy
Aris

1997. The well-distributed American M113 APC is amphibious to the extent that it can swim slowly in calm water, propelled by its tracks. The Italian Aris company have developed an add-on kit which can be applied to any M113 and which vastly improves its capabilities to the point where it can confidently be used for off-shore operations in average seas. The kit consists mainly of bolt-on nose and tail units which give additional buoyancy and a better shape to the front of the vehicle. The tail sections fit on each side of the rear door, and contain propeller units to give additional thrust and also, being independently operable, improve the steering and general agility in the water. The vehicle roof is modified to improve the cooling system, add extension exhaust and air intakes and improve the sealing. A number of units have been ordered by the Italian Army and marines for extended trial.

Armament: 1 × HMG
Armour: 38mm
Crew: 2 + 11
Weight: 12.65 tons (12,856kg)
Length: 22ft 6in (6.87m)
Width: 9ft 8in (2.95m)
Height: 6ft 9in (2.05m)
Engine: GMC 6-cylinder, diesel, 215bhp at 2,800rpm
Speed: 42mph (68km/hr)
Range: 300 miles (480km)

Armadillo Guatemala
SMG

1983. Although the Armadillo was entirely designed and produced in Guatemala, there can be little doubt that the designers had taken a good look at the Cadillac Gage Commando armoured cars before sharpening their pencils. The Armadillo has similar sloped sides, 4 x 4 drive, and wheels recessed into the lower slope of the body. The rear engine has a prominent radiator at the rear of the body, and there are vision and firing ports down each side. Driver and commander are at the front, and the troop compartment has seats for 14, one man being the third crewman, who attends upon the roof-mounted heavy machine gun. There are side doors for the occupants, plus roof hatches.

Armament: 1 × HMG
Armour: 15mm
Crew: 3 + 13
Weight: 9.84 tons (10,000kg)
Length: 20ft 2in (6.15m)
Width: 9ft 2in (2.80m)
Height: 8ft 3in (2.50m)
Engine: Detroit Diesel V-6, 212bhp at 2,800rpm
Speed: 62mph (100km/hr)
Range: 745 miles (1,200km)

Armored Infantry Fighting Vehicle (AIFV) USA/Netherlands
FMC

1973. This vehicle originated as a US Army request for an M113 APC with the addition of a turret-mounted gun and firing ports for the occupants, and two such vehicles were developed and tested. The US Army then modified the specification and went on to promote a different vehicle, while the FMC Corporation, who had made the two test vehicles, continued to develop the original idea and produced the AIFV. Though not adopted by the US Army, a quantity were bought by the Netherlands government.

The vehicle body was of aluminium/steel laminated armour. The driver sat in front, the commander behind him; the gunner manned the turret gun, and the rest of the compartment held seven fully-equipped infantrymen. Access to the interior was by a power-operated door in the rear face of the hull. Five firing ports, each with periscope, were arranged around the hull. The turret was armed with an Oerlikon 25mm cannon and a 7.62mm machine gun. The vehicle was fully amphibious, being propelled in the water by its tracks.

After the Netherlands purchase, sales were also made to Belgium, the Philippines and Turkey, and it was evaluated by several other countries.

Armament: 1 × 25mm cannon; 1 × MG
Armour: not disclosed
Crew: 3 + 7
Weight: 13.25 tons (13,470kg)
Length: 17ft 3in (5.25m)
Width: 9ft 3in (2.81m)

Height: 8ft 7in (2.61m)
Engine: Detroit Diesel, V-6, turbocharged, 264bhp at 2,800rpm
Speed: 37mph (60km/hr)
Range: 300 miles (480km)

Ascod MICV Austria/Spain
Steyr-Daimler-Puch, Santa Barbara

1990. This is a cooperative venture by the two companies to produce a new MICV for the Austrian and Spanish Armies. It is a tracked vehicle, with a conventional layout of driver at the left front with engine alongside, turret with commander and gunner offset to the right, at the front of the hull roof, and a troop compartment for eight men occupying the rest of the vehicle, with two access doors at the rear. The infantry squad have firing ports and a roof hatch, and their section leader has a vision cupola at the left rear of the hull giving him all-round observation. A number of variant models have been designed, but it is probable that they will wait until some experience has been gained with the basic vehicle before developing these. A total of 112 vehicles were ordered by the Austrian Army in 2000, at a cost of $249 million.

Armament: 1 × 30mm cannon; 1 × coaxial MG
Armour: not disclosed
Crew: 3 + 8
Weight: 24.4 tons (24,800kg)
Length: 20ft 4in (6.19m)
Width: 9ft 10in (3.00m)
Height: 8ft 7in (2.62m)
Engine: MTU V-8 diesel, 600bhp
Speed: 43mph (70km/hr)
Range: 370 miles (600km)

AT-104 APC UK
GKN

1970. This vehicle was developed in 1970 as a private venture by GKN-Sankey, who saw the need for a specialized internal security vehicle. It was purchased by Brunei and by the Dutch State Police, and a small number were used by the British Army. The chassis and suspension were those of the standard Bedford MK commercial truck, and the Bedford engine was retained, coupled to an Allison automatic transmission. The driver sat in the usual position, behind the engine, and behind him was the troop compartment, access to which was by doors each side of the body and twin doors at the rear. The sides and rear were also provided with firing or vision slots, and a cupola on the roof allowed the commander all-round vision. This cupola could be fitted with a light machine gun or grenade discharger. A variety of equipment options were offered, including obstacle-removing blade, searchlights, smoke and tear-gas projectors and winch.

Armament: various options
Armour: 12mm
Crew: 2 + 9
Weight: 8.75 tons (8,900kg)
Length: 18ft 0in (5.48m)
Width: 8ft 0in (2.43m)
Height: 8ft 2in (2.48m)
Engine: Bedford, 6-cylinder, petrol, 134bhp at 3,300rpm
Speed: 50mph (80km/hr)
Range: 400 miles (640km)

AT-105 Saxon APC UK
GKN

1976. This is more or less an improved AT-104, with better armour protection for the engine, radiator and transmission, a re-designed floor to provide better protection against mines, a shorter wheelbase and a more powerful engine. Originally known as the AT-105 if was christened Saxon in 1982, and shortly after the British Army brought the first of about 600 vehicles into service. This includes a small number used as command posts by field artillery regiments. In general, Saxon has been issued to infantry battalions in infantry divisions, whilst the Warrior APC has gone to battalions in armoured divisions. There are a number of variant models, including ambulance, recovery, water cannon and internal security types.

Armament: 1 x MG
Armour: not disclosed
Crew: 2 + 8
Weight: 11.47 tons (11,660kg)
Length: 17ft 0in (5.17m)
Width: 8ft 2in (2.49m)
Height: 8ft 7in (2.63m)
Engine: Bedford 6-cylinder, diesel, 164bhp at 2,800rpm
Speed: 60mph (96km/hr)
Range: 300 miles (480km)

Auverland AV-3 France
Auverland

1992. This is a lightweight armoured carrier intended for police and internal security tasks rather than the hurly-burly of the battlefield. It is based upon the chassis of the company's 4 x 4 utility vehicle, which is fitted with a welded steel body of conventional shape. The engine is at the front,

driver and commander in the front seats, and the remaining occupant is in the rear compartment. Bullet-proof windows are provided, there is a roof hatch with a machine gun mount, and there is a vision block and firing port facing to the rear. Various weapon fits, and options such as air conditioning, 24-volt electrics, power steering and so forth are offered.

Armament: 1 x MG
Armour: not disclosed
Crew: 3
Weight: 2.22 tons (2,260kg)
Length: 12ft 8in (3.85m)
Width: 5ft 1in (1.54m)
Height: 5ft 7in (1.70m)
Engine: Peugeot 4-cylinder diesel, 85bhp at 4,600rpm
Speed: 80mph (130km/hr)
Range: 310 miles (500km)

AV-90 Italy/West Germany
OTO-Melara, MaK

1978. This was an Italo-German joint venture which really amounted to no more than taking the hull of the OTO-Melara C13 APC (*qv*) and replacing the engine, cooling system, transmission and tracks with German-designed components. The result was a low-set, somewhat cramped, APC carrying a driver, commander and ten men. Armament was confined to a cupola with a heavy machine gun. The usual wide range of variants to cover every conceivable role was postulated but in the event the project never got beyond the first handful of prototypes.

Armament: 1 x HMG
Armour: not disclosed
Crew: 2 + 10
Weight: 18.2 tons (18,500kg) (estimated)
Length: 19ft 8in (6.00m)
Width: 8ft 11in (2.71m)
Height: 8ft 6in (2.59m)
Engine: MTU V-8 turbocharged diesel, 450bhp at 2,100rpm
Speed: 40mph (65km/hr)
Range: 350 miles (565km)

BDX APC Belgium
Beherman Demoen

1977. This is actually an improved version of the 4 x 4 Timoney APC, the Belgian firm having obtained a licence from Timoney in 1976. It remains the same slope-fronted, box-bodied vehicle with side and rear doors, driver in the front and ring-mounted machine gun over one of the hatches.

The improvements are in minor details and do not substantially change the vehicle. They were taken into service by the Belgian Gendarmerie and the Belgian Air Force and numbers were also sold to Argentina.

Armament: 1 × MG
Armour: 13mm
Crew: 2 + 10
Weight: 10.53 tons (10,700kg)
Length: 16ft 7in (5.05m)
Width: 8ft 3in (2.50m)
Height: 9ft 4in (2.84m)
Engine: Chrysler V-8, petrol, 180bhp at 4,000rpm
Speed: 63mph (100km/hr)
Range: 465 miles (750km)

Berliet VXB-170 APC France
Berliet
1971. The Berliet was a 4 x 4 APC originally built as a private venture in the hope of capturing part of the expanding market for reasonably priced APCs. It was not taken by the French Army, but a number were bought for the Gendarmerie and others were sold to Gabon, Senegal and Guatemala. An attraction of the vehicle was that it used many commercial components from the Berliet range of heavy trucks and it also carried rather more men than did most other APCs, a useful feature for police operations. The driver and commander sat together in the front and the troop compartment was directly behind them. Unusually, the engine was at the rear, on the left side, with a rear access door beside it. The main access doors were in the sides of the hull. The basic vehicle had no specific armament, but almost any combination of guns and turrets could be fitted at the user's request. The vehicle was amphibious, using its wheels for propulsion in the water.

Armament: 1 × MG
Armour: 7mm
Crew: 1 + 11
Weight: 12.50 tons (12,700kg)
Length: 19ft 7in (6.00m)
Width: 8ft 3in (2.52m)
Height: 6ft 6in (2.01m)
Engine: Berliet V-8, diesel, 170bhp at 3,000rpm
Speed: 53mph (85km/hr)
Range: 465 miles (750km)

Bionix 25 MICV Singapore
Singapore Technologies
1997. The Bionix 25 is a tracked carrier, with five roadwheels on each side, front drive and rear idler,

the upper track run covered by a skirt. It is of the usual slope-front boxy shape. The driver is at the left front, the engine compartment to his right; behind are the commander and gunner, sharing a two-man turret carrying a 25mm cannon and coaxial machine gun, and an air defence machine gun is carried externally. The troop compartment is entered from the rear via a power-operated ramp door and has space for seven men. The compartment has a large roof hatch and mounts for an additional machine gun on both sides of the roof. The Bionix 25 is now in production and the first units should be in use by Singapore forces by 2000.

Armament: 1 × 25mm cannon; 3 × MG
Armour: not disclosed
Crew: 3 + 7
Weight: 22.63 tons (23,000kg)
Length: 19ft 4in (5.90m)
Width: 8ft 10in (2.70m)
Height: 8ft 6in (2.60m)
Engine: Detroit Diesel V-6, 475bhp
Speed: 43mph (70km/hr)
Range: not disclosed

Bionix 40/50 MICV Singapore
Singapore Technologies
1997. This is exactly the same vehicle as the Bionix 25 described above but is fitted with a turret which carries a 40mm automatic grenade launcher and a .50-inch heavy machine gun. Dimensions, etc., are exactly the same, although there may be a very slight difference in weight.

Bison APC Canada
GM Canada
1988. This was developed as a private venture, proved successful, and went into service with the Canadian and Australian Armies in the 1990s. It is based upon the 8 x 8 chassis of the Light Armoured Vehicle, and is generally of the same sort of appearance, with the contemporary 'squashed lozenge' shape of slope-sided hull with the wheels inset into the under-slope. The rear part of the upper hull is built up into a more boxy shape to give better headroom for the occupants, and the outside is liberally provided with stowage brackets, racks and attachments, to the point where it becomes difficult to see what shape the vehicle is when all the occupants have hung their belongings all over it. There is a prominent cupola for the commander, and the crew compartment has roof hatches and a rear power-operated ramp door. It is fully amphibious, propelled by two propeller units at the rear of the hull.

Armament: I × MG
Armour: not disclosed
Crew: 2 + 8
Weight: 12.50 tons (12,936kg)
Length: 19ft 7in (6.45m)
Width: 8ft 3in (2.52m)
Height: 6ft 6in (2.21m)
Engine: Detroit Diesel, V-6, 275bhp at 2,800rpm
Speed: 63mph (100km/hr)
Range: 400 miles (645km)

BLR APC Spain
Santa Barbara
1985. This vehicle was designed to a Spanish Army specification but it is obviously intended more for use as an internal security and border patrol vehicle than as a 'battle taxi'. The boxy 4 x 4 body with sloped front is conventional enough, but the square bullet-proof glass windows in the sides are unusual, and are apparently intended so that the occupants can observe the terrain in their travels. It probably has the additional virtue of reducing the chance of disorientation, always a hazard with closed-in vehicles. Armament is confined to a simple machine gun ring mount. There are doors on each side of the crew compartment and also two rear doors

Armament: I × MG
Armour: not disclosed
Crew: I + 12
Weight: 11.81 tons (12,000kg)
Length: 18ft 6in (5.65m)
Width: 8ft 2in (2.50m)
Height: 6ft 7in (2.0m)
Engine: Pegaso, 6-cylinder turbocharged diesel, 210bhp at 2,100rpm
Speed: 58mph (93km/hr)
Range: 355 miles (570km)

BMD-I Airborne IFV Russia
State factories
1970. This is the usual BMD family shape, with a low hull and wedge-like nose. It is tracked, with five roadwheels, but has an unusual adjustable suspension which can be used to lower the hull and reduce the overall height for rail transport. This effectively brings the front idler and rear drive sprocket down to the ground, so giving an impression of seven roadwheels. There is a small turret in the forward part of the hull, mounting a 73mm low-pressure gun, a coaxial machine gun and a 'Sagger' or other anti-tank missile launcher. The driver is in front, centrally, with a machine gunner sitting alongside him and controlling two guns mounted above the tracks. The troop compartment

has a concertina-type roof cover which opens to the front; this is the only means of entry and exit for the occupants.

Armament: I × 73mm gun; I × ATGW launcher; 3 × MG
Armour: 23mm
Crew: 3 + 4
Weight: 6.59 tons (6,700kg)
Length: 17ft 9in (5.40m)
Width: 9ft 3in (2.83m)
Height: 6ft 6in (1.97m)
Engine: V-6-cylinder, diesel, 240bhp
Speed: 43mph (70km/hr)
Range: 200 miles (320km)

BMD-3 Airborne IFV Russia
State factories
1990. This is probably the only armoured vehicle which can be dropped by parachute with its crew inside it; one wonders whether they start the engine before or after landing. It is generally similar to the BMD-1 but is said to have more interior room, better firepower, a completely new chassis, and better amphibious performance. The turret is that of the BMP-2 MICV and carries a 30mm automatic cannon with coaxial machine gun and an anti-tank missile launcher; there is also a 30mm automatic grenade launcher mounted in the left front of the hull, and an RPK-S machine gun on the right front, each of which are operated by one of the infantry squad carried in the vehicle.

Armament: I × 30mm cannon; I × ATGW launcher; I × 30mm grenade launcher; 2 × MG
Armour: not disclosed
Crew: 3 + 4
Weight: 12.95 tons (13,200kg)
Length: 20ft 0in (6.10m)
Width: 10ft 3in (3.13m)
Height: 7ft 1in (2.17m)
Engine: V-6, diesel, 450bhp
Speed: 43mph (70km/hr)
Range: 310 miles (500km)

BMP-I MICV Russia
State factories
1967. The BMP-1 is a derivative of the PT-76 light tank and is most comprehensively equipped and heavily armed. The hull is of lightweight magnesium alloy, with the driver seated alongside the engine and transmission in the front. Immediately behind him is the commander, on the left side of the hull and well provided with periscopes and night-vision devices. In the centre is a low turret mounting a smoothbore 73mm gun

with a 'Sagger' anti-tank missile mounted on a rail above the barrel. The gun has an auto loader and the turret holds only the gunner. The eight infantrymen are carried in a cramped compartment at the rear, with four roof hatches and a firing port for each occupant. The normal entry is through two rear doors. The vehicle will swim without preparation, propelling itself by its tracks

Armament: I × 73mm; I × MG; I × ATGW
Armour: 23mm
Crew: 3 + 8
Weight: 13.28 tons (13,500kg)
Length: 22ft 2in (6.75m)
Width: 9ft 8in (2.94m)
Height: 7ft 1in (2.15m)
Engine: Model V-6, 6-cylinder, diesel, 280bhp at 2,000rpm
Speed: 40mph (65km/hr)
Range: 340 miles (550km)

BMP-2 MICV Russia
State factories
1980. This is more or less the same as the earlier BMP-1 (*above*) but with better armour and more modern fire control and vision equipment. The turret is a new, all-welded pattern mounting a 30mm cannon, coaxial machine gun, and an anti-tank missile launcher, usually an AT-4 or AT-5.

There are variants; the **BMP-2D** has additional armour attached to the hull and turret and was the final production model; the **BMP-2L** was the command version with additional communications equipment; and there was also a BMP-2 with mine plough equipment.

Armament: I × 30mm cannon; I × MG; I × ATGW
Armour: not disclosed
Crew: 3 + 7
Weight: 14.07 tons (14,300kg)
Length: 22ft 1in (6.73m)
Width: 10ft 4in (3.15m)
Height: 8ft 0in (2.45m)
Engine: Model UTD-20 V-6, 6-cylinder, diesel, 300bhp at 2,000rpm
Speed: 40mph (65km/hr)
Range: 340 miles (550km)

BMP-3 MICV Russia
State factories
1990. This was a completely new design based upon the more desirable features of the BMP-2 and the BMD airborne IFV. It appears that financial restrictions have prevented the design being produced in the huge numbers necessary to replace

the earlier BMPs, although a substantial quantity have been built for and sold to Abu Dhabi.

The hull is of the usual BMP wedge-fronted shape, and the tracks have six roadwheels and three return rollers. The turret carries a 100mm gun with automatic loader, a 30mm high-velocity cannon, and a machine gun, all three being coaxial. The 100mm gun fires conventional projectiles and is also said to fire a laser-guided projectile. There are also two machine guns mounted in the hull front, operated by crew members seated alongside the driver.

Armament: I × 100mm; I × 30mm cannon; 3 × MG
Armour: not disclosed
Crew: 3 + 7
Weight: 18.40 tons (18,700kg)
Length: 23ft 7in (7.20m)
Width: 10ft 7in (3.23m)
Height: 7ft 7in (2.30m)
Engine: Model UDT-29M, 10-cylinder, diesel, 500bhp
Speed: 43mph (70km/hr)
Range: 370 miles (600km)

BMP-23 MICV Bulgaria
State factories
1984. This was based upon the Russian MT-LB multi-purpose vehicle, which was altered to suit the Bulgarian views on fighting vehicles. The MT-LB was being built in Bulgaria for other reasons, so there was little difficulty in building-in the desired changes. The turret is placed further back on the hull than is customary with Russian MICVs, and mounts a 23mm cannon with a coaxial machine gun; there is also an infra-red searchlight and an anti-tank missile launcher on the turret roof. The troop compartment at the rear of the hull has the six infantrymen seated back-to-back and facing outward, with eight firing ports for their personal weapons. A seventh infantryman mans a machine gun in a hatch. Entry and exit is by two doors at the rear of the hull.

Armament: I × 23mm cannon; I × MG fitted; I × ATGW
Armour: not disclosed
Crew: 3 + 7
Weight: 14.95 tons (15,200kg)
Length: 23ft 11in (7.29m)
Width: 9ft 4in (2.85m)
Height: 8ft 4in (2.53m)
Engine: V-6, diesel, 315bhp
Speed: 40mph (65km/hr)
Range: 340 miles (600km)

BMP-30 MICV Bulgaria
State factories
1995. This is an improved BMP-23, using the same hull and running gear but with a new turret which closely conforms to the turret on the Russian BMP-2 MICV. It carries a 30mm cannon and a machine gun, and, on the roof, a launcher for an anti-tank guided missile, which may be the AT-4 or AT-5. It is also fairly liberally outfitted with day and night sights and surveillance equipment. Six fully-equipped infantrymen can be seated in the troop compartment, another one sits next to the driver, and the section commander and his gunner occupy the turret.

Armament: 1 × 30mm cannon; 1 × MG; 1 × ATGW
Armour: not disclosed
Crew: 3 + 7
Weight: 14.78 tons (15,000kg)
Length: 23ft 4in (7.13m)
Width: 9ft 5in (2.86m)
Height: 6ft 11in (2.12m)
Engine: Diesel, 302bhp at 2,100rpm
Speed: 37mph (60km/hr)
Range: 372 miles (600km)

BMR-600 APC Spain
Santa Barbara
1979. This is a 6 x 6 vehicle of conventional form, a boxy body with sloped front and sides and with the wheels inset into the under-slope of the body. A drop-down ramp acts as a rear door to the troop compartment, and there is an observation cupola for the vehicle commander with a remote-controlled machine gun on top of it. The driver is seated forward, on the left, with the engine and transmission on his right side and the cupola behind him. The vehicle is fully amphibious, using water jets. There are a number of variant models, including an ambulance, a recovery and repair vehicle, a mortar carrier and a version mounting a 90mm gun. In addition to the Spanish Army, these vehicles are also used by Egypt and Saudi Arabia.

Armament: 1 × MG
Armour: not disclosed
Crew: 2 + 11
Weight: 13.78 tons (14,000kg)
Length: 20ft 2in (6.15m)
Width: 8ft 3in (2.50m)
Height: 7ft 9in (2.36m)
Engine: Pegaso 6-cylinder diesel, 310bhp at 2,200rpm
Speed: 65mph (105km/hr)
Range: 620 miles (1,000km)

Boragh APC Iran
DIO
1997. This is generally similar to the Russian BMP-1 in outline, though it is not, by any means, an exact or licensed copy. Fully tracked, with six roadwheels each side, front drive and rear idler, it has a similar low hull with prow-like front, and is fully amphibious. Instead of a turret, it has merely a hatch with a heavy machine gun on a ring mount. and it does not appear to have very sophisticated night vision or fire control equipment.

Armament: 1 × HMG
Armour: not disclosed
Crew: 2 + 8 or 12
Weight: 12.80 tons (13,000kg)
Length: 22ft 0in (6.72m)
Width: 10ft 2in (3.10m)
Height: 5ft 3in (1.60m)
Engine: V-8 air-cooled turbocharged diesel, 330bhp at 2,300rpm
Speed: 40mph (65km/hr)
Range: 370 miles (600km)

BOV APC Yugoslavia/Slovenia
MPP Vozila
1983. This vehicle was designed and manufactured in Yugoslavia for both military and police use, and several of them are still in use. It is a 4 x 4 vehicle which resembles a Mowag or Cadillac Gage armoured car in having a well-sloped body with the wheels recessed into the lower hull and a prow-like front end. The engine is at the rear of the hull, the commander and driver sit alongside each other at the front, and the troop compartment is in the middle. The APC version has a hatch with machine gun, but variants with turrets mounting multiple anti-aircraft cannon were built in some quantity.

Armament: 1 × MG
Armour: not disclosed
Crew: 2 + 8
Weight: 5.60 tons (5,700kg)
Length: 18ft 9in (5.70m)
Width: 8ft 3in (2.53m)
Height: 7ft 8in (2.33m)
Engine: Deutz 6-cylinder, diesel, 148bhp at 2,650rpm
Speed: 60mph (95km/hr)
Range: 465 miles (750km)

Bradley M2/M3 MICV USA
FMC
1982. This vehicle appears in two forms: as the **M2 Infantry Fighting Vehicle**, or as the **M3 Cavalry Fighting Vehicle**. The difference lies in their

equipment and crew, the M2 being intended for an infantry fighting patrol, and the M3 for a cavalry scout and reconnaissance vehicle. The basic vehicle and armament remain the same for both types. The hull is is a mixture of aluminium and laminated, spaced, armour and is topped by a turret carrying a 25mm cannon and a TOW missile launcher. The driver is at the left front with the engine and transmission alongside him, and the rear of the vehicle is taken up by the crew compartment and storage space. The M2 has a crew of three (driver, commander, gunner) and carries six fully-equipped infantrymen; the M3 has the same crew and carries two additional men to assist with the observation and scouting duties.

The designation has now advanced; the **M2A1** and **M3A1** have Improved TOW equipment, Dragon ATGW sights and several minor improvements. The **M2A2** and **M3A2** have additional appliqué armour and provision for fitting explosive reactive armour; this increases the weight to about 15 tons and a 600bhp engine was therefore installed. The **/A3** version has improved fire control, communications and electronics, and many of the earlier vehicles are in the course of conversion to the /A3 standard.

Armament: 1 × 25mm; 1 × coaxial MG; 2 × ATGW
Armour: not disclosed
Crew, M2: 3 + 6
Crew, M3: 3 + 2
Weight, M2: 22.23 tons (22,590kg)
Weight, M3: 22.10 tons (22,445kg)
Length: 21ft 2in (6.45m)
Width: 10ft 6in (3.20m)
Height: 8ft 5in (2.57m)
Engine: Cummins 8-cylinder turbocharged diesel, 500bhp at 2,600rpm
Speed: 40mph (65km/hr)
Range: 300 miles (485km)

Bravia Commando Portugal
Bravia

1977. This vehicle was developed at the request of the Guarda Nacional for border patrolling and internal security tasks and is simple a light 4 x 4 truck chassis with an armoured body. Its general appearance is similar to the many armoured Land Rover conversions which have appeared. The windscreen is provided with a top-hinged armoured shutter, as are the cab side-windows, and there is a small turret carrying two machine guns. The crew compartment is cut short so that there is a small cargo trunk with the spare wheel mounted on top. The vehicle can be provided with two or four doors.

Alternatively, the body can be extended to the rear of the vehicle and given a rear door, making it easier for entry and exit.

Armament: 2 × MG
Armour: 8mm
Crew: 3 + 5
Weight: 4.77 tons (4,855kg)
Length: 16ft 4in (4.98m)
Width: 6ft 4in (1.93m)
Height: 7ft 11in (2.42m)
Engine: V-8 petrol, 180bhp at 3,600rpm; or V-8 diesel, 155bhp at 3,600rpm
Speed: 55mph (90km/hr)
Range: 370 miles (600km)

Bravia Tigre Portugal
Bravia

1990. This large and ungainly vehicle is simply a 6 x 6 military truck chassis with a plain slab-sided armoured body. The normal truck configuration remains, with the engine under an armoured hood, driver and commander in an armoured cab, and the rear of the vehicle formed into a spacious open-topped troop compartment. There is a raised shield around the forward end of the roof, protecting a machine gun on a ring mount, and a skate rail inside the rear portion of the roof for mounting another machine gun. As with other Bravia vehicles, numerous variants have been proposed, with additional machine guns, anti-tank missiles, air defence cannon and mortars, but none appear to have got beyond the drawing board.

Armament: 2 × MG
Armour: not disclosed
Crew: 20
Weight: 9.34 tons (9,500kg)
Length: 22ft 3in (6.80m)
Width: 7ft 10in (2.40m)
Height: 7ft 6in (2.30m)
Engine: V-9 petrol, 210bhp at 4,000rpm; or V-8 diesel, 210bhp at 3,000rpm
Speed: 63mph (100km/hr)
Range: 600 miles (960km)

Bravia V-200 APC Portugal
Bravia

1990. This is an improved model of the Chaimite, armoured car which itself was a modification of the Cadillac Gage Commando, and the family likeness remains. It is a 4 x 4 vehicle with side doors and a turret, the sides being well sloped and the wheels recessed into the lower hull. A number of variations have been postulated and some built, ranging from

ATGW carriers to a 90mm gun version, but it is not clear which, if any, have been adopted for service other than the basic APC. 6 x 6 and 8 x 8 versions have also been designed but have never been put into production.

Armament: 2 x MG in turret
Armour: 8mm
Crew: 2 + 4
Weight: 17.18 tons (7,300kg)
Length: 18ft 5in (5.61m)
Width: 7ft 5in (2.26m)
Height: 7ft 5in (2.26m)
Engine: Detroit Diesel V-6, turbocharged, 210bhp at 3,000rpm
Speed: 60mph (95km/hr)
Range: 805 miles (1,300km)

Bren Gun Carrier UK
Thornycroft, Morris, Sentinel, Aveling Barford, Ford UK

1934–60. This ubiquitous vehicle began as a spin-off from the 1930s Vickers development of a light tracked gun tractor. In 1934 the company developed a tracked vehicle which could act either as a gun-tower or as a machine-gun carrier; in the latter role it could mount a Vickers medium machine gun so as to fire on the move, and also carry a four-man gun squad and tripod so that the gun could be dismounted for ground action independently of the carrier.

A prototype was built, and after tests a fresh version appeared in which the crew was reduced to three men. A small number of these were built in 1936, but in the following year the Bren light machine gun was introduced and therefore the concept of the carrier was slightly changed. The Vickers gun was replaced by the Bren gun and the superstructure and interior arrangements suitably modified. Some were built to carry the .55-inch Boys anti-tank rifle in place of the machine gun. After some improvements to the armour, this became the 'Carrier, Bren' and issues began in 1938 on the scale of 10 carriers per infantry battalion.

Other units of the army saw possibilities in the carrier, and some variant models were developed. The 'Carrier, Scout', of 1938, was intended for use by mechanized cavalry regiments and carried a radio installation. It was followed by the 'Carrier, Cavalry', which had accommodation for six men and reduced armour, a canvas tilt cover and various racks for equipment; it was intended to carry dismounted personnel of cavalry light tank regiments. The 'Carrier, Armoured, OP' was provided for Royal Artillery field regiments, to carry

forward observation officers. It was fitted with radio and also with a telephone cable drum at the rear.

In addition to these official variants, the carrier was used as a basis for several experimental vehicles, including self-propelled mountings for 2-pounder, 6-pounder and 25-pounder guns, mortars of various types and multiple machine gun mountings. None was accepted for service.

Armament: 1 x MG
Armour: 10mm
Crew: 2
Weight: 3.75 tons (3,810kg)
Length: 12ft 0in (3.65m)
Width: 6ft 9in (2.05m)
Height: 4ft 9in (1.45m)
Engine: Ford, V-8, petrol, 3,923cc, 85bhp at 3,500rpm
Payload: 1,200lb (545kg)
Speed: 30mph (48km/hr)
Range: 130 miles (210km)

BTR-40 APC Russia
State factories

World War II showed the Russians the value of the armoured personnel carrier, and a design was begun in mid-1944, using the chassis of the GAZ-63 light 4 x 4 truck as the starting point. This was stretched, given a more powerful engine and an armoured body, and the first prototypes were tested in 1947. After modifications and further trials, it was accepted into service in 1950 and was originally employed as both an APC and as an armoured reconnaissance vehicle.

The armoured steel body has a sloped front, in which are windscreens for the driver and commander, with armour shutters, and the rear section is open-topped, with seats for eight men. Entry to the troop compartment is by double doors at the rear, while the driver and commander each have a side door. There are mounts for three machine guns, one on each side of the troop compartment and one behind the driving position, but normal armament is only one machine gun, usually fitted on the front mount. Early vehicles had no firing ports, but later production had three ports on each side.

Variants included a version carrying twin air defence machine guns, another carrying an anti-tank guided missile, and an improved APC version with an armoured roof with hatches and accommodation for only six men in the troop compartment.

Armament: 1 x MG
Armour: 8mm
Crew: 2 + 8

Weight: 5.22 tons (5,300kg)
Length: 16ft 5in (5.0m)
Width: 6ft 3in (1.9m)
Height: 5ft 9in (1.75m)
Engine: GAZ-40, 6-cylinder, petrol, 80bhp at
  3,400rpm
Speed: 50 mph (80km/hr)
Range: 177 miles (285km)

BTR-50P APC Russia
State factories
1957. This was developed directly from the PT-76 light tank (*qv*) and is now an obsolescent design, although it is still in service with many of the former satellite countries. The layout follows the tank fairly closely with the driver and commander side by side in front and a heavy machine gun between and behind them. Instead of the tank turret there is a large armoured box in which the troops ride in rather cramped conditions. This box projects well above the original hull top and is cut flat at the back, giving a distinctive side silhouette. The engine and transmission are at the rear and all crew members have to climb over the sides to get in or out. Early versions had no roof, but most production models were fitted with large hatch covers over the troop compartment. Like the PT-76 the vehicle swims with minimal preparation and drives itself by water jets.

Armament: 1 × MG
Armour: 14mm
Crew: 2 + 14
Length: 22ft 4in (6.82m)
Width: 10ft 1in (3.07m)
Height: 6ft 6in (2.00m)
Weight: 13.97 tons (14,200kg)
Engine: Model V-6, 6-cylinder, diesel, 240bhp at
  1,800rpm
Speed: 27mph (44km/hr)
Range: 160 miles (260km)

BTR-60P APC Russia
State factories
1960. The 8 x 8 BTR-60P is probably the most widespread carrier in the old Warsaw Pact bloc and the numbers in use must rival the M113; at least 18 armies outside Russia have used it. The design is now obsolescent, but it is still a useful vehicle. All eight wheels are driven and the front four are steered. The driver and commander are in the extreme front with a machine-gun hatch behind them, but in the **60PB** model there is a small turret instead of a hatch. The troop compartment is behind this turret and the engines are in the extreme rear. The troops can get in and out only by scrambling over the roof and using the hatches, and this is a poor feature of the design. On the other hand it means that there are the fewest possible openings in the sides and the only preparation needed for swimming is to raise the bow vane. It is driven in the water by a single water jet. There are many variants of the basic APC and different users specify different fittings. All models have a central tyre-pressure system, infra-red driving aids and NBC protection. Most have a winch and an infra-red searchlight for the commander. Although no longer in production, the BTR-60P will survive for many years yet.

Armament: 1 × MG
Armour: 14mm
Crew: 2 + 14
Weight: 10.14 tons (10,300kg)
Length: 24ft 10in (7.56m)
Width: 9ft 3in (2.85m)
Height: 7ft 7in (2.31m)
Engine: two GAZ-49B, 6-cylinder, petrol, 90bhp each
  at 3,400rpm
Speed: 50mph (80km/hr)
Range: 310 miles (500km)

BTR-70 APC Russia
State factories
1976. This 8 x 8 vehicle appears to be an improved version of the BTR-60P, built to much the same design but with slightly different hull contours. It has a similar prow and is amphibious, with a single water-jet unit at the rear, The small turret carries a heavy machine gun, with a rifle-calibre machine gun mounted coaxially. Variant models include a command version, a communications version with the usual proliferation of antennas, a recovery version with a small jib crane mounted on the glacis plate, and a model fitted with the turret of the BTR-80 (*below*). Many of the standard vehicles have had AGS-17 automatic grenade launchers fitted to the roof.

Armament: 2 × MG
Armour: not disclosed
Crew: 2 + 9
Weight: 11.31 tons (11,500kg)
Length: 24ft 9in (7.54m)
Width: 9ft 2in (2.80m)
Height: 7ft 4in (2.23m)
Engine: 2 × 8-cylinder petrol, total 240bhp
Speed: 50mph (80km/hr)
Range: 370 miles (600km)

BTR-80 APC Russia
State factories

This is a further improvement on the BTR-60 and -70 series, the most significant changes being the substitution of a single diesel engine for the two petrol engines of the previous models, and the provision of side doors in the hull instead of requiring the occupants to scramble in and out over the side and through the roof. Firing ports in the hull side are angled so as to be able to fire towards the front of the vehicle. The turret remains armed with the KPV heavy machine gun plus a rifle-calibre coaxial machine gun. A command version is also in service, with additional radio equipment, and the hull is used as the basis for the 2S23 SP gun.

Armament: 2 × MG
Armour: not disclosed
Crew: 3 + 7
Weight: 13.38 tons (13,600kg)
Length: 24ft 7in (7.50m)
Width: 9ft 6in (2.90m)
Height: 8ft 0in (2.45m)
Engine: V-8 diesel, 210bhp
Speed: 50mph (80km/hr)
Range: 370 miles (600km)

BTR-90 APC Russia
Azamash

1994. This 8 x 8 wheeled APC was briefly seen in 1994 and appears to have been a private venture, though whether aimed at the home or the export market is unclear. It appears to be a cleaned-up version of the BTR-80, using a similar slope-sided hull and prow-shaped nose, but with the addition of a rather more complicated turret installation mounting a 30mm cannon and an anti-tank guided missile launcher.

Armament: 1 × 30mm cannon; 1 × MG; 1 × ATGM (AT-5 'Spandrel')
Armour: not disclosed
Crew: 3 + 7
Weight: 16.73 tons (17,000kg)
Length: 25ft 1in (7.64m)
Width: 10ft 6in (3.20m)
Height: 9ft 9in (2.98m)
Engine: diesel, *ca* 500bhp
Speed: 55mph (90km/hr)
Range: 310 miles (500km)

BTR-152 APC Russia
State factories

1950. The BTR-152 was the first Soviet APC to be built after World War 2 and it is rather remarkable that it is still in service with many countries. The original version was based on a 6 x 6 ZIL truck, but later models used a special chassis, albeit from the same family. In design it is now obsolete as it follows the layout of pre-war armoured cars. The engine is inside a prominent armoured bonnet with the driver and commander sitting side by side in an armoured cab. The troop compartment takes up the remainder of the hull, with two doors at the back for the troops to enter and leave. Some versions have no roof, others have one with hatches. There are many variants, every user country adapting the vehicle to suit its own particular needs, and it can be seen carrying a wide variety of armament and equipment.

Armament: see text
Armour: 12mm
Crew: 2 + 14
Weight: 8.64 tons (8,950kg)
Length: 22ft 5in (6.85m)
Width: 7ft 7in (2.32m)
Height: 6ft 9in (2.10m)
Engine: ZIL-123, 6-cylinder, petrol, 110bhp at 2,900rpm
Speed: 46mph (75km/hr)
Range: 400 miles (650km)

BTR-T APC Russia
State factories

1997. The Russians appear to have taken a leaf from the Israeli book in this design, since, like the Israeli Achzarit, this is based upon the chassis of the T-55 tank and is intended as a heavyweight APC to protect infantry accompanying main battle tanks. The tank's turret has been discarded, the hull built up to give headroom, and a remotely controlled 30mm automatic cannon is mounted on the roof. But, given that the combat weight is said to be 38.5 tonnes, the payload is derisory – commander/gunner, driver, and five fully-equipped infantry, one of whom mans a turret over the crew compartment equipped with an AT-4 anti-tank missile launcher. Moreover, their only means of entry and exit is via roof hatches. It may be a cheap solution, but it seems doubtful that the army will accept it.

Armament: 1 × 30mm cannon; 1 × HMG; 1 × ATGW
Armour: not disclosed
Crew: 2 + 5
Weight: 37.9 tons (38,500kg)
Length: 21ft 2in (6.45m)
Width: 10ft 9in (3.27m)
Height: 5ft 8in (1.72m)
Engine: V-12 diesel, 580bhp at 2,000rpm
Speed: 35mph (55km/hr)
Range: 400 miles (650km)

Buffalo UK

Name given by British troops in North-West Europe in 1944–45, to the LVT(A)-2 (**Buffalo Mark 2**) and LVT-4 (**Buffalo Mark 4**), which see.

Buffalo APC France
Panhard et Levassor

1985. This is a wheeled 4 x 4 vehicle of conventional form, with sloped front and a roomy troop compartment with rear doors. The engine is behind the driver, and there are storage compartments above the wheels which can be blown off by a mine and still leave the armour of the vehicle in place. This gives the side doors a recessed effect, useful for disembarking in a bullet-swept environment. There are numerous hatches, some of which can be used as firing ports, and it is possible to fit a turret or other weapon arrangements on the hull roof.

Armament: to choice
Armour: 12mm
Crew: 2 + 10
Weight: 6.50 tons (6,600kg)
Length: 15ft 1in (4.59m)
Width: 7ft 10in (2.40m)
Height: 6ft 6in (2.0m)
Engine: Peugeot V-6, petrol, 145bhp at 5,500rpm
Speed: 56mph (90km/hr)
Range: 370 miles (600km)

BVP-M80A MICV Yugoslavia/Serbia
State factories

1980. This was an improved version of the M80 MICV which was intended to replace that vehicle, but less than two years after production had begun it was halted by the outbreak of the Third Balkan War and does not appear to have been resumed. The tracked vehicle is to the same general design as the M80 but is slightly larger in all dimensions, has thicker armour, a better engine, and weighs more. The standard turret carries a 20mm cannon and coaxial machine gun, but there was an **M80AK** variant which had a turret mounting a 30mm cannon, coaxial machine gun and twin ATGW launcher.

Other variants were the **M80AKB** commander's vehicle with additional radio equipment; **M80AKC** company commander's vehicle; **M80AL** anti-tank vehicle with no turret but six ATGW launchers on the roof; **M80ASn** ambulance; and **M30/2** AA vehicle with two 30mm air defence cannon.

Armament: 1 × 20mm cannon; 1 × coaxial MG; 2 × ATGW
Armour: not disclosed
Crew: 3 + 7

Weight: 13.78 tons (14,000kg)
Length: 21ft 1in (6.42m)
Width: 9ft 10in (2.99m)
Height: 7ft 3in (2.20m)
Engine: FAMOS V-10 diesel, 315bhp at 2,500rpm
Speed: 40mph (65km/hr)
Range: 310 miles (500km)

BWP-2000 MICV Poland
Bumar-Labedy

1996. This had its beginnings in a Soviet-Polish design office which collapsed with the Soviet Empire. The Polish team continued working on the MICV design and arrived at this, which they fitted with an Italian turret (by OTO-Melara) carrying an Italo-Swiss (Oerlikon-Contraves) 25mm cannon. There seems some doubt as to whether they will be able to afford such a luxurious specification if and when the vehicle goes into production, and will probably have to settle for something more pedestrian but cheaper. The vehicle itself is of the conventional slope-fronted box form, tracked, with six roadwheels per side, front drive and rear idler. In addition to the 25mm gun the turret also carries a coaxial machine gun and two TOW anti-tank missile launch pods. The troop compartment has two hatches and is entered by means of a powered ramp door in the rear.

Armament: 1 × 25mm cannon; 1 × MG; 2 × ATGW
Armour: not disclosed
Crew: 3 + 9
Weight: 28.54 tons (29,000kg)
Length: 24ft 1in (7.34m)
Width: 10ft 8in (3.25m)
Height: 8ft 3in (2.51m)
Engine: diesel, 700bhp
Speed: 43mph (70km/hr)
Range: 310 miles (500km)

Cardoen BMS-1 Alacran Multi-Purpose Vehicle Chile
Cardoen

1983. This interesting vehicle was an attempt to revive the half-track, a system which has been sadly neglected since 1945. It was of the now-conventional shape, a boxy body with a sloping front and sides sloping inwards from a point just above the wheel level. The front was like any other vehicle of its type, but the rear end was supported on a half-track unit. The driver sat at the front, with the engine alongside him; the commander had a small cupola behind the driver, and there was a large (for this class of vehicle) turret ring so that a variety of weapon fits could be accommodated. A large rear door gave entry to the troop compartment, which had firing ports and vision blocks along each side, plus two roof hatches close to the rear door and clear of the turret ring. An ambitious design, it was vigorously promoted for a few years with various experimental weapon fits, but evinced no serious interest, never went into production, and the makers had dropped it from their books by 1990.

Armament: see text
Armour: not disclosed
Crew: 2 + 12
Weight: 10.33 tons (10,500kg)
Length: 20ft 11in (6.37m)
Width: 7ft 10in (2.38m)
Height: 6ft 8in (2.03m)
Engine: Cummins V-555, V-8 turbocharged diesel, 225bhp at 3,000rpm
Speed: 43mph (70km/hr)
Range: 560 miles (900km)

Cardoen VTP-1 Orca Chile
Cardoen

1983. This is virtually a 6 x 6 (in 'two-and-four' style) armoured truck, insofar as the configuration has the engine in front, driver and commander behind, and then an open-topped compartment forming the remainder of the vehicle and which can be adapted to whatever purpose the user requires. With seats it is a troop carrier, but it can easily become an ambulance, cargo vehicle, weapons carrier, mortar vehicle or anything else. The hull shape is more or less similar to the Mowag/Cadillac Gage pattern with a wedge-like front and the sides sloping inwards at top and bottom. It is believed that not many were produced and it was dropped in the early 1990s.

Armament: none fitted; personal weapons
Armour: 16mm
Crew: 2 + 16
Weight: 17.71 tons (18,000kg)
Length: 25ft 9in (7.84m)
Width: 8ft 3in (2.50m)
Height: 8ft 3in (2.50m)
Engine: GM V-6 diesel, 260bhp at 2,400rpm
Speed: 75mph (120km/hr)
Range: 620 miles (1000km)

Cardoen VTP-2 APC Chile
Cardoen

1982. The VTP-2 was a small 4 x 4 vehicle which was developed as a private venture; it found no takers in military circles, but was adopted in small numbers by the Chilean police as an internal

security vehicle. It was of conventional form with the engine in front, driver and commander behind, and a crew compartment with rear door. There was a roof hatch at the front end of the compartment into which a simple ring mount for a machine gun was fitted.

Armament: 1 x MG
Armour: 8mm
Crew: 2 + 10
Weight: 7.68 tons (7,800kg)
Length: 17ft 7in (5.37m)
Width: 7ft 7in (2.32m)
Height: 7ft 3in (2.22m)
Engine: Mercedes-Benz 6-cylinder diesel, 120bhp at 2,800rpm
Speed: 63mph (100km/hr)
Range: 370 miles (600km)

Car, Half-Track, M2 USA
Autocar, White

1940. This, the first of the wartime American half-tracks, was little more than the existing Combat Car M3 with a half-track unit replacing the rear axle and wheels. The lower part of the bodywork had to be re-shaped to provide space the the tracks, but apart from that there was very little difference. The half-track unit was based broadly upon the Kégresse system which had been developed in France in the 1920s and consisted of four small dual roadwheels with large skeleton drive and idler wheels, the front wheels being the drivers. The cab had a shatterproof windscreen protected by drop-down shutters, but it and the crew compartment at the rear were open topped and merely provided with a canvas cover to keep out the rain. There was a 'skate rail' around the rear compartment along which mountings for a .50-inch and a .30-inch machine gun could slide.

Armament: 1 x HMG; 1 x MG
Armour: 12mm
Crew: 2 + 8
Weight: 8.83 tons (8,980kg)
Length: 19ft 7in (5.97m)
Width: 6ft 5in (1.95m)
Height: 7ft 5in (2.26m)
Engine: White 160AX, 6-cylinder petrol, 128bhp at 2,800rpm
Speed: 45mph (72km/hr)
Range: 175 miles (280km)

Car, Half-Track, M2A1 USA
Autocar, White

1940. This was the same as the M2 except that the gun arrangements were different. Instead of the skate rail, there was a ring mounting over the assistant driver's position, allowing a 360° field of fire and also permitting anti-aircraft fire. Three fixed pedestal mounts were fitted in the crew compartment to which the .30-inch machine gun could be attached when required. The addition of the gun mounting raised the height to 8ft 10in (2.69m). Both the M2 and M2A1 could be found with rollers on the front of the body, to assist in clambering out of trenches, or with winches instead of the roller.

Car, Half-Track, M3A2 USA
Autocar, Diamond-T, White
1944. The M3A2 was exactly the same vehicle as the Carrier, Personnel, Half-Track, M3A1 (*qv*) but was designed so that the stowage and crew accommodation could be rapidly and easily changed to suit the vehicle to a variety of applications, the object in view being to replace all other models of M2 and M3 with one single production item which units could then adjust to their own requirements. Dimensions were as for the M3A1.

Car, Half-Track, M9A1 USA
International Harvester
1941. This was the International Harvester version of the M2A1 design, the short-bodied member of the tribe. This appeared at the same time as the M5/M5A1 models and it is difficult to understand why this design was perpetuated; possibly because it was a little more compact that the other models.

Armament: 2 × MG
Armour: 16mm
Crew: 2 + 8
Weight: 9.46 tons (9616kg)
Length: 20ft 2in (6.15m)
Width: 7ft 3in (2.20m)
Height: 9ft 0in (2.74m)
Engine: International Harvester RED-450B, 6-cylinder, petrol, 148 bhp at 2,700 rpm
Speed: 42 mph (68km.hr)
Range: 220 miles (355km)

Carrier, Armoured, Wheeled, IP UK
Tata, East Indian Railway
1940. The notation 'IP' indicates 'Indian Pattern' and this was developed for manufacture in India, as being more suited to the available industries than a tracked vehicle. The first or **Mark 1** version was a front-engined, high-set vehicle built on a Ford truck chassis and fitted with the Marmon-Herrington four-wheel drive conversion. It was

rapidly replaced by **Mark 2**, a rear-engined model built upon a Ford four-wheel drive rear-engined chassis supplied from Canada. This had a sloping front with driver and gunner side-by-side, and was open-topped with a simple machine gun mount. A later **Mark 3** version had the roof covered in and a simple turret added, and the final **Mark 4** changed the shape of the front, sat the driver centrally and moved the rest of the crew back.

Mark 2
Armament: 2 × MG
Armour: 14mm
Crew: 3
Weight: 5.7 tons (5,800kg)
Length: 15ft 6in (4.72m)
Width: 7ft 6in (2.29m)
Height: 6ft 6in (2.01m)
Engine: Ford V-8 petrol, 95bhp at 3600rpm
Speed: 50mph (80km/hr)
Range: not known

Carrier, Personnel, Half-Track, M3 USA
ACF, Autocar, Diamond-T, White
1940. The M3 was to the same general design as the M2 but the body was lengthened so as to carry more cargo or passengers and the armament was reduced to a single .30-inch machine gun on a fixed pedestal mount in the rear crew compartment. It was also given a door at the rear.

Armament: 1 × MG
Armour: 12mm
Crew: 2 + 11
Weight: 8.93 tons (9,072kg)
Length: 20ft 9in (6.32m) with winch
Width: 6ft 5in (1.95m)
Height: 7ft 5in (2.26m)
Engine: White 160AX, 6-cylinder, petrol, 128bhp at 2,800rpm
Speed: 45mph (72km/hr)
Range: 175 miles (280km)

Carrier, Personnel, Half-Track, M3A1
USA
ACF, Autocar, Diamond-T, White
1940. This is the lengthened M2A1, or an M3 with a .50-inch machine gun mount over the assistant driver's seat and three fixed pedestals in the crew compartment, between which the .30-inch machine gun could be shifted as required. Dimensions as for the M3, except that the height became 8ft 10in (2.69m) due to the machine gun mount.

Carrier, Personnel, Half-Track, M5 USA
International Harvester

1941. In order to increase output, the International Harvester Company were brought into the half-track production plans, and for convenience they were allowed to use their own engine and other components, which resulted in new models. The M5 was more or less the same as the M3 except for the International Harvester components (engine, front axle, transfer box and minor changes in the dash and driving controls). The engine delivered more power and torque but was governed to 2,700rpm, thus restricting the maximum speed.

Armament: 1 × MG
Armour: 16mm
Crew: 2 + 11
Weight: 9.15 tons (9,300kg)
Length: 20ft 9in (6.33m)
Width: 7ft 3in (2.20m)
Height: 7ft 7in (2.31m)
Engine: International Harvester RED-450B, 6-cylinder, petrol, 143bhp at 2,700rpm
Speed: 38mph (61km/hr)
Range: 125 miles.(200km)

Carrier, Personnel, Half-Track, M5A1 USA
International Harvester

1941. This was the M3A1 to International Harvester standards, or the M5 with the addition of the ring machine gun mount above the car; The only dimensional difference is the increase of height to 9ft 0in (2.74m).

Carrier, Personnel, Half-Track, M5A2 USA
International Harvester

Like the M3A2, this was intended as a modular design in which the interior fittings could be changed around as required by the vehicle's intended role. This model was 'intended for International Aid Requirements only' according to the Ordnance Catalog, and it is doubtful if many were ever made. Dimensions as for the M5A1.

Carrier, Personnel, Half-Track, M14 USA
International Harvester

1943. This actually began its career as the Gun Motor Carriage M14 (details of which can be found in the SP Gun section) but by 1943 there was a sufficiency of light air defence GMCs, so that when a British requirement for half-tracks arose, it was found convenient to continue manufacturing the GMC M14 but omit the gun mounting and guns, fitting the rear compartment with seats instead. The end result was virtually an M9A1 but without rear doors to the crew compartment. There is some doubt as to whether this was ever standardised within the US Army; it seems certain that the entire production run was sent to Britain in 1943–44. Dimensions as for the M9A1, except length, which was 21ft 3in (6.50m) due to the fitting of a front winch instead of the M9A1 roller.

Cashuat Light Assault Vehicle El Salvador
National armoury

1985. This vehicle was designed by the US Tank and Automotive Command in order to provide El Salvador with a cheap but effective light APC. It uses the 4 x 4 chassis of a standard US military truck (the M37B1) with a steel and Kevlar armoured body fitted to it. The chassis and body components were prepared in the USA in kit form and shipped to El Salvador for assembly. About 70 were made. The vehicle is of simple form, with front engine, driver and commander in a cab, and a crew compartment at the rear. A small turret with machine gun is fitted into the roof of the compartment.

Armament: 1 × MG
Armour: not disclosed
Crew: 2 + 8
Weight: 4.38 tons (4,454kg)
Length: 17ft 8in (5.38m)
Width: 6ft 0in (1.83m)
Height: 8ft 8in (2.63m)
Engine: Detroit Diesel, 110bhp
Speed: 50mph (80km/hr)
Range: 300 miles (480km)

Charrua APC Brazil
Moto Peças

1988. This was developed as a private venture and as part of a complete tracked vehicle family, some elements of which have been adopted by various South American military forces. The Charrua is full-tracked, the hull extending over the tracks. The driver is at the left front, with the engine and transmission on his right. Immediately behind him is a gunner's hatch with heavy machine gun and shields. The troop compartment forms the rear of the hull and has the hull sides sloped inwards at the top, with firing ports in each side. Entrance and exit is by a power-operated ramp door at the rear, and there are back-to-back seats for nine men. There are two roof hatches in the troop compartment. The vehicle is fully amphibious, using two jet units for propulsion. Several variants have been designed, including command vehicle, ambulance, IFV with turret and 25mm cannon, mortar carrier and recovery vehicle.

Armament: 1 × MG
Armour: not disclosed
Crew: 2 + 9
Weight: 17.71 tons (18,000kg)
Length: 21ft 1in (6.43m)
Width: 10ft 6in (3.20m)
Height: 6ft 5in (1.95m)
Engine: 6-cylinder turbocharged diesel, 395bhp at 2,100rpm
Speed: 43mph (70km/hr)
Range: 310 miles (500km)

Cobra APC Belgium
ACEC

1971. This tracked APC was developed as a private venture by ACEC, and was more or less built around an electric drive system the firm had developed. The vehicle used a diesel engine to drive a generator which then drove electric motors for normal propulsion, and also electric jet units for water propulsion, the vehicle being amphibious. A mild steel prototype, demonstrated in 1978, was favourably received by various military observers, and the company went on to develop several more prototypes and also to postulate a number of variations, including rocket launchers and 90mm gun carriers. But in spite of showing completed vehicles at various military exhibitions in the 1980s, nothing came of it and the Cobra was quietly abandoned.

Armament: 2 × MG
Armour: not disclosed
Crew: 2 + 10
Weight: 8.36 tons (8,500kg)
Length: 14ft 10in (4.52m)
Width: 9ft 0in (2.75m)
Height: 7ft 7in (2.32m)
Engine: Cummins VT-190 turbocharged diesel, 190bhp at 3,300rpm
Speed: 46mph (75km/hr)
Range: 372 miles (600km)

Cobra APC Turkey
See Otokar Cobra

Condor APC Germany
Thyssen-Henschel

1978. Condor is a private venture 4 x 4 vehicle which was designed to use as many commercial parts as possible in order to keep the cost down and make maintenance and the procurement of spares much easier. The design is quite conventional but for a driver's compartment with relatively large bullet-proof glass windows with hinged steel shutters. The engine is alongside the driver, and the crew compartment has doors on each side and at the rear. Armament is to the buyer's choice, and may be anything from a rifle-calibre machine gun mounted in a hatch over the crew compartment to a 20mm cannon in a power-driven turret. Several hundred were built and sold to Malaysia, Portugal, Turkey and several other countries.

Armament: 1 × MG, or to choice
Armour: not disclosed
Crew: 3 + 9
Weight: 9.05 tons (9,200kg)
Length: 21ft 3in (6.47m)
Width: 8ft 1in (2.47m)
Height: 9ft 2in (2.78m)
Engine: Daimler Benz 6-cylinder supercharged diesel, 168bhp
Speed: 63mph (100km/hr)
Range: 560 miles (900km)

Cougar Wheeled Fire Support Vehicle Canada
GM Canada

1979. This is basically the Swiss Mowag Piranha in 6 x 6 configuration, with the turret of the British Scorpion light tank mounted on top of the hull, and carrying a 76mm gun. A total of 195 were built during the 1980s. Fundamentally, this is really no more than a light self-propelled gun.

Armament: 1 × 76mm gun; 1 × MG
Armour: not disclosed
Crew: 3
Weight: not known
Length: 21ft 1in (5.97m)
Width: 10ft 6in (2.53m)
Height: 6ft 5in (2.53m)
Engine: Detroit Diesel V-6, 215bhp
Speed: 62mph (100km/hr)
Range: 375 miles (600km)

CV-90 Sweden

The term CV-90 covers a family of Swedish armoured vehicles, which can lead to a good deal of confusion. In view of this, reference should be made to 'CV-90-xx' in the different sections of this book for the different variant models.

CV-90-40 IFV Sweden
Bofors, Hagglund

This vehicle gets its title from being the Combat Vehicle 90, armed with a 40mm Bofors gun. Although the gun is basically the same weapon as the well-known L/70 AA gun, it is not, in this case, being used in the air defence role and has some significant mechanical differences. It is turret mounted and feeds from below, ejecting the cases upwards, through the roof. The magazine holds 24 rounds, and a further 216 rounds are carried in the vehicle. The exterior is fairly conventional, a tracked carrier with sloped front, with the turret immediately behind the driver and the engine and transmission alongside him under the glacis plate. The troop compartment behind the turret holds eight men, and is entered by a large door in the rear of the hull. There are also roof hatches, hinged on the centre line, allowing the occupants to stand and fire over the hull sides.

Armament: 1 × 40mm gun; 1 × MG
Armour: not disclosed
Crew: 3 + 8
Weight: 22.04 tons (22,400kg)
Length: 21ft 3in (6.47m)
Width: 9ft 10in (3.01m)
Height: 8ft 3in (2.5m)
Engine: Scania DS14, 4-cylinder, diesel, 550bhp
Speed: 43mph (70km/hr)
Range: not disclosed

Daewoo K200 IFV South Korea
Daewoo

1985. This is a tracked vehicle of the usual boxy shape with sloped front, and rear doors. The hull is of welded aluminium armour with an additional layer of steel to give extra protection without undue weight. The driver is at the left front, with the engine compartment to his right. The gunner is behind the engine and has a hatch with a ring-mounted heavy machine gun; a second hatch behind the driver mounts a light machine gun. The rear of the vehicle forms the troop compartment, entered by a ramp rear door and with seats for nine men. There is a roof hatch and firing ports are provided. Five roadwheels on each side are suspended on torsion bars. Several variant models have been developed, particularly a 107mm mortar carrier, an air defence version with a Gatling-type 20mm gun, and an NBC reconnaissance vehicle. As well as the South Korean Army, the K200 is also used by the Malaysian Army and has seen active service in Bosnia.

Armament: 1 × HMG; 1 × MG
Armour: not disclosed
Crew: 3 + 9
Weight: 12.69 tons (12,900kg)
Length: 18ft 0in (5.49m)
Width: 9ft 4in (2.85m)
Height: 6ft 4in (1.93m) to hull top
Engine: MAN V-8 diesel, 280bhp at 2,300rpm
Speed: 47mph (75km/hr)
Range: 300 miles (480km)

Daewoo K200A1 IFV South Korea
Daewoo

1998. This is the same basic vehicle as the K200 but with a far more powerful engine and a fully automatic transmission with torque converter instead of the previous semi-automatic transmission. The usual type of tiller steering is replaced by a steering wheel which is said to reduce driver fatigue and probably makes training somewhat easier as well. It is anticipated that service K200 vehicles will, upon overhaul, be upgraded to the K200A1 standard by replacement of the complete power pack.

Armament: 1 × HMG; 1 × MG
Armour: not disclosed
Crew: 3 + 9
Weight: 13.0 tons (13,200kg)
Length: 18ft 0in (5.49m)
Width: 9ft 4in (2.85m)
Height: 6ft 4in (1.93m)
Engine: MAN turbocharged V-8 diesel, 350bhp at 2,300rpm
Speed: 47mph (75km/hr)
Range: 300 miles (480km)

DAF Multi-Purpose Carrier (MPC)
Netherlands
DAF

The MPC was developed by DAF as a 4 x 4 light wheeled carrier which could be configured more or less as the purchaser desired. The object was to meet a demand by the Dutch Army, and, later, a similar one from Germany. The resulting vehicle built for the Dutch was known as the **Light Armoured Transport Vehicle** (LATV) and was a simple slope-sided vehicle with the driver at the front and the engine at the rear. Entrance is by two side hatches in the lower section of the hull and two roof hatches. An unusual feature is the provision of a large windscreen and side windows of bulletproof glass for the driver, giving him exceptionally good vision but suggesting that the thick of the battle might not be the intended place for the MPC. Up to five people can be carried, and there is said to be ample room for equipment.

The DAF company was later absorbed into a new consortium known as SP Aerospace and Vehicle Systems, and the vehicle was named **Fennek**. As the 20th century ended the Fennek was being evaluated by the German and Netherlands Armies in the reconnaissance role.

Armament: as desired; normally 1 × MG
Armour: not disclosed
Crew: 3 + 5
Weight: 7.87 tons (8,000kg)
Length: 15ft 9in (4.8m)
Width: 8ft 3in (2.5m)
Height: 5ft 7in (1.7m)
Engine: DAF 6-cylinder turbocharged diesel, 210bhp
Speed: 68mph (110km/hr)
Range: 435–620 miles (700–1,000km)

Dardo IFV Italy
Iveco

1998. This was originally developed as the VCC-80 (*qv*) but after trials it was decided to fit a different turret capable of mounting TOW missiles, and adopt a less expensive fire control system. In the event, all turrets are fitted for the TOW system attachment but only those vehicles designated for the anti-tank role actually have the launchers fitted. The vehicle is otherwise similar to the VCC-80, with six roadwheels on each side, skirts over the upper run of track, sloped front, flat roof with small turret and troop compartment with rear door. As with most vehicles of this type, a host of variations have been proposed, but few will ever get past the drawing board. A total of 200 IFV and anti-tank versions have been ordered by the Italian Army.

Armament: 1 × 25mm cannon; 1 × MG; 2 × TOW ATGW
Armour: not disclosed
Crew: 2 + 7
Weight: 22.63 tons (23,000kg)
Length: 22ft 0in (6.70m)
Width: 9ft 10in (3.0m)
Height: 8ft 8in (2.64m)
Engine: Iveco turbocharged V-8 diesel, 520bhp at 2,300rpm
Speed: 44mph (70km/hr)
Range: 310 miles (500km)

Dragoon LFV-90 USA
AV Technology

This vehicle first appeared as the **Dragoon 300** in the mid-1970s. It met with some success, and the

two companies involved in its manufacture amalgamated. Development continued, with minor improvements and changes being added, and it has been proposed in various forms, most of which appear to have got no further. The APC and LFV (Light Forces Vehicle) went into production and numbers have been bought by the US Army and by some South American countries.

The basic Dragoon is a 4 x 4 armoured car in the same mould as the Cadillac Gage or Mowag or Thyssen types, with sloped-out sides and recessed wheels, side doors and rear engine. The LFV-90 also has a power-driven turret carrying a 90mm gun and a coaxial machine gun. The APC version merely has a flat roof with hatches and with a light machine gun in a shielded hatch mount.

Armament: 1 × 90mm gun; 1 × coaxial MG
Armour: not disclosed
Crew: 5
Weight: 12 tons (12,700kg)
Length: 19ft 4in (5.89m)
Width: 8ft 0in (2.44m)
Height: 9ft 3in (2.82m)
Engine: Detroit Diesel V-6 turbocharged diesel, 300bhp at 1,800rpm
Speed: 72mph (116km/hr)
Range: 425 miles (685km)

Engesa EE-11 Urutu APC Brazil
Engesa

1972. The EE-11 is a wheeled APC which was specially designed for the Brazilian Army; the Brazilian Marines use a slightly different version capable of swimming in the open sea. The vehicle is a 6 x 6 with the rear wheels mounted on the Engesa Boomerang suspension unit. Engine and driver are in the extreme front of the hull, and centrally behind them is the circular hatch for the commander/gunner. He can be given one of a wide variety of armament fittings up to a 20mm cannon turret; and there is also a 90mm gun turret which can be squeezed in. The roof over the troop compartment has six hatches, which allow the occupants to fire out, but they also have eleven firing ports in the hull sides and end which allow them to use their personal weapons from under armour. The vehicle is fully amphibious and propels itself by its wheels when in the water. The Marine version has two propellers and a more powerful engine.

Armament: various; see text
Armour: 12mm
Crew: 2 + 13
Weight: 8.85 tons (9,000kg)

Length: 18ft 9in (5.76m)
Width: 8ft 0in (2.44m)
Height: 8ft 1in (2.45m)
Engine: Mercedes-Benz OM-352-A, 6-cylinder turbocharged diesel, 165bhp at 2,800rpm
Speed: 60mph (96km/hr)
Range: 370 miles (600km)

Engesa EE-T4 Light Tracked Vehicle Brazil
Engesa
1986. In the mid-1980s several countries expressed a wish for a light armoured vehicle which could be configured for various roles, and the Engesa company produced the EE-T4. It was extensively tested in the Middle East in 1986–87, but as suddenly as the demand had arisen, so did it vanish, and the EE-T4 never got beyond the prototype stage. It was full-tracked, with the engine at the right front and the driver on its left. Behind them was the fighting compartment with a small turret which could be one of several different models depending upon the desired armament. Various machine guns, anti-tank missile launchers and 20mm cannon were proposed; there was also a proposal to have a simple remote-control machine gun on the roof and use the interior as a troop compartment in the APC role.

Armament: to choice
Armour: not disclosed
Crew: 2 or 3
Weight: 4.33 tons (4,400kg)
Length: 12ft 4in (3.75m)
Width: 7ft 1in (2.15m)
Height: 4ft 6in (1.36m) to hull top
Engine: BMW 4-cylinder turbocharged diesel, 130bhp at 4,800rpm
Speed: 48mph (75km/hr)
Range: 225 miles (360km)

Fahd APC Egypt
Kadr Factory
The Fahd is a local design somewhat out of the usual run, with a bluff-fronted cab-over-engine layout having a considerable overhang, and a rectangular body with four firing ports and a rack of smoke dischargers down each side. There is a rear door for entry to the troop compartment (which holds 10 men) and side doors for the driver and commander. The cab has windscreens and side windows, with armoured steel shutters which can be dropped to cover them. Although the manufacturers have suggested this vehicle as a suitable carrier for anti-tank missiles and mortars, the general layout suggests that its principal

employment will be internal security tasks.

Armament: none fitted
Armour: not disclosed
Crew: 2 + 10
Weight: 11.07 tons (11,250kg)
Length: 19ft 8in (6.0m)
Width: 8ft 10in (2.69m)
Height: 6ft 11in (2.10m)
Engine: Mercedes-Benz 6-cylinder turbocharged diesel, 168bhp at 2,800rpm
Speed: 52mph (84km/hr)
Range: 500 miles (800km)

FAMAE Piranha Chile
FAMAE
1994. The FAMAE organisation obtained a licence from Mowag to manufacture the Piranha in Chile, and this 8 x 8 vehicle is generally the same as the Swiss product but for some small local preferences. It has a commander's cupola behind the driver's position which is armed with a .50-inch machine gun, the twin rear doors have been replaced by a single bottom-hinged, power-operated ramp/door, and the water jet units have been removed and replaced by stowage boxes since there is no requirement for the vehicle to be amphibious. The manufacturers have also proposed prototype support vehicles with 60mm or 90mm guns in turrets, but these do not appear to have been put into production.

Armament: 1 x MG
Armour: not disclosed
Crew: 1 + 14
Weight: 12.30 tons (12,500kg)
Length: 20ft 10in (6.36m)
Width: 8ft 3in (2.50m)
Height: 7ft 9in (2.37m)
Engine: Mowag V-6, petrol, 300bhp at 2,800rpm
Speed: 62mph (100km/hr)
Range: 435 miles (700km)

Fantail UK
Name given in 1944–45 by British troops in Italy to the LVT(A)-2 and LVT-4, which see.

FIAT-OTO 6614 APC Italy
Fiat
1977. The Fiat-OTO 6614 is a fairly compact wheeled vehicle with 4 x 4 drive and a useful specification. It originated from the 6614 BM, which was smaller and could carry only six infantry in the troop compartment. The larger vehicle found a ready market among those forces needing a light

and strong armoured carrier with minimum complications. It has the usual layout of driver and engine in front with turret behind them and troop compartment to the rear. There are doors in the sides and a powered ramp at the back. The Italian police adopted a small number, after which several hundred were sold to Somalia, South Korea, Peru, Libya and Tunisia before production ended in the early 1990s.

Armament: 1 × MG
Armour: 8mm
Crew: 2 + 8
Weight: 6.88 tons (7,000kg)
Length: 18ft 3in (5.56m)
Width: 7ft 8in (2.37m)
Height: 5ft 6in (1.68m)
Engine: Fiat Model 8062, 6-cylinder, diesel, 128bhp at 3,200rpm
Speed: 60mph (96km/h)
Range: 435 miles (700km)

Fuchs APC Germany
Thyssen-Henschel

1979. Also known as **Transportpanzer 1**, this is a 6 x 6 wheeled carrier with a slope-sided body and the wheels tucked under the recessed lower part of the hull. All wheels drive and the front four steer. There is a large bullet-proof windscreen at the front which can be covered by an armoured shutter. The driver and commander occupy the cab, while ten infantrymen can be accommodated in the troop compartment. The engine is in a compartment between the cab and the troop area, though there is a narrow alleyway along one side giving access between the two spaces. A large rear door gives entry to the troop compartment, which is also provided with roof hatches. As well as serving with the German Army, numbers were sold to Saudi Arabia, Israel, the Netherlands and Turkey, and a special version, equipped as an NBC Reconnaissance vehicle, was also adopted by Britain and the USA.

Armament: none
Armour: not disclosed
Crew: 2 + 10
Weight: 16.73 tons (17,000kg)
Length: 22ft 5in (6.83m)
Width: 9ft 9in (2.98m)
Height: 7ft 7in (2.30m)
Engine: Mercedes-Benz V-8 diesel, 320bhp at 2,500rpm
Speed: 65mph (105km/hr)
Range: 500 miles (800km)

FV420 family UK
FVRDE

FV420 was the designation for a family of light armoured vehicles designed in Britain during the late 1950s. They included the **FV421** load carrier, **FV422** APC, **FV423** command vehicle, **FV424** engineer vehicle, **FV425** recovery vehicle and **FV426** guided missile launcher. The whole project appears to have got out of hand and was cancelled before even prototypes could be built. It was replaced by the GV430 project in the 1960s, the principal result of which was the FV432, *below*.

FV432 APC UK
GKN

1962. The FV432 was approved in 1962 and built from then until 1971. Originally called **Trojan**, this name was dropped from official use, but was still used among the troops.

It was a boxy, tracked vehicle of similar appearance to the American M113 of the same era. The driver was at the right front, with the engine to his left. Behind the driver was the commander, with a hatch carrying a machine gun. The remainder of the vehicle body formed the crew compartment, which could accommodate 10 fully equipped infantrymen. Over the crew compartment was a large circular hatch, and the rear of the compartment was closed by a full-width door. A flotation screen around the hull could be erected in 10 minutes and allowed the vehicle to swim. Full NBC protection was given by filtering air to the interior.

The 432 was modified to suit varying roles: as a mortar carrier, with an 81mm mortar carried inside and firing through the main hatch; as an ambulance, capable of lifting four stretchers; as a command vehicle with additional radios, map-boards, etc. It could also carry the Wombat 120mm recoilless anti-tank gun; be connected to a minelaying plough to lay the Barmine anti-tank mine mechanically; or be used as a surveillance vehicle, carrying the ZB298 radar or Green Archer mortar-locating radar. It was also used by artillery regiments to carry fire-control equipment.

Armament: 1 × MG
Armour: 12mm
Crew: 2 + 10
Weight: 15.04 tons (15,280kg)
Length: 17ft 3in (5.25m)
Width: 9ft 2in (2.80m)
Height: 6ft 2in (1.87m)
Engine: Rolls-Royce, 6-cylinder, multi-fuel, 240bhp at 3,750rpm

Speed: 32mph (52km/hr)
Range: 360 miles (580km)

FV438 UK
GKN

1965. A variant of the FV432 family, this was exactly the same vehicle in dimensions and general appearance, but carried a launcher unit for the Swingfire anti-tank guided missile on the roof, and the necessary aiming and guidance equipment inside the vehicle. It was removed from service in 1986 after being replaced by the Striker ATGW vehicle.

General Dynamics Advanced Amphibious Assault Vehicle USA
General Dynamics

1999. General Dynamics having been awarded a contract for a new amphibious assault vehicle for the US Marines, this is their proposed design. At the time of writing it is no more than lines on paper, computer graphics and a provisional specification, but the concept is for a tracked vehicle with aluminium armour reinforced by Kevlar and ceramics. The tracks will be retractable to give a better shape in the water, and an extendable prow will also improve its sailing capabilities. The hull will be shaped to permit planing and thus a high speed in the water. A turret armed with a 30mm cannon will be on top of the hull. Propulsion in the water will be by two jet units mounted at the rear.

Armament: 1 × 30mm cannon; 1 × MG
Armour: not disclosed
Crew: 3 + 18
Weight: 31.86 tons (32,170kg)
Length: 29ft 5in (8.97m) on land,
        34ft 5in (10.50m) in water
Width: 12ft 0in (3.66m)
Height: 19ft 6in (3.20m) on tracks
Engine: MTU V-8 diesel; 2,700 shp in water,
        850bhp on land
Speed, land: 45mph (72km/hr)
Speed, water: 28mph (46km/hr)
Range, land: 400 miles (645km)
Range, water: 75 miles (120km)

Grizzly APC Canada
GM Canada

1979. The Grizzly is based on the same vehicle as the Cougar (*qv*), in other words it is a Canadian copy of the Mowag 6 x 6 Piranha. It has the usual slope-sided body with prow-like front end. On top of the hull is a Cadillac-Gage turret with a .50-inch

Browning and a coaxial 7.62mm MG. The troop compartment can take eight infantrymen, who have firing ports and vision blocks in the sides and rear.

Armament: 2 × MG
Armour: 10mm
Crew: 3 + 8
Weight: 10.33 tons (10,500kg)
Length: 19ft 7in (5.97m)
Width: 8ft 3in (2.53m)
Height: 8ft 4in (2.53m)
Engine: Detroit Diesel, 6-cylinder, 215bhp
Speed: 62mph (100km/hr)
Range: 375 miles (600km)

Half-Track Vehicles Germany
See entries under 'Sonder Kraftfahrzeug (Sd Kfz)'

Half-Track Vehicles USA
See entries under 'Car, Half-Track' and 'Carrier, Personnel, Half-Track'

HS-30 APC Switzerland/West Germany
Hispano-Suiza, British Leyland, Henschel, Hanomag

1955. When the Federal German Bundeswehr was set up in 1954, they instituted development which eventually produced the Marder MICV (*qv*) but as an interim measure adopted this APC which had originally been developed for the Swiss Army. A tracked vehicle, with five roadwheels and rear drive, the hull is low, flat-topped, and sloped at both ends. There is a small turret at the front left, carrying a 20mm cannon, and the troop compartment has overhead hatches and a double door in the rear face of the hull. Manufacture was licensed to British Leyland, Henschel and Hanomag for a total of 3,625 vehicles, but this was later halved.

Armament: 1 × 20mm cannon
Armour: 30mm
Crew: 1 + 9
Weight: 12 tons (12,195kg)
Length: 17ft 7in (5.25m)
Width: 8ft 2in (2.48m)
Height: 6ft 4in (2.03m)
Engine: Rolls-Royce
Speed: 40mph (65km/hr)
Range: not known

Hotchkiss Light APC West Germany
Hanomag

1958. When the HS-30 (*above*) began delivery to the German Army, there were so many faults and defects that the order was immediately halved. To fulfill the balance, a fresh design, based upon the TT-6 (*below*) was put in hand and from 1958 was issued as an APC-cum-reconnaissance vehicle. A full-tracked vehicle, it differed from the TT-6 by having the roof line lowered, the body lengthened, an extra pair of roadwheels added, and a small turret mounting a 20mm cannon placed on the left side of the hull.

Armament: I × 20mm cannon
Armour: 15mm
Crew: 4
Weight: 8.20 tons (8,330kg)
Length: 14ft 7in (4.44m)
Width: 7ft 5in (2.26m)
Height: 6ft 7in (2.00m)
Engine: Talbot 6-cylinder petrol, 170bhp at 3,900rpm
Speed: 40mph (65km/hr)
Range: 220 miles (350km)

Humber FV302 Armoured Truck UK
Humber (chassis), GKN (body)
1955. In the early 1950s a range of specially designed military cargo vehicles was developed with particularly good cross-country performance. Among these was a one-ton 4 x 4 truck by Humber, and a number of these were fitted with armoured bodies in order to provide the infantry with a protected vehicle as an interim measure until the Saracen APC was in general issue. Its increased weight, allied to the relatively soft independent suspension, led to the troops nicknaming it the 'Armoured Pig' from the way it wallowed on rough ground. Once sufficient Saracens were provided, the Humber truck was withdrawn from service and most were either sold or scrapped.

When the civil troubles broke out in Northern Ireland in the 1960s, most of the remaining vehicles were repurchased and issued as internal security trucks. They were later reworked with additional armour and stronger suspension. The vehicle is simply an armoured box on a truck chassis; the engine is at the front, with the driver in the normal right-hand position. The remainder of the vehicle can be adapted as a cargo carrier, personnel carrier or ambulance. It is roofed, and has vision and firing slits down each side. It is not normally armed.

Armament: none
Armour: not disclosed
Crew: 2 + 8
Weight: 6.84 tons (6,950kg)
Length: 16ft 2in (4.92m)
Width: 6ft 8in (2.04m)
Height: 6ft 11in (2.12m)

Engine: Rolls-Royce, 6-cylinder, petrol, 120bhp at 3,750rpm
Speed: 40mph (65km/hr)
Range: 250 miles (400km)

HWK-II APC West Germany
Henschel
1964. In the late 1950s the company of Henschel-Werke developed a light tracked chassis as a basis for a number of military vehicles, including an APC, anti-tank missile carrier, anti-tank gun carrier, armoured ambulance and mortar carrier. They were primarily aimed at the export market, but apart from some 40 APCs sold to Mexico in 1964 only two prototype reconnaissance vehicles were built. The company then abandoned the project. The HWK-11 APC was a tracked vehicle with torsion-bar suspension, and used a boxy body with sloping front. The engine was at the right front, with the driver and vehicle commander on its left. The commander had a small hatch, which was provided with a light machine gun. The main part of the body was covered by two large hatches which could be opened to give access or partly opened to provide cover while allowing the occupants to fire their personal weapons. Two doors at the rear were normally used for access. The vehicle had no amphibious capability.

Armament: I × MG
Armour: 15mm
Crew: 2 + 10
Weight: 10.82 tons (11,000kg)
Length: 16ft 7in (5.05m)
Width: 8ft 4in (2.53m)
Height: 5ft 2in (1.58m)
Engine: Chrysler, V-8, petrol, 211bhp at 4,000rpm
Speed: 40mph (65km/hr)
Range: 200 miles (320km)

Iron Eagle Infantry Support Vehicle South Africa
Denel
1993. This is a light 4 x 4 vehicle carrying a 106mm recoilless rifle and intended to be air-droppable as a support vehicle for airborne or parachute infantry. Although this was the primary intent it can, of course, be used in other roles where lightness and agility are demanded. Three can be carried inside one C-130 Hercules aircraft. The hull is designed to minimise blast damage from mines, and has the engine at the rear and the open crew compartment, with driver, to the front. The 106mm is mounted on the left side of the crew compartment and is on a removable pallet base so that it can be replaced by

other weapons as desired. There is also a light machine gun on a pedestal mounting on the other side of the compartment.

Armament: 1 × 106mm RCL; 1 × MG
Armour: not disclosed
Crew: 3
Weight: 3.94 tons (4,000kg)
Length: 11ft 10in (3.6m)
Width: 6ft 11in (2.1m)
Height: 5ft 9in (1.74m)
Engine: diesel, 6-cylinder, 123bhp
Speed: 62mph (100km/hr)
Range: 280 miles (450km)

Kadr Fahd Egypt
See Fahd APC

Kadr Walid Egypt
See Walid APC

Kangaroo APC UK
Field workshops
In August 1944 the First Canadian Army launched Operation Totalize to break out from Caen through a very strongly defended German line. Tactical surprise was virtually impossible and the Commander II Canadian Corps, General Simonds, decided to drive the infantry through by placing them in armoured carriers. At the end of July the three field artillery regiments of 3rd Canadian Division had exchanged their American M7 Priest 105mm SP howitzers for towed 25-pounder guns, and General Simonds now obtained permission from the Americans, to whom the M7s should have been returned, to convert them into carrier vehicles for the infantry.

An advanced workshop detachment, code-named Kangaroo, was given the task of conversion, which they did by removing the howitzer, seats and ammunition racks and welding a piece of armour plate over the front opening. Some of the armour, it is said, was removed from stranded landing craft on the Normandy beaches. By the morning of 6 August 75 Priests had been converted, the infantry had a day in which to practise embarking and disembarking, and on the 7th the the Kangaroos (the unit name now attached to the vehicles) went into action. The drivers were taken from the artillery units that had previously used the vehicles.

The Kangaroos were an unqualified success in the battle and were used on several subsequent occasion. The conversion was later applied to Sherman and Ram tanks by removing the turrets

and much of the internal stowage, and Kangaroos were used by British and American units as the idea spread. These extemporized carriers undoubtedly had an effect on post-war thinking and led to the development of armoured personnel carriers.

Kentaurus MICV Greece
ELBO
1998. This has been developed as a private venture, and is intended to form the basis of a proposed family of light armoured vehicles. It is a conventional-looking tracked machine with sloping front and flat-roofed hull upon which is a turret carrying a 30mm Mauser cannon (made under licence in Greece) and a coaxial machine gun. A launcher for Stinger AA missiles is an optional fitment for the turret. The troop compartment normally holds 8 men but the interior can be configured to make room for 10 if required. The prototype is currently undergoing trials and evaluation.

Armament: 1 × 30mm; 1 × MG; 2 × SAM (optional)
Armour: not disclosed
Crew: 3 + 8 (or 3 + 10)
Weight: 19.0 tons (19,300kg)
Length: 19ft 8in (5.98m)
Width: 8ft 4in (2.55m)
Height: 8ft 0in (2.45m)
Engine: MTU V-6 diesel, 420bhp at 2,300rpm
Speed: 47mph (75km/hr)
Range: 310 miles (500km)

LAV Canada/USA
See Light Armoured Vehicle

Leonidas Greece
ELBO
Leonidas 1 was the Steyr 4K 7FA (*qv*) built under licence in Greece; about 20 were built between 1984 and 1989. **Leonidas 2** is the same vehicle but with the addition of an automatic fire-suppression system, night vision equipment for the driver and improved smoke dischargers Development of this model began in 1987 and some 200 were built. It is believed that some time in the near future these may be upgraded by the addition of turrets with 25mm cannon.

Armament: 1 × MG
Armour: 25mm
Crew: 1 + 8
Weight: 14.56 tons (14,800kg)
Length: 17ft 3in (5.87m)
Width: 8ft 2in (2.50m)

Height: 5ft 3in (1.61m)
Engine: Steyr 7FA 6-cylinder turbocharged diesel,
  320bhp at 2,300rpm
Speed: 40mph (64km/hr)
Range: 325 miles (520km)

Light Armored Vehicle (LAV) Canada/USA
GM Canada

The Light Armored Vehicle (LAV) is a Canadian-built 8 x 8 Mowag Piranha , fitted with a turret carrying a 25mm cannon, and originally supplied to the US Marine Corps in 1982. This became the **LAV-25**. A second design had a turret carrying a 90mm Cockerill gun, and this became the **AGV** or **Assault Gun Vehicle**, also supplied to the USMC. Subsequently GM Canada received a contract to supply several hundred vehicles to the USMC and US Army. Some vehicles were built as 81mm mortar carriers, others carried rocket launchers, and the manufacturers also proposed a wide variety of variants, some of which were built, and some of which may yet be built. Vehicles have also been supplied to Australia and to the Canadian Army.

Armament: 1 × 25mm M242 cannon; 1 × coaxial MG;
  1 × AA MG
Armour: not disclosed
Crew: 3 + 6
Weight: 12.59 tons (12,792kg)
Length: 21ft 9in (6.39m)
Width: 8ft 3in (2.50m)
Height: 8ft 10in (2.69m)
Engine: Detroit Diesel V-6, 275bhp at 2,800rpm
Speed: 62mph (100km/hr)
Range: 400 miles (650km)

Lohr RPX 3000 France
Lohr

1985. This 4 x 4 'light armoured vehicle' was privately developed by Lohr, but although evaluated by various agencies never went into production. It was a simple and small car, with the commander and driver seated at the front, the engine behind them, and a small compartment at the rear for two men. The driver and commander had large windscreens with bottom-hinged armoured shutters, and side doors. There was a hatch over the commander with a light machine gun. There was also a hatch over the rear compartment, where a second weapon – a Milan or HOT missile for example – could be fitted.

Armament: 1 × MG plus missiles or other weapon
Armour: not disclosed
Crew: 4
Weight: 3.44 tons (3,500kg)

Length: 12ft 4in (3.75m)
Width: 7ft 2in (2.18m)
Height: 5ft 5in (1.65m)
Engine: BMW 6-cylinder turbocharged diesel, 125bhp
  at 4,800rpm
Speed: 68mph (110km/hr)
Range: 370 miles (600km)

Lohr VPX 5000 France
Lohr

1981. This is described as a 'light armoured tracked vehicle' and might be thought of as a sort of mini-MICV. The same could be said of the shape, a slope-fronted, flat-topped hull with skirted tracks revealing six roadwheels and a front drive sprocket. The driver is at the front, alongside the engine, and the rear forms a troop compartment. There is a hatch in the roof allowing a soldier to man a missile launcher, and there is also a remote-controlled machine gun which can be aimed and fired by a crew member under armour. This armament is not mandatory, merely an example of possibilities. So far as is known it has not yet been accepted for service.

Armament: to choice
Armour: not disclosed
Crew: 4
Weight: 4.52 tons (4,600kg)
Length: 13ft 9in (4.20m)
Width: 6ft 7in (2.0m)
Height: 5ft 3in (1.60m)
Engine: BMW 6-cylinder petrol, 180bhp at 5,500rpm
Speed: 50mph (80km/hr)
Range: 215 miles (350km)

LVT-1 (Landing Vehicle, Tracked, Mark 1) USA
FMC, Roebling, Graham-Paige, Ingersoll, St Louis Car

1940. In the 1930s a Mr Donald Roebling, a retired engineer, designed an amphibious vehicle to operate in the flooded Florida Everglades. By 1940, when he had perfected his 'Alligator', the US Marines were looking for a suitable vehicle to carry troops ashore and then operate on land with them. After examining Roebling's design they then asked for some modifications and placed an order for 300 late in 1940. This became the LVT-1; made of steel, it was not armoured, and was intended solely as a supply vehicle to back up a landing. It had a driver's compartment at the forward end and the remainder of the body was used for cargo space except for a small engine room at the rear. The tracks had oblique shoes, which were Roebling's patented method of water propulsion as well as giving the vehicle good grip on land. The rest of the hull was divided into watertight compartments and provided with a bilge pump. The cargo compartment was encircled by a skate rail upon which machine guns could be mounted.

Armament: 1 or more MGs
Armour: none
Crew: 3
Weight: 9.73 tons (9,888kg)
Length: 21ft 6in (6.55m)
Width: 9ft 10in (2.99m)
Height: 8ft 1in (2.46m)
Engine: Hercules 6-cylinder petrol, 146bhp at 2,400rpm
Speed, land: 12mph (19km/hr)
Speed, water: 6mph (9.5km/hr)
Range: 210 miles (240km)

LVT(A)-1 (Landing Vehicle, Tracked, Armored, Mark I) USA
FMC, Roebling
1942. In spite of the nomenclature this is not a modified LVT-1 (*above*) but a totally different model. It was, in strict fact, an amphibious tank based on the LVT-2 hull. It was armoured to the same standard as the LVT(A)-2, but had the addition of an M3 light tank turret and gun behind the driver's cab. The cargo compartment was covered in armour so as to approximate to a tank hull, and there was sufficient space for a reduced amount of cargo to be carried if needed.

Armament: 1 × 37mm gun, 3 × MG
Armour: 12mm
Crew: 6
Weight: 14.64 tons (14,877kg)
Length: 26ft 1in (7.95m)
Width: 10ft 8in (3.25m)
Height: 10ft 1in (3.07m)
Engine: Continental W670-9A, 7-cylinder, radial, air-cooled, petrol, 262bhp at 2,400rpm
Speed, land: 25mph (40km/hr)
Speed, water: 6.5mph (10.5km/hr)
Range: 125 miles (200km)

LVT-2 and LVT(A)-2 USA
FMC, Graham-Paige, Ingersoll, St Louis Car
1943. After experience with the LVT-1 the US Marines set about designing an improved model. The primary defect with the LVT-1 had been the rigid suspension and track system, which led to frequent breakdowns and poor riding on land. The LVT-2 used an improved track with W-shaped

shoes, which could be quickly replaced when they wore down. It also featured a sprung suspension which improved the ride quality. To save time and simplify production the engine and major transmission components of the M3 light tank were incorporated in the design. Apart from these mechanical changes the general layout of the craft was the same as that of the LVT-1. Total production of the LVT-2 amounted to some 2,600, and they were extensively used in the South Pacific.

It became obvious that more protection was needed and this gave rise to the **LVT(A)-2**, the (A) indicating it was armoured. The cab of this pattern was protected with half-inch (12.7mm) armour plate and the rest of the hull with quarter-inch (6mm) armour plate. The added weight meant that the craft sat slightly deeper in the water, but apart from that its dimensions and performance were the same as the LVT-2.

Armament: 1 × MG
Armour: see text
Crew, LVT-2: 6
Crew, LVT(A)-2: 4
Weight, LVT-2: 10.82 tons (11,000kg)
Weight, LVT(A)-2: 12.05 tons (12,245kg)
Length: 26ft 1in (7.95m)
Width: 10ft 8in (3.25m)
Height: 8ft 1in (2.46m)
Engine: Continental W-670-9A, 7-cylinder, radial, air-cooled, petrol, 262bhp at 2,400rpm
Speed, land: 20mph (32km/hr)
Speed, water: 7.5mph (12km/hr)
Range: 150 miles (240km)

LVT-3 USA
Graham-Paige, Ingersoll
1945. One of the drawbacks of the LVT-1 and -2 was that the cargo had to be lifted in and out over the side. The Borg-Warner Corporation set about improving matters by moving the engine forward and placing a bottom-hinged door at the rear of the hull which acted as a loading and unloading ramp. This became the LVT-3; it was made slightly wider than the earlier models so that a standard Jeep could be driven up the ramp and carried in the cargo space, and it could be used to carry 30 men. Some 3,000 or so were built, and it was first used at Okinawa in 1945. This model used the engine and transmission of the obsolescent M5 series of light tanks (*qv*), and it continued in use until replaced in the mid-1950s.

Armament: 1 × MG
Armour: none
Crew: 3

Weight: 11.87 tons (12,065kg)
Length: 24ft 6in (7.46m)
Width: 11ft 2in (3.40m)
Height: 9ft 11in (3.02m)
Engine: 2 × Cadillac, V-8, petrol, each 148bhp at 3,200rpm
Speed, land: 17mph (27km/hr)
Speed, water: 6mph (9.6km/hr)
Range: 150 miles (240km)

LVT-4 and LVT(A)-4 USA
FMC, Graham-Paige, St Louis Car

1945. This was developed by FMC in the same manner as the LVT-3, by moving the engine forward so as to allow for a ramp door at the rear of the hull. Since no major changes of engine were made, the design was faster to completion and the first LVT-4 were in action at Saipan in June 1944. Its superiority over the earlier models, due to it being easier and quicker to load and unload, led to it being produced in greater numbers; over 8,300 were built.

A modified version was the LVT(A)-4, which, like the LVT(A)-1, was virtually an amphibious tank. The cargo compartment was covered, the entire vehicle armoured, and the turret of the M8 HMC, with 75mm howitzer, was installed. This vehicle was used as a close-support equipment for US Marine landings and was highly effective. This also had its debut at Saipan. After the war a number had the turrets removed and replaced by those of the M24 light tank, complete with 75mm gun.

Armament, LVT-4: 1 × MG
Armament, LVT(A)-4: see text
Armour: 13mm
Crew: 6
Weight: 12.23 tons (12,428kg) LVT-4
Weight: 17.61 tons (17,898kg) LVT(A)-4
Length: 26ft 1in (7.95m)
Width: 10ft 8in (3.25m)
Height: 8ft 1in (2.46m)
Engine: Continental W670-9A, 7-cylinder, radial, petrol, air-cooled, 262bhp at 2,400rpm
Speed, land: 20mph (32km/hr) LVT-4
Speed, land: 16mph (25km/hr) LVT(A)-4
Speed, water: 7mph (12km/hr) both versions
Range: 150 miles (240km)

LVTP-5 (Landing Vehicle, Tracked, Personnel, Mark 5) USA

LVTH-6 (Landing Vehicle, Tracked, Howitzer, Mark 6) USA
FMC, Ingersoll, Pacific Car, St Louis Car

1955. Once the war ended the US Marines drew up a specification for a fully armoured and more powerful landing vehicle and these came into service in the middle 1950s. The LVTP-5 and LVTH-6 were basically similar. They both had a squared-off armoured body with the tracks set low in the sides and with a ramp door at the forward end, roof hatches to give additional means of entry to the cargo space, and the driver in a slightly raised cab with cupola at the forward end of the hull. The engine compartment was at the rear. They used the same hull and track unit, but the LVTH-6 had a turret with a 105mm howitzer mounted centrally, slightly behind the driver. In spite of (or perhaps because of) their advanced design the vehicles proved unsuccessful, due to heavy maintenance demands and frequent breakdowns. They were eventually replaced in the 1970s by the LVTP-7 series and sold abroad.

Armament: 1 × 105mm howitzer + 2 × MG LVTH-6
1 × MG LVTP-5
Armour: 16mm
Crew: 3 + 25
Weight: 31.15 tons (31,650kg)
Length: 29ft 8in (9.04m)
Width: 11ft 8in (3.55m)
Height: 10ft 0in (3.06m)
Engine: Continental, V-12, petrol, 810bhp at 2,400rpm
Speed, land: 30mph (48km/hr)
Speed, water: 7mph (11km/hr)
Range: 190 miles (300km)

LVTP-7A1 USA
FMC

1971. Development of this vehicle began in 1964, it was issued in 1971, and in 1985 it was re-titled the **Amphibious Assault Vehicle 7A1** (or **AAV-7A1**). As well as being used by the US Navy it has been sold to several other countries. A fully amphibious tracked vehicle, it has better 'sea-keeping' qualities than the average floatable APC. The hull is of aluminium armour. The driver is at the left front with a small cupola with vision blocks and an infra-red periscope. The commander has a similar cupola just behind him. The engine is central at the front, and is in power pack form allowing it to be changed in 45 minutes. Behind the engine and to the right of the hull is a turret which usually carries a .50-inch machine gun. The remainder of the vehicle accommodates 25 full-equipped marines. Propulsion in the water is by two jet units at the rear of the hull.

Minor variations of this design are the **LVTR-7** recovery vehicle with winch and repair equipment and the **LVTC-7** command vehicle with additional communications equipment. The **LVTE-7**, an engineer vehicle with bulldozer blade and minefield clearing equipment, and the **LVTH-7** with a 105mm howitzer in a turret, were also developed but neither was accepted for service.

Armament: 1 × MG
Armour: 45mm
Crew: 3 + 25
Weight: 22.47 tons (22,838kg)
Length: 26ft 0in (7.94m)
Width: 10ft 9in (3.27m)
Height: 10ft 8in (3.26m)
Engine: Detroit Diesel V-8 turbocharged diesel, 400bhp at 2,800rpm
Speed, land: 40mph (64km/hr)
Speed, water: 8.5mph (13.6km/hr)
Range: 300 miles (480km)

m/42 SKPF APC Sweden
Scania-Vabis

1954. The SKPF was an interim vehicle for the Swedish Army and was scarcely a practical proposition for modern battlefields. It was little more than an armoured truck and it was built on a 4 × 4 commercial chassis with twin rear wheels. Large flat sheets of armour surrounded the front, enclosing the front wheels, and the driver and commander sat in a conventional cab behind the engine. The troop compartment had sloping sides and was open on top, though there was a canvas cover for winter. The troops entered by doors at the back, but the limitations of the vehicle were severe and its cross-country performance was negligible. It was used in the infantry brigades only, after which they were given to United Nations peacekeeping troops in different parts of the world.

Armament: 2 × MG
Armour: 10mm
Crew: 2 + 13
Weight: 8.50 tons (8,638kg)
Length: 22ft 3in (6.78m)
Width: 7ft 6in (2.28m)
Height: 7ft 5in (2.26m)
Engine: Scania-Vabis, 4-cylinder petrol, 115bhp
Speed: 45mph (70km/hr)
Range: 250 miles (400km)

M59 APC USA
FMC

1953. The M75 APC (*below*) was too expensive and lacked an amphibious capability, and so in 1953 the M59 was introduced to replace it. Although made to a cheaper specification it was a better vehicle, was

amphibious and was less vulnerable, but it turned out to be underpowered and placed a considerable load on the maintenance services. The M59 generally resembled the M75 in being a simple steel box on tracks with a sloped front, but it was a 'cleaner' design. The driver sat at the front, leaving the rest of the vehicle for the crew and passengers. Entry was by a large hydraulically operated ramp in the rear, and there were also two hatches over the crew compartment. The vehicle commander had a cupola with periscopes and a .50-inch machine gun. The engines were mounted one at each side of the crew compartment. Variant models included an armoured ambulance version, a command vehicle, and a 4.2-inch mortar carrier, in which the mortar could be fired from the vehicle through the open roof or dismounted and used away from the vehicle.

Armament: 1 × MG
Armour: 16mm
Crew: 2 + 10
Weight: 19.01 tons (19,325kg)
Length: 19ft 5in (5.61m)
Width: 10ft 8in (3.26m)
Height: 10ft 4in (3.14m)
Engine: two GMC, 6-cylinder, petrol, each 127bhp at 3,350rpm
Speed: 32mph (52km/hr)
Range: 100 miles (160km)

M60-P APC Yugoslavia
State factories

1965. This was a local design which followed the contemporary fashion and was simply a rectangular box on tracks, with a sloped front. The tracked suspension was copied from the Soviet SU-76 assault gun, numbers of which had been acquired by Yugoslavia in the late 1940s. The engine was an imported Austrian Saurer. The driver is at the left front, with a co-driver on his right who also mans the bow machine gun. The commander is behind the driver, and has an observation cupola, whilst the machine gunner sits behind the co-driver and has a hatch with a ring-mounted heavy machine gun. The remainder of the hull is the troop compartment, for ten men, with firing ports on both sides and double doors at the rear. A variant model was the **M60-PB** which had two 82mm recoilless guns on a rotating mounting on the roof.

Armament: 2 × MG
Armour: 25mm
Crew: 4 + 10
Weight: 10.82 tons (11,000kg)
Length: 16ft 6in (5.02m)
Width: 9ft 1in (2.77m)

Height: 6ft 1in (1.86m)
Engine: Saurer 6-cylinder diesel, 140bhp
Speed: 28mph (45km/hr)
Range: 240 miles (400km)

M75 APC USA
International Harvester, FMC

1952. During the last year of World War II the US Army realised the shortcomings of the M3 half-track (*qv*) as an infantry carrier, and in September 1945 issued a specification for a fully enclosed, tracked, personnel carrier. The resulting vehicle was standardized as the M75 in December 1952, and some 1,700 vehicles were built. The hull was a steel armoured box built on to running gear assembled from components of the M41 light tank. The driver sat at the front, with the engine and transmission on his right side in a package that could be removed through the hull front. The commander had a vision cupola and a .50-inch machine gun, while the 10 infantrymen carried could enter by twin doors in the rear of the hull. Two hatches were also provided over the passenger compartment. The vehicle was not amphibious and since it was largely built from tank components and in small numbers, was extremely expensive. It was replaced in US service by the M59 (*qv*), after which numbers of M75s were supplied to the Belgian Army.

Armament: 1 × MG
Armour: 25mm
Crew: 2 + 10
Weight: 18.53 tons (18,828kg)
Length: 17ft 0in (5.19m)
Width: 9ft 4in (2.84m)
Height: 9ft 0in (2.75m)
Engine: Continental, 6-cylinder, horizontally-opposed petrol, 295bhp at 2,660rpm
Speed: 44mph (70km/hr)
Range: 115 miles (185km)

M80 MICV Yugoslavia
State factories

1974. This was originally called the **M980** but had its designation changed in 1981. It was designed in Yugoslavia but used a number of foreign components and borrowed features from various foreign designs. The corrugated small-wheel suspension of the tracks was vaguely Soviet in inspiration, the engine was French, the anti-tank missile was a Yugoslav copy of the Soviet 'Sagger' and the 20mm cannon was closely related to the Hispano-Suiza HS 404. The general appearance was similar to the Soviet BMP-1 though it had only five roadwheels instead of six. A noteworthy feature

was the mounting of the cannon and coaxial machine gun in slots in the turret, enabling them to elevate and fire in the air defence role.

Armament: 1 × 20mm; 1 × MG; 2 × ATGW
Armour: 30mm
Crew: 3 + 7
Weight: 13.48 tons (13,700kg)
Length: 21ft 0in (6.4m)
Width: 8ft 6in (2.59m)
Height: 7ft 6in (2.3m)
Engine: Hispano-Suiza HS115, V-8 turbocharged diesel, 260bhp at 3,000rpm
Speed: 37mph (60km/hr)
Range: 320 miles (500km)

M80A MICV Yugoslavia
See BVP-M80A

M113 APC USA
FMC, OTO-Melara (licence)

1955. In 1954 the US Army demanded an air-portable APC, resulting in the **M113**, made of aluminium armour, a considerable step forward in armoured vehicle design, and manufacture began in 1960. The first batch was built with petrol engines, but in 1963 a fresh model, the **M113A1**, with a diesel engine, became the production standard. Well over 74,000 of the two models had been built in the USA by the time production ended in 1992, as well as several thousand made in Italy under licence. It is still in use by over 35 countries and must rank as one of the most successful armoured vehicles ever made.

The M113 is simply a box with a sloped front and tracked suspension. Driver and engine are at the front of the hull, leaving the rest clear as a crew compartment. The commander is located centrally and has a cupola with vision devices and a .50-inch machine gun. Ten infantrymen can sit in the hull, along the sidewalls, and entry to the compartment is by a large hydraulically operated ramp in the rear of the hull or via a hatch over the crew area. The vehicle is fully amphibious, being propelled in water by its tracks, and the only preparation required is the erection of a 'trim board' at the hull front. There have been innumerable variants of the M113, either projected or actually produced and used.

M113A1
Armament: 1 × MG
Armour: 38mm
Crew: 3 + 10
Weight: 10.97 tons (11,156kg)

Length: 15ft 11in (4.86m)
Width: 8ft 10in (2.68m)
Height: 8ft 2in (1.82m)
Engine: GMC, 6-cylinder, diesel, 215bhp at 2,800rpm
Speed: 42mph (68km/hr)
Range: 300 miles (485km)

M980 MICV Yugoslavia
See M80 MICV

Makina Carancho 180 APC Chile
Makina

1978. This is a light 4 x 4 armoured utility vehicle, numbers of which were adopted by the Chilean armed forces, probably for internal security tasks. Commercial automotive components have been used wherever possible in order to keep the cost down and simplify spares provision. The layout was conventional, with the engine under an armoured hood, driver and commander in the cab behind it, and the rest of the vehicle taken up by an open-topped troop compartment holding four men. Driver and commander have bulletproof screens with armoured shutters, and there are three pivot mountings for machine guns, one above the commander and the other two on each side of the troop compartment. Double doors at the rear offer exit and entry, and the cab has doors on each side.

Armament: up to 3 x MG
Armour: 'protection against 7.62mm AP';
     8mm estimated
Crew: 2 + 4
Weight: 4.23 tons (4,300kg)
Length: 16ft 1in (4.9m)
Width: 7ft 3in (2.2m)
Height: 6ft 3in (1.9m)
Engine: Chrysler V-8 petrol, 180bhp at 4,000rpm
Speed: 75mph (120km/hr)
Range: 280 miles (450km)

Makina Multi 163 APC Chile
Makina

1983. Doubtless flushed by their success with the Carancho 180, the Makina company next developed this vehicle, also intended for internal security tasks. Built on a commercial chassis, this 4 x 4 was a large rectangular vehicle with a sloping front face and with the wheels recessed within the sloped-in lower hull sides. The engine was in front, with the driver and commander behind it; each had a bullet-proof screen with an armoured shutter. Behind them was the troop compartment, with two large rectangular roof hatches and two rear doors; there was also a

circular hatch to the forward end, in which a machine gun mount could be fitted. There were firing ports along the sides. The vehicle does not appear to have been a success and was dropped by the late 1980s.

Armour: 1 x MG
Armour: 8mm
Crew: 2 + 8
Weight: 4.92 tons (5,000kg)
Length: 16ft 6in (5.05m)
Width: 7ft 3in (2.23m)
Height: 6ft 11in (2.10m)
Engine: Chrysler V-8 petrol, 180bhp at 4,000rpm
Speed: 68mph (110km/hr)
Range: 280 miles (450km)

Marder MICV Germany
Rheinstahl, Atlas MaK

1971. The German Army were among the pioneers of armoured personnel carriers, and in 1959 the reconstituted Bundeswehr made such a vehicle their top priority. However, with the experience of the Russian campaign behind them, they insisted that the occupants had to be able to fight from the vehicle and not be merely passengers. Moreover it was to be well protected and carry powerful armament, all of which turned the requirement into one for a mechanized infantry combat vehicle. After long and careful development, the Marder was first issued in May 1971. It has a welded steel hull capable of withstanding 20mm cannon attack at the front, and the driver and engine are side by side in the hull front. Behind this is the troop compartment in which the vehicle commander and two gunners operate and where six infantrymen can be accommodated. On the vehicle top is a remote-controlled turret unit mounting an Rh202 20mm cannon with a coaxial machine gun; early versions had a smaller remote-control mount carrying a machine gun fitted over the rear of the troop compartment. At the rear of the hull a bottom-hinged door gives access and acts as a disembarkation ramp. Suspension is by torsion bars, and with a snorkel fitted it can wade in depths of up to 8ft (2.5m) of water.

Armament: 1 x 20mm cannon; 1 x MG
Armour: not disclosed
Crew: 4 + 6
Weight: 28.75 tons (29,200kg)
Length: 22ft 3in (6.79m)
Width: 10ft 7in (3.24m)
Height: 9ft 9in (2.98m)
Engine: Mercedes-Benz 833, 6-cylinder, diesel, 600bhp at 2,200rpm

Speed: 46mph (75km/hr)
Range: 325 miles (520km)

Marder 2 MICV Germany
Krauss-Maffei

This was a proposal for an improved Marder which would be ready for production in the mid-1990s, Krauss-Maffei having been selected in 1987 to produce a prototype. No firm details were released except that it would be more powerful, would have a larger troop compartment, and would use a newly-developed 35/50mm cannon from Rheinmetall in a power-operated turret. Shortly after Krauss-Maffei designers had sharpened their pencils the Berlin Wall came down, East and West Germany were re-united, and several defence contracts and proposals were forthwith scrapped. Among them was Marder 2.

MARS-15 IFV France
Creusot-Loire

1990. MARS was a proposal for a family of light armoured vehicles developed by Creusot-Loire. As well as this MICV, a light tank with a 90mm gun was also built in prototype form. The basic vehicle was a tracked machine with five roadwheels per side, front drive and rear idler and with the engine and transmission under the sloped glacis plate. The rear of the vehicle was formed into a box which could then be configured as a troop compartment or as a fighting compartment. In the MICV role the compartment carried a small turret with a 25mm Chain Gun; in the light tank role a larger turret could be provided with various types of armament up to 105mm calibre. Other variations were proposed, but the project never got beyond the prototype stage and was abandoned in the 1990s.

APC version

Armament: variable
Armour: not disclosed
Crew: 1 + 12
Weight: 15.05 tons (15,300kg)
Length: 19ft 8in (5.99m)
Width: 9ft 9in (2.98m)
Height: 6ft 4in (1.93m)
Engine: Baudouin diesel, 400bhp
Speed: 47mph (76km/hr)
Range: 370 miles (600km)

MLI-84 Romania
State factories

1983. This is a Romanian copy of the Soviet BMP-1 IFV, though the dimensions differ somewhat and it

has a permanently-mounted 12.7mm machine gun in an air defence mounting attached to the hull roof alongside a circular hatch which replaces one of the four rectangular hatches normally found on the BMP-1.

Armament: 1 × 73mm gun; 1 × ATGW; 1 × coaxial MG; 1 × AAMG
Armour: not disclosed
Crew: 2 + 9
Weight: 16.34 tons (16,600kg)
Length: 24ft 0in (7.32m)
Width: 10ft 3in (3.15m)
Height: 6ft 6in (1.97m)
Engine: V-8 turbocharged diesel, 350bhp
Speed: 40mph (65km/hr)
Range: 375 miles (600km)

ML-VM Romania
State factories

1985. This is described as a combat vehicle for mountain troops, though what particular features it has which justify this, apart from being short and light, are not apparent; in appearance it is very similar to the MLI-84 described above, though the wheels are spoked rather than the usual Soviet-style corrugated metal discs. There is a low, conical turret with a 14.5mm heavy machine gun and a 7.62mm machine gun mounted coaxially. The layout is the standard front engine and rear troop compartment, the turret being central; six men are seated down the sides and the seventh mans the turret. The troop compartment has a rear door, two roof hatches and firing ports. A variant model carries a 120mm mortar in the troop compartment, firing through a hatch and with a baseplate to permit deployment out of the vehicle.

Armament: 2 × MG
Armour: not disclosed
Crew: 2 + 7
Weight: 9.65 tons (9,800kg)
Length: 19ft 2in (5.85m)
Width: 9ft 5in (2.87m)
Height: 6ft 5in (1.95m)
Engine: turbocharged diesel
Speed: 31mph (50km/hr)
Range: 435 miles (700km)

Mowag Grenadier APC Switzerland
Mowag

1977. The 4 x 4 Grenadier was one of the many Mowag vehicles offered on the open market. This one was much like the Piranha (*qv*), but it was smaller and had a better power/weight ratio. In all other respects it seems to have been very similar and could be fitted with the usual range of armaments on the central roof hatch. It was fully amphibious, using a single propeller in the water. It was produced in the 1970s and sold in some numbers to undisclosed countries.

Armament: see text
Armour: not disclosed
Crew: 1 + 8
Weight: 6.0 tons (6,100kg)
Length: 15ft 9in (4.84m)
Width: 7ft 3in (2.22m)
Height: 5ft 6in (1.70m)
Engine: Mowag, 8-cylinder, petrol, 202bhp at 3,900rpm
Speed: 62mph (100km/hr)
Range: 342 miles (550km)

Mowag MR8-01 'Wotan' APC Switzerland
Büssing-NAG, Henschel (under licence)
1958. This vehicle was a very simple police armoured 4 x 4 carrier and it only saw service with the West German Border Police. Several prototypes were bought from Switzerland and about 600 were then built under licence in Germany. It had the engine at the left rear of the hull and the remainder of the interior was free space for the crew. There were two basic models. The **SW1** carried no armament, though some were seen fitted with an obstacle-clearing blade on the front. The **SW2** was a support vehicle and exactly the same as the SW1 but with a 20mm cannon in a small turret at the front of the hull. The Mowag company proposed one or two other variants with multiple rocket projectors, 130mm mortars and even a 90mm gun, but none were manufactured.

Armament, SW1: none
Armament, SW2: 1 x 20mm cannon
Armour: 10mm
Crew: 3–5
Weight: 8.07 tons (8,200kg)
Length: 17ft 4in (5.30m)
Width: 7ft 3in (2.22m)
Height: 6ft 3in (1.92m)
Engine: Chrysler R361, 6-cylinder, petrol, 160bhp
Speed: 50mph (80km/h)
Range: 248 miles (400km)

Mowag Piranha APC Switzerland
Mowag
1977. The Piranha was a private venture by Mowag and was intended for export. It has been supplied in three sizes, 4 x 4, 6 x 6 and 8 x 8, all having almost

exactly the same performance. All models have a simple welded hull with sloping sides and a sharply sloped glacis. The driver and engine are in front with a weapon installation behind him. A variety of turrets and weapons can be fitted, going up to 30mm cannon, 90mm anti-tank guns or 120mm mortars. The 8 x 8 is large enough to mount twin anti-aircraft 30mm cannon if needed, and it can also have a remotely-controlled machine gun on the rear roof. The usual hull has two firing ports in the sides and two more in the rear doors, so that the infantry can fire from under armour. The suspension is by torsion bar with special provision for long wheel travel, and for swimming there are two propellers under the rear doors. There is full NBC protection for all models and additional operating range can be achieved by fitting an extra external fuel tank. The 4 x 4 and 6 x 6 APC versions are in use by several countries, and the 8 x 8 version is used by Ghana and the US Marine Corps.

4 x 4 Version
Armament: variable, up to 1 x 20mm cannon
Armour: 10mm
Crew: 1 + 9
Weight: 6.89 tons (7,000kg)
Length: 17ft 3in (5.26m)
Width: 8ft 2in (2.50m)
Height: 6ft 1in (1.85m)
Engine: Mowag V-6 petrol, 216bhp at 2,900rpm
Speed: 62mph (100km/hr)
Range: 465 miles (750km)

6 x 6 Version
Armament: variable, up to 1 x 90mm
Armour: 10mm
Crew: 1 + 13
Weight: 10.33 tons (10,500kg)
Length: 19ft 6in (5.97m)
Width: 8ft 2in (2.50m)
Height: 6ft 1in (1.85m)
Engine: Mowag V-6 petrol, 300bhp at 2,800rpm
Speed: 62mph (100km/hr)
Range: 370 miles (600km)

8 x 8 Version
Armament: variable, up to 1 x 90mm
Armour: 10mm
Crew: 1 + 14
Weight: 12.10 tons (12,300kg)
Length: 20ft 10in (6.36m)
Width: 8ft 2in (2.50m)
Height: 6ft 1in (1.85m)
Engine: Mowag V-6 petrol, 300bhp at 2,800rpm
Speed: 62mph (100km/hr)
Range: 485 miles (780km)

Mowag Piranha 10 x 10 MICV Switzerland
Mowag

1995. This is dealt with separately from the earlier Piranhas since it is an entirely new vehicle. Although keeping to the same general formula it does not have the individual wheel recesses of the smaller vehicles and groups the wheels into four and six, with a prominent gap between the two groups. With a larger payload capability and larger internal space, nevertheless it will fit into a C-130 aircraft and can be air-lifted. The standard configuration uses a GIAT turret with 105mm gun, but virtually any desired armament or equipment can be fitted. The vehicle has been adopted by Sweden as an armoured command vehicle, with a large slab-sided superstructure and as a surveillance and target acquisition vehicle carrying a radar on the end of an articulated arm.

Armament: 1 x 105mm; 2 x MG; or variations
Armour: not disclosed
Crew: 4–6 according to role
Weight: 17.71 tons (18,000kg)
Length: 24ft 5in (7.45m)
Width: 8ft 6in (2.60m)
Height, with turret: 9ft 10in (2.99m)
Engine: Detroit Diesel, 350bhp
Speed: 62mph (100km/hr)
Range: 500 miles (800km)

Mowag Roland APC Switzerland
Mowag

1970. The Roland is a simple 4 x 4 armoured vehicle intended for use a an internal security vehicle rather than a military personnel carrier for modern battle. It is in service with several South American countries and it has been made under licence in Argentina. The engine is at the rear on the left side, so that there is only one rear door and the troops have a door on each side under the turret. The turret can accept a variety of light armaments, but it usually mounts a single machine gun. The basic vehicle is kept simple so that the user can add the special equipment that he needs. No attempt has been made to give an amphibious capability.

Armament: 1 x MG
Armour: 8mm
Crew: 3 + 4
Weight: 4.62 tons (4,700kg)
Length: 14ft 6in (4.45m)
Width: 6ft 7in (2.01m)
Height: 6ft 8in (2.03m)
Engine: Chrysler, V-8, petrol, 202bhp at 3,900rpm
Speed: 68mph (110km/hr)
Range: 340 miles (550km)

Mowag Shark Weapons Carrier
Switzerland
Mowag

1981. In spite of the title, this was an 8 x 8 fighting vehicle which could carry a variety of potent armament, such as 90mm or 105mm tank guns in suitable turrets. The hull was of the sloped-plate form used in all the Mowag range, with a turret ring such that it could accept a number of proprietary turrets and guns. Demonstration models were displayed using the French FL-20 turret with 105mm gun, a Rheinmetall turret and gun, a Bofors turret with 40mm Trinity AA gun, and various missile fits including ADATS. No orders resulted, and Mowag withdrew the design in the early 1990s in order to improve it.

Armament: variable, up to 1 x 105mm
Armour: not disclosed
Crew: 3 or 4
Weight: 21.65 tons (22,000kg)
Length: 24ft 8in (7.52m)
Width: 9ft 10in (3.0m)
Height: 6ft 3in (1.90m) to hull top, without turret
Engine: Detroit Diesel, V-8 turbocharged diesel, 530bhp at 2,500rpm
Speed: 62mph (100km/hr)
Range: 310 miles (500km)

Mowag Spy Reconnaissance Vehicle
Switzerland
Mowag

1980. The Spy was developed as a spin-off from the Piranha series and is basically a 4 x 4 Piranha with additions. The driver and engine are at the front of the sloped-plate hull, and there is a turret at the rear end of the troop compartment; this can be a one-man or a remote-controlled type, and is usually armed with a heavy machine gun and possibly a coaxial rifle-calibre machine gun as well. In fact, the Spy is a small armoured car, and reconnaissance is a function of the crew, and nothing to do with the vehicle or its equipment. Numbers have been sold, but Mowag never say to whom they sell; you just have to watch out for them.

Armament: 1 or 2 MG
Armour: not disclosed
Crew: 3
Weight: 7.38 tons (7,500kg)
Length: 14ft 10in (4.52m)
Width: 8ft 3in (2.50m)
Height: 5ft 5in (1.66m) to hull roof
Engine: Cummins diesel, V-6 195bhp at 2,800rpm
Speed: 68mph (110km/hr)
Range: 435 miles (700km)

Mowag Taifun MICV Italy
OTO-*Melara*

1977. The Taifun was an experimental 6 x 6 vehicle by Oto Melara and it was largely based on the Swiss Mowag. It was intended to be a highly mobile MICV capable of being adapted to several different roles. The basic layout was slightly altered from that of the Mowag in that the driver has the gun turret beside him and the power pack immediately behind him, in the middle of the vehicle. This arrangement allowed the gunner and driver to be close together, which is an important point when the infantry have dismounted and left the vehicle in their charge. However, it brings difficulties in servicing the engine, though it was claimed that this was easily hoisted out. The standard armament fit used a turret of the same type as is fitted to the Fiat-OTO 6616 armoured car plus two machine guns on remote mountings at the rear and ball mounts in the sides for personal weapons. The infantry sat facing outwards and had a powered ramp at the rear instead of a door. The suspension used six roadwheels sprung by torsion bars. Three variants were proposed, one of them having a 76mm gun in a turret the same as is on the Scorpion armoured vehicle. However, the Italian Army evinced little or no interest, the vehicles proved to be expensive and complex, and the project was abandoned in the early 1980s in favour of simpler designs.

Armament: 1 x 20mm cannon; 3 x MG
Armour: 30mm
Crew: 3 + 6
Weight: 22.43 tons (22,800kg)
Length: 22ft 4in (6.82m)
Width: 10ft 4in (3.15m)
Height: 7ft 8in (2.37m)
Engine: V-8, 2-stroke turbocharged diesel, 530bhp
Speed: 43mph (70km/hr)
Range: 310 miles (500km)

Mowag Tornado MICV Switzerland
Mowag

1980. The Tornado is another of the Mowag range which was offered to several governments through the 1980s. It was a very sophisticated and well-equipped tracked vehicle with an impressive specification and in many ways was not unlike the German Marder. The driver and engine sat beside each other in the front with the commander behind the driver. The gunner was in the middle of the vehicle in a small turret with a remote controlled 25mm cannon above it. This unusual arrangement allowed the gunner's turret to be little more than a large observation cupola and the externally

mounted gun did not significantly add to the silhouette. There were two firing ports in each side of the troop compartment which allowed the troops to fire sub-machine guns, and there were two more in the rear doors. The standard vehicle had two remotely-controlled external machine gun mounts on the rear roof, both of them identical to that used on the early Marder. There was full NBC protection, night-driving aids and an automatic fire-extinguishing system. It was not amphibious as it was too heavy, but it could wade to a depth of 4ft 3in (1.30m). Nevertheless, there were no takers and it was dropped from the Mowag catalogue in the early 1990s.

Armament: 1 x 25mm cannon; 2 x MG
Armour: not disclosed
Crew: 2 + 8
Weight: 16.92 tons (17,200kg)
Length: 19ft 9in (6.05m)
Width: 10ft 4in (3.15m)
Height: 6ft 3in (1.92m)
Engine: Mowag M8 DV-TLK, 8-cylinder, multi-fuel, 430bhp at 2,100rpm
Speed: 44mph (70km/hr)
Range: 372 miles (600km)

MT-LB Russia
State factories

1980. This was originally developed as a tracked towing vehicle for heavy artillery, but thereafter it was adapted to innumerable purposes, from being a command car to a logistic supply truck, a self-propelled radar station, a mortar carrier or an engineer vehicle. It is a fairly standard PT-76 derivative, with the driver and engine in the front of the hull, behind a well-sloped glacis plate. There is a single machine gun in a turret and a commander's cupola, both well forward in the hull, leaving the rear clear for the cargo and troop compartment. The suspension has six roadwheels and no return rollers, and the springing is by torsion bars. It can carry up to 11 passengers, a payload of 2,000kg and tow a 6,500kg trailer. The vehicle is fully amphibious, being propelled in the water by its tracks. In addition to Russian service, it is in use by Bulgaria, Czech Republic, Finland, Hungary, Iraq, Poland, Slovak Republic and Serbia.

Armament: 1 x MG
Armour: 10mm
Crew: 2 + 11
Weight: 11.71 tons (11,900kg)
Length: 21ft 2in (6.45m)
Width: 9ft 5in (2.86m)
Height: 6ft 1in (1.86m)

Engine: V-8 diesel, 240bhp at 2,100rpm
Speed: 38mph (62km/hr)
Range: 320 miles (500km)

Multi-Role Armoured Vehicle (MRAV)
UK/France/Germany
ARTEC
1998. This is a tripartite venture to produce a Multi-Role Armoured Vehicle – primarily as a wheeled APC – for use by the three countries concerned and, possibly, for export thereafter. Contracts were issued in 1998 for the production of 14 prototype vehicles. At the present time only artist's impressions and general arrangement drawings have been divulged, showing proposed 6 x 6 and 8 x 8 vehicles. They are of conventional form, with sloped front, boxy superstructure, and large, evenly-spaced wheels recessed into the hull sides. Armament is suggested as a remote-control cupola with a machine gun and possibly a 40mm grenade launcher. Whether this results in a serviceable vehicle or whether the project goes the way of most multi-national projects of the last forty years, remains to be seen. The following specifications are entirely provisional.

MRAV 6 x 6
Armament: 1 x MG, 1 x grenade launcher
Armour: not disclosed
Crew: 10
Weight: 26.08 tons (26,500kg)
Length: 23ft 9in (7.23m)
Width: 9ft 10in (2.99m)
Height: 7ft 10in (2.38m)
Engine: diesel, 530bhp
Speed: 65mph (105km/hr)
Range: 680 miles (1,100km)

MRAV 8 x 8
Armament: 1 x MG, 1 x grenade launcher
Armour: not disclosed
Crew: 11
Weight: 32.48 tons (33,000kg)
Length: 25ft 10in (7.88m)
Width: 9ft 10in (2.99m)
Height: 7ft 10in (2.38m)
Engine: diesel, 710bhp
Speed: 65mph (105km/hr)
Range: 680 miles (1,100km)

NFV-1 IFV China/USA
Norinco, FMC
1986. This is another of the many abortive cooperative designs which appeared in the 1980s. In this case it was a combination of the hull and chassis of the Chinese WZ501 IFV (which was a copy of the Russian BMP-1) with a turret designed by the FMC Company and mounting a 25mm M242 Chain Gun and a coaxial FN MAG machine gun. The turret was a one-man design, electrically operated, and with day and night sights, laser rangefinding and all mod. cons. In most respects it was similar to the earlier NVH-1 MICV (*qv*) which was an Anglo-Chinese effort using different components, and one has a suspicion that there was some competitive element at work. The prototype was exhibited, then put through its paces by the Egyptian Army in 1987, after which no more was heard of it.

Armament: 1x 25mm; 1 x MG
Armour: not disclosed
Crew: 3 + 8
Weight: 13.39 tons (13,600kg)
Length: 22ft 2in (6.74m)
Width: 9ft 9in (2.97m)
Height: 8ft 2in (2.48m)
Engine: V-5 diesel, 293bhp at 2,300rpm
Speed: 40mph (65km/hr)
Range: 285 miles (460km)

NVH-1 MICV China/UK
Norinco, Vickers
1984. This appeared at a military exhibition in China in late 1984 and was a combination of the body of the Chinese YW-531 (or Type 85, or H-1 as it was then called) modified to carry a two-man turret which had been designed by Vickers. This was fitted with a 25mm Chain Gun and a coaxial 7.62mm Chain Gun, together with day and night sights, laser rangefinding and various other technical novelties. A prototype was built and exhibited, but no interest was aroused and no more were ever produced.

Armament: 1 x 25mm; 1 x MG
Armour: not disclosed
Crew: 2 + 9
Weight: 15.75 tons (16,000kg)
Length: 19ft 9in (6.03m)
Width: 10ft 0in (3.06m)
Height: 9ft 1in (2.77m)
Engine: Deutz V-8 turbocharged air-cooled diesel, 320bhp at 2,500rpm
Speed: 40mph (65km/hr)
Range: 310 miles (500km)

Orca Chile
See Cardoen VTP-1

OT-62 APC Czechoslovakia
State factories

1964. The OT-62 was the Czechoslovakian version of the Soviet BTR-50P, but there were some differences. The Czech vehicle was completely closed-in and so resembled the command vehicle rather than the APC. It also had a more powerful engine and a better performance. In all other respects it resembled the Soviet vehicle and the details will not be repeated here. The **OT-62A** was the basic model and normally carried no armament, relying on the personal weapons of the crew. It was sometimes fitted with a recoilless gun on the rear deck. The **OT-62B** had a small turret at the right front, armed with a machine gun, and an 82mm recoilless gun alongside the turret. The **OT-62C** was supplied to the Polish Army and had a centrally mounted turret with a 14.5mm machine gun. There were also a number of models designated **OT-62R** which carried various communications options.

OT-62B

Armament: 1 x MG; optional 82mm RCL
Armour: 14mm
Crew: 2 + 18
Weight: 15.74 tons (16,000kg)
Length: 22ft 10in (7.00m)
Width: 10ft 6in (3.20m)
Height: 7ft 2in (2.20m)
Engine: Model PV-6, 6-cylinder, supercharged, diesel, 300bhp at 2,000rpm
Speed: 37mph (60km/hr)
Range: 310 miles (500km)

OT-64 APC Czechoslovakia
State factories

1962. The OT-64 dates from a design study of 1959, which was undertaken jointly by Poland and Czechoslovakia, and both continue to use the vehicle together with at least eight other countries. It is large, fairly heavy and probably rather complicated. It is an 8 x 8 with semi-automatic transmission and a central air system to all wheels and tyres. The hull is built up round a tubular frame, suggesting Tatra origins. Driver and commander are at the extreme front, with the engine between them and the infantry compartment. Over this latter compartment there are six hatches and in most models two of them are replaced with a turret, usually the one used on the Russian BRDM-2. The vehicle is fully NBC protected, and is amphibious, being propelled by two screw propellers in the rear of the hull. There are several variants in service: one carries 'Sagger' ATGW on launchers on each side of the turret.

Armament: 1 or 2 MG
Armour: 10mm
Crew: 2 + 18
Weight: 14.07 tons (14,300kg)
Length: 24ft 5in (7.44m)
Width: 8ft 3in (2.50m)
Height: 6ft 6in (2.00m)
Engine: Tatra Model T 928-14, V-8, air-cooled, diesel, 180bhp at 2,000rpm
Speed: 37mph (60km/hr)
Range: 310 miles (500km)

OT-90 Czechoslovakia
State factories

1985. This is the Russian BMP-1 MICV built under licence in Czechoslovakia and with a few modifications to suit the Czech preferences. The principal change is the removal of the Russian turret and its replacement by that of the OT-64 APC, using a 14.5mm machine gun as the main weapon and a 7.62mm machine gun as the coaxial weapon. The reason for this was that the BMP-1 vehicles originally operated by the Czechs were armed with the 73mm gun and consequently rated as tanks for the purposes of Conventional Forces Limitation agreements. Changing the turrets and reclassifying them as MICVs evaded this limitation, but by the mid-1990s it had been decided not to pursue the conversions, and the OT-90 will be allowed to die out by natural wastage.

OT-810 APC Czechoslovakia
State factories

1948. This was a remarkable hang-over from World War Two, since it was actually the German three-quarter-tracked armoured carrier Sd Kfz 251, which had been built by Skoda during the war. After the war they continued making them for the Czech Army, and in the 1950s they improved the design by fitting a Tatra engine and some extra armour. The general layout immediately dates the design: the engine is in front under a long hood, the driver and commander sit side by side in the cab, and the troop compartment is behind them, above the tracked suspension, with doors at the rear. There was no fixed armament, but it was usual to see these cars with a machine gun on the commander's hatch. The only known variant was an anti-tank vehicle with an 82mm recoilless gun in the rear of the car and with the sides capable of being folded down to allow for traverse. Numbers were also supplied to Romania in the 1950s. They remained in use in both countries well into the late 1980s.

Armament: 1 × MG
Armour: 12mm
Crew: 2 + 10
Weight: 8.36 tons (8,500kg)
Length: 19ft 1in (5.92m)
Width: 6ft 9in (2.10m)
Height: 5ft 8in (1.75m)
Engine: Tatra, 6-cylinder, air-cooled, diesel, 120bhp
Speed: 32mph (52km/hr)
Range: 198 miles (320km)

Otokar Cobra APC Turkey
Otokar

1997. This 4 x 4 wheeled APC has an interesting parentage. The steel body is made in Turkey and then fitted to a chassis which is built from components of the American General Motors Expanded Capacity Vehicle, which is based upon the chassis and running gear of the HMMWV High Mobility Vehicle. The result is a slope-sided vehicle with large bullet-proof windscreens for driver and commander, a small troop compartment behind them and a turret carrying a machine gun, spotlight and smoke discharger. There is a rear door, as well as side doors for the cab occupants. The Cobra can also be configured as an ambulance, a command post or a reconnaissance vehicle, and a number of each of these variations are in service with the Turkish Army.

Armament: 1 × MG
Armour: not disclosed
Crew: 2 + 7
Weight: 5.90 tons (6,000kg)
Length: 17ft 6in (5.32m)
Width: 7ft 1in (2.16m)
Height: 6ft 3in (1.90m) to hull top
Engine: GMC V-8 turbocharged diesel, 190bhp at 3,400rpm
Speed: 68mph (110km/hr)
Range: 340 miles (550km)

OTO-Melara C13 IFV Italy
OTO-Melara

1983. The C13 was developed as an export sales item, intending to improve upon existing IFVs by giving the vehicle better armour and better mobility. Fully tracked, with six roadwheels each side suspended by torsion bars, it had the engine at the right front, with the driver on the left, a sloping nose and a flat-topped hull with a turret capable of mounting a variety of ordnance. The rear section was the troop compartment, entered by means of a power-operated ramp door in the rear. The compartment was provided with vision blocks and

firing ports down each side. A number of prototypes were built between 1983 and 1990 and the design was completed, but no production took place.

Armament: 1 × HMG; other options
Armour: aluminium 50mm; steel 13mm
Crew: 3 + 9
Weight: 14.41 tons (14,650kg)
Length: 17ft 5in (5.65m)
Width: 8ft 11in (2.71m)
Height: 8ft 1in (2.47m)
Engine: Isotta-Fraschini V-6 supercharged diesel, 360bhp at 2,800rpm
Speed: 43mph (70km/hr)
Range: 310 miles (500km)

Oxford Carrier UK
Morris

1944. Wartime experience led to a number of suggestions for improving the design of the Universal carrier, and in 1944 work began on the **Carrier, Tracked, CT20**, which became known as the Oxford Carrier. This vehicle used the same type of suspension as its predecessors, but had a greatly improved body design incorporating a double-plate floor for protection against mines. The front was built up to give better protection and the driver was provided with periscope vision equipment. The transmission and steering arrangements were also improved, with the adoption of automatic transmission and controlled differential steering. Armoured plates protected the track upper run, storage capacity was improved and seating was in a crew compartment behind the driver, with the engine at the rear. For all its virtues the Oxford had a short life; by the time production began, the war was over and production contracts were severely reduced. It was employed for some years after the war as an infantry machine-gun or mortar carrier and as a towing vehicle for various anti-tank guns.

Armament: none; crew personal weapons only
Armour: 20mm
Crew: 2 + 4
Weight: 7.84 tons (7,975kg)
Length: 14ft 9in (4.49m)
Width: 7ft 7in (2.28m)
Height: 5ft 7in (1.70m)
Engine: Cadillac V-8, petrol, 110bhp at 3,200rpm
Speed: 31mph (50km/hr)
Range: 125 miles (200km)

Panhard EBR ETT APC France
Panhard et Levassor

1959. This vehicle was a variant of the Panhard EBR-75 armoured car and only 30 were built. They were specifically intended for the French colonies and all were sent to Africa, and in subsequent years they passed into other hands. The vehicle has the same chassis as the EBR, but the rear driver's position is taken out and two rear doors put in place of it. The hull is built up into a long troop compartment in which the infantry sit back to back facing outwards. The sloping sides of the compartment lift up to give a good field of fire and also to let in cooling air. Two small turrets for machine guns are placed at each end of the troop compartment and the two centre wheels have pneumatic tyres instead of steel rims. Cross-country mobility is said to be good, but the vehicle was obviously not a success, perhaps because it was too expensive for a mere troop taxicab.

Armament: none fitted, turrets could take 2 × MG
Armour: 15mm
Crew: 1 + 14
Weight: 13.29 tons (13,500kg)
Length: 18ft 3in (5.56m)
Width: 7ft 11in (2.42m)
Height: 7ft 7in (2.32m)
Engine: Panhard, 12-cylinder, horizontally-opposed, petrol, 200bhp at 3,700rpm
Speed: 65mph (105km/hr)
Range: 404 miles (650km)

Panhard M3 APC France
Panhard et Levassor

1971. The M3 has been a most successful APC and very large numbers have been built and sold all over the world. It is in service with at least 12 armies and many more police forces and is still in production. It is a straightforward and relatively simple design and is capable of being adapted to many uses without great expense. The driver is in the extreme front of the welded hull with the engine and gearboxes directly behind him. The remainder of the vehicle is taken up by the rather chunky troop compartment, which has four doors, eight firing ports and two hatches. A wide variety of armaments can be fitted to either or both of the hatches, and there are several kinds of turret which drop on. The number of variants is at least nine, and there are more if the types of armament are considered as separate models. The vehicle swims, propelling itself by its wheels, but there is no NBC protection.

Armament: see text
Armour: 12mm

Crew: 2 + 10
Weight: 5.98 tons (6,080kg)
Length: 14ft 6in (4.45m)
Width: 7ft 9in (2.40m)
Height: 8ft 2in (2.48m)
Engine: Panhard 4HD, 4-cylinder, horizontally-opposed, petrol, 90bhp at 4,700rpm
Speed: 62mph (100km/hr)
Range: 372 miles (600km)

Panhard VBC APC
See Ultrav M11

Panhard VCR (6 x 6) APC France
Panhard et Levassor

1975. Developed as a possible export venture, this wheeled APC was sold to several countries during the 1970s. It is rather unusual in its design, since it has six wheels, but uses only the outer four on hard surfaces, only lowering the centre pair of wheels to the ground when preparing to move across rough country. A boxy vehicle with a sloping nose, it has the driver centrally in front, the commander behind to his left and the engine behind to his right. The troop compartment holds ten men, seated five each side on bench seats. They enter and leave by a large rear door, and have two hatches in the roof. The usual armament was one machine gun on the roof, behind the commander; but other armament could be fitted, up to and including 20mm cannon, though the more involved the armament, the fewer the men that could be carried.

Armament: 1 × MG
Armour: 12mm
Crew: 3 + 9
Weight: 7.77 tons (7,900kg)
Length: 16ft 0in (4.88m)
Width: 8ft 2in (2.48m)
Height: 7ft 0in (2.13m)
Engine: Peugeot V-6, petrol, 155bhp at 5,500rpm
Speed: 62mph (100km/hr)
Range: 500 miles (800km)

Panhard VCR (4 x 4) APC France
Panhard et Levassor

1979. This was essentially a 4 x 4 version of the 6 x 6 VCR above, over 90% of the components being common to both. Indeed, the only essential difference is the absence of the central pair of wheels and their associated mechanical arrangements, the length of hull being the same. A small number were sold to Argentina, but beyond that there do not appear to have been any other adoptions.

Armament: I × MG
Armour: not disclosed
Crew: 3 + 9
Weight: 6.69 tons (6,800kg)
Length: 16ft 0in (4.88m)
Width: 8ft 2in (2.48m)
Height: 7ft 0in (2.13m)
Engine: Peugeot V-6, petrol, 155bhp at 5,500rpm
Speed: 62mph (100km/hr)
Range: 500 miles (800km)

Panhard VCR-TT2 APC France
Panhard et Levassor
1985. This was another private venture by Panhard, intended as a possible future replacement for the original VCR. It is a 6 x 6 wheeled vehicle, in two-and-four configuration, with a slope-sided hull and sloped front. The driver sits centrally and the engine compartment is behind him. There are side doors in the hull, behind the first roadwheels, and also a large rear door and four roof hatches. The troop compartment seats 12 men, and the main armament is located at the forward end of the compartment. This can be anything from a light machine gun to a 25mm cannon, according to what the customer desires. The vehicle is amphibious, and has two propeller units at the rear of the hull.

Armament: as desired, up to 25mm
Armour: not disclosed
Crew: 2 + 12
Weight: 9.45 tons (9,600kg)
Length: 20ft 2in (6.14m)
Width: 8ft 10in (2.70m)
Height: 7ft 5in (2.27m)
Engine: Peugeot: 2 × V-6 petrol, total 290bhp,
        or 2 × VXD3 diesel, total 196bhp
Speed: 68mph (110km/hr)
Range: 620 miles (1000km) (diesel)

Panhard VCR-2 France
Panhard et Levassor
1998. This was a development of the VCR-TT2 described above, converting the design into an 8 x 8 configuration It was primarily produced to meet a demand from Poland for a suitable wheeled APC, but although the Poles have received submissions from several makers, no selection has yet been made. The proposed VCR-2 is little more than the VCR-TT2 with the hull extended and another pair of wheels added; and until the Poles make up their minds it will remain a paper project. The following specification is entirely provisional.

Armament: I × 25mm cannon; I × MG
Armour: not disclosed

Crew: 2 + up to 10
Weight: not more than 14.75 tons (15,000kg)
Length: 19ft 8in (6.0m)
Width: 8ft 10in (2.70m)
Height: 5ft 11in (1.80m)
Engine: twin Peugeot V-6 diesels, total 290bhp
Speed: 62mph (100km/hr)
Range: 500 miles (800km)

Panserbandvagn (Pbv) 301 APC Sweden
Hagglund
1961. *Panserbandvagn* = 'armoured tracked vehicle'. The Pbv 301 was unusual in that it was one of the very few post-war conversions of a tank to an APC. The basis was the Strv m/41 light tank, which was really the 1938 Czechoslovak TNH built under licence in Sweden. These tanks were quite obsolete by the mid-1950s, but were in excellent condition and capable of running on for many more years, so the Hagglund company completely rebuilt them into APCs, a conversion which required a fundamental restructuring of the entire vehicle. The engine was moved from the rear to the front, a new transmission was installed and the superstructure was built up to make a suitable troop compartment. A rear door was fitted and a domed cupola put on the roof with an external machine gun on top of that. The finished APC was very good, although it only carried eight infantry. It had no swimming capability, but was otherwise fully equipped. It was replaced by the Pbv 302 (*qv*).

Armament: I × MG
Armour: 12mm
Crew: 2 + 8
Weight: 11.32 tons (11,500kg)
Length: 15ft 2in (4.66m)
Width: 7ft 4in (2.23m)
Height: 8ft 7in (2.64m)
Engine: Scania-Vabis, 6-cylinder, petrol, 160bhp
Speed: 26mph (45km/h)
Range: 120 miles (200km)

Pbv 302 APC Sweden
Hagglund
1966. The Pbv 302 was introduced to give the Swedish infantry a carrier that could operate in conjunction with the S Tank, and the design was completely new and owed nothing to previous vehicles in military service. The layout follows the general practice of putting the engine in front with the driver, but in this case it is under the floor and the driver sits above it. There is a turret mounting a 20mm cannon on the front left side of the hull, and the commander has a cupola on the right. From the

start of the design it was intended that vehicle should be capable of fighting and protecting itself in an armoured battle. Although the sides are flat and high, the vision is good and the infantry can open two long hatch covers and fire their weapons over the roof. There are no firing ports and the vehicle is amphibious without preparation apart from raising the bow vane. The troop compartment is roomy and well heated in winter.

Armament: 1 × 20mm cannon
Armour: 20mm
Crew: 2 + 10
Weight: 13.29 tons (13,500kg)
Length: 17ft 7in (5.35m)
Width: 9ft 5in (2.86m)
Height: 8ft 2in (2.49m)
Engine: Volvo-Penta 6-cylinder, turbocharged diesel, 280bhp at 2,200rpm
Speed: 41mph (66km/hr)
Range: 186 miles (300km)

Pbv 401 APC Sweden
Neubrandenburg
These are actually the Russian MT-LB multi-purpose vehicle which originally were part of the equipment of the East German Army. After the re-unification of Germany they were offered for sale; Sweden bought a few to test, liked them, and contracted for 1,000, doubtless at fire-sale prices. They further asked for 450 to be refurbished in Germany to suit their requirements, and these became the Pvb 401; the refurbishment involves improved lighting systems, changes to the hatches, storage arrangements and other minor conveniences. Dimensions and performance remain the same as the basic MT-LB vehicle, and reference should be made to that entry.

Patria XA-180 APC Finland
See Sisu XA-180

Pizarro IFV Spain
Steyr-Daimler-Puch, Santa Barbara
1998. This is the Spanish name for the Ascod MICV (*qv*) produced by collaboration between Steyr-Daimler-Puch and Santa Barbara. Over 400 are required by the Spanish Army and the first batch of 125 began production in 1998.

PSZH-4 APC Hungary
State factories
1970. This light 4 x 4 wheeled APC is derived from the FUG scout car and uses the same basic hull and running gear, differing in having the forward end of the hull built up into a higher structure and topped with a small turret carrying a 14.5mm machine gun with a 7.62mm coaxial gun. The engine is in the rear of the vehicle, and access to the troop compartment and turret is by means of doors in each side of the hull. The vehicle is amphibious, NBC-protected, and equipped with infra-red driving lights.

Armament: 2 × MG
Armour: not disclosed
Crew: 3 + 6
Weight: 7.48 tons (7,600kg)
Length: 18ft 8in (5.7m)
Width: 8ft 3in (2.5m)
Height: 7ft 6in (2.3m)
Engine: Csepel 4-cylinder diesel, 100bhp at 2,300rpm
Speed: 50mph (80km/hr)
Range: 310 miles (500km)

Puma APC Israel
Israeli Defence Force Workshops
1994. This is rather unusual, being an APC dedicated to the combat engineer rather than the infantryman. It is based upon a redundant Centurion tank chassis from which the turret has been removed and the superstructure built up to give the occupants rather more room. There are two hatches in the roof, and a remote-controlled heavy machine gun mount. There are also various clamps and brackets for engineer equipment, and doubtless the interior is re-arranged to facilitate storage of the specialist equipment. The vehicle is exceptionally well armoured, using additional composite armour and with the ability to fit explosive reactive armour if required.

Data: none disclosed

Puma APC Italy
Iveco
1990. This was developed as a wheeled APC to accompany the Centauro tank destroyer (*qv*). Two basic models, 4 x 4 and 6 x 6, were developed, together with designs for a variety of different versions carrying missiles, mortars, air defence guns and so forth. So far as is known, only the basic model has been accepted for service. In either configuration, the vehicle is a conventional slope-side, slope-front box, with the engine at the front and the troop compartment at the rear, surmounted by a machine gun mount on one of the roof hatches. Access is by the usual rear door plus doors in each side.

4 x 4 Version
Armament: 1 x MG
Armour: not disclosed
Crew: 1 + 6
Weight: 5.41 tons (5,500kg)
Length: 15ft 3in (4.65m)
Width: 6ft 10in (2.08m)
Height: 5ft 6in (1.67m)
Engine: Iveco 4-cylinder diesel, 180bhp at 3,000rpm
Speed: 65mph (105km/hr)
Range: 500 miles (800km)

6 x 6 Version
Armament: 1 x MG
Armour: not disclosed
Crew: 1 + 8
Weight: 7.38 tons (7,500kg)
Length: 16ft 5in (5.0m)
Width: 7ft 6in (2.3m)
Height: 5ft 7in (1.7m)
Engine: Iveco 4-cylinder diesel, 180bhp at 3,000rpm
Speed: not disclosed
Range: not disclosed

Ratel MICV South Africa
Sandcock-Austral
1976. This is a 6 x 6 wheeled vehicle, arranged two-and-four, designed in South Africa to suit environmental conditions there. Like most South African vehicles of that period, special attention has been paid to protection from mine explosions. The hull is of armour steel; the driver sits centrally at the front; behind him is the turret, with the commander, main gunner and anti-aircraft gunner. The troop compartment is entered by means of side doors, and has seats for six men. The engine compartment is at the rear of the vehicle. The basic vehicle was the **Ratel 90**, armed with a 90mm gun in the turret; later variants were the **Ratel 60**, with a 60mm gun-mortar in the turret, the **Ratel 20** with a 20mm cannon, and the **Ratel Command**, with a 12.7mm machine gun.

Ratel 90
Armament: 1 x 90mm gun; 3 x MG
Armour: 20mm
Crew: 4 + 6
Weight: 18.70 tons (19,000kg)
Length: 23ft 8in (7.21m)
Width: 8ft 5in (2.52m)
Height: 9ft 7in (2.92m)
Engine: 6-cylinder turbocharged diesel, 282bhp at 2,200rpm
Speed: 65mph (105km/hr)
Range: 620 miles (1,000km)

Renault VAB APC France
Renault
1977. The Renault VAB (*Véhicule de l'Avant Blindé*) arose from a French Army decision to equip mechanized infantry with a tracked MICV and the rest with a wheeled vehicle. The tracked vehicle was the AMX-10P. A competitive trial of three designs was held to select the wheeled vehicle, which produced this model from Saviem, a company which was part of the Renault group. Renault then became the prime contractor. Several thousand have been built, and as well as equipping the French Army they have been sold widely in both 4 x 4 and 6 x 6 models.

As far as possible commercial components have been used in the design to keep costs down. The hull is the usual welded box with driver and commander in front and the power pack behind them in one unit. There are hatches and vision ports in the troop compartment, all of which close and seal so that the vehicle can swim without preparation apart from raising the bow vane. Water propulsion is by water jets and NBC protection is standard. Armament is optional, but the basic vehicle has no turret. About 30 variant models have been developed, for military and police purposes, though not all these have found customers. The French Army use more 4 x 4 than 6 x 6 models, but overseas sales seem to be equally divided.

4 x 4 Version
Armament: see text
Armour: not disclosed
Crew: 2 + 10
Weight: 13.38 tons (13,600kg)
Length: 20ft 0in (6.10m)
Width: 8ft 2in (2.50m)
Height: 6ft 11in (2.10m)
Engine: Renault, 6-cylinder, turbocharged diesel, 250bhp at 2,500rpm
Speed: 62mph (110km/hr)
Range: 800 miles (1,00km)

6 x 6 Version
Armament: see text
Armour: not disclosed
Crew: 2 + 10
Weight: 14.57 tons (14,800kg)
Length: 20ft 0in (6.10m)
Width: 8ft 2in (2.50m)
Height: 6ft 11in (2.10m)
Engine: Renault, 6-cylinder, turbocharged diesel, 250bhp at 2,500rpm
Speed: 62mph (110km/hr)
Range: 800 miles (1,00km)

Renault WERE Carrier France
Renault
1931. This was another of the many two-man machine-gun carriers spawned by the Carden-Loyd designs of the late 1920s, though most of these Renault vehicles were unarmed and used as cargo carriers for forward infantry. Some were given a machine-gun for the co-driver, and most were given a tracked trailer to tow, since the actual load-carrying space on the vehicle was limited. A surprising number found their way to Britain in 1940 where they were mostly used by the Polish Army as tank-driver training vehicles.

Armament: 1 × MG
Armour: 7mm
Crew: 2
Weight: 2.10 tons (2,135kg)
Length: 8ft 10in (2.69m)
Width: 5ft 7in (1.79m)
Height: 3ft 5in (1.04m)
Engine: Renault 4-cylinder, petrol, 35bhp
Speed: 18mph (30km/hr)
Range: 62 miles (100km)

RN-94 APC Turkey/Romania
Nurol, Romarm
1995. This is a 6 x 6 wheeled APC developed as a joint venture by a Turkish and a Romanian company, with a view to adoption by the Turkish Army. Of conventional form, with slope-sided hull and sharp prow, it may be fitted with a small turret with cannon or heavy machine gun, or merely have a machine gun in a hatch mounting. Driver and commander are at the front of the vehicle, and the engine compartment is behind them, with a passageway alongside to give access to the troop compartment. This has double doors at the rear and can accommodate 11 fully-equipped men. The vehicle currently exists in pre-production form, with various armament fits, and is undergoing trials in Turkey, after which the final form and armament will be decided and production will commence.

Armament: 1 × 25mm cannon + 1 × MG;
 or 1 × HMG + 1 × MG
Armour: not disclosed
Crew: 2 + 11
Weight: 12.80 tons (13,000kg)
Length: 22ft 0in (6.72m)
Width: 9ft 2in (2.80m)
Height: 9ft 0in (2.74m)
Engine: Cummins diesel, 240bhp at 2,400rpm
Speed: 68mph (110km/hr)
Range: 310 miles (500km)

Saracen APC UK
Alvis
1953. The Saracen APC was basically the same vehicle as the Saladin armoured car, using a welded steel hull carried on six independently-sprung and driven wheels, the front four of which were steerable. The suspension was such that the loss of any one wheel, as, for example, by running over a mine, would not immobilize the vehicle. The engine was at the front, under an armored hood, with the driver seated centrally behind it. Behind the driver were the vehicle commander and the radio operator. The crew compartment was roofed and had seats for 10 men, and on top was a hand-operated turret mounting a machine gun. Entry to the crew compartment was by doors in the rear face of the hull, and firing ports were provided. In addition to its basic role as an APC, some were modified to act as command vehicles, and a number were used by the Royal Artillery as Troop Command Post vehicles. An ambulance version was built in small numbers.

Armament: 1 or 2 × MG
Armour: 16mm
Crew: 2 + 10
Weight: 10 tons (10,170kg)
Length: 17ft 2in (5.23m)
Width: 8ft 4in (2.53m)
Height: 8ft 1in (2.46m)
Engine: Rolls-Royce, 8-cylinder, petrol, 160bhp at:
 3,750rpm
Speed: 45mph (72km/hr)
Range: 250 miles (400km)

Sarath MICV India
IOF
1987. The Sarath is simply the Russian BMP-2 manufactured in India under licence. The basic vehicles is identical to the Russian product and similarly armed; the Indian Ordnance Factory has, however, developed some variants, including a 105mm SP field gun, an air defence missile carrier, an anti-tank missile carrier, and an armoured ambulance. It is unclear which, if any, of these variants have been adopted for service.

Saurer 4K 4FA APC Austria
Saurer, Steyr-Daimler-Puch
1956. The Saurer was the standard APC of the Austrian Army and was never in service with any other army. Issues began in about 1959, production ended in 1969 after about 450 had been made, and it has since been replaced almost entirely by the later Steyr 4K 7FA described below. The basic

vehicle had a welded hull with the driver in front and the engine on his right. The commander was directly behind him, in a small turret, and he also fired the main armament. The troop compartment was at the rear and had two rear doors and two long hatch covers in the roof, which allowed the passengers to stand up and fire over the top if necessary. When closed down they had no firing ports. There were many variants in service, including ambulance, command, anti-aircraft, mortar and rocket-launcher models. There was, however, no NBC protection, nor could the vehicle swim.

Armament: 1 x 20mm cannon
Armour: 20mm
Crew: 2 + 8
Weight: 13.26 tons (13,500kg)
Length: 17ft 8in (5.42m)
Width: 8ft 2in (2.50m)
Height: 7ft 2in (2.20m)
Engine: Saurer, 6-cylinder, diesel, 250bhp at 2,400rpm
Speed: 40mph (65km/hr)
Range: 190 miles (300km)

Sd Kfz Series
See Sonder Kraftfahrzeug

SIBMAS APC Belgium
Cockerill

1980. This was developed as a private venture in the late 1970s, with the intention of producing a basic vehicle which could be tailored to suit a wide variety of roles. The original company was taken over shortly after production for a Malaysian order began, and after completion of the order they announced that it would no longer be marketed. There was then no further development or manufacture. It was a 6 x 6 wheeled vehicle in two-and-four arrangement, and could be provided with a wide range of armament; the standard appears to have been a 90mm Cockerill gun with coaxial and air defence machine guns. The troop compartment held 11 men and was behind the turret, and the engine compartment was at the left rear of the body. The vehicle was amphibious; it was normally propelled by paddle action of its wheels, but for faster water speed it could be fitted with propeller units.

Armament: 1 x 90mm; 2 x MG
Armour: not disclosed
Crew: 3 + 11
Weight: 18.20 tons (18,500kg)
Length: 24ft 0in (7.32m)

Width: 8ft 3in (2.50m)
Height: 9ft 1in (2.77m)
Engine: MAN 6-cylinder turbocharged diesel, 320bhp at 1,900rpm
Speed: 62mph (100km/hr)
Range: 620 miles (1,000km)

Simba LCV UK
GKN

1986. This is described as a 'Light Combat Vehicle' and is more or less a wheeled 4 x 4 APC capable of being configured as an IFV by the addition of quite sizeable armament. It was designed specifically for the export market and the only sales were in APC configuration to the Philippine forces, manufacture being done in the Philippines under licence. The Simba has unusually high ground clearance and large square recesses for the wheels, giving it a spindly appearance but also giving it good cross-country performance. The driver sits alongside the engine, with the troop compartment behind him; entry to this is by a large rear door or a second door on the left side. The compartment is provided with vision blocks and firing ports. A cupola carries a light machine gun. Other versions with armament up to 90mm were developed but do not appear to have attracted any sales.

Armament: variable; 1 x MG on APCs
Armour: not disclosed
Crew: 2 + 10
Weight: 9.84 tons (10,000kg)
Length: 17ft 7in (5.35m)
Width: 8ft 3in (2.50m)
Height: 7ft 2in (2.19m)
Engine: Perkins 6-cylinder turbocharged diesel, 210bhp at 2,100rpm
Speed: 62mph (100km/hr)
Range: 410 miles (660km)

SISU XA-180 APC Finland
SISU-Auto

1983. This is a 6 x 6 wheeled vehicle of conventional pattern with a boxy body and a sharp nose, though the body appears very shallow above the wheels, giving it a slender appearance. Driver and commander sit in the front cab, with bullet-proof wind- and side-screens which also have armoured shutters. The engine compartment is behind the driver, and there is a narrow passageway connecting the cab with the troop compartment. The compartment holds ten men, is entered from the rear, and is provided with firing ports and vision blocks. In the roof are two rectangular hatches and a mount for a heavy machine gun. Ambulance and command versions have also been manufactured and are in Finnish service.

SISU-Auto AB became Patria Vehicles Oy in 1998 and the SISU XA-180 has been officially known as the **Patria XA-180** since that time.

Armament: 1 × MG
Armour: not disclosed
Crew: 2 + 10
Weight: 15.25 tons (15,500kg)
Length: 24ft 2in (7.35m)
Width: 9ft 6in (2.9m)
Height: 7ft 6in (2.3m)
Engine: Valmet 6-cylinder turbocharged diesel, 236bhp
Speed: 62mph (100km/hr)
Range: 500 miles (800km)

SKPF M42 Sweden
See m/42 SKPF

Sonder Kraftfahrzeug (Sd Kfz) Germany
German vehicles of the Nazi era built to military specifications were given an identification number preceded by the letters Sd Kfz for *Sonder Kraftfahrzeug* or 'Special Motor Vehicle'. Tanks and other vehicles rarely use these numbers, but they are the standard method of referring to armoured cars and APCs. A complete listing of Sd Kfz numbers appears in the Appendices, pages 353–7.

Sonder Kraftfahrzeug (Sd Kfz) 247 APC
Germany
Daimler-Benz
1941. Usually overlooked when considering the history of the armoured personnel carrier, this is among the earliest examples of the class. It was intended as an armoured vehicle for commanders and their staffs and was an open-topped armoured body mounted on the chassis of a 6 x 6 Krupp truck. No armament was fitted, the occupants being expected to avoid contact with an enemy.

Armament: none
Armour: 8mm
Crew: 6
Weight: 4.46 tons (4,530kg)
Length: 16ft 5in (5.0m)
Width: 6ft 7in (2.0m)
Height: 5ft 11in (1.8m)
Engine: Horch 3.5 litre, V-8 petrol, 75bhp at 3,600rpm
Speed: 50mph (80km/hr)
Range: 250 miles (400km)

Sd Kfz 250 (alte) APC Germany
Büssing-NAG, Demag and others
1939. After experience with the standard half-track vehicles, the German Army asked for an armoured machine to carry an infantry section to accompany reconnaissance armoured cars on patrols. The design was based on the existing Sd Kfz 10 one-ton vehicle, with a new armoured body by Demag, but various production delays meant that the first of over 4,200 which were eventually built did not appear until June 1941. There was a long series of variants and sub-variants which were simply the basic vehicle adapted to some particular role or weapon and which are listed, in abbreviated form, in the list of Sd Kfz numbers elsewhere in this book. Production of this first model ended in October 1943 and was replaced by the new model below.

Armament: various; usually 1 or 2 × MG
Armour: 15mm
Crew: 3
Weight: 5.80 tons (5,890kg)
Length: 15ft 0in (4.56m)
Width: 6ft 5in (1.95m)
Height: 5ft 5in (1.66m)
Engine: Maybach HL42 TRKM, 6-cylinder petrol, 100bhp at 3,000rpm
Speed: 37mph (60km/hr)
Range: 200 miles (320km)

Sd Kfz 250 (neue) APC Germany
Deutsche Werke and others
1943. The body of the Sd Kfz 250 (*alte*) was given a degree of ballistic shaping, and this meant some precise cutting and careful fitting, which meant the production was slow. In 1943 it was felt that flat armour would do just as well and would simplify, speed up and cheapen production, and this redesign became the Sd Kfz 250 (*neue*). It replaced the old model in production in October 1943 and 2,376 were built before the war ended. It is distinguished by the flat sides with the upper portion sloped inward, and a wedge-shaped engine compartment.

Armament: various; usually 1 × MG
Armour: 15mm
Crew: 2
Weight: 5.38 tons (5,465kg)
Length: 15ft 2in (4.61m)
Width: 6ft 5in (1.95m)
Height: 5ft 5in (1.66m)
Engine: Maybach LM42 TUKRM, 6-cylinder petrol, 120bhp at 3,000rpm
Speed: 37mph (60km/hr)
Range: 185 miles (300km)

Sd Kfz 251 Medium APC Germany
Hanomag, and others

1939. As early as 1935 the planners of Germany's Panzer divisions stated a requirement for an armoured carrier to take the accompanying infantry into battle, and suggested armouring one of the then-new half-track vehicles. The idea took some time to germinate but in 1937 design work began, using the 3-ton half-track as the foundation. The result was a slope-sided body of good ballistic shape, open-topped, with a machine gun mounted at the front of the crew compartment, and with double doors at the rear. There were several contractors, and minor differences – some were welded, some riveted, some had vision slots, some had only one for the commander, some had none – but they were all the same vehicle in different interpretations. As with the 250 there was a shoal of variants and sub-variants which are tabulated elsewhere, since apart from their armament or fittings for special tasks, they were all the same vehicle. A total of 2,650 were built between June 1939 and September 1943, when they were superseded in production by the Ausf D model (*below*).

Armament: various; generally 1 or 2 × MG
Armour: 15mm
Crew: 2
Weight: 7.81 tons (7,935kg)
Length: 19ft 0in (5.8m)
Width: 6ft 10in (2.1m)
Height: 5ft 9in (1.75m)
Engine: Maybach HL42 TUKRM, 6-cylinder petrol, 120bhp at 3,000rpm
Speed: 33mph (53km/hr)
Range: 185 miles (300km)

Sd Kfz 251 Ausf D APC Germany
Hanomag, and others

1943. This 'D Model' was, like the Sd Kfz 250 (*neue*), an economy model using slab-sided armour rather than ballistically-shaped plates in the interests of cheaper and quicker production. Where the body sides of the original vehicle were abruptly sloped inwards and had stores boxes on the mudguards above the tracks, this had flat sides built out over the tracks to contain the storage space, and the upper section sloping inwards at the top. In fact it was a much cleaner design than the original, and almost 11,000 were built between September 1943 and the war's end. Those variants which were still required were formed from the new vehicle and retained their old designation.

Armament: normally 1 or 2 × MG, but variants up to 75mm guns
Armour: 15mm
Crew: 2
Weight: 8 tons (8,130kg)
Length: 19ft 7in (5.98m)
Width: 6ft 11in (2.1m)
Height: 5ft 9in (1.75m)
Engine: Maybach HL42 TUKRM, 6-cylinder petrol, 120bhp at 3,000rpm
Speed: 33mph (53km/hr)
Range: 185 miles (300km)

Sd Kfz 252 Munitions Carrier Germany
Demag, Deutsche Werke

1940. This half-tracked carrier was developed at the same time as the Sd Kfz 253 (*below*) and is a fully-armoured and roofed-in vehicle with a sharply-sloped back. There was a roof hatch over the co-driver's position, rear doors, and pistol ports beneath the side windows of the cab. It was usually seen towing an armoured trailer, to increase its payload, and was organic to assault gun batteries.

Armament: 1 × MG
Armour: 18mm
Crew: 2
Weight: 5.73 tons (5,875kg)
Length: 15ft 5in (4.7m)
Width: 6ft 5in (1.95m)
Height: 5ft 11in (1.8m)
Engine: Maybach HL42 TRKM, 6-cylinder petrol, 100bhp at 3,000rpm
Speed: 40mph (65km/hr)
Range: 200 miles (320km)

Sd Kfz 253 Armoured Observation Post
Germany
Demag

1940. This was a similar all-armoured half-track to the Sd Kfz 252 but with the rear sloped less sharply. There was a large circular hatch in the roof from which the artillery observers could use their instruments. It was provided to assault gun batteries, but after about 250 had been built production stopped; it was considered uneconomical to devote so much attention to a small-quantity specialist vehicle, and the standard Sd Kfz 250 was adopted in the Armoured OP role instead.

Data: as for the Sd Kfz 252

Sd Kfz 254 Armoured Observation Post
Germany
Saurer
1940. This remarkable vehicle is probably the only wheel-and-track design which ever actually went into combat. Wheel-and-track designs were very popular with inventors in the 1925–35 period, less popular with the military because they were generally eccentric brain-children, highly unreliable and grossly impractical. But Saurer got this one exactly right; they began by trying to make a tank and the Austrian Army persuaded them to settle for a rather useful tractor. When the Germans moved in in 1938 they encouraged the idea as a potential APC but eventually saw it as an armoured OP and had 128 of them built and issued to artillery batteries accompanying Panzer divisions. They appear to have been principally used on the Eastern Front. The body was similar to the bodies of the half-track vehicles, with sloped-out sides, but with a full-length track unit beneath. Outside the track, at the four corners of the vehicle, were rubber-tyred wheels which could be lowered, lifting the tracks clear of the ground, for travelling on hard surfaces.

Armament: 1 × MG
Armour: 15mm
Crew: 6
Weight: 6.4 tons (6,500kg)
Length: 21ft 0in (6.4m)
Width: 15ft 0in (4.56m)
Height: 6ft 8in (2.02m) on tracks;
      7ft 3in (2.20m) on wheels
Engine: Saurer CRDV 4-cylinder diesel, 70bhp
Speed: 37mph (60km/hr) on wheels
Range: 310 miles (500km) on wheels

SPZ 12-3 APC Germany
Henschel, Hanomag, Leyland
1955. This vehicle was originally designed by Hispano-Suiza in Switzerland as one of a family of combat vehicles. At that time the Bundeswehr was reforming, needed a tracked APC, and also wanted 'educational' contracts to inaugurate the building of armoured vehicles in Germany once again. As a result of all this, Hispano-Suiza were given a contract to develop the vehicle to meet the German requirement, and production contracts were placed with two German firms and, in order to speed the vehicle into service, with Leyland Motors of England. Production was completed by 1962, about 1,800 vehicles having been built.

The SPZ 12-3 (SPZ = *Schutzenpanzer*) was a low-set full-tracked vehicle with the engine placed at the right rear. The driver was at the left front, and alongside him was the gunner with a turret-mounted 20mm cannon. The vehicle commander had a small hatch in the crew compartment which is usually provided with a machine gun. Two long hatches covered the crew compartment and were thrown open to allow the passengers to dismount; the only other access is by a small door in the hull rear, alongside the engine. It was not a good design, and had numerous mechanical defects; these were mostly cured during its service, but it was rapidly discarded as soon as Marder was in production.

Armament: 1 × 20mm cannon, 1 × MG
Armour: 30mm
Crew: 3 + 5
Weight: 14.38 tons (14,600kg)
Length: 18ft 3in (5.56m)
Width: 8ft 4in (2.54m)
Height: 6ft 1in (1.85m)
Engine: Rolls-Royce, 9-cylinder, petrol, 235bhp at 3,800rpm
Speed: 36mph (58km/hr)
Range: 175 miles (280km)

Spartan APC UK
Alvis
1978. Although classed as an APC, Spartan carries only four infantrymen and has been employed more as a missile carrier for various hand-held AA missiles, as a resupply vehicle for anti-tank missile launchers, a ground reconnaissance radar carrier, and as an engineer reconnaissance vehicle. It is one of the Alvis CVR(T) family, derived from the Scorpion tank, and is a simple box body with sloped front behind which are the driver and engine, while the vehicle commander/gunner and radio operator ride behind him. The four infantrymen fit into the troop compartment, which is provided with vision periscopes on the sides, and two roof hatches and a rear door. The commander's cupola has a remote controlled machine gun mounted on the right side, which can be aimed and fired from under armour.

Armament: 1 × MG
Armour: not disclosed
Crew: 3 + 4
Weight: 8.04 tons (8,128kg)
Length: 16ft 11in (5.13m)
Width: 7ft 4in (2.24m)
Height: 7ft 5in (2.26m)
Engine: Jaguar 100B 6-cylinder, petrol, 190bhp at 4,750rpm
Speed: 50mph (81km/hr)
Range: 300 miles (485km)

Steyr 4K 7FA APC Austria
Steyr-Daimler-Puch

1977. This is little more than the Saurer 4K 4FA (*above*) up-armoured and provided with a more powerful engine. Some of the shortcomings of the earlier design have been rectified; it now has ventilation and heating for the interior, NBC protection and night vision equipment as standard. The main armament is now standardized as the .50-inch Browning MG, but other weapon fits can be mounted. There are a number of variants, most of which have never got beyond the proposal stage, and the vehicle has been sold in some numbers to Nigeria, Bolivia and Greece.

Armament: 1 × MG
Armour: 25mm
Crew: 1 + 8
Weight: 14.56 tons (14,800kg)
Length: 17ft 3in (5.87m)
Width: 8ft 2in (2.50m)
Height: 5ft 3in (1.61m)
Engine: Steyr 7FA 6-cylinder turbocharged diesel, 320bhp at 2,300rpm
Speed: 40mph (64km/hr)
Range: 325 miles (520km)

Steyr Kampfschutzenpanzer 90 MICV
Austria
Steyr-Daimler-Puch

This was privately developed by S-D-P in the late 1980s with a view to producing what they considered to be a suitable vehicle for the 1990s which would meet the requirements of the Austrian Army whenever it eventually decided on a new MICV. In essence it was the existing 4K 7FA (*above*) improved and modernized, the principal change being the adoption of a new two-man power-operated turret armed with a 30mm Mauser Model F cannon and a coaxial machine gun Other types of armament could be catered for, and plans were drawn up for various weapon fits, up 105mm guns. A prototype was built in the early 1990s, but the project was cancelled by 1992.

Armament: 1 × 30mm; 1 × MG
Armour: not disclosed
Crew: 3 + 8
Weight: 18.9 tons (19,200kg)
Length: 20ft 3in (6.17m)
Width: 8ft 8in (2.65m)
Height: 8ft 6in (2.58m)
Engine: S-D-P 6-cylinder diesel, 470bhp
Speed: 43mph (70km/hr)
Range: 310 miles (500km)

Steyr Pandur Austria
Steyr-Daimler-Puch

1986. This was a private venture by Steyr which was adopted by the Austrian Army in 1994, has also been adopted by Belgium and Kuwait, and is under evaluation by the Czech Army. The basic vehicle is a 6 x 6 wheeled carrier with the driver at the left front and the engine on his right. The commander is behind the driver and has an observation cupola The rear of the vehicle is the troop compartment, with doors at the rear and seating for eight troops. There are two long hatches in the roof and firing ports on each side. Variant models which have been proposed include 30mm and 90mm gun carriers, missile carriers, air defence gun carriers and mortar carriers. There is also an amphibious version of the APC.

Armament: variable; APC with 1 × MG
Armour: not disclosed
Crew: 2 + 8
Weight: 13.28 tons (13,500kg)
Length: 18ft 8in (5.7m)
Width: 8ft 3in (2.5m)
Height: 6ft 0in (1.82m)
Engine: Steyr 6-cylinder turbocharged diesel, 260bhp at 2,400rpm
Speed: 62mph (100km/hr)
Range: 435 miles (700km)

Stormer APC UK
Alvis

This was originally designed by the British MVEE (Military Vehicles Engineering Establishment) and the manufacturing rights sold to Alvis in 1980. The original APC configuration was somewhat modified by Alvis, who applied much of their Scorpion technology to it. Variants with different turrets, minelaying equipment, engineer equipment, artillery observation equipment and missiles were developed. The version carrying Starstreak air defence missiles was adopted by the British Army, and APC versions of slightly different configuration have been sold abroad. In basic form it is a tracked vehicle with a boxy body having a well-sloped front; there are six roadwheels on each side, with forward drive sprocket and rear idler.

Armament: variable; usually one MG
Armour: not disclosed
Crew: 3 + 8
Weight: 12.50 tons (12,700kg)
Length: 17ft 6in (5.33m)
Width: 8ft 10in (2.69m)
Height: 7ft 5in (2.27m) to top of cupola

Engine: Perkins 6-cylinder turbocharged diesel, 250bhp at 2,600rpm
Speed: 50mph (80km/hr)
Range: 400 miles (650km)

SU-60 APC Japan
See Type SU-60

TAB-71 APC Romania
RATMIL
1971. The TAB-71 was a licensed copy of the 8 x 8 Soviet BTR-60P and was first seen in public in late 1972. The principal difference between this and the original BTR-60P is that the Romanians used two 140bhp engines in place of the original Russian 90bhp motors, giving it a better turn of speed and improved cross-country agility.

Armament: 1 x HMG; 1 x MG
Armour: 9mm
Crew: 3 + 8
Weight: 10.82 tons (11,000kg)
Length: 23ft 8in (7.22m)
Width: 9ft 3in (2.83m)
Height: 8ft 10in (2.70m)
Engine: 2 x V-8 petrol, each 140bhp
Speed: 60mph (95km/hr)
Range: 310 miles (500km)

TAB-72 APC Romania
RATMIL
1973. This replaced the TAB-71 after a relatively small number of that type had been built. It is, again, a licensed copy of a Soviet design, this time of the BTR-60PB, differing in some dimensions and in the shape of the gun turret. They have been replaced in first-line service by the TAB-77 APC and the MLI-84 MICV, but numbers remain in the hands of militia and police units in Romania and Serbia.

Armament: 2 x MG
Armour: 9mm
Crew: 3 + 8
Weight: 10.82 tons (11,00kg)
Length: 23ft 8in (7.22m)
Width: 9ft 4in (2.83m)
Height: 8ft 10in (2.70m)
Engine: 2 x V-6 petrol, 140bhp each
Speed: 60mph (95km/hr)
Range: 310 miles (500km)

TAB-77 APC Romania
RATMIL
As with the other TAB models, this is a licensed copy of a Russian design, in this case the BTR-70 8 x 8 APC. The only significant difference is that instead of using two petrol engines, it uses two diesel engines.

TABC-79 APC Romania
RATMIL
The TABC-79 is a 4 x 4 APC of local design, though some of the components of the TAB-77 are employed to take advantage of existing manufacture. It appears to have been based on the Swiss Mowag vehicles and uses a similarly slope-sided hull. A one-man turret carries a heavy machine gun and the occupants can fire their personal weapons through firing ports in the sides. The driver and commander/gunner are at the front, with the troop compartment behind them, and the engine is at the left rear. Access to the troop compartment is by a single rear door alongside the engine compartment, and one door on each side of the vehicle. It is amphibious and is propelled in the water by a water jet unit at the rear.

Armament: 1 x HMG; 1 x MG
Armour: not disclosed
Crew: 3 + 4
Weight: 9.13 tons (9,275kg)
Length: 17ft 5in (5.61m)
Width: 9ft 3in (2.81m)
Height: 8ft 8in (2.64m)
Engine: Saviem 6-cylinder turbocharged diesel, 154bhp
Speed: 53mph (85km/hr)
Range: 435 miles (700km)

TAMSE VCTP MICV Argentina
TAMSE
In the later 1970s the German company Thyssen-Henschel developed the TAM medium tank for manufacture in Argentina, and the hull of this vehicle was also developed into various other forms, including this MICV. It is vaguely reminiscent of the German Marder, a full-tracked vehicle with well-sloped armour and a small two-man turret at the front end of the troop compartment carrying a 20mm cannon and a coaxial machine gun. The troop compartment has roof hatches and a remote-controlled machine gun mounting at the rear. Variant models include a 120mm mortar carrier, command vehicle, recovery vehicle, multiple rocket launcher carrier and 155mm SP gun carrier.

Armament: 1 × 20mm cannon; 2 × MG
Armour: not disclosed
Crew: 2 + 19
Weight: 27.56 tons (28,000kg)
Length: 22ft 5in (6.83m)
Width: 10ft 11in (3.32m)
Height: 8ft 9in (2.68m)
Engine: MTU V-8 diesel, 720bhp at 2,400rpm
Speed: 50mph (80km/hr)
Range: 375 miles (600km)

THE439 APC Germany
Thyssen-Henschel

1988. This was developed by Thyssen-Henschel as a private venture and is intended to be a specialist vehicle for negotiating difficult terrain such as swamps, snowfields and other soft surfaces. The basis is a civilian all-terrain chassis with wide tracks and a low-pressure footprint, to which an armoured body has been added. The basic vehicle is simply a box which can then be modified into whatever configuration the purchaser needs. The engine is at the front, driver and vehicle commander behind it, and the rest is a troop or cargo compartment, to which access can be gained by side and rear doors.

Armament: to choice
Armour: not disclosed
Crew: 2 + 8
Weight: 6.40 tons (6,500kg)
Length: 13ft 9in (4.20m)
Width: 7ft 9in (2.37m)
Height: 7ft 10in (2.38m)
Engine: Mercedes-Benz OM352 6-cylinder
  turbocharged diesel, 152bhp
Speed: 31mph (50km/hr)
Range: 155 miles (250km)

Timoney Mark 6 APC Ireland
Timoney

1982. The Mark 6 4 × 4 APC was an improved model of the earlier Timoney design which was built under licence in Belgium as the BDX (*qv*). The hull was a welded box, with driver and engine in front behind the rather large sloping front plate. The engine and transmission were similar to those in the M113 APC, making the provision of spares and servicing a simple matter. A one-man turret was centrally mounted behind the engine and in the rear was the troop compartment. There were firing ports in the sides and hatches in the roof. The vehicle was amphibious and propelled itself by its wheels in the water. There was comprehensive electrical equipment and the basic hull was adaptable to a number of different roles.

Armament: 1 × MG
Armour: 8mm estimated
Crew: 3 + 9
Weight: 9.82 tons (9,980kg)
Length: 16ft 3in (4.95m)
Width: 8ft 3in (2.50m)
Height: 9ft 0in (2.75m)
Engine: Detroit Diesel 4-53T 4-cylinder diesel,
  180bhp at 2,800rpm
Speed: 60mph (95km/hr)
Range: 620 miles (1000km)

Timoney 6 × 6 APC Ireland
Timoney

This was little more than the Timoney Mark 6 (*above*) with the troop compartment stretched and with four wheels at the rear instead of two. It was capable of carrying turrets mounting guns up to cannon calibre, and the troop compartment held ten fully-equipped infantrymen, access being by a rear door/ramp with hydraulic operation. Two prototypes were built in the early 1990s but no subsequent production took place.

Armament: to choice
Armour: not disclosed
Crew: 2 + 10
Weight: 14.76 tons (15,000kg)
Length: 21ft 2in (6.45m)
Width: 8ft 10in (2.70m)
Height: 6ft 8in (2.04m)
Engine: Cummins 6-cylinder diesel, 350bhp at
  2,500rpm; or Perkins 6-cylinder diesel 300bhp at
  2,600rpm
Speed: 62mph (100km/hr)
Range: 455 miles (730km)

TM-170 APC Germany
Thyssen-Henschel

1978. This was really an armoured utility vehicle, being capable of performing a variety of roles from internal security to ambulance, APC, command, communications or missile carrier. It was a light 4 × 4 with with the usual wedge-sloped sides and recessed wheels and recognisable by the large full-width windscreen, which could be covered by two armoured shutters which folded down to lie on the glacis plate in front of the driver and vehicle commander. A turret could be fitted, or an observation cupola, over the troop compartment which held ten men. Access was gained by doors on each side or by means of a roof hatch. The engine was in front of the driver, and it was possible to shift from 4 × 4 to 4 × 2 mode when operating on hard roads.

Numbers were used by the Bundesgrenzschutz and various German police and security forces, as well as being sold to several countries.

Armament: to choice
Armour: not disclosed
Crew: 2 + 10
Weight: 11.17 tons (11,650kg)
Length: 20ft 1in (6.12m)
Width: 8ft 0in (2.45m)
Height: 7ft 7in (2.32m) to hull top
Engine: Daimler-Benz OM352 6-cylinder turbocharged diesel, 168bhp at 2,800rpm
Speed: 62mph (100km/hr)
Range: 450 miles (720km)

TPK 4.20 VBL France
See ACMAT

Trojan APC UK
See FV432

TT-6 APC France
Hotchkiss-Brandt
1952. The TT-6 was the first tracked carrier for the French infantry and it was the forerunner of the Hotchkiss Reconnaissance Vehicle which the Federal German Army adopted. The TT-6 was small and not very powerful, it carried only six infantrymen and there was little room for extra equipment, but it taught some useful lessons and led to greatly improved designs. The driver of the TT-6 sat alongside the engine in the front of the hull, and behind him the commander had a hatch on which he could mount a machine gun. The squad sat back to back in the troop compartment and had small openings to shoot through. They entered by two rear doors. A cargo variant had an open load bay and no roof for the driver.

Armament: 1 × MG
Armour: 15mm
Crew: 1 + 6
Weight: 6.39 tons (6,490kg)
Length: 13ft 0in (3.96m)
Width: 7ft 6in (2.29m)
Height: 6ft 1in (1.85m)
Engine: Hotchkiss, 6-cylinder, petrol, 164bhp at 3,900rpm
Speed: 40mph (65km/hr)
Range: 220 miles (355km)

Type 55 APC China
State factories
1960. The Type 55 is the Chinese version of the Soviet BTR-40 (*qv*) and its physical features are almost identical. The internal differences are that the Chinese version probably uses locally built engines and transmissions.

Type 56 APC China
State factories
1958. The Type 56 is the Chinese version of the Soviet BTR-152 (*qv*), a six-wheeled carrier which is now obsolete. However, it still survives in use with the Chinese reserve forces and it is suspected that there are variants in service in such configurations as light anti-aircraft self-propelled mountings, and perhaps some command vehicles.

Type 73 APC Japan
Mitsubishi
1973. The Type 73 was the successor to the Type SU-60; it is a larger and heavier vehicle, and more sophisticated. There is a hull machine-gunner beside the driver and this forces the engine to be near the middle of the hull. It is on the left side with the main armament beside it, either mounted in a turret or on an external mounting. It would be simple to class this as merely an improved Type SU-60, but it is rather more than that, and there are few components that are common to both, though the crew positions are similar. The infantry have a powered ramp at the back, and in case of failure of the mechanism there is door in the ramp which can be opened by hand. The vehicle is fully amphibious with minimal preparation and has full NBC protection.

Armament: 1 × MG turret, 1 × MG hull
Armour: not disclosed
Crew: 2 + 10
Weight: 13.08 tons (13,300kg)
Length: 19ft 0in (5.80m)
Width: 9ft 2in (2.80m)
Height: 7ft 3in (2.20m)
Engine: Mitsubishi, V-4 supercharged diesel, 300bhp at 2,200rpm
Speed: 43mph (70km/hr)
Range: 185 miles (300km)

Type 77 APC China
State factories
1977. This vehicle is similar to the Russian BTR-50P, a tracked carrier with the driver and commander at the front, troop compartment

behind them, and the engine at the rear of the vehicle. The commander has a heavy machine gun mounted on his hatch; the troops enter the vehicle through a door in the right side, and there are also roof matches in their compartment and firing ports. The vehicle is amphibious, and is propelled by two jet units in the water. Variant models include an armoured ambulance, command vehicle and logistic cargo carrier.

Armament: I × MG
Armour: not disclosed
Crew: 2 + 16
Weight: 15.26 tons (15,500kg)
Length: 24ft 3in (7.4m)
Width: 10ft 6in (3.2m)
Height: 8ft 0in (2.44m)
Engine: 4-cylinder diesel, 400bhp at 2,000rpm
Speed: 38mph (60km/hr)
Range: 230 miles (370km)

Type 82 Command Vehicle Japan
Mitsubishi

1978. This is a 6 x 6 wheeled vehicle which shares the same body and running gear as the Type 87 Reconnaissance/Patrol vehicle (*see* Reconnaissance Vehicles section), and in general it is similar to the better-known Renault VAB. This command vehicle, though, has a peculiar hull stepped up at the rear so as to give ample headroom inside the command compartment and also to permit two forward-facing windows. The driver and co-driver sit in the front cab, the co-driver having a roof hatch with a machine gun. The engine compartment is behind them separating them from the remainder of the vehicle, which is entirely given over to radio equipment, maps and the trappings of command. It is also liberally provided with periscopes and roof hatches and a second machine gun. A side door and a large rear door give access to the command compartment.

Armament: 2 × MG
Armour: not disclosed
Crew: 8
Weight: 13.38 tons (13,600kg)
Length: 18ft 9in (5.72m)
Width: 8ft 2in (2.48m)
Height: 7ft 10in (2.38m)
Engine: Isuzu V-10 diesel, 308bhp at 2,700rpm
Speed: 62mph (100km/hr)
Range: 310 miles (500km)

Type 85 APC China
State factories

This is actually the YW-531 (*below*) which was renamed the Type 85 some time in the late 1980s in order to conform with a revised system of nomenclature. It has also had various other names, detailed in the main entry.

Type 89 MICV Japan
Mitsubishi

1991. This is a full-track vehicle looking like a small tank, with a low hull, sloping glacis, six roadwheels on each side, skirted tracks, and a turret which mounts an Oerlikon 35mm automatic gun, a coaxial machine gun and two wire-guided anti-tank missiles. The driver and engine are in the front of the vehicle, the fighting compartment behind, and the rear of the vehicle, with the roof level a few inches higher than the forepart, forms the troop compartment. This has two rear doors, six firing ports at sides and rear, and a roof hatch.

Armament: I × 35mm; I × MG; 2 × ATGW
Armour: not disclosed
Crew: 3 + 7
Weight: 20.17 tons (20,500kg)
Length: 22ft 4in (6.80m)
Width: 10ft 6in (3.20m)
Height: 9ft 0in (2.75m)
Engine: diesel, 600bhp at 2,000rpm
Speed: 43mph (70km/hr)
Range: 185 miles (300km)

Type 90 APC China
State factories

1991. This is a full-track vehicle very reminiscent of the Russian BMP family, with a low hull, skirted tracks and a sharp prow. The driver sits in the front, with the engine and transmission alongside him beneath the glacis plate, and the vehicle commander sits to his right rear, with an observation cupola above him. The remainder of the vehicle is the troop compartment, with entry by a large door in the rear face of the hull. This compartment has four roof hatches, and three firing ports on each side; it has seating for 13 men. One of the forward hatches gives access to the roof-mounted heavy machine gun which has protecting shields. There are five roadwheels on each side, with torsion bar suspension, and the vehicle is amphibious, propelled in the water by its tracks.

Armament: I × MG
Armour: not disclosed
Crew: 2 + 13

Weight: 14.17 tons (14,400kg)
Length: 21ft 9in (6.63m)
Width: 10ft 4in (3.15m)
Height: 7ft 9in (2.37m)
Engine: 8-cylinder turbocharged diesel, 320bhp
Speed: 40mph (65km/hr)
Range: 310 miles (500km)

Type SU-60 APC Japan
Mitsubishi

1960. Despite a superficial likeness, the SU-60 was not a copy of the M113 but is quite different. The driver had a bow machine-gunner beside him, an unusual throwback to World War 2 practice, and the engine was behind him, on the left of the hull. The commander had a cupola directly behind the driver and hull machine-gunner, and an external machine gun was above a hatch to his right. The troop accommodation in the rear of the vehicle was somewhat cramped, and the occupants entered and left by two doors in the rear face of the hull. The tracks had five roadwheels, but there were three return rollers which distinguish the vehicle immediately from the M113. There were three variants, though one, an SP mounting, never went into service. The SU-60 was replaced with the Type 73 (*qv*), but several are still in use with the Self-Defence Force.

Armament: 2 × MG
Armour: 20mm
Crew: 2 + 8
Weight: 11.61 tons (11,800kg)
Length: 15ft 10in (4.85m)
Width: 7ft 9in (2.4m)
Height: 7ft 6in (2.31m)
Engine: Mitsubishi Model HA-21, V-8, turbocharged diesel, 220bhp at 2,400rpm
Speed: 28mph (45km/hr)
Range: 142 miles (230km)

Ultrav M11 APC France
Panhard et Levassor

1990. Having had considerable success with their VBL armoured car (*qv*) the Panhard company decided that by lengthening the wheelbase it could be more easily converted into a number of different configurations, from ambulances to missile launchers. The first, and most common, version was this APC, originally called the VBL APC, but very quickly Panhard gave the development a completely different name, the Ultrav M11, which covered the entire range of vehicles which were produced for the French Army and police forces as well as for export. The APC has room for a four-man crew with a variety of other stores, and has four roof hatches and a rear door. The French Army also employ a reconnaissance and scout version with a three-man crew and a machine gun on a circular mount on a roof hatch; a similar vehicle but with a heavy machine gun; an anti-tank version with MILAN missile launcher and this APC, which is also widely employed by the Gendarmerie Nationale.

Armament: 1 × MG
Armour: not disclosed
Crew: 4
Weight: 3.54 tons (3,600kg)
Length: 12ft 6in (3.80m)
Width: 6ft 8in (2.02m)
Height: 5ft 7in (1.70m)
Engine: Peugeot XD3T turbocharged diesel, 95bhp at 2,250rpm
Speed: 60mph (95km/hr)
Range: 375 miles (600km)

United Defense IFV (Light) USA
United Defense

1997. In the 1970s, the FMC company developed the Armored Infantry Fighting Vehicle (AIFV) (*qv*) which they sold to the Netherlands and other forces. In the early 1990s they were approached by the Egyptian Army for a similar vehicle and produced this IFV (Light). (During the development period FMC Corporation became United Defense LP.) The resulting vehicle is based on the M113 APC and used some components of that vehicle but is a completely new design. Full-tracked, with six roadwheels each side, front drive and rear idler, it is of a similar slab-sided, slope-front shape to the M113 but had the track skirted, and is fitted with a large turret carrying a 25mm Chain Gun cannon, a coaxial machine gun and a twin TOW ATGW launcher. The prototype was built in 1996, but no further progress has been made.

Armament: 1 × 25mm; 1 × MG; 2 × TOW ATGW
Armour: not disclosed
Crew: 3 + 6
Weight: 17.85 tons (18,140kg)
Length: 19ft 4in (5.89m)
Width: 9ft 0in (2.75m)
Height: 9ft 1in (2.78m)
Engine: Detroit Diesel V-6, 400bhp at 2,800rpm
Speed: 40mph (65km/hr)
Range: 300 miles (480km)

United Defense MTV (Light) USA
United Defense

1997. The makers see this as a replacement for the ageing M113 APC, but instead of being an APC this is a Mobile Tactical Vehicle (Light). It is virtually the same as the IFV (Light) described above except that it does not have a turret, merely a hatch-mounted heavy machine gun. It has more interior space and a better cross-country performance than the old M113. It has six roadwheels on each side instead of five, giving a better ride, and the hull is of welded aluminium armour, though add-on steel plates can be fitted to the frontal arc. The MTV(L) can be built new, or it can be a conversion of existing M113 vehicles by changing the power pack and suspension and various lesser details. It is currently being evaluated here and there.

Armament: 1 × HMG
Armour: not disclosed
Crew: 2 + 12
Weight: 17.85 tons (18,144kg)
Length: 19ft 2in (5.84m)
Width: 8ft 10in (2.69m)
Height: 9ft 6in (2.90m)
Engine: Detroit Diesel V-6, 400bhp at 2,800rpm
Speed: 40mph (65km/hr)
Range: 300 miles (450km)

Universal Carrier UK
Thornycroft, Morris, Sentinel, Aveling Barford, Ford UK, Ford Canada, GM NZ, NZ Rail

1940. The popularity of the Bren carrier (*qv*) led to a number of derivatives, and it was obviously uneconomic and wasteful of effort to build several near copies in small numbers. In 1940, therefore, design of a 'Universal' carrier was begun, a basic vehicle which could, by the incorporation of small modification kits during the manufacturing stage, be adapted to almost any required role. This became the standard carrier for the rest of the war, though in spite of its official title it remained the Bren carrier to almost everybody. The new design incorporated improved armour plating to cover all round the vehicle and the top of the engine compartment; mud deflectors over the tracks; steps for entry at the rear; and room for three men.

Numbers of existing Bren carriers were modified to bring them up to 'Universal' standard, while modification kits allowed the Universal to function as an Artillery OP, mortar carrier or flamethrower. There were a number of marks and sub-marks, but the only essential differences were in the engines – some having British, some Canadian and some American engines – and in the arrangement of fittings to carry a mortar at the rear of the body.

Carriers were built in Britain, Canada, Australia and New Zealand, but the US Army, considering the Universal to be overloaded and underpowered, set about improving it. They developed the **Carrier T16**, with a longer body and track and more powerful engine; over 2,600 were built, but for once the Americans had got it wrong and the T16 could not carry as much payload as the standard Universal, nor was it as reliable, so that few were put to use.

Armament: various
Armour: 10mm
Crew: 3
Weight: 4.25 tons (4,318kg)
Length: 12ft 4in (3.75m)
Width: 6ft 11in (2.10m)
Height: 5ft 3in (1.60m)
Engine: Ford, V-8 petrol, 85bhp
Speed: 20mph
Range: 125 miles (200km)

Urutu APC Brazil
See Engesa EE-11

VAB France
See Renault VAB

Valkyr UK
Vickers

1985. The Valkyr is a 4 x 4 wheeled vehicle which is an improved and developed version of the Belgian BDX APC (*qv*). Vickers collaborated with Beherman-Demoen, makers of the BDX, to develop a fire support vehicle and then an APC. As with many such vehicles, the APC became the basic model from which a number of possible variants have been proposed. The vehicle is a boxy structure with well-sloped front and side armour, and with prominent front and side windows for the driver. The commander, behind and to the left of the driver, has an observation cupola; to his right is the engine compartment. The rear of the vehicle forms the troop compartment, with entry by a side door on the left side or by a large rear door. A variety of weapon fits are offered. The **Fire Support Vehicle** variant uses the same hull but mounts a larger turret with a 90mm gun or a 60mm gun-mortar.

Armament: 1 × MG
Armour: not disclosed
Crew: 2 + 8
Weight: 11.32 tons (11,500kg)

Length: 18ft 4in (5.60m)
Width: 8ft 3in (2.50m)
Height: 7ft 5in (2.27m)
Engine: Detroit Diesel V-8, 300bhp at 2,800rpm
Speed: 62mph (100km/hr)
Range: 435 miles (700km)

VCC-1 MICV Italy
OTO-Melara
1980. This was developed by the Italian Army as a means of improving the efficiency of the standard M113 APC; this vehicle had been made under licence in Italy by OTO-Melara for several years, and the army now proposed improving the armament and interior arrangements and up-armouring the hull so as to turn it into a fighting vehicle and not simply a battle taxi. The main hatch was given a ring mount with armour shields for a .50-inch machine gun, and the crew compartment provided with firing ports and vision blocks. The front and sides of the hull had an additional layer of steel armour applied over the basic aluminium armour. The vehicle is, of course, fully amphibious. This basic model was supplied to the Italian Army and numbers are still in use. A second version, armed with the Improved TOW anti-tank missile system in a retracting roof mounting, was purchased by Saudi Arabia in the mid-1980s and is also still in service.

Armament: 2 × MG
Armour: not disclosed
Crew: 2 + 7
Weight: 11.41 tons (11,600kg)
Length: 16ft 6in (5.04m)
Width: 8ft 10in (2.69m)
Height: 6ft 8in (2.03m)
Engine: GMC V-6 diesel, 210bhp at 2,800rpm
Speed: 40mph (65km/hr)
Range: 340 miles (550km)

VCC-80 MICV Italy
Iveco/OTO-Melara
1988. This was a large full-tracked vehicle with six roadwheels each side and track skirts, a flat-topped comparatively tall hull with sloping glacis plate front, and a large turret carrying a 25mm cannon, coaxial machine gun and air defence machine gun. The engine was at the right front, driver at the left, and the troop compartment, behind the turret, held six men and was entered through a rear door. Vision equipment and firing ports were provided for the occupants. The vehicle was not amphibious but could ford to a depth of 1.5m without preparation. After evaluation and trials it was decided to make

some changes, and the resulting vehicle emerged as the Dardo IFV (*qv*).

Armament: 1 × 25mm cannon; 2 × MG
Armour: not disclosed
Crew: 3 + 6
Weight: 21.36 tons (21,700kg)
Length: 22ft 0in (6.71m)
Width: 9ft 10in (3.0m)
Height: 8ft 10in (2.70m)
Engine: Fiat V-6 turbocharged diesel, 520bhp at 2,300rpm
Speed: 44mph (70km/hr)
Range: 310 miles (500km)

VP-90 Carrier France
Lohr
1975. The Lohr company specialises in small, agile carriers which can be configured to carry a variety of weapons or equipment, and the VP-90 was one of its earlier designs. It was no more than an open-topped box, with seats for two men, on a tracked chassis. The object was to provide a low, easily-concealed and hard to hit vehicle which could whisk about the battlefield in moderate safety, delivering ammunition and other vital stores. It is believed that the French airborne troops purchased some.

Armament: none fitted; can be adapted as required
Armour: not disclosed
Crew: 2
Weight: 2.65 tons (2,700kg)
Length: 11ft 9in (3.58m)
Width: 6ft 1in (1.85m)
Height: 3ft 5in (1.05m)
Engine: Citroën CX2000, 4-cylinder, petrol, 102bhp at 5,500rpm
Road speed: 55mph (90km/hr)
Range: 250 miles (400km)

VTT-323 APC North Korea
State factories
1973. This is a full-tracked carrier which is believed to have been based upon the Chinese YW 531 APC, a number of which were supplied to the North Korean forces. It is of steel armour, to the usual boxy shape with sloped front, with five roadwheels on each side, front drive and rear idler. The driver and commander sit at the front; the engine is behind the commander, on the right side, and behind the driver is a crewman with an observation cupola and hatch. Behind them is the troop compartment with space for 8–10 men; in the roof is a one-man turret with a heavy machine gun and

with fittings for an SA-16 air defence missile launcher.

Armament: 1 × HMG; 1 × SAM
Armour: not disclosed
Crew: 3 + 8 or 10
Weight: 12.50 tons (12,700kg)
Length: 29ft 4in (6.20m)
Width: 10ft 0in (3.06m)
Height: 8ft 3in (2.50m)
Engine: 6-cylinder diesel, 320bhp
Speed: not disclosed
Range: not disclosed

VXB-170 France
See Berliet VXB-170

Walid APC Egypt
Kadr Factory

1960. This was designed and built in Egypt, using the chassis of a licence-built German Magirus-Deutz truck as the foundation and putting an armoured body on it. The result looks very similar to the Soviet BTR vehicles of the same period, and was, for some years, thought to be a simple copy. The design was overhauled and improved in 1981, the manufacture now being based upon Mercedes-Benz mechanical components. The layout is simple, with the engine at the front, driver and commander in the front cab, and the remainder of the welded steel body devoted to the open-topped troop compartment. A rear door give entry to this, and there are three firing ports in each side. The Walid has been bought by a number of other countries in the Middle East, including Israel.

Armament: 1 × MG
Armour: 9mm estimated
Crew: 2 + 8
Weight: 5.31 tons (5,400kg)
Length: 20ft 1in (6.12m)
Width: 8ft 5in (2.57m)
Height: 7ft 6in (2.30m)
Engine: Mercedes Benz, V-8, 160bhp (formerly Deutz, 90bhp)
Speed: 53mph (85km/hr)
Range: 500 miles (800km)

Warrior MICV UK
GKN

1985. Originally known as **MCV-80**, this was the first British MICV and has proved very successful. The basic vehicle has a two-man turret with 30mm Rarden cannon and Chain Gun machine gun and has room for seven infantrymen. The driver is at the

left front, the engine to his right beneath the sloping glacis plate. The commander and gunner are in the turret, just behind the driver and on the centre line. The troop compartment is entered via a power-operated door in the hull rear face, but there are no firing ports or vision devices for the occupants. There are two roof hatches. The hull is of welded aluminium armour, and there are six roadwheels with torsion bar suspension. Alternative versions which have been produced include a command vehicle, a repair and recovery vehicle, armoured artillery OP, artillery battery commander's vehicle, and a combat repair vehicle. A number of further options have been developed by the manufacturer.

Armament: 1 × 30mm Rarden cannon; 1 × 7.62mm Chain Gun
Armour: not disclosed
Crew: 3 + 7
Weight: 24.11 tons (24,500kg)
Length: 20ft 10in (6.34m)
Width: 9ft 11in (3.03m)
Height: 9ft 2in (2.79m)
Engine: Perkins CV8, V-8 diesel, 550bhp at 2,300rpm
Speed: 47mph (75km/hr)
Range: 410 miles (660km)

Warrior 2000 UK
Alvis

1999. As might be imagined by the name, this is a modernised version of the Warrior described above. However, it is not merely an update of the existing vehicle but was developed as an entirely new design to meet a Swiss Army requirement. It was tested by the Swiss early in 1999, but the results have not yet been announced.

The general layout is the usual one of driver on the left, engine on the right, turret central and troop compartment at the rear with a rear door. Fully tracked, it has six roadwheels each side, skirted, with front drive and rear idler. The frontal slope is flatter than that of the original Warrior and the turret has pronounced ballistic shaping and carries a 30mm automatic cannon. There is a complete suite of electro-optical sighting and fire control equipment, including automatic tracking for engagement of aerial targets.

Armament: 1 × 30mm cannon; 1 × MG
Armour: not disclosed
Crew: 3 + 7
Weight: 29.92 tons (30,400kg)
Length: 22ft 10in (6.97m)
Width: 11ft 1in (3.38m)
Height: 9ft 8in (2.95m)
Engine: Perkins Condor V-8 diesel, 650bhp

Speed: 47mph (75km/hr)
Range: 372 miles (600km)

Wasp Flamethrower UK

1942. Late in 1940 work began in Britain on development of a flamethrower that could be fitted into the Universal Carrier. Eventually the gas-pressure-operated device known as Ronson was selected, and this was fitted by mounting two tanks for fuel on the rear of the carrier hull, the nitrogen pressure cylinders inside the hull, and the flame projector on a swivel above the co-driver's position. Whilst this worked adequately, it was unacceptable because the flame fuel was outside the carrier, dangerously exposed to enemy fire. A fresh design was produced in which all the pressure and fuel system was inside the carrier hull, with the flame gun mounted rigidly above the co-driver. This gave a range of about 100 yards/metres and had to be aimed by pointing the whole vehicle at the target. This design was accepted for service as the **Wasp Mark 1**.

While these were being built, an improved version of the flame gun was designed, which could be fitted inconspicuously into the normal machine-gun housing in front of the co-driver, thus making the vehicle less obviously a flame-thrower. This became **Wasp Mark 2** and went into production late in 1943. The Mark 1 vehicles were relegated to training and the Mark 2 was extensively used in combat. A slight variation was the **Mark 2C**, built in Canada; in this model the fuel capacity was reduced and moved out on to the rear of the carrier so as to leave room inside for a third crew man operating a light machine gun.

Wiesel Germany
MaK

1989. The Wiesel is well-named, a small, lively, go-anywhere tracked carrier which went into German Army service principally as a carrier of anti-tank missile launchers. There are, however, several further variants which MaK have developed, though whether they attain military service remains to be seen.

The basic vehicle is like a miniature APC, with a long slope to the nose and a low hull surmounted usually by a HOT or TOW missile launcher. The tracks have three roadwheels, a front sprocket and a trailing rear idler, and a single return roller. The driver sits at the right front with the engine on his left; behind him the crew compartment is open and access is by climbing over the sides.

An alternative version, which is also used by the German Army, has the compartment roofed over and fitted with a turret mounting a 20mm RH202 cannon.

Armament: TOW launcher with 7 missiles
Armour: not disclosed
Crew: 3
Weight: 2.75 tons (2,800kg)
Length: 10ft 10in (3.31m)
Width: 6ft 0in (1.82m)
Height: 6ft 3in (1.9m)
Engine: Volkswagen 5-cylinder turbocharged diesel, 86bhp at 4,500rpm
Speed: 47mph (75km/hr)
Range: 186 miles (300km)

WZ-501 IFV China
State factories

1980. This is a copy of the Russian BMP-1 MICV which, according to some sources, is not a licensed copy but-reverse engineered from a BMP-1 bought from Egypt.

There are slight differences in dimensions and armament, but otherwise the two are identical.

Armament: 1 x 73mm gun; 1 x MG; 1 x ATGW
Armour: not disclosed
Crew: 3 + 8
Weight: 13.09 tons (13,300kg)
Length: 22ft 1in (6.74m)
Width: 9ft 9in (2.97m)
Height: 7ft 1in (2.16m)
Engine: V-6 diesel, 298bhp
Speed: 48mph (65km/hr)
Range: 310 miles (500km)

Variant WZ-501 models

WZ-501A MICV
As for the 501, but with a new turret carrying a 25mm cannon.

WZ-503 MICV
As for the 501, but the hull is higher and has a single rear door instead of two.

WZ-504
Carries four 'Red Arrow' anti-tank missiles on the roof.

WZ-505
Armoured ambulance.

WZ-506
Command vehicle.

WZ-523 APC China
State factories

1984. This is a 6 x 6 wheeled vehicle, arranged as 'two-and-four', and very similar to others of the same class such as the SIBMAS and the Ratel. A rather boxy body with a short and sharp prow at the front, windscreens for driver and commander with shutters, and long roof hatches with a heavy machine gun are the salient features. There is a rear door for access to the troop compartment. It is amphibious, using water jets for propulsion.

Armament: 1 x MG
Armour: not disclosed
Crew: 2 + 10
Weight: 11.02 tons (11,200kg)
Length: 19ft 9in (6.02m)
Width: 7ft 4in (2.55m)
Height: 9ft 0in (2.73m)
Engine: petrol, 165bhp
Speed: 50mph (80km/hr)
Range: 375 miles (600km)

WZ-551 APC China
State factories

1986. The Chinese purchased a Renault VAB in the mid-1970s, and the WZ-551 appears to have been designed using the VAB as the model; the dimensions differ, as do some of the mechanical details, but the similarity is beyond question. This is an armoured 6 x 6 vehicle, amphibious by means of propeller units at the rear (instead of the VAB's water jets) and with a large rear door giving access to the troop compartment. Driver and commander sit at the front, with bullet-proof screens and armoured shutters and each has a circular roof hatch. Behind them is the engine compartment, and then the troop compartment with seats down each side and four roof hatches. There is also a round hatch for the 12.7mm machine gun mount. A number of variants have been discussed, including an armoured ambulance, and 25mm cannon, air defence and anti-tank missile carriers, but the basic vehicle remains the same.

Armament: 1 x MG
Armour: not disclosed
Crew: 3 + 9
Weight: 15.05 tons (15,300kg)
Length: 21ft 10in (6.65m)
Width: 9ft 2in (2.80m)
Height: 6ft 5in (1.95m)
Engine: V-8 air-cooled diesel, 250bhp at 2,500rpm
Speed: 53mph (85km/hr)
Range: 375 miles (600km)

YP-408 APC Netherlands
DAF

1964. The YP-408 was designed to a specification raised by the Dutch Army and it has only been used by them. About 750 were built between 1964 and 1968 and production then ceased. It was a large 8 x 6 vehicle with the engine compartment in front and the driver and commander seated side by side behind it. The commander also fired the externally mounted heavy machine gun on his hatch. Behind this was the troop compartment with the 10 infantry seated facing inwards. There were no firing ports in the sides, but six hatches in the roof allowed them to stand up to shoot. There were two doors in the rear for entry and exit. The vehicle was made from as many commercial components from the DAF truck range as possible. The two front pairs of wheels were steered, but the second pair was not driven. It was not amphibious but could wade to a depth of 4ft (1.20m) without preparation. There were a number of variants, including one for the Brandt 120mm mortar. The YP-408 was replaced in military service by the AIFV, the last being removed in 1990, but a number are still used by the Dutch military police for airport security patrolling and similar tasks.

Armament: 1 x MG
Armour: 15mm
Crew: 2 + 10
Weight: 11.81 tons (12,000kg)
Length: 20ft 4in (6.20m)
Width: 7ft 9in (2.40m)
Height: 5ft 11in (1.55m) to hull top
Engine: DAF Model DS 575, 6-cylinder, turbocharged, diesel, 165bhp at 2,400rpm
Speed: 50mph (80km/hr)
Range: 310 miles (500km)

YW-531 APC China
State factories

1968. This is a light tracked carrier which was widely exported in the 1970s and is still in use in many African countries. Originally called the Type K-63, this vehicle has had several changes of nomenclature to Type 63, M1967, M1970, H-1 and Type 85 before settling down as the YW-531. It has a boxy hull with sloped front plate and with the sides sloped inwards to the roof. The driver and commander sit on the front, on left and right, with the engine compartment behind the commander. A third crewman sits behind the driver and has an observation hatch. The remainder of the vehicle forms the troop compartment, which has a gunner's hatch with 12.7mm machine gun towards the rear end. A large door on the rear face of the hull gives access to the compartment. There are four roadwheels on each side, sprung by torsion bars. Several variant models have been identified, for 82mm or 120mm mortars, anti-tank missile launchers, command cars and armoured ambulances among them, but the basic dimensions remain the same.

Armament: 1 × MG
Armour: not disclosed
Crew: 4 + 10
Weight: 12.30 tons (12,500kg)
Length: 18ft 0in (5.48m)
Width: 9ft 9in (2.98m)
Height: 6ft 0in (1.84m)
Engine: V-8 turbocharged diesel, 320bhp at 2,500rpm
Speed: 40mph (65km/hr)
Range: 310 miles(500km)

YW-534 APC China
State factories

1987. The YW-534 is a tracked carrier with a deep and well-sloped hull, flat roofed. The engine is under the right front of the sloping glacis plate, with the driver on the left and the commander behind him. The remainder of the vehicle forms the troop compartment, entered by a large single door in the rear face of the hull. Towards the front end of the compartment is a circular hatch with a mount for a 12.7mm machine gun; behind this are two rectangular roof hatches. There are firing ports with vision blocks and periscopes on both sides of the compartment. There are five irregularly spaced roadwheels, sprung by torsion bars, and the vehicle is amphibious, using its tracks as paddles.

Armament: 1 × MG
Armour: not disclosed
Crew: 2 + 13
Weight: 14.07 tons (14,300kg)
Length: 20ft 1in (6.15m)
Width: 10ft 3in (3.13m)
Height: 6ft 2in (1.88m)
Engine: 4-cylinder air-cooled diesel, 320bhp
Speed: 40mph (65km/hr)
Range: 320 miles (500km)

COMPARATIVE TABLES

IN ASCENDING ORDER OF WEIGHT

Name	Wheels	Weight	Length	Crew	Armour	Armament		Engine	Power	Speed	Range	Country
Renault WERE	FT	2.10	8.83	2	7	–	1	P/4	35	18	62	France
Auverland AV-3	4 × 4	2.22	12.67	3	*	–	1	D/4/L	85	80	310	France
VP90	FT	2.65	11.75	2	*	options		P/4/L	102	55	250	France
Wiesel	FT	2.75	10.83	3	*	GW	–	D/5/T/L	86	47	186	Germany
Lohr RPX 3000	4 × 4	3.44	12.33	4	*	GW	1	D/6/T/L	125	68	370	France
Ultrav M11	4 × 4	3.54	12.5	4	*	–	1	D/T	95	60	375	France
Bren Carrier	FT	3.75	12.0	2	10	–	1	P/V/8/L	85	30	130	UK
Iron Eagle	4 × 4	3.94	11.83	3	*	106	1	D/6/L	123	62	280	S Africa
Makina Carancho 180	4 × 4	4.23	16.08	2 + 4	8	–	3	P/V/8/L	180	75	280	Chile
Universal Carrier	FT	4.25	12.33	3	10	options		P/V/8/L	85	20	125	UK
Engesa EE-T4	FT	4.33	12.33	3	*	options		D/4/T	130	48	225	Brazil
Cashuat	4 × 4	4.38	17.67	2 + 8	*	–	1	D/6/L	110	50	300	El Salvador
Sd Kfz 247 APC	6 × 6	4.46	16.42	6	8	–		P/V/8/L	75	50	250	Germany
Lohr VPX 5000	FT	4.52	13.75	4	*	options		P/6/L	180	50	215	France
Mowag Roland	4 × 4	4.62	14.5	3 + 4	8	–	1	P/V/8/L	202	68	340	Switzerland
Bravia Commando	4 × 4	4.77	16.33	3 + 5	8	–	2	P/V/8/L	180	55	370	Portugal
Makina Multi 163 APC	4 × 4	4.92	16.5	2 + 8	8	–	1	P/V/8/L	180	68	280	Chile
Walid APC	4 × 4	5.31	20.08	2 + 8	9	–	1	P/V/8/L	160	53	500	Egypt
Sd Kfz 250 (neue) APC	HT	5.38	15.17	2	15	–	1	P/6/L	120	37	185	Germany
Puma	4 × 4	5.41	15.25	1 + 6	*	–	1	D/4/L	180	65	500	Italy
BOV APC	4 × 4	5.60	18.75	2 + 8	*	–	1	D/6/L	148	60	465	Yugoslavia
Carrier, Arm'd, Wheel IP	4 × 4	5.7	15.5	3	14	–	2	P/V/8	95	50	?	UK
Sd Kfz 252	HT	5.73	15.42	2	18	–	1	P/6/L	100	40	200	Germany
Sd Kfz 250 (alte) APC	HT	5.80	15.0	3	15	–	1	P/6/L	100	37	200	Germany
Otokar Cobra	4 × 4	5.90	17.5	2 + 7	*	–	1	D/V/8/T	190	68	340	Turkey
Panhard M3	4 × 4	5.98	14.5	2 + 10	12	options		P/HO/4/L	90	62	373	France
Mowag Grenadier	4 × 4	6.0	15.75	1 + 8	*	options		P/V/8/L	202	62	342	Switzerland
TT6 APC	FT	6.39	13.0	1 + 6	15	–	1	P/6/L	164	40	220	France
Sd Kfz 254 Arm'd OP	W&T	6.40	21.0	6	15	–	1	D/4/L	70	37	310	Germany
THE439	FT	6.40	13.75	2 + 8	*	options		D/6/T	152	31	155	Germany
Buffalo APC	4 × 4	6.50	15.08	2 + 10	12	options		P/V/6/L	145	56	370	France
BMD-1 Airborne IFV	FT	6.59	17.75	3 + 4	23	73 + GW	3	D/V/6/L	240	43	200	Russia
Panhard VCR	4 × 4	6.69	15.0	3 + 9	*	–	1	P/V/6/L	155	62	500	France
Humber FV 302	4 × 4	6.84	16.17	2 + 8	*	–	–	P/6/L	120	40	250	UK
Fiat-OTO 6614 APC	4 × 4	6.88	18.25	2 + 8	8	–	1	D/6/L	128	60	435	Italy
Mowag Piranha	4 × 4	6.89	17.25	1 + 9	10	options		P/V/6/L	216	62	465	Switzerland
ACMAT TPK 4.20	4 × 4	7.18	19.58	2 + 10	8	–	1	D/6/L	135	60	1000	France
Mowag Spy	4 × 4	7.38	14.83	3	*	–	2	D/V/6/L	195	68	435	Switzerland
Puma	6 × 6	7.38	16.42	1 + 8	*	–	1	D/4/L	180	*	*	Italy
PSZH-4 APC	4 × 4	7.48	18.67	3 + 6	*	–	2	D/4/L	100	50	310	Hungary

Name	Wheels	Weight	Length	Crew	Armour	Armament		Engine	Power	Speed	Range	Country
Cardoen VTP-2 APC	4 × 4	7.68	17.58	2 + 10	8	–	1	D/6/L	120	63	370	Chile
Panhard VCR APC	6 × 6	7.77	16.0	3 + 9	12	–	1	P/V/6/L	155	62	500	France
Sd Kfz 251 APC	HT	7.81	19.0	2	15	–	2	P/6/L	120	33	185	Germany
Oxford Carrier	FT	7.84	14.75	2	10	–	1	P/V/8/L	110	31	125	UK
DAF MPC	4 × 4	7.87	15.75	3 + 5	*	options		D/6/T/L	210	68	500	Neth'lands
Sd Kfz 251 Ausf D	HT	8.00	19.58	2	15	–	2	P/6/L	120	33	185	Germany
Spartan APC	FT	8.04	16.92	3 + 4	*	–	1	P/6/L	190	50	300	UK
Mowag MR8-01 SW2	4 × 4	8.07	17.33	5	10	20	–	P/6/L	160	50	248	Switzerland
Hotchkiss Light	FT	8.20	14.58	4	15	20	–	P/6	170	40	220	Germany
Cobra	FT	8.36	14.83	2 + 10	*	–	2	D/V/6/T/L	190	46	372	Belgium
OT-810	HT	8.36	19.08	2 + 10	12	–	1	D/6/A	120	32	198	Czech
m/42 SKPF	4 × 4	8.50	22.25	2 + 13	10	–	2	P/4/L	115	45	250	Sweden
BTR-152	6 × 6	8.64	22.42	2 + 14	12	options		P/6/L	110	46	400	Russia
AT-104 APC	4 × 4	8.75	18.0	2 + 9	12	options		P/6/L	134	50	400	UK
Car, Half-Track, M2	HT	8.83	19.58	2 + 8	12	–	2	P/6/L	128	45	175	USA
Engesa EE-11 APC	6 × 6	8.85	18.75	2 + 13	12	options		D/6/T/L	165	60	370	Brazil
Carrier, Half-Track, M3	HT	8.93	20.75	2 + 11	12	–	1	P/6/L	128	45	175	USA
Condor	4 × 4	9.05	21.25	3 + 9	*	–	1	D/6/S/L	168	63	560	Germany
TABC-79	4 × 4	9.13	17.42	3 + 4	*	–	2	D/6/T	154	53	435	Romania
Carrier, Half-Track, M5	HT	9.15	20.75	2 + 11	16	–	1	P/6/L	143	38	125	USA
Bravia Tigre	6 × 6	9.34	22.25	20	*	–	2	P/V/8/L	160	55	370	Portugal
Panhard VCR-TT2	6 × 6	9.45	20.17	2 + 12	*	options		2 × P/V/6/L	290	68	620	France
Car, Half-Track M9A1	HT	9.46	20.17	2_8	16	–	2	P/6/L	148	42	220	USA
ML-VM	FT	9.65	19.17	2 + 7	*	–	2	D/T/L	?	31	435	Romania
LVT-1	FT	9.73	21.5	3	–	–	1+	P/6/L	146	12	210	USA
Timoney Mk 6	4 × 4	9.82	16.25	3 + 9	8	–	1	D/4/L	180	60	620	Ireland
Armadillo	4 × 4	9.84	20.17	3 + 13	15	–	1	D/V/6/L	212	62	745	Guatemala
Simba LCV	4 × 4	9.84	17.58	2 + 10	*	–	1	D/6/T	210	62	410	UK
Saracen	6 × 6	10.0	17.17	2 + 10	16	–	2	P/V/8/L	160	45	250	UK
BTR-60P	8 × 8	10.14	24.83	2 + 14	14	–	1	2 × P/6/L	180	50	310	Russia
Cardoen BMS-1 Alacran	HT	10.33	20.92	2 + 12	*	options		D/V/8/T/L	225	43	560	Chile
Grizzly APC	6 × 6	10.33	19.58	3 + 8	10	–	2	D/V/6/L	215	62	375	Canada
Mowag Piranha	6 × 6	10.33	19.5	1 + 13	10	90	1	P/V/6/L	300	62	370	Switzerland
BDX	4 × 4	10.53	16.58	2 + 10	13	–	1	P/V/8/L	180	63	465	Belgium
HWK-11 APC	FT	10.82	16.58	2 + 10	15	–	1	P/V/8/L	210	40	200	Germany
M60-P	FT	10.82	16.5	4 + 10	25	–	2	D/6/L	140	28	240	Yugoslavia
LVT-2	FT	10.82	26.08	6	–	–	1	P/R/7/A	262	20	150	USA
TAB-71	8 × 8	10.82	23.67	3 + 8	9	–	2	2 × P/V/8	280	60	310	Romania
TAB-72 APC	8 × 8	10.82	23.67	3 + 8	9	–	2	2 × P/V/6/L	280	60	310	Romania
M113 APC	FT	10.97	15.92	3 + 10	38	–	1	D/6/L	215	42	300	USA
WZ-523	6 × 6	11.02	19.75	2 + 10	*	–	1	P	165	50	375	China
Fahd APC	4 × 4	11.07	19.67	2 + 10	*	options		D/6/T/L	168	52	500	Egypt
TM-170	4 × 4	11.17	20.08	2 + 10	*	options		D/6/T	168	62	450	Germany
BTR-70 APC	8 × 8	11.31	24.75	2 + 9	*	–	2	2 × P/V/8/L	240	50	370	Russia
Pbv 301 APC	FT	11.32	15.17	2 + 8	12	–	1	P/6/L	160	26	120	Sweden
Valkyr	4 × 4	11.32	18.33	2 + 8	*	–	1	D/V/8/L	300	62	435	UK
VCC-1 MICV	FT	11.41	16.5	2 + 7	*	–	2	D/V/6/L	210	40	340	Italy
AT-105 Saxon APC	4 × 4	11.47	17.0	2 + 8	*	–	1	D/6/L	164	60	300	UK
Type SU-60 APC	FT	11.61	15.83	2 + 8	20	–	2	D/V/8/T/L	220	28	142	Japan
MT-LB	FT	11.71	21.17	2 + 11	10	–	1	D/V/8/L	240	38	320	Russia
BLR APC	4 × 4	11.81	18.5	1 + 12	*	–	1	D/6/T/L	210	58	355	Spain

Name	Wheels	Weight	Length	Crew	Armour	Armament		Engine	Power	Speed	Range	Country
YP-408 APC	8 × 8	11.81	20.33	2 + 10	15	–	1	D/6/T/L	165	50	310	Neth'lands
LVT-3	FT	11.87	24.5	3	–	–	1	2 × P/V/8/L	296	17	150	USA
Dragoon LFV 90	4 × 4	12.0	19.33	5	*	90	1	D/V/6/T/L	300	72	425	USA
HS-30	FT	12.0	17.58	1 + 9	30	20	–	?	?	40	?	Switz/Ger
LVT(A)-2	FT	12.05	26.08	4	13	–	1	P/R/7/A	262	20	150	USA
Mowag Piranha	8 × 8	12.10	20.83	1 + 14	10	90	1	P/V/8/L	300	62	485	Switzerland
LVT-4	FT	12.23	26.08	6	13	–	1	P/R/7/A	262	20	150	USA
FAMAE Piranha	8 × 8	12.30	20.83	1 + 14	*	–	1	P/V/6/L	300	62	435	Chile
YW-531 APC	FT	12.30	18.0	4 + 10	*	–	1	D/V/8/T/L	320	40	310	China
Berliet VXB-170	4 × 4	12.50	19.58	1 + 11	7	–	1	D/V/8/L	170	53	465	France
Bison APC	8 × 8	12.50	19.58	2 + 8	*	–	1	D/V/6/L	275	63	400	Canada
VTT-323	FT	12.50	29.33	3 + 8	*	SAM	1	D/6	320	*	*	N Korea
Stormer	FT	12.50	17.5	3 + 8	*	–	1	D/6/T	250	50	400	UK
LAV-25	8 × 8	12.59	21.75	3 + 6	*	25	1	D/V/6/L	275	62	400	Canada
Arisgator	FT	12.65	22.5	2 + 11	38	–	1	D/6/L	215	42	300	Italy
Daewoo K200	FT	12.69	18.0	3 + 9	*	–	2	D/V/8	280	47	300	S Korea
Boragh	FT	12.80	22.0	2 + 8	*	–	1	D/V/8/A	330	40	370	Iran
RN-94	6 × 6	12.80	22.0	2 + 11	*	25		D	240	68	310	Turk/Rom
BMD-3 Airborne IFV	FT	12.95	20.0	3 + 4	*	30 + GW	2	D/V/6/L	450	43	310	Russia
Daewoo K200A1	FT	13.0	18.0	3 + 9	*	–	2	D/V/8	350	47	300	S Korea
Type 73 APC	FT	13.08	19.0	2 + 10	*	–	2	D/V/4/S/L	300	43	185	Japan
WZ-501 APC	FT	13.09	22.08	3 + 8	*	73 + GW	1	D/V/6/L	298	48	310	China
Armored Infantry FV	FT	13.25	17.25	3 + 7	*	25	1	D/V/6/T/L	264	37	300	US/Neth
Saurer 4K-4FA APC	FT	13.26	17.67	2 + 8	20	20	–	D/6/L	250	40	190	Austria
BMP-1 MICV	FT	13.28	22.17	3 + 8	23	75 + GW	1	D/V/6/L	280	40	340	Russia
Steyr Pandur	6 × 6	13.28	18.67	2 + 8	*	–	1	D/6/T/L	260	62	435	Austria
Panhard EBR ETT	8 × 8	13.29	18.25	1 + 14	15	options		P/HO/12/L	200	65	400	France
Pbv 302 APC	FT	13.29	17.58	2 + 10	20	20	–	D/6/T/L	280	41	186	Sweden
BTR-80 APC	FT	13.38	24.58	3 + 7	*	–	2	D/V/8/L	270	50	370	Russia
Renault VAB	4 × 4	13.38	20.0	2 + 10	*	options		D/6/T/L	250	62	800	France
Type 82 Command	6 × 6	13.38	18.75	8	*	–	2	D/V/10/L	300	62	310	Japan
NFV-1	FT	13.39	22.17	3 + 8	*	25	1	D/V/5	293	40	285	China
M80 MICV	FT	13.48	21.0	3 + 7	30	20 + GW	1	D/V/8/T/L	260	37	320	Yugoslavia
AMX-10P	FT	13.58	18.08	2 + 9	30	20	1	D/V/8/S/L	276	40	370	France
AMX-VCI MICV	FT	13.77	18.17	1 + 12	30	–	1	P/V/8/L	250	40	250	France
BMR-600 APC	6 × 6	13.78	20.17	2 + 11	*	–	1	D/6/L	310	65	620	Spain
BVP M-80A MICV	FT	13.78	21.08	3 + 7	*	20 + GW	1	D/V/10/L	315	40	310	Yugoslavia
BTR-50P	FT	13.97	22.33	2 + 14	14	–	1	D/V/6/L	240	27	160	Russia
BMP-2 MICV	FT	14.07	22.08	3 + 7	*	30 + GW	1	D/V/6/L	300	40	340	Russia
OT-64 APC	8 × 8	14.07	24.42	2 + 18	10	–	2	D/V/8/A	180	37	310	Czech
YW-534 APC	FT	14.07	20.08	2 + 13	*	–	1	D/4/A	320	40	320	China
Type 90 APC	FT	14.17	21.75	2 + 13	*	–	1	D/V/8/T/L	320	40	310	China
SPZ 12-3	FT	14.38	18.25	3 + 5	30	20	1	P/9	235	36	175	Germany
OTO-Melara C13	FT	14.41	17.42	3 + 9	63	–	1	D/V/6/S	360	43	310	Italy
Renault VAB	6 × 6	14.57	20.0	2 + 10	*	options		D/6/T/L	250	62	800	France
LVT(A)-1	FT	14.64	26.08	6	12	37	3	P/R/7/A	262	25	125	USA
Leonidas APC	FT	14.56	17.25	1 + 8	25	–	1	D/6/T/L	325	40	325	Greece
Steyr 4K 7FA	FT	14.56	17.25	1 + 8	25	–	1	D/6/T	320	40	325	Austria
Panhard VCR-2	8 × 8	14.75	19.67	2 + 10	*	25	1	2 × D/V/6	290	62	500	France
Timoney 6 × 6	6 × 6	14.76	21.17	2 + 10	*	options		D/6	350	62	455	Ireland
BMP-30	FT	14.78	23.33	3 + 7	*	30 + GW	1	D	302	37	372	Bulgaria

Name	Wheels	Weight	Length	Crew	Armour	Armament		Engine	Power	Speed	Range	Country
BMP-23	FT	14.95	23.92	3 + 7	*	23 + GW	1	D/V/6/L	315	40	340	Bulgaria
FV432 Trojan APC	FT	15.04	17.25	2 + 10	12	–	1	M/6/L	240	32	360	UK
MARS-15	FT	15.05	19.75	1 + 12	*	options		D	400	47	370	France
WZ-551	6 × 6	15.05	21.83	3 + 9	*	–	1	D/V/8/A	250	53	375	China
Sisu XA-180 APC	6 × 6	15.25	24.17	2 + 10	*	–	1	D/6/T/L	236	62	500	Finland
Type 77 APC	FT	15.26	24.25	2 + 16	*	–	1	D/4/L	400	38	230	China
OT-62 APC	FT	15.74	22.83	2 + 18	14	82RCL	1	D/V/6/S/L	300	37	310	Czech
NVH-1	FT	15.75	19.75	2 + 9	*	25	1	D/V/8/T/A	320	40	310	China
MLI-84	FT	16.34	24.0	2 + 9	*	73 + GW	1	D/V/8/T/L	350	40	375	Romania
Fuchs APC	6 × 6	16.73	22.42	2 + 10	*	–	–	D/V/8/L	320	65	500	Germany
Mowag Tornado	FT	16.92	19.75	2 + 8	*	25	2	M/V/8/L	430	44	372	Switzerland
Bravia V-200 APC	4 × 4	17.18	18.42	2 + 4	8	–	2	D/V/6/T/L	210	60	805	Portugal
LVT(A)-4	FT	17.61	26.08	6	30	75	2	P/R/7/A	262	16	150	USA
Cardoen VTP-1 Orca	6 × 6	17.71	25.75	2 + 16	16	–	–	D/V/6/L	260	75	620	Chile
Charrua	FT	17.71	21.08	2 + 9	*	–	1	D/V/6/T/L	395	43	310	Brazil
Mowag Piranha	10 × 10	17.71	24.42	6	*	105	2	D	350	62	500	Switzerland
United Def IFV Light	FT	17.85	19.33	3 + 6	*	25 + GW	1	D/V/6	400	40	300	USA
United Def MTV Light	FT	17.85	19.17	2 + 12	*	–	1	D/V/6	400	40	300	USA
AV-90	FT	18.20	19.67	2 + 10	*	–	1	D/V/8/T/L	450	40	350	Italy/Ger
SIBMAS APC	6 × 6	18.20	24.0	3 + 11	*	90	2	D/6/T/L	320	62	620	Belgium
BMP-3 MICV	FT	18.40	23.58	3 + 7	*	100 + 30	3	D/V/10/L	500	43	370	Russia
M75 APC	FT	18.53	17.0	2 + 10	25	–	1	P/HO/6/A	295	44	115	USA
Ratel 90	6 × 6	18.70	23.67	4 + 6	20	90	3	D/6/T/L	282	65	620	S Africa
Steyr KmpfSchPz 90	FT	18.9	20.25	3 + 8	*	30	1	D/6	470	43	310	Austria
Kentaurus	FT	19.0	19.67	3 + +8	*	30 + GW	1	D/V/6	420	47	310	Greece
M59 APC	FT	19.01	19.42	2 + 10	16	–	1	2 × P/6/L	254	32	100	USA
Type 89 MICV	FT	20.17	22.33	3 + 7	*	35 + GW	1	D	600	43	185	Japan
VCC-80	FT	21.36	22.0	3 + 6	*	25	2	D/V/6/T/L	520	44	310	Italy
Mowag Shark	8 × 8	21.65	24.67	4	*	105	1	D/V/8/T/L	530	62	310	Switzerland
CV-90-40 IFV	FT	22.04	21.25	3 + 8	*	40	1	D/4/L	550	43	*	Sweden
Bradley M3 CFV	FT	22.10	21.17	3 + 2	*	25 + GW	1	D/8/T/L	500	40	300	USA
Bradley M2 IFV		22.23		3 + 6								
Mowag Taifun	6 × 6	22.43	22.33	3 + 6	30	20	3	D/V/8/T/L	530	43	310	Italy
LVTP-7	FT	22.47	26.0	3 + 25	45	–	1	D/V/8/T/L	400	40	300	USA
Bionix 25	FT	22.63	19.33	3 + 7	*	25	3	D/V/6	475	43	*	Singapore
Dardo	FT	22.63	22.0	2 + 7	*	25 + GW	1	D/V/8/T	520	44	310	Italy
Warrior (MCV-80)	FT	24.11	20.83	3 + 7	*	30	1	D/V/8/L	550	47	410	UK
Ascod MICV	FT	24.40	20.33	3 + 8	*	30	1	D/V/8/L	600	43	370	Austria/Spn
Multi-Role AV	6 × 6	26.08	23.75	10	*	–	1	D	530	65	680	UK/Fr/Ger
TAMSE VCTP APC	FT	27.56	22.42	2 + 19	*	20	2	D/V/8/L	720	50	375	Argentina
BWP-2000	FT	28.54	24.08	3 + 9	*	25 + GW	1	D	700	43	310	Poland
Marder MICV	FT	28.75	22.25	4 + 6	*	20	1	D/6/L	600	46	325	Germany
Warrior 2000	FT	29.92	22.83	3 + 7	*	30	1	D/V/8	650	47	372	UK
LVTP-5	FT	31.15	29.67	3 + 34	16	–	1	P/V/12/L	810	30	190	USA
Gen Dynamics AAAV	FT	31.86	29.42	3 + 18	*	30	1	D/V/8	850	45	400	USA
Multi-Role AV	8 × 8	32.48	25.83	11	*	–	1	D	710	65	680	UK/Fr/Ger
BTR–T	FT	37.9	21.17	2 + 5	*	30 + GW	1	D/V/12	580	35	400	Russia

SELF-PROPELLED GUNS

Self-propelled field guns, assault guns, tank destroyers, SP anti-aircraft guns and similar types. Close support tanks, 20mm cannons on the back of half-tracks, wheeled anti-tank guns carried portée in the back of 3-ton trucks and similar devices do not qualify.

Definitions

Self-Propelled Gun: for the purposes of this book, this is an artillery piece (gun or howitzer) on a mobile mounting, tracked, wheeled or semi-tracked, and used in its normal role. The mobile mounting is there purely to move the gun from here to there quicker than by towing.

Assault Gun: an artillery piece or a tank gun, mounted into a modified tank chassis, usually with restricted traverse and elevation, for the purpose of accompanying either infantry or tank assaults and providing heavy fire support.

Tank Destroyer: a vehicle equipped with a high velocity tank or anti-tank gun and designed purely as a gun carrier; it is a specialised SP gun and is sometimes called an SPAT (Self-Propelled Anti-Tank) gun.

Specifications

The specifications are divided into two sections; the first covers the gun and its performance, the second the vehicle.

Gun Data Most of the items are self-explanatory, but there are certain conventions. *Length of barrel* is the length from the face of the breech block to the muzzle; *Weight of shell* is the weight of the standard projectile around which the gun was designed; other projectiles may differ. Where there is a significant difference for tactical reasons, this is given – e.g. specialist anti-tank projectiles. *Muzzle velocity* is that obtained by firing the highest charge with the standard projectile; exceptions are noted. *Maximum range* is that obtained against ground targets with the standard projectile and maximum charge. *Operational range* (for anti-tank guns) is that range at which fire can be opened with a reasonable certainty that a hit will be obtained and the armour of a typical MBT of the relevant period defeated. *Effective ceiling* is the greatest altitude at which effective fire can be brought to bear on an aircraft. *Ammunition types* gives the major types; the listing is not comprehensive. *Ammunition load* is the number of rounds for the main armament carried on the vehicle ready for use

Vehicle data *All-up weight* is the combat-loaded weight, with fuel, ammunition, radios, crew, rations, water and all the authorised paraphernalia. It does not include loot, extra rations and illegal spare parts. *Armour* is the greatest thickness of plate, generally the hull or turret front. In the case of current service equipments, this may not be known. *Dimensions* are to the extremities of the hull, including skirting plates and such additions, when in march order; unfolded loading platforms and recoil spades are not taken into account. *Height* is to the highest part of the hull and gun, or to the top of the turret, ignoring any machine gun fitted to the roof. *Speed* and *Range* are normally maker's figures for a new vehicle in perfect condition on a hard road with premium fuel and a following wind; they are rarely achieved in service

Nomenclature is that attached to the weapon when introduced; in several cases the manufacturer of the gun has been absorbed into a new company or consortium and the gun, if still in production, may be given a new title. In such cases the new title will be listed, but referred back to the original form.

2S1 122mm SP Howitzer M1974 Russia
State factories
1971. This equipment went into Soviet and Polish service in 1971 at the same time as the 2S3 (*below*) to inaugurate a fresh generation of Soviet SP guns. The vehicle is based very obviously on the MT-LB multi-purpose vehicle chassis, and is provided with a low turret carrying the 122mm howitzer, which has a fume extractor and muzzle brake. The gun is a development of the towed D-30 weapon.

Armament: 1 × 122mm D-30A
Barrel length: 16ft 0in (4.86m)
Weight of shell: 47lb 14oz (21.72kg)
Muzzle velocity: 2,264ft/sec (690m/sec)
Maximum range: 16,730yd (15,300m)
Ammunition types: HR, HEAT, smoke, illuminating
Ammunition load: 40

Vehicle: Based on MT-LB
Crew: 6
All-up weight: 15.45 tons (15,700kg)
Armour: 20mm
Hull length: 23ft 9in (7.25m)
Width: 9ft 4in (2.85m)
Height: 8ft 11in (2.72m)
Engine: V-8 diesel, 240bhp
Road speed: 37mph (60km/hr)
Range: 310 miles (500km)

2S3 152mm SP Gun M1973 Russia
State factories
1971. This was one of the first of the 'new generation' of Soviet SP artillery, a neat and simple, if somewhat cramped design. The chassis was specially designed, and not a made-over tank chassis as is the usual SP gun, and there are six irregularly-spaced roadwheels on each side, with front drive and rear idlers. There is also a bulldozer blade under the hull nose to allow the driver to dig an emplacement for his vehicle. There is no recoil spade, the vehicle being substantial enough to absorb much of the firing shock. The gun is mounted in a turret placed at the rear of the hull and is recognisable by a prominent recoil cylinder above the barrel.

Armament: 1 × 152mm
Barrel length: 17ft 0in (5.195m)
Weight of shell: 95lb 14oz (43.5kg)
Muzzle velocity: 2,150ft/sec (655m/sec)
Maximum range: 20,230yd (18,500m)
Ammunition types: HE/Frag, HEAT, AP, smoke, nuclear
Ammunition load: 46

Vehicle
Crew: 4 (+2 in ammunition carrier)

All-up weight: 27.06 tons (27,500kg)
Armour: not disclosed
Hull length: 25ft 6in (7.76m)
Width: 10ft 8in (3.25m)
Height: 10ft 0in (3.05m)
Engine: V-12 diesel, 520bhp
Road speed: 43mph (70km/hr)
Range: 500 miles (800km)

2S4 240mm SP Mortar Russia
State factories
For reasons best known to themselves the Russians have always set great store by a breech-loading 240mm mortar which has been in service for many years. This is the SP version, introduced in the early 1970s (it is also called the **M-1975**), and it is believed that there are about 400 in Russian service. The tracked chassis shares a number of components with other SP guns and missile carriers, and carries the mortar, complete with its standard baseplate, in such a manner than it can be erected by hydraulic means simply by lowering the rear end and baseplate and then forcing the barrel back until it actually points rearward and the baseplate sits just behind the rear end of the vehicle and remains connected during firing.

Armament: 1 × 240mm mortar Model 2B8
Barrel length: 17ft 6in (5.34m)
Weight of shell: 288lb 7oz (130.85kg)
Muzzle velocity: 1,125ft/sec (343m/sec)
Maximum range: 10,610yd (9,700m)
Ammunition types: HE/Frag, smoke, nuclear
Ammunition load: 40

Vehicle
Crew: 4 (+5 on ammunition carrier)
All-up weight: 27.06 tons (27,500kg)
Armour: not disclosed
Hull length: 27ft 10in (8.50m)
Width: 10ft 6in (3.20m)
Height: 10ft 6in (3.20m)
Engine: V-12 diesel, 520bhp
Road speed: 37mph (60km/hr)
Range: 310 miles (500km)

2S5 152mm SP Gun Russia
State factories
This uses the same chassis as the 2S3 152mm equipment described above, and in this application is very reminiscent of the US 155mm M40 in outline, with the same flat-topped hull sloping down at the front, and with the gun mounted at the rear end and steadied in action by the usual sort of blade. The gun is provided with a large multi-baffle

muzzle brake, which no doubt reduces the firing shock to the chassis, and with a mechanical ramming system.

Armament: 1 × 152mm
Barrel length: 26ft 10in (8.19m)
Weight of shell: 101lb 7oz (46kg)
Muzzle velocity: 2,657ft/sec (810m/sec)
Maximum range: 31,060yd (28,400m)
Ammunition types: HE/Frag, CP, ICM, smoke, nuclear, chemical
Ammunition load: 30

Vehicle: Based on T-72 tank chassis
Crew: 7
All-up weight: 27.75 tons (28,200kg)
Armour: not disclosed
Length with gun: 27ft 4in (8.33m)
Width: 10ft 8in (3.25m)
Height: 9ft 1in (2.76m)
Engine: supercharged multi-fuel, 520bhp
Road speed: 39mph (63km/hr)
Range: 310 miles (500km)

2S6 SP Air Defence System Russia
State factories
1986. This vehicle carries four 30mm cannon, eight missile launchers, a surveillance radar, a tracking radar, and the associated fire control computer systems. In many respects, particularly in the positioning of the radar antennae and the guns outboard of the turret, it appears to have been influenced by the German Gepard. The missile launchers are in two blocks of four, below the cannons on each side of the turret. The surveillance radar antenna is at the back of the turret, the tracker antenna on the turret front face. The chassis is a special tracked utility chassis adopted for various missile launchers and other vehicles.

Armament: 4 × 30mm; 8 × SA-19 SAM
Barrel length: not disclosed
Weight of shell: 29.5oz (840g)
Muzzle velocity: 3,150ft/sec (960m/sec)
Rate of fire: 1,000rpg/min
Effective ceiling: 9,840ft (3,000m) gun
11,490ft (3,500m) missile
Ammunition types: HE, AP, APDS
Ammunition load: 1,900 × 30mm; 8 missiles

Vehicle
Crew: 4
All-up weight: 35.43 tons (36,000kg)
Armour: not disclosed
Hull length: 23ft 1in (7.03m)
Width: 10ft 8in (3.24m)
Height: 11ft 0in (3.36m) radar folded

Engine: diesel
Road speed: 40mph (65km/hr)
Range: 280 miles (450km)

2S7 203mm SP Gun Russia
State factories
1975. Like some other Russian equipments, this is known from photographs, and a specimen, claimed to be an early model, is on show in the Artillery Museum, but it has never been seen in any public parade or with any army formation during exercises, although something in excess of 1,000 are said to have been taken into service. It has a long, low, hull with seven roadwheels and six return rollers on each side, and the gun is mounted on top of the hull, at the rear end, with the exceptionally long barrel reaching out well in front of the vehicle. The driver's cab is at the very front, overhanging the front tracks. The usual type of hydraulic spade is fitted at the rear of the vehicle.

Armament: 1 × 203mm M1975
Barrel length: not known
Weight of shell: 242lb 8oz (110kg)
Muzzle velocity: 3,150ft/sec (960m/sec)
Maximum range: 40,775yd (37,285m)
Ammunition types: HE
Ammunition load: 4

Vehicle
Crew: 7
All-up weight: 45.76 tons (46,500kg)
Armour: not known
Length, with gun: 43ft 0in (13.10m)
Width: 11ft 1in (3.38m)
Height: 9ft 10in (3.0m)
Engine: V-12 diesel, 745bhp
Road speed: 31mph (50km/hr)
Range: 420 miles (675km)

2S9 120mm SP Mortar Russia
State factories
This vehicle was first seen in 1981 and was later deployed during the Soviet intervention in Afghanistan. It appears to be designed as a support assault gun for airborne troops and uses a breech-loading smoothbore 120mm mortar as its main armament. It can fire at high angles in the conventional mortar role, or it can fire in a flat trajectory using either a HEAT shaped-charge anti-tank round or a gun-launched anti-tank missile. The chassis is a lengthened version of that of the BMD-1 airborne MICV, with the mortar carried in a revolving turret over the central fighting compartment.

Armament: 1 x 120mm breech-loading mortar
Barrel length: 6ft 1in (1.85m)
Weight of shell: 35lb 4oz (16.0kg)
Muzzle velocity: 985ft/sec (300m/sec)
Maximum range: 9,685yd (8,855m)
Ammunition types: HE/Frag, HEAT, 'Gran' gun-launched missile
Ammunition load: 60

Vehicle: Based on BMD MICV
Crew: 4
All-up weight: 8.56 tons (8,700kg)
Armour: not disclosed
Hull length: 19ft 9in (6.02m)
Width: 8ft 8in (2.63m)
Height: 7ft 6in (2.30m)
Engine: diesel, 240bhp
Road speed: 37mph (60km/hr)
Range: 310 miles (500km)

2S19 152mm SP Gun Russia
State factories
1989. The 2S19 is a 152mm gun-howitzer carried on a chassis which is basically that of the T-80 MBT but which has the power pack of the T-72 MBT. The turret is a special construction to carry the gun and crew and is much larger and taller, with rounded edges, and reaches almost to the rear of the hull. The suspension has six roadwheels on each side but there is no form of recoil spade. It is possible that the torsion bar suspension can be locked when firing, but it is also possible that there is no form of restraint and the weight of the vehicle absorbs most of the recoil shock.

Armament: 1 x 152mm gun-howitzer M1976
Barrel length: 26ft 10in (8.19m)
Weight of shell: 101lb 7oz (46kg)
Muzzle velocity: 2,658ft/sec (810m/sec)
Maximum range: 31,060yd (28,400m)
Ammunition types: HE/Frag, CP, ICM, smoke, nuclear, chemical
Ammunition load: 50

Vehicle
Crew: 5
All-up weight: 41.33 tons (42,000kg)
Armour: not disclosed
Hull length: 24ft 3in (7.40m)
Width: 11ft 1in (3.38m)
Height: 9ft 10in (2.99m)
Engine: V-12 multi-fuel, 780bhp
Road speed: 37mph (60km/hr)
Range: 310 miles (500km)

2S23 120mm SP Mortar Russia
State factories
1989. This is the same weapon as that used on the 2S9, a 120mm smoothbore breech-loaded mortar, but mounted in a turret on the hull of the 8 x 8-wheeled BTR-80 APC. Just what tactical function this vehicle is intended to fulfil is not entirely clear; it is unlikely to be used by the airborne force, since it weighs almost twice as much as the BMD-based model. It does, though, have the advantage of being amphibious.

Armament: 1 x 120mm breech-loading mortar
Barrel length: 6ft 1in (1.85m)
Weight of shell: 35lb 4oz (16.0kg)
Muzzle velocity: 985ft/sec (300m/sec)
Maximum range: 9,685yd (8,855m)
Ammunition types: HE/Frag, HEAT, 'Gran' gun-launched missile
Ammunition load: 30

Vehicle: BTR-80 APC
Crew: 4
All-up weight: 14.27 tons (14,500kg)
Armour: not disclosed
Hull length: 24ft 7in (7.50m)
Width: 9ft 6in (2.90m)
Height: 9ft 2in (2.80m)
Engine: V-8 diesel, 210bhp
Road speed: 50mph (80km/hr)
Range: 370 miles (600km)

2S25 125mm SP AT Russia
Volgograd
1999. This is a direct-fire assault/anti-tank gun which uses a 125mm smoothbore gun based upon that used in the T-72 and later MBTs. The vehicle is a lightweight machine with minimal armour protection in order to give it high mobility; it is also amphibious, which opens up an interesting area of speculation about future anti-tank tactics. It is largely based upon components of the BMP-3 MICV, and is tracked, with seven roadwheels per side, and has a similar low hull with frontal prow. The driver sits centrally in front, the turret with gun is central, and the engine and transmission are at the rear. The gun is provided with an auto-loader. Full details are not yet available.

Armament: 1 x 125mm smoothbore; 1 x MG
Barrel length: 20ft 0in (6.1m)
Weight of shot: 15.75lb (7.15kg) APFSDS
Muzzle velocity: 5,415ft/sec (1,650m/sec) APFSDS
Maximum range: 13,340yd (12,200m) HE
Ammunition types: HE, HEAT, APFSDS
Ammunition load: 40

Vehicle: BMP-3
Crew: 3
All-up weight: 17.7 tons (18,000kg)
Engine: diesel, 510bhp
Road speed: 45mph (70km/hr)
Range: 310 miles (500km)
Other details: not disclosed

2S31 120mm SP Gun/Mortar Russia
State factories

1997. This equipment, which currently exists only in prototype form, is a tracked chassis based upon the BMP-3 IFV, carrying an armoured turret which mounts a new 120mm gun/mortar. It is amphibious, though this is more probably a by-product of using that particular chassis than an actual tactical requirement. It is said to be completely autonomous, having its own fire control computer and positioning system.

Armament: 1 × 120mm gun/mortar
Barrel length: not disclosed
Weight of shell: 43lb 10oz (19.8kg)
Muzzle velocity: 1,270ft/sec (387m/sec)
Maximum range: 9,685yd (8,855m)
Ammunition types: HE, HERA, HEAT, smoke
Ammunition load: 70

Vehicle: BMP-3
Crew: 4
All-up weight: 19.19 tons (19,500kg)
Armour: not disclosed
Hull length: 22ft 0in (6.72m)
Width: 10ft 4in (3.15m)
Height: not known
Engine: diesel, 515bhp
Road speed: 43mph (70km/hr)
Range: 372 miles (600km)

Abbot UK
Vickers

1964. The British Army, in the 1950s, were on the point of adopting the 87mm Garrington Gun as their new towed artillery piece, when NATO standardisation demanded that they adopt the 105mm calibre for their close support gun. The quick solution was the Italian 105mm M56 pack howitzer; the long term solution was this 105mm SP gun, Abbot. It was based on the FV432 APC chassis and mounted an entirely new gun firing entirely new ammunition and not, as almost every other 105mm howitzer in NATO, the American M1 family. The layout of the vehicle had the driver and engine in the front, with a full-powered rotating turret at the rear. The barrel had a fume extractor and muzzle brake, and loading was assisted by a power rammer and semi-automatic breech. A flotation screen was permanently fitted to the hull. Shortly after adoption, a replacement barrel, capable of firing American M1 ammunition, was made for use in areas where supply of US ammunition would be easier than supplying British. Abbot was also adopted by the Indian Army.

Armament: 105mm QF Gun L13
Barrel length: 12ft 9in (3.89m)
Weight of shell: 35lb 6oz (16.06kg)
Muzzle velocity: 2,313ft/sec (705m/sec)
Maximum range: 18,920yd (17,300m)
Ammunition types: HE, HESH, smoke, illuminating
Ammunition load: 40

Vehicle: FV432 basis
Crew: 4
All-up weight: 17.19 tons (17,4625kg)
Armour: 12mm maximum
Hull length: 18ft 9in (5.70m)
Width: 8ft 8in (2.64m)
Height: 8ft 2in (2.48m)
Engine: Rolls-Royce K60, multi-fuel, 6-cylinder vertically-opposed, 250bhp at 2,750rpm
Road speed: 30mph (50km/hr)
Range: 245 miles (395km)

Achilles UK
Woolwich

1944. Achilles was the British name for the US M10 Gun Motor Carriage (*qv*) when fitted with the British 17-pounder anti-tank gun. The performance of this gun was far superior to that of the American 3-inch M7 gun originally fitted to the M10, and as soon as supplies of the 17-pounder were available the conversions began. The Achilles can always be distinguished from the M10 or M36 by the presence of a muzzle brake on the gun. A slight adjustment had to be made to the turret counterweight, but apart from that there was no physical difference except the weight and length of the gun.

Armament: Ordnance QF 17-pdr Mark 1
Barrel length: 13ft 9in (4.20m)
Weight of shot: 17.0lb (7.71kg) APC
7.65lb (3.47kg) APDS
Muzzle velocity: 2,900ft/sec (884m/sec) APC
3,950ft/sec (1,204m/sec) APDS
Maximum range: 10,000yd (9,145m) HE
Penetration: 231mm/1,000yd/90° APDS
Ammunition types: HE, APC, APDS
Ammunition load: 50

Vehicle: M10 GMC
Crew: 5
All-up weight: 29.47 tons (29,937kg)
Armour: 64mm maximum
Hull length: 19ft 7in (5.96m)
Width: 10ft 0in (3.04m)
Height: 8ft 2in (2.49m)
Engine: 2 x GMC diesel, total 375bhp at 2,100rpm;
    or Ford V-8 petrol, 450bhp at 2,600rpm
Road speed: 30mph (48km/hr)
Range: 200 miles (320km)

Alecto UK

1942. This was intended to be a light close support gun for accompanying infantry, but finding a suitable chassis and developing a suitable gun were performed slowly and it was not until 1944 that the combination of the Harry Hopkins tank chassis and a 95mm infantry howitzer was decided on. The tank's turret was removed and the hull modified so as to mount the howitzer in the front plate. The driver sat behind the gun, slightly raised, in a cupola on the vehicle's centre-line. The remainder of the crew were somewhat cramped, and protection was scanty, but by the time the design was completed the war was over and Alecto was never produced. Another version, with a 25-pounder gun, was proposed but never even reached prototype stage.

Armament: 95mm QF SP Howitzer Mark 3
Barrel length: 6ft 11in (2.10m)
Weight of shell: 25lb 0oz (11.34kg)
Muzzle velocity: 1,111ft/sec (339m/sec)
Maximum range: 6,800yd (6,217m)
Ammunition types: HE, smoke, flare
Ammunition load: 20 rounds

Vehicle: Carrier, Alecto, SP 95mm howitzer, Mark 1
Crew: 4
All-up weight: 8 tons (8,128kg)
Armour: 10mm maximum
Hull length: 14ft 3in (4.34m)
Width: 8ft 10in (2.69m)
Height: 8ft 2in (2.48m)
Engine: Meadows, 12-cylinder, horizontally-opposed, petrol, 165bhp at 2,700rpm
Road speed: 30mph (48km/hr)
Range: not known

Al Fao 210mm SP Gun Iraq
State factories

1989. This was unveiled at the same time as the 155mm Majnoon SP gun and is precisely the same vehicle but mounting a 21cm (8.26-inch) gun. The two equipments look very similar, but the Al Fao can be distinguished by its longer gun and much larger muzzle brake. As for the 155mm gun, the mounting is a 6 x 6 wheeled chassis divided into two units which are linked by a rolling joint and hydraulic rams. The front unit carries the driver and engine, the rear section, with four wheels, carries the turreted gun. Although prototypes were publicly displayed in 1989 the subsequent history of this weapon is unclear and it is probable that few, if any, were produced for service.

Armament: 1 x 210mm gun
Barrel length: 36ft 6in (11.13m)
Weight of shell: 241lb (109.4kg)
Muzzle velocity: 3,140ft/sec (997m/sec) ERFB
Maximum range: 49,210yd (45,000m) ERFB
Ammunition types: HE, smoke, conventional and ERFB
Ammunition load: not disclosed

Vehicle
Crew: 6
All-up weight: 47.74 tons (48,500kg)
Armour: not disclosed
Length overall: 49ft 3in (15.0m)
Width: 11ft 6in (3.50m)
Height: 11ft 10in (3.60m)
Engine: Mercedes-Benz diesel, 560bhp
Road speed: 55mph (90km/hr)
Range: not disclosed

AMS (Armoured Mortar System)
Canada/UK/USA
Delco, GM Canada, United Defense, Royal Ordnance

1995. This is a co-operative venture by the four companies shown above, and the result is that the 120mm breech-loading mortar developed in the mid-1980s by Royal Ordnance is fitted into a turret developed by Royal Ordnance and Delco, which then goes on to a Canadian 8 x 8 Light Armoured Vehicle built by General Motors of Canada. United Defense were associated with Royal Ordnance in the early development of the turret and its testing in the Middle East, as a result of which Saudi Arabia ordered 72 equipments in 1996, the first of which was delivered in 1998.

Armament: 1 x 120mm BL mortar; 1 x MG
Barrel length: 9ft 10in (3.0m)
Weight of shell: 29.1lb (13.20kg)
Muzzle velocity: not disclosed
Maximum range: 9,840yd (9,000m)
Ammunition types: HE, smoke, illuminating
Ammunition load: not disclosed

Vehicle: LAV
Crew: 3

All-up weight: *ca* 12.90 tons (13,000kg)
Armour: not disclosed
Hull length: 21ft 0in (6.39m)
Width: 8ft 3in (2.50m)
Height: 9ft 4in (2.85m)
Engine: Detroit Diesel V-6, 275bhp at 2,800rpm
Road speed: 62mph (100km/hr)
Range: 415 miles (670km)

AMX-13 DCA France
Thomson-CSF

1962. This was a self-propelled AA gun (DCA = *Défense Contre Avions*) based on the chassis of the AMX-13 light tank. It was completely autonomous, with its own radar and fire control computer in the turret together with the twin 30mm cannon. The French Army, after prolonged testing, bought 60 of them, after which the makers made some minor modifications to the turret and fitted it on to an AMX-30 chassis. This became the AMX-30 DCA, but the only army to adopt it was the Saudi Arabian, and that largely for logistic reasons, since they were already using the AMX-30 tank.

AMX-13 DCA

Armament: 2 × 30mm Hispano-Suiza HS 831 cannon
Barrel length: 8ft 5in (2.57m)
Weight of shell: 12.7oz (360gm)
Muzzle velocity: 3,543ft/sec (1,080m/sec)
Effective ceiling: 14,760ft (4,500m)
Ammunition types: HE, APHE
Ammunition load: not known

Vehicle: AMX-13 tank
Crew: 3
All-up weight: 14.76 tons (15,000kg)
Armour: 30mm maximum
Hull length: 16ft 11in (5.15m)
Width: 8ft 8in (2.64m)
Height: 8ft 10in (2.69m) radar dish folded
Engine: SOFAM 8-cylinder, horizontally-opposed, petrol, 270bhp at 3,200rpm
Road speed: 37mph (60km/hr)
Range: 215 miles (350km)

AMX-30 DCA

Armament: 2 × 30mm Hispano-Suiza HS831 cannon
Barrel length: 8ft 5in (2.57m)
Weight of shell: 12.7oz (360g)
Muzzle velocity: 3,543ft/sec (1,080m/sec)
Effective ceiling: 14,760ft (4,500m)
Ammunition types: HE, APHE
Ammunition load: not known

Vehicle: AMX-30 tank
Crew: 3
All-up weight: 35.43 tons (36,000kg)

Armour: not known
Hull length: 22ft 4in (6.80m)
Width: 10ft 2in (3.1m)
Height: 9ft 10in (3.0m)
Engine: Hispano-Suiza 110, flat-12, multi-fuel, 700bhp at 2,400rpm
Road speed: 40mph (65km/hr)
Range: 400 miles (640km)

AMX-40 DCA France
AMX

1953. This was an AMX-13 tank chassis with a large turret in which was mounted a standard 40mm L/60 Bofors light anti-aircraft gun. It appeared at military shows for a few years but was not adopted for service. A variant model mounting four 20mm Oerlikon cannon was also produced and tested in 1956, but this, too, failed to find a buyer and the design was abandoned. Do not confuse this with the AMX-40 MBT project of the 1990s, detailed in the Tanks section.

Armament: 1 × Bofors 40mm L/60 gun
Barrel length: 9ft 10in (3.00m)
Weight of shell: 2lb 0oz (0.91kg)
Muzzle velocity: 2,800ft/sec (854m/sec)
Effective ceiling: 10,200ft (3,110m)
Ammunition types: HE, AP
Ammunition load: not known

Vehicle
Crew: 3
All-up weight: 15 tons (15,240kg)
Armour: 40mm
Hull length: 16ft 10in (5.13m)
Width: 8ft 8in (2.54m)
Height: 7ft 10in (2.39m)
Engine: Sofam 8GKB, 8-cylinder petrol, 250bhp at 3,200rpm
Road speed: 25mph (40km/hr)
Range: 130 miles (210km)

AMX GCT-155 France
Roanne

1980. This self-propelled 155mm gun was an extremely advanced design for its day and is still in the forefront of its class. Based on the AMX-30 tank hull and chassis, the massive turret is fully automated and can be operated by two men, the commander/gunner and loader. It is completely autonomous, with its own navigation system and fire control computer, so that it does not require a command post to follow it around. Ammunition is carried in a magazine at the rear of the turret and is automatically fed to the gun breech and loaded by push-button commands from the loader. The cartridge is in a combustible case and is ignited by an induction coil inside the breech block. There is therefore no necessity to load primers and no requirement for anyone to go near the gun breech, and it can be separated from the crew, thus not exposing them to fumes. It is in service with the French, Saudi Arabian and Iraqi armies.

Armament: 1 x 155mm howitzer
Barrel length: 20ft 4in (6.20m)
Weight of shell: 96lb 7oz (43.75kg)
Muzzle velocity: 2,493ft/sec (760m/sec)
Maximum range: 30,620yd (28,000m)
Ammunition types: HE, smoke, rocket-assisted, base bleed
Ammunition load: 42

Vehicle: AMX-30 tank
Crew: 4
All-up weight: 41.33 tons (42,000kg)
Armour: 30mm maximum
Hull length: 22ft 0in (6.70m)
Width: 10ft 4in (3.15m)
Height: 10ft 8in (3.25m)
Engine: Hispano-Suiza HS 110, multi-fuel, horizontally opposed 12-cylinder, supercharged, 720bhp at 2,000rpm
Road speed: 37mph (60km/hr)
Range: 280 miles (450km)

AMX 105 Mark 61 France
Roanne

1952. This was designed in the late 1940s and was among the first post-war designs to appear in the French Army. The hull and chassis are those of the AMX-13 light tank, upon which was built a fixed superstructure mounting the standard field artillery Modèle 50 105mm howitzer. The result is a sound and simple design which stayed in service into the late 1980s and is probably still in use by Morocco and Indonesia, the only two other countries which bought it. The fighting compartment is closed, with a commander's cupola on top, and the vehicle is unique in having a separate gun shield in front of the usual mantlet. Not also that this chassis differs from other AMX-13 derivatives by having the rear idler off the ground.

Armament: 1 x 105mm howitzer M1950
Barrel length: 10ft 4in (3.15m)
Weight of shell: 35lb 4oz (16.0kg)
Muzzle velocity: 2,200ft/sec (670m/sec)
Maximum range: 16,400yd (15,000m)
Ammunition types: HE, HEAT, smoke, illuminating
Ammunition load: 56

Vehicle: AMX-13 tank
Crew: 5
All-up weight: 16.24 tons (16,500kg)
Armour: 20mm maximum
Hull length: 16ft 10in (5.13m)
Width: 8ft 8in (2.65m)
Height: 8ft 10in (2.70m)
Engine: SOFAM V-8 petrol, 250bhp at 3,200rpm
Road speed: 37mph (60km/hr)
Range: 215 miles (350km)

Archer UK
Vickers

1943. The 17-pounder gun, adopted in 1942, was the master of any tank in the world, but it was only available in towed form; the British Army had no tank capable of mounting the gun, and no immediate prospect of one. A solution was found by taking redundant Valentine tanks, removing the turret, building up the hull and mounting the 17-pounder gun to fire to the rear, over the engine deck. The result was low, compact and agile, was a success in North-West Europe in 1944–45, and stayed in service until the mid-1950s.

Armament: Ordnance QF 17-pdr Gun Mark 1
Barrel length: 13ft 9.5in (4.20m)
Weight of shot: 17.0lb (7.71kg) APC
　　　　　　　7.65lb (3.47kg) APDS
Muzzle velocity: 2,900ft/sec (884 m/sec) APC
　　　　　　　3,950ft/sec (1,204m/sec) APDS
Maximum range: 10,000yd (9,145m) HE
Penetration: 231mm/1,000yd/90° APDS
Ammunition types: HE, APC, APDS
Ammunition load: 39 rounds

Vehicle: Carrier, Valentine, SP 17-pdr Gun Mark 1
Crew: 4
All-up weight: 14.75 tons (14,990kg)
Armour: 60mm maximum
Hull length: 17ft 9in (5.41m)
Width: 9ft 0in (2.75m)
Height: 7ft 4in (2.23m)
Engine: GMC diesel, 6 cylinder, 192bhp at 1,900rpm
Road speed: 20mph (32km/hr)
Range: 100 miles (160km)

AS-90 UK
Vickers

Vickers Armstrong, carrying out sub-contract work on the SP-70 project, could see the defects in that design and quietly set about preparing a design of their own. At first it was developed as a turret and gun unit which could be dropped into a suitable tank hull so as to produce an SP gun, but as SP-70 became more and more impractical, a complete vehicle was designed and developed. When SP-70 was finally knocked on the head, the British had the choice between the US M109 in its latest version, or the Vickers AS-90. The former was, by this time, stretching its design to the limits, whereas the latter was new and with a long upgrading life ahead of it. It was selected and went into service in 1993. As originally built it mounts a 39-calibre howitzer, but it is capable of mounting 45- and 52-calibre weapons and will probably standardise on the latter in the near future.

Armament: Ordnance BL, 155mm Howitzer
Barrel length: 19ft 10in (6.045m)
Weight of shell: 100lb 5oz (42.55kg)
Muzzle velocity: 2,713ft/sec (827m/sec)
Maximum range: 27,012yd (24,700m) with
  conventional ammunition
Ammunition types: HE, smoke, illuminating, ICM
Ammunition load: 48

Vehicle: Carrier, Vickers, 155mm SP Howitzer
Crew: 5
All-up weight: 44.29 tons (45,000kg)
Armour: 17mm maximum
Hull length: 23ft 8in (7.20m)
Width: 11ft 2in (3.40m)
Height: 9ft 10in (3.00m)
Engine: Cummins V-8 diesel, 660bhp at 2,800rpm
Road speed: 34mph (55km/hr)
Range: 150miles (240km)

ASU-57 Russia
State factories
1957. This was a self-propelled anti-tank gun specifically designed for carriage by air and operations with airborne troops. To save weight the armour was thin and the hull open-topped, and as a result it was capable of being dropped by parachute. It remained in service well into the 1980s even though the gun was obsolete by anyone else's standards and incapable of harming modern heavy armour. Low-set, it had four roadwheels on each side, the last one on the ground and acting as the track idler.

Armament: 1 × 57mm gun
Barrel length: 13ft 8in (4.167m)
Weight of shell: 6lb 13oz (3.1kg)
Muzzle velocity: 3,280ft/sec (1,000m/sec)
Maximum range: 9,185yd (8,400m)
Ammunition types: HEAP, APDS

Vehicle
Crew: 3
All-up weight: 7.28 tons (7,400kg)

Armour: 10mm maximum
Hull length: 12ft 3in (3.73m)
Width: 7ft 3in (2.20m)
Height: 4ft 8in (1.42m)
Engine: ZIL-123, 6-cylinder, petrol, 110bhp
Road speed: 40mph (65km/hr)
Range: 200 miles (320km)

ASU-85 Russia
State factories
1960. This, like the ASU-57, was designed for use by airborne units, but this was air landed by heavy transport aircraft. A far more effective vehicle than the ASU-57, it would usually have landed in the first reinforcing wave, the ASU-57 being used in the initial capture of a suitable airfield. It had better protection, being fully enclosed and even had NBC protection for the crew. Much of the mechanical components are those of the PT-76 amphibious tank, and the hull is a simple sloped-front superstructure with the 85mm gun in the front plate, the driver alongside and below it. Night vision equipment is fitted.

Armament: 1 × 85mm gun D-70
Barrel length: 21ft 4in (6.49m)
Weight of shell: 11lb 2oz (5.07kg) HVAP
            21lb 3oz (9.62kg) HE
Muzzle velocity: 3,510ft/sec (1,070m/sec) HVAP
            2,600ft/sec (793m/sec) HE
Maximum range: 10,935yd (10,000m)
Ammunition types: HE, HEAT, HVAP
Ammunition load: 40

Vehicle: Based on PT-76 tank
Crew: 4
All-up weight: 15.25 tons (15,500kg)
Armour: 40mm maximum
Hull length: 19ft 8in (6.0m)
Width: 9ft 2in (2.8m)
Height: 6ft 10in (2.1m)
Engine: V-6 diesel, 240bhp at 1,800rpm
Road speed: 28mph (45km/hr)
Range: 160 miles (260km)

Avenger UK
Although employed as a tank destroyer this was originally designed as a tank, and formed part of the A30 Cromwell tank family. For that reason it is listed in the tank section under 'Avenger A30'.

Bandkanon Sweden
Bofors
1966. Also known as the VK/155, this was the first highly-automated SP gun; design work began in

1950, it appeared in 1966, and it is still in first line use by the Swedish Army. Built by Bofors it has an automated firing system, capable of delivering 15 rounds per minute. The gun itself is quite conventional, but behind it is a magazine containing 14 complete rounds, loaded in 5-round clips. (This is the only 155mm ammunition using a brass cartridge case and fixed round.) The mechanism is spring driven, the recoil of the gun cocking the springs for the next round. Ammunition feeds to a tray from where it is rammed into the chamber and the breech closes automatically. The gun can normally be operated by 4 men, but in the event of mechanical failure, 3 more men are added and the entire system can then be operated manually.

The tracked mounting is quite conventional, with six roadwheels on each side and a front drive sprocket. Rear stabilising jacks are lowered before firing, and turret traverse is restricted to 15° each side. An unusual feature is the presence of two engines; the diesel is for normal running, and the gas turbine can be brought in when extra bursts of power are required when moving across difficult terrain.

Armament: 1 × 155mm gun
Barrel length: 25ft 5in (7.75m)
Weight of shell: 105lb 13oz (48kg)
Muzzle velocity: 2,838ft/sec (865m/sec)
Maximum range: 26,900yd (24,600m)
Ammunition types: HE
Ammunition load: 14

Vehicle
Crew: 5
All-up weight: 52.17 tons (53,000kg)
Armour: 20mm maximum
Hull length: 21ft 6in (6.55m)
Width: 11ft 0in (3.37m)
Height: 11ft 0in (3.35m)
Engine: 1 × Rolls-Royce K60 6-cylinder opposed-piston, two-stroke multi-fuel, 240bhp at 3,750rpm; + 1 × Boeing 502-10MA gas turbine, 300shp at 38,000rpm
Road speed: 17mph (28km/hr)
Range: 140 miles (230km)

Birch Gun UK
Woolwich

1925. The first British SP gun, this was developed by Woolwich Arsenal using a Vickers medium tank chassis as the starting point and an 18-pounder field gun as the armament. The first model has the gun mounted in an enlarged turret which replaced the normal tank turret. A second model, developed in 1926, had a much wider hole in the hull and a specially-built rotating platform with a gun mounting which allowed the gun to elevate to 85° so that it could function as either a field, anti-tank or anti-aircraft gun. In 1927 one battery of six guns was issued to the Experimental Mobile Force and appears to have been successful. In 1928 a third version was proposed in which the gun was to be in an open shielded rotating platform and used in the field or anti-tank roles only, but shortly afterwards the Experimental Mobile Force was disbanded, and the SP gun project abandoned. The name came from Sir Noel Birch, Master-General of the Ordnance, who authorised its manufacture.

Armament: Ordnance QF 18-pdr Gun Mark 5
Barrel length: 8ft 3in (2.514m)
Weight of shell: 18lb 8oz (8.39kg)
Muzzle velocity: 1,625ft/sec (495m/sec)
Maximum range: 10,500yd (9,600m)
Ammunition types: HE, shrapnel, smoke
Ammunition load: 20 rounds

Vehicle: Mounting, SP, 18-pdr Mark 1
Crew: 5
All-up weight: 12.45 tons (12,645kg)
Armour: 6mm maximum
Hull length: 18ft 4in (5.58m)
Width: 8ft 4in (2.54m)
Height: 6ft 9in (2.05m)
Engine: Armstrong-Siddeley air-cooled V-8, 90bhp
Road speed: 28mph (45km/hr)
Range: not known

Bishop UK
Vickers

1942–44. The first British SP gun of World War II, this was the standard 25-pounder gun mounted in a large armoured box on top of a Valentine tank chassis. The box was fixed, so that the gun could only traverse 4° either side of zero, and it could not elevate to its maximum so that the range was restricted to 6,400 yards. The official verdict after the North African campaign was 'Nothing good can be said of the Valentine SP, though the crews were efficient.' It was replaced first by the American M7 Pries' and then later by the British Sexton 25-pounder SP.

Armament: Ordnance QF, 25-pdr Gun Mark 2
Barrel length: 8ft 1in (2.47m)
Weight of shell: 25lb (11.34kg)
Muzzle velocity: 1,450ft/sec (442m/sec)
Maximum range: 6,400yd (5,850m)
Ammunition types: HE, smoke, flare, illuminating, AP shot
Ammunition load: 32

Vehicle: Carrier, Valentine, SP 25-pdr Gun Mark I
Crew: 4
All-up weight: 17.16 tons (17,440kg)
Armour: 60mm maximum
Hull length: 18ft 2in (5.53m)
Width: 8ft 7in (2.61m)
Height: 9ft 1in (2.76m)
Engine: GMC, 6-cylinder, diesel, 162bhp at 1,900rpm
Road speed: 15mph (24km/hr)
Range: 100 miles (160km)

BMY/ARE 122 SPH USA/Egypt
BMY

Like the Royal Ordnance SP122 described elsewhere, this was developed in response to an Egyptian request. In this case the chassis was that of the well-known M109, onto which a fixed superstructure had been built in place of the usual turret. In the front face of this was mounted the standard 122mm D-30 field howitzer. A prototype was provided for evaluation in 1985–87, and after long contemplation, the Egyptian Army finally ordered 76 in 1992. The vehicles were built in the USA and shipped to Egypt, where the guns were added. A further 24 were built in 1996.

Armament: 1 × 122mm D-30 howitzer
Barrel length: 14ft 0in (4.27m)
Weight of shell: 54lb 14oz (24.9kg)
Muzzle velocity: 2,350ft/sec (716m/sec)
Maximum range: 16,840yd (15,400m)
Ammunition types: HE, HEAT, smoke
Ammunition load: 85

Vehicle: Based on M109
Crew: 5
All-up weight: 22.82 tons (23,182kg)
Armour: not disclosed
Hull length: 20ft 4in (6.20m)
Width: 10ft 4in (3.15m)
Height: 9ft 3in (2.82m)
Engine: Detroit Diesel turbocharged V-8, 405bhp at 2,350rpm
Road speed: 35mph (56km/hr)
Range: 220 miles (350km)

Bofors FH-77 SP Howitzer Sweden
Bofors

1995. Like the French Caesar (*below*) this is a standard service 155mm howitzer mounted on the rear of a 6 x 6 heavy-duty truck. The cab is armoured, and large enough to take all six members of the gun detachment, and the rear of the chassis is provided with substantial recoil spades which relieve the suspension of firing shock. The spades are splayed so as to permit the gun to traverse and fire up to 30° right and left of the centre line. Travelling and firing trials have proved the viability of the design, but development is still in progress.

Armament: 1 × 155mm howitzer FH-77
Barrel length: 19ft 4in (5.89m)
Weight of shell: 93lb 8oz (42.4kg)
Muzzle velocity: 2,540ft/sec (774m/sec)
Maximum range: 24,060yd (22,000m)
Ammunition types: HE, smoke, illuminating
Ammunition load: 24

Vehicle
Crew: 6
All-up weight: 29.52 tons (30,000kg)
Armour: not disclosed
Hull length: 39ft 4in (12.0m)
Width: 8ft 6in (2.6m)
Height: 10ft 2in (3.1m)
Engine: diesel, 6-cylinder, turbocharged, 255bhp
Road speed: 43mph (70km/hr)
Range: not disclosed

BOV-3 Triple 20mm SPAA Gun Yugoslavia
State factories

1982. This is a 4 x 4 wheeled vehicle carrying three 20mm cannon. The carrier has the driver in front, engine at the rear, and has an open-topped turret mounted centrally and carrying the three guns. This configuration is necessary since the guns are magazine fed and the crew have to be able to reach them easily and quickly in action. Sights are optical, and there is no provision for receiving data from outside sources such as radars. The weapon has been seen in the air defence and ground support roles during the fighting in the Balkans since 1990.

Armament: 3 × 20mm M55 cannon
Barrel length: 4ft 7in (1.40m)
Weight of shell: 4.3oz (122g)
Muzzle velocity: 2,740ft/sec (835m/sec)
Rate of fire: 800rpg/min
Maximum ceiling: 3,940ft (1,200m)
Ammunition types: HE-I, AP-I
Ammunition load: 1,500

Vehicle
Crew: 4
All-up weight: 9.25 tons (9,400kg)
Armour: not known
Hull length: 22ft 4in (6.79m)
Width: 8ft 4in (2.53m)
Height: 10ft 6in (3.21m)
Engine: Deutz V-6 diesel, 148bhp at 2,650rpm
Road speed: 56mph (90km/hr)
Range: 310 miles (500km)

Brummbär Germany
Deutsche Eisenwerke

1943. Brummbär ('Grizzly bear') was called an assault infantry gun although the weapon was actually a short howitzer. The equipment was based upon the hull and running gear of the Pz Kpfw 4 and had the superstructure built up from sloping plates, with the stubby howitzer in the front plate. Late production had a slightly different shape to the superstructure and had skirting plates over the suspension. It also had a hull-mounted machine gun on the front plate alongside the howitzer. A total of 306 were built or converted from Pz Kpfw 4 tanks in 1943.

Armament: 1 x 15cm Stürmhaubitze 43
Barrel length: 5ft 11in (1.80m)
Weight of shell: 55lb 2oz (25kg)
Muzzle velocity: 920ft/sec (280m/sec)
Maximum range: 5,240yd (4,700m)
Ammunition types: HE, APHE, HEAT
Ammunition load: 38

Vehicle: Based on Panzer 4
Crew: 5
All-up weight: 28.2 tons (28,650kg)
Armour: 100mm maximum
Hull length: 19ft 5in (5.93m)
Width: 9ft 5in (2.88m)
Height: 8ft 3in (2.52m)
Engine: Maybach, petrol, V-12, 300bhp at 3,000rpm
Road speed: 24mph (40km/hr)
Range: 130 miles (210km)

BTR-40A Twin 14.5mm SPAA Gun Russia
State factories

1948. This was probably inspired by the American multiple gun motor carriages sent to Russia during the war; it is claimed that the original intention was for it to be a support weapon for the infantry company, with air defence as an afterthought, but this seems doubtful. Twin 14.5mm machine guns are not much of an anti-personnel weapon. The guns were mounted in the crew compartment of a BTR-40P, a fairly basic sort of armoured scout car.

Armament: 2 x 14.5mm KPV machine guns
Barrel length: 4ft 5in (1.346m)
Weight of bullet: 2.26oz (64.1g)
Muzzle velocity: 3,238ft/sec (987m/sec)
Rate of fire: 600rpg/min
Maximum ceiling: 6,560ft (2,000m)
Ammunition types: AP-I
Ammunition load: not known

Vehicle: BTR-40P
Crew: 5

All-up weight: 5.71 tons (5,800kg)
Armour: 8mm maximum
Hull length: 16ft 5in (5.0m)
Width: 6ft 3in (1.9m)
Height: 8ft 3in (2.5m)
Engine: GAZ-40 6-cylinder petrol, 80bhp at 3,400rpm
Road speed: 50mph (80km/hr)
Range: 170 miles (280km)

BTR-152 Twin 14.5mm SPAA Gun Russia
State factories

1952. This appeared somewhat later than the BTR-40A and was intended to fill the same role; experience had shown that the BTR-40 was too cramped to be operated for any length of time, and was not robust enough to carry the weight. It is precisely the same twin 14.5mm machine gun mount, but in the cargo compartment of a 6 x 6 BTR-152 APC. This is the standard vehicle; variants have been seen, including four-gun 14.5mm mountings, 23mm cannon in place of the normal twin 14.5mm machine guns, and quadruple 12.7mm DShK machine guns.

Armament: 2 x 14.5mm KPV machine guns
Barrel length: 4ft 5in (1.35m)
Weight of bullet: 2.26oz (64.1g)
Muzzle velocity: 3,238ft/sec (987m/sec)
Rate of fire: 600rpg/min
Maximum ceiling: 6,560ft (2,000m)
Ammunition types: AP-I
Ammunition load: not known

Vehicle: BTR-152
Crew: 5
All-up weight: 9.45 tons (9,600kg)
Armour: 13.5mm maximum
Hull length: 22ft 5in (6.83m)
Width: 7ft 7in (2.32m)
Height: 9ft 2in (2.8m)
Engine: ZIL-123 6-cylinder petrol, 110bhp at 3,000rpm
Road speed: 40mph (65km/hr)
Range: 465 miles (750km)

Caesar 155mm SP Gun France
GIAT

1994. This is an unusual design, insofar as it is a 155mm gun mounted on the back of a truck; an armoured, cross-country truck, but a truck nonetheless. The intention is to cover the perceived gap between the heavy, tracked, armoured SP gun and the light, unprotected, towed gun. The truck is based on the Mercedes-Benz Unimog 6 x 6 chassis, with an armoured cab large enough for the gun detachment. The gun is mounted over the rear wheels, together with a retractable recoil spade which can take most of the firing shock off the vehicle's suspension. There is also an efficient muzzle brake to cut down further on the stress. The gun can traverse 17° either side and can be elevated to 65°. Evaluation and development are complete; all that remains is to convince the army that they need it.

Armament: 1 × 155mm gun
Barrel length: 26ft 5in (8.06m)
Weight of shell: 103lb (46.7kg) ERFB-BB
Muzzle velocity: 2,936ft/sec (895m/sec)
Maximum range: 45,930yd (42,000m)
Ammunition types: HE, HE-ERFB, -BB, smoke, cargo, illuminating
Ammunition load: 18

Vehicle
Crew: 6
All-up weight: 17.4 tons (17,680kg)
Armour: not disclosed
Hull length: 32ft 10in (10.0m)
Width: 8ft 4 in (2.55m)
Height: 12ft 0in (3.65m)
Engine: Mercedes-Benz 6-cylinder turbocharged diesel, 240bhp at 2,600rpm
Road speed: 62mph (100km/hr)
Range: 372 miles (600km)

Catapult SP 130mm Gun India
IOF

Ca 1987. This is an ingenious conversion, using the hull and running gear of a Vijayanta tank (*see* Vickers MBT), removing the turret and building an open superstructure, and then mounting an ex-Russian 130mm M-46 field gun so as to fire across the rear deck of the tank. Numbers were later given a simple overhead cover to the superstructure, mostly for the sake of weather protection. It is reported that some 140 were built, of which 100 are in service and the remainder in reserve.

Armament: 1 × 130mm M-46
Barrel length: 24ft 11in (7.60m)
Weight of shell: 84.6lb (33.4kg)
Muzzle velocity: 3,050m/sec (930m/sec)
Maximum range: 29,700yd (27,150m)
Ammunition types: HE, APC-T, smoke
Ammunition load: 30

Vehicle: Vijayanta tank
Crew: 6
All-up weight: not known
Armour: 80mm
Hull length: 26ft 0in (7.92m)

Width: 10ft 5in (3.17m)
Height: not known
Engine: Leyland 6-cylinder multi-fuel, 535bhp
Road speed: 31mph (50km/hr)
Range: 250 miles (400km)

Centauro B1 Tank Destroyer Italy
Iveco

1988. The Centauro is an 8 x 8 wheeled gun carrier with no other purpose than tank hunting. The hull is of typical 'APC' shape, with sloping sides and wheels set into the lower hull; all eight wheels drive and the front four steer. The hull is half-covered by the large, low-set turret into which goes a NATO-standard 105mm gun. The armour is said to be proof against 20mm and .50-inch attack, which suggests that the tactics of this equipment must be to lie in ambush and get in the first shot. The turret holds the commander, gunner and loader, and is provided with a computerised fire control system, night vision equipment, laser rangefinding and other modern devices.

Armament: 1 × 105mm 52-cal gun; 1 × co-axial MG; 1 × AA MG
Barrel length: 17ft 11in (5.46m)
Weight of shot: 7.50lb (3.40kg)
Muzzle velocity: 4,757ft/sec (1,450m/sec)
Operational range: 2,000yd/m
Ammunition types: APFSDS
Penetration: not disclosed, but probably about 750mm/2000m/90°
Ammunition load: 40

Vehicle
Crew: 4
All-up weight: 23.62 tons (24,000kg)
Armour: not disclosed
Hull length: 24ft 3in (7.40m)
Width: 9ft 8in (2.94m)
Height: 8ft 0in (2.43m)
Engine: IVECO V-6 turbocharged diesel, 520bhp at 2,300rpm
Road speed: 63mph (100km/hr)
Range: 500 miles (800km)

Char Canon 75 France
Renault

1918. The French regarded the tank as a gun-carrier from the start, but they gradually realised you could move a gun without having to take a tank along as well. This represents the ultimate in that point of view; it is simply the Renault two-man FT17 tank with the hull stripped away and replaced by a superstructure just sufficient to support the gun. Even the driver is out in the open air. One gunner remained on the vehicle with the driver, the other three members of the crew rode in the ammunition carrier. A handful of these were made for tests during the 1920s, and one was even fitted with a 105mm howitzer, but the army were not impressed and the idea was abandoned.

Armament: 1 × 75mm M1897 gun
Barrel length: 8ft 11in (2.72m)
Weight of shell: 16lb 1oz (7.23kg)
Muzzle velocity: 1,735ft/sec (529m/sec)
Maximum range: 9,295yd (8,500m)
Ammunition types: HE, smoke
Ammunition load: not known

Vehicle: Modified Renault FT17
Crew: 5
All-up weight: 7.19 tons (7,300kg)
Armour: 8mm maximum
Hull length: 13ft 5in (4.09m)
Width: 5ft 8in (1.72m)
Height: 5ft 6in (1.67m)
Engine: Renault, 4-cylinder, petrol, 35bhp at 1,400rpm
Road speed: 4.5mph (7km/hr)
Range: 22 miles (35km)

Charioteer UK
Leyland

In 1954 the Royal Artillery gave up its anti-tank role, which was then divided between the infantry, with the 120mm recoilless gun, and the Royal Armoured Corps. To fulfil their side of the bargain, the RAC were given Charioteer, which replaced the A30 Avenger and the remaining Archers as the SP anti-tank equipment. Charioteer was a refurbished Cromwell tank with a new and larger turret mounting the 20-pounder gun of the Centurion tank. It soon became apparent that whatever the Charioteer could do, the Centurion could do it better, and after 1958, when the Centurion adopted the 105mm L7 gun, the Charioteer was gradually phased out of service and sold to Austria and Jordan.

Armament: Ordnance QF 20-pdr Gun
Barrel length: 18ft 4in (5.58m)
Weight of shot: 9lb 13oz (4.44kg) APDS
Muzzle velocity: 4,850ft/sec (1,478m/sec)
Operational range: 2,000yd/m
Ammunition types: HE, APC, APDS
Ammunition load: 25

Vehicle
Crew: 4
All-up weight: 28.5 tons (28,960kg)
Armour: 60mm
Hull length: 21ft 1in (6.43m)
Width: 10ft 0in (3.05m)

Height: 8ft 0in (2.44m)
Engine: Rolls-Royce Meteor, V-12, petrol, 600bhp at 2,250rpm
Road speed: 31mph (50km/hr)
Range: 165 miles (265km)

China: 155/45 SP Gun China
Norinco

1988. This equipment is of conventional form, a tracked chassis with the driver and engine forward, leaving space at the rear of the hull for a fighting compartment surmounted by a large turret carrying a 45-calibre 155mm gun. The gun has a muzzle brake and fume extractor, and is provided with mechanical assistance for loading and ramming at any angle of elevation. Since 155mm is not a Chinese service calibre, it is assumed that this was produced for export, but there is no information available about possible purchasers.

Armament: 1 × 155mm gun WAC-21
Barrel length: 22ft 10in (6.97m)
Weight of shell: 100lb 5oz (45.5kg)
Muzzle velocity: 2,943ft/sec (897m/sec)
Maximum range: 32,800yd (30,000m)
Ammunition types: ERFB, ERFB-BB
Ammunition load: 30

Vehicle
Crew: 5
All-up weight: 31.50 tons (32,000kg)
Armour: not disclosed
Hull length: 20ft 0in (6.10m)
Width: 10ft 6in (3.20m)
Height: 8ft 6in (2.59m)
Engine: diesel, 525bhp
Road speed: 35mph (56km/hr)
Range: 20 miles (450km)

CV-90 AAV 40mm SPAA Gun Sweden
Bofors, Hagglund

1995. This is the air defence element of the Swedish Combat Vehicle 90 family and consists of the CV-90 MICV chassis mounting a 40mm Bofors automatic gun, with electro-optical sights, target acquisition radar, laser rangefinder and fire control computer. Full details of the fire control system and sights have not been divulged, but it is interesting that this equipment requires six men to operate it; driver; commander and gunner in the turret; radar operator, combat controller and external co-ordinator in the crew compartment behind the turret. The vehicle is full-tracked, with six roadwheels on each side; it is more fully described in the CV-90 MICV entry.

Armament: 1 x 40mm L/70 Bofors gun
Barrel length: 9ft 2in (2.80m)
Weight of shell: 2lb 2oz (960g)
Muzzle velocity: 3,297ft/sec (1,005m/sec)
Maximum ceiling: *ca* 8,200ft (2,500m)
Ammunition: HE
Ammunition load: not disclosed

Vehicle: CV-90 MICV
Crew: 6
All-up weight: 21.76 tons (22,000kg)
Armour: not disclosed
Hull length: 31ft 3in (6.47m)
Width: 10ft 2in (3.1m)
Height: 8ft 3in (2.5m)
Engine: Scania diesel, 550bhp
Road speed: 43mph (70km/hr)
Range: 185 miles (300km)

Dana 152mm SP Howitzer *Czechoslovakia*
ZTS Dubnica
1980. This innovative equipment introduced the idea of a wheeled SPG to a wider audience. Wheels have advantages in simplicity and economy but it required the expertise of the earthmoving industry to develop heavy wheels and tyres capable of bearing the load. This eight-wheeler has a bifurcated turret: the gun moves up and down in a central slot, while the gunners sit in armoured boxes on each side and the weapon is loaded mechanically. It is stabilised by jacks before firing.

Armament: 1 x 152mm howitzer
Barrel length: 19ft 11in (6.08m)
Weight of shell: 96lb 0oz (43.56kg)
Muzzle velocity: 2,273ft/sec (693m/sec)
Maximum range: 20,450yd (18,700m)
Ammunition types: HE
Ammunition load: 60

Vehicle
Crew: 5
All-up weight: 28.78 tons (29,250kg)
Armour: not known
Length: 36ft 7in (11.15m) with gun
Width: 9ft 10in (3.0m)
Height: 9ft 4in (2.85m)
Engine: Tatra diesel, 345bhp
Road speed: 50mph (80km/hr)
Range: 435 miles (700km)

Dassault M3 VDA Twin 20mm SPAA Gun
France
Panhard et Levassor, Dassault Électronique
1986. VDA = *Véhicule de Défense Antiaerienne*. This equipment consists of the Dassault Electronique

TA-20 turret, carrying two 20mm cannon, electro-optical sights, and a surveillance/acquisition radar, all carried on a Panhard 4 x 4 M3 APC. The radar is used to detect incoming targets, and is so connected to the electro-optical sight that it will direct the sight on to the point where the aircraft can be expected to appear. It also constantly measures the range and informs the gunner when the target is within the effective range of the guns. About sixty equipments were sold to various Middle Eastern countries.

Armament: 2 x 20mm Hispano-Suiza HS 820 cannon
Barrel length: 7ft 7in (2.32m)
Weight of shell: 4.4oz (125g)
Muzzle velocity: 3,412ft/sec (1,040m/sec)
Rate of fire: 1,000rpg/min
Maximum ceiling: 4,320ft (1,500m)
Ammunition types: HE-I, AP-I
Ammunition load: not disclosed

Vehicle: Panhard M3 APC
Crew: 3
All-up weight: 7.09 tons (7,200kg)
Armour: 12mm maximum
Hull length: 14ft 7in (4.45m)
Width: 7ft 10in (2.40m)
Height: 9ft 10in (2.99m)
Engine: Panhard 4HD, 4-cylinder, petrol, 90bhp at 4,700rpm
Road speed: 56mph (90km/hr)
Range: 620 miles (1,000km)

Dassault VDAA Twin 20mm SPAA Gun
France
Dassault Électronique, Renault
1986. VDAA = *Véhicule d'Auto-Défense Antiaerienne*. This is the same TA-20 turret as described in the previous entry, but in this case it is mounted into a 6 x 6 Renault VAB APC. A small number of these were sold to Oman in the late 1980s.

Armament: 2 x 20mm Hispano-Suiza HS 820 cannon
Barrel length: 7ft 7in (2.32m)
Weight of shell: 4.4oz (125g)
Muzzle velocity: 3,412ft/sec (1,040m/sec)
Rate of fire: 1,000rpg/min
Maximum ceiling: 4,920ft (1,500m)
Ammunition types: HE-I, AP-I
Ammunition load: not disclosed

Vehicle
Crew: 3
All-up weight: 13.98 tons (14,200kg)
Armour: not disclosed
Hull length: 19ft 8in (5.98m)
Width: 8ft 2in (2.49m)

Height: 6ft 10in (2.06m)
Engine: MAN HM72 6-cylinder diesel, 235bhp at 2,200rpm
Road speed: 53mph (85km/hr)
Range: 620mph (1,000km)

Deacon UK
AEC
1942. A primitive tank destroyer consisting of a standard 6-pounder anti-tank gun inside an armoured shield, mounted on to the cargo bed of an AEC Matador 4 x 4 medium gun tractor which was then given a light armour skin. Some 175 of them were built and issued to divisional anti-tank regiments in the North African desert in 1942, and they saw considerable use in the closing stages of the desert campaign. As guns went, they were serviceable enough, but the Matador was a high-set vehicle which was difficult to conceal and had indifferent cross-country performance. They were withdrawn at the end of the campaign in Tunisia and were subsequently sold to Turkey.

Armament: Ordnance QF 6-pdr Gun Mark 2
Barrel length: 8ft 5in (2.565m)
Weight of shot: 6.25lb (2.83kg)
Muzzle velocity: 2,693ft/sec (820m/sec) AP shot
2,665ft/sec (910m/sec) APCBC
Maximum range: 5,500yd (5,030m)
Ammunition types: AP, APC, APCBC, HE
Ammunition load: 24
Penetration: 74mm/1,000m/30° AP
146mm/1,000m/0° APDS

Vehicle: AEC Matador 4 x 4 truck chassis
Crew: 4
All-up weight: 12 tons (12,190kg)
Armour: 10mm maximum
Hull length: 21ft 6in (6.55m)
Width: 8ft 0in (2.43m)
Height: 10ft 2in (3.09m)
Engine: AEC 6-cylinder diesel, 95bhp at 1,780rpm
Road speed: 25mph: (40km/hr)
Range: not known

Doher 155mm SP Howitzer Israel
This is the Israeli nomenclature for the M109 155mm SP howitzer which has been improved in such things as fire control and communications equipment. The essential dimensions and data remain the same as the standard M109A2.

Escorter 35 SPAA Gun Switzerland
Oerlikon-Contraves
1990. This unusual equipment was developed by Oerlikon-Contraves as a private venture. The basis was a commercial heavy-duty giant-tyre chassis with four-wheel steering and remarkable manoeuvrability. The cab was over the front wheels and contained not only the driver but also the gunner. The twin 35mm guns were on a rotating platform in the centre of the vehicle, and the tracking radar was also on this platform, slaved to the gun. Each gun had a large rotary magazine carrying 215 rounds of ammunition. Once the gunner, in the cab, had acquired a target on his radar, the subsequent action was almost entirely automatic, tracking, opening fire when within range and correcting on observation. There was a good deal of interest in the equipment, but no firm orders, and as Oerlikon-Contraves were having a difficult time, they wisely abandoned the idea and concentrated on their ADATS missile system.

Armament: 2 x 35mm GDF
Barrel length: 10ft 4in (3.15m)
Weight of shell: 1lb 3oz (0.55kg)
Muzzle velocity: 3,822ft/sec (1,165m/sec)
Maximum ceiling: 13,120ft (4,000m)
Ammunition types: HE-A, AP-I, APDS
Ammunition load: 430

Vehicle: HYKA
Crew: 3
All-up weight: 23.62 tons (24,000kg)
Armour: not disclosed
Hull length: 28ft 9in (8.75m)
Width: 9ft 9in (2.98m)
Height: 12ft 11in (3.93m)
Engine: diesel, 450bhp
Road speed: 75mph (120km/hr)
Range: 372 miles (600km)

F3 155 SP Howitzer France
Creusot-Loire
1955. One of the smallest and neatest of 155mm SP equipments, this served the French for many years until superseded by the AMX GCT-155 in the middle 1980s. It was simply the hull and chassis of the AMX-13 tank with a clear area at the rear on the hull into which the top carriage of the service towed howitzer was bolted down. Two folding spades at the rear corners completed the conversion. There was no armour protection for the detachment and most of them rode on the ammunition carrier. To go into action the spades were dropped, and the ammunition carrier backed up to the rear of the gun; the men dismounted and stood on the ground to serve the gun. Simple and effective; it must have been designed by gunners.

Armament: 1 × 155mm howitzer
Barrel length: 16ft 9in (5.11m)
Weight of shell: 98lb 7oz (43.75kg)
Muzzle velocity: 2,379ft/sec (725m/sec)
Maximum range: 21,825yd (20,047m)
Ammunition types: HE, smoke, illuminating; all US
  M107 types
Ammunition load: none

Vehicle: Based on the AMX-13 tank
Crew: 2
All-up weight: 17.12 tons (17,400kg)
Armour: 20mm maximum
Hull length: 14ft 3in (4.338m)
Width: 8ft 10in (2.70m)
Height: 6ft 10in (2.09m)
Engine: SOFAM, V-8 petrol, 250bhp at 3,200rpm;
  or Detroit Diesel, V-8 turbocharged, 280bhp at
  2,800rpm
Road speed: 37mph (60km/hr)
Range: 186 miles (300km)

Falcon UK
Vickers, BMARC

1976. This was an attempt by Vickers to interest the British Army in an SPAA gun. It failed, as usual; the British Army has a Thing about SPAA guns, alternating between useless ones and none at all. Falcon was an adaptation of the successful Abbot SP gun design, replacing the 105mm gun with two high-velocity 30mm AA cannon which fired at a combined rate of 1,300 rounds per minute. It carried optical sights coupled to a laser rangefinder and a fire control computer, and it was capable of receiving radar data and injecting it into the sighting system. But in spite of being evaluated by several military forces it was never put into production.

Armament: 2 × Hispano-Suiza HS 831L 30mm
  cannon
Barrel length: 8ft 4in (2.555m)
Weight of shell: 12.7oz (360g)
Muzzle velocity: 3,543ft/sec (1,080m/sec)
Effective ceiling: 14,760ft (4,500m)
Ammunition types: HE, APHE
Ammunition load: 620

Vehicle: Modified Abbot SP gun chassis
Crew: 3
All-up weight: 15.60 tons (15,850kg)
Armour: 12mm maximum
Hull length: 17ft 6in (5.33m)
Width: 8ft 8in (2.64m)
Height: 8ft 3in (2.51m)
Engine: Rolls-Royce K60, 6-cylinder, vertically-
  opposed, petrol, 213bhp at 3,750rpm
Road speed: 30mph (48km/hr)

Range: 250 miles (400km)

Ferdinand Germany
Niebelungenwerke

1943; Also called **Elefant**. This design originated as a contestant for the 'Tiger' tank, and Porsche, in an excess of optimism, had built 90 chassis before the competing design from Henschel was selected; whereupon Porsche had 90 redundant vehicles on his hands. It was decided to turn them into tank destroyers, and the superstructure was built up to give a sloped front into which an 88mm PaK 43 gun was inserted. The transmission was petrol electric, and a notable omission was the lack of any local defence machine gun, which meant that the tank was easily stalked by a man on foot who could then take his time about wrecking it with a suitable charge. Their first battle was Kursk; those which survived were withdrawn and, provided with a machine gun, sent to Italy and later to other parts of the Eastern Front. But they remained mechanically unreliable and tactically vulnerable, and by the end of 1944 all had been either destroyed or withdrawn.

Armament: 1 × 88mm PaK 43/2
Barrel length: 19ft 9in (6.01m)
Weight of shell: 22lb 15oz (10.40kg)
Muzzle velocity: 3,280ft/sec (1,000m/sec)
Operational range: 3,280yd (3,000m)
Ammunition types: APHE, HE
Ammunition load: 50

Vehicle: Sd Kfz 184
Crew: 6
All-up weight: 63.97 tons (65,000kg)
Armour: 200mm maximum
Hull length: 26ft 9in (8.14m)
Width: 10ft 10in (3.38m)
Height: 9ft 9in (2.97m)
Engine: 2 × Maybach HL120TRM, V-12, petrol, total
  600bhp at 3,000rpm
Road speed: 18mph (30km/hr)
Range: 93 miles (150km)

G6 South Africa
LIW

1983. This was the second wheeled SP to astonish the world in the early 1980s (the other being the Czech Dana), and although the South African Army has used it effectively and speaks well of it, nobody else appears willing to take the plunge and adopt it. It uses a specially-designed 6 × 6 chassis, well armoured, and with ample working space at the rear carrying a turret mounting the same 155mm gun used in the towed role as the G5. Jacks are provided to support the vehicle and keep it steady while firing, and the large-wheel suspension absorbs the worst cross-country conditions. A massive wedge-shaped prow acts as a magazine containing shells as well as holding the driver's cab.

Armament: 1 × 155mm
Barrel length: 22ft 11in (6.975m)
Weight of shell: 100lb 5oz (45.5kg)
Muzzle velocity: 2,943ft/sec (897m/sec)
Maximum range: 32,800yd (30,000m)
Ammunition types: HE, ERFB, ERFB-BB, illuminating, smoke
Ammunition load: 50

Vehicle
Crew: 6
All-up weight: 46.25 tons (47,000kg)
Armour: not disclosed
Hull length: 30ft 2in (9.20m)
Width: 11ft 2in (3.40m)
Height: 10ft 10in (3.30m)
Engine: diesel, 525bhp
Road speed: 56mph (90km/hr)
Range: 435 miles (700km)

Gepard Germany
Krauss-Maffei

1975. *Gepard* = 'Cheetah'. Experience in World War II had shown the German Army the desirability of a self-propelled anti-aircraft gun for the protection of armoured columns, and the demand was raised in 1960. Several designs were examined, but the final choice was based on the Leopard 1 tank chassis carrying a special turret upon which were two 35mm Oerlikon guns in external pods, a surveillance radar at the rear of the turret and a tracking radar on the front of the turret. The fire control computing system was inside the turret. The guns fire at 550 rounds per minute each and can fire single shots, five-round bursts, or continuous fire.

Armament: 2 × 35mm Oerlikon GDF
Barrel length: 10ft 4in (3.15m)
Weight of shell: 1lb 3oz (0.55kg)
Muzzle velocity: 3,855ft/sec (1,175m/sec)
Maximum ceiling: 13,120ft (4,000m)
Ammunition types: HE-I, SAP-HE, APDS
Ammunition load: 660

Vehicle: Based on Leopard 1 tank
Crew: 3
All-up weight: 44.29 tons (45,000kg)
Armour: 70mm maximum
Hull length: 23ft 10in (7.26m)
Width: 10ft 8in (3.25m)

Height: 10ft 1in (3.07m)
Engine: Mercedes V-10 multi-fuel, 830bhp at 2,200rpm
Road speed: 40mph (65km/hr)
Range: 370 miles (600km)

Hetzer Germany
BMKD, Skoda

1944. *Hetzer* = 'Harasser'. With a total of 2,584 built, this must have been the most popular German assault gun of World War II. It was a neat and efficient design, based on the chassis of the Czech TNH/PS (PzKpfw 38(*t*)) light tank. A well-sloped superstructure was built up from the basic hull and the front plate carried the 75mm tank gun in a well protected ball mount. Agile and presenting a difficult small target, it went into service in mid-1944.

After the war the Swiss Army acquired 158 of them and the Czech Army also kept them in service for many years.

Armament: 1 × 75mm PaK 39 L/48
Barrel length: 11ft 10in (3.60m)
Weight of shell: 14lb 15oz (6.80kg)
Muzzle velocity: 3,556ft/sec (790m/sec)
Maximum range: 8,400yd (7,680m)
Ammunition types: APHE, HVAP
Ammunition load: 41

Vehicle: Modified PzKpfw 38 tank chassis
Crew: 4
All-up weight: 15.50 tons (15,750kg)
Armour: 60mm maximum
Hull length: 21ft 0in (6.38m)
Width: 8ft 8in (2.63m)
Height: 7ft 2in (2.17m)
Engine: Praga AC/2, petrol, 160bhp at 2,800rpm
Road speed: 26mph (42km/hr)
Range: 110 miles (180km)

Hornisse Germany
See Nashorn

Hummel Germany
Alkett

1943. *Hummel* = 'Bumblebee'. This equipment was built to provide heavy support for the armoured divisions, and it is surprising that only 100 were ever made, since it appears to have been a useful piece of equipment. Like the Nashorn, it was based on a special chassis derived from the Panzer 3 and Panzer 4, basically a Panzer 4 with an extra wheel on each side. Above this was a slope-sided superstructure with a working space big enough to accommodate the 150mm heavy field howitzer (sFH 18) and its recoil system. A similar vehicle, but without the gun, was used as an ammunition carrier.

Armament: 1 × 150mm sFH 18/1
Barrel length: 13ft 6in (4.13m)
Weight of shell: 95lb 14oz (43.50kg)
Muzzle velocity: 1,624ft/sec (495m/sec)
Maximum range: 13,670yd (12,500m)
Ammunition types: HE, HEAT, HERA, smoke
Ammunition load: 18

Vehicle: Sd Kfz 165
Crew: 6
All-up weight: 23.82 tons (24,000kg)
Armour: 30mm maximum
Hull length: 23ft 6in (7.17m)
Width: 9ft 9in (2.97m)
Height: 9ft 3in (2.81m)
Engine: Maybach HL120TRM, V-12, petrol, 300bhp at 3,000rpm
Road speed: 26mph (42km/hr)
Range: 133 miles (215km)

IKV-91 Sweden
Hägglund

1970. This looks like a tank, and is sometimes classed as one, but in fact it is too lightly armoured to allow it to act like a tank. It is a self-propelled anti-tank gun, relying upon concealment for firing and agility to move from one firing position to another. It has a roomy hull in order to carry a reasonable amount of ammunition, and a turret well-shaped to deflect shot. It mounts a powerful 90mm gun with a fume extractor but no muzzle brake.

Armament: 1 × 90mm smoothbore; 2 × MG
Barrel length: 16ft 8in (5.08m)
Weight of shell: 14lb 12oz (6.70kg)
Muzzle velocity: 3,083ft/sec (940m/sec)
Maximum range: 8,000m (2,000m effective)
Ammunition types: HE, HEAT
Ammunition load: 59 + 4,250

Vehicle
Crew: 4
All-up weight: 16.04 tons (16,300kg)
Armour: not known
Hull length: 21ft 0in (6.41m)
Width: 9ft 10in (3.0m)
Height: 7ft 7in (2.32m)
Engine: Volvo-Penta 6-cylinder turbocharged diesel, 360bhp at 2,200rpm
Road speed: 40mph (65km/hr)
Range: 340 miles (550km)

IKV-103 Assault Howitzer Sweden
Landsverk

1956. This simple but effective infantry support howitzer started out in 1952 with a 75mm gun, but this was soon seen to be quite useless, and it was re-designed to take a 105mm howitzer and reissued in 1956. The tracked chassis has six roadwheels each side, and has the hull built up into a superstructure with a sloping front in which the howitzer is mounted in a ball mantlet. The superstructure then slopes down to the engine deck at the rear. It was employed both as an assault gun and as a normal SP field artillery piece.

Armament: 1 × 105mm howitzer
Barrel length: 11ft 1in (3.38m)
Weight of shell: 33lb 12oz (15.30kg)
Muzzle velocity: 2,100ft/sec (640m/sec)
Maximum range: *ca* 8,750yd (8,000m)
Ammunition types: HE, smoke
Ammunition load: not known

Vehicle
Crew: 4
All-up weight: 8.8 tons (8940kg)
Armour: 20mm maximum
Hull length: 16ft 0in (4.87m)
Width: 7ft 2in (2.18m)
Height: 8ft 6in (2.59m)
Engine: Ford V-8, petrol, 145bhp
Road speed: 35mph (56km/hr)
Range: 155 miles (250km)

Jagdpanther Germany
MIAG, Niedersachsen

1944. In late 1942 the German Army demanded a tank destroyer based on the Panther tank, carrying an 88mm gun, but the response was slow and it was not until January 1944 that production of the Jagdpanther began. The basic Panther chassis was given a built-up superstructure in which the front glacis plate was simply carried up to the roof and the 88mm gun fitted into a ball mounting in the centre. It was probably the best tank destroyer of the war, being well armoured, agile and powerfully armed, but it came too late and only 392 were built.

Armament: 1 × 88mm PaK 43/3
Barrel length: 19ft 9in (6.01m)
Weight of shell: 22lb 14oz (10.40kg) APHE
16lb 1oz (7.30kg) HVAP
Muzzle velocity: 3,280ft/sec (1,000m/sec) APHE
3,700ft/sec (1,130m/sec) HVAP
Operational range: 3,280yd (3,000m)
Maximum range: 19,140yd (17,500 m)
Ammunition types: APHE, HVAP, HE, HEAT
Ammunition load: 57

Vehicle: Sd Kfz 173
Crew: 5
All-up weight: 45.27 tons (46,000kg)
Armour: 100mm maximum
Hull length: 22ft 11in (6.98m)
Width: 11ft 5in (3.47m)
Height: 8ft 11in (2.72m)
Engine: Maybach HL230P30 V-12, petrol, 700bhp at 3,000rpm
Road speed: 28mph (46km/hr)
Range: 100 miles (160km)

Jagdpanzer 4 Germany
Vormag
1944. 769 built. This was actually an improved model of the Sturmgeschütz 4 and was properly known as the 'Sturmgeschütz neuer Art', since it broke away from the previous Sturmgeschütz standard pattern of two low superstructures separated by the central gun. The new pattern had a boxy, slope-sided superstructure and a sloping front plate carrying the gun slightly offset to the right so as to give the driver elbow-room. The result was low-slung with well sloped armour and a high survivability chance. The running gear was still the same Panzer 4 style with eight roadwheels per side.

Armament: 1 x 75mm PaK 39 L/48
Barrel length: 11ft 10in (3.60m)
Weight of shell: 14lb 15oz (6.80kg)
Muzzle velocity: 3,556ft/sec (790m/sec)
Maximum range: 8,400yd (7,680m)
Ammunition types: APHE, HVAP
Ammunition load: 79

Vehicle: Sd Kfz 162
Crew: 4
All-up weight: 23.86 tons (24,250kg)
Armour: 80mm maximum
Hull length: 19ft 5in (5.92m)
Width: 10ft 5in (3.17m)
Height: 6ft 1in (1.85m)
Engine: Maybach HL120TRM V-12, petrol, 300bhp at 3,000rpm
Road speed: 25mph (40km/hr)
Range: 130 miles (210km)

Jagdpanzer 6 Germany
See *Jagdtiger*

Jagdpanzer 38(t) Germany
See *Hetzer*

Jagdpanzer 638 Germany
1945. This was a proposal to built the Czech TNH tank in Germany, with a few modifications, and arm it with either the long 75mm PaK 39 gun or the 105mm Sturm Haubitze 42. This idea was in line with Hitler's general instruction to reduce tank manufacture and increase assault guns. But the proposal was not formulated until late in 1944 and it is doubtful if it ever got as far as the prototype stage. The effect would have been more or less to duplicate the existing Hetzer.

Jagdpanzer Jaguar Germany
Henschel, Hanomag
1963. These vehicles were designed in the days when the fire-and-forget missile seemed to be just around the corner, and the prospect of cruising around the battlefield loosing these off against the enemy seemed a very good one. Unfortunately the missile engineers were not quite as far ahead as they had thought, and the anti-tank missile vehicle has remained anchored to the end of a control wire for as long as it takes the missile to reach the target, thus presenting a stationary target to the enemy. As a result, the plethora of anti-tank missile carriers which were once promised, never appeared. This is one of the few survivors, and is simply the German Jagdpanzer Kanone (*below*) with the gun removed and a suitable missile launcher – SS-11, HOT, Milan and TOW have all appeared at various times, though HOT appears to have become the standard – mounted on the roof.

Armament: 1 x HOT missile launcher; 2 x MG
Weight of missile: 51lb (23kg)
Maximum velocity: 770ft/sec (235m/sec)
Maximum range: 4,375yd (4,000m)
Ammunition types: HEAT
Ammunition load: 20 missiles + 3,200 MG

Vehicle: Modified Jagdpanzer Rakete
Crew: 4
All-up weight: 25.1 tons (25,500kg)
Armour: not known
Hull length: 21ft 8in (6.61m)
Width: 10ft 3in (3.12m)
Height: 8ft 4in (2.54m)
Engine: MTU MT837, V-8 diesel, 500bhp at 2,000rpm
Road speed: 44mph (70km/hr)
Range: 250 miles (400km)

Jagdpanzer Kanone Germany
Rheinstahl, Thyssen-Henschel
1960. When Germany re-armed in the 1950s, one of the army's first demands was for an assault gun;

they probably knew more about the tactics, handling and general worth of assault guns than anyone else, and they knew what they wanted. The first prototypes appeared in 1960 and after various trials and modifications, the JpzK went into production in 1965, 750 being built. Apart from the suspension, there is not a great deal of difference between this and the wartime Sturmgeschütz 4; a low-set machine with a powerful gun mounted in a ball mantlet in the centre of the sloping front plate. There are five roadwheels on each side, with rear drive and front idler. Refinements in fire control and night vision equipment have been added from time to time.

Armament: 1 × 90mm; 2 × MG
Barrel length: 16ft 1in (4.91m)
Weight of shell: 16lb 7oz (7.45kg) HESH
    12lb 10oz (5.74kg) HEAT
Muzzle velocity: 2,608ft/sec (795m/sec) HESH
    3,756ft/sec (1,145m/sec) HEAT
Maximum effective range: 2,190yd (2,000m)
Ammunition types: HESH, HEAT, HE
Ammunition load: 51 + 4,000

Vehicle
Crew: 4
All-up weight: 27.06 tons (27,500kg)
Armour: 50mm maximum
Hull length: 20ft 6in (6.24m)
Width: 9ft 9in (2.98m)
Height: 6ft 10in (2.08m)
Engine: MTH MB837, V-8 diesel, 500bhp at 2,000rpm
Road speed: 43mph (70km/hr)
Range: 250 miles (400km)

Jagdpanzer Rakete Germany
Hanomag, Henschel

1967 A tracked carrier, based on a common chassis which was also used for the Jagdpanzer Jaguar and, with modifications, the Marder MICV, carrying an anti-tank guided missile launcher on the roof above and behind the driver. Slope-fronted and flat-roofed, the vehicle is quite low-set and only the missile launcher and the sights protrude above the roof. Originally fitted with two SS-11 missile launchers it was later upgraded to use a single Euromissile HOT system.

Jagdtiger Germany
Niebelungenwerke

1944. Design of a heavy tank destroyer began in mid-1943, and the first prototypes appeared in April 1944. Two types of suspension were tried, one by Henschel and one by Porsche, but the latter was unsatisfactory and production with Henschel torsion-bar suspension began in mid-1944, the first vehicles being issued in October. They were used in the Ardennes battle and in others against the western Allied forces. 77 were built before production ceased in 1945. The vehicle was based upon the King Tiger chassis but with lengthened hull and with the hull sides continued up in the front to form a superstructure in the front face of which was a 128mm gun. This was the most powerful tank or tank destroyer gun to be employed during the war.

Armament: 128mm PaK 44; 1 × MG
Barrel length: 21ft 8in (6.62m)
Weight of shell: 63lb 12oz (28.30kg)
Muzzle velocity: 3,280ft/sec (1,000m/sec)
Maximum range: *ca* 13,125yd (12,000m)
Ammunition types: APHE
Ammunition load: 40

Vehicle: Sd Kfz 186
Crew: 6
All-up weight: 68.90 tons (70,000kg)
Armour: 250mm maximum
Hull length: 24ft 3in (7.39m)
Width: 11ft 11in (3.63m)
Height: 9ft 8in (2.95m)
Engine: Maybach HL230P30, V-12, petrol, 700bhp at 3,000rpm
Road speed: 24mph (38km/hr)
Range: 70 miles (110km)

JPK Belgium
Henschel

This is the German Jagdpanzer Kanone as employed by the Belgian Army. A total of 80 were acquired, from 1975 onwards. The vehicles have the same hull, armament and engine as the German equipment but use a different transmission and different fire control equipment. The dimensions are the same.

JSU-122 Russia
Tankograd

1943. After the first of the JS-1 tanks entered service, it was thought necessary to provide a heavy SP gun to support them, and the JS-1 hull was adapted to take a 122mm gun by simply removing the turret and building up a boxy superstructure with a sloping front. The gun was mounted into this front plate by means of an enormous square mantlet. A variety of guns were fitted, the final model being the D25S, with a long slender barrel and a prominent muzzle brake.

Armament: 1 × 122mm
Barrel length: 17ft 11in (5.49m)
Weight of shell: 54lb 14oz (24.9kg)
Muzzle velocity: 2,625ft/sec (800m/sec)
Maximum range: *ca* 10,935yd (10,000m)
Ammunition types: HE, APHE, HEAT, smoke
Ammunition load: 40

Vehicle: Based on JS-1 tank
Crew: 5
All-up weight: 41.14 tons (41,800kg)
Armour: 120mm maximum
Hull length: 22ft 4in (6.80m)
Width: 10ft 0in (3.07m)
Height: 8ft 1in (2.46m)
Engine: V2-JS V-12 diesel, 520bhp at 2,100rpm
Road speed: 23mph (37km/hr)
Range: 150 miles (240km)

JSU-152 Russia
Tankograd

1943. This is the same basic vehicle as the JSU-122 (*above*) but configured for a bigger gun, the 152mm ML-20S. The design began with an adapted KV-1 tank chassis, but this was soon changed for that of the Josef Stalin tank. Like the JSU-122, the -152 was exported to other countries in the postwar Communist bloc and remained in use until the late 1970s.

Armament: 152mm gun-howitzer ML-20S
Barrel length: 9ft 2in (2.80m)
Weight of shell: 95lb 11oz (43.4kg)
Muzzle velocity: 2,150ft/sec (655m/sec)
Maximum range: *ca* 10,935yd (10,000m)
Ammunition types: HE, APHE
Ammunition load: 25

Vehicle: Based on JS-1 tank
Crew: 5
All-up weight: 41.14 tons (41,800kg)
Armour: 110mm maximum
Length: 29ft 7in (9.05m) including gun
Width: 10ft in (3.07m)
Height: 8ft 1in (2.46m)
Engine: V2-JS, V-12, diesel, 520bhp at 2,100rpm
Road speed: 23mph (37km/hr)
Range: 150 miles (240km)

K9 Thunder 155mm SP Howitzer South
Korea
Samsung

1996. This is a heavy full-tracked vehicle carrying an armoured turret which mounts a 52-calibre 155mm howitzer. The barrel is fitted with a fume extractor and muzzle brake, and an automatic loading system permits a burst of three rounds to be fired in 15 seconds. A family of ammunition has been developed for the weapon, including rocket-assisted and base-bleed projectiles. Fire control systems include azimuth and position determination which, with a data computer, gives the weapon full autonomy.

Armament: 1 × 155mm howitzer
Barrel length: 26ft 5in (8.06m)
Weight of shell: 100.7lb (45.7kg)
Muzzle velocity: 2,920ft/sec (890m/sec)
Maximum ceiling: 43,745yd (40,000m)
Ammunition types: HE-ERFBB, HERA
Ammunition load: 45

Vehicle
Crew: 5
All-up weight: 46.25 tons (47,000kg)
Armour: not disclosed
Hull length: 24ft 5in (7.44m)
Width: 11ft 2in (3.40m)
Height: 10ft 9in (3.28m)
Engine: MTU V-8 diesel, 1,000bhp at 2,700rpm
Road speed: 40mph (65km/hr)
Range: 225 miles (360km)

Karl Gerät Germany
Rheinmetall-Borsig

1940. A massive 60cm self-propelled howitzer developed to provide heavy siege artillery in places which did not admit of railway guns getting within range – which, quite simply, meant the Eastern Front. Development commenced in 1936, the equipment being named for General Karl Becker, Chief of the German Army Weapons Office. A prototype was built in 1940, modified, and production of six service equipments took place in 1940–42. The design was simple: a rectangular box with a 60cm howitzer on top. The howitzer had a conventional recoil system, and the carriage also recoiled along the top of the hull. The original 60cm howitzer had a maximum range of 6,580 metres; the army demanded more range and an interchangeable 54cm barrel was provided in 1943. The prototype vehicle can be identified by its eight roadwheels on swinging arm suspension. Production models had eleven roadwheels on torsion bar suspension.

Armament: 1 × 54cm or 1 × 60cm howitzer
Barrel length, 54cm: 23ft 3in (7.10m)
            60cm: 16ft 8in (5.07m)
Weight of shell, 54cm: 2,756lb (1,250kg)
              or 3,483lb (1,580kg)
         60cm: 4,783lb (2,170kg)
              or 3,748lb (1,700kg)

Muzzle velocity, **54cm:** 984ft/sec (300m/sec)
 60cm: 458ft/sec (208m/sec)
Maximum range, **54cm:** 11,482yd (10,500m)
 60cm: 7,196yd (6,580m)
Ammunition types: HECP heavy or light, HE
Ammunition load: none; separate ammunition carrier

Vehicle

Crew: 18
All-up weight: 122.04 tons (124,000kg)
Armour: none; mild steel construction
Hull length: 37ft 4in (11.37m)
Width: 10ft 5in (3.18m)
Height: 15ft 8in (4.78m)
Engine: Daimler-Benz MB503, V-12, petrol, 580bhp at 2,000rpm
Road speed: 6mph (10km/hr)
Range: not known

Kentron ZA-35 Twin 35mm SPAA Gun
 South Africa
LIW

1992. The South Africans startled everybody by adopting a wheeled 155mm SP gun in 1983 (*see* G6), and they did the same again when they announced this wheeled SPAA gun in 1992. The vehicle is a specially-designed 8 x 8 with an armoured body and it mounts a revolving turret carrying two 35mm GA-35 belt-fed automatic cannon. There is also an electro-optical tracking sight, laser rangefinder, and acquisition radar. The turret carries its own diesel engine and generator for supplying the electrical power required, so that it can be inserted into any suitable vehicle. The radar can detect targets at 12km range and align the optical sight with the oncoming aircraft, after which the gunner switches in the automatic tracking system and opens fire. Due to the changed political situation in South Africa the army was denied funds for the adoption of this weapon, but development has continued at a low priority and the turret assembly has been tested in various tracked vehicles.

Armament: 2 x 35mm GA-35 cannon
Barrel length: 10ft 4in (3.14m)
Weight of shell: 1lb 3oz (550g)
Muzzle velocity: 3,855ft/sec (1,175m/sec)
Maximum ceiling: 13,125ft (4,000m)
Ammunition types: HE-I, SAP-HE-I, APC-I
Ammunition load: 460

Vehicle

Crew: 3
All-up weight: 31.45 tons (32,000kg)
Armour: not disclosed
Hull length: 23ft 7in (7.20m)
Width: 9ft 6in (2.90m)

Height: 10ft 2in (3.1m) with radar folded
Engine: V-10 diesel, 565bhp
Road speed: 75mph (120km/hr)
Range: 435 miles (700km)

King Kong USA
Nickname applied to the T92 240mm SP Howitzer.

L-33 Israel
Soltam

1973. This is a 155mm field gun on a self-propelled mounting which is based on the running gear of the Sherman M4A3E8 tank (with horizontal volute spring suspension) topped by a large boxy superstructure to accommodate the large crew and their ammunition. There is no power assistance, elevation, traverse and loading all being done by hand.

Armament: 1 x 155mm M68 howitzer
Barrel length: 16ft 9in (5.11m)
Weight of shell: 96lb 6oz (43.70kg)
Muzzle velocity: 2,379ft/sec (725m/sec)
Maximum range: 23,540yd (21,525m)
Ammunition types: HE, smoke, illuminating
Ammunition load: 54

Vehicle: Modified M4A3E8 Sherman
Crew: 8
All-up weight: 41.58 tons (42,250kg)
Armour: 60mm maximum
Hull length: 21ft 4in (6.50m)
Width: 10ft 9in (3.27m)
Height: 8ft 1in (2.46m)
Engine: Cummins VTA-903 V-8 diesel, 460bhp at 2,600rpm
Road speed: 22mph (36km/hr)
Range: 160 miles (260km)

LVKV Sweden
Landsverk

1955. Instead of scrapping their obsolete tanks, the Swedes re-work them into SP gun platforms; this particular specimen is a rebuilt Strv m/40 Light Tank (*qv*) with two 40mm Bofors AA guns mounted in a square, open-topped turret. The tank hull was lengthened and an additional roadwheel on each side gave the equipment a more stable platform. Only a small number were built and they were withdrawn in the early 1970s.

Armament: 2 x 40mm Bofors L/70
Barrel length: 9ft 2in (2.80m)
Weight of shell: 2lb 3oz (1.0kg)
Muzzle velocity: 3,280ft/sec (1,000m/sec)
Effective ceiling: 3,935ft (1,200m)

Ammunition types: HE
Ammunition load: not known

Vehicle
Crew: 4
All-up weight: 17 tons (17,277kg)
Armour: 20mm maximum
Hull length: 19ft 0in (5.79m)
Width: 7ft 10in (2.39m)
Height: 7ft 10in (2.39m)
Engine: Scania-Vabis, 6-cylinder, petrol. 290bhp
Road speed: 31mph (50km/hr)
Range: 215 miles (350km)

M3 75mm GMC USA
Autocar
1941–44. This has the distinction of being the first US self-propelled gun to be used in combat, in the Philippines in 1941–42. The M3 was designed by the Aberdeen Proving Ground staff early in 1941, to meet demand for a mobile equipment for the tank destroyer battalions being formed. Their solution was to put the standard M1897A4 field gun into the cargo space of the standard half-track scout car. Approved for issue in November 1941, a handful were sent to the Philippines, where they soon showed their worth against the small Japanese tanks. They were then sent to North Africa in Operation Torch in 1942, where they discovered that German tanks were another story. They did their best, but the basic fact was that the gun was designed in 1897 and no amount of improvement would ever make it a practical anti-tank gun against modern armour.

Armament: Gun, 75mm, M1897A4 on Mount, Gun, 75mm M3 or M5
Barrel length: 110.6in (2.81m)
Weight of shell: 14.60lb (6.62kg)
Muzzle velocity: 2,000ft/sec (609m/sec)
Maximum range: 13,300yd (12,162m)
Ammunition types: HE, AP, smoke
Ammunition load: 59

Vehicle: Modified Carrier, Half-Track, Personnel, M3
Crew: 5
All-up weight: 8.48 tons (8,618kg)
Armour: 7mm
Hull length: 19ft 8in (6.013m)
Width: 6ft 6in (1.98m)
Height: 8ft 6in (2.59m)
Engine: White 160AX, 6-cylinder petrol, 128bhp at 2,800rpm
Road speed: 41mph
Range: 200 miles (320km)

M4 81mm Mortar Carrier USA
White
1940. This was designed in 1940 primarily as a means of carrying the 81mm mortar and its crew, but the mounting was fitted into the forward part of the cargo space and could be fired from the vehicle in an emergency. The basic vehicle was the standard White half-track M2. The **M4A1**, standardised in December 1942 (whereupon the M4 was declared Limited Standard), was the same combination but with some improvements to the mortar mount to allow it to be taken out of the vehicle and emplaced more rapidly. The M4A1 was replaced as standard by the Mortar Carrier M21 in July 1943.

Armament: Mortar, 81mm, M1 on Mounting, Vehicle & Ground M1
Barrel length: 4ft 1.5in (1.26m)
Weight of shell: 6lb 15oz (3.14kg)
Muzzle velocity: 700ft/sec (214m/sec)
Maximum range: 3,288yd (3,000m)
Ammunition types: HE, smoke, illuminating
Ammunition load: 120

Vehicle: Car, Half-Track, Scout, M2
Crew: 6
All-up weight: 7.85 tons (7,985kg)
Armour: 7mm
Hull length: 19ft 6in (5.96m)
Width: 6ft 3in (1.96m)
Height: 6ft 0in (1.84m)
Engine: White 160AX, 6-cylinder, petrol, 128bhp at 2,800rpm
Road speed: 41mph (66km/hr)
Range: 200 miles (320km)

M6 37mm GMC USA
Fargo, Dodge
1942. In the early months of the war the US automobile industry threw itself into the business of putting wheels or tracks underneath guns, and some of their designs were quite impractical. The M6 was better than most, but exhibits the dangers of enthusiasm. It was intended to be an inexpensive tank destroyer, using the existing 37mm anti-tank gun bolted down into the existing Dodge 4 x 4 ¾-ton truck. The theory was that it would dash to some suitable point, open a rapid fire against the enemy's light tanks, and then dash off 'before heavy return fire could be directed against it.' But by 1942, when it appeared, the 37mm gun was no longer of any use, since nobody was using light tanks on the battlefield. Moreover, as the M6 had no armour beyond the gun shield, it didn't need heavy return fire to incapacitate it; any fire would do. No fewer than 5,380 were built, but by November 1943 all

but 100 had been recalled, their guns removed, and the vehicles re-converted to being cargo trucks.

Armament: Gun, 37mm, M3 on Mount, Pedestal, M25 or M26
Barrel length: 6ft 11in (2.09m)
Weight of shell: 1.92lb (0.86kg)
Muzzle velocity: 2,900ft/sec (884m/sec)
Operational range: 500yd/m
Ammunition types: HE, AP, APC, Canister
Ammunition load: 80

Vehicle: Modified ¾-ton Dodge 4 × 4 Weapons Carrier
Crew: 4
All-up weight: 3.28 tons (3334kg)
Armour: 0.25in gun shield only
Hull length: 14ft 10in (4.52m)
Width: 7ft 4in (2.24m)
Height: 6ft 11in (2.11m)
Engine: Dodge T-214, 6-cylinder, petrol, 76bhp at 3,200rpm
Road speed: 55mph: (88km/hr)
Range: 240 miles (385km)

M7 105mm HMC USA
Alco, Federal Machine
1942. This design was begun in October 1941, and the pilot model, built by the Baldwin Locomotive Company, was tested in February 1942. Very few modifications were required and it went into production as the M7 in April 1942. Some of the first were sent to Egypt to be used by the British Army, who christened it Priest because of the pulpit-like AA machine gun mounting at the right front of the hull. It was based on the running gear of the M3 medium tank, with an open-topped superstructure and the standard 105mm Field Howitzer M2A1 on a modified version of its ordinary split-trail carriage. This restricted the elevation to 35° and hence limited the maximum range.

Armament: Howitzer, 105mm, M2A1 on Mount M4 or M4A1
Barrel length: 8ft 6in (2.59m)
Weight of shell: 33.0lb (14.97kg)
Muzzle velocity: 1,250ft/sec (381m/sec)
Maximum range: 11,400yd (10,425m)
Ammunition types: HE, HEAT, smoke, illuminating
Ammunition load: 69

Vehicle: Based on the M3 Medium Tank
Crew: 7
All-up weight: 22.60 tons (22,968kg)
Armour: 108mm maximum
Hull length: 19ft 9in (6.02m)

Width: 8ft 6in (2.59m)
Height: 8ft 4in (2.54m)
Engine: Continental R-975-C1, 9-cylinder radial, petrol, 340bhp at 2,100rpm
Road speed: 25mph (40km/hr)
Range: 120 miles (195km)

M7B1 105mm HMC USA
Alco
1943. This was the same vehicle as the M7 but based upon the M4 tank chassis, since the M3 had gone out of production. The dimensions were the same, the only difference being in the engine, since it used the Ford GAA V-8 petrol engine. Later production models used soft steel for the lower hull sides as an economy measure. These vehicles remained in service after 1945 and were brought into use again in Korea in 1951. Here they were modified by raising the gun mounting so as to permit the barrel to be elevated to 65° and thus achieve the full range of 11,150 metres. Vehicles so converted were known as the **M7B2**, and after they had been retired from US service they were sold to the Austrians, who used them for several years.

M8 75mm HMC USA
Cadillac (1)
1942. This was developed to act as a close support tank to provide a bombardment weapon for dealing with field fortifications and similar obstacles. The first attempt was a scaled-down M7, which was refused on the grounds of lack of crew protection. So the eventual answer was to take the turret off the M5 Light tank and put on a new turret carrying a modified 75mm field howitzer. When you remember that the shells used by the 75mm howitzer were exactly the same as those used by the contemporary tank guns, one wonders why they bothered. Over 1,700 were built, and they saw wide use in every theatre of war. The only serious problem was the lack of ammunition space, cured by fitting a towing hook and giving each tank an ammunition trailer.

Armament: Howitzer, 75mm, M2 or M3 in Mount, Howitzer, 75mm M1
Barrel length: 54.18in (1.37m)
Weight of shell: 14lb 11oz (6.66kg)
Muzzle velocity: 1,250ft/sec (381m/sec)
Maximum range: 9,760yd (8,925m)
Ammunition types: HE, HEAT, smoke
Ammunition load: 46

Vehicle: Modified M5 Light Tank chassis
Crew: 4
All-up weight: 15.45 tons (15,695kg)

Armour: 45mm maximum
Hull length: 14ft 7in (4.44m)
Width: 7ft 5in (2.26m)
Height: 7ft 7in (3.31m)
Engine: 2 × Cadillac V-8, petrol, total 220bhp at 4,000rpm
Road speed: 40mph (65km/hr)
Range: 130 miles (210km)

M9 3-inch GMC USA

1942. In their search for a specialist tank destroyer, the US Army thought they had found it in the M9, which was a conversion of the M3 tank chassis in very similar manner to the conversion which produced the M7 HMC. The only real difference was that the armament was a 3-inch AA gun M1918 installed in a similar manner to the 105mm howitzer in the M7. All was well, though there were doubts about its agility, and the design was standardised as the M9. At this point it was discovered that there were only 27 M1918 3-inch guns available for the conversion, so the idea was forthwith abandoned.

M10 3-inch GMC USA
Fisher Body, Ford

While the M9 was pursuing its pointless way, the Tank Destroyer Board demanded a vehicle with 360° arc of fire, sloped armour to deflect shot and very high mobility, which sounds a very common-sense specification. It was achieved by taking the diesel-engined M4A2 tank chassis and fitting it with an open-topped turret mounting a 3-inch M7 anti-tank gun. The length of gun had to be balanced by counter-weighting the rear of the turret, and this overhanging lip makes a useful identification feature. The result was everything the TD Board wanted, and it went into production in time to be deployed in Tunisia in March 1943. Such was the demand that the **M10A1** was also standardised, the same vehicle but based on the Ford-engined M4A3 tank chassis. 1,648 were supplied to the British Army, most of which were refitted with the 17-pounder gun and christened **Achilles** (*qv*).

Armament: Gun 3in M7 in Mount, Gun, 3in M5
Barrel length: 13ft 2in (4.01m)
Weight of shell: 12lb 14oz (5.84kg)
Muzzle velocity: 2,800ft/sec (853m/sec)
Maximum range: 16,100yd (14,720m)
Ammunition types: HE, APC
Ammunition load: 54

Vehicle

Crew: 5
All-up weight: 29.47 tons (29,937kg)

Armour: 64mm maximum
Hull length: 19ft 7in (5.96m)
Width: 10ft 0in (3.04m)
Height: 8ft 2in (2.49m)
Engine: 2 × GMC diesel, 375hp at 2,100rpm; or Ford V-8 petrol, 450bhp at 2,600rpm
Road speed: 30mph (48km/hr)
Range: 200 miles (320km)

M12 155mm GMC USA
Pressed Steel Car, Baldwin

1943. The US Ordnance Department designed this vehicle in 1941 and, after testing it, the Field Artillery accepted the idea and had 100 built. After which the newly-constituted Army Ground Forces stepped in and, seeing no tactical purpose for them, had them placed in store. In 1943, when plans were being laid for the invasion of Europe, somebody remembered them, found that 74 were capable of being cleaned up and refurbished, and they were finally issued for service.

The M12 consisted of an elderly M1917 or M1918 155mm gun mounted on to a modified M3 tank chassis which had the engine shifted forwards so as to leave room at the rear for the gun and some working space. It also inaugurated the idea of a bulldozer-like blade, lowered to the ground, to act as a spade and resist the recoil thrust when the gun fired. Six gunners rode on the carriage; the remainder rode on the Ammunition Carrier M30 which was simply an M12 without a gun. The weapon was effective within its limitations, but the gun was obsolete before it ever got on to the carriage, and no more were ever made.

Armament: Gun, 155mm, M1918M1, 1917A1 or 1917, in Mount, Gun, 155mm, M4
Barrel length: 19ft 5in (5.92m)
Weight of shell: 95lb (43.09kg)
Muzzle velocity: 2,410ft/sec (735m/sec)
Maximum range: 18,700yd (17,100m)
Ammunition types: HE, APHE
Ammunition load: 10

Vehicle

Crew: 6
All-up weight: 25.89 tons (26,310kg)
Armour: 51mm maximum
Hull length: 22ft 1in (6.73m)
Width: 8ft 9in (2.67m)
Height: 8ft 10in (2.69m)
Engine: Continental R-975-C1, 9-cylinder radial, 353bhp at 2,400rpm
Road speed: 24mph (39km/hr)
Range: 140 miles (225km)

M13–17 Multiple GMCs USA
White, International Harvester, Autocar

1941. Very sensibly, the US Army decided that if it was to have mechanised columns, it needed mechanised air defence as well, and proceeded to develop a range of multiple machine gun carriages based upon the ubiquitous M3 half-track. Most relied upon a power-driven mounting developed by the W.L. Maxson Company which carried two .50-inch M2HB Browning machine guns, though there were other variations and combinations of weapon used from time to time.

M13

The M13 was the first to appear, in September 1942, with twin .50-inch Brownings. The Maxson Mount allowed 360° of traverse and an elevation of 90°, so that a target could be engaged anywhere. Each gun fired at about 500 rounds per minute and had a maximum ground range of 7,000 yards.

M14

The M14 was the same two-gun mounting but carried in the M5 half-track, which differed from the M3 only by being manufactured by the International Harvester Company rather than by White, Autocar or Diamond-T who made the M3.

M15

The M15 began with an M3 half-track and then stripped away the sides behind the cab to leave a flat platform upon which was placed an armoured revolving barbette with a Combination Gun Mount M42 carrying one 37mm AA gun M1A2 and two .50-inch M2HB Browning machine guns. This was a deadly combination which added high explosive shells to the solid bullets of the machine guns. It was replaced by the **M15A1** which had a better-designed mounting for the guns, but was otherwise the same equipment.

M16

The M16 introduced the four-gun Maxson mount, similar to the earlier model but modified to carry four machine guns. The vehicle was still the M3 half-track.

M17

Finally, the M17 was simply an M16 four-gun system but on an M5 half-track.

Of all these, the M16 was perhaps the most common, and remained in service through the Korean War where it frequently showed its versatility by acting as an infantry support gun.

M15

Armament: 1 × 37mm Gun M1A2; 2 × .50in M2HB MG
Barrel length: 78.2in (1.97m)

Weight of shell: 1lb 10oz (730g)
Muzzle velocity: 2,600ft/sec (792m/sec)
Maximum range: 8,875yd (8,115m)
Effective ceiling: 11,700ft (3,566m)
Rate of fire: 120rd/min
Ammunition types: HE, Canister
Ammunition load: 200 × 37mm; 1,200 × .50in

Vehicle: Carrier, Half-Track, Personnel, M3
Crew: 7
All-up weight: 8.93 tons (9,072kg)
Armour: 7mm maximum
Hull length: 20ft 4in (6.19m)
Width: 7ft 5in (2.26m)
Height: 7ft 10in (2.38m)
Engine: White 160AX, 6-cylinder, petrol, 128bhp at 2,800rpm
Road speed: 40mph (65km/hr)
Range: 175 miles (280km)

M18 76mm GMC USA
Buick

1943. In December 1941 the US Army put in a request for a fast, light, tank destroyer using Christie suspension and carrying a 37mm gun. By April 1942 the Ordnance Department had managed to convince the Staff that the 37mm gun was a waste of time, and that a 57mm gun should be fitted. After seeing the pilot model, the Tank Destroyer Board said they would consider nothing less than a 75mm gun. By this time the Buick company had developed a torsion-bar suspended chassis capable of high speeds, and the idea of mounting a 76mm gun into an open-topped turret on this chassis was accepted, as the M18.

A total of 2,507 were built, and it was used in NW Europe in 1944–45; it was nicknamed **Hellcat**, which was optimistic since the 76mm gun could not do much damage to the heavier German tanks except when suicidally close.

Armament: Gun, 76mm M1A1C or M1A2 on Mount, Gun, 76mm
Barrel length: 13ft 8in ((4.16m)
Weight of shell: 12lb 14oz (5.83kg) HE
9lb 6oz (2.86kg) HVAP
Muzzle velocity: 2,700ft/sec. (822m/sec) HE
3,400ft/sec (1,036m/sec) HVAP-T
Maximum range: HE: 14,200yd (12,985m)
Ammunition types: HE, APC-T, HVAP-T, smoke, illuminating
Ammunition load: 45

Vehicle: Gun Motor Carriage M18
Crew: 5
All-up weight: 17.85 tons (18,144kg)
Armour: 25mm maximum

Hull length: 17ft 4in (5.28m)
Width: 9ft 2in (2.79m)
Height: 8ft 5in (2.56m)
Engine: Continental R-975-C4 9-cylinder, radial, petrol, 460bhp at 2,400rpm
Road speed: 50mph (80km/hr)
Range: 150 miles (240km)

M19 Twin 40mm GMC USA
Cadillac (1), Massey-Harris

1944. The various Multiple GMCs were valuable weapons but as aircraft improved, it became necessary to think about a mobile gun with more power, and this was the result. It consists of the chassis of the M24 light tank, with the engine and transmission moved forward so as to leave space at the rear end to mount a revolving barbette carrying two 40mm Bofors light AA guns. The mount was power-operated and the guns could elevate to 80°. They were also provided with anti-tank ammunition and frequently accompanied infantry as a sort of assault gun when nothing much was doing in the air defence business.

Armament: Gun, Dual Automatic, 40mm, M2 on Mount, Gun, Twin, 40mm M4
Barrel length: 8ft 8in (2.64m)
Weight of shell: 2lb 1oz (935g)
Muzzle velocity: 2,870ft/sec (875m/sec)
Effective ceiling: 12,900ft (3,930m)
Ammunition types: HE, AP-T
Ammunition load: 336

Vehicle: Based on Light Tank M24 chassis
Crew: 6
All-up weight: 17.19 tons (17,464kg)
Armour: 8mm maximum
Hull length: 17ft 11in (5.21m)
Width: 9ft 4in (2.84m)
Height: 9ft 10in (2.85m)
Engine: 2 x Cadillac V-8, net 220bhp at 3,400rpm
Road speed: 35mph (56km/hr)
Range: 160 miles (250km)

M21 81mm Mortar Carrier USA
White

1943. This was generally the same as the 81mm Mortar Carrier M4A1, a half-track scout car with an 81mm mortar carried in the cargo space and capable of being either removed for emplacement on the ground in the normal manner or fired forward out of the vehicle in extremis. The only difference between this and the M4A1 is that the basic vehicle is the Half-Track Scout Car M3 instead of the M2, which by then was obsolescent. The principal distinction between the two vehicles was that the M3 had a winch mounted at the front.

Armament: Mortar, 81mm, M1 on Mounting, Vehicle & Ground M1
Barrel length: 4ft 1.5in (1.25m)
Weight of bomb: 6lb 15oz (3.14kg)
Muzzle velocity: 700ft/sec (213m/sec)
Maximum range: 3,288yd (3,000m)
Ammunition types: HE, smoke, illuminating
Ammunition load: 97

Vehicle: Carrier, Half-Track, Personnel, M3
Crew: 6
All-up weight: 8.26 tons (8,392kg)
Armour: 13mm maximum
Hull length: 20ft 10in (6.35m)
Width: 7ft 4in (2.23m)
Height: 7ft 5in (2.26m)
Engine: White 160AX, 6-cylinder, 128hp at 2,800rpm
Road speed: 40mph (65km/hr)
Range: 175 miles (280km)

M36 90mm GMC USA
Fisher Body, Massey-Harris, Alco, Montreal

1944. By late 1942 it was apparent that the newer varieties of German tank would tax the 3-inch gun to the utmost, and a tank destroyer with a better gun was urgently needed. The existing 90mm anti-aircraft gun was modified and fitted into the turret of an M10 tank destroyer; it worked, but it was not entirely satisfactory, and a completely new turret with power operation was developed and fitted into the existing M10A1 hull to produce the M36. This proved to be invaluable in NW Europe, since it was the only US tank destroyer with a chance against the German Tiger and Panther tanks. More were ordered to be built, but a shortage of M10A1 chassis led to them being built on to modified M4A3 tanks, becoming the **M36B1**. Later still, more were needed and the supply of M10A1 vehicles had dried up; they were therefore converted from refurbished diesel-engined M10s, and these became the **M36B2**.

Armament: Gun, 90mm, M3 on Mount, Gun, 90mm, M4 or M4A1
Barrel length: 15ft 6in (4.72m)
Weight of shell: 23lb 7oz (10.61kg) HE
16lb 13oz (7.63kg) HVAP-T
Muzzle velocity: 2,700ft/sec (823m/sec) HE
3,350ft/sec (1,021m/sec) HVAP-T
Maximum range: 19,560yd (17,885m) HE
Ammunition types: HE, APC, HVAP, smoke
Ammunition load: 47

Vehicle: Improved Gun Motor Carriage M10A1
Crew: 5
All-up weight: 27.68 tons (28,123kg)
Armour: 50mm maximum
Hull length: 20ft 2in (6.15m)
Width: 10ft 0in (3.04m)
Height: 8ft 11in (2.72m)
Engine: Ford GAA, V-8, petrol, 450bhp at 2,600rpm
Road speed: 30mph (48km/hr)
Range: 150 miles (240km)

M37 105mm HMC USA
Cadillac (1)

1945. The M7 105mm howitzer carriage did sterling work, but it was a design which had been put together from what was available at the time. Later analysis indicated that it was far too ponderous and heavy for the gun it carried, and in 1944 work began on a fresh design using the M24 light tank as the basis. The hull was built so that there was no need to move the engine and transmission, and the Howitzer M4, already designed for fitting into tank turrets, was adopted and mounted into the front plate of the hull. The result was shorter but wider than the M7 and gave the gunners more room to work around the gun. It began replacing the M7 in January 1945 and remained in use until replaced by the M52 in the mid-1950s.

Armament: Howitzer, 105mm, M4 on Mount M5
Barrel length: 8ft 6in (2.59m)
Weight of shell: 33lb 0oz (14.97kg) HE
Muzzle velocity: 1,250ft/sec (381m/sec)
Maximum range: 12,205yd (11,160m)
Ammunition types: HE, HEAT, smoke, illuminating
Ammunition load: 90

Vehicle: Modified M24 Light Tank chassis
Crew: 7
All-up weight: 17.86 tons (18,144kg)
Armour: 12mm maximum
Hull length: 18ft 2in (5.53m)
Width: 9ft 11in (3.02m)
Height: 7ft 4in (2.23m)
Engine: 2 × Cadillac V-8, Series 42 petrol; total 220bhp at 3,400rpm
Road speed: 35mph (56km/hr)
Range: 150 miles (240km)

M40 155mm GMC USA
Pressed Steel Car

1945. The effectiveness of the 155mm SP gun M12 led to demands for more of them, but both the gun and the chassis were now obsolete, and therefore a fresh design using the in-service M1 gun had to be developed. Components of the M4A3E8 tank, with horizontal volute spring suspension, were used to build a special hull, with the engine in a compartment behind the driver so as to leave the rear end open for the gun mounting and a flat working platform. A further folding platform was arranged so that it extended rearward over the spade, but folded up as the spade was hauled up to its travelling position. An excellent weapon, except for a tendency to catch fire in the engine compartment from time to time, it remained in use for many years after the war.

Armament: Gun, 155mm M2 on Mount, Gun, 155mm M13
Barrel length: 23ft 2in (7.06m)
Weight of shell: 96lb 1oz (43.13kg)
Muzzle velocity: 2,800ft/sec (853m/sec)
Maximum range: 25,715yd (23,514m)
Ammunition types: HE, AP, smoke, illuminating
Ammunition load: 20

Vehicle: developed from components of the M4 Medium Tank
Crew: 8
All-up weight: 36.16 tons (36,742kg)
Armour: 108mm maximum
Hull length: 23ft 4in (7.11m)
Width: 10ft 4in (3.15m)
Height: 10ft 10in (3.30m)
Engine: Continental R-975-C4, 9-cylinder, radial, petrol, 400bhp at 2,400rpm
Road speed: 24mph (38km/hr)
Range: 100 miles (160km)

M41 155mm HMC USA
Massey-Harris

1945. When you think of the enormous number of 155mm towed howitzers the US Army employed, and their valuable supporting fire, it is surprising that it took until 1943 before anyone thought of putting them on to tracks. The first proposal was to use the chassis of the M5 light tank, but as M5 production was scheduled to end, this was changed to use the M24 tank chassis, and the hull unit which had already been developed for the M19 40mm GMC was adopted. The howitzer was the standard field howitzer in a special mounting, a thin shield in front of it, with a working platform and a recoil spade fitted at the rear end. It was a good and sound design but only 60 were ever built; they were used in Korea and remained in service until the middle 1950s.

Armament: Howitzer, 155mm, M1 on Mount, Howitzer, 155mm M14
Barrel length: 12ft 5in (3.78m)

Weight of shell: 94lb 12oz (42.98kg)
Muzzle velocity: 1,850ft/sec (564m/sec)
Maximum range: 16,355yd (14,955m)
Ammunition types: HE, smoke, illuminating
Ammunition load: 22

Vehicle
Crew: 5
All-up weight: 18.30 tons (18,597kg)
Armour: 12mm maximum
Hull length: 19ft 2in (5.84m)
Width: 9ft 4in (2.84m)
Height: 7ft 10in (2.38m)
Engine: 2 × Cadillac V-8, petrol, net 220bhp at 3,400rpm
Road speed: 35mph (56km/hr)
Range: 100 miles (160km)

M42 Twin 40mm GMC USA
Cleveland, ACF
1945. The Allied air superiority of 1944–45 had led to AA gun tanks being under-employed and there were doubts as to whether there was any need for them. The opening weeks of the Korean War pointed out the flaws in that argument and the hunt was on for a new AA tank. The twin 40mm gun still seemed to be the optimum choice, and the chassis of the M41 Walker Bulldog tank was selected as the foundation. To simplify matters, the 40mm barbette was redesigned so that it could be fitted into the turret ring of the M41 without requiring any modification to the tank. Over 3,000 were built and they were widely adopted by other countries besides the USA.

Armament: 2 × 40mm Gun M2A1 on Mount T12E1
Barrel length: 8ft 8in (2.44m)
Weight of shell: 2lb 1oz (935g)
Muzzle velocity: 2,870ft/sec (875m/sec)
Effective ceiling: 12,900ft (3930m)
Ammunition types: HE-T
Ammunition load: 336

Vehicle
Crew: 6
All-up weight: 22.10 tons (22,452kg)
Armour: 25mm maximum
Hull length: 19ft 1in (5.82m)
Width: 10ft 7in (3.22m)
Height: 9ft 4in (2.84m)
Engine: Continental AOS-895-3, 6-cylinder, air-cooled, supercharged, petrol, 500bhp at 2,800rpm
Road speed: 45mph (72km/hr)
Range: 100 miles (160km)

M43 8-inch HMC USA
Pressed Steel Car
1945. The towed 155mm Gun M1 shared the same carriage with the 8-inch Howitzer M1, and it seemed logical, therefore, that they should be able to share the same self-propelled carriage as well. Some minor adjustments had to be made to the gun mounting, since the weight, balance and recoil forces were different. One pilot model was made early in 1945 and shipped to Europe to be battle-tested, after which the design was standardised and production began in November 1945. A total of 576 had been proposed, but the end of the war saw that severely reduced and only 48 were ever built, of which 24 were conversions from M40s by removing the 155mm gun and replacing it with an 8-inch howitzer. They remained in use until the mid-1950s.

Armament: Howitzer, 8in, M2 on Mount, Howitzer, 8in M17
Barrel length: 16ft 10in (5.13m)
Weight of shell: 200lb (90.82kg)
Muzzle velocity: 1,950ft/sec (595m/sec)
Maximum range: 18,510yd (16,925m)
Ammunition types: HE
Ammunition load: 16

Vehicle: developed from components of the M4 Medium Tank
Crew: 8
All-up weight: 35.71 tons (36,285kg)
Armour: 108mm maximum
Hull length: 25ft 11in (7.90m)
Width: 11ft 9in (3.58m)
Height: 11ft 8in (3.55m)
Engine: Continental R-975-C4, 9-cylinder, radial, petrol, 400bhp at 2,400rpm
Road speed: 21mph (33km/hr)
Range: 160 miles (260km)

M44 HMC USA
Massey-Harris
1953. In 1947 work commenced on a new family of vehicles on a common chassis, that of the M41 light tank. Work on a new 155mm SP howitzer was given priority since the utility of that calibre had been particularly noted during the Korean War. The engine and transmission went to the front, the driver sat up in the left front corner of the fighting compartment, alongside the howitzer, the howitzer had power elevation and ramming, and the fighting compartment was closed at the rear by two swinging cartridge compartments. These opened and a folding platform rested on top of the usual recoil spade. The idler wheel of each track was placed on

the ground to give additional resistance to the firing shock.

The M44 was also taken into British service in the later 1950s, and when modified to meet British safety standards became the **155mm Howitzer L8A1**.

Armament: 1 × 155mm howitzer M45
Barrel length: 11ft 10in (3.60m)
Weight of shell: 94lb 9oz (42.9kg)
Muzzle velocity: 1,866ft/sec (569m/sec)
Maximum range: 15,965yd (14,600m)
Ammunition types: HE, smoke, illuminating, nuclear
Ammunition load: 24

Vehicle: Based on M41 tank
Crew: 5
All-up weight: 27.90 tons (28,350kg)
Armour: 12.7mm maximum
Hull length: 20ft 3in (6.16m)
Width: 10ft 8in (3.24m)
Height: 10ft 3in (3.11m)
Engine: Continental AOS-895-3 6-cylinder, air-cooled, petrol, 500bhp at 2,800rpm
Road speed: 35mph (56km/hr)
Range: 76 miles (122km)

M44-T Germany
MTU, Rheinmetall
1986. This is a conversion of the original US M44 vehicle by changing the petrol engine for an MTU diesel delivering 450bhp, increasing the fuel capacity so as to give the vehicle a range of 385 miles (620km), moving the driver down into the hull, alongside the engine compartment, and strengthening the suspension. The most obvious change is the removal of the original M45 howitzer and its replacement by a new howitzer with a 39-calibre barrel 19ft 10 in (6.05m long) with a large double-baffle muzzle brake, giving the weapon a maximum range of 27,000 yards (24,700m) with conventional ammunition and 32,800 yards (30,000m) with enhanced ammunition. This conversion was requested by the Turkish Army and was designed by a German consortium of GLS and Rheinmetall. 168 M44s of the Turkish Army were subsequently modified to this standard.

M50 Multiple GMC (Ontos) USA
Allis-Chalmers
1963–70. In 1951 work began in the USA on developing a new tank destroyer, and once the lightweight chassis had been designed, there were plans to develop a complete range of lightweight armoured vehicles around it. However, by the time the chassis appeared, the Army had changed its mind and policies and had lost interest. But the US Marine Corps could see a need for a light vehicle capable of being air-transported and landed, so work continued. To keep the weight low, recoilless guns were suggested, and this meant mounting them outside the hull because of the back-blast on firing. Eventually Ontos appeared, six 106mm RCL rifles arranged on a very light chassis and with limited traverse. They were used to some extent in Vietnam and the Dominican Republic, but the back blast always revealed their position when they fired, and re-loading had to be done in full view of the enemy. They were withdrawn and scrapped in 1970.

Armament: 6 × 106mm RCL Rifles M40A1C with Spotting Rifle M8C
Barrel length: 11ft 2in (3.40m)
Weight of shell: 17lb 9oz (7.96kg)
Muzzle velocity: 1,650ft/sec (503m/sec)
Maximum range: 7,500yd (6,860m)
Ammunition types: HEAT, HEP
Ammunition load: 18

Vehicle
Crew: 3
All-up weight: 8.50 tons (8,641kg)
Armour: 13mm maximum
Hull length: 12ft 6in (3.81m)
Width: 9ft 6in (2.89m)
Height: 6ft 11in (2.11m)
Engine: Chrysler, V-8, petrol, 180bhp at 2,450rpm
Road speed: 30mph (48km/hr)
Range: 150 miles (240km)

M50 155mm Howitzer Israel
EFAB
1963. This was designed and built in the French gun factory at Bourges for the Israeli Army and is simply the French Army's standard 155mm howitzer Modèle 1950 fitted into a chassis based on the Sherman M4 tank. The turret and the hull top were removed and the engine moved forward to the right front, alongside the drive, so as to leave a working platform and space for the gun mounting at the rear of the hull. The superstructure was then simply built up at the sides to offer some protection to the gunners.

Armament: 1 × 155mm howitzer Mle 50
Barrel length: 11ft 8in (3.56m)
Weight of shell: 96lb 5oz (43.7kg)
Muzzle velocity: 2,115ft/sec (645m/sec)
Maximum range: 19,410yd (17,750m)
Ammunition types: HE, smoke, illuminating
Ammunition load: not known

Vehicle: Based on M4 Sherman tank
Crew: 8
All-up weight: 30.51 tons (31,000kg)
Armour: not known
Hull length: 20ft (6.10m)
Width: 9ft 9in (2.98m)
Height: 9ft 2in (2.80m)
Engine: dependent upon the model of Sherman converted
Road speed: 28mph (45km/hr)
Range: 220 miles (350km)

M52 105mm HMC USA
Allis-Chalmers

1954. In the 1950s the Perceived Threat was nuclear, and therefore the US Army decided that everybody had to be under cover; no more open-topped SP guns, for a start. So the M52 was the first of a completely new family of self-propelled equipments all armoured, roofed or turreted so as to give the crews the maximum protection on the nuclear battlefield. This was another vehicle which was based upon the M41 tank chassis and, like the M44, had its rear idler on the ground for additional firing stability, though in this case no rear spade was fitted. Engine and transmission were in the hull front, and the gun was carried in a large turret capable of traversing to 60° either side of zero. The driver was also in the turret, with his controls connected by flexible cables; this was acceptable because, unlike a tank, an SP gun never needs to move its turret when travelling. The M52 was also adopted by the German, Greek, Japanese and Turkish Armies.

Armament: 1 × 105mm Howitzer M49
Barrel length: 7ft 11.5in (2.73m)
Weight of shell: 33.0lb (14.97kg)
Muzzle velocity: 1,548ft/sec (472m/sec)
Maximum range: 12,325yd (11,270m)
Ammunition types: HE, HEP, HERA, chemical, smoke, illuminating
Ammunition load: 102

Vehicle
Crew: 5
All-up weight: 23.66 tons (24,040kg)
Armour: 12.7mm maximum
Hull length: 19ft (5.80m)
Width: 10ft 4in (3.15m)
Height: 10ft 1in (3.06)
Engine: Continental, 6-cylinder, air cooled, petrol, 500bhp at 2,800rpm
Road speed: 35mph (56km/hr)
Range: 100 miles (160km)

M52T 155mm SP Howitzer Turkey
MKEK

1995. By the late 1980s the M52 105mm howitzer was virtually obsolete, and the Turkish Army set about improving their stock. The vehicles were refurbished and given new diesel engines and automatic transmissions, and the 105mm howitzer was discarded and replaced by a 155mm howitzer copied from the German M109A3. This is 39 calibres long and has a chamber to NATO standard dimensions. It was necessary to fit a folding recoil spade at the rear in order to relieve the suspension of most of the increased firing shock, but the result is a very serviceable weapon.

Armament: 1 × 155mm howitzer
Barrel length: 22ft 6in (6.87m)
Weight of shell: 100.7lb (45.7kg)
Muzzle velocity: 2,936ft/sec (895m/sec)
Maximum range: 32,800yd (30,000m) ERFB-BB
Ammunition types: HE, HE-ERFB, -BB
Ammunition load: 30

Vehicle
Crew: 5
All-up weight: 29.03 tons (29,500kg)
Armour: 12.7mm
Hull length: 19ft 0in (5.80m)
Width: 10ft 6in (3.20m)
Height: 10ft 10in (3.30m)
Engine: MTUV-6 diesel, 460bhp at 2,300rpm
Road speed: 37mph (60km/hr)
Range: 260 miles (420km)

M53 155mm GMC USA
Pacific Car

1953. Although the M40 155mm SP gun was a sound enough weapon, the US Army were dissatisfied on the ground of lack of protection for the crew and lack of power assistance for working such a large gun in a confined space. So by the late 1940s they were asking for a new design; this, of course, coincided with the nuclear scare, and the result was the next all-protected design. This was like a scaled-up M52, with the gun, crew and driver all carried in a massive turret capable of swinging 30° either side of zero. Rear doors on the turret opened up and down to form a working platform and shelter, a massive recoil spade was fitted, and power operation of the gun, ramming and shell handling were provided. Issued in 1952, they soon acquired a reputation for unreliability and almost all had to be withdrawn and returned to the factory to be overhauled and modified. It was then decided to convert them to M55 8-inch howitzers by re-barrelling, and this was completed in the mid-

1960s, except for a number which were retained by the US Marine Corps.

Armament: 1 × 155mm Gun M46
Barrel length: 22ft 11in (6.97m)
Weight of shell: 94.71lb (42.96kg)
Muzzle velocity: 2,800ft/sec (853m/sec)
Maximum range: 23,225yd (21,236m)
Ammunition types: HE
Ammunition load: 20

Vehicle
Crew: 6
All-up weight: 42.85 tons (43,545kg)
Armour: 15mm maximum
Hull length: 25ft 11in (7.90m)
Width: 11ft 9in (3.58m)
Height: 11ft 8in (3.55m)
Engine: Continental, V-12 petrol, 704bhp at 2,800rpm
Road speed: 30mph (48km/hr)
Range: 160 miles (258km)

M55 8-inch HMC USA
Pacific Car
The M40 155mm GMC was partnered by the M43 8-inch howitzer carriage, and the same sort of shared mounting resulted in the M55 HMC which was the 8-inch howitzer mounted on to the carriage of the M53 155mm gun. This appears to have been more reliable than the 155mm gun vehicle, probably because it was less highly stressed on firing, and, as noted above, most M53s were competed into M55s in the early 1960s.

Armament: 1 × 8in Howitzer M47
Barrel length: 16ft 8in (5.08m)
Weight of shell: 200lb (90.70kg)
Muzzle velocity: 1,950ft/sec (595m/sec)
Maximum range: 18,372yd (16,800m)
Ammunition types: HE
Ammunition load: 10

Vehicle
Crew: 6
All-up weight: 40.18 tons (40,823kg)
Armour: not known
Hull length: 25ft 11in (7.90m)
Width: 11ft 9in (3.58m)
Height: 11ft 8in (3.55m)
Engine: Continental, V-12 petrol, 704bhp at 2,800rpm
Road speed: 30mph (48km/hr)
Range: 160 miles (258km)

M56 90mm SPAT USA
Cadillac (2)
1953. This was a tank destroyer for airborne units, based on the chassis of the M76 amphibious cargo

carrier. A minimal design, it consisted of a 90mm anti-tank gun on a low pedestal mount on top of an unarmoured aluminium body carried on four roadwheels each side, suspended by torsion bars. The driver and engine took up all the remaining space in the hull, and the gunlayer could ride on top. Where the rest of the detachment went is not certain; they probably travelled with an ammunition vehicle and if the gun moved during an action, held on wherever they could. It saw some use in Vietnam but was eventually replaced by the M551 tank.

Armament: 1 × 90mm Gun M54 on Mount, Gun, M80
Barrel length: not known
Weight of shell: 16.8lb (7.62kg) HVAP-T
Muzzle velocity: 3,650ft/sec (1,112m/sec)
Operational range: 2,500yd/m
Ammunition types: HE, HVAP
Ammunition load: 29

Vehicle
Crew: 4
All-up weight: 5.69 tons (5783kg)
Armour: none
Hull length: 19ft 2in (5.84m)
Width: 8ft 6in (2.59m)
Height: 6ft 9in 2.06m)
Engine: Continental, 6-cylinder horizontally-opposed, petrol, 200bhp at 3,000rpm
Road speed: 28mph (45km/hr)
Range: 140 miles (225km)

M89 122mm SP Howitzer Romania
Romarm
1988. This is somewhat unusual, an amphibious SP gun, the vehicle using elements of the Romanian MLI-84 MICV in its construction and retaining that vehicle's water-jet propulsion system. The turret is of armour steel and carries a 2A31 122mm howitzer. The track is carried on seven roadwheels on each side, with front drive and rear idler, suspended by torsion bars.

Armament: 1 × 122mm D-30A
Barrel length: 16ft 0in (4.86m)
Weight of shell: 47lb 14oz (21.72kg)
Muzzle velocity: 2,264ft/sec (690m/sec)
Maximum range: 16,730yd (15,300m)
Ammunition types: HR, HEAT, smoke, illuminating
Ammunition load: 40

Vehicle: Based on MLI-84 MICV
Crew: 5
All-up weight: 17.22 tons (17,500kg)
Armour: not disclosed
Length: 24ft 0in (7.31m)

Width: 10ft 4in (3.15m)
Height: 8ft 9in (2.66m)
Engine: diesel, V-8 turbocharged, 360bhp
Road speed: 40mph (65km/hr)
Range: 310 miles (500km)

M107 175mm SPG USA
BMY, FMC, Pacific Car

1961. After the nuclear threat had subsided, the next concern of the US Army was to get as much as possible air-portable, and from ponderous turreted bulldogs, they changed overnight to stripped-down whippets. Replacements for the 155mm gun and 8-inch howitzer were called for, but instead of the 155mm gun a new calibre was to be adopted, 175mm, since it promised greater range and also a nuclear projectile. The carriage was simply a hull with space for the engine and driver, five roadwheels each side, and the gun mounting, together with hydraulic shell-handling machinery. There was the usual hydraulically operated recoil spade at the rear.

Armament: 1 × 175mm Gun M113
Barrel length: 35ft 8in (10.86m)
Weight of shell: 147lb 4oz (66.78kg)
Muzzle velocity: 3,028ft/sec (923m/sec)
Maximum range: 35,760yd (32,700m)
Ammunition types: HE
Ammunition load: 2

Vehicle
Crew: 5
All-up weight: 27.72 tons (28,168kg)
Hull length: 18ft 9in (5.72m)
Width: 10ft 4in (3.15m)
Height: 12ft 0in (3.67m)
Engine: Detroit Diesel, V-8, turbocharged, 405bhp at 2,300rpm
Road speed: 34mph (55km/hr)
Range: 450 miles (725km)

M108 105mm SP Howitzer USA
Cadillac (2)

In the 1950s the US Army decided to develop an entirely new field howitzer in 100mm calibre, to replace the 105mm. To go with it they also developed a new carriage, using components and running gear of the M113 APC, and this and the M109, also based on the same chassis, are easily distinguished by their seven small roadwheels and no return rollers. In the event, the 100mm failed to come up to expectations, and the design reverted to using a 105mm howitzer with a fume extractor. This is fitted into a large turret above a roomy fighting compartment which has rear doors for the supply of ammunition.

Armament: 1 × 105mm Howitzer M103
Barrel length: 11ft 8in (3.55m)
Weight of shell: 33lb (14.98kg)
Muzzle velocity: 1,620ft/sec (494m/sec)
Maximum range: 12,575yd (11,500m)
Ammunition types: HE, HEP, HERA, chemical, smoke, illuminating
Ammunition load: 102

Vehicle
Crew: 7
All-up weight: 22.10 tons (22,453kg)
Armour: not known
Hull length: 20ft 9in (6.11m)
Width: 10ft 10in (3.30m)
Height: 10ft 4in (3.14m)
Engine: Detroit Diesel, V-8, turbocharged, 405bhp at 2,300rpm
Road speed: 35mph (56km/hr)
Range: 220 miles (350km)

M109 155mm SP Howitzer USA
Allison, Cadillac (2), Chrysler

This was developed at the same time as the M108 and uses the same chassis, hull and turret. The howitzer, however, was entirely new, with a fume extractor and a large muzzle brake, though it fired the same ammunition as its predecessors. It has proved surprisingly long-lived; it entered service in 1963, was adopted by almost every NATO army and several others, has gone through a series of improvements and is still in widespread use.

In the 1970s various improvements in artillery ammunition led to improvements in some of the guns, and the 155mm howitzer began to grow; in 1972 the **M109A1** appeared, with a longer, more slender barrel having a longer fume extractor and a muzzle brake. This increased the maximum range from 15,970 to 19,795 yards (14,600 to 18,100m).

In 1978 the **M109A2** went into production; this used the same ordnance as the A1 but improved such things as the rammer, the ammunition stowage, the hull doors and so forth. It also redesigned the rear of the turret to form a bustle which would hold an additional 22 rounds of ammunition.

The **M109A3** is an M109A1 which has been converted to M109A2 standard. The **M109A4** is an A2 or A3 which has been upgraded by the addition of NBC protective equipment and various 'Reliability and Maintainability' improvements. The **M109A5** in an A4 upgraded by replacing the gun with an improved model which can fire rocket-assisted and other unconventional ammunition, raising the maximum range to 18.6 miles (30km).

The M109A6 is an entirely new equipment also called Paladin, described below.

M109A2
Armament: 1 × 155mm Howitzer M185
Barrel length: 21ft 11in (6.67m) including muzzle brake
Weight of shell: 94lb 9oz (42.91kg)
Muzzle velocity: 2,244ft/sec (684m/sec)
Maximum range: 19,795yd (18,100m)
Ammunition types: HE, HERA, smoke, illuminating, ICM
Ammunition load: 36

Vehicle
Crew: 6
All-up weight: 24.55 tons (24,948kg)
Armour: 20mm maximum
Hull length: 20ft 4in (6.19m)
Width: 10ft 2in (3.1m)
Height: 9ft 2in (2.8m)
Engine: Detroit Diesel, V-8, turbocharged, 405bhp at 2,300rpm
Road speed: 35mph (56km/hr)
Range: 220 miles (350km)

M109A3G Germany
Rheinmetall
In 1983 the German Army purchased several hundred conversion kits from the USA which enabled them to upgrade their M109Gs to M109A3 standard. At the same time they changed the barrel for a new 32-calibre type developed by Rheinmetall which gives a maximum range of 26,250 yards (24,000m).

M109A6 Paladin USA
BMY
1993. This has the same hull and suspension as the previous M109s, but everything else has been changed. The turret is larger and with a full-width bustle, the new 39-calibre M284 howitzer has a new chamber contour and several detail improvements to the breech ring and mechanism, a reinforced muzzle and muzzle brake and a new firing mechanism. There is an entirely new fire control system allied to a position-finding system which permits the automatic pointing of the gun when supplied with target data.

Armament: 1 × 155mm Howitzer M284
Barrel length: 19ft 10in (6.05m)
Weight of shell: 96lb 12oz (43.88kg)
Muzzle velocity: 2,723ft/sec (830m/sec)

Maximum range: 26,246yd (24km) conventional)
32,810yd (30km) HERA
Ammunition types: HE, smoke, HERA
Ammunition load: 39

Vehicle
Crew: 4
All-up weight: 28.28 tons (28,738kg)
Armour: not disclosed
Hull length: 20ft 4in (6.19m)
Width: 10ft 4in (3.149m)
Height: 10ft 7in (3.236m)
Engine: Detroit Diesel 8V-71T, V-8 turbocharged two-stroke diesel, 405bhp at 2,300rpm
Road speed: 35mph (56km/hr)
Range: 252 miles (405km)

M109G Germany
Rheinmetall
This was the standard M109, purchased from the USA, but the Germans were not impressed by the performance, nor by the obsolete slow-coned breech-block used by the howitzer. They therefore made some modifications, incorporating a sliding block breech, similar to that used on the FH-70, which increased the maximum range to 19,085 yards (18,000m).

M109L Italy
OTO-Melara
The Italian Army purchased some 221 M109s from the USA in the 1960s; in the 1970s OTO-Melara developed a long-barrelled conversion to increase their maximum range, but the Italian Army were not, at that time, interested. In the mid-1980s, though, they called for a demonstration of this improvement, which was a success, and subsequently modified all their M109s by fitting this 39-calibre barrel. It is recognisable by its considerable length and by the double-baffle muzzle brake. Adoption of this barrel raised the maximum range to 14.9 miles (24km) with conventional ammunition and 18.6 miles (30km) with rocket-assistance.

M110 8-inch SP Howitzer USA
BMY, FMC, Pacific Car
1962. When the M107 was designed, the usual partnership with the 8-inch howitzer was also taken into consideration, and the same carriage was used for the M110 8-inch HMC. It was, though, a much lighter and more reliable weapon than the 175mm which was somewhat temperamental, and eventually most M107s had their 175mm barrels

removed and were converted into M110s by putting the 8-inch howitzer barrel on them.

Armament: 1 × 8in Howitzer M2A1E1
Barrel length: 17ft 5in (5.31m)
Weight of shell: 200lb (90,7kg)
Muzzle velocity: 1,950ft/sec (594m/sec)
Maximum range: 17,275yd (15,800m)
Ammunition types: HE, ICM, chemical, nuclear
Ammunition load: 2

Vehicle
Crew: 5
Weight: 23.93 tons (24,313kg)
Hull length: 18ft 9in (5.72m)
Width: 10ft 4in (3.14m)
Height: 9ft 8in (2.93m)
Engine: Detroit Diesel, V-8, turbocharged, 405bhp at 2,300rpm
Road speed: 34mph (56km/hr)
Range: 450 miles (725km)

M110A1 and A2 8-inch HMC USA
BMY, FMC, Pacific Car

1970. The loss of the 175mm gun meant that there was no heavy SP gun capable of reaching well into enemy territory, and as a quick solution a new longer barrel was developed for the 8-inch howitzer, turning it into the M110A1. By 1970 all M110s had been converted or taken out of service. In 1978 a further improvement was the addition of a muzzle brake, allowing the use of a more powerful propelling charge and increasing the maximum range to 14.2 miles (22.9km) with conventional ammunition, 18.6 miles (30km) with rocket assistance.

Armament: 1 × 8in Howitzer M12A2
Barrel length: 26ft 8in (8.12m)
Weight of shell: 203lb 12oz (92.43kg)
Muzzle velocity: 2,333ft/sec (711m/sec)
Maximum range: 25,045yd (22,900m)
Ammunition types: HE, HE/ICM
Ammunition load: 2

Vehicle
Crew: 5
All-up weight: 27.91 tons (28,350kg)
Armour: not disclosed
Hull length: 18ft 9in (5.72m)
Width: 1-ft 4in (3.14m)
Height: 9ft 8in (2.93m)
Engine: Detroit Diesel, V-8, turbocharged, 405bhp at 2,300rpm
Road speed: 34mph (56km/hr)
Range: 325 miles (520km)

M163 Vulcan Air Defense System USA
General Electric (USA)

1968. The development of the General Electric multi-barrel Gatling-type gun offered a means of getting a great deal of metal into the sky in a short time and had obvious attractions as a short-range air defence weapon. The M163 system was quickly put together by building a turret carrying a GE Vulcan 20mm 6-barrel gun, an optical computing sight and a rangefinding radar and then dropping this into the roof of a standard M113 APC. It was adopted enthusiastically and replaced the M42 twin 40mm equipment in the late 1960s. It was also taken up by several other countries, and saw combat in the Middle East, but was withdrawn from US service by the mid-1990s as too expensive to maintain and not sufficiently effective in its designated role.

Armament: 1 × GE 20mm Gatling gun M168
Barrel length: 5ft 0in (1.524m)
Weight of shell: 3.5oz (100g)
Muzzle velocity: 3,380ft/sec (1,030m/sec)
Rate of fire: 1,000 or 3,000rd/min, selectable
Maximum ceiling: 3,950ft (1,200m)
Ammunition types: HE-I, AP-I
Ammunition load: 2280

Vehicle: M113 APC
Crew: 4
Weight: 12.12 tons (12,310kg)
Armour: 39mm maximum
Hull length: 15ft 11in (4.86m)
Width: 9ft 4in (2.85m)
Height: 9ft 0in (2.74m)
Engine: Detroit Diesel V-6, 215bhp at 2,800rpm
Road speed: 42mph (68km/hr)
Range: 300 miles (480km)

Majnoon 155mm SP Gun Iraq
State factories

1989. This was a remarkably advanced design, though there is room to suspect that some of the technicalities were there simply to prove they could be done. It was a wheeled chassis in two units, the front end with the driver and engine and the rear end with the gun; the two sections were connected by a rolling joint and hydraulic rams so that the chassis could bend in the middle to assist the steering and could roll independently to conform to the terrain. In some respects it resembles the South African G6, with a prominent prow and driver's compartment, 6 x 6 wheels arranged as two and four, and a rear turret with double doors at the back. The subsequent history of this vehicle is not fully known, but it does not appear to have been produced in any quantity.

Armament: 1 x 155mm
Barrel length: 26ft 5in (8.06m)
Weight of shell: 100lb 5oz (45.5kg)
Muzzle velocity: 2,952ft/sec (900m/sec) with ERFB
Maximum range: 42,100yd (38,500m) with ERFB
Ammunition types: HE, smoke, illuminating, conventional and ERFB
Ammunition load: not disclosed

Vehicle
Crew: 6
All-up weight: 42.32 tons (43,000kg)
Armour: not disclosed
Length overall: 39ft 4in (12.0m)
Width: 11ft 6in (3.50m)
Height: 11ft 10in (3.60m)
Engine: Mercedes-Benz diesel, 560bhp
Road speed: 55mph (90km/hr)
Range: not disclosed

Marder 1 Germany
Becker
1942. When the German Army occupied France it scooped up a mass of military vehicles of which it made good use. Among these were some 300 Lorraine tracked cargo carriers, and these became the basis for a number of self-propelled gun designs. Marder 1 was the German 75mm PaK 40 anti-tank gun mounted in a slope-sided superstructure so as to have 32° of traverse to either side of zero. The gun's normal shield was retained as a form of mantlet. Suspension was by six roadwheels on each side, in three pairs, with front drive and rear idler.

Armament: 1 x 75mm PaK 40; 1 x MG
Barrel length: 10ft 6in (3.20m)
Weight of shell: 15lb 0oz (6.80kg) APHE
Muzzle velocity: 2,598ft/sec (792m/sec)
Maximum range: 8,400yd (7,680m)
Ammunition types: HE, APHE, HVAP, HEAT
Ammunition load: not known

Vehicle: Lorraine Schlepper
Crew: 5
All-up weight: 8 tons (8,128kg)
Armour: 12mm maximum
Hull length: 17ft 5in (5.31m)
Width: 6ft 0in (1.81m)
Height: 7ft 5in (2.25m)
Engine: Delahaye, 6-cylinder petrol, 70bhp at 2,800rpm
Road speed: 22mph (35km/hr)
Range: 84 miles (135km)

Marder 2 Germany
FAMO, MAN, Daimler-Benz
1942. Marder is the German for 'marten', a vicious little animal of the weasel tribe; the German Army appear to have thought it a good name for a tank destroyer, so they used it three times. Marder 2 was a lively little vehicle built on the chassis of the Panzer 2 tank, onto which a boxy fighting compartment was built. Inside this was the top carriage of the standard PaK 40 anti-tank gun, supported on girders and firing forward across the front of the vehicle. A total of 671 of these were built by June 1943 and they remained in use until the end of the war.

Armament: 1 x 75mm PaK 40
Barrel length: 10ft 6in (3.20m)
Weight of shell: 15lb 0oz (6.80kg) APHE
Muzzle velocity: 2,598ft/sec (792m/sec)
Maximum range: 8,400yd (7,680m)
Ammunition types: HE, APHE, HVAP, HEAT
Ammunition load: 37

Vehicle: Sd Kfz 131
Crew: 3
All-up weight: 10.63 tons (10,800kg)
Armour: 30mm maximum
Hull length: 15ft 3in (4.65m)
Width: 7ft 6in (2.28m)
Height: 7ft 3in (2.20m)
Engine: Maybach HL62TRM, 6-cylinder, petrol, 140bhp at 2,000rpm
Road speed: 25mph (40km/hr)
Range: 120 miles (190km)

Marder 3 Germany
BMKD
1942. This was more or less the Marder 2 (above) but using the Panzer 38(t) (TNH/PS) tank as the basis. The tank turret was removed and the hull top modified to carry the 76.2mm PaK 36(r), which was a weapon captured in large numbers from the Russians. The gun was on a pedestal, giving 21° traverse on either side of zero, and behind it was a shielded working platform for the gun crew. The result was nimble and carried a useful punch, but was somewhat vulnerable due to its height and lack of crew protection. 363 were built.

Armament: 1 x 76.2mm PaK 36(r)
Barrel length: 13ft 10in (4.20m)
Weight of shell: 10lb 10oz (7.54kg) APHE
8lb 15oz (4.05kg) HVAP
Muzzle velocity: 2,426ft/sec (740m/sec) APHE
3,248ft/sec (990m/sec) HVAP
Maximum range: 9,840yd (9,000m)

Ammunition types: APHE, HVAP, HE
Ammunition load: 30

Vehicle: Sd Kfz 139
Crew: 4
All-up weight: 10.50 tons (10,670kg)
Armour: 50mm maximum
Hull length: 16ft 3in (4.65m)
Width: 7ft 1in (2.16m)
Height: 8ft 3in (2.50m)
Engine: Praga EPA, 6-cylinder, petrol, 125bhp at 2,200rpm
Road speed: 26mph (42km/hr)
Range: 120 miles (190km)

Möbelwagen Germany
Deutsche Eisenwerke

1944. Möbelwagen ('Furniture van') was a mobile anti-aircraft gun developed in Germany in 1944 as an interim solution pending the development of a more advanced equipment. In the event, this never appeared and 240 Möbelwagen were built and served until the war ended. The basis was the hull and running gear of the Panzer 4 tank, upon which a flat-topped superstructure carried a 3.7cm FlaK 43 gun. The rotating gun platform was surrounded by a steel box, the walls of which were hinged so as to fold down and provide a working platform for the gun detachment. (It should be noted that the original design for this vehicle was that it should carry a quadruple 20mm FlaK 38 mounting; prototypes were built but the design was turned down and the 3.7cm gun adopted instead.)

Armament: 1 × 37mm FlaK 43
Barrel length: 7ft 0in (2.13m)
Weight of shell: 1lb 6oz (635g)
Muzzle velocity: 2,690ft/sec (820m/sec)
Maximum range: 7,200yd (6,585m)
Effective ceiling: 13,780ft (4,200m)
Ammunition types: HE-T, HEI-T, APHE-T, APHE-I-T
Ammunition load: 416

Vehicle: Sd Kfz 161/3
Crew: 6
All-up weight: 23.62 tons (24,000kg)
Armour: 80mm maximum
Hull length: 19ft 5in (5.92m)
Width: 9ft 7in (2.93m)
Height: 9ft 0in (2.73m)
Engine: Maybach HL120TRM, V-12, petrol, 300bhp at 3,000rpm
Road speed: 24mph (38km/hr)
Range: 120 miles (200km)

Nashorn Germany
Deutsche Eisenwerke

1943. Nashorn ('Rhinoceros') was a heavy tank destroyer which armed a number of specialist tank-hunting units and which proved to be a most effective weapon. It consisted of the Panzer 2/4 combination chassis developed for the Hummel SP gun, and which was a Panzer 4 hull lengthened and with the engine moved forward to a central position. The suspension was basically Panzer 4 but with some Panzer 3 components. The hull was opened up into a slope-sided open-topped superstructure with the PaK 43 88mm gun firing forward. 494 of these weapons were built. Originally called Nashorn from the prominent central gun, it was thought that this was not sufficiently aggressive and it was changed to **Hornisse** ('Hornet') some time in 1944.

Armament: 1 × 88mm PaK 43/1
Barrel length: 12 ft 8in (6.61m)
Weight of shell: 22lb 14oz (10.4kg) APHE
16lb 20z (7.3kg) HVAP
Muzzle velocity: 3,280ft/sec (1,000m/sec) APHE
3,710ft/sec (1,130m/sec) HVAP
Maximum range: 19,140yd (17,500m)
Ammunition types: APHE, HVAP, HE
Ammunition load: 25

Vehicle: Sd Kfz 164
Crew: 4
All-up weight: 23.62 tons (24,000kg)
Armour: 30mm maximum
Hull length: 23ft 6in (7.17m)
Width: 9ft 2in (2.80m)
Height: 8ft 8in (2.65m)
Engine: Maybach HL120TRM, V-12, petrol, 300bhp at 3,000rpm
Road speed: 26mph (42km/hr)
Range: 125 miles (200km)

NORA Yugoslavia

1992. NORA was a proposal for a self-propelled 155mm howitzer on an 8 x 8 wheeled chassis. It was announced by the Yugoslavian Federal Directorate of Supply and Procurement in 1992, and was to consist of the barrel of their existing M48/84 towed howitzer allied to a locally-manufactured 8 x 8 truck which was already used as the carrier for a multiple rocket system sold to Iraq. The gun was based on one of Dr Gerald Bull's Space Research Corporation designs, was purely an export venture and probably never got beyond a prototype, and the NORA project probably never got beyond a set of drawings before Yugoslavia collapsed.

Ostwind Germany
Ostbau

1944. This was designed to replace Wirbelwind with a more effective weapon having a higher ceiling and more destructive power. It used the same Panzer 4 chassis and running gear and hexagonal turret but mounted a single 37mm FlaK 43 in place of the quadruple 20mm mounting. This put less metal into the sky but pushed the ceiling up.

Armament: I × 37mm FlaK 43
Barrel length: 7ft 0in (2.13m)
Weight of shell: Ilb 6oz (635g)
Rate of fire: 250rd/min
Muzzle velocity: 2,690ft/sec (820m/sec)
Maximum range: 7,200yd (6,585m)
Effective ceiling: 13,775ft (4,200m)
Ammunition types: HE-T; HEI-T; APHE-T; APHE-I-T
Ammunition load: 1,000

Vehicle: FlaK Panzerwagen 604
Crew: 6
All-up weight: 25 tons (25,400kg)
Armour: 80mm maximum
Hull length: 19ft 5in (5.92m)
Width: 9ft 7in (2.95m)
Height: 9ft 10in (3.0m)
Engine: Maybach HL120 TRM112, V-12, petrol, 272bhp at 2,800rpm
Road speed: 24mph (38km/hr)
Range: 125 miles (200km)

Otomatic 76mm Air Defence Tank Italy
OTO-Melara

1992. This was developed by OTO-Melara primarily as a weapon for keeping helicopters and ground attack aircraft off the back of ground troops, and secondarily as a useful weapon against light armoured vehicles should they also appear. The Otomatic System consists of a turret assembly with a 76mm gun, surveillance and tracking radars, electro-optical sights, fire control computer and all the sundry fixtures and fittings that tie these items together. This complete unit can then be dropped into any tank with a large enough turret ring; for the purposes of the Italian Army trials the Leopard 1 was selected and the whole ensemble fits together well and has performed successfully in trials.

Armament: I × 76mm
Barrel length: 15ft 6in (4.72m)
Weight of shell: 14lb 0oz (6.35kg)
Muzzle velocity: 3,035ft/sec (925m/sec)
Maximum range: 17,500yd (16,000m)
Effective ceiling: 19,685ft (6,000m)
Ammunition types: HEPF, APFSDS
Ammunition load: 78 AA; 12 AT

Vehicle
Crew: 4
All-up weight: 46.26 tons (47,000kg)
Armour: not disclosed
Hull length: 23ft 3in (7.08m)
Width: 10ft 8in (3.25m)
Height: 10ft 1in (3.07m) radar stowed
Engine: MTU V-10 multi-fuel, 830bhp at 2,200rpm
Road speed: 37mph (60km/hr)
Range: 310 miles (500km)

Palmaria Italy
OTO-Melara

1980. This 155mm SP howitzer was developed by OTO-Melara of Italy as a private export venture, and numbers were sold to Argentina, Libya, Nigeria and other countries. When the SP-70 project collapsed the design took on new significance as a likely contender for the Italian Army; it may yet do so, but not until the Italians are satisfied that there is no more mileage in their M109s. The hull and chassis of the vehicle are derived from the OF-40 MBT, though the engine is special to this vehicle. The hull is very 'square' and simple in outline, and the gun turret fits into the hull in place of the tank turret, leaving the engine in the rear of the hull. The howitzer is 41 calibres long and fitted with a fume extractor and a double-baffle muzzle brake.

Armament: I × 155mm howitzer
Barrel length: 20ft 10in (6.35m)
Weight of shell: 95lb 14oz (43.5kg)
Muzzle velocity: 3,060ft/sec (933m/sec)
Maximum range: 27,010yd (24,700m) conventional
32,819yd (30,000m) HERA
Ammunition types: HE, HERA, HE/ICM
Ammunition load: 30

Vehicle
Crew: 5
All-up weight: 44.29 tons (45,000kg)
Armour: not disclosed
Hull length: 23ft 10in (7.26m)
Width: 11ft 0in (3.35m)
Height: 9ft 5in (2.87mm)
Engine: MTU MB837 turbocharged multi-fuel, 1,000bhp
Road speed: 37mph (60km/hr)
Range: 310 miles (500km)

Panhard AML S530 Twin 20mm SPAA Gun France
Panhard et Levassor, SAMM

1973. This equipment was devised by Panhard and SAMM (Société d'Application des Machines

Motrices) for export sale. They sold about a dozen to Venezuela and that was all. It consists of a standard Panhard 4 x 4 AML armoured car with a SAMM turret carrying two GIAT M621 20mm cannon with optical sights. It is, therefore, a fair-weather-only system.

Armament: 2 x GIAT M621 20mm cannon
Barrel length: 5ft 1in (1.54m)
Weight of shell: 3.5oz (100g)
Muzzle velocity: 3,248ft/sec (990m/sec)
Rate of fire: 740rpg/min
Maximum ceiling: 4,920ft (1,500m)
Ammunition types: HE-I, AP-I
Ammunition load: 600

Vehicle: Panhard AML
Crew: 3
All-up weight: 5.41 tons (5,500kg)
Armour: 14mm maximum
Hull length: 12ft 5in (3.79m)
Width: 6ft 6in (1.97m)
Height: 7ft 4in (2.24m)
Engine: Panhard 4HD, 4-cylinder petrol, 90bhp at 4,700rpm
Road speed: 56mph (90km/hr)
Range: 370 miles (600km)

Panzerhaubitze 2000 Germany
Wegmann/MaK

1990. As a result of the collapse of the SP-70 project, Germany had to find a new SP howitzer. Designs were solicited from two groups of companies, and after examination that offered by Wegmann/MaK was accepted and contracts for its further development were issued. Development was completed and the first of 185 equipments was delivered to the army in mid-1998. The hull and running gear are based on those of the Leopard 2 tank, with the engine and transmission at the front of the hull. The rear is surmounted by a large turret containing the 52-calibre length gun which has a sliding block breech and a large multi-baffle muzzle-brake. The gun and turret are entirely power-operated and there is an automatic mechanical loading system which will permit the firing of three rounds in ten seconds.

Armament: 1 x 155mm howitzer
Barrel length: 26ft 5in (8.06m)
Weight of shell: 97lb 0oz (44kg)
Muzzle velocity: not known
Maximum range: 35,880yd (30km) conventional
43,745yd (40km) assisted
Ammunition types: HE, HE/ICM, HERA
Ammunition load: 60

Vehicle
Crew: 5
All-up weight: 54.46 tons (55,330kg)
Armour: not disclosed
Hull length: 23ft 11in (7.30m)
Width: 11ft 0in (3.37m)
Height: 11ft 2in (3.40m)
Engine: MTU 881 V-12 diesel, 1,000bhp
Road speed: 27mph (60km/hr)
Range: 260 miles (420km)

Panzerjäger SK105 Austria
Steyr-Daimler-Puch

1971. Also known as the **Kurassier**, this vehicle was originally designed as a tank destroyer but it appears to function well as a light tank and could be classed under either head. The hull is derived from the Saurer 4K 7FA APC (*qv*); the running gear has five roadwheels and three return rollers on each side, rear drive and front idlers. The prime feature is the turret, which is the oscillating type first seen on the AMX-13 tank. This allows the fitting of a powerful 105mm gun complete with automatic loading.

The **SK105/A1** is an improved model with new fire control and sighting systems. The **SK105/A2** has the turret stabilised, a new fire control computer and a passive night vision sight for the gunner. The **SK105/A3** is a substantial re-design and is dealt with separately below.

SK105/A1

Armament: 1 x 105mm gun 105G1
Barrel length: 15ft 2in (4.62m)
Weight of shell: 26lb 11oz (12.1kg) HE
Muzzle velocity: 2,625ft/sec (800m/sec)
Operational range: 2,952yd (2,700m)
Ammunition types: HE, HEAT, APFSDS
Ammunition load: 42

Vehicle
Crew: 3
All-up weight: 17.42 tons (17,700kg)
Armour: 40mm maximum
Hull length: 18ft 4in (5.58m)
Width: 8ft 3in (2.50m)
Height: 8ft 4in (2.53m)
Engine: Steyr 7FA 6-cylinder turbocharged diesel, 320bhp at 2,300rpm
Road speed: 43mph (70km/hr)
Range: 320 miles (520km)

Panzerjäger SK105/A3
Steyr-Daimler-Puch

This amounts to a major overhaul of the SK105 design, by fitting the American M68 105mm tank gun with a new and improved recoil system. The gun has a fume extractor, a high efficiency muzzle brake and a thermal sleeve. The auto-loading system has been electrically powered, and a new electric rammer is included. Turret traversing and elevating is by electric power, with manual backup. A more powerful engine has been fitted, together with a new six-speed transmission.

Armament: 1 x 105mm M68
Barrel length: 17ft 6in (5.34m)
Weight of shell: 12lb 12oz (5.79kg) APFSDS-T
Muzzle velocity: 4,920ft/sec (1,500m/sec)
Operational range: 3,280yd (3,000m)
Ammunition types: APFSDS-T, HE-T, APDS-T, HEP-T, HEAT-T
Ammunition load: not known

Vehicle
Crew: 3
All-up weight: 20.37 tons (20,700kg)
Armour: not known
Hull length: 18ft 4in (5.58m)
Width: 8ft 3in (2.50m)
Height: 9ft 0in (2.76m)
Engine: Steyr 9FA 6-cylinder turbocharged diesel, 360bhp at 2,300rpm
Road speed: 43mph (70km/hr)
Range: 340 miles (550km)

PRAM-S 120mm SP Mortar Czech
Republic
ZTS Dubnica
1990. Most armies use heavy mortars, but not many go to the trouble of developing a self-propelled mounting for them. This equipment is based on the hull and running gear of the Soviet BMP-2 MICV, the chassis having been lengthened and an extra roadwheel added on each side. The roof of the rear troop-carrying section has been raised slightly in order to fit the fire control equipment in, and the mortar protrudes at 45° from the front of this compartment. The 120mm mortar is a breech-loading weapon, and has limited traverse but the full range of elevation. The hull has a sharp, flat prow and a folding trim vane, indicating that the vehicle is amphibious.

Armament: 1 x 120mm mortar
Barrel length: 6ft 1in (1.85m)
Weight of shell: 33lb 13oz (15.33kg)
Muzzle velocity: 902ft/sec (275m/sec)
Maximum range: 6,290yd (5,750m)
Ammunition types: HE/Frag, smoke
Ammunition load: 60

Vehicle: Based on BMP-2
Crew: 4
All-up weight: 16.70 tons (16,970kg)
Armour: not disclosed
Hull length: 24ft 4in (7.41m)
Width: 9ft 8in (2.94m)
Height: 8ft 3in (2.50m)
Engine: diesel, 300bhp
Road speed: 37mph (60km/hr)
Range: 340 miles (550km)

PVKV Sweden
Landsverk
1950–70. This was a mobile anti-tank equipment based upon the chassis of the obsolescent Strv m/42 tank. The turret was removed and a tall rectangular superstructure built on to the hull. A long-barrelled 75mm gun was fitted into this compartment, pointing forward through a ball mounting. It was not a particularly good design, but it sufficed for defensive purposes until more advanced vehicles could be developed.

Armament: 1 x 75mm; 1 x MG
Crew: 4
All-up weight: 23.0 tons (23,375kg)
Armour: 40mm maximum
Hull length: 16ft 1in (4.90m)
Width: 7ft 9in (2.36m)
Height: 8ft 6in (2.59m)
Engine: Scania-Vabis, diesel, 370bhp
Road speed: 28mph (45km/hr)
Range: 125 miles (200km)

Rascal Light 155mm SP Howitzer Israel
Soltam
1993. The Rascal was a private venture by Soltam, the Israel manufacturers, and represents an entirely new design of SP gun. The object was to produce a gun light enough not be restricted by the carrying capacity of country bridges, and also light enough to be air-lifted. The vehicle is not based upon any existing tank or carrier; the hull has a raised driver's compartment at the left front, with the engine behind the driver. There is a central compartment for the commander and two gunners. There are six dual roadwheels on each side, with a pronounced gap between the first and second, two return rollers, large front drive sprockets and rear idlers. The 155mm howitzer is installed on a platform at the rear of the vehicle and is power operated; the gun may be either 39- or 52-calibres length. 40 rounds of ammunition are carried, the shells in racks alongside the gun and the cartridges in an armour-protected compartment in the hull.

Armament: 1 × 155mm howitzer
Barrel length: 19ft 10in (6.04m) 39-cal
    26ft 5in (8.06m) 52-cal
Weight of shell: 98lb 2oz (44.5kg)
Muzzle velocity: not disclosed
Maximum range: 26,250yd (24,000m) 52-calibre
Ammunition types: HE, HE/ICM
Ammunition load: 40

Vehicle
Crew: 4
All-up weight: 10.19 tons (19,500kg)
Armour: not disclosed
Hull length: 24ft 7in (7.50m)
Width: 8ft 1in (2.46m)
Height: 7ft 6in (2.30m)
Engine: diesel, 350bhp
Road speed: not disclosed
Range: 218 miles (350km)

Romach 175mm SP Gun Israel

This is the Israeli nomenclature for the M107 175mm gun; there are some minor modifications to the automotive aspects, but essential dimensions and data are the same.

Royal Ordnance SP122 UK
ROF Nottingham

In the 1980s some Middle Eastern countries upgraded their Soviet-supplied artillery with modern fire control equipment from Western sources. This led to a burst of optimistic designs for putting these ex-Soviet weapons on to Western carriages, and this was one such, developed to the prototype stage by RO to meet an Egyptian enquiry. It was a fairly pedestrian design of roofed superstructure set at the rear on a tracked chassis derived from the then-current development of the RO 2000 series of tracked vehicles. The engine was in the right front, the driver in the left front of the vehicle. The 122mm D-30 howitzer was selected as the weapon. Translated into Imperial measure, this meant a 20-ton vehicle carrying a 4.7-inch gun, which was no sort of a bargain in the 1980s. Not surprisingly there were no takers, and in the 1990s, when the RO 2000 project collapsed, the SP122 vanished with it.

Armament: 1 × 122mm D-30 howitzer
Barrel length: 14ft 0in (4.27m)
Weight of shell: 54lb 14oz (24.9kg)
Muzzle velocity: 2,350ft/sec (716m/sec)
Maximum range: 16,840yd (15,400m)
Ammunition types: HE, HEAT, smoke
Ammunition load: not known

Vehicle
Crew: 5
All-up weight: 19.68 tons (20,000kg)
Armour: not disclosed
Hull length: 25ft 3in (7.70m)
Width: 9ft 3in (2.81m)
Height: 8ft 10in (2.70m)
Engine: Perkins V-8 turbocharged diesel, 300bhp
Road speed: 34mph (55km/hr)
Range: not known

S-3 37mm Light SP Gun Czechoslovakia
Skoda

1936–39. The belief that small-calibre anti-tank guns would suffice against all possible future tanks led to a number of designs of lightweight tank destroyers in the 1930s, of which the S-3 is a prize example. The design was based upon the hull and running gear of the LT-35 light tank. The turret was removed, the hull top flattened, and a rectangular space walled off by hinged thin plates so as to make an area into which a 37mm anti-tank gun on a pedestal, with shield, was fitted. The side plates could be dropped to allow the gun to swing in any direction and form a platform for the gunners to operate. A variant model had a 66mm infantry gun instead of the 37mm, and a third variant reverted to the 37mm gun but covered the shield top to form a rudimentary sort of turret. By 1939 they were too light to damage any existing tank, and too flimsy to survive for long on the battlefield, and the German Army simply scrapped them.

Armament: 1 × 37mm + 2 × MG;
    or 1 × 66mm + 2 × MG
Crew: 5
All-up weight: 10.03 tons (10,200kg)
Armour: 12mm maximum
Hull length: 16ft 1in (4.90m)
Width: 7ft 1in (2.16m)
Height: 7ft 6in (2.28m)
Engine: Skoda, 6-cylinder petrol, 120bhp at 1,800rpm
Road speed: 25mph (40km/hr)
Range: 118 miles (190km)

St Chamond France
FAMH

1918. This unusual equipment consists of two vehicles; one is the '*affut à chenilles*', the tracked chassis carrying the gun; the other is the '*avant-train chenilles*', a similar tracked chassis containing the power supply. Propulsion is done by a petrol engine driving an electrical generator which supplies power to electric motors driving the tracks of the 'avant-train' and, by means of a cable and towbar connection, the motors driving the gun carriage. The gun carriage portion is controlled by a steersman, while the entire unit is driven by the avant-train driver, who controls the speed of the train by varying the current to the electric motors. The avant-train unit also carried a supply of ammunition and some of the gun crew. On arriving at the firing point, the gun unit was uncoupled and placed in the firing position, while the tractor unit unloaded its ammunition and departed to some safer place. The system was cumbersome but at least it had the merit of providing plenty of traction power for difficult terrain. About a dozen were built, and briefly used in 1918, but they did not survive for long after the war ended.

Armament: 1 x 194mm GPF gun
Barrel length: 21ft 6in (6.57m)
Weight of shell: 176lb 6oz (80.0kg)
Muzzle velocity: 2,100ft/sec (640m/sec)
Maximum range: 20,015yd (18,300m)
Ammunition types: HE

Vehicle
Crew: 8
All-up weight: 27.56 tons (28,000kg)
Armour: none
Hull length: 26ft 8in (8.12m)
Width: 8ft 9in (2.67m)
Height: 7ft 8in (2.35m)
Engine: Panhard, 6-cylinder, petrol, 110bhp at 1,500rpm, driving Crochat-Collardeau electric dynamos and motors
Road speed: 6mph (10km/hr)
Range: 31 miles (50km)

Schneider France
Schneider
1917. This was produced to the same specification as the St Chamond design described above, but was less complicated and rather more successful. It consisted of a tracked chassis, derived, like most tracked vehicles of that period, from the American Holt agricultural tractor, and driven by a conventional petrol engine and gearbox arrangement. On top of the hull was a simple carriage with a 22cm gun; at the front end was the driver, with his controls, and at the rear end was a raised compartment containing the engine and transmission. The gunners apparently hung on where they could, and ammunition and more gunners came along in a supporting vehicle. The design was simple, numbers were built, and it was used with some success in the St Mihiel sector in 1918. Some even survived to be captured by the Germans in 1940 and sent to the Eastern Front.

Armament: 1 x 220mm gun M1917
Barrel length: 25ft 2in (7.67m)
Weight of shell: 231lb (104.75kg)
Muzzle velocity: 2,513ft/sec (766m/sec)
Maximum range: 24,935yd (22,800m)
Ammunition types: HE
Ammunition load: not known

Vehicle
Crew: 8
All-up weight: 25.59 tons (26,000kg)
Armour: none
Hull length: 28ft 0in (8.52m)
Width: 8ft 3in (2.52m)
Height: 10ft 0in (3.04m)
Engine: Panhard, 6-cylinder, petrol, 110bhp at 1,500rpm
Road speed: 5mph (8km/hr)
Range: 31 miles (50km)

Sd Kfz Series Germany
See Sonder Kraftfahrzeug, below

Semovente 47/32 Italy
Fiat/Ansaldo
1941. This was a light anti-tank equipment derived from the Fiat-Ansaldo L 6-40 light tank by removing the turret and extending the hull sides up for about a foot so as to form a cramped crew compartment. A 47mm anti-tank gun was installed on the left front, and the two gunners and the driver shared the space around it. In spite of its many faults, it was all that was available to provide the anti-tank defence for the Italian Army in Libya in 1941.

Armament: 1 x 47mm; 1 x MG
Barrel length: 5ft 6in (1.68m)
Weight of shell: 3lb 5oz (1.5kg) APHE
Muzzle velocity: 2,067ft/sec (630m/sec)
Maximum range: 3,830yd (3,500m)
Ammunition types: HE, APHE
Ammunition load: 89

Vehicle
Crew: 3
All-up weight: 6.40 tons (6,500kg)
Armour: 30mm maximum
Hull length: 12ft 5in (3.78m)
Width: 6ft 4in (1.92m)
Height: 5ft 5in (1.63m)
Engine: Fiat 18D, 4-cylinder, petrol, 70bhp at 2,500rpm
Road speed: 26mph (42km/hr)
Range: 125 miles (200km)

Semovente 75/18 Italy
Fiat/Ansaldo

1941. This was based on the chassis of the CA M13/40 and M15/42 tanks as each came into service, since the conversion was a simple matter and could be applied to almost any tank. The turret was removed and a square box put in its place, with the stub-barrelled 75mm gun protruding through the front face of the box. For such a vehicle it was very low and easily concealed and hard to spot, which aided its survival. The space inside was cramped, but they were effective enough to be retained and used by the German Army after the Italian surrender.

Armament: 1 x 75mm gun Breda Mod 35; 2 x MG
Barrel length: 4ft 5in (1.35m)
Weight of shell: 14lb 0oz (6.35kg)
Muzzle velocity: 1,427ft/sec (435m/sec)
Maximum range: 5,685yd (5,400m)
Ammunition types: HE
Ammunition load: 48

Vehicle
Crew: 4
All-up weight: 13.78 tons (14,000kg)
Armour: 30mm maximum
Hull length: 16ft 2in (4.92m)
Width: 7ft 3in (2.20m)
Height: 6ft 4in (1.92m)
Engine: SPA 15-TA41, 8-cylinder diesel, 145bhp at 1,900rpm
Road speed: 22mph (35km/hr)
Range: 125 miles (200km)

Semovente 90/53 Italy
Fiat/Ansaldo

1940. This was probably the most potent SP anti-tank gun of its day, having been a conversion from a useful anti-aircraft gun, but only 24 were ever made and they were all destroyed during the battle for Sicily in 1943. The size of the gun made it necessary to mount it in the open air, at the rear end of the hull of a Model 13/40 tank chassis, which made life hazardous for the gunners. Another drawback was the limited amount of ammunition it could carry.

Armament: 1 x 90mm gun 90/53 Mod 39
Barrel length: 17ft 5in (5.30m)
Weight of shell: 24lb 13oz (11.25kg) APHE
Muzzle velocity: 2,723ft/sec (830m/sec)
Maximum range: 10,936yd (10,000m)
Ammunition types: HE, APHE
Ammunition load: 6

Vehicle
Crew: 4

All-up weight: 16.73 tons (17,000kg)
Armour: 40mm maximum
Hull length: 17ft 4in (5.28m)
Width: 7ft 4in (2.26m)
Height: 7ft 1in (2.15m)
Engine: SPA 15-Tm, 8-cylinder diesel, 145bhp at 1,800rpm
Road speed: 18mph (30km/hr)
Range: 93 miles (150km)

Semovente 149/40 Italy
Ansaldo

1943. The 149mm Mod 35 was the Italian Army's most modern medium gun, with a respectable performance, and this was a project to mount it on a tracked chassis constructed from components of the experimental CA P26/40 heavy tank. It was simply a box with a driver and engine, on a complex two-double-bogie suspension. The gun was mounted at the rear end of the hull and was low-set so that it lay along the hull top at zero elevation. It would probably have been a useful and effective piece of equipment in the mobile field artillery role, but the Italian surrender in 1943 put an end to the development.

Armament: 1 x 149mm gun 149/40 Mod 35
Barrel length: 19ft 6in (5.96m)
Weight of shell: 112lb 0oz (50.80kg)
Muzzle velocity: 2,625ft/sec (800m/sec)
Maximum range: 24,060yd (22,000m)
Ammunition types: HE
Ammunition load: 6

Vehicle
Crew: 2
All-up weight: 23.62 tons (24,000kg)
Armour: 25mm maximum
Hull length: 21ft 4in (6.50m)
Width: 9ft 8in (3.00m)
Height: 6ft 7in (2.01m)
Engine: SPA, petrol, 240bhp
Road speed: 22mph (35km/hr)
Range: 93 miles (150km)

Sexton UK/Canada
Montreal

1943. The British Army adopted the US M7 SP gun but disliked the 105mm howitzer for its lack of range and because it required a special supply of ammunition. Could they please have the same conversion but with a 25-pounder gun instead of a 105mm? No, said the US authorities, we will only build what we can use, and we don't use the 25-pounder. (They did, eventually, but that's another story.) So the British went to Canada and adapted the Ram tank, which was a Canadian version of the US M4 Medium, by doing a similar conversion to the M7. The hull was opened up and a working space created, with the 25-pounder gun mounted in the front of the compartment so as to give full elevation.

Production began in 1943, the first models being known as **Ram Carriers**; they were soon re-christened Sexton, there being a tradition of clerical nicknames for British SP guns, and these became Sexton **Mark 1**. Sexton **Mark 2** differed in having large square battery and auxiliary generator boxes on the rear corners of the hull. A total of 2,150 were built, and some remained in use with the Portuguese and South African Armies until the middle 1980s, when the supply of spare parts finally dried up.

Armament: Ordnance QF, 25-pdr Gun Mk 2C
Barrel length: 8ft 1in (3.92m)
Weight of shell: 25lb (11.34kg)
Muzzle velocity: 1,700ft/sec (518m/sec)
Maximum range: 13,400yd (12,250m)
Ammunition types: HE, smoke, flare, illuminating, AP Shot
Ammunition load: 112

Vehicle: Carrier, Ram, SP 25-pdr Gun, Mark 1
Crew: 6
All-up weight: 25.45 tons (25,853kg)
Armour: 108mm maximum
Hull length: 20ft 1in (6.12m)
Width: 8ft 11in (2.71in)
Height: 8ft 0in (2.43m)
Engine: Continental, 9-cylinder, radial, petrol, 400bhp at 2,400rpm
Road speed: 24mph (38km/hr)
Range: 125 miles (200km)

SIDAM-25 SPAA Gun System Italy
OTO-Melara
1989. Like the Otomatic system described previously, the Sidam-25 is a complete turret unit, with four 25mm cannon, optical sights, low-light video sights, laser rangefinder and fire control computer. This is fitted into the roof of a standard M113 APC, and has been tested in various other vehicles. The Italian Army has adopted the M113 version. It has also been tested with an add-on missile assembly, firing the French Mistral SAM, and with thermal imaging sights and radar input to the fire control system, all of which appear to have been satisfactory.

Armament: 4 x Oerlikon 25mm KBA cannon
Barrel length: 7ft 1in (2.17m)

Weight of shell: 6.3oz (180g)
Muzzle velocity: 3,610ft/sec (1,100m/sec)
Effective ceiling: 8,200ft (2,500m)
Ammunition types: HE, SAPHE, APDS
Ammunition load: 640 AA; 30 AT

Vehicle
Crew: 3
All-up weight: 14.27 tons (14,500kg)
Armour: 44mm maximum
Hull length: 20ft 0in (4.86m)
Width: 8ft 10in (2.69m)
Height: not known
Engine: Detroit Diesel V-6, 265bhp at 2,800rpm
Road speed: 40mph (65km/hr)
Range: 310 miles (500km)

sIG 33 15cm Infantry Assault Gun
Germany
BMKD
1940. German infantry battalions were always provided with their own direct support artillery, and the schwere Infanterie Geschütz 33 (heavy Infantry Gun) was the backbone of this force, firing a useful shell to a moderate range. As early as 1938 the infantry had asked for this gun to be mounted on a tracked chassis so that it could accompany the troops, probably the first suggestion for an assault gun, and after much experimenting the first design appeared in February 1940. It was based on the chassis and hull of the Panzer 1 tank, the turret being removed and a flat platform for the gun installed, surrounded by a tall sloping shielded barbette, which gave the vehicle a grossly top-heavy appearance. The sIG33 gun was then fitted inside this shield on its normal field carriage. Cumbersome and primitive it may have been, but it worked well in the 1940 campaigns and confirmed the infantry in their theory of assault gun support.

In 1941 a more ambitious design appeared based on the Panzer 3 chassis; the turret was removed and the hull opened up, with the gun mounted behind a small shield at the front of this fighting compartment. Protection for the gunners was minimal, and only 12 were built, all of which went to North Africa. And stayed there.

Next, also in 1941, came the third attempt, the **Sturm Infanterie Geschütz 33B**, also based on the Panzer 3 chassis. This had a slope-sided superstructure with the gun in the front face, but offered far better protection to the gunners since the compartment was fully enclosed. The vehicle was designed in the latter part of 1941 but nothing much happened until late 1942 when 24 were urgently demanded for use in the fighting in Stalingrad. No more were built, the design being considered too expensive.

Finally, what became the ultimate sIG33 design, was the version built in the ex-Czech TNH/PS chassis. This made a compact and reliable vehicle which was also economic to build, using the Czech chassis and running gear and surmounting it with a simple open-topped fighting compartment with the gun in the front face. 91 of these were built during 1943, and with these and the more nimble Sturmgeschütz, the infantry were content.

TNHP version
Armament: 1 × 15cm sIG 33
Barrel length: 5ft 5in (1.650m)
Weight of shell: 83lb 12oz (38.0kg)
Muzzle velocity: 787ft/sec (240m/sec)
Maximum range: 5,140yd (4,700m)
Ammunition types: HE, smoke
Ammunition load: 18

Vehicle: Modified Czech TNH/PS tank, Sd Kfz 138/1
Crew: 4
All-up weight: 11.81 tons (12,000kg)
Armour: 20mm maximum
Hull length: 16ft 3in (4.95m)
Width: 7ft 1in (2.15m)
Height: 8ft 1in (2.47m)
Engine: Praga AC, 6-cylinder petrol, 160bhp at 2,800rpm
Road speed: 21mph (35km/hr)
Range: 125 miles (200km)

Sinai 23 SPAA Gun Egypt
Dassault Électronique
1990. This light air defence weapon system was produced in France to meet an Egyptian Army requirement and consists of a Dassault TA-20 turret mounting two 23mm ex-Russian cannon, electro-optical sights and a surveillance/acquisition radar, all mounted on top of an M113 APC. The radar is used to detect an oncoming target; it is slaved to the electro-optical sight and thus the gunner can pick the target up quickly and easily. A signal indicates when the target is within range and the gunner can then open fire. Six 'Sakr Eye' ground-to-air missiles are also mounted on the turret, in two sets of three alongside each cannon. These are the Egyptian-made version of the Russian SA-7 'Grail' shoulder-fired missile.

Armament: 2 × 23mm ZU-23 cannon; 6 × SAM
Barrel length: 6ft 7in (2.01m)
Weight of shell: 6.5oz (185g)
Muzzle velocity: 3,182ft/sec (970m/sec)
Rate of fire: 800rpg/min
Maximum ceiling: 4,929ft (1,500m)

Ammunition types: HE-I
Ammunition load: 1,200 23mm; 6 missiles

Vehicle: M113A2 APC modified
Crew: 3
All-up weight: not known
Armour: 44mm maximum
Hull length: 16ft 0in (4.86m)
Width: 8ft 10in (2.69m)
Height: not known
Engine: Detroit Diesel V-6, 212bhp at 2,800rpm
Road speed: 27mph (60km/hr)
Range: 295 miles (475km)

Slammer 155mm SP Howitzer Israel
Soltam
1985. This was a venture by Soltam which consisted of mounting a 52-calibre howitzer into a newly-designed turret fitted into a Merkava MBT chassis in place of the original turret. Two prototypes were made and submitted to the Israeli Defence Force but no production was ever undertaken.

Armament: 1 × 155mm howitzer
Barrel length: 26ft 5in (8.06m)
Weight of shell: 99.8lb (45.3kg)
Muzzle velocity: 2,936ft/sec (895m/sec)
Maximum range: 43,750+yd (40,000+m)
Ammunition types: HE-ERFBB
Ammunition load: 75

Vehicle
Crew: 4
All-up weight: 63 tons (64,000kg)
Armour: not disclosed
Hull length: 24ft 5in (7.45m)
Width: 12ft 2in (3.70m)
Height: 11ft 2in (3.40m)
Engine: diesel, 900bhp
Road speed: 28mph (45km/hr)
Range: 250 miles (400km)

SM-240 SP Mortar Russia
See 2S4

Sonder Kraftfahrzeug (Sd Kfz) 6/2
Germany
Büssing-NAG
1940. This was the standard 37mm FlaK 35 anti-aircraft gun bolted down to the cargo bed of the Büssing-NAG 5-ton semi-tracked carrier. The sides of the cargo area (or troop compartment) were hinged so as to drop outwards and make a platform for the gunners as the gun traversed. The gun mounting generally retained its normal shield. Ammunition was carried in a trailer towed behind

the vehicle. A total of 349 were built before manufacture of the basic vehicle ceased in September 1943, which brought manufacture of the conversions to a halt as well; the 8-ton carrier was then adopted as the basis (*see* Sd Kfz 7/2).

Armament: I × 37mm FlaK 18 or 36
Barrel length: 9ft 5in (3.63m)
Weight of shell: 1.4lb (635g)
Muzzle velocity: 2,690ft/sec (820m/sec)
Effective ceiling: 6,560ft (2,000m)
Ammunition types: HE, HE-I, APHE
Ammunition load: none

Vehicle: Fahrgestell Zugkraftwagen 5-tonne
Crew: 7
All-up weight: 10.4 tons (10,565kg)
Armour: 10mm
Hull length: 20ft 9in (6.32m)
Width: 7ft 5in (2.26m)
Height: 8ft 3in (2.5m)
Engine: Maybach HL54, 6-cylinder petrol, 180bhp at 4,000rpm
Road speed: 31mph (50km/hr)
Range: 200 miles (320km)

Sd Kfz 7/2 Germany
Borgward, Krauss-Maffei, Saurer
When manufacture of the Sd Kfz 6/2 was forced to stop in 1943, this 8-tonne carrier was adopted as the vehicle upon which to mount the 3.7cm FlaK gun. Some vehicles had the driver's cab encased in armour, most did not. Details of the gun and its performance as the same as for the Sd Kfz 6/2; details for the vehicle follow.

Vehicle: Fahrgestell Zugkraftwagen 8-tonne
Crew: 10
All-up weight: 11.55 tons (11,735kg)
Armour: 8mm
Hull length: 20ft 10in (6.85m)
Width: 7ft 10in (2.40m)
Height: 8ft 7in (2.62m)
Engine: Maybach HL62
Road speed: 31mph (50km/hr)
Range: 155 miles (250km)

Sd Kfz 8 Germany
Daimler-Benz
1939. The most ambitious of the German semi-tracked SP guns, this was the standard 8.8cm FlaK 18 or 36 gun mounted on the cargo bed of the Daimler-Benz 12-ton semi-tracked carrier. Ten were built in 1939, their object being two-fold, as an anti-tank vehicle and also as a high-velocity gun for direct shooting at field fortifications, for which

reason the vehicle was quite well armoured. It appears to have proved useful in the Polish campaign, and in 1940 a further 15 were built as the Sd Kfz 9 using the 18-tonne carrier. Interest in these 12-tonners appears to have lapsed, and they were never heard of again after 1940.

Armament: I × 88mm FlaK 18 or 35 gun
Barrel length: 16ft 2in (4.93m)
Weight of shell: 20lb 15oz (9.50kg) APHE
Muzzle velocity: 2,690ft/sec (820m/sec)
Operational range: 2,750yd (2,500m)
Ammunition types: APHE, HE
Ammunition load: 40

Vehicle: Zugkraftwagen 12-tonne
Crew: 9
All-up weight: 20 tons (20,320kg)
Armour: 14mm
Hull length: 24ft 2in (7.35m)
Width: 8ft 3in (2.5m)
Height: 9ft 2in (2.8m)
Engine: Maybach HL85, V-12 petrol, 185bhp at 2,500rpm
Road speed: 31mph (50km/hr)
Range: 160 miles (260km)

Sd Kfz 9 Germany
FAMO
1940. After the success of the Sd Kfz 8 a further 15 guns were ordered to be built on the chassis of the FAMO 18-tonne carrier, to be employed primarily as anti-aircraft guns. It was apparently thought that the larger carrier would allow the crew a little more room to operate and would also withstand the recoil forces rather better. These were duly built, and a further order for another 112 was prepared; but this ran foul of the *Führerbefehl* in which Hitler had ruled that defensive weapons were not to be developed. The order was cancelled and interest in these vehicles evaporated.

Armament: I × 88mm FlaK 18 or 36 gun
Barrel length: 16ft 2in (4.93m)
Weight of shell: 20lb 12oz (9.40kg)
Muzzle velocity: 2,690ft/sec (820m/sec)
Effective ceiling: 26,250ft (8,000m)
Ammunition types: HE, HE/I, HEAP
Ammunition load: 40

Vehicle: Zugkraftwagen 18-tonne
Crew: 10
All-up weight: 25 tons (25,400kg)
Armour: 14mm
Hull length: 30ft 7in (9.32m)
Width: 8ft 9in (2.65m)
Height: 12ft 0in (3.67m)

Engine: Maybach HL108, V-12 petrol, 250bhp at 3,000rpm
Road speed: 31mph (50km/hr)
Range: 160 miles (260km)

SP-70 UK/Germany/Italy
Royal Ordnance, Rheinmetall, OTO-Melara
1973-88. This project was initiated shortly after the start of development of the FH-70 155mm howitzer, and was simply a question of putting the FH-70 on to a tracked mounting. It then escalated, with the adoption of the German Leopard tank as the vehicle base, and with the addition of very advanced sighting and laying systems and a highly automated magazine and automatic loading system. Other bells and whistles were added from time to time, the cost went into the stratosphere, nothing ever worked properly, and it over-ran its schedule by so much that scornful gunners referred to it as 'SP-2000'. It was eventually terminated in 1988 and the various partners went their own ways.

Armament: 1 × 155mm howitzer FH-70
Barrel length: 19ft 9in (6.02m)
Weight of shell: 95lb 14oz (43.50kg)
Muzzle velocity: 2,885ft/sec (880m/sec)
Maximum range: 32,810yd (30,000m)
Ammunition types: HE, HERA, ICM
Ammunition load: not known

Vehicle: Modified Leopard MBT
Crew: 5
All-up weight: 42.83 tons (43,524kg)
Armour: not known
Hull length: 25ft 0in (7.64m)
Width: 10ft 8in (3.25m)
Height: not known
Engine: MTU MB871 V-8 diesel, turbocharged, 650bhp
Road speed: not known
Range: not known

SP122 SPH Egypt
See BMY/ARE 122

Sturmgeschütz 3 Germany
Alkett, MIAG
1942. The idea of an infantry-accompanying tank mounting a low-velocity support gun was first broached in 1936. It took some time to settle the form that the machine should take and it was not until the spring of 1940 that the first trials models were produced. They soon showed their worth and there then began a series of designs, all of them called StuG 3 and all more or less the same, but each

one improving upon its predecessor in various details. Broadly, the StuG 3 was the hull and running gear of the Panzer 3 tank but with a superstructure divided into two halves with the gun trunnioned between them, the breech being under armour. As the design progressed, so the armament improved, from a short low-powered howitzer to a long-barrelled high velocity gun in the final versions. About 9,000 of the various models were produced, with 7,720 of the final (Ausf G) version.

Ausf G
Armament: 1 × 75mm StuK 40
Barrel length: 10ft 6in (3.20m)
Weight of shell: 15lb (6.80kg) APHE
7lb (3.18kg) HVAP
Muzzle velocity: 2,600ft/sec (792m/sec) APHE
3,248ft/sec (990m/sec) HVAP
Maximum range: 8,400yd (7,680m)
Operational range: 1,970yd (1,800m)
Ammunition types: APHE, HVAP, HE, smoke
Ammunition load: 54

Vehicle: Sd Kfz 142/1
Crew: 4
All-up weight: 23.52 tons (23,900kg)
Armour: 50mm maximum
Hull length: 17ft 9in (5.40m)
Width: 9ft 8in (2.95m)
Height: 6ft 11in (2.16m)
Engine: Maybach HL12-TRM, V-12, petrol, 300bhp at 3,000rpm
Road speed: 25mph (40km/hr)
Range: 96 miles (155km)

Sturmgeschütz 4 Germany
Krupp
1943. 1,139 built. The success of the StuG 3 led the designers to try the same thing with the Panzer 4 chassis, a process which was speeded up by the Allied bombing of the factory which was producing StuG 3. The hull and running gear of the Panzer 4 were taken as the starting point, and the upper hull, superstructure and gun of the StuG 3 were simply grafted on. The result differed from the StuG 3 only in the suspension and lower hull, and had a similar performance. Eventually manufacture of the Panzer 4 stopped and all Krupp's production line was put to work on the StuG 4.

Armament: 1 × 75mm PaK 40 L/48
Barrel length: 10ft 6in (3.20m)
Weight of shell: 15lb (6.80kg)
Muzzle velocity: 3,250ft/sec (990m/sec) HVAP
Maximum range: 8,400yd (7680m)
Ammunition types: HE, APHE, HVAP, HEAT
Ammunition load: 79

Vehicle: Sd Kfz 167
Crew: 4
All-up weight: 22.64 tons (23,000kg)
Armour: 80mm maximum
Hull length: 19ft 5in (5.92m)
Width: 9ft 8in (2.95m)
Height: 7ft 3in (2.20m)
Engine: Maybach HL120TRM V-12, petrol, 300bhp at 3,000rpm
Road speed: 25mph (40km/hr)
Range: 130 miles (210km)

Sturmhaubitze 42 Germany
Alkett
1943. 1,211 built. This was generally similar to the Sturmgeschütz 3 but was armed with the standard 105mm howitzer 18M, giving it a heavier shell and rather more versatility than the assault guns. It was demanded in 1941 when the assault guns carrying 75mm weapons were finding it hard to make an impression on well-built field defences. Development was slow and the first production vehicles did not appear until March 1943. The chassis was that of the Panzer 3 with the superstructure of the StuG 3, with two raised elements for the crew and the howitzer placed between them.

Armament: 1 × 105mm leFH18M
Barrel length: 8ft 11in (2.71m)
Weight of shell: 32lb 10oz (14.81kg)
Muzzle velocity: 1,542ft/sec (470m/sec)
Maximum range: ca 8,750yd (8,000m)
Ammunition types: HE, HEAT, APHE, HE-I, smoke, coloured smoke, leaflet, illuminating
Ammunition load: 36

Vehicle: Sd Kfz 142/2
Crew: 4
All-up weight: 23.62 tons (24,000kg)
Armour: 50mm maximum
Hull length: 17ft 9in (5.40m)
Width: 9ft 8in (2.95m)
Height: 7ft 1in (2.16m)
Engine: Maybach HL120TRM, V-12 petrol, 300bhp at 3,000rpm
Road speed: 25mph (40km/hr)
Range: 100 miles (160km)

Sturmmörser 38cm Tiger Germany
Alkett
1944. This remarkable weapon was built for the purpose of demolishing strongpoints using an extremely powerful and destructive rocket projectile. In order to get this weapon close enough

to guarantee accurate shooting, it needed to be inside an armoured vehicle, but the only way to fire a rocket from an armoured vehicle was to fire it out of a gun. But firing rockets out of guns was normally a grossly inaccurate process due to the action and interaction of the gases trapped inside the gun barrel behind the rocket. The Germans solved this dilemma by building a gun barrel with a double skin and allowing the blast from the rocket to enter this double skin and thus be vented to the front, through holes around the muzzle. The gun was breech-loaded inside the tank, but the blast was discharged outside and there was no gas pressure problem behind the rocket as it left the barrel.

The vehicle was simply the chassis of the Tiger tank, with a slope-sided superstructure and with the rocket gun mounted in the front face, and with a machine gun on one side and the driver on the other. 18 were built, in the latter half of 1944, but by that time their assault function was forgotten and they were entirely involved in defending Germany.

Armament: 38cm rocket launcher
Barrel length: 6ft 9in (2.05m)
Weight of shell: 760lb 8oz (345kg)
Muzzle velocity: 984ft/sec (300m/sec)
Maximum range: 6,180yd (5,650m)
Ammunition types: HE
Ammunition load: 14

Vehicle
Crew: 4
All-up weight: 63.97 tons (65,000kg)
Armour: 150mm maximum
Hull length: 20ft 7in (6.28m)
Width: 11ft 6in (3.51m)
Height: 9ft 4in (2.85m)
Engine: Maybach HL230 P45, V-12, petrol, 700bhp at 3,000rpm
Road speed: 25mph (40km/hr)
Range: 75 miles (120km)

SU-76 Russia
GAZ
1943. After seeing the German assault guns, the Russians thought they were worth copying, and began by developing this design using the obsolescent T-70 light tank as the basis. The turret was removed and the hull lengthened by putting an extra roadwheel on each side. An open-topped box was built on to the hull, with a large enough working platform to take the 76mm field gun on a modified carriage. Traverse was limited, and the early models were unreliable, but the mechanical side was rapidly improved and eventually over 12,500 were built.

Armament: 1 × 76.2mm gun M1942 (ZIS-3)
Barrel length: 10ft 4in (3.15m)
Weight of shell: 13lb 11oz (6.2kg)
Muzzle velocity: 2,230ft/sec (680m/sec)
Maximum range: 12,575yd (11,500m)
Ammunition types: HE, APHE, HVAP
Ammunition load: not known

Vehicle
Crew: 4
All-up weight: 11.02 tons (11,200kg)
Armour: 35mm maximum
Hull length: 16ft 5in (5.00m)
Width: 9ft 0in (2.74m)
Height: 7ft 3in (2.20m)
Engine: V-12, diesel, 500bhp at 1,800rpm
Road speed: 27mph (44km/hr)
Range: 165 miles (265km)

SU-85 Russia
Uralmashzavod, Kirov
1943. This was designed to counter the Tiger and Panther tanks, which outranged the T-34 with its 76mm gun. It was based on the T-34 chassis but with a simple armoured superstructure and a powerful 85mm gun mounted in the front plate. It was put together very quickly and production was under way by the middle of 1943. Once the T-34/85 tank, with the same gun, was in service, the SU-85 stopped production, but they stayed in service until the war ended.

Armament: 1 × 85mm Gun M1943
Barrel length: 15ft 4in (4.68m)
Weight of shell: 21lb (9.5kg)
Muzzle velocity: 2,620ft/sec (795m/sec)
Maximum range: 16,950yd (15,500m)
Ammunition types: HE, APHE, HVAP
Ammunition load: not known

Vehicle
Crew: 4
All-up weight: 29.13 tons (29,600kg)
Armour: 54mm maximum
Hull length: 21ft 7in (6.58m)
Width: 9ft 10in (2.99m)
Height: 8ft 4in (2.54m)
Engine: V-12, diesel, 500bhp at 1,800rpm
Road speed: 30mph (48km/hr)
Range: 200 miles (320km)

SU-100 Russia
Uralmashzavod
1944. When the T-34/85 tank went into service, it was necessary to produce a self-propelled heavy gun for its support, and the SU-100 was built by taking

a 100mm naval gun and shoe-horning it into the SU-85 chassis. It was a tight fit, and the body had to take some peculiar contours to accommodate the mounting, but the whole thing went together and worked well. It dealt effectively with the heaviest German tanks and was retained in Russian service until the late 1950s.

Armament: 1 × 100mm gun M1944
Barrel length: 19ft 8in (5.99m)
Weight of shell: 35lb (15.88kg)
Muzzle velocity: 2,936ft/sec (895m/sec)
Maximum range: 22,580yd (20,650m)
Ammunition types: HE, APHE, HVAP
Ammunition load: not known

Vehicle
Crew: 4
All-up weight: 32.0 tons (32,515kg)
Armour: hull front 75mm; gun mantlet 110mm
Hull length: 19ft 5in (5.92m)
Width: 9ft 10 in (3.0m)
Height: 8ft 4in (2.54m)
Engine: V-12 diesel, 500bhp at 1,800rpm
Road speed: 35mph (56km/hr)
Range: 186 miles (300km)

T19 105mm HMC USA
Diamond-T
1942–44. Development of this weapon began in September 1941, when just about every weapon in the American armoury was being tried out on top of a half-track. The success of the 75mm M3 GMC led the Ordnance Department to try fitting the 105mm howitzer, but the more powerful weapon demanded the strengthening of the vehicle chassis before it became acceptable. In March 1942 an order for the building of 342 equipments was placed, and the T19 (it was never standardised) went into action in North Africa later that year. It was found effective as a mobile field gun, less effective as a tank destroyer, but, like the British Bishop of the same period, it gave useful lessons in the tactics of SP field artillery. It was replaced by the M7 GMC and became obsolete late in 1944.

Armament: 1 × 105mm Howitzer M2A1
Barrel length: 8ft 5.5in (2.58m)
Weight of shell: 33lb (14.97kg)
Muzzle velocity: 1,550ft/sec (472m/sec)
Maximum range: 11,700yd (10,698m)
Ammunition types: HE, HEAT, smoke, illuminating
Ammunition load: 8

Vehicle
Crew: 6
All-up weight: 8.92 tons (9,072kg)

Armour: 13mm maximum
Hull length: 19ft 9in (6.03m)
Width: 6ft 5in (1.96m)
Height: 7ft 8in (2.33m)
Engine: White, 6-cylinder, petrol, 128bhp at 2,800rpm
Road speed: 45mph (72km/hr)
Range: 200 miles (320km)

T48 GMC USA
Diamond-T

1942. Designed by the US Ordnance Department, this was seen as a fast and agile tank destroyer, just what would be needed in desert warfare. It consisted of the 57mm anti-tank gun (the British 6-pounder) mounted in the back of an M3 half-track. It seemed simple and effective, and orders for 1,000 were given. By the time production got under way the US Tank Destroyer Board had changed their minds and were awaiting a full-tracked vehicle. The British, too, had second thoughts, since they had adopted the 17-pounder and the desert war was over. All 1,000 were delivered to Britain, from where they were promptly re-directed to Russia.

Armament: 1 × 57mm Gun M1 on Mount T5
Barrel length: 9ft 9in (2.97m)
Weight of shell: 6.28lb (2.85kg)
Muzzle velocity: 2,800ft/sec (853m/sec)
Maximum range: 10,250yd (9,370m)
Ammunition types: AP, APC, HE
Ammunition load: 99

Vehicle: Carrier, Half-Track, Personnel, M3
Crew: 5
All-up weight: 8.48 tons (8,618kg)
Armour: 16mm maximum
Hull length: 21ft 1in (6.42m)
Width: 7ft 1in (2.16m)
Height: 7ft 0in (2.13m)
Engine: White, 6-cylinder, petrol, 128bhp at 2,800rpm
Road speed: 45mph (72km/hr)
Range: 200 miles (320km)

T92 HMC USA

1944. In preparation for Operation Olympic, the invasion of mainland Japan planned for 1946, it was decided that the heaviest artillery must be made available in self-propelled form, and in January 1944 work began on designing a motor carriage for the 240mm howitzer M1. The chassis and running gear of the T26E3 tank (which later became the M26 Pershing) were used as the foundation; the barrel and recoil system of the 240mm howitzer were mounted into a working space at the rear of the vehicle (the engine having been shifted forward) and a massive recoil spade fitted to the rear end. The equipment was tested and worked successfully, and in March 1945 orders were given for the production of 112 weapons. Five were built before the war ended and the project was cancelled.

Armament: 1 × 240mm Howitzer M1
Barrel length: 27ft 7in (8.41m)
Weight of shell: 360lb (163.3kg)
Muzzle velocity: 2,300ft/sec (701m/sec)
Maximum range: 25,225yd (23,065m)
Ammunition types: HE
Ammunition load: not known

Vehicle
Hull length: 24ft 0in (7.32m)
No other data available

T93 GMC USA

1944. The towed 240mm Howitzer M1 shared its mounting with the 8-inch Gun M1, and therefore it was logical to try and fit the gun on to the T93 mounting which had been designed for the howitzer. Since the actual recoil cradle was the same, the mechanical problems were easily solved, though balancing the great length of barrel caused a few headaches. Orders were given for the production of 58 complete equipments, but only two were ever built.

Armament: 1 × 8in Gun M1
Barrel length: 34ft 1.5in (10.40m)
Weight of shell: 240.37lb (109.03kg)
Muzzle velocity: 2,840ft/sec (866m/sec)
Maximum range: 35,635yd (32,585m)
Ammunition types: HE
Ammunition load: not known

Vehicle
Hull length: 24ft 0in (7.32m)
No other data available

T95 GMC USA
See T28 Super Heavy Tank

TAMSE VCA 155mm SP Gun Argentina
TAMSE

1993. This is a hybrid equipment which has been arrived at by taking the chassis of the Argentine TAM tank, lengthening it by adding another roadwheel on each side, and then adding the turret and gun of the Italian Palmaria 155mm SP gun. OTO-Melara of Italy sold 20 complete turret assemblies to Argentina in 1993 and presumably all have now been installed.

Armament: 1 x 155mm howitzer
Barrel length: 20ft 10in (6.355m)
Weight of shell: 95lb 14oz (43.5kg)
Muzzle velocity: 3,060ft/sec (933m/sec)
Maximum range: 27,012yd (24,700m) conventional
　　　　　　　32,810yd (30,000m) HERA
Ammunition types: HE, HERA, HE/ICM
Ammunition load: 30

Vehicle
Crew: 5
All-up weight: 39.37 tons (40,000kg)
Armour: not disclosed
Hull length: 25ft 3in (7.69m)
Width: 10ft 10in (3.30m)
Height: 10ft 6in (3.20m)
Engine: MTU 6-cylinder diesel, 720bhp at 2200rpm
Road speed: 34mph (55km/hr)
Range: 435 miles (700km)

Thunder 155mm SP Howitzer South Korea
See K9 Thunder

Tortoise UK
Nuffield
1944. Super-heavy tank destroyer proposed as a means of getting the 32-pounder anti-tank gun into the field. Similar to the German Jagdtiger, it had a massively armoured superstructure carrying the gun in the sloping front face. Traverse was restricted to a few degrees either side of the centreline. The gun was a re-worked 3.7-inch AA gun and was designed with discarding sabot ammunition in mind, though none was ever made for it. Six prototypes were completed in 1947, trials were conducted which proved the vehicle impractical due to its weight and bulk, four were scrapped and the other two went to museums.

Armament: 1 x 32-pdr gun; 2 x MG
Barrel length: 15ft 5in (4.69m)
Weight of shell: 32lb (14.52kg) APCBC
Muzzle velocity: 2,880ft/sec (878m/sec)
Effective range: 3,000yd/m estimated
Ammunition types: APCBC, HE, APDS

Vehicle
Crew: 7
All-up weight: 78 tons (79,250kg)
Armour: 225mm
Hull length: 33ft 0in (10.05m)
Width: 12ft 10in (3.91m)
Height: 10ft 0in (3.05m)
Engine: Rolls-Royce Meteor, 600bhp
Road speed: 12mph (20km/hr)

Type 38 Tank Destroyer Switzerland
Skoda
1946. When World War II ended, there was a good deal of German equipment scattered about Europe with no owner. The astute Czechs rounded up large number of German Hetzer 75mm SP anti-tank guns, refurbished them (since they were on Czech chassis) and then sold 158 of them to Switzerland. The Swiss called them the Type 38. For further details and dimensions, *see* Hetzer.

Type 54-1 122mm SP Howitzer China
Norinco
This is a simple and inexpensive weapon which has been constructed by removing the roof of the YW-531 APC crew compartment and installing the top carriage, ordnance and shield of the Type 54-1 122mm towed howitzer. There is little protection for the crew, apart from the driver, but for the simple field artillery role this seems a perfectly adequate solution.

Armament: 1 x 122mm howitzer Type 54-1
Barrel length: 9ft 2in (2.80m)
Weight of shell: 47lb 15oz (21.75kg)
Muzzle velocity: 1,690ft/sec (515m/sec)
Maximum range: 12,905yd (11,800m)
Ammunition types: HE, HEAT, smoke, illuminating
Ammunition load: 40

Vehicle: Based on Type 531 APC
Crew: 6
All-up weight: 15.06 tons (15,300kg)
Armour: 12mm maximum
Hull length: 18ft 5in (5.60m)
Width: 10ft 1in (3.07m)
Height: 8ft 6in (2.68m)
Engine: 6150L 6-cylinder diesel, 260bhp at 2,000rpm
Road speed: 36mph (56km/hr)
Range: 280 miles (450km)

Type 60 Japan
Komatsu
1975. This unusual vehicle was developed at the request of the Japanese Self-Defence Force and consist of a lightweight carrier with two 106mm recoilless rifles (with a spotting rifle) mounted on an elevating mount on the right side of the hull. The crew (driver, commander and loader) are on the left side. The guns can be fired from their retracted position, on top of the hull, though this limits the elevation and traverse. They can be elevated by hydraulic means to a position about 20 inches (50cm) above the hull, which allows greater elevation and traverse. As the gun unit is raised, so

the commander (who is also the gunner) is raised with it. The loader needs to be something of a contortionist to load the guns without dismounting from the vehicle.

Armament: 2 x 106mm RCL
Barrel length: 10ft 11in (3.32m)
Weight of shell: 17lb 6oz (7.90kg)
Muzzle velocity: 1,650ft/sec (503m/sec)
Maximum range: 7,655yd (7,000m)
Operational range: 1,430yd (1,300m)
Ammunition types: HEAT
Ammunition load: 8

Vehicle
Crew: 3
All-up weight: 7.48 tons (7,600kg)
Armour: 15mm maximum
Hull length: 14ft 1in (4.30m)
Width: 7ft 4in (2.23m)
Height: 5ft 3in (1.59m)
Engine: Komatsu 6TM 6-cylinder diesel, 120bhp at 2,400rpm
Road speed: 34mph (55km/hr)
Range: 43 miles (130km)

Type 74 Japan
Mitsubishi

1974. This equipment was developed in the late 1960s and went into production in the middle 1970s. The steel hull and chassis were specially developed for the vehicle, and have the driver and engine in front, leaving the rear of the hull clear for the fitting of a turret which carries the 105mm howitzer. This has a muzzle brake and fume extractor, but no ballistic details have ever been released, and it is assumed that it conforms to the 105mm howitzer which was then in use in the towed role. However, only 20 were built before it was decided to standardise on the 155mm howitzer, and production of the Type 74 ceased.

Armament: 1 x 105mm howitzer
Barrel length: not known
Weight of shell: 33lb (14.96kg)
Muzzle velocity: 1,550ft/sec (472m/sec)
Maximum range: 12,325yd (11,270m)
Ammunition types: HE, HEAT, smoke, illuminating
Ammunition load: not known

Vehicle
Crew: 5
All-up weight: 16.24 tons (16,500kg)
Armour: not known
Hull length: 19ft 4in (5.90m)
Width: 9ft 6in (2.90m)
Height: 7ft 10in (2.39m)

Engine: Mitsubishi V-4 diesel, 300bhp at 2,200rpm
Road speed: 31mph (50km/hr)
Range: 185 miles (300km)

Type 75 Japan
Mitsubishi

1978. This was the equipment which was developed to replace the Type 74 (*above*) as the standard close support weapon for the Japanese Self Defence Force.

It was designed from scratch, not being an adaptation of any existing vehicle. The tracked suspension has six roadwheels, the rear roadwheel acting as the idler, and the hull has the driver and engine set forward to leave a clear working area at the rear end, over which the turret is installed. The ordnance is generally similar to that used on the US M109, even to the muzzle brake and fume extractor, and fired the same ammunition, though it also fired Japanese projectiles to a greater range.

Armament: 1 x 155mm howitzer
Barrel length: 15ft 3in (4.650m)
Weight of shell: 99lb 4oz (43.2kg)
Muzzle velocity: 1,840ft/sec (561m/sec)
Maximum range: 20,775yd (19,000m)
Ammunition types: HE, HERA, smoke, illuminating
Ammunition load: 28

Vehicle
Crew: 6
All-up weight: 24.90 tons (25,300kg)
Armour: not known
Hull length: 21ft 9in (6.64m)
Width: 10ft 2in (3.09m)
Height: 8ft 4in (2.54m)
Engine: Mitsubishi 6-cylinder air-cooled diesel, 450bhp at 2,200rpm
Road speed: 29mph (47km/hr)
Range: 186 miles (300km)

Type 80 Twin 57mm SPAA China
Norinco

At first glance this appears to be simply the Russian ZSU-57-2, but a second look reveals five roadwheels instead of four. It is, in fact, the chassis and running gear of the Chinese Type 69 MBT, with, on top of the hull, a large in-curved, open-topped turret copied from the Russian ZSU and mounting two Chinese 57mm guns, which are Chinese copies of the Russian weapons. There are, therefore, some differences in performance and dimensions, but they are not very great. Like the Russian equipment, this is a fair-weather-only weapon with optical sights.

Armament: 2 x 57mm Type 59
Barrel length: 14ft 3in (4.39m)
Weight of shell: 6lb 3oz (2.81kg)
Muzzle velocity: 3,280ft/sec (1,000m/sec)
Maximum ceiling: 18,045ft (5,500m)
Ammunition types: HE/Frag, APC
Ammunition load: 300

Vehicle: Based on Type 69 tank
Crew: 6
All-up weight: 30.51 tons (31,000kg)
Armour: 45mm maximum
Hull length: 27ft on 98.24m)
Width: 10ft 10in (3.30m)
Height: 9ft 0in (2.75m)
Engine: diesel, 580bhp at 2,000rpm
Road speed: 31mph (50km/hr)
Range: 260 miles (420km)

Type 83 152mm SP Howitzer China
Norinco

1983. This vehicle uses an entirely new chassis which is identifiable by the oddly-spaced six roadwheels on each side, with gaps between wheels 1 & 2, 3 & 4 and 5 & 6. The drive sprocket is at the front, idler at the rear. Driver and engine are forward, with a large turret and working compartment at the rear, with rear doors for ammunition loading and crew access. The ordnance is similar to the towed Type 66 but is fitted with muzzle brake and fume extractor.

Armament: 1 x 152mm Howitzer Type 66-1
Barrel length: 17ft 0in (5.19m)
Weight of shell: 96lb (43.56kg)
Muzzle velocity: 2,150ft/sec (655m/sec)
Maximum range: 18,840yd (17,230m)
Ammunition types: HE, smoke
Ammunition load: 30

Vehicle
Crew: 5
All-up weight: 29.52 tons (30,000kg)
Armour: not disclosed
Hull length: 22ft 7in (6.88m)
Width: 10ft 7in (3.24m)
Height: 8ft 9in (2.68m)
Engine: diesel, 520bhp
Road speed: 35mph (55km/hr)
Range: 280 miles (450km)

Type 85 122mm SP Howitzer China
Norinco

This is based on the chassis and basic hull of the Type 85 APC (see YW-531), fitted with the 122mm howitzer Type D-30, which is simply a copy of the

Russian weapon of the same designation. As with the Type 54 it has been arrived at by opening up the roof of the APC and installing the top carriage, shield and ordnance of the towed D-30 into the crew space. There is no protection for the gunners, but as a divisional support weapon it does the job and is no doubt cheap and easy to maintain. It also has amphibious ability.

Armament: 1 x 122mm D-30 howitzer
Barrel length: 16ft 0in (4.87m)
Weight of shell: 47lb 15oz (21.75kg)
Muzzle velocity: 2,263ft/sec (690m/sec)
Maximum range: 16,405yd (15,000m)
Ammunition types: HE, HEAT, ERFB, ICM
Ammunition load: 40

Vehicle
Crew: 6
All-up weight: 16.24 tons (16,500kg)
Armour: not disclosed
Hull length: 20ft 1in (6.12m)
Width: 9ft 10in (3.0m)
Height: 9ft 4in (2.85m)
Engine: diesel, 320bhp
Road speed: 37mph (60km/hr)
Range: 310 miles (500km)

VCA-155 SP Gun Argentina
See TAMSE

Vulcan Commando Air Defense System
USA
General Electric (USA)

1985. This was a private construction by the General Electric company to meet a Saudi Arabian requirement, and it consisted of fitting the turret, gun and fire control system of the US M163 Vulcan Air Defense System into the roof of a Cadillac Gage V-150 Commando armoured car. The vehicle is fitted with three levelling and stabilising jacks which can be operated from inside.

Armament: 1 x GE 20mm Gatling gun M168
Barrel length: 5ft 0in (1.52m)
Weight of shell: 3.5oz (100g)
Muzzle velocity: 3,380ft/sec (1,030m/sec)
Rate of fire: 1,000 or 3,000rd/min, selectable
Maximum ceiling: 3,935ft (1,200m)
Ammunition types: HE-I, AP-I
Ammunition load: 2,280

Vehicle
Crew: 4
All-up weight: 10.04 tons (10,210kg)
Armour: not disclosed
Hull length: 18ft 8in (5.69m)

Width: 7ft 5in (2.26m)
Height: 9ft 5in (2.88m)
Engine: Chrysler V-8, petrol, 202bhp at 3,300rpm
Road speed: 55mph (88km/hr)
Range: 600 miles (965km)

Wespe Germany
FAMO

1943. Wespe ('Wasp') was the German equivalent of the American M7 or British Sexton – their standard divisional field piece on tracks. The chassis of the obsolescent Panzer 2 was taken as the foundation and given an open-topped superstructure with the 105mm light field howitzer 18 mounted firing forwards. The conversion was done at some speed, and instead of relocating the engine, the fighting platform was built on top of it, giving the vehicle a rather high profile and making it somewhat unstable across rough ground. But it served well enough and almost 700, plus 150 or so ammunition carriers, were built.

Armament: 1 × 105mm leFH 18M howitzer
Barrel length: 8ft 6in (2.61m)
Weight of shell: 32lb 10oz (14.81kg)
Muzzle velocity: 1,542ft/sec (470m/sec)
Maximum range: 11,675yd (10,675m)
Ammunition types: HE, APHE, HEAT, smoke, coloured smoke, leaflet, incendiary, illuminating
Ammunition load: 32

Vehicle: Sd Kfz 124
Crew: 5
All-up weight: 10.82 tons (11,000kg)
Armour: 30mm maximum
Hull length: 15ft 9in (4.81m)
Width: 7ft 6in (2.28m)
Height: 7ft 7in (2.30m)
Engine: Maybach HL62TR, 6-cylinder, petrol, 140bhp at 2,600rpm
Road speed: 25mph (40km/hr)
Range: 87 miles (140km)

Wirbelwind Germany
Ostbau

1944. 86 built. Also known as **Flakpanzer 4**, the 'Whirlwind' was a Panzer 4 with the standard turret removed and replaced by a larger, angular, type carrying a quadruple 20mm cannon mounting. The equipments were made by converting Panzer 4 tanks returned for overhaul, and it was a stopgap measure to increase the number of AA tanks until a larger-calibre model (the Möbelwagen) was in production. Once the Möbelwagen was in full production, the Wirbelwinds would be withdrawn

and refitted with a quadruple 37mm mounting, whereupon they would become the **Zerstörer** ('Destroyer'). The prototype Zerstörer was never completed before the war ended.

Armament: 4 × 20mm FlaK 38
Barrel length: 6ft 6in (2.0m)
Weight of shell: 4.05oz (115g)
Muzzle velocity: 2,952ft/sec (900m/sec)
Maximum range: 2,940yd (2,690m)
Effective ceiling: 1,000ft (300m)
Rate of fire: 420rpg/min
Ammunition types: AP, APHE, HE, HE-I
Ammunition load: 3,200

Vehicle: Converted PzKpfw 4 chassis
Crew: 5
All-up weight: 21.65 tons (22,000kg)
Armour: 80mm maximum
Hull length: 9ft 4in (5.92m)
Width: 9ft 7in (2.92m)
Height: 9ft 1in (2.76m)
Engine: Maybach HL120TRM, V-12, petrol, 300bhp at 3,000rpm
Road speed: 24mph (38km/hr)
Range: 125 miles (200km)

Zerstörer 45 Germany
See Wirbelwind

ZSU-23-4 Russia
State factories

1964. This was one of the earliest designs of integrated gun/radar equipment on a self-propelled carriage, and was generally conceded to be one of the most formidable air defence weapons of its day. It consisted of four 23mm cannon mounted in a large revolving turret which also carried the acquisition and tracking radar set and antenna. The chassis is special to this vehicle, although the suspension resembles that of the PT-76 light tank. The hull is conventional, with the driver in the front and engine at the rear, leaving a large central fighting compartment on which the turret is placed.

Armament: 4 × 23mm ZSU automatic cannon
Barrel length: 6ft 7in (2.01m)
Weight of shell: 6.5oz (185g)
Muzzle velocity: 3,182ft/sec (970m/sec)
Rate of fire: 800rpg/min
Maximum ceiling: 4,920ft (1,500m)
Ammunition types: HE-I
Ammunition load: 500 per gun

Vehicle
Crew: 4
All-up weight: 13.78 tons (14,000kg)

Armour: 20mm maximum
Hull length: 20ft 8in (6.29m)
Width: 9ft 8in (2.95m)
Height: 7ft 5in (2.25m) radar folded
Engine: V-6 diesel, 240bhp at 1,900rpm
Road speed: 27mph (44km/hr)
Range: 160 miles (260km)

ZSU-57-2 Russia
State factories
1956. Among the earliest of Soviet air defence equipments, this uses two guns which are based upon a German wartime development. There is no form of radar or other electronic assistance; the guns use optical sights. The chassis is based upon that of the T-54 tank, with the addition of a large rectangular open-topped turret carrying the guns. The guns are hand-loaded with clips of five rounds and fire at about 120 rounds per gun per minute. The ZSU-57 was widely distributed to Warsaw Pact and other Communist-inclined countries, but it is doubtful if any now remain in service.

Armament: 2 × 57mm S-60
Barrel length: 14ft 5in (4.39m)
Weight of shell: 6lb 3oz (2.80kg)
Muzzle velocity: 3,280ft/sec (1,000m/sec)
Maximum ceiling: 13,125ft (4,000m)
Ammunition types: HE/Frag, AP
Ammunition load: 300

Vehicle
Crew: 6
All-up weight: 27.65 tons (28,100kg)
Armour: 15mm maximum
Hull length: 20ft 5in (6.22m)
Width: 10ft 9in (3.27m)
Height: 8ft 11in (2.71mm)
Engine: V-12, diesel, 520bhp at 2,000rpm
Road speed: 30mph (48km/hr)
Range: 250 miles (400km)

Zuzana ZTS 155mm SP Gun-howitzer
Czech Republic
ZTS Dubnica
1992. This is simply the 152mm Dana equipment, described elsewhere, fitted with a NATO-standard 45-calibre 155mm ordnance. It uses the same 8 x 8 wheeled chassis, but there are some minor changes to accommodate the different gun. It is anticipated that the Czech Army, once integrated into NATO, will require to change from 152mm to 155mm as their standard, and this design has been prepared in readiness. A small number have been built and have been successfully tested by the Czechs.

Armament: 155mm gun-howitzer
Barrel length: 22ft 10in (6.97m)
Weight of shell: 104.7lb (47.5kg) ERFB
Muzzle velocity: 2,942ft/sec (897m/sec)
Maximum range: 43,305yd (39,600m)
Ammunition types: HE-ERFB
Ammunition load: 40

Vehicle
Crew: 4
All-up weight: 27.55 tons (28,000kg)
Armour: not disclosed
Hull length: 29ft 1in (8.87m)
Width: 9ft 11in (3.02m)
Height: 11ft 7in (3.53m)
Engine: Tatra V-12 air-cooled diesel, 355bhp
Road speed: 56mph (90km/hr)
Range: 466 miles (750km)

Zuzana T-72M1 155mm SP Gun-howitzer
Czech Republic
ZTS Dubnica
1995. This is the same turret, gun-howitzer and automatic loading system used on the Zuzana wheeled carriage and described above, but mounted on to a T-72 tank hull and chassis. It was prepared, using an Indian-built chassis, for trials in India but was not selected by the Indian Army. It is believed that the Czechs are currently looking at the possibility of putting the turret on to a T-55 hull, of which there are several thousand scattered about the world, some of whose owners might be attracted by an SP conversion.

Armament: 155mm gun-howitzer
Barrel length: 22ft 10in (6.97m)
Weight of shell: 104.7lb (47.5kg) ERFB
Muzzle velocity: 2,942ft/sec (897m/sec)
Maximum range: 43,305yd (39,600m)
Ammunition types: HE-ERFB
Ammunition load: 40

Vehicle
Crew: 4
All-up weight: 37.4 tons (38,000kg)
Armour: not disclosed
Hull length: 22ft 6in (6.86m)
Width: 11ft 9 in (3.59m)
Height: 11ft 4in (3.45m)
Engine: V-12 diesel, 780bhp at 2,000rpm
Road speed: 37mph (60km/hr)
Range: 400 miles (650km)

COMPARATIVE TABLES

CONVENTIONS

These follow the pattern used in earlier chapters with the addition of the following:

Range: ^^ indicates maximum effective ceiling of air defence guns; ^AT^ indicates maximum effective range of anti-tank guns.

Units of measurement: calibres are in mm, barrel lengths in inches, shell weights in pounds, velocity in ft/sec, ranges and ceilings in yards, weight is total in tons, vehicle lengths in feet, speeds in mph.

Shell weights: 57mm calibre and greater have been rounded to whole pounds.

IN ASCENDING ORDER OF CALIBRE

Model	Calibre	Barrel length	Shell weight	Velocity	Range	Total weight	Vehicle length	Road speed	Country
BTR-40A Twin AA	14.5	53	0.14	3238	2190 ^^	5.71	16.42	50	Russia
BTR-152 Twin AA	14.5	53	0.14	3238	2190 ^^	9.45	22.42	40	Russia
BOV-3 Triple 20mm AA	20	55	0.27	2740	1312 ^^	9.25	22.33	56	Yugoslavia
Dassault M3 VDA Twin AA	20	91	0.28	3412	1440 ^^	7.09	14.58	56	France
Dassault VDAA Twin AA	20	91	0.28	3412	1440 ^^	13.98	19.67	53	France
M163 VADS	20	60	0.22	3380	1315 ^^	12.12	15.92	42	USA
Panhard AML S530 Twin	20	61	0.22	3248	1640 ^^	5.41	12.42	56	France
Vulcan Commando ADS	20	60	0.22	3380	1315 ^^	10.04	18.67	55	USA
Wirbelwind SPAA Quad	20	78	0.25	2952	330 ^^	21.65	9.33	24	Germany
Sinai 23 SP AA Twin	23	79	0.4	3182	1645 ^^	?	16.0	27	Egypt
ZSU-23-4 SP AA Quad	23	79	0.4	3182	1645 ^^	13.78	20.67	27	Russia
SIDAM-25 SP AA Quad	25	85	0.40	3610	2735 ^^	14.27	20.0	40	Italy
2S6 AD System	30	?	1.75	3150	3280 ^^	35.43	23.08	40	Russia
AMX-13DCA	30	101	0.79	3543	4920 ^^	14.76	16.92	37	France
AMX-30DCA	30	101	0.79	3543	4920 ^^	35.43	22.33	40	France
Falcon Twin AA	30	100	0.79	3543	4920 ^^	15.60	17.5	30	UK
Escorter 35 SP AA Gun	35	124	1.21	3822	4373 ^^	23.62	28.75	75	Switzerland
Gepard 35mm SP AA Gun	35	124	1.21	3855	4373 ^^	44.29	23.83	40	Germany
Kentron ZA-35 Twin AA	35	124	1.21	3855	4375 ^^	31.45	27.58	75	S Africa
M6 37mm GMC	37	83	1.92	2900	500 ^AT^	3.28	14.83	55	USA
M15 Multiple GMC	37	78	1.62	2600	8875	8.93	20.33	40	USA
Möbelwagen	37	84	1.40	2690	4595 ^^	23.62	19.42	24	Germany
Ostwind	37	84	1.40	2690	4595	25.0	19.42	24	Germany
Sd Kfz 6/2	37	113	1.40	2690	2185 ^^	10.4	20.75	31	Germany
Sd Kfz 7/2	37	113	1.40	2690	2185 ^^	11.55	20.83	31	Germany
AMX-40 DCA	40	118	2.0	2800	10200 ^^	15.0	16.83	25	France
CV-90 AAV 40mm Gun	40	110	2.12	3297	2730 ^^	21.76	31.25	43	Sweden
LVKV Twin 40mm AA	40	110	2.20	3280	1310 ^^	17.0	19.0	31	Sweden
M19 Twin 40mm GMC	40	104	2.1	2870	4300 ^^	17.19	17.92	35	USA
M42 Twin 40mm GMC	40	104	2.1	2870	4300	22.10	19.08	45	USA
Semovente 47/32 SP AT	47	66	3.31	2067	3830	6.40	12.5	26	Italy

Model	Calibre	Barrel length	Shell weight	Velocity	Range	Total weight	Vehicle length	Road speed	Country
ASU-57 gun	57	164	7	3280	9185	7.28	12.25	40	Russia
Deacon 6-pdr	57	101	6	2693	5500	12.0	21.5	25	UK
T48 57mm GMC	57	117	6	2800	10250	8.48	21.08	45	USA
Type 80 Twin SP AA	57	171	6	3280	6015 AA	30.51	27.0	31	China
ZSU-57-2 SP AA Twin	57	173	6	3280	4375 AA	27.65	20.42	30	Russia
Char Canon 75	75	107	16	1735	9295	7.19	13.42	4.5	France
Hetzer SP AT Gun	75	142	15	3556	8400	15.50	21.0	26	Germany
Jagdpanzer 4	75	142	15	3556	8400	23.86	19.42	25	Germany
M3 75mm GMC	75	111	15	2000	13300	8.48	19.67	41	USA
M8 75mm HMC	75	54	15	1250	9760	15.45	14.58	40	USA
Marder 1	75	126	15	2598	8400	8.0	17.42	22	Germany
Marder 2	75	126	15	2598	8400	10.63	15.25	25	Germany
Semovente 75/18	75	53	14	1427	5685	13.78	16.17	22	Italy
Sturmgeschütz 3	75	126	15	2600	1970 AT	23.5	17.75	25	Germany
Sturmgeschütz 4	75	126	7	3250	8400	22.64	19.42	25	Germany
Achilles	76	165	17	2900	10000	29.47	19.58	30	UK
Archer 17-pdr Gun	76	165	17	2900	10000	14.75	17.75	20	UK
M10 3-in GMC	76	158	13	2800	16100	29.47	19.58	30	USA
M18 76mm GMC	76	164	13	2700	14200	17.85	17.33	50	USA
Marder 3	76	166	11	2426	9840	10.50	16.25	26	Germany
Otomatic 76mm AD Tank	76	186	14	3035	6560 AA	46.26	23.25	37	Italy
SU-76	76	124	14	2230	12575	11.02	16.42	27	Russia
M4 Mortar Carrier	81	49.5	7	700	3288	7.85	19.5	41	USA
M21 Mortar Carrier	81	49.5	7	700	3288	8.26	20.83	40	USA
Birch 18-pdr Gun Mk 5	84	99	18	1625	10500	12.45	18.33	28	UK
Charioteer SP 20-pdr Gun	84	220	10	4850	2000	28.5	21.1	31	UK
ASU-85 gun	85	256	11	3510	10935	15.25	19.67	28	Russia
SU-85	85	184	21	2620	16950	29.13	21.58	30	Russia
Bishop 25-pdr Gun Mk 2	87	97	25	1450	6400	17.16	18.17	15	UK
Sexton 25-pdr Gun Mk 2	87	97	25	1700	13400	25.45	20.08	24	UK/Canada
Ferdinand Tank Destroyer	88	237	23	3280	3280 AT	63.97	26.75	18	Germany
Jagdpanther Tank Destroyer	88	237	23	3280	3280 AT	45.27	22.92	20	Germany
Nashorn	88	260	23	3280	3280 AT	23.62	23.5	26	Germany
Sd Kfz 8 Tank Destroyer	88	194	21	2690	2750 AT	20.0	24.17	31	Germany
Sd Kfz 9 SP AA gun	88	194	21	2690	8750 AA	25.0	30.58	31	Germany
IKV-91 Tank Destroyer	90	200	15	3083	2000 AT	16.04	21.0	40	Sweden
Jagdpanzer Kanone	90	193	16	2608	2190 AT	27.06	20.5	43	Germany
M36 90mm GMC	90	186	23	2700	19560	27.68	20.17	30	USA
M56 90mm SP AT	90	?	17	3650	2500 AT	5.69	19.17	28	USA
Semovente 90/53	90	209	25	2723	10936	16.73	17.33	18	Italy
Tortoise SP 32-pdr Gun	94	185	32	2880	3000 AT	78.00	33.0	12	UK
Alecto 95mm Howitzer	95	83	25	1111	6800	8.0	14.25	30	UK
SU-100	100	236	35	2936	22580	32.0	19.42	35	Russia
Abbot 105mm Gun	105	153	35	2313	18920	17.19	18.75	30	UK
AMX 105 Mk 61 How	105	124	35	2200	16400	16.24	16.83	37	France
Centauro B1 Tank Dest	105	215	7	4757	2000 AT	23.62	24.25	63	Italy
IKV-103 Assault Howitzer	105	133	34	2100	8750	8.80	16.0	35	Sweden
M7 Priest 105mm SO How	105	102	33	1250	11400	22.60	19.75	25	USA
M37 105mm HMC	105	102	33	1250	12205	17.86	18.17	35	USA
M52 105mm HMC	105	107	33	1548	12325	23.66	19.0	35	USA
M108 105mm SP How	105	140	33	1620	12575	22.10	20.75	35	USA
Panzerjäger SK105/A1	105	182	27	2625	2952 AT	17.42	18.33	43	Austria
Panzerjäger SK105/A3	105	210	13	4920	3280 AT	20.37	18.33	43	Austria

Model	Calibre	Barrel length	Shell weight	Velocity	Range	Total weight	Vehicle length	Road speed	Country
Sturmhaubitze 42	105	107	33	1542	8750	23.62	17.75	25	Germany
T19 105mm HMC	105	102	33	1550	11700	8.92	19.75	45	USA
Type 74 105mm SPH	105	?	33	1550	12325	16.24	19.33	31	Japan
Wespe 105mm SPH	105	102	33	1542	11675	10.82	15.75	25	Germany
M50 Multiple GMC Ontos	106	134	18	1650	7500	8.50	12.5	30	USA
Type 60 SPAT	106	131	17	1650	1430 ᴬᵀ	7.48	14.08	34	Japan
2S9 120mm Mortar	120	73	35	985	9685	8.56	19.75	37	Russia
2S23 120mm Mortar	120	73	35	985	9685	14.27	24.58	50	Russia
2S31 120mm Mortar	120	?	44	1270	9685	19.19	22.0	43	Russia
AMS Arm'd Mortar System	120	118	29	?	9840	12.90	21.0	62	Can/UK/USA
PRAM-S 120mm Mortar	120	73	34	902	6290	16.70	24.33	37	Czech
2S1 122mm How M1974	122	192	48	2264	16730	15.45	23.75	37	Russia
BMY/ARE 122 SP How	122	168	55	2350	16840	22.82	20.33	35	USA/Egypt
JSU-122 Assault Gun	122	215	55	2625	10935	41.14	22.33	23	Russia
M89 122mm Howitzer	122	192	47	2264	16730	17.22	24.0	40	Romania
Royal Ordnance SP122	122	168	55	2350	16840	19.68	25.25	34	Egypt/UK
Type 54-1 122mm SPH	122	110	48	1690	12905	15.06	18.42	36	China
Type 85 122mm SPH	122	192	48	2263	16405	16.24	20.08	37	China
2S25 SPAT	125	240	16	5415	13340	17.70	?	43	Russia
Jagdtiger	128	260	64	3280	13125	68.90	24.25	24	Germany
Catapult 130mm SP Gun	130	299	85	3050	29700	?	26.0	31	India
Semovente 149/40	149	234	112	2625	24060	23.62	21.33	22	Italy
Brummbär 150mm How	150	71	55	920	5240	28.20	19.42	24	Germany
Hummel 150mm How	150	162	96	1624	13670	23.82	23.5	26	Germany
sIG33 Infantry Assault Gun	150	65	84	787	5140	11.81	16.25	21	Germany
2S3 152mm Gun M1973	152	204	96	2150	20230	27.06	25.5	43	Russia
2S5 152mm Gun	152	322	101	2657	31060	27.75	27.33	39	Russia
2S19 152mm Gun	152	322	101	2658	31060	41.33	24.25	37	Russia
Dana 152mm SP How	152	239	96	2273	20450	28.78	36.58	50	Czech
JSU-152 assault gun	152	110	96	2150	10935	41.14	29.58	23	Russia
Type 83 152mm SPH	152	204	96	2150	18840	29.52	22.58	35	China
AMX GCT-155 Gun	155	244	96	2493	30620	41.33	22.0	37	France
AS-90 155mm Gun	155	238	100	2713	27012	44.29	23.67	34	UK
Bandkanon 155mm Gun	155	305	106	2838	26900	52.17	21.5	17	Sweden
Bofors FH-77 SP How	155	232	93	2540	24060	29.52	39.33	43	Sweden
Caesar 155 SP Gun	155	317	103	2936	45930	17.40	32.83	62	France
China 155/45 SP Gun	155	274	100	2943	32800	31.5	20.0	35	China
F3 155mm Howitzer	155	201	98	2379	21825	17.12	14.25	37	France
G6 155mm SP Gun	155	275	100	2943	32800	46.25	30.17	56	S Africa
K-9 Thunder 155 SP How	155	317	101	2920	43745	46.25	24.5	40	S Korea
L-33 155mm SP How	155	201	96	2379	23540	41.58	21.33	22	Israel
M12 155mm GMC	155	233	95	2410	18700	25.89	22.08	24	USA
M40 155mm GMC	155	278	96	2800	25715	36.16	23.33	24	USA
M41 155mm HMC	155	149	95	1850	16355	18.30	19.17	35	USA
M44 155mm HMC	155	142	95	1866	15965	27.90	20.25	35	USA
M50 155mm Howitzer	155	140	96	2115	19410	30.51	20.0	28	Israel
M52T 155mm Howitzer	155	270	101	2936	32800	29.03	19.0	37	Turkey
M53 155mm GMC	155	275	95	2800	23225	42.85	25.92	30	USA
M109A1 155mm SP How	155	263	95	2244	19795	24.55	20.33	35	USA
M109A6 Paladin SP How	155	238	97	2723	26246	28.28	20.33	35	USA
Majnoon 155mm SP Gun	155	317	100	2952	42100	42.32	39.33	55	Iraq
Palmaria 155mm SP How	155	250	96	3060	27010	44.29	23.83	37	Italy
Panzerhaubitze 2000	155	317	97	?	35880	54.46	23.92	27	Germany

Self-Propelled Guns • Comparative Tables

Model	Calibre	Barrel length	Shell weight	Velocity	Range	Total weight	Vehicle length	Road speed	Country
Rascal (52-cal)	155	317	98	?	26250	10.19	24.58	?	Israel
Slammer 155 SPH	155	317	100	2936	43750	63	24.5	28	Israel
SP-70	155	237	96	2885	32810	42.83	25.0	?	UK/Ger/Ital
TAMSE VCA	155	250	96	3060	27012	39.37	25.25	34	Argentina
Type 75 155mm SPH	155	183	99	1840	20775	24.90	21.75	29	Japan
Zuzana 155mm Gun-How	155	274	105	2942	43305	27.55	29.08	56	Czech
Zuzana T-72M1 Gun-How	155	274	105	2942	43305	27.55	29.08	56	Czech
M107 175mm SP Gun	175	428	147	3028	35760	27.72	18.75	34	USA
St Chamond 194 GPF	194	258	176	2100	20015	27.56	26.67	6	France
2S7 203mm Gun	203	?	242	3150	40775	45.76	43.0	31	Russia
M43 8-in HMC	203	202	200	1950	18510	35.71	25.92	21	USA
M55 8-in HMC	203	200	200	1950	18372	40.18	25.92	30	USA
M110 8-in SP Howitzer	203	209	200	1950	17275	23.93	18.75	34	USA
M110A1/A2 8-in SP How	203	320	204	2333	25045	27.91	18.75	34	USA
T93 8-in GMC	203	410	240	2840	35635	?	24.0	?	USA
Al Fao	210	438	241	3140	49210	47.74	49.25	55	Iraq
Schneider	220	302	231	2513	24935	25.59	28.0	5	France
2S4 240mm Mortar	240	210	288	1125	10610	27.06	27.83	37	Russia
T92 240mm HMC	240	331	360	2300	25225	?	24.0	?	USA
Sturmmörser 38cm Tiger	380	81	761	984	6180	63.97	20.58	25	Germany
Karl Gerät 054	540	279	2756	984	11482	122.04	37.33	6	Germany
Karl Gerät 060	600	200	4783	458	7196	122.04	37.33	6	Germany

No Calibre Applicable

Model	Calibre	Barrel length	Shell weight	Velocity	Range	Total weight	Vehicle length	Road speed	Country
Jagdpanzer Jaguar	GW	n/a	51	770	4375	25.10	21.67	44	Germany

Appendix 1

Sd Kfz Numbers

German vehicles of the World War II era built to military specifications were given an identification number preceded by the letters Sd Kfz, the abbreviation for Sonder Kraft Fahr Zeug or 'Special Motor Vehicle'. The classification covered all types of vehicle from tanks to motorcycles, and in order to assist readers in finding a particular number, this list shows exactly what kind of vehicle each number is associated with. If the machine concerned is covered by our definition of 'armoured fighting vehicle' it can then be found in the appropriate section of this book.

Sd Kfz 2
Semi-tracked motor cycle.

Sd Kfz 2/1, 2/2
Semi-tracked motor cycle adapted for field cable laying.

Sd Kfz 3a
2-ton semi-tracked cargo truck, Opel Maultier.

Sd Kfz 3b
2-ton semi-tracked cargo truck, Ford Maultier.

Sd Kfz 3c
2-ton semi-track cargo truck, Klockner-Humboldt-Deutz, diesel.

Sd Kfz 4
4.5-ton semi-tracked cargo truck.

Sd Kfz 4/1
As for 3a but carrying a 10-barrel 150mm rocket projector.

Sd Kfz 6
5-ton semi-tracked tractor (pioneer version).

Sd Kfa 6/1
As for 6 but artillery version.

Sd Kfz 6/2
As for 6 but carrying a 37mm FlaK gun.

Sd Kfz 7
8-ton semi-tracked tractor.

Sd Kfz 7/1
As for 7 but carrying a quadruple 20mm cannon.

Sd Kfz 7/2
As for 7 but carrying a 37mm FlaK gun.

Sd Kfz 7/6
As for 7 but carrying AA artillery predictor and height finder.

Sd Kfz 8
Armoured 88mm Flak 18 gun on 12-ton semi-tracked tractor.

Sd Kfz 9
Armoured 88mm Flak 18 gun on 18-ton semi-tracked tractor.

Sd Kfz 9/1
As for 9 but equipped with a 6-ton crane.

Sd Kfz 9/2
As for 9 but equipped with a 10-ton crane.

Sd Kfz 10
1-ton semi-track tractor.

Sd Kfz 10/1
As for 10 but equipped for gas detection and analysis.

Sd Kfz 10/2
1-ton semi-tracked decontamination vehicle.

Sd Kfz 10/3
1-ton semi-tracked decontamination vehicle with spraying equipment.

Sd Kfz 10/4
1-ton semi-tracked tractor mounting 20mm FlaK 30.

Sd Kfz 10/5
1-ton semi-tracked tractor mounting 20mm FlaK 38 in armoured cab.

Sd Kfz 11
3-ton semi-tracked tractor.

Sd Kfz 11/1
3-ton semi-tracked smoke-generator vehicle, also used as an ammunition carrier for the 150mm Nebelwerfer.

Sd Kfz 11/2
3-ton semi-tracked decontamination vehicle

Sd Kfz 11/3
3-ton semi-tracked decontamination vehicle with spraying equipment.

Sd Kfz 11/4
3-ton semi-tracked smoke-generator vehicle.

Sd Kfz 11/5
3-ton semi-tracked gas-detector vehicle.

Sd Kfz 101
PzKpfw 1, models A and B.

Sd Kfz 111
PzKpfw 1 converted to munitions carrier.

Sd Kfz 121
PzKpfw 2 series.

Sd Kfz 122
PzKpfw 2 models D and E converted to flame-throwing tank

Sd Kfz 123
Reconnaissance vehicle, also known as Panzerspähwagen Luchs.

Sd Kfz 124
Wespe. 105mm leFH 18/2 mounted on PzKpfw 2 chassis.

Sd Kfz 131
Marder 2. 75mm anti-tank gun mounted on PzKpfw 2 chassis.

Sd Kfz 132
76.2mm Russian anti-tank gun mounted on PzKpfw 2 chassis D and E.

Sd Kfz 135
Marder 1. 75mm anti-tank gun mounted on French Lorraine tractor.

Sd Kfz 135/1
150mm howitzer mounted on Lorraine tractor.

Sd Kfz 138
75mm PaK 40 mounted on Czech tank chassis.

Sd Kfz 138/1
150mm howitzer mounted on Czech tank chassis.

Sd Kfz 139
Marder 3. 76.2mm Russian anti-tank gun mounted on 38(*t*) tank chassis.

Sd Kfz 140
20mm FlaK gun mounted on Czech tank chassis.

Sd Kfz 140/1
Tracked reconnaissance vehicle based on 38(*t*) tank chassis.

Sd Kfz 141
PzKpfw 3 series, Models A to H.

Sd Kfz 141/1
PzKpfw 3 series, Models J, L and M.

Sd Kfz 141/2
PzKpfw 3 series, Model N, armed with 75mm L/24 gun.

Sd Kfz 141/3
Pz KPfw 3 Model M, converted to flame-throwing tank.

Sd Kfz 142
A blanket designation covering a variety of conversions of the PzKpfw 3 chassis into assault guns..

Sd Kfz 142/1
Sturmgeschütz 3. Assault guns based on PzKpfw 3 and armed with the 75mm L/43 or L/48.

Sd Kfz 142/2
Assault howitzer based on PzKpfw 3 armed with 105mm StuH 42 L/28.

Sd Kfz 143
PzKpfw 3 converted for artillery forward observer duties.

Sd Kfz 161
PzKpfw 4 series, models A–F1.

Sd Kfz 161/1
PzKpfw 4 series, Models F2, G.

Sd Kfz 161/2
PzKpfw 4 series, Models H and J.

Sd Kfz 161/ 3
Möbelwagen. 37mm FlaK 43 mounted on the chassis of PzKpfw 4.

Sd Kfz 162
Jagdpanzer 4. Tank destroyer based on the PzKpfw 4 chassis, armed with 75mm PaK 39 L/48.

Sd Kfz 162/1
Improved version of the Jagdpanzer 4 to mount the 75mm L/70.

Sd Kfz 164
Nashorn. 88mm PaK 43 mounted on the PzKpfw 38(*t*) chassis as a tank destroyer.

Sd Kfz 165
Hummel. Self-propelled carriage for field howitzer sFH 18.

Sd Kfz 166
Brummbär. Self-propelled carriage for 150mm heavy infantry howitzer.

Sd Kfz 167
Sturmgeschütz 4. Assault gun based on PzKpfw 4 chassis and armed with the 75mm L/48.

Sd Kfz 171
Panther series, Models A, D and G.

Sd Kfz172
Assault gun project based on PzKpfw 5 chassis with 88mm gun.

Sd Kfz 173
Jagdpanther. Tank destroyer based on the PzKpfw 5 chassis, armed with the 88mm PaK 43/3 L/71.

Sd Kfz 179
Armoured tank recovery vehicle based on Panther chassis.

Sd Kfz 181
Tiger 1 Model E, formerly Model H.

Sd Kfz 182
King Tiger. Tiger 2 Model B.

Sd Kfz 184
Ferdinand. Tank destroyer based on the Porsche Tiger chassis, armed with the 88mm PaK 43/2.

Sd Kfz 186
Jagdtiger. Tank destroyer based on the Tiger 2 chassis and with 128mm PaK 44.

Sd Kfz 221
Light Auto-Union/Horch armoured car.

Sd Kfz 222
As for 221 but with more powerful engine and armament.

Sd Kfz 223
Light 4-wheeled armoured car, with radio equipment.

Sd Kfz 231
6- or 8-wheeled armoured car.

Sd Kfz 232
6- or 8-wheeled armoured car.

Sd Kfz 233
As for 8-wheeled 232 but with more powerful armament.

Sd Kfz 234
As for 232 but tropicalised and with air-cooled engine.

Sd Kfz 234/1
As for 234 but with 20mm turret gun.

Sd Kfz 234/2
As for 234 but with 50mm gun in turret.

Sd Kfz 234/3
As for 234/2 but with short 75mm gun in open topped turret.

Sd Kfz 234/4
As for 234 but with 75mm Pak 40 gun.

Sd Kfz 247
Arrmoured staff car on 4- or 6-wheeled chassis.

Sd Kfz 250
Light armoured semi-tracked personnel carrier (basic model).

Sd Kfz 250/1-I
As for 250 but with intercom facilities.

Sd Kfz 250/1-II
As for 250 but with radio equipment.

Sd Kfz 250/2
As for 250 but equipped for telephone cable laying.

Sd Kfz 250/3-I, 3/II, 3/III, 3/IV
As for 250 but fitted in various ways for radio.

Sd Kfz 250/4
Anti-aircraft vehicle armed with two machine guns.

Sd Kfz 250/5-I
Artillery forward observer's vehicle.

Sd Kfz 250/5-II
As for 250/5-1 but different radio equipment.

Sd Kfz 250/6
Ammunition carrier for assault guns.

Sd Kfz 250/7
Light armoured semi-tracked mortar carrier.

Sd Kfz 250/7
Ammunition-carrier for mortar carrier.

Sd Kfz 250/8
Light armoured semi-tracked vehicle mounting short 75mm gun.

Sd Kfz 250/9
Light armoured semi-tracked vehicle with 20mm gun and MG mounted in turret.

Sd Kfz 250/10
Light armoured semi-tracked vehicle armed with 37mm PaK 35/36 gun.

Sd Kfz 250/11
Light armoured semi-tracked vehicle armed with the schwere Panzerbüchse 41 taper-bore anti-tank gun.

Sd Kfz 250/12
Light armoured semi-tracked artillery survey vehicle.

Sd Kfz 251
Medium armoured semi-tracked personnel carrier, basic model.

Sd Kfz 251/1-I
As 251 but with intercommunication facilities.

Sd Kfz 251/1-II
As for 251 but fitted for radio.

Sd Kfz 251/2
Medium amoured semi-tracked mortar vehicle.

Sd Kfz 251/3
As for 251 but fitted for radio.

Sd Kfz 251/3-I
As for 251 but fitted for radio.

Sd Kfz 251/3-II
As for 251 but fitted for radio.

Sd Kfz 251/3-III
As for 251 but fitted for radio.

Sd Kfz 251/3-IV
Mobile command post.

Sd Kfz 251/3-V
As for 251 but fitted for radio.

Sd Kfz 251/4
Munition-carrier and tractor for the IG 18 close-support gun.

Sd Kfz 251/5
Command vehicle for engineers in armoured divisions.

Sd Kfz 251/6
Mobile command post.

Sd Kfz 251/7-I
Medium semi-tracked vehicle for engineer equipment.

Sd Kfz 251/7-II
As for 7-I but with different radio equipment.

Sd Kfz 251/8-I
Medium semi-tracked armoured ambulance.

Sd Kfz 251/8-II
As for 8-I but with different radio equipment.

Sd Kfz 251/9
Medium semi-tracked vehicle mounting short 75mm gun.

Sd Kfz 251/10
Medium semi-tracked vehicle mounting 37mm PaK 35/36 gun.

Sd Kfz 251/11
Medium semi-tracked armoured telephone vehicle.

Sd Kfz 251/12
Medium semi-tracked armoured artillery survey vehicle.

Sd Kfz 251/13
Medium semi-tracked armoured artillery sound-ranging microphone vehicle.

Sd Kfz 251/14
Medium semi-tracked armoured artillery sound-ranging plotting vehicle.

Sd Kfz 251/15
Medium semi-tracked armoured artillery flash-spotting vehicle.

Sd Kfz 251/16
Medium semi-tracked armoured flame-throwing vehicle.

Sd Kfz 251/17
Medium semi-tracked armoured vehicle mounting 20mm FlaK 38.

Sd Kfz 251/18-I
Mobile armoured observation post.

Sd Kfz 251/18-Ia
Airmobile armoured observation post.

Sd Kfz 251/18-II
Mobile armoured observation post.

Sd Kfz 251/18-IIa
Mobile armoured observation post.

Vehicles 18-I to 18-IIa differed only in the type of radio equipment.

Sd Kfz 251/19
Mobile armoured telephone exchange.

Sd Kfz 251/20
Medium semi-tracked armoured vehicle carrying infra-red searchlight.

Sd Kfz 251/21
Medium semi-tracked armoured vehicle mounting triple 15mm or 20mm AA MGs.

Sd Kfz 251/22
Medium semi-tracked armoured vehicle mounting 75mm PaK 40 anti-tank gun.

Sd Kfz 251/23
Medium semi-tracked reconnaissance vehicle.

Sd Kfz 252
Light semi-tracked armoured ammunition-carrier.

Sd Kfz 253
Light semi-tracked armoured observation vehicle.

Sd Kfz 254
Medium wheel and track armoured observation vehicle.

Sd Kfz 260

Light 4-wheeled armoured car with radio equipment.

Sd Kfz 261

Light 4-wheeled armoured car with radio equipment, and frame antenna.

Sd Kfz 263

6- or 8-wheel armoured car, long-range command car version.

Sd Kfz 265

PzKpfw 1 converted to armoured command vehicle.

Sd Kfz 266

PzKpfw 3, Ausf E converted to armoured command vehicle.

Sd Kfz 266

PzKpfw 3, Ausf H converted to armoured command vehicle.

Sd Kfz 266

PzKpfw 3, Ausf J converted to armoured command vehicle.

Sd Kfz 266

PzKpfw 3, Ausf M converted to armoured command vehicle.

Sd Kfz 267

PzKpfw 3, Ausf D converted to armoured command vehicle.

Sd Kfz 267

PzKpfw 5 Panther commander's tank with additional radio equipment.

Sd Kfz 267

PzKpfw 6 Tiger commander's tank with additional radio equipment.

Sd Kfz 268

The 268 vehicles varied from the 266 and 267 versions in the different radio equipment carried.

Sd Kfz 268

PzKpfw 3, Ausf D converted to armoured command vehicle.

Sd Kfz 268

PzKpfw 3, Ausf E converted to armoured command vehicle.

Sd Kfz 268

PzKpfw 3, Ausf H converted to armoured command vehicle.

Sd Kfz 268

PzKpfw 3, Ausf J converted to armoured command vehicle.

Sd Kfz 268

PzKpfw 3, Ausf M converted to armoured command vehicle.

Sd Kfz 268

PzKpfw 5 Panther commander's tank with additional radio equipment.

Sd Kfz 268

PzKpfw 6 Tiger commander's tank with additional radio equipment.

Sd Kfz 280

Armoured ammunition carier (VK 501).

Sd Kfz 300

Borgward B1 and B2. Remote-controlled mine-clearing and demolition vehicles.

Sd Kfz301

Demolition Vehicle B4 Models A and B.

Sd Kfz301

Demolition Vehicle B4 Model C.

Sd Kfz 302

Demolition Vehicle Goliath Type E.

Sd kfz 303

Demolition Vehicle Goliath Type V.

Sd Kfz 304

Demolition Vehicle NSU Springer.

Appendix 2

Names and Nicknames

This table is designed to list alternative names commonly found for various equipments. The item in bolder type gives the location chosen for the vehicle's entry in this book.

Name/ Nickname	Country	Official nomenclature	Name/ Nickname	Country	Official nomenclature
Abrams	USA	M1	**King Tiger**	Germany	PzKpfw 6, Ausf B
Achilles	UK	M10 GMC	Lee	USA	**M3 Medium**
Al Khalid	Pakistan	MBT2000	Locust	USA	**M22 Light**
Avenger	UK	A30	Luchs (WW2)	Germany	**PzKpfw 2, Ausf L**
Black Prince	UK	A43	**Luchs** (1970s)	Germany	Spähpanzer
Boarhound	UK	**T18E2**	Ontos	USA	**M50 MGMC**
Cavalier	UK	A24; Cruiser Mk 7	**Osorio**	Brazil	EE-T1
Centaur	UK	A27; Cruiser Mk 8	**Panther**	Germany	PzKpfw 5
Centurion	UK	A41	Patton	USA	**M46, M47**
Chaffee	USA	**M24**	Pershing	US	**M26**
Challenger	UK	A30	Royal Tiger	Germany	**King Tiger**
Churchill	UK	A20/A22			(Königstiger)
Comet	UK	A34	Scorpion	USA	**M56**
Covenanter	UK	**Cruiser Mk 5**	**Sentinel**	Australia	AC1
Cromwell	UK	**Cruiser Mark 8**	Sheridan	USA	**M551**
Crusader	UK	A15; **Cruiser Mk 6**	Sherman	USA	**M4**
Duck	UK	**Tank Mk 9 Amphib**	Skink	Canada	AA Tank (C) Mk 1
Elefant, **Ferdinand**	Germany	Pz Jäg Tiger	Staghound	USA	**T17E1**
Excelsior	UK	**A33**	Stuart	USA	**M3, M5 Light**
Firefly	UK	Sherman 5C	**Tetrarch**	UK	Light Tank Mk 7
Gorilla	USA	**M41 HMC**	**Tiger**	Germany	PzKpfw 6
Grant	UK	**M3 Medium Tank**	**Tortoise**	UK	A39
Greyhound	UK	**M8**	Tritton Chaser	UK	**Medium A**
Grizzly	Canada	**M3A1 Medium**	**Valiant**	UK	A38
Harry Hopkins	UK	Light Tank Mk 8	Vickers 16-tonner	UK	**A6E1**
Hellcat	USA	**M18 GMC**	**Vickers Three-Man**	UK	A5E1
Honey	UK	**M5 Stuart**	Walker Bulldog	USA	**M41 Light**
Hornet	UK	**Medium C**	Whippet	UK	**Medium A**
Independent	UK	A1E1	Wolfhound	USA	**M38**
King Kong	USA	**T92 HMC**			

Index

This lists all individual entries and references. Where variants of a basic model – e.g. Challenger 1 and Challenger 2 – have separate entries, they are separately listed here. Where the variants are included in the entry for the basic tank – e.g. the M3A1, M3A2, M3A3 etc – they are not given individual listings here and should be sought under the entry for the basic vehicle, in this case under M3 Medium USA.